Lecture Notes in Computer Science 2274

Edited by G. Goos, J. Hartmanis, and J. van Leeuwen

Springer-Verlag Berlin Heidelberg GmbH

David Naccache   Pascal Paillier (Eds.)

Public Key Cryptography

5th International Workshop on Practice and Theory
in Public Key Cryptosystems, PKC 2002
Paris, France, February 12-14, 2002
Proceedings

 Springer

Series Editors

Gerhard Goos, Karlsruhe University, Germany
Juris Hartmanis, Cornell University, NY, USA
Jan van Leeuwen, Utrecht University, The Netherlands

Volume Editors

David Naccache
Pascal Paillier
Gemplus International, Cryptography and Security Group
34 Rue Guynemer, 92447 Issy-le-Moulineaux, France
E-mail: {David.Naccache/Pascal.Paillier}@gemplus.com

Cataloging-in-Publication Data applied for

Die Deutsche Bibliothek - CIP-Einheitsaufnahme

Public key cryptography : proceedings / 5th International Workshop on
Practice and Theory in Public Key Cryptosystems, PKC 2002, Paris, France,
February 12 - 14, 2002. David Naccache ; Pascal Paillier (ed.).

(Lecture notes in computer science ; Vol. 2274)
ISBN 978-3-540-43168-8   ISBN 978-3-540-45664-3 (eBook)
DOI 10.1007/978-3-540-45664-3

CR Subject Classification (1998): E.3, F.2.0, C.2.0

ISSN 0302-9743
ISBN 978-3-540-43168-8

Typesetting: Camera-ready by author, data conversion by Steingräber Satztechnik GmbH, Heidelberg
Printed on acid-free paper   SPIN 10846181   06/3142   5 4 3 2 1 0

Preface

The International Workshop on Practice and Theory in Public Key Cryptography PKC 2002 was held at the Maison de la Chimie, situated in the very center of Paris, France from February 12 to 14, 2002. The PKC series of conferences yearly represents international research and the latest achievements in the area of public key cryptography, covering a wide spectrum of topics, from cryptosystems to protocols, implementation techniques or cryptanalysis. After being held in four successive years in pacific-asian countries, PKC 2002 experienced for the first time a European location, thus showing its ability to reach an ever wider audience from both the industrial community and academia.

We are very grateful to the 19 members of the Program Committee for their hard and efficient work in producing such a high quality program. In response to the call for papers of PKC 2002, 69 papers were electronically received from 13 different countries throughout Europe, America, and the Far East. All submissions were reviewed by at least three members of the program committee, who eventually selected the 26 papers that appear in these proceedings. In addition to this program, we were honored to welcome Prof. Bart Preneel who kindly accepted to give this year's invited talk. The program committee gratefully acknowledges the help of a large number of colleagues who reviewed submissions in their area of expertise: Masayuki Abe, Seigo Arita, Olivier Baudron, Mihir Bellare, Emmanuel Bresson, Eric Brier, Mathieu Ciet, Alessandro Conflitti, Jean-Sébastien Coron, Roger Fischlin, Pierre-Alain Fouque, Matt Franklin, Rosario Genarro, Marc Girault, Louis Granboulan, Goichiro Hanaoka, Darrel Hankerson, Eliane Jaulmes, Ari Juels, Jinho Kim, Marcos Kiwi, Kazukuni Kobara, Francois Koeune, Byoungcheon Lee, A. K. Lenstra, Pierre Loidreau, Wenbo Mao, Gwenaelle Martinet, Yi Mu, Phong Nguyen, Satoshi Obana, Guillaume Poupard, Yasuyuki Sakai, Hideo Shimizu, Tom Shrimpton, Ron Steinfeld, Katsuyuki Takashima, Huaxiong Wang, and Yuji Watanabe. Julien Brouchier deserves special thanks for skillfully maintaining the program committee's website and patiently helping out during the refereeing process.

Finally, we wish to thank all the authors who committed their time by submitting papers (including those whose submissions were not successful), thus making this conference possible, as well as the participants, organizers, and contributors from around the world for their kind support.

December 2001   David Naccache, Pascal Paillier

PKC 2002

Fifth International Workshop on Practice and Theory in Public Key Cryptography

Maison de la Chimie, Paris, France
February 12–14, 2002

Program Committee

David Naccache (Program Chair) ....Gemplus, France

Daniel Bleichenbacher ....Bell Labs, Lucent Technologies, USA
Yvo Desmedt ....Florida State University, USA
Marc Fischlin ....Goethe-University of Frankfurt, Germany
Shai Halevi ....IBM T. J. Watson Research Center, USA
Markus Jakobsson ....RSA Laboratories, USA
Antoine Joux ....DCSSI, France
Burt Kaliski ....RSA Laboratories, USA
Kwangjo Kim ....Information and Communications University, Korea
Eyal Kushilevitz ....Technion, Israel
Pascal Paillier ....Gemplus, France
David Pointcheval ....École Normale Supérieure, France
Jean-Jacques Quisquater ....Université Catholique de Louvain, Belgium
Phillip Rogaway ....UC Davis, USA
Kazue Sako ....NEC Corporation, Japan
Bruce Schneier ....Counterpane Internet Security, USA
Junji Shikata ....University of Tokyo, Japan
Igor Shparlinski ....Macquarie University, Australia
Moti Yung ....Certco, USA
Jianying Zhou ....Oracle Corporation, USA

Table of Contents

Encryption Schemes

Signature Schemes

Protocols I

Invited Talk

ECC Implementations

Applications

New Semantically Secure Public-Key Cryptosystems from the RSA-Primitive

Kouichi Sakurai[1] and Tsuyoshi Takagi[2]

[1] Kyushu University
Department of Computer Science and Communication Engineering
Hakozaki, Fukuoka 812-81, Japan
sakurai@csce.kyushu-u.ac.jp
[2] Technische Universität Darmstadt,
Fachbereich Informatik,
Alexanderstr.10, D-64283 Darmstadt, Germany
ttakagi@cdc.informatik.tu-darmstadt.de

Abstract. We analyze the security of the simplified Paillier (S-Paillier) cryptosystem, which was proposed by Catalano et al. We prove that the one-wayness of the S-Paillier scheme is as intractable as the standard RSA problem. We also prove that an adversary, which breaks the semantic security, can compute the least significant bits of the nonce. This observation is interesting, because the least significant bit of the nonce is the hard core bit of the encryption function. Moreover, we proposed a novel semantically secure cryptosystem, based on the one-way function $f_{MSBZ(l)}^{e,n}(r) = (r - MSB_l(r))^e \bmod n$, where (e, n) is the RSA public-key and $r - MSB_l(r)$ means that the l most significant bits of r are zeroed. We proved that the one-wayness of the proposed scheme is as intractable as the standard RSA problem. An adversary, which breaks the semantic security of the proposed scheme, can break the least significant bits of the nonce. These security results of the proposed scheme are similar to those of the S-Paillier cryptosystem. However, the proposed scheme is more efficient than the S-Paillier cryptosystem.

1 Introduction

One of the requirements for a secure public-key cryptosystem is the semantic security, which is assorted the indistinguishability against the chosen plaintext attack (IND-CPA) and the indistinguishability against the chosen ciphertext attack (IND-CCA) [BDPR98]. Although there is an IND-CCA public-key cryptosystem from the discrete logarithm primitive in a standard model, namely the Cramer-Shoup cryptosystem [CS98], there is no IND-CCA public-key cryptosystem from the RSA primitive in a standard model. It is an interesting problem to find such a public-key cryptosystem. The Cramer-Shoup cryptosystem is converted a standard IND-CPA ElGamal cryptosystem to be an IND-CCA scheme using hash functions. The security of the IND-CPA ElGamal cryptosystem relies on the decisional Diffie-Hellman (DDH) assumption. On the contrary, the RSA

D. Naccache and P. Paillier (Eds.): PKC 2002, LNCS 2274, pp. 1–16, 2002.

primitive has no standard IND-CPA cryptosystem corresponding to the standard ElGamal. We first have to consider an IND-CPA public-key cryptosystem from the RSA primitive in order to construct an IND-CCA public-key cryptosystem from the RSA primitive in a standard model. Because there is no decisional RSA problem, we need a contrivance for exploring a suitable decisional problem from the RSA primitive. In this paper, we investigate the security of an IND-CPA cryptosystem from the RSA primitive and we call IND-CPA as semantically secure in the following. The Pointcheval cryptosystem [Poi99] and the simplified version of Paillier cryptosystem [CGHN01] are known as semantically secure public-key cryptosystems from the RSA primitive. However, the security of these cryptosystems is not well studied comparing with the standard ElGamal cryptosystem. It is unknown that the one-wayness of these cryptosystem is as hard as solving the standard problem, e.g. the RSA problem or factoring problem. Although the semantic security of these scheme is proved equivalent to a decisional number-theoretic problem, the decisional problem has not been well studied, and no non-trivial relationship between the computational problem and its corresponding decisional problem is known.

The Paillier cryptosystem is a probabilistic encryption scheme over the ring $\mathbb{Z}/n^2\mathbb{Z}$, where n is the RSA modulus [Pai99]. It encrypts a message $m \in \mathbb{Z}/n\mathbb{Z}$ by computing $E(m, r) = g^m r^n \bmod n^2$, where r is a random integer in $\mathbb{Z}/n\mathbb{Z}$, and g is an element whose order in $\mathbb{Z}/n^2\mathbb{Z}$ is divisible by n. The encryption function $E(m, r)$ has a homomorphic property: $E(m_1, r_1)E(m_2, r_2) = E(m_1 + m_2, r_1 r_2)$. Therefore, the Paillier cryptosystem can be used as the primitives for voting systems, commitment schemes, threshold schemes, etc [DJ01] [CGHN01]. The security of the Paillier cryptosystem has been investigated in [Pai99]. The one-wayness of the Paillier cryptosystem is related to the computational composite residuosity (C-CR) problem, which finds m from its encryption $g^m r^n \bmod n^2$. It is known that an algorithm, which solves the RSA problem with the encryption exponent $e = n$, can solve the C-CR problem. The semantic security of the Paillier cryptosystem is based on the decisional composite residuosity (D-CR) problem, which determines whether an integer x of $\mathbb{Z}/n^2\mathbb{Z}$ is represented as $x = a^n \bmod n^2$ for an integer a of $\mathbb{Z}/n^2\mathbb{Z}$. Then, Catalano et al. proved that $n - b$ least significant bits of the message are simultaneously secure under the 2^b-hard C-CR assumption, where the 2^b-hard C-CR assumption uses the short message space such that $m \in \{0, 1, .., 2^b\}$ [CGH01]. The Paillier cryptosystem is a generalization of the Goldwasser-Micali cryptosystem based on the quadratic residuosity problem [GM84]. [1] Okamoto and Uchiyama proposed a similar construction over the integer ring $\mathbb{Z}/(p^2 q)\mathbb{Z}$, where p, q are primes [OU98].

The simplified version of the Paillier cryptosystem is proposed by Catalano et al. [CGHN01]. We call it the S-Paillier cryptosystem in this paper. The S-Paillier cryptosystem is strongly related to the RSA cryptosystem modulo n^2, where n is the RSA modulus. They choose the public key g as $g = (1+n)$, whose order in $\mathbb{Z}/n^2\mathbb{Z}$ is n. Then $g^m \bmod n^2$ is represented by $g^m = (1 + n)^m = $

---

[1] Recently, Cramer and Shoup proposed IND-CCA cryptosystems based on the Paillier cryptosystem or the Goldwasser-Micali cryptosystem [CS01].

$(1 + mn) \bmod n^2$. The encryption of the S-Paillier scheme is carried out by $E(m, r) = r^e(1 + mn) \bmod n^2$ for a random integer $r \in (\mathbb{Z}/n\mathbb{Z})^\times$, where e is an integer. They proved that the one-way security of the S-Paillier scheme is at least as hard as the computational small e-root problem (C-SR) problem, which computes $x \in \mathbb{Z}/n\mathbb{Z}$ from given $x^e \bmod n^2$. They also proved that the semantic security of the S-Paillier scheme is as hard as to solve the decisional small e-root problem (D-SR) problem, which decides whether $y \in \mathbb{Z}/n^2\mathbb{Z}$ is represented as $y = x^e \bmod n^2$ for $x \in \mathbb{Z}/n\mathbb{Z}$.

Contributions of This Paper

In this paper we investigate the security of the S-Paillier cryptosystem. At first we prove that the one-way security of the S-Paillier cryptosystem is as intractable as the standard RSA problem. Let an adversary A be an algorithm that breaks the one-wayness of the S-Paillier cryptosystem. We construct an adversary, which can compute the least significant bit of x for given $x^e \bmod n$, where $x \in_R (\mathbb{Z}/n\mathbb{Z})^\times$. An integer c of $\mathbb{Z}/n^2\mathbb{Z}$ is uniquely represented as $c = [c]_0 + n[c]_1$, where $0 \le [c]_0, [c]_1 < n$. The adversary A can compute $[x^e \bmod n^2]_1$ for a given $x^e \bmod n$. Then the difference between $[2^{-e}x^e \bmod n^2]_1$ and $A(2^{-e}x^e \bmod n)$ gives us the information about the least significant bit of x. Moreover, we prove that an adversary, which breaks the semantic security of the S-Paillier cryptosystem, can compute the least significant bits of the nonce r. This observation is interesting, because the least significant bit of the nonce r is the hard core bit of $E(m, r) \bmod n$. The adversary is equivalent to solving the D-SR problem and can learn the least significant bit of r by multiplying $2^{-e} \bmod n^2$ with y.

We also propose a general conversion technique, which enhances the RSA cryptosystem to be semantically secure using a one-way function f, where f is a function $\mathbb{Z}/n\mathbb{Z} \to \mathbb{Z}/n\mathbb{Z}$. A message m is encrypted by $(c_0 = r^e \bmod n, c_1 = f(r) + mc_0 \bmod n)$. We analyze the requirements for the one-way function. The computational RSA + one-way function (C-RSA+OW) problem is to find $f(r)$ for a given $r^e \bmod n$. The decisional RSA+OW (D-RSA+OW) problem is to distinguish the distribution $(r^e \bmod n, f(r))$ from the uniform distribution. The converted scheme is one-way if and only if the C-RSA+OW problem of f is hard, and it is semantically secure if and only if the D-RSA+OW of f is hard. The S-Paillier cryptosystem uses the one-way function $f(r) : r \bmod n \to [r^e]_1$. We also discuss the relationship between the converted scheme and the Pointcheval cryptosystem using the dependent RSA problem [Poi99]. The Pointcheval cryptosystem encrypts a message m by $(c_0 = r^e \bmod n, c_1 = m(r + 1)^e \bmod n)$. We generalized this encryption to $(c_0 = r^e \bmod n, c_1 = mf(r) \bmod n)$ and its security has the same properties as the above conversion.

Moreover, we propose a novel one-way function $f^{e,n}_{MSBZ(l)}(r) = (r - MSB_l(r))^e$ $\bmod n$, where $r - MSB_l(r)$ makes the l most significant bits of r zero for a large enough l. The computational RSA+MSBZ problem is to find the $f^{e,n}_{MSBZ(l)}(r)$ from a given $r^e \bmod n$. The RSA+MSBZ problem is different from the dependent RSA problem, because we do not know the $MSB_l(r)$ of $(r - MSB(r))^e \bmod$

n and there is no dependence between $r^e \bmod n$ and $f_{MSBZ(l)}^{e,n}(r)$. The decisional RSA+MSBZ problem is to distinguish $(r^e \bmod n, f_{MSBZ(l)}^{e,n}(r))$ from the uniform distribution. We prove that the computational RSA+MSBZ is as intractable as the standard RSA problem. An adversary, which breaks the decisional RSA+MSBZ problem, can break the least significant bits of the computational RSA+MSBZ problem. These security results are similar to those of the S-Paillier, but the encryption/decryption of our proposed cryptosystem are more efficient than those of the S-Paillier.

Notation. In this paper we choose $\{0, 1, 2, .., m-1\}$ as the reduced residue class of modulo m, namely the elements of $\mathbb{Z}/m\mathbb{Z}$ are $\{0, 1, 2, .., m-1\}$.

2   Simplified Paillier Cryptosystem

In this section we review the simplified Paillier (S-Paillier) cryptosystem proposed by Catalano et al. [CGHN01]. The S-Paillier cryptosystem is related to the RSA cryptosystem over $\mathbb{Z}/n^2\mathbb{Z}$. The description of the S-Paillier cryptosystem in this paper is a little different from the paper [CGHN01]. Indeed we use the standard RSA key. Let RSA_{public} be the set of the RSA modulus n and the RSA encryption exponent e of n, respectively.

$$RSA_{public} = \{(n, e) | n \leftarrow \text{RSA modulus}, e \leftarrow \mathbb{Z}_{>2}, s.t. \gcd(e, \varphi(n)) = 1\} \quad (1)$$

We explain the S-Paillier cryptosystem in the following.

> **Key generation:** Let $(n, e) \leftarrow_R RSA_{public}$. The integer d is computed by $ed = 1 \bmod \varphi(n)$. Then (n, e) is the public key and d is the secret key.
> **Encryption:** Let $m \in \mathbb{Z}/n\mathbb{Z}$ be a message. We generate a random integer $r \in (\mathbb{Z}/n\mathbb{Z})^\times$ and encrypt the message m by $c = r^e(1 + mn) \bmod n^2$.
> **Decryption:** At first r is recovered with computing $r = c^d \bmod n$. Then the message m is decrypted by $m = L(cr^{-e} \bmod n^2)$, where $L(k) = (k-1)/n$.

Remark 1. In the key generation we do not assume $\gcd(e, \varphi(n^2)) = 1$ as described in the paper [CGHN01], which guarantees that the function $r \to r^e \bmod n^2$ is a permutation function over $\mathbb{Z}/n^2\mathbb{Z}$. The difference to the RSA exponent e is the condition $\gcd(e, n) = 1$. This condition is not necessary for the decryption of the S-Paillier cryptosystem and does not affect its security, as we will prove in the next section. Moreover, the probability that an integer is relatively prime to the primes p or q is upper-bounded $1/p + 1/q$, where $n = pq$. When we randomly choose the exponent e from RSA_{public}, the probability is negligible in $\log n$.

The problem of breaking the one-wayness of the S-Paillier cryptosystem is to find the integer m for given $(n, e) \leftarrow RSA_{public}$, $r \leftarrow (\mathbb{Z}/n\mathbb{Z})^\times$, and $r^e(1 + mn) \bmod n^2$. The one-wayness assumption of the S-Paillier cryptosystem is that for any probabilistic polynomial time algorithm $A_{S-Paillier}^{OW}$ the probability

$$Pr_{m \in_R \mathbb{Z}/n\mathbb{Z}}[(n, e) \leftarrow RSA_{public}, r \leftarrow_R (\mathbb{Z}/n\mathbb{Z})^\times,$$
$$c = r^e(1 + mn) \bmod n^2 : A_{S-Paillier}^{OW}(c) = m]$$

is negligible in $\log n$. Catalano et al. proposed a number theoretic problem in order to investigate the one-wayness of the S-Paillier cryptosystem. They defined the computational small e-roots (C-SR) problem, which is to find the integer $r \in (\mathbb{Z}/n\mathbb{Z})^{\times}$ for given $(n, e) \leftarrow RSA_{public}$ and $r^e \bmod n^2$. The computational small e-root (C-SR) assumption is as follows: for any probabilistic polynomial time algorithm $A_{C\text{-}SR}$ the probability

$$Pr_{r \in_R (\mathbb{Z}/n\mathbb{Z})^{\times}} \left[(n, e) \leftarrow RSA_{public}, c = r^e \bmod n^2 : A_{C\text{-}SR}(c) = r \right]$$

is negligible in $\log n$. It is clear that the one-wayness of the S-Paillier cryptosystem can be solved by the oracle that solves the C-SR problem. However the opposite direction is unknown and there is possibility of breaking the one-wayness of the S-Paillier scheme without solving the C-SR problem.

We explain the semantic security of the S-Paillier cryptosystem. A semantic security adversary $A_{S\text{-}Paillier}^{SS}$ consists of the find stage $A_{S\text{-}Paillier}^{SS1}$ and the guess stage $A_{S\text{-}Paillier}^{SS2}$. The $A_{S\text{-}Paillier}^{SS1}$ outputs two messages m_0, m_1 and a state information st for a public-key n. Let c be a ciphertext of either m_0 or m_1. The $A_{S\text{-}Paillier}^{SS1}$ guesses whether the ciphertext c is the encryption of $m_b (b \in \{0, 1\})$ for given (c, m_0, m_1, st) and outputs b. The semantic security of the S-Paillier cryptosystem is that for any probabilistic polynomial time algorithm $A_{S\text{-}Paillier}^{SS}$ the probability

$$2Pr \; [(n, e) \leftarrow RSA_{public}, (m_0, m_1, st) \leftarrow A_{S\text{-}Paillier}^{SS1}(e, n), b \leftarrow \{0, 1\},$$
$$r \leftarrow_R (\mathbb{Z}/n\mathbb{Z})^{\times}, c = r^e(1 + m_b n) \bmod n^2 : A_{S\text{-}Paillier}^{SS2}(c, m_0, m_1, st) = b] - 1$$

is negligible in $\log n$. The semantic security of the S-Paillier cryptosystem is related to the decisional version of the C-SR problem, which distinguishes whether an element of $\mathbb{Z}/n^2\mathbb{Z}$ comes from the distribution $\{r^e \bmod n^2 | r \in (\mathbb{Z}/n\mathbb{Z})^{\times}\}$. The decisional small e-residue (D-SR) assumption is defined as follows: for any probabilistic polynomial time algorithm $A_{D\text{-}SR}$ the probability of distinguishing the two distributions

$$|Pr[x \leftarrow (\mathbb{Z}/n^2\mathbb{Z})^{\times} : A_{D\text{-}SR}(x) = 1]$$
$$-Pr[x \leftarrow (\mathbb{Z}/n\mathbb{Z})^{\times}, y = x^e \bmod n : A_{D\text{-}SR}(y) = 1]|$$

is negligible in $\log n$. Catalano et al. proved that the S-Paillier cryptosystem is semantically secure if and only if the D-SR assumption holds.

2.1 One-Wayness of the S-Paillier Scheme

The one-wayness is the simplest requirement for public-key cryptosystems. We prove that the one-way security of the S-Paillier scheme is as intractable as the RSA problem. The RSA problem is to find the integer $r \in (\mathbb{Z}/n\mathbb{Z})^{\times}$ for given $(n, e) \leftarrow RSA_{public}$ and $r^e \bmod n$. The RSA assumption is as follows: for any probabilistic polynomial time algorithm A_{RSA}, the probability

$$Pr_{r \in_R (\mathbb{Z}/n\mathbb{Z})^{\times}} \left[(n, e) \leftarrow RSA_{public}, c = r^e \bmod n : A_{RSA}(c) = r \right] \qquad (2)$$

is negligible in $\log n$.

We define a novel problem in order to investigate the security of the S-Paillier cryptosystem. We denote an element c of $\mathbb{Z}/n^2\mathbb{Z}$ by the unique n-adic representation so that $c = [c]_0 + n[c]_1$, where $0 \le [c]_0, [c]_1 < n$. The RSA approximation (RSAaprx) problem is to find the integer $[r^e]_1$ for given $(n, e) \leftarrow RSA_{public}$ and $[r^e]_0 = r^e \bmod n$. The value $[r^e]_1$ is the first approximation of the n-adic representation of $r^e \bmod n^2 = [r^e]_0 + n[r^e]_1$. A similar problem is discussed for the ESIGN [Oka90].

The RSA approximation (RSAaprx) assumption is as follows: for any probabilistic polynomial time algorithm $A_{RSAaprx}$ the probability

$$Pr_{r \in_R (\mathbb{Z}/n\mathbb{Z})^\times} [(n, e) \leftarrow RSA_{public}, c = r^e \bmod n : A_{RSAaprx}(c) = [r^e]_1] \quad (3)$$

is negligible in $\log n$.

The RSAaprx problem and the S-Paillier cryptosystem are nicely related. Indeed, we prove the following theorem.

Theorem 1. *The encryption function of the S-Paillier cryptosystem is one-way if and only if the RSAaprx assumption holds.*

Proof. Note that we can compute the value $[r^e]_0 = r^e \bmod n$ from the ciphertext $c = r^e(1 + mn) \bmod n^2$. If the RSAaprx assumption is not true, we can find the first approximation $[r^e]_1$ from $[r^e]_0$ and we obtain $r^e \bmod n^2 = [r^e]_0 + n[r^e]_1$. Thus we can break the one-wayness of the S-Paillier cryptosystem by computing $m = k/n, k = c(r^e)^{-1} - 1 \bmod n^2$. On the contrary, assume that there is an algorithm $A_{S-Paillier}^{OW}$, which breaks the one-wayness of the S-Paillier cryptosystem. We will construct an algorithm $A_{RSAaprx}$, which breaks the RSAaprx problem using the algorithm $A_{S-Paillier}^{OW}$. Let $b = a^e \bmod n$ be a random ciphertext of the RSA cryptosystem for (n, e) as the input of the algorithm $A_{RSAaprx}$. The algorithm $A_{RSAaprx}$ works as follows:

1. $A_{RSAaprx}$ generates a random t in $\mathbb{Z}/n\mathbb{Z}$ and computes $c = b + nt$.
2. $A_{RSAaprx}$ runs $A_{S-Paillier}^{OW}(c)$ and obtains the message m of c.
3. $A_{RSAaprx}$ outputs $t - bm \bmod n$.

In step 1, the algorithm $A_{RSAaprx}$ generates a random number $t \in \mathbb{Z}/n\mathbb{Z}$ and computes $c = b + nt$. The distribution of c is equivalent to that of the ciphertext of the S-Paillier cryptosystem. Indeed, the ciphertext of the S-Paillier cryptosystem is represented by $[r^e]_0 + ([r^e]_1 + [r^e]_0 m)n$, and the value $([r^e]_1 + [r^e]_0 m)$ is uniformly distributed over $\mathbb{Z}/n\mathbb{Z}$, because the message m is uniformly distributed over $\mathbb{Z}/n\mathbb{Z}$ and $\gcd([r^e]_0, n) = 1$. Thus, in step 2, the algorithm $A_{RSAaprx}$ finds the message m for input $c = b + nt$. Finally, in step 3, the algorithm $A_{RSAaprx}$ outputs $[a^e]_1$ by computing $[a^e]_1 = t - [a^e]_0 m = t - bm \bmod n$, which is the first approximation of $a^e \bmod n^2$.

It is obvious that the RSAaprx problem can be solved by the oracle that solves the RSA problem. Indeed, for inputs $r^e \bmod n$ and $(e, n) \leftarrow RSA_{public}$, the oracle can find the integer r. Then $[r^e]_1$ can be easily computed by $[r^e]_1 = k/n$ for $k = (r^e \bmod n^2) - r^e \bmod n$. The opposite direction is not trivial. However, we prove the following theorem.

Theorem 2. *The RSAaprx assumption holds if and only if the RSA assumption holds.*

Proof. Let $A_{RSAaprx}$ be an algorithm, which solves the RSAaprx problem with advantage ε in time t. We will construct an algorithm $A_{RSA-LSB}$, which finds the least significant bit of the RSA problem with advantage ε^2 in time $2t+\mathcal{O}((\log n)^3)$ using the algorithm $A_{RSAaprx}$. Let $b_0 = r^e \bmod n$ be a random ciphertext of the RSA cryptosystem for (n, e) as the input of the algorithm $A_{RSA-LSB}$. The algorithm $A_{RSA-LSB}$ works as follows:

1. $A_{RSA-LSB}$ runs $A_{RSAaprx}(b_0)$ and obtains the first approximation b_1 of b_0.
2. $A_{RSA-LSB}$ computes $a_0 = b_0 2^{-e} \bmod n$, runs $A_{RSAaprx}(a_0)$, and obtains the first approximation a_1 of a_0.
3. $A_{RSA-LSB}$ returns 1 as the least significant bit of r, if $a_0 + na_1 = 2^{-e}(b_0 + nb_1) \bmod n^2$ holds, otherwise it returns 0.

In step 1, the algorithm $A_{RSA-LSB}$ obtains the first approximation b_1 of b_0, so that it knows $r^e \bmod n^2$. In step 2, the algorithm $A_{RSA-LSB}$ computes $a_0 = b_0 2^{-e} \bmod n$ and obtains the first approximation a_1 of a_0, so that it knows $a_0 + na_1$. In step 3, the algorithm $A_{RSA-LSB}$ compares the two values $(2^{-1}r)^e \bmod n^2$ and $a_0 + na_1$. Note that $2^{-1} \equiv \frac{n^2+1}{2} \bmod n^2$ and $\frac{n^2+1}{2} = \frac{n+1}{2} + n\frac{n-1}{2}$. Thus if $\gcd(e, n) = 1$ we have the following relations:

$$LSB(r) = 0 \Leftrightarrow (2^{-1}r)^e \bmod n^2 = (r/2)^e \bmod n^2$$
$$\Leftrightarrow a_0 + na_1 = (r/2)^e \bmod n^2,$$
$$LSB(r) = 1 \Leftrightarrow (2^{-1}r)^e \bmod n^2 = \left(\frac{r+n}{2} + n\frac{n-1}{2}\right)^e \bmod n^2$$
$$\Leftrightarrow a_0 + na_1 = \left(\frac{r+n}{2}\right)^e \bmod n^2,$$

where $LSB(r)$ is the least significant bit of r. The probability $\gcd(n, e) = 1$ is upper-bounded by the negligible probability $(1/p + 1/q)$. Thus, in the step 3, we have $2^{-e}(b_0 + nb_1) \bmod n^2 = a_0 + na_1$ if and only if the least significant bit of r is equal to 0.

We estimate the advantage and the time of the algorithm $A_{RSA-LSB}$ in the following. In step 1 and step 2 the algorithm $A_{RSAaprx}$ is used as an oracle, and in step 2 and step 3 two modular exponentiations are computed. The advantage and the time of the algorithm $A_{RSA-LSB}$ are ε^2 and $2t + \mathcal{O}((\log n)^3)$, respectively. Next, Fishlin and Schnorr proved that the RSA problem is solved in time $\mathcal{O}((\log n)^2\varepsilon^{-2}t + (\log n)^2\varepsilon^{-6})$ using an oracle that predicts the least significant bit with advantage ε and in time t [FS00]. Thus the algorithm $A_{RSA-LSB}$ solves the RSA problem in time $\mathcal{O}((\log n)^2\varepsilon^{-4}t + (\log n)^5\varepsilon^{-4} + (\log n)^2\varepsilon^{-12})$. When we choose ε^{-1} as the polynomial of $\log n$, the time becomes the polynomial time in $\log n$. Thus we have proven the theorem.

From theorem 1 and theorem 2 we have proven that the encryption function of the S-Paillier cryptosystem is one-way if and only if the standard RSA assumption holds.

2.2   Semantic Security of the S-Paillier Cryptosystem

Let c be the ciphertext of either the message m_0 or m_1. Loosely speaking, if the cryptosystem is semantically secure, any adversary can not distinguish whether the ciphertext c is the encryption of m_0 or m_1 with more than negligible probability. Several public-key cryptosystems have been proven semantically secure under a standard model [OU98], [CS98], [Pai99], [Poi99]. The reduced number-theoretic problems are not computational problems but decisional problems, e.g. the decisional p-subgroup problem, the decisional Diffie-Hellman problem, the decisional n-residue problem, and the decisional dependent-RSA problem. The difficulties of these decisional problems have not been studied well. Then a new number-theoretic problem, the so called Gap problem, has been proposed [OP01]. The Gap problem is a problem to solve the computational problem with the help of its decisional problem. Several fundamental security problems can be reduced to the Gap problem. To investigate the relation between the computational problem and its decisional problem is an important problem.

Catalano et al. proved that the semantic security of the S-Paillier cryptosystem is as hard as the decisional small e-root problem (D-SR) problem [CGHN01]. In this section we study how to relate the D-SR problem with the C-SR problem. We can prove the following theorem:

Theorem 3. *Let $(n, e) \leftarrow RSA_{public}$ and $c = r^e \bmod n^2 (0 \leq r < n)$ be the inputs of the computational small e-root problem. An adversary, which breaks the decisional small e-root problem, can compute the least significant bit of r. If the least significant bits of r are zero, the next bit after the zeros can be compute by the adversary.*

Proof. Let $A_{D\text{-}SR}$ be an adversary, which solves the D-SR problem. We can assume that with non-negligible probability the adversary $A_{D\text{-}SR}$ answers $A_{D\text{-}SR}(y) = 1$ if y is the small e-root residue, and it answers $A_{D\text{-}SR}(y) = 0$ otherwise. We will construct an algorithm A_{LSB}, which computes the least significant bit of r using algorithm $A_{D\text{-}SR}$. The algorithm A_{LSB} works as follows:

1. A_{LSB} computes $y = 2^{-e}c^e \bmod n^2$.
2. A_{LSB} runs algorithm $A_{D\text{-}SR}(y)$, and obtains $b = A_{D\text{-}SR}(y)$
3. A_{LSB} returns $\bar{b}$.

In step 1 the integer y is computed as $y = 2^{-e}c \bmod n^2$. As we showed in the proof of theorem 2, the least significant bit of r is 0 if and only if $2^{-1}r \bmod n^2 = r/2$, and it is 1 if and only if $2^{-1}r \bmod n^2 = \frac{r+n}{2} + \frac{n-1}{2}n$. Therefore, the least significant bit of r is 0 if and only if y is the small e-root residue, and it is 1 if and only if y is not the small e-root residue. Thus, the output $\bar{b}$ of the A_{LSB} is the least significant bit of r. If the k least significant bits r are zero, $(r/2^k)^e = 2^{-ke}r^e \bmod n^2$ is the small e-root residue. We can detect the $(k+1)$-th bit of r using the above algorithm.

The S-Paillier cryptosystem encrypts a message m by $c = r^e(1+mn) \bmod n^2$ where $r \in (\mathbb{Z}/n\mathbb{Z})^\times$. By the result of Catalano et al., the adversary $A_{D\text{-}SR}$, which breaks the D-SR problem, can break the semantic security of the S-Paillier cryptosystem [CGHN01]. Then, we can obtain the $r^e \bmod n^2$. With the theorem the least significant bit of the nonce r can be computed by invoking $A_{D\text{-}SR}$. Thus the least significant bit of r can be computed. If the k-th least significant bits of r is zero, then we learn the $(k+1)$-th bit of r. Thus, we have proven the following corollary.

Corollary 1. *An adversary, which breaks the decisional small e-root problem, can compute the least significant bit of the nonce r of the S-Paillier cryptosystem. If the least significant bits of r are zero, then the adversary can compute the next bit after the zeros.*

This observation is interesting because the least significant bits of the nonce r is the hard core bit of the ciphertext $c \bmod n$.

3 General Conversion of the RSA Cryptosystem

In this section we generalize the encryption mechanism of the S-Paillier cryptosystem to a general RSA-type encryption scheme. We discuss the one-way security and the semantic security of the general RSA-type encryption scheme. The scheme is also related to the dependent RSA cryptosystem proposed by Pointcheval [Poi99]. Moreover, we propose a novel cryptosystem based on the most significant bits zero problem.

The S-Paillier cryptosystem encrypts a message m by $c = r^e(1+mn) \bmod n^2$ where $(n, e) \leftarrow RSA_{public}$ and r is a random integer in $(\mathbb{Z}/n\mathbb{Z})^\times$. If we represent the ciphertext c as the n-adic expansion $c = [c]_0 + [c]_1 n$, where $0 \le [c]_0, [c]_1 < n$, we have the following relationship:

$$[c]_0 = r^e \bmod n, \quad [c]_1 = [r^e]_1 + mr^e \bmod n. \tag{4}$$

The message is randomized by the value $[r^e]_1$. Let f be a function $f : r \to [r^e]_1$ for $r \in (\mathbb{Z}/n\mathbb{Z})^\times$. We proved that computing the value $f(r)$ from $r^e \bmod n$ is as hard as breaking the RSA problem.

Our proposed scheme uses a general one-way function $f : \mathbb{Z}/n\mathbb{Z} \to \mathbb{Z}/n\mathbb{Z}$ instead of the function $r \to [r^e]_1$. The proposed scheme is as follow:

Key generation: Let $(n, e) \leftarrow_R RSA_{public}$. The integer d is computed by $ed = 1 \bmod \varphi(n)$. Then (n, e) is the public key and d is the secret key. Moreover, we use a one-way function $f : \mathbb{Z}/n\mathbb{Z} \to \mathbb{Z}/n\mathbb{Z}$ as a system parameter.
Encryption: Let $m \in \mathbb{Z}/n\mathbb{Z}$ be a message. We generate a random integer $r \in (\mathbb{Z}/n\mathbb{Z})^\times$ and encrypt the message m by $c_0 = r^e \bmod n$ and $c_1 = f(r) + mc_0 \bmod n$. The ciphertext is (c_0, c_1).
Decryption: At first r is recovered by $r = c_0^d \bmod n$. Then the message m is decrypted by $m = (c_1 - f(r))c_0^{-1} \bmod n$.

We call this scheme the G-RSA cryptosystem in this paper and define several assumptions of this G-RSA cryptosystem. Let OW be a class of the one-way function $\mathbb{Z}/n\mathbb{Z} \to \mathbb{Z}/n\mathbb{Z}$. The one-wayness assumption of the G-RSA cryptosystem is that, for any probabilistic polynomial time algorithm $A_{G\text{-}RSA}^{OW}$, the probability

$$Pr_{m \in_R (\mathbb{Z}/n\mathbb{Z})}[(n,e) \leftarrow RSA_{public}, f \leftarrow \mathsf{OW}, r \leftarrow_R (\mathbb{Z}/n\mathbb{Z})^{\times},$$
$$c_0 = r^e \bmod n, c_1 = f(r) + mc_0 \bmod n : A_{G\text{-}RSA}^{OW}((c_0, c_1)) = m]$$

is negligible in $\log n$. A semantic security adversary $A_{G\text{-}RSA}^{SS}$ against the G-RSA cryptosystem consists of the find stage $A_{G\text{-}RSA}^{SS1}$ and the guess stage $A_{G\text{-}RSA}^{SS2}$. The semantic security of the G-RSA cryptosystem is that, for any probabilistic polynomial time algorithm $A_{G\text{-}RSA}^{SS}$, the probability

$$2Pr \ [(n,e) \leftarrow RSA_{public}, f \leftarrow \mathsf{OW}, (m_0, m_1, st) \leftarrow A_{G\text{-}RSA}^{SS1}(e, n),$$
$$b \leftarrow \{0,1\}, r \leftarrow_R (\mathbb{Z}/n\mathbb{Z})^{\times}, c_0 = r^e \bmod n,$$
$$c_1 = f(r) + m_b c_0 \bmod n^2 : A_{G\text{-}RSA}^{SS2}((c_0, c_1), m_0, m_1, st) = b] - 1$$

is negligible in $\log n$.

3.1 Security of the G-RSA Cryptosystem

We define the following two problems in order to investigate the security of the G-RSA cryptosystem based on a one-way function $f : \mathbb{Z}/n\mathbb{Z} \to \mathbb{Z}/n\mathbb{Z}$. The computational RSA + one-way function (C-RSA+OW) problem is to compute the value $f(r)$ for a given RSA public-key (e, n) and a ciphertext $r^e \bmod n$. The C-RSA+OW assumption is as follows: for any probabilistic polynomial time algorithm $A_{C\text{-}RSA+OW}$, the probability

$$Pr_{r \in_R (\mathbb{Z}/n\mathbb{Z})^{\times}} \ [(n,e) \leftarrow RSA_{public}, f \leftarrow \mathsf{OW},$$
$$c = r^e \bmod n^2 : A_{C\text{-}RSA+OW}(c) = f(r)]$$

is negligible in $\log n$. The decisional version of the C-RSA+OW problem is to distinguish whether an element $(x, y) \in \mathbb{Z}/n\mathbb{Z} \times \mathbb{Z}/n\mathbb{Z}$ comes from the distribution $(r^e \bmod n, f(r))$ for $r \in (\mathbb{Z}/n\mathbb{Z})^{\times}$. The decisional RSA + one-way function (D-RSA+OW) assumption is defined as follows: for any probabilistic polynomial time algorithm $A_{D\text{-}RSA+OW}$, the probability of distinguishing the two distributions

$$|Pr[(x, y) \leftarrow \mathbb{Z}/n\mathbb{Z} \times \mathbb{Z}/n\mathbb{Z} : A_{D\text{-}RSA+OW}(x, y) = 1] - Pr[r \leftarrow (\mathbb{Z}/n\mathbb{Z})^{\times},$$
$$x = r^e \bmod n, f \leftarrow \mathsf{OW}, y = f(r) : A_{D\text{-}RSA+OW}(x, y) = 1]|$$

is negligible in $\log n$.

The one-way security and the semantic security are as intractable as the C-RSA+OW problem and the D-RSA+OW problem, respectively. These properties can be proved by applying the same techniques used in theorem 1 and for the S-Paillier cryptosystem [CGHN01], respectively. The statements are as follows:

Theorem 4. *The encryption function of the G-RSA cryptosystem is one-way if and only if the C-RSA+OW assumption holds.*

Theorem 5. *The G-RSA cryptosystem is semantically secure if and only if the D-RSA+OW assumption holds.*

We can recognize that the G-RSA cryptosystem is a conversion technique, which enhances the security of the RSA cryptosystem to be semantically secure. If we find a one-way function, whose C-RSA+OW problem and D-RSA+OW problem are intractable, then we can construct a semantically secure encryption scheme. The S-Paillier cryptosystem is an example of the G-RSA cryptosystem, whose security is based on the RSA+RSAaprx problem.

To find another one-way function for the G-RSA cryptosystem is a quite difficult problem. Consider the function $f : r \to r^2 \bmod n$. Computing $f(r)$ for a given $r^e \bmod n$ is as hard as the RSA problem, because $r = (r^e)^x (r^2)^y \bmod n$ holds for integers x, y such that $ex + 2y = 1$. Therefore this C-RSA+OW problem of the function f is as intractable as the RSA problem. However, the distribution (r^e, r^2) can be distinguished from the random distribution using the same gcd computation, and this D-RSA+OW problem is easily broken.

3.2   Relation to the Pointcheval Cryptosystem

The Pointcheval public-key cryptosystem encrypts a message m by $c_0 = r^e \bmod n$ and $c_1 = m(r + 1)^e \bmod n$ [Poi99]. The one-way security of the Pointcheval scheme is based on the difficulty of computing $(r + 1)^e \bmod n$ for given $(n, e) \leftarrow RSA_{public}$ and $r^e \bmod n$, which is called the computational dependent RSA (C-DpdRSA) problem. The semantic security of the Pointcheval scheme is as hard as to distinguishes the distribution $(r^e \bmod n, (r+1)^e \bmod n)$ from the uniform distribution, which is called the decisional dependent RSA (D-DpdRSA) problem. The one-way function that the Pointcheval scheme uses is $r \to (r + 1)^e \bmod n$ for $r \in (\mathbb{Z}/n\mathbb{Z})^\times$.

We can generalize the Pointcheval scheme using a general one-way function $f : \mathbb{Z}/n\mathbb{Z} \to \mathbb{Z}/n\mathbb{Z}$ instead of the function $r \to (r+1)^e \bmod n$. The encryption is carried out as follows:

$$c_0 = r^e \bmod n, \quad c_1 = mf(r) \bmod n. \tag{5}$$

The difference to the G-RSA cryptosystem is to mask the message m using $c_1 = mf(r) \bmod n$ instead of $c_1 = f(r) + mc_0 \bmod n$. In the same manner as in the previous section, we can prove that the one-way security and semantic security of the generalized Pointcheval scheme is as intractable as solving the C-RSA+OW problem and the D-RSA+OW problem, respectively. Our generalized Pointcheval cryptosystem is another conversion technique, which depends on the same security requirements as the G-RSA cryptosystem.

We can also choose different conversion forms like $c_1 = m(f(r) + c_0) \bmod n$ or $c_1 = f(r) + m \bmod n$, whose one-way and semantic security are equivalent to the

C-RSA+OW and the D-RSA+OW, respectively. Let g be a function, which can efficiently compute both $c_1 = g(m, f(r), c_0)$ and $m = g^{-1}(c_1, f(r), c_0)$. Then we can generate the secure conversion analogue to the G-RSA cryptosystem using the function g.

If we apply the one-way function of the S-Paillier cryptosystem to the Point-cheval conversion, the converted encryption scheme encrypts a message m by $c_0 = r^e \bmod n$ and $c_1 = m[r^e]_1 \bmod n$. This encryption method is also observed by Catalano et al. [CGHN01].

3.3 A New One-Way Function

We propose a new one-way function, which is provably secure in the sense of the RSA+OW problem. We prove that the C-RSA+OW problem of the proposed one-way function is as intractable as the standard RSA problem. We prove that an adversary, which breaks the D-CRSA+OW problem of the proposed one-way function, can break the least significant bits of the C-RSA+OW problem.

We explain our new one-way function in the following. Let r be a k-bit random integer in $(\mathbb{Z}/n\mathbb{Z})^{\times}$. The binary presentation of r is $r = r_0 2^0 + r_1 2^1 + ... + r_{k-1} 2^{k-1}$, where $r_{k-1} = 1$. Denote by $MSB_l(r)$ the l-bit upper part of r such that $r_{k-l} 2^{k-l} + r_{k-l+1} 2^{k-l+1} + ... + r_{k-1} 2^{k-1}$. The proposed one-way function is defined by

$$f^{e,n}_{MSBZ(l)}(r) = (r - MSB_l(r))^e \bmod n, \tag{6}$$

where l is large enough. The l most significant bits of r are chosen as zeros by $r - MSB_l(r)$. We call the one-way function the RSA most significant bits zero (MSBZ) function. Micali and Schnorr proposed a similar one-way function, which is used for a parallel generation of a pseudo random number generator [MS88].

The computational RSA+MSBZ (C-RSA+MSBZ) problem is to compute $f^{e,n}_{MSBZ(l)}(r)$ for a given $r^e \bmod n$, where r is a random integer r in $(\mathbb{Z}/n\mathbb{Z})^{\times}$. The C-RSA+MSBZ assumption is that, for any probabilistic polynomial time algorithm $A_{C\text{-}RSA+MSBZ}$, the probability

$$Pr_{r \in_R (\mathbb{Z}/n\mathbb{Z})^{\times}} \ [(n, e) \leftarrow RSA_{public}, c = r^e \bmod n :$$
$$A_{C\text{-}RSA+MSBZ}(c) = f^{e,n}_{MSBZ(l)}(r)]$$

is negligible in $\log n$.

The RSA+MSBZ problem is different from the DpdRSA problem by the Pointcheval cryptosystem [Poi99], because $MSB_l(r)$ of the $f^{e,n}_{MSBZ(l)}(r) = (r - MSB_l(r))^e \bmod n$ is unknown. We have no known dependences between $r^e \bmod n$ and $(r - MSB_l(r))^e \bmod n$. A possible attack to break the C-RSA+MSBZ problem is to use the Coppersmith algorithm [Cop96]. The Coppersmith algorithm can find the integer r from two values $r^e \bmod n$ and $(r + t)^e \bmod n$, where t is a unknown random integer with $|t| < n^{1/e^2}$. Therefore, if l is small for small exponent e, the Coppersmith attack finds the r. When n is 1024 bits, we have to choose $l > 114$ for $e = 3$ and $l > 21$ for $e = 7$. The other attack is the low exponent attack with known related messages from Coppersmith et al. [CFPR96]. In this case an attacker computes $\gcd(x^e, (x + t)^e)$ over the polynomial ring $\mathbb{Z}/n\mathbb{Z}[x]$ for all possible t. If l is small, the attacker can find the r. Therefore, we have to make l enough large. For example, we recommend $l = 160$ for a 1024-bit RSA modulus n.

The decisional RSA+MSBZ (D-RSA+MSBZ) problem is to distinguish

$$(r^e \bmod n, f_{MSBZ(l)}(r))$$

from the uniform distribution. The D-RSA+MSBZ assumption is defined as follows: for any probabilistic polynomial time algorithm $A_{D\text{-}RSA+MSBZ}$, the probability to distinguish the two distributions

$$|Pr[x, y \leftarrow \mathbb{Z}/n\mathbb{Z} \times \mathbb{Z}/n\mathbb{Z} : A_{D\text{-}RSA+MSBZ}(x, y) = 1] - Pr[r \leftarrow (\mathbb{Z}/n\mathbb{Z})^\times,$$
$$c = r^e \bmod n, z = f_{MSBZ(l)}^{e,n}(r) \bmod n : A_{D\text{-}RSA+MSBZ}(c, z) = 1]|$$

is negligible in $\log n$. We prove the following theorem:

Theorem 6. *The C-RSA+MSBZ assumption holds if and only if the RSA assumption holds*

Proof. The proof of the theorem is similar to that of theorem 2. We compare $2^{-e} f_{MSBZ(l)}^{e,n}(r) \bmod n$ with $f_{MSBZ(l)}^{e,n}(2^{-1}r \bmod n)$. Let $A_{C\text{-}RSA+MSBZ}$ be an adversary, which breaks the C-RSA+MSBZ assumption. Then we construct an algorithm $A_{RSA\text{-}LSB}$, which breaks the least significant bit of the RSA problem using $A_{C\text{-}RSA+MSBZ}$. Let $y = r^e \bmod n$ be a random input for the RSA problem. At first, the algorithm $A_{RSA\text{-}LSB}$ runs the adversary $A_{C\text{-}RSA+MSBZ}$ and obtains $f_{MSBZ(l)}^{e,n}(r)$. Second, it computes $w = y2^{-e} \bmod n$, runs the adversary $A_{C\text{-}RSA+MSBZ}$, and obtains $f_{MSBZ(l)}^{e,n}(2^{-1}r \bmod n)$. Finally, the algorithm $A_{RSA\text{-}LSB}$ outputs 0 if $2^{-e} f_{MSBZ(l)}^{e,n}(r) \bmod n = f_{MSBZ(l)}^{e,n}(2^{-1}r \bmod n)$ holds, and it outputs 1 otherwise.

The least significant bit of r (we denote it by $LSB(r)$) is zero if and only if $r/2 = 2^{-1}r \bmod n$. The $LSB(r)$ is one if and only if $(r+n)/2 = 2^{-1}r \bmod n$. Let $r' = r - MSB_l(r)$, so that $r'^e \bmod n = f_{MSBZ(l)}^{e,n}(r)$ holds. Note that $LSB(r') = LSB(r)$ and $MSB_l(a/2) = MSB_l(a)/2$ for all at least $(l + 2)$-bit integers a. Here, for $LSB(r) = 0$, we have

$$2^{-1}r' \bmod n = r'/2 = (r - MSB_l(r))/2 = r/2 - MSB_l(r/2). \tag{7}$$

On the contrary, for $LSB(r) = 1$, we have $2^{-1}r' \bmod n = (r - MSB_l(r) + n)/2$, which is not equivalent to $2^{-1}r \bmod n - MSB_l(2^{-1}r \bmod n) = (r + n)/2 - MSB_l((r + n)/2)$, because of $MSB_l(r) \neq MSB_l(r + n)$. Therefore, the least significant bit of r is zero if and only if $2^{-e} f_{MSBZ(l)}^{e,n}(r) \bmod n = f_{MSBZ(l)}^{e,n}(w)$ holds.

Let ε and t be the advantage and the time of the adversary $A_{C\text{-}RSA+MSBZ}$, respectively. Then the advantage and time of algorithm $A_{RSA\text{-}LSB}$ are ε^2 and $2t + \mathcal{O}((\log n)^3)$, respectively. By the result of [FS00], the algorithm $A_{RSA\text{-}LSB}$ can solve the RSA problem. Thus we have proven the theorem.

There is a relation between the D-RSA+MSBZ problem and C-RSA+MSBZ problem. It is similar with that of the D-RSAaprx problem and the C-RSAaprx problem. We prove the following theorem.

Theorem 7. *Let $(n,e) \leftarrow RSA_{public}$ and $c = r^e \bmod n$ be the input of the computational RSA+MSBZ problem. An adversary, which breaks the decisional RSA+MSBZ problem, can compute the least significant bit of r. If the least significant bits of r are zero, the next bit after the zeros can be computed by the adversary.*

Proof. The proof of the theorem is similar to that of theorem 3. Let $A_{D\text{-}RSA+MSBZ}$ be an adversary, which solves the D-RSA+MSBZ problem. We can assume that, with non-negligible probability, the adversary $A_{D\text{-}RSA+MSBZ}$ answers $A_{D\text{-}RSA+MSBZ}(y) = 1$ if y comes from the distribution $(x^e \bmod n, f_{MSBZ(l)}^{e,n}(x))$ for an integer $x \in (\mathbb{Z}/n\mathbb{Z})^{\times}$, and it answers $A_{D\text{-}RSA+MSBZ}(y) = 0$ otherwise. We will construct an algorithm A_{LSB}, which computes the least significant bit of r using algorithm $A_{D\text{-}RSA+MSBZ}$. At first the algorithm A_{LSB} computes $y = (2^{-e}c \bmod n, 2^{-e}f_{MSBZ(l)}^{e,n}(r) \bmod n)$. Second, A_{LSB} runs algorithm $A_{D\text{-}RSA+MSBZ}(y)$ and obtains $b = A_{D\text{-}RSA+MSBZ}(y)$. Finally, A_{LSB} returns b. As we showed in the proof of theorem 6, the least significant bit of r is 0 if and only if y comes from the distribution $(x^e \bmod n, f_{MSBZ(l)}^{e,n}(x))$ for an integer $x \in (\mathbb{Z}/n\mathbb{Z})^{\times}$. If the k least significant bits of r are zero, $(r/2^k)^e = 2^{-ke}r^e \bmod n$ is the image of $f_{MSBZ(l)}^{e,n}(r/2^k)$. We can detect the $(k+1)$-th bit of r using the above algorithm.

By these theorems, the G-RSA cryptosystem using the one-way function $f_{MSBZ(l)}^{e,n}$ has similar security conditions as the S-Paillier cryptosystem. An adversary, which breaks the D-RSA+MSBZ problem, can compute the least significant bits of the nonce of the G-RSA cryptosystem with $f_{MSBZ(l)}^{e,n}$.

3.4   Comparison

We compare the public-key cryptosystems discussed in this paper, i.e., the Paillier cryptosystem, the S-Paillier cryptosystem, the Pointcheval cryptosystem, and the proposed cryptosystem. The security and the efficiency of these cryptosystems are compared. For the efficiency we count the number of modular exponentiations in the encryption and decryption process, because the computation of the modular exponents is dominant for the efficiency. Denote by $ME(k)$ a modular exponentiation modulo k. We assume that these cryptosystems use the same length RSA keys n. In table 1 we indicate the comparison.

The Paillier cryptosystem encrypts a message m by $c = g^m r^n \bmod n^2$ and decrypts it by $m = L(c^{\varphi(n)} \bmod n^2)/L(g^{\varphi(n)} \bmod n^2)$, where $L(u) = (u-1)/n$. The encryption and the decryption of the Paillier cryptosystem require two $ME(n^2)$ and two $ME(n^2)$, respectively. If we use the key $g = 1 + n$, the encryption requires only one $ME(n^2)$. If we precompute the g, the decryption needs only one $ME(n^2)$. The one-way security and the semantic security are as hard as the C-CR problem and the D-CR problem, respectively.

Table 1. Comparison of security and efficiency among several schemes

	Paillier	S-Paillier	Pointcheval	Proposed scheme
One-wayness	C-CR	**RSA**	C-DpdRSA	**RSA**
Semantic security	D-CR	**D-RSA+RSAaprx**	D-DpdRSA	**D-RSA−MSBZ**
Encryption	$1\ ME(n^2)$	$1\ ME(n^2)$	$2\ ME(n)$	$\mathbf{2\ ME(n)}$
Decryption	$1\ ME(n^2)$	$1\ ME(n^2) + 1\ ME(n)$	$2\ ME(n)$	$\mathbf{2\ ME(n)}$

The S-Paillier cryptosystem requires one $ME(n^2)$ for the encryption $c = r^e(1 + nm) \bmod n^2$, and one $ME(n)$ and one $ME(n^2)$ for the decryption $m = L(cr^{-e} \bmod n^2)$ and $r = c^d \bmod n$. Note that a small encryption exponent e can be used. We proved that the one-way security and the semantic security are as hard as the RSA problem and the D-RSA+RSAaprx problem, respectively. We also proved that an adversary, which breaks the semantic security, can compute the least significant bits of the nonce r.

The Pointcheval cryptosystem requires two $ME(n)$ for the encryption $c_0 = r^e \bmod n$ and $c_1 = m(r + 1)^e \bmod n$, and two $ME(n)$ for the decryption $m = c_1(r + 1)^{-e} \bmod n$ and $r = c_0^d \bmod n$. Note that a small exponent e is not secure for this scheme because of the message related attack and e must be at least 32 bits [CFPR96]. The one-way security and the semantic security are as hard as the C-DpdRSA problem and the D-DpdRSA problem, respectively.

The proposed cryptosystem encrypts a message m by $c_0 = r^e \bmod n, c_1 = f_{MSBZ(l)}^{e,n}(r) - mc_0 \bmod n$ and decrypts it by $m = (c_1 - f_{MSBZ(l)}^{e,n}(r))c_0^{-1} \bmod n, r = c_0^d \bmod n$, where $f_{MSBZ(l)}^{e,n}(r) = (r - MSBZ_l(r))^e \bmod n$. Therefore, the encryption and the decryption of the proposed cryptosystem require two $ME(n)$ and two $ME(n)$, respectively. The computation time of the function $f_{MSBZ(l)}^{e,n}(r)$ is about 4 times faster than that of the S-Paillier cryptosystem $r^e \bmod n^2$. Thus the encryption/decryption of the proposed cryptosystem are more efficient than those of the S-Paillier cryptosystem. Because a small exponent key e can be used for a enough large l, the proposed cryptosystem is more efficient than the Pointcheval cryptosystem. We proved that the one-way security and the semantic security are as hard as the RSA problem and the D-RSA+MSBZ problem, respectively. An adversary, which breaks the semantic security, can break the least significant bits of the nonce r. The proposed cryptosystem has the similar security properties as the S-Paillier cryptosystem.

Acknowledgments

We would like to thank Holger Vogt for his valuable comments, and the anonymous referees of PKC 2002 for their helpful comments.

References

BDPR98. M. Bellare, A. Desai, D. Pointcheval, and P. Rogaway, Relations among notions of security for public-key encryption schemes," CRYPTO'98, LNCS 1462, (1998), pp.26-45.

CGH01. D. Catalano, R. Gennaro, and N. Howgraw-Graham; "The bit security of Paillier's encryption scheme and its applications," Eurocrypt 2001, LNCS 2045, pp.229-243, 2001.

CGHN01. D. Catalano, R. Gennaro, N. Howgrave-Graham, and P. Nguyen; "Paillier's cryptosystem revisited," to appear in the ACM conference on Computer and Communication Security, 2001.

Cop96. D. Coppersmith, "Finding a small root of a univariate modular equation," EUROCRYPT '96, LNCS 1070, pp.155–165, 1996.

CFPR96. D. Coppersmith, M. Franklin, J. Patarin, M. Reiter, "Low-exponent RSA with related messages," EUROCRYPT '96, LNCS 1070, (1996), pp.1-9.

CS98. R. Cramer and V. Shoup, "A practical public key cryptosystem provably secure against adaptive chosen ciphertext attack," CRYPTO'98, LNCS 1462, pp.13-25, 1998.

CS01. R. Cramer and V. Shoup, "Universal hash proofs and a paradigm for adaptive chosen ciphertext secure public-Key encryption ," Cryptology ePrint Archive, IACR, http://eprint.iacr.org/, 2001.

DJ01. I. Damgård and M. Jurik; "A generalization, a simplification and some applications of Paillier's probabilistic public-Key system," PKC 2001, LNCS 1992, pp.119-136, 2001.

FS00. R. Fischlin and C.P. Schnorr; "Stronger security proofs for RSA and Rabin bits," Journal of Cryptology, 13 (2), pp.221-244, 2000.

GM84. S. Goldwasser and S. Micali; "Probabilistic encryption," Journal of Computer and System Science, Vol.28, No.2, pp.270-299, 1984.

MS88. S. Micali and C. Schnorr, "Efficient, perfect random number generators," Crypto'88, LNCS 403, pp.173-199, 1988.

Oka90. T. Okamoto; "A fast signature scheme based on congruential polynomial operations," IEEE Transactions on Information Theory, IT-36, pp.47-53, 1990.

OP01. T. Okamoto and D. Pointcheval, "The Gap-Problems: a new class of problems for the security of cryptographic schemes," PKC 2001, LNCS 1992, pp.104-118, 2001.

OU98. T. Okamoto and S. Uchiyama; "A new public-key cryptosystem as secure as factoring," Eurocrypt'98, LNCS 1403, pp.308-318, 1998.

Pai99. P. Paillier; "Public-key cryptosystems based on composite degree residuosity classes," Eurocrypt'99, LNCS 1592, pp.223-238, 1999.

Poi99. D. Pointcheval, "New public key cryptosystems based on the dependent-RSA problems," Eurocryt'99, LNCS 1592, pp. 239-254, 1999.

Tak97. T. Takagi, "Fast RSA-type cryptosystems using n-adic expansion," CRYPTO '97, LNCS 1294, pp.372-384, 1997.

Optimal Chosen-Ciphertext Secure Encryption of Arbitrary-Length Messages

Jean-Sébastien Coron[1], Helena Handschuh[1], Marc Joye[2], Pascal Paillier[1],
David Pointcheval[3], and Christophe Tymen[1,3]

[1] Gemplus Card International
34 rue Guynemer, 92447 Issy-les-Moulineaux, France
{jean-sebastien.coron,helena.handschuh}@gemplus.com
{pascal.paillier,christophe.tymen}@gemplus.com
[2] Gemplus Card International
Parc d'Activités de Gémenos, B.P. 100, 13881 Gémenos Cedex, France
marc.joye@gemplus.com – http://www.geocities.com/MarcJoye/
[3] École Normale Supérieure, Computer Science Department
45 rue d'Ulm, 75230 Paris Cedex 05, France
david.pointcheval@ens.fr – http://www.di.ens.fr/~pointche/

Abstract. This paper considers arbitrary-length chosen-ciphertext secure asymmetric encryption, thus addressing what is actually needed for a practical usage of strong public-key cryptography in the real world. We put forward two generic constructions, GEM-1 and GEM-2 which apply to explicit *fixed-length* weakly secure primitives and provide a strongly secure (IND-CCA2) public-key encryption scheme for messages of unfixed length (typically computer files). Our techniques optimally combine a single call to any one-way trapdoor function with repeated encryptions through some weak block-cipher (a simple XOR is fine) and hash functions of fixed-length input so that a minimal number of calls to these functions is needed. Our encryption/decryption throughputs are comparable to the ones of standard methods (asymmetric encryption of a session key + symmetric encryption with multiple modes). In our case, however, we *formally* prove that our designs are secure in the strongest sense and provide complete security reductions holding in the random oracle model.

1 Introduction

A real-life usage of public-key encryption requires three distinct ideal properties. *Security* is a major concern: a cryptosystem should be secure against any attack of any kind, should the attack be realistic in the context of use or only theoretical. *Performance* has to be risen to upmost levels to guarantee high speed encryption *and* decryption rates in communication protocols and real time applications. At last, *design simplicity* is desirable to save time and efforts in software or hardware developments, increase modularity and reusability, and facilitate public understanding and scrutiny.

D. Naccache and P. Paillier (Eds.): PKC 2002, LNCS 2274, pp. 17–33, 2002.

Designing an encryption scheme which meets these criteria is quite a challenging work, but methodologies and tools exist, at least for the first property. Our knowledge of security features inherent to cryptographic objects and of the relations connecting them has intensively evolved lately, driving us to a growing range of powerful generic constructions, both simple and provably secure [FO99a,FO99b,Poi00,OP01a]. Among these constructions, Okamoto and Pointcheval's REACT [OP01a] is certainly the one that offers most flexibility: unlike Bellare and Rogaway's long-lived OAEP [BR95], REACT applies to any trapdoor function, *i.e.* any asymmetric encryption scheme presenting such a weak level of security as being OW-PCA (see further), to provide a cryptosystem of strongest level IND-CCA2 in the random oracle model.

1.1   Our Results

This paper considers arbitrary-length chosen-ciphertext secure (IND-CCA2) asymmetric encryption schemes, thus addressing what is actually needed for a practical usage of strong public-key cryptography in the real world. We propose two generic constructions which apply to fixed-length weakly secure primitives and provide a strongly secure public-key cryptosystem for messages of unfixed length, such as computers files or communication streams. In our schemes, the encryption and decryption processes may start and progress without even knowing the overall input blocklength; they also may stop at any time. Besides, our designs are one-pass only, meaning that each message block will be treated exactly once.

Our techniques combine a *single* call to any one-way trapdoor function with repeated encryptions through some weak block-cipher (a simple XOR will do) and hash functions of fixed-length input. Contrarily to previous generic conversions, each message block will require only *one* call to a hash function so that the overall execution cost for an n-block plaintext is exactly 1 call to the one-way trapdoor encryption, followed by n calls to the block-cipher and $n + 1$ (or $n + 2$) calls to a hash function[1]. Besides, the storage of the whole plaintext file in memory is completely unnecessary and encryption/decryption procedures use a memory buffer of only ~ 3 blocks, thus allowing on-the-fly treatments of communication streams. We believe that our schemes are the first that combine these practical properties simultaneously while keeping total genericity.

The first construction applies to any OW-PCA probabilistic trapdoor function and incorporates two extra fields of fixed length in the ciphertext, one at each end. The second construction we give only works for deterministic OW trapdoor functions but adds only one extra field at the end of the ciphertext. Our performances are similar to the ones of standard methods, which usually encrypt some random session key under an asymmetric scheme and then feed that key into some block-cipher running under an appropriate multiple mode. In our case, however, we can formally prove that our designs are secure in the strongest sense IND-CCA2. Indeed, we provide complete security reductions holding in the random oracle model.

---

[1] an extra hash call is needed for message authenticity.

1.2   Outline of the Paper

The paper is organized as follows. Section 2 briefly recalls security notions for encryption schemes in both symmetric and asymmetric settings. We also review Okamoto and Pointcheval's plaintext checking attacks in connection with computational gap problems [OP01b]. Then, Sections 3.1 and 3.2 introduce our new generic conversions, GEM-1 and GEM-2, whose reduction proofs are given in the extended version of this paper [CHJ$^+$01]. Furthermore, typical examples of practical usage of these systems are given in Section 4. We conclude by giving some possible extensions of our work in Section 5.

2   Security Notions for Encryption Schemes

2.1   Asymmetric Encryption

We now introduce a few standard notations. An asymmetric encryption scheme is a triple of algorithms $(\mathcal{K}, \mathcal{E}, \mathcal{D})$ where

- $\mathcal{K}$ is a probabilistic key generation algorithm which returns random pairs of secret and public keys (sk, pk) depending on the security parameter κ,
- $\mathcal{E}$ is a probabilistic encryption algorithm which takes on input a public key pk and a plaintext $m \in \mathcal{M}$, runs on a random tape $u \in \mathcal{U}$ and returns a ciphertext c,
- $\mathcal{D}$ is a deterministic decryption algorithm which takes on input a secret key sk, a ciphertext c and returns the corresponding plaintext m or the symbol $\perp$. We require that if $(sk, pk) \leftarrow \mathcal{K}$, then $\mathcal{D}_{sk}(\mathcal{E}_{pk}(m, u)) = m$ for all $(m, u) \in \mathcal{M} \times \mathcal{U}$.

Adversarial Goals

ONE-WAYNESS. The first secrecy notion required from an encryption scheme is its *one-wayness*, meaning that one should not be able to recover a plaintext given its encryption. More formally, the scheme is said to be (τ, ε)-OW if for any adversary $\mathcal{A}$ with running time bounded by τ, the probability that $\mathcal{A}$ inverts $\mathcal{E}$ is less than ε:

$$\mathsf{Succ}^{\mathsf{ow}}(\mathcal{A}) = \Pr_{\substack{m \xleftarrow{R} \mathcal{M} \\ u \xleftarrow{R} \mathcal{U}}} [(sk, pk) \leftarrow \mathcal{K}(1^{\kappa}) : \mathcal{A}(\mathcal{E}_{pk}(m, u)) = m] < \varepsilon \,,$$

where the probability is taken over the random choices of the adversary.

SEMANTIC SECURITY. Formalizing another security criterion that an encryption scheme should verify beyond one-wayness, Goldwasser and Micali [GM84] introduced the notion of *semantic security*. Also called *indistinguishability of encryptions* (or IND for short), this property captures the idea that an adversary should not be able to learn any information whatsoever about a plaintext, its length excepted, given its encryption. More formally, an asymmetric encryption scheme is said to be (τ, ε)-IND if for any adversary $\mathcal{A} = (\mathcal{A}_1, \mathcal{A}_2)$ with running time upper-bounded by τ,

$$\mathsf{Adv}^{\mathsf{ind}}(\mathcal{A}) = 2 \times \Pr_{\substack{b \xleftarrow{R} \{0,1\} \\ u \xleftarrow{R} \mathcal{U}}} \left[\begin{array}{l} (sk, pk) \leftarrow \mathcal{K}(1^\kappa), (m_0, m_1, \sigma) \leftarrow \mathcal{A}_1(pk) \\ c \leftarrow \mathcal{E}_{pk}(m_b, u) : \mathcal{A}_2(c, \sigma) = b \end{array} \right] - 1 < \varepsilon \,,$$

where the probability is taken over the random choices of $\mathcal{A}$. The two plaintexts m_0 and m_1 chosen by the adversary in $\mathcal{M}$ have to be of identical length.

NON-MALLEABILITY. The property of *non-malleability* (NM), independently proposed by Dolev, Dwork and Naor [DDN00], supposes that, given the encryption of a plaintext m, the attacker cannot produce the encryption of a related plaintext m'. Here, rather than learning some information about m, the adversary will try to output the encryption of m'. These two properties are related in the sense that non-malleability implies semantic security for any adversarial model, as pointed out in [DDN00] and [BDPR99].

Adversarial models. On the other hand, there exist several types of adversaries, or attack models. In a chosen-plaintext attack (CPA), the adversary has access to an encryption oracle, hence to the encryption of any plaintext she wants. Clearly, in the public-key setting, this scenario cannot be avoided. Naor and Yung [NY90] considered non-adaptive chosen-ciphertext attacks (CCA1) (also known as lunchtime or midnight attacks), wherein the adversary gets, in addition, access to a decryption oracle before being given the challenge ciphertext. Finally, Rackoff and Simon [RS92] defined adaptive chosen-ciphertext attacks (CCA2) as a scenario in which the adversary queries the decryption oracle before and *after* being challenged; her only restriction here is that she may not feed the oracle with the challenge ciphertext itself. This is the strongest known attack scenario.

Various security levels are then defined by pairing each goal (OW, IND or NM) with an attack model (CPA, CCA1 or CCA2), these two characteristics being considered separately. Interestingly, it has been shown that IND-CCA2 and NM-CCA2 were strictly equivalent notions [BDPR99]. This level is now considered as standard and referred to as IND-CCA2 security or chosen-ciphertext security. The security of a cryptosystem is thus measured as the ability to resist an adversarial goal in a given adversarial model. Whenever possible, the scheme is proven IND-CCA2 secure by exhibiting a polynomial reduction: if some adversary can break the IND-CCA2 security of the system, then the same adversary can be invoked (polynomially many times) to solve some related hard problem.

2.2   Symmetric Encryption Schemes

A symmetric encryption scheme with key bit-length k and message bit-length m is a pair of algorithms (E, D) where

- E is a deterministic encryption algorithm which takes a key $k \in \{0,1\}^k$ and a plaintext $m \in \{0,1\}^m$ and returns a ciphertext $c \in \{0,1\}^m$,
- D is a deterministic decryption algorithm which takes a key $k \in \{0,1\}^k$ and a ciphertext $c \in \{0,1\}^m$ and returns a plaintext $m \in \{0,1\}^m$. We require that $D_k(E_k(m)) = m$ for all $m \in \{0,1\}^m$ and $k \in \{0,1\}^k$.

In this setting, again, various security notions are defined; most are adaptations from the asymmetric notions. In this work, however, we only need to define indistinguishability. A symmetric encryption scheme is said (τ, ε)-IND if for any adversary $\mathcal{A} = (\mathcal{A}_1, \mathcal{A}_2)$ with running time bounded by τ,

$$\mathsf{Adv}^{\mathsf{ind}}(\mathcal{A}) = 2 \times \Pr_{\substack{k \xleftarrow{R} \{0,1\}^k \\ b \xleftarrow{R} \{0,1\}}} [(m_0, m_1, \sigma) \leftarrow \mathcal{A}_1(k), c \leftarrow E_k(m_b) : \mathcal{A}_2(c, \sigma) = b] - 1 < \varepsilon \,,$$

where the probability is also taken over the random choices of $\mathcal{A}$. Both plaintexts m_0 and m_1 are chosen by the adversary in $\{0,1\}^k$. Although other attack scenarios may be considered, passive attacks are enough for our purposes. Note that this notion is a very weak requirement. Note also that the one-time pad encryption is perfectly indistinguishable, *i.e.* , it is $(\tau, 0)$-IND for any τ.

2.3   Plaintext-Checking Security

Okamoto and Pointcheval recently introduced an intermediate adversarial model called plaintext checking attacks [OP01a]. In this model, the adversary has access to a *plaintext-checking* oracle $\mathcal{O}^{\mathrm{PCA}}$ which detects plaintext-ciphertext correspondences: the oracle takes as input a pair (m, c) and tells whether c encrypts m or not. Clearly, this oracle remains weaker than a decryption oracle because it is generally easier to check the solution of a problem (scheme inversion here) than to compute it. Obviously in the case of a deterministic encryption scheme, PCA and CPA are strictly equivalent attack scenarios. More specifically, any trapdoor permutation is OW-PCA if and only if it is OW (e.g., RSA).

From a complexity viewpoint, breaking a scheme's OW-PCA-security exactly consists in breaking its OW-security (*i.e.* its one-wayness) with the help of an oracle solving a weaker problem. That kind of problems, *i.e.* solving P_1 with access to $\mathcal{O}^{P_2}$ and $P_2 \Leftarrow P_1$, are called *gap problems* [OP01b] and define some notion of complexity distance between problems in a hierarchy.

A typical example is ElGamal encryption, for which breaking OW is equivalent to CDH and having access to $\mathcal{O}^{\mathrm{PCA}}$ allows to solve DDH trivially (and conversely). OW-PCA-security is in this case equivalent to the gap problem separating CDH from DDH, which is called *Gap Diffie-Hellman Problem* and noted GDH (see [OP01b] for insights).

2.4   Generic Conversions

In [BR95], Bellare and Rogaway proposed OAEP, a specific hash-based treatment applicable to any *partial-domain* [Sho01,FOPS01] one-way trapdoor permutation to provide an IND-CCA2 secure encryption scheme in the random oracle model [BR93]. Later, Fujisaki and Okamoto [FO99a] presented a way to transform, still in the random oracle model, any IND-PCA trapdoor function into an IND-CCA2 encryption scheme. They improved their results in [FO99b] where they gave a generic method to convert a *one-way* trapdoor function into an IND-CCA2 secure encryption scheme in the random oracle model[2]. A similar result was independently discovered by Pointcheval [Poi00]. More recently, Okamoto and Pointcheval [OP01a] proposed a more efficient generic conversion, called REACT. Contrarily to [FO99a,FO99b,Poi00], a complete re-encryption is unnecessary in the decryption process of REACT to ensure IND-CCA2 security, thus yielding a low running time overhead. Besides, REACT applies to any trapdoor function *i.e.* any asymmetric encryption scheme presenting such a weak level of security as being OW-PCA. Until now, however, no generic conversion has been explicitly defined[3] to encrypt messages of variable length based on fixed-length functions. The next section describes our arbitrary-length generic conversions.

3   Arbitrary-Length IND-CCA2 Encryption

The most popular and usual way of ensuring confidentiality of unfixed-length messages consists in public-key encrypting a random session key and then encrypting the message under that session key by the means of a block-cipher used within a suitable encryption mode. This approach has never been shown secure; in particular, the use of an IND-CCA2 asymmetric scheme to encrypt the session key is obviously insufficient to ensure any security whatsoever about the whole construction.

In comparison, our conversions are based on the same primitives, *i.e.* some asymmetric scheme $\mathcal{E}_{pk}$ and some symmetric scheme E_k. But we additionally use hash functions to make the session key evolve permanently as the encryption progresses. Our important result here is that the two cryptosystems we propose are IND-CCA2-secure provided that $\mathcal{E}_{pk}$ is OW-PCA or OW and E_k is indistinguishable. Independently, they provide different security/performance tradeoffs that we analyze in section 4.

3.1   Relying on a OW-PCA Trapdoor Function: GEM-1

Our first construction $\mathbb{E}^1_{pk}$ applies to any OW-PCA probabilistic trapdoor function $\mathcal{E}_{pk}$ and incorporates two extra fields of fixed length in the ciphertext, one at each end. To make the security proof easier, we will assume that the message blocklength is upper-bounded by some very large number n_{max} which value is discussed in section 4. The encryption and decryption procedures are as depicted below.

---

[2] the conversion cost is however quite heavy as a complete re-encryption is needed during decryption.

[3] note that [OP01a] considers the case of variable-length encryption without providing any explicit construction for fixed-length primitives.

Encryption

Input   plaintext $(m_1, \ldots, m_n)$, $1 \le n \le n_{max}$, random $\rho = w\|u$.
Output   ciphertext $(t_1, c_1, \cdots, c_n, t_2)$ given by

$$\mathbb{E}^1_{pk}(m, \rho) = (\underbrace{\mathcal{E}_{pk}(w, u)}_{t_1}, \underbrace{\mathrm{E}_{k_1}(m_1)}_{c_1}, \underbrace{\mathrm{E}_{k_2}(m_2)}_{c_2}, \cdots, \underbrace{\mathrm{E}_{k_n}(m_n)}_{c_n}, \underbrace{\mathrm{F}(k_n, m_n, w)}_{t_2})$$

where $k_1 = \mathrm{H}_1(w, t_1)$, $k_2 = \mathrm{H}_2(k_1, m_1, w)$, ..., $k_n = \mathrm{H}_n(k_{n-1}, m_{n-1}, w)$.

Decryption

Input   ciphertext $(t_1, c_1, \cdots, c_n, t_2)$ with $1 \le n \le n_{max}$.
Output   plaintext $(\hat{m}_1, \cdots, \hat{m}_n)$ or $\perp$ according to

$$\mathbb{D}^1_{sk}(t_1, c_1, \cdots, c_n, t_2) = \begin{cases} \hat{m}_1 = \mathrm{D}_{\hat{k}_1}(c_1), \ldots, \hat{m}_n = \mathrm{D}_{\hat{k}_n}(c_n) & \text{if } t_2 = \mathrm{F}(\hat{k}_n, \hat{m}_n, \hat{w}) \\ \perp & \text{otherwise} \end{cases}$$

where $\hat{w} = \mathcal{D}_{sk}(t_1)$, $\hat{k}_1 = \mathrm{H}_1(\hat{w}, t_1)$ and $\hat{k}_i = \mathrm{H}_i(\hat{k}_{i-1}, \hat{m}_{i-1}, \hat{w})$ for $i = 2, n$.

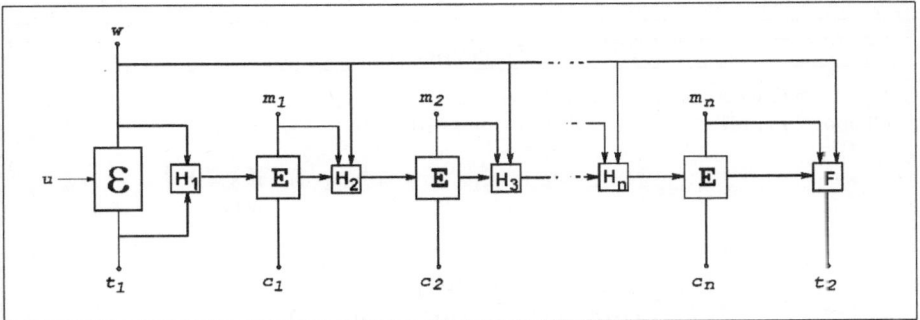

Fig. 1. Synopsis of GEM-1.

We claim that for any **OW-PCA** asymmetric encryption $\mathcal{E}_{pk}$ and any **IND**-secure symmetric encryption scheme E_k, our converted scheme $\mathbb{E}^1_{pk}[\mathcal{E}_{pk}, \mathrm{E}_k]$ is **IND-CCA2** in the random oracle model. To be more precise:

Theorem 1. *Suppose there exists an adversary $\mathcal{A}$ which distinguishes $\mathbb{E}^1_{pk}[\mathcal{E}_{pk}, \mathrm{E}_k]$ within a time bound τ with advantage ε in less than q_{F}, $q_{\mathrm{H}} = \sum_{i \in \langle 1, n_{max} \rangle} q_{\mathrm{H}_i}$, $q_{\mathbb{D}^1_{sk}}$ oracle calls. Suppose also that E_k is (τ, ν)-indistinguishable. Then there exists an algorithm $\mathcal{B}$ which inverts $\mathcal{E}_{pk}$ with probability ε' greater than*

$$\varepsilon' \ge \frac{\varepsilon}{2} - q_{\mathbb{D}^1_{sk}} \left(\frac{1}{\sharp t_2} + \frac{3}{\sharp k} \right) - n_{max} \left(\frac{\nu}{2} + \frac{q_{\mathbb{D}^1_{sk}}}{\sharp k} \right),$$

with a total number of calls to $\mathcal{O}^{\mathrm{PCA}}$ upper-bounded by $q_{\mathcal{O}^{\mathrm{PCA}}} \le q_{\mathrm{F}} + q_{\mathrm{H}}$ and in time

$$\tau_{\mathcal{B}} = \tau + (q_{\mathbb{D}^1_{sk}} + 1)(q_{\mathrm{F}} + q_{\mathrm{H}}) \cdot (\tau_{\mathrm{PCA}} + O(1)).$$

Here, $\sharp a$ denotes the number of all possible values of a (hence $\sharp k = 2^k$).

We refer the reader to the (extensive) reduction proof given in appendix A.

3.2   Relying on a OW Trapdoor Function: GEM-2

Our second construction $\mathbb{E}_{pk}^2$ only works with a deterministic OW trapdoor function $\mathcal{E}_{pk}$ (such as RSA) but adds only one extra field at the end of the ciphertext. Here again, we will assume that the message blocklength is upper-bounded by some large number n_{max}. The encryption and decryption procedures follow.

Encryption

Input   plaintext $(m_1, \ldots, m_n)$, $1 \leq n \leq n_{max}$, random r.

Output   ciphertext $(c_1, \cdots, c_n, t)$ given by

$$\mathbb{E}_{pk}^2(m, r) = (\underbrace{\mathrm{E}_{k_1}(m_1)}_{c_1}, \underbrace{\mathrm{E}_{k_2}(m_2)}_{c_2}, \cdots, \underbrace{\mathrm{E}_{k_n}(m_n)}_{c_n}, \underbrace{\mathcal{E}_{pk}(s\|v)}_{t})$$

where $\begin{cases} k_1 = \mathrm{G}_1(r), k_i = \mathrm{G}_i(k_{i-1}, m_{i-1}, r) \text{ for } i = 2, \ldots n, \\ s = \mathrm{F}(k_n, m_n, r), \text{ and } v = r \oplus \mathrm{H}(s). \end{cases}$

Decryption

Input   ciphertext $(c_1, \cdots, c_n, t)$ with $1 \leq n \leq n_{max}$.

Output   plaintext $(\hat{m}_1, \cdots, \hat{m}_n)$ or $\bot$ according to

$$\mathbb{D}_{sk}^2(c_1, \cdots, c_n, t) = \begin{cases} \hat{m}_1 = \mathrm{D}_{\hat{k}_1}(c_1), \ldots, \hat{m}_n = \mathrm{D}_{\hat{k}_n}(c_n) & \text{if } \hat{s} = \mathrm{F}(\hat{k}_n, \hat{m}_n, \hat{r}), \\ \bot & \text{otherwise.} \end{cases}$$

where $\begin{cases} \hat{s}\|\hat{v} = \mathcal{D}_{sk}(t), \hat{r} = \hat{v} \oplus \mathrm{H}(\hat{s}), \\ \hat{k}_1 = \mathrm{G}_1(\hat{r}), \text{ and } \hat{k}_i = \mathrm{G}_i(\hat{k}_{i-1}, \hat{m}_{i-1}, \hat{r}) \text{ for } i = 2, \ldots n. \end{cases}$

We claim that for any OW asymmetric encryption $\mathcal{E}_{pk}$ and any IND-secure symmetric encryption scheme E_k, the converted scheme $\mathbb{E}_{pk}^2[\mathcal{E}_{pk}, \mathrm{E}_k]$ is IND-CCA2 in the random oracle model. To be more precise:

Theorem 2. *Suppose there exists an adversary $\mathcal{A}$ which distinguishes $\mathbb{E}_{pk}^2[\mathcal{E}_{pk}, \mathrm{E}_k]$ within a time bound τ with advantage ε in less than q_{F}, q_{H}, $q_{\mathrm{G}} = \sum_{i \in \langle 1, n_{max} \rangle} q_{\mathrm{G}_i}$, $q_{\mathbb{D}_{sk}^2}$ oracle calls. Suppose also that E_k is (τ, ν)-indistinguishable. Then there exists an algorithm $\mathcal{B}$ which inverts $\mathcal{E}_{pk}$ with probability ε' greater than*

$$\varepsilon' \geq \frac{\varepsilon}{2} - \frac{q_{\mathrm{F}} + q_{\mathrm{G}}}{\sharp r} - q_{\mathbb{D}_{sk}^2}(q_{\mathrm{F}} + 1)\left(\frac{1}{\sharp s} + \frac{1}{\sharp r}\right) - \frac{q_{\mathbb{D}_{sk}^2}}{\sharp k} - n_{max}\left(\frac{\nu}{2} + \frac{q_{\mathbb{D}_{sk}^2}}{\sharp k}\right),$$

within a time bounded by

$$\tau_{\mathcal{B}} = \tau + \left(q_{\mathbb{D}_{sk}^2} + 1\right)\left(q_{\mathrm{F}} + q_{\mathrm{G}}\right) q_{\mathrm{H}} \cdot \left(\tau_{\mathcal{E}} + O(1)\right),$$

where $\tau_{\mathcal{E}}$ denotes the maximum time needed by $\mathcal{E}_{pk}$ for a single encryption.

The reader is invited to find the reduction proof given in the extended version of this work [CHJ+01].

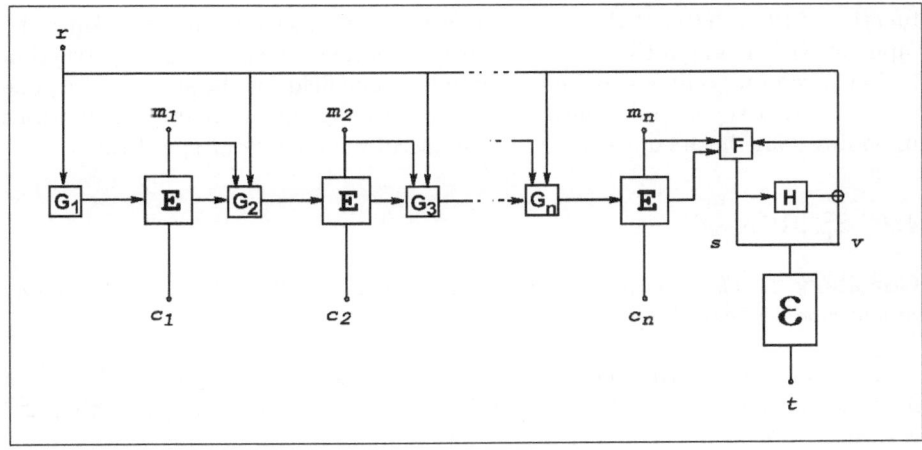

Fig. 2. Synopsis of GEM-2.

4   Applications

Numerous applications are possible when embodying $\mathcal{E}_{pk}$ and E_k. Due to lack of space, we will only consider the typical case $\mathcal{E}_{pk} = \text{RSA}$ and $E_k = \oplus$ (for which $\nu = 0$). The instantiations of random oracles F, H_i, H and G_i in one scheme or another by hash functions can be done by setting for instance $H_i(\cdot) = \text{SHA}(\cdot\|i)$ where the counter $i \in \langle 1, n_{max}\rangle$ is incremented at each block treatment. Special values of i such as 0 or -1 may be used to implement F and H.

4.1 $\mathbb{E}_{pk}^1[\mathbf{RSA}, \oplus]$

Corollary 1. *The encryption scheme* $\mathbb{E}_{pk}^1[\text{RSA}, \oplus]$ *is* IND-CCA2 *in the random oracle model under the RSA assumption.*

For concrete security parameters, we suggest to use 1024-bit RSA keys with public exponent $e = \mathbb{F}_4 = 2^{16} + 1$. We set for instance $\log_2 \sharp t_2 = \mathsf{m} = \mathsf{k} = 160$ (hash functions F, H_i being derived from SHA-1 using a counter $i \in \langle 1, n_{max}\rangle$ like described above), $\sharp w = 2^{160}$ and $n_{max} = 2^{32}$. Assuming that the probability ε' to invert RSA lies around $\varepsilon' = 2^{-60}$, then an attaquer could distinguish $\mathbb{E}_{pk}^1[\text{RSA}, \oplus]$ with $q_{\mathbb{D}_{sk}^1} = 2^{50}$ decryptions with advantage no more than $\varepsilon = 2^{-58}$.

From an implementation viewpoint, note that as soon as the RSA encryption has been done, the encryption procedure may directly output ciphertexts blocks one after the other without having to wait that all blocks are encrypted to transmit them all together. Definitely, this is a major advantage compared to previously proposed constructions. This property allows on-the-fly encryption of communication streams. Three-tuples (w, y, k_1) may also be computed in advance to let the encryption device or software deal with hash computations only. The suggested setting allows to replace oracles $H_2, \ldots, H_n$, F by the compression function ($512 \mapsto 160$) of SHA-1, driving us to $n+3$ calls to this function since the input of H_1 is made of three 512-bit blocks. Another benefit of our construction is that it requires only a small memory buffer (one field for the storage of w, one for the current key k_i and a third one for m_i). Finally, hardware implementations providing some hash coprocessor may drastically increase our speed rates.

4.2 $\mathbb{E}_{pk}^2[\mathbf{RSA}, \oplus]$

Corollary 2. *The encryption scheme* $\mathbb{E}_{pk}^2[\mathrm{RSA}, \oplus]$ *is* IND-CCA2 *in the random oracle model under the RSA assumption.*

For concrete security bounds, the same suggestions as previously lead to a maximal advantage of $\varepsilon = 2^{-58}$ if we take $\log_2 \sharp s = \log_2 \sharp r = 512$, $q_\mathrm{F} = q_\mathrm{G} = 2^{50}$ and $n_{max} = 2^{32}$.

Here again, any smart implementation allows on-the-fly encryption. The memory requirements are similar to the one of $\mathbb{E}_{pk}^1$. Here too, a coprocessor devoted to hash computations would increase speed rates.

5   Conclusion

We devised new generic constructions which apply to fixed-length weakly secure primitives and provide a strongly secure (IND-CCA2) public-key encryption scheme for messages of unfixed length like computer files or communications streams. An open question resides in investigating whether simpler and/or faster designs could exist, or whether the security requirements on the primitives could be shrunk further. Another challenging topic would be to come up with a construction holding only one additional field in the ciphertext but still employing a probabilistic encryption $\mathcal{E}_{pk}$ as in $\mathbb{E}_{pk}^1$. Finally, one could try to include a *signature* scheme in the encryption process to simultaneously authenticate the sender's identity, the plaintext and the ciphertext itself. Such an extension would ideally lead to fast and secure (according to one-more decryption attacks) signcryption schemes for arbitrary-length messages.

References

[BBM00]   Mihir Bellare, Alexandra Boldyreva, and Silvio Micali. Public-key Encryption in a Multi-User Setting: Security Proofs and Improvements. In *Advances in Cryptology – EUROCRYPT '00*, LNCS 1807, pages 259–274. Springer-Verlag, Berlin, 2000.

[BDPR99] Mihir Bellare, Anand Desai, David Pointcheval, and Phillip Rogaway. Relations Among Notions of Security for Public-Key Encryption Schemes. Full paper (30 pages), February 1999. An extended abstract appears in H. Krawczyk, ed., Advances in Cryptology – CRYPTO '98, volume 1462 of Lecture Notes in Computer Science, pages 26–45, Springer-Verlag, 1998.

[BPS00]   Olivier Baudron, David Pointcheval, and Jacques Stern. Extended Notions of Security for Multicast Public Key Cryptosystems. In *Proc. of the 27th ICALP*, LNCS 1853, pages 499–511. Springer-Verlag, Berlin, 2000.

[BR93]   Mihir Bellare and Phillip Rogaway. Random Oracles are Practical: A Paradigm for Designing Efficient Protocols. In *First ACM Conference on Computer and Communications Security*, pages 62–73. ACM Press, 1993.

[BR95]   Mihir Bellare and Phillip Rogaway. Optimal Asymmetric Encryption. In A. De Santis, editor, *Advances in Cryptology – EUROCRYPT '94*, volume 950 of *Lecture Notes in Computer Science*, pages 92–111. Springer-Verlag, 1995.

[CHJ+01]   Jean-Sébastien Coron, Helena Handschuh, Marc Joye, Pascal Paillier, David Pointcheval, and Christophe Tymen.   Optimal Chosen-Ciphertext   Secure   Encryption   of   Arbitrary-Length   Messages. http://eprint.iacr.org/, 2001.

[DDN00]   Danny Dolev, Cynthia Dwork, and Moni Naor. Non-Malleable Cryptography. *SIAM Journal on Computing*, 30(2):391–437, 2000.

[FO99a]   Eiichiro Fujisaki and Tatsuaki Okamoto. How to Enhance the Security of Public-Key Encryption at Minimum Cost. In H. Imai and Y. Zheng, editors, *Public Key Cryptography*, volume 1560 of *Lecture Notes in Computer Science*, pages 53–68. Springer-Verlag, 1999.

[FO99b]   Eiichiro Fujisaki and Tatsuaki Okamoto. Secure Integration of Asymmetric and Symmetric Encryption Schemes. In M. Wiener, editor, *Advances in Cryptology – CRYPTO '99*, volume 1666 of *Lecture Notes in Computer Science*, pages 537–554. Springer-Verlag, 1999.

[FOPS01]   Eiichiro Fujisaki, Tatsuaki Okamoto, David Pointcheval, and Jacques Stern. RSA–OAEP is Secure under the RSA Assumption. In *Advances in Cryptology – CRYPTO '01*, Lecture Notes in Computer Science. Springer-Verlag, 2001.

[GM84]   Shafi Goldwasser and Silvio Micali. Probabilistic Encryption. *Journal of Computer and System Sciences*, 28:270–299, 1984.

[NY90]   Moni Naor and Moti Yung. Public-Key Cryptosystems Provably Secure against Chosen Ciphertext Attacks. In *22nd ACM Annual Symposium on the Theory of Computing (STOC '90)*, pages 427–437. ACM Press, 1990.

[OP01a]   Tatsuaki Okamoto and David Pointcheval. REACT: Rapid Enhanced-security Asymmetric Cryptosystem Transform. In D. Naccache, editor, *RSA 2001 Cryptographers' Track*, volume 2020 of *Lecture Notes in Computer Science*, pages 159–175. Springer-Verlag, 2001.

[OP01b]   Tatsuaki Okamoto and David Pointcheval. The Gap-Problems: a New Class of Problems for the Security of Cryptographic Schemes. In *PKC*, volume 1992 of *Lecture Notes in Computer Science*, pages 104–118. Springer-Verlag, 2001.

[Poi00]   David Pointcheval. Chosen-Ciphertext Security for any One-Way Cryptosystem. In H. Imai and Y. Zheng, editors, *Public Key Cryptography*, volume 1751 of *Lecture Notes in Computer Science*, pages 129–146. Springer-Verlag, 2000.

[RS92]   Charles Rackoff and Daniel R. Simon. Non-Interactive Zero-Knowledge Proof of Knowledge and Chosen Ciphertext Attack. In J. Feigenbaum, editor, *Advances in Cryptology – CRYPTO '91*, volume 576, pages 433–444. Springer-Verlag, 1992.

[Sho01]   Victor Shoup.   OAEP Reconsidered.   In *Advances in Cryptology – CRYPTO '01*, Lecture Notes in Computer Science. Springer-Verlag, 2001.

A   Security Analysis of GEM-1

A.1   Notations

It is useful to introduce some notations. If a is some random variable, then $\sharp a$ denotes the number all possible values of a. For integers a and b, $\langle a, b \rangle$ denotes the set on integers ranging from a to b. For any predicate $R(x)$, $R(*)$ will stand for $\exists x$ s.t. $R(x)$. If $\mathcal{O}$ is an oracle to which $\mathcal{A}$ has access, we denote by $query \mapsto response$ the correspondance $\mathcal{O}$ establishes between $\mathcal{A}$'s request $query$ and the value $response$ returned to $\mathcal{A}$. $\text{HIST}\,[\mathcal{O}]$ stands for the set of correspondances established by $\mathcal{O}$ as time goes on: $\text{HIST}\,[\mathcal{O}]$ can be seen as a memory which gets updated each time $\mathcal{A}$ makes a query to $\mathcal{O}$. We denote by $q_{\mathcal{O}}$ the number of calls $\mathcal{A}$ made to $\mathcal{O}$ during the simulation.

A.2   Extending Indistinguishability to Scheme Products

Let E^1 and E^2 be two symmetric encryption schemes. We define the scheme product of E^1 and E^2, $\mathrm{E} = \mathrm{E}^1 \times \mathrm{E}^2$ by

$$\mathrm{E}_k(m) = (\mathrm{E}^1 \times \mathrm{E}^2)_{(k_1, k_2)}(m_1, m_2) = (\mathrm{E}^1_{k_1}(m_1), \mathrm{E}^2_{k_2}(m_2)) \,,$$

where all values stand in their respective sets. Then

Lemma 1. *If E^1 is (τ, ν_1)-IND and E^2 is (τ, ν_2)-IND then E is $(\tau, \nu_1 + \nu_2)$-IND.*

Note that [BPS00] and [BBM00] provide similar results for asymmetric encryption schemes. By immediate induction of lemma 1, we get that if E^i is (τ, ν_i)-IND for $i \in \langle 1, n \rangle$, then $\mathrm{E} = \prod_i \mathrm{E}^i$ is $(\tau, \sum_i \nu_i)$-IND. In particular, if E is (τ, ν)-IND, then $(\mathrm{E})^n$ is $(\tau, n\nu)$-IND.

A.3   Description of the Reduction Algorithm

$\mathcal{B}$ is given an encryption $y = \mathcal{E}_{pk}(\widetilde{w}, *)$, an oracle $\mathcal{O}^{\text{PCA}}$ which checks plaintexts for $\mathcal{E}_{pk}$, and an adversary $\mathcal{A} = (\mathcal{A}_1, \mathcal{A}_2)$ that breaks the IND-CCA2 security of $\mathbb{E}^1_{pk}$. The goal of the reduction $\mathcal{B}$ is to retrieve the total knowledge of $\widetilde{w}$. Each time the reduction $\mathcal{B}$ needs to check whether a plaintext-ciphertext correspondance holds between y and w (which we denote $y = \mathcal{E}_{pk}(w, *)$), the query (y, w) is implicitly sent to $\mathcal{O}^{\text{PCA}}$ which returns a boolean value. We assume for simplicity that $\mathcal{O}^{\text{PCA}}$ responds to any of $\mathcal{B}$'s requests with no error and within a time bound τ_{PCA}.

Overview of $\mathcal{B}$. $\mathcal{B}$ runs $\mathcal{A}_1$ and provides a simulation for H_i with $i \in \langle 1, n_{max} \rangle$, F and $\mathbb{D}^1_{sk}$ as described later (find stage). $\mathcal{A}_1$ outputs a pair of message sequences (m^0, m^1) of identical blocklength $n \leq n_{max}$ after a certain time. $\mathcal{B}$ then randomly chooses $b \in \{0, 1\}$ and proceeds to the following operations:

- if there exists $(w, y) \mapsto k_1 \in \text{HIST}\,[\mathrm{H}_1]$ with $y = \mathcal{E}_{pk}(w, *)$ then $\widetilde{w} := w$ and $\widetilde{k}_1 := k_1$ (event E_1) otherwise $\widetilde{k}_1$ is set to a random value,

- for $i \in \langle 2, n \rangle$, if there exists $(\widetilde{k}_{i-1}, m_i^b, w) \mapsto k_i \in \text{HIST}[\text{H}_i]$ with $y = \mathcal{E}_{pk}(w, *)$ then $\widetilde{w} := w$ and $\widetilde{k}_i := k_i$ (event E_i); otherwise $\widetilde{k}_i$ is set to a random value,

- if there exists $(\widetilde{k}_n, m_n^b, w) \mapsto t_2 \in \text{HIST}[\text{F}]$ with $y = \mathcal{E}_{pk}(w, *)$ then $\widetilde{w} := w$ and $\widetilde{t}_2 := t_2$ (event E_F); otherwise $\widetilde{t}_2$ is set to a random value.

$\mathcal{B}$ then computes $\widetilde{c}_i = \text{E}_{\widetilde{k}_i}(m_i^b)$ for $i \in \langle 1, n \rangle$ and builds

$$\widetilde{c} = (y, \widetilde{c}_1, \ldots, \widetilde{c}_n, \widetilde{t}_2) \ .$$

This challenge is given to $\mathcal{A}_2$ which outputs some bit after another certain time (guess stage). Once finished, $\mathcal{B}$ will actually check whether some value $\widetilde{w}$ was defined during the game. If so, $\widetilde{w}$ is returned as the inversion of $\mathcal{E}_{pk}$ on y. Otherwise, the challenge y is simply rejected i.e. $\mathcal{B}$ sets $\widetilde{w} := \bot$ and stops. The simulation of random oracles as well as the simulation of the decryption oracle $\mathbb{D}^1_{\varepsilon k}$ are detailed hereafter. Wlog, we assume that all simulated oracles keep tracks of their past queries throughout the game so that, if a query has been presented before and responded with some recorded output, then the same output is returned. In the sequel, all probabilities are taken over the random choices of $\mathcal{A}$ and $\mathcal{B}$ if not otherwise mentioned.

Simulation of H_1. For each new query (w, t_1),
(event E_1') if $t_1 = y$ and $y = \mathcal{E}_{pk}(w, *)$ then H_1 sets $\widetilde{w} := w$, returns $\widetilde{k}_1$ and updates its history,
(event E_1'') else if $y = \mathcal{E}_{pk}(w, *)$ then H_1 sets $\widetilde{w} := w$, outputs a random value and updates its history,
(no event) else H_1 outputs a random value and updates its history.

Simulation of H_i for $i \in \langle 2, n \rangle$. For each new query (k, m, w),
(event E_i') if processing guess stage and $k = \widetilde{k}_{i-1}$, $m = m_{i-1}^b$ and $y = \mathcal{E}_{pk}(w, *)$ then H_i sets $\widetilde{w} := w$, returns $\widetilde{k}_i$ and updates its history,
(event E_i'') else if $y = \mathcal{E}_{pk}(w, *)$ then H_i sets $\widetilde{w} := w$, outputs a random value and updates its history,
(no event) else H_i outputs a random value and updates its history.

Simulation of H_i for $i \in \langle n + 1, n_{max} \rangle$. For each new query (k, m, w),
(event E_i) if $y = \mathcal{E}_{pk}(w, *)$ then H_i sets $\widetilde{w} := w$, outputs a random value and updates its history,
(no event) else H_i outputs a random value and updates its history.

Simulation of F. For each new query (k, m, w),
(event E_F') if processing guess stage and $k = \widetilde{k}_n$, $m = m_n^b$ and $y = \mathcal{E}_{pk}(w, *)$ then F sets $\widetilde{w} := w$, returns $\widetilde{t}_2$ and updates its history,
(event E_F'') else if $y = \mathcal{E}_{pk}(w, *)$ then F sets $\widetilde{w} := w$, outputs a random value and updates its history,
(no event) else F outputs a random value and updates its history.

Simulation of $\mathbb{D}_{sk}^1$ (plaintext extractor). For each new query $(t_1, c_1, \ldots, c_d, t_2)$, $\mathbb{D}_{sk}^1$ first checks (this verification step only stands while the guess phase $\mathcal{A}_2$ is running) that $(t_1, c_1, \ldots, c_d, t_2) \neq (y, \widetilde{c}_1, \ldots, \widetilde{c}_n, \widetilde{t}_2)$ since if this equality holds, the query must be rejected as $\mathcal{A}$ attempts to decrypt its own challenge ciphertext. Then, $\mathbb{D}_{sk}^1$ tries to find the only (if any) message sequence $(m_1, \ldots, m_d)$ matching the query. To achieve this, $\mathbb{D}_{sk}^1$ invokes the simulations of the random oracles provided by $\mathcal{B}$ as follows:

- search for the unique $w \in \text{HIST}\,[\mathrm{H}_1] \cup \ldots \cup \text{HIST}\,[\mathrm{H}_d] \cup \text{HIST}\,[\mathrm{F}]$ such that $t_1 = \mathcal{E}_{pk}(w, *)$. If such a w exists,
  - query H_1 to get $k_1 = \mathrm{H}_1(w, t_1)$,
  - letting $m_1 = \mathsf{D}_{k_1}(c_1)$, query H_2 to get $k_2 = \mathrm{H}_2(k_1, m_1, w)$,
  - letting $m_2 = \mathsf{D}_{k_2}(c_2)$, query H_3 to get $k_3 = \mathrm{H}_3(k_2, m_2, w)$,
    $\vdots$
  - letting $m_{d-1} = \mathsf{D}_{k_{d-1}}(c_{d-1})$, query H_d to get $k_d = \mathrm{H}_d(k_{d-1}, m_{d-1}, w)$,
  - letting $m_d = \mathsf{D}_{k_d}(c_d)$, query F to check if $\mathrm{F}(k_d, m_d, w) = t_2$. If the equality holds, return $(m_1, \ldots, m_d)$; otherwise reject the query (event RJ_1).
- if the search for w is unsuccessful, reject the query (event RJ_2).

A.4   Soundness of $\mathcal{B}$

Simulation of Random Oracles

SOUNDNESS OF H_1. The simulation is perfect.

SOUNDNESS OF H_i FOR $i \in \langle 2, n \rangle$. The simulation is perfect.

SOUNDNESS OF H_i FOR $i \in \langle n+1, n_{max} \rangle$. The simulation is perfect.

SOUNDNESS OF F. The simulation is perfect.

Plaintext extraction. The simulation of $\mathbb{D}_{sk}^1$ fails when $\perp$ is returned although the query $c = (t_1, c_1, \ldots, c_d, t_2)$ is a valid ciphertext. Let w and m_i, k_i for $i \in \langle 1, d \rangle$ denote the unique random variables associated to c in this case. Further define

$$\mathcal{H}_d = \bigcup_{i \in \langle 1, d \rangle} \text{HIST}\,[\mathrm{H}_i] \cup \text{HIST}\,[\mathrm{F}] \ .$$

Obviously, c was rejected through event RJ_2, because a rejection through RJ_1 refutes the validity of c. Therefore, if $\mathbb{D}_{sk}^1$ is incorrect for c, we must have

$$(\mathbb{D}_{sk}^1 \text{ incorrect for } c) \wedge (c \text{ valid}) \quad \Rightarrow \quad w \notin \mathcal{H}_d \ .$$

We now decompose the failure event into several disjoint cases covering all possible situations.

ASSUME $(k_d \neq \widetilde{k}_n) \vee (m_d \neq m_n^b) \vee (w \neq \widetilde{w})$. Since $w \notin \mathrm{HIST}\,[\mathrm{F}] \subset \mathcal{H}_d$, $\mathrm{F}(k_d, m_d, w)$ is a uniformly distributed random value unknown to $\mathcal{A}$. The fact that c is a valid ciphertext implies that $\mathrm{F}(k_d, m_d, w) = t_2$, which happens with probability

$$\Pr_{\mathrm{F}} \left[\mathrm{F}(k_d, m_d, w) = t_2 \right] = \frac{1}{\sharp t_2} \ .$$

ASSUME $(k_d, m_d, w) = (\widetilde{k}_n, m_n^b, \widetilde{w})$ AND $d > n$. Since $w \notin \mathrm{HIST}\,[\mathrm{H}_d] \subset \mathcal{H}_d$, $\mathrm{H}_d(k_{d-1}, m_{d-1}, w)$ is a uniformly distributed random value unknown to $\mathcal{A}$. The fact that c is a valid ciphertext implies that $\mathrm{H}_d(k_{d-1}, m_{d-1}, w) = k_d = \widetilde{k}_n$, which happens with probability

$$\Pr_{\mathrm{H}_d} \left[\mathrm{H}_d(k_{d-1}, m_{d-1}, w) = \widetilde{k}_n \right] = \frac{1}{\sharp k} \ .$$

ASSUME $w = \widetilde{w}$, $d < n$ AND $(k_i, m_i) = (\widetilde{k}_{n-d+i}, m_{n-d+i}^b)$ FOR $i \in \langle 1, d \rangle$. If $t_1 = y$, we must have $\widetilde{k}_{n-d+1} = k_1 = \mathrm{H}_1(w, t_1) = \mathrm{H}_1(\widetilde{w}, y) = \widetilde{k}_1$ and this only happens with probability

$$\Pr_{\widetilde{k}_1, \widetilde{k}_{n-d+1}} \left[\widetilde{k}_1 = \widetilde{k}_{n-d+1} \right] = \frac{1}{\sharp k} \ .$$

Now suppose $t_1 \neq y$. This imposes $\mathrm{H}_1(w, t_1) = \widetilde{k}_{n-d+1}$. Because $w = \widetilde{w}$ was never queried to H_1, this situation occurs with probability

$$\Pr_{\mathrm{H}_1} \left[\mathrm{H}_1(w, t_1) = \widetilde{k}_{n-d+1} \right] = \frac{1}{\sharp k} \ .$$

ASSUME $w = \widetilde{w}$, $d = n$ AND $(k_i, m_i) = (\widetilde{k}_i, m_i^b)$ FOR $i \in \langle 1, n \rangle$. Obviously $t_1 \neq y$, since otherwise $c = \widetilde{c}$. Now we must have $\widetilde{k}_1 = k_1 = \mathrm{H}_1(w, t_1) = \mathrm{H}_1(\widetilde{w}, t_1)$, which happens with probability

$$\Pr_{\mathrm{H}_1} \left[\mathrm{H}_1(\widetilde{w}, t_1) = \widetilde{k}_1 \right] = \frac{1}{\sharp k} \ .$$

ASSUME $w = \widetilde{w}$, $d \leq n$ AND $(k_i, m_i) \neq (\widetilde{k}_{n-d+i}, m_{n-d+i}^b)$ FOR SOME $i \in \langle 1, d-1 \rangle$. Let us consider H_{j+1} where $j = \max_{i \leq d-1} \{ (k_i, m_i) \neq (\widetilde{k}_{n-d+i}, m_{n-d+i}^b) \}$. We have $k_{j+1} = \mathrm{H}_{j+1}(k_j, m_j, w) = \widetilde{k}_{n-d+j+1}$, which, because w was never asked to H_{j+1}, occurs with probability

$$\Pr_{\mathrm{H}_{j+1}} \left[\mathrm{H}_{j+1}(k_j, m_j, w) = \widetilde{k}_{n-d+j+1} \right] = \frac{1}{\sharp k} \ .$$

CONCLUSION. Gathering all preceding bounds, we get

$$\Pr\left[c \text{ is valid} \wedge \mathbb{D}_{sk}^1 \text{ incorrect for } c\right] \leq \frac{1}{\sharp t_2} + \frac{4}{\sharp k} + \sum_{j<d\leq n} \frac{1}{\sharp k} \leq \frac{1}{\sharp t_2} + \frac{n+3}{\sharp k} \,,$$

which, taken over all queries of $\mathcal{A}_2$, leads to

$$\Pr\left[\mathbb{D}_{sk}^1 \text{ incorrect}\right] \leq q_{\mathbb{D}_{sk}^1}\left(\frac{1}{\sharp t_2} + \frac{n+3}{\sharp k}\right) \,.$$

We further define $\dot{\Pr}\left[\cdot\right] = \Pr\left[\cdot \mid \neg(\mathbb{D}_{sk}^1 \text{ incorrect})\right]$.

A.5   Reduction Cost

Success probability. Let us suppose that $\mathcal{A}$ distinguishes $\mathbb{E}_{pk}^1$ within a time bound τ with advantage ε in less than q_F, $q_H = \sum_{i \in \langle 1, n_{max}\rangle} q_{H_i}$, $q_{\mathbb{D}_{sk}^1}$ oracle calls. This means that

$$\dot{\Pr}\left[\mathcal{A} = b\right] \geq \frac{1}{2} + \frac{\varepsilon}{2} \,.$$

Suppose also that $\mathbb{E}_k$ is (τ, ν)-indistinguishable. Assuming that the plaintext extractor is correctly simulated, if none of the events E_i, E_i', E_i'' or E_F occurs, then $\mathcal{A}$ never asked $\widetilde{w}$ to any of the random oracles and so could not learn any information whatsoever about the keys $\widetilde{k}_i$ under which the m_i^b were encrypted in $\widetilde{c}$ due to the randomness of the H_i. By virtue of lemma 1, this upper-limits the information leakage on b by $n\nu$, since $\mathcal{A}$'s running time is bounded by τ. Noting $\mathsf{E}_{win} = \mathsf{E}_F \bigvee_{i \in \langle 1, n_{max}\rangle} \mathsf{E}_i \bigvee_{i \in \langle 1, n\rangle} \mathsf{E}_i' \vee \mathsf{E}_i''$, this means

$$\dot{\Pr}\left[\mathcal{A} = b \mid \neg\mathsf{E}_{win}\right] \leq \frac{1}{2} + \frac{n\nu}{2} \,.$$

We then get

$$\frac{1}{2} + \frac{\varepsilon}{2} \leq \dot{\Pr}\left[\mathcal{A} = b\right] \leq \dot{\Pr}\left[\mathcal{A} = b \mid \neg\mathsf{E}_{win}\right] + \dot{\Pr}\left[\mathsf{E}_{win}\right] \leq \frac{1}{2} + \frac{n\nu}{2} + \dot{\Pr}\left[\mathsf{E}_{win}\right] \,,$$

wherefrom $\dot{\Pr}\left[\mathsf{E}_{win}\right] \geq (\varepsilon - n\nu)/2$. But $\dot{\Pr}\left[\mathcal{B} = \widetilde{w}\right] = \dot{\Pr}\left[\mathsf{E}_{win}\right]$ and finally,

$$\Pr\left[\mathcal{B} = \widetilde{w}\right] \geq \dot{\Pr}\left[\mathcal{B} = \widetilde{w}\right] - \Pr\left[\mathbb{D}_{sk}^1 \text{ incorrect}\right]$$

$$\geq \frac{\varepsilon - n\nu}{2} - q_{\mathbb{D}_{sk}^1}\left(\frac{1}{\sharp t_2} + \frac{n+3}{\sharp k}\right) \,.$$

Since the blocklength n of the message sequences (m^0, m^1) output by $\mathcal{A}_1$ cannot exceed n_{max}, $\mathcal{B}$ inverts $\mathcal{E}_{pk}$ on y with probability greater than

$$\frac{\varepsilon}{2} - q_{\mathbb{D}_{sk}^1}\left(\frac{1}{\sharp t_2} + \frac{3}{\sharp k}\right) - n_{max}\left(\frac{\nu}{2} + \frac{q_{\mathbb{D}_{sk}^1}}{\sharp k}\right) \,,$$

i.e. succeeds with non-negligible probability.

Total number of calls to $\mathcal{O}^{\text{PCA}}$. Each simulated oracle H_i (resp. F) makes at most q_{H_i} (resp. q_F) queries to the plaintext-checking oracle. Note that the queries required by $\mathbb{D}^1_{sk}$ were already asked to $\mathcal{O}^{\text{PCA}}$ by either F or one of the H_i. By keeping tracks of all queries to $\mathcal{O}^{\text{PCA}}$, it is easy to see that the total number of calls actually needed by $\mathcal{B}$ is upper-bounded by

$$q_{\mathcal{O}^{\text{PCA}}} \leq q_F + q_H \quad \text{where} \quad q_H = \sum_{i \in \langle 1, n_{max} \rangle} q_{H_i} \; .$$

Total running time. The reduction algorithm runs in time bounded by

$$\tau_{\mathcal{B}} = \tau + (q_{\mathbb{D}^1_{sk}} + 1)\,(q_F + q_H) \cdot (\tau_{\text{PCA}} + O(1)) \; .$$

On Sufficient Randomness
for Secure Public-Key Cryptosystems

Takeshi Koshiba

Secure Computing Lab., Fujitsu Laboratories Ltd.,
4-1-1 Kamikodanaka, Nakahara-ku, Kawasaki 211-8588, Japan
koshiba@acm.org

Abstract. In this paper, we consider what condition is sufficient for random inputs to secure probabilistic public-key encryption schemes. Although a framework given in [16] enables us to discuss uniformly and comprehensively security notions of public-key encryption schemes even for the case where cryptographically weak pseudorandom generator is used as random nonce generator to encrypt single plaintext messages, the results are rather theoretical. Here we naturally generalize the framework in order to handle security for the situation where we want to encrypt many messages with the same key. We extend some results w.r.t. single message security in [16] – separation results between security notions and a non-trivial sufficient condition for the equivalence between security notions – to multiple messages security. Besides the generalization, we show another separation between security notions for k-tuple messages and for $(k+1)$-tuple messages. The natural generalization, obtained here, rather improves to understand the security of public-key encryption schemes and eases the discussion of the security of practical public-key encryption schemes. In other words, the framework contributes to elucidating the role of randomness in public-key encryption scheme. As application of results in the generalized framework, we consider compatibility between the ElGamal encryption scheme and some sequence generators. Especially, we consider the applicability of the linear congruential generator (LCG) to the ElGamal encryption scheme.

1 Introduction

One of the important goals in computational cryptography is to provide a public-key encryption scheme that achieves a security level as strong as possible under various circumstances. For this purpose, several security notions have been introduced. In particular, we will discuss in this paper the notions of "semantic security" and "ciphertext indistinguishability" introduced in [14], which have been shown to be equivalent [14,20]. For another major security notion, we have "non-malleability" introduced in [8]. These notions are basically defined in terms of an adversary who is given only a challenge ciphertext. This attack model is called *ciphertext only attack* (abbreviated COA). Besides COA, three major attack models have been studied in the literature. One is called *chosen plaintext*

D. Naccache and P. Paillier (Eds.): PKC 2002, LNCS 2274, pp. 34–47, 2002.
© Springer-Verlag Berlin Heidelberg 2002

attack (abbreviated CPA) model, in which the adversary can encrypt any plaintext messages of his choice. For more stronger attack models, chosen ciphertext attack and adaptive chosen ciphertext attack have been also considered in the literature [21,22].

Although these security notions have been studied quite well (see, e.g., [1,3]), we think that there are still some important issues that have not been addressed in the previous research. Security when used with a "pseudorandom" resource is one of such issues. Usually, security notions are defined assuming that ideal (i.e., true) random resource is available. Furthermore, it has been shown that one can safely use any "cryptographically strong polynomial-time pseudorandom" generator (see, e.g., [4,26]) for the substitute of the true random resource; that is, most security notions do not change by using the polynomial-time pseudorandomness for the true randomness. Although we have several "cryptographically strong" polynomial-time pseudorandom generators, they are unfortunately not fast enough for practical use, and much faster but less reliable pseudorandom generators have been used in many practical situations. Then the above security notions (and their relations) may be no longer valid with such weak pseudorandomness. In fact, it has been shown [2] that if DSS is used with the linear congruential generator, then its secret key can be easily detected after seeing a few signatures. Though this result indicates that the linear congruential generator is unsuitable for cryptographic purposes, it does not mean that the linear congruential generator is useless at all for *all* cryptographic systems. It is certainly important to study more carefully which aspect of the randomness is indeed important for discussing several security levels.

A framework introduced in [16] enables to discuss uniformly and comprehensively "semantic security" and "ciphertext indistinguishability" notions even for the case where some cryptographically weak pseudorandom generator is used as random nonce generator to encrypt plaintext messages. It has been shown that semantic security and ciphertext indistinguishability in the framework are not equivalent and a non-trivial sufficient condition for the equivalence has been given. Unfortunately, security notions only for the situation where we encrypt a single message per key generated can be handled in the framework. Clearly, in reality, we want to encrypt many messages with the same key. Nevertheless, security for multiple messages has not been intensively studied except results in [11]. In [11], security notions for multiple messages have been shown to coincide with their respective security notions for single messages. We note that such coincidence is proved only when cryptographically strong pseudorandom generators are used.

Here we naturally generalize the framework, proposed in [16], in order to handle security for multiple messages. We extend results w.r.t. single message security in [16] to multiple messages security. That is, we show that semantic security for k-tuple messages and ciphertext indistinguishability for k-tuple messages are not equivalent for any $k \geq 1$ and give a sufficient condition for the equivalence. Since these generalized results are easily derived from the original results, we stress that the generalization improves to understand the security of public-key encryption schemes and eases the discussion of the security of practical public-key encryption schemes. Besides the generalization, we show another separation between security notions for k-tuple messages and for $(k + 1)$-tuple messages. Moreover, the generalized framework enables us to discuss compatibility between public-key encryption schemes and practical pseudorandom generators. We stress that though the generalization is a natural extension, it may have an impact upon designing pseudorandom generators within practical public-key cryptosystems. In the single message security setting, it is hard to grasp the practical meaning of the results. On the other hand, generalized results with respect to the multiple message security help us to figure out involvement with practical systems. As application of results in the generalized framework, we consider compatibility between the ElGamal encryption scheme and some sequence generators. Especially, we show that linear congruential generator (LCG) is applicable to the ElGamal encryption scheme without losing security on some new and acceptable assumption.

The main contribution of this paper is rather providing a framework in which we can easily discuss security notions of practical public-key encryption schemes under more various circumstances than theoretical results. In addition, we stress that the framework elucidates the role of randomness in public-key encryption scheme.

Notations and Conventions

We introduce some useful notations and conventions for discussing probabilistic algorithms. If A is a probabilistic algorithm, then for any input x, the notation $A(x)$ refers to the probability space which assigns to the string y the probability that A, on input x, outputs y. If S is a probability space, denote by $\Pr_{e \leftarrow S}[e]$ (or $\Pr_S[e]$) the probability that S associates with element e. When we consider finite sample sets, it is convenient to consider separately a sample set and probability distribution on the set. If S is a finite set and D is a probability distribution on S, denote by $\Pr_{e \in_D S}[e]$ the probability that element $e \in S$ is chosen according to D. If S is a finite set, denote by $\Pr_{e \in_U S}[e]$ the probability that element $e \in S$ is chosen uniformly.

By 1^n we denote the unary representation of the integer n. A function $f : \{0,1\}^* \to \{0,1\}^*$ is *polynomially-bounded* if there exists a polynomial $p(\cdot)$ such that $|f(x)| \le p(|x|)$ for all $x \in \{0,1\}^*$.

2   New Framework

In this section, we prepare a framework in which we can uniformly and comprehensively discuss "semantic security" and "ciphertext indistinguishability" notions for multiple messages even for the case where some cryptographically weak pseudorandom generator is used as random nonce generator to encrypt messages. This framework is a slightly generalized version of the framework proposed in [16]. We stress that the generalization improves to understand the security of public-key encryption schemes and eases the discussion of the security of practical public-key encryption schemes thought the generalization itself is slight.

2.1   *R*-sequence for Random Inputs to Encryption Algorithms

We begin with introducing the notion of "*R*-sequence" and some notations. An *R*-sequence is just a sequence of strings (of certain length ℓ) randomly and uniformly chosen from some (finite) subset of initial segments of sequences of strings (of length ℓ). More specifically, we consider the following set family of string sequences.

Definition 1. Let $q(\cdot)$ be a polynomial. A $q(n)$-*R-sequence set family* (abbreviated RSSF) $\{R_n\}_{n\in\mathbb{N}}$ is a set family of sequences of strings of length $q(n)$.

Below we usually use $\{R_n\}$ to denote some RSSF. On the other hand, we consider a special $q(n)$-RSSF, where $q(n)$-RSSF $\{T_n\}$ is just a collection of sets of all infinite sequences of strings of length $q(n)$, and denote the special RSSF by TSSF. We sometimes use TSSF instead of true randomness in the sequel. Note that, in order to regard sequences in R_n as infinite ones, we sometimes consider the concatenation of the finite sequence in R_n and some infinite sequences of constant dummy strings. Although each element in R_n is possibly infinite, we use its finite initial segments only. So, we prepare some operation $Pref(\cdot,\cdot)$ on R_n; $Pref(R_n, i)$ denotes a set $\{(r_1, \ldots, r_i) : (r_1, \ldots, r_i)$ is the initial segment of a sequence in $R_n\}$. This is because we avoid a tedious discussion of random variables of infinite domain.

Our ultimate purpose is to give a taxonomy of RSSF from a viewpoint of the security of public-key encryption schemes. We will enumerate some conditions over RSSF to begin with.

While the well-known fact can be restated in our framework as the polynomial-time pseudorandomness (see, e.g., [4,26]) is *sufficient* to have the equivalence between semantic security and ciphertext indistinguishability, we show that the polynomial-time pseudorandomness is not necessary to have the equivalence. This implies that there may be more usable sufficient conditions for the equivalence. It is easy to consider separately "efficient samplability" and 'indistinguishability from true randomness" as some properties on *R*-sequences. We call the former property *samplability* simply and the latter *semi-randomness* to distinguish from pseudorandomness. "Samplability" is quite a natural property because generators without samplability is, in general, difficult to use algorithmically. Especially in Monte-Carlo simulation, far efficient samplability is required much. On the other hand, "semi-randomness" is also one of important properties. Semi-random sequences pass many feasible statistical tests. Some sequences that are obtained from physical sources such as electronic noise or the quantum effects in a semiconductor. When the sequences pass all known feasible statistical tests, it is often that such sequences may have the semi-randomness property. So, in this paper, we study these two properties on RSSF.

We begin with definition of "semi-randomness." Semi-random sequences are ones which are not distinguished from the true randomness by any polynomial-size circuit. More specifically, we consider the following definition.

Definition 2. A $q(n)$-RSSF $\{R_n\}$ is said to be $t(n)$-*semi-random* if for any polynomial-size circuit family $\{C_n\}_{n\in\mathbb{N}}$, any polynomial $p(\cdot)$, all sufficiently large n,

$$\left| \Pr_{\substack{(r_1,\ldots,r_{t(n)})\in_U \\ Pref(R_n,t(n))}} \left[C_n(r_1,\ldots,r_{t(n)}) = 1 \right] - \Pr_{\substack{(r'_1,\ldots,r'_{t(n)})\in_U \\ Pref(T_n,t(n))}} \left[C_n(r'_1,\ldots,r'_{t(n)}) = 1 \right] \right| < \frac{1}{p(n)},$$

where $\{T_n\}$ is TSSF.

We note that semi-random sequences are different from output sequences by polynomial-time pseudorandom generators. Semi-random sequences need not to be recursive nor generated efficiently.

Next, we give a definition of "samplability." For any samplable sequence, there exists a (polynomial-size) generator $\{S_n\}_{n\in\mathbb{N}}$ whose output is statistically close to the samplable sequence. More specifically, we consider the following definition.

Definition 3. A $q(n)$-RSSF $\{R_n\}$ is said to be $t(n)$-*samplable* if there exists a polynomial-size circuit family $\{S_n\}_{n\in\mathbb{N}}$ so that for every polynomial $p(\cdot)$ and all sufficiently large n,

$$\max_A \left\{ \left| \Pr_{r\in_U\{0,1\}^{q(n)}} \left[S_n(r) \in A \right] - \Pr_{\substack{(r_1,\ldots,r_{t(n)})\in_U \\ Pref(R_n,t(n))}} \left[(r_1,\ldots,r_{t(n)}) \in A \right] \right| \right\} < \frac{1}{p(n)},$$

where the maximum is taken all over the subsets A of $Pref(T_n,t(n))$.

We note that the maximum value in the above definition is so called "statistical difference" between two probability distributions: $\{S_n(r)\}_{r\in_U\{0,1\}^{q(n)}}$ and the uniform distribution on $Pref(R_n,t(n))$.

We extend the notion of public-key encryption scheme in order to cope with RSSF instead of true randomness. The following is our treatment for public-key encryption schemes in the new framework. The following definition seems to be cumbersome. Since nonces in encryption are not necessarily independent of each other, the definition below seems to be more complex than the original (simplified) definition.

Definition 4 (public-key encryption scheme, revisited). A *public-key encryption scheme* is a quadruple (G, M, E, D), where the following conditions hold.

1. G, called the *key generator*, is a probabilistic polynomial-time algorithm which, on input 1^n, outputs a pair of binary strings. (Although the key generator also uses randomness, we disregard it here in order to cast light on roles of randomness in encrypting. So, we assume that randomness in key generator is always ideal.)

2. $M = \{M_n\}_{n \in \mathbb{N}}$ is a family of message spaces from which all plaintext messages will be drawn. In order to make our notation simpler (but without loss of generality), we will assume that $M_n = \{0,1\}^n$.
3. For every polynomial $q(\cdot)$, every $q(n)$-RSSF $\{R_n\}$, every n, every pair (e, d) in the support of $G(1^n)$, for any integer $k \geq 1$ and for any $\alpha_1, \ldots, \alpha_k \in M_n$, (*encryption*) "deterministic" polynomial-time algorithm E and (*decryption*) deterministic polynomial-time algorithm D satisfy

$$\Pr_{\substack{(r_1,\ldots,r_k) \in_U \\ Pref(R_n,k)}} \left[\bigwedge_{i=1}^{k} D(d, E(e, \alpha_i; r_i)) = \alpha_i \right] = 1,$$

where the probability is over the uniform distribution on $Pref(R_n, k)$.

Hereafter, we write $E_e(\alpha; r)$ instead of $E(e, \alpha; r)$ and $D_d(\beta)$ instead of $D(d, \beta)$. We note that the argument r in the term $E_e(\alpha; r)$ denotes the random input to the encryption algorithm E. Also, we let $G_1(1^n)$ denote the first element (i.e., encryption key) in the pair $G(1^n)$. Without loss of generality, we treat the encryption algorithm as deterministic one fed with a plaintext message and a (random) supplementary input of length $q(n)$.

2.2   Security Notions in the New Framework

In this subsection, we reformulate the notions of semantic security and indistinguishability to suit the new framework.

Since Goldwasser and Micali defined semantic security and ciphertext indistinguishability (a.k.a. polynomial security), several ways to define such notions are shown. In this paper, we adopt a non-uniform formulation as in [11] in order to simplify the exposition. We note that employing such a non-uniform formulation (rather than a uniform one) may strengthen the definitions; yet, it does weaken the implications proven between the definitions, since proofs make free usage of non-uniformity.

A transformation is a uniform algorithm which, on inputs $\overline{C_n}$, outputs $\overline{C'_n}$, where $\overline{C_n}$ (resp., $\overline{C'_n}$) is the representation of a circuit C_n (resp., C'_n) in some standard encoding. Without loss of generality, we identify a circuit with its representation (in the standard encoding).

Definition 5. A public-key encryption scheme (G, M, E, D) is *semantically secure for $t(n)$-tuple messages w.r.t. $q(n)$-RSSF* $\{R_n\}$ if there exists a probabilistic polynomial-time transformation T so that every polynomial-size circuit family $\{C_n\}_{n \in \mathbb{N}}$, for every probability ensemble $\{\bar{X}_n\}_{n \in \mathbb{N}}$ satisfying that $\bar{X}_n$ is a probability distribution on $M_n^{t(n)}$, every pair of polynomially-bounded functions $f, h : \{0,1\}^* \to \{0,1\}^*$, every polynomial $p(\cdot)$ and all sufficiently large n,

$$\Pr_{\substack{G,\bar{X};(r_1,\ldots,r_{t(n)}) \in_U \\ Pref(R_n,t(n))}} \left[C_n(G_1(1^n), \bar{E}_{G_1(1^n)}(\bar{X}_n; \bar{r}), 1^n, h(\bar{X}_n)) = f(\bar{X}_n) \right]$$

$$< \Pr_{T,G,\bar{X}_n} \left[C'_n(G_1(1^n), 1^n, h(\bar{X}_n)) = f(\bar{X}_n) \right] + \frac{1}{p(n)}$$

where $C_n' = T(C_n)$, $\bar{X}_n = (X_n^{(1)}, \ldots, X_n^{(t(n))})$, and $\bar{E}_e(\bar{X}_n; \bar{r}) = E_e(X_n^{(1)}; r_1), \ldots, E_e(X_n^{(t(n))}; r_{t(n)})$.

Some explanation on the attack model is needed here. In the above definition, an adversary C_n is given only an encryption key $G_1(1^n)$ and a ciphertext message $E_{G_1(1^n)}(X_n; r)$ (and some supplementary information $h(X_n)$). Thus, it is considered as ciphertext only attack (COA) model. But note here that we may consider any polynomial-size circuit C_n for the adversary; hence, we may assume that the encryption algorithm is also included in C_n. In the situation where the true randomness is available, this immediately includes the chosen plaintext attack (CPA) model where the adversary can encrypt any plaintext messages of his choice. This is not true any more in the new framework because there is no guarantee that some (randomized) polynomial-size circuit can generate R-sequences in R_n uniformly at random. Moreover, we consider our revised COA model. For our COA model, we consider the situation where an adversary cannot directly access to R-sequence generators. The situation means that those who use public-key encryption scheme have their own *private* R-sequence generators. In general, they do not have to publicize their R-sequence generators which are used in public-key encryption scheme. In addition, the case where R-sequence generators are *privately* used is more secure than the case where R-sequence generators are *publicly* used. Thus, we can say that our COA model makes sense.

Definition 6. A public-key encryption scheme (G, M, E, D) is *ciphertext indistinguishable for $t(n)$-tuple messages w.r.t. $q(n)$-RSSF* $\{R_n\}$ if for every polynomial-size circuit family $\{C_n\}_{n \in \mathbb{N}}$, every polynomial $p(\cdot)$, all sufficiently large n and every $x_1, \ldots, x_{t(n)}, y_1, \ldots, y_{t(n)} \in M_n$,

$$\left| \Pr_{\substack{G; (r_1, \ldots, r_{t(n)}) \in_U \\ Pref(R_n, t(n))}} \left[C_n(G_1(1^n), \bar{E}_{G_1(1^n)}(\bar{x}; \bar{r})) = 1 \right] \right.$$

$$\left. - \Pr_{\substack{G; (r_1', \ldots, r_{t(n)}') \in_U \\ Pref(R_n, t(n))}} \left[C_n(G_1(1^n), \bar{E}_{G_1(1^n)}(\bar{y}; \bar{r}')) = 1 \right] \right| < \frac{1}{p(n)}$$

where $\bar{x} = (x_1, \ldots, x_{t(n)})$, $\bar{y} = (y_1, \ldots, y_{t(n)})$, $\bar{E}_e(\bar{x}; \bar{r}) = E_e(x_1; r_1), \ldots, E_e(x_{t(n)}; r_{t(n)})$, and $\bar{E}_e(\bar{y}; \bar{r}') = E_e(y_1; r_1'), \ldots, E_e(y_{t(n)}; r_{t(n)}')$.

The following notion is somewhat artificial. However, it is useful to characterize the notions of semantic security and ciphertext indistinguishability.

Definition 7. A public-key encryption scheme (G, M, E, D) is *ciphertext skew-indistinguishable for $t(n)$-tuple messages w.r.t. $q(n)$-RSSF* $\{R_n\}$ if for every polynomial-size circuit family $\{C_n\}_{n \in \mathbb{N}}$, every polynomial $p(\cdot)$, all sufficiently large n and every $x_1, \ldots, x_{t(n)}, y_1, \ldots, y_{t(n)} \in M_n$,

$$\left| \Pr_{\substack{G;(r_1,\ldots,r_{t(n)}) \in_U \\ Pref(R_n,t(n))}} \left[C_n(G_1(1^n), \bar{E}_{G_1(1^n)}(\bar{x}; \bar{r})) = 1 \right] \right.$$

$$\left. - \Pr_{\substack{G;(r'_1,\ldots,r'_{t(n)}) \in_U \\ Pref(T_n,t(n))}} \left[C_n(G_1(1^n), \bar{E}_{G_1(1^n)}(\bar{y}; \tilde{r})) = 1 \right] \right| < \frac{1}{p(n)}$$

where $\bar{x} = (x_1, \ldots, x_{t(n)})$, $\bar{y} = (y_1, \ldots, y_{t(n)})$, $\bar{E}_e(\bar{x}; \bar{r}) = E_e(x_1; r_1), \ldots,$ $E_e(x_{t(n)}; r_{t(n)})$, and $\bar{E}_e(\bar{y}; \tilde{r}) = E_e(y_1; r'_1), \ldots, E_e(y_{t(n)}; r'_{t(n)})$.

We note that, in three definitions above, any adversary does not directly access to RSSF but gets ciphertext messages encrypted using the RSSF as inputs.

We have seen some security notions for public-key encryption schemes. Here we mention known results w.r.t. multiple messages security by our terminology.

Theorem 1 ([11,14,20]). *Let (G, M, E, D) be a public-key encryption scheme. The following statements are equivalent.*

1. *(G,M,E,D) is semantically secure for single message w.r.t. TSSF.*
2. *(G,M,E,D) is ciphertext indistinguishable for single message w.r.t. TSSF.*
3. *(G,M,E,D) is semantically secure for polynomial-tuple messages w.r.t. TSSF.*
4. *(G,M,E,D) is ciphertext indistinguishable for polynomial-tuple messages w.r.t. TSSF.*

Recall that TSSF is a special case of RSSF. So, the equivalence is satisfied if the true randomness (say, TSSF) is used as random inputs. In what follows, we discuss general cases.

3   Results

3.1   Separation Results

In this subsection, we consider classes of pairs of RSSF and public-key encryptions scheme w.r.t. the RSSF. We especially show that semantic security and ciphertext indistinguishability for multiple messages are separable from each other.

We denote by $\mathcal{SS}_r^{t(n)}$ the class of pairs of encryption scheme (G, M, E, D) and RSSF $\{R_n\}$ satisfying that (G, M, E, D) w.r.t. $\{R_n\}$ is semantically secure for $t(n)$-tuple messages. We also denote $\langle (G, M, E, D), \{R_n\} \rangle \in \mathcal{SS}_r^{t(n)}$ if an encryption scheme (G, M, E, D) which is semantically secure for $t(n)$-tuple messages w.r.t. a RSSF $\{R_n\}$. We denote by $\mathcal{IND}_{rr}^{t(n)}$ the class of pairs of encryption schemes (G, M, E, D) and RSSF $\{R_n\}$ satisfying that (G, M, E, D) w.r.t. RSSF $\{R_n\}$ is ciphertext indistinguishable for $t(n)$-tuple messages. We denote by $\mathcal{IND}_{rt}^{t(n)}$ the class of pairs of encryption scheme (G, M, E, D) and

RSSF $\{R_n\}$ satisfying that (G, M, E, D) w.r.t. RSSF $\{R_n\}$ is ciphertext skew-indistinguishable for $t(n)$-tuple messages.

In [16], some relations among security notions for single message have been already shown. In case of multiple messages, we can obtain similar results to the case of single message.

Theorem 2. *Suppose that there exists a public-key encryption scheme w.r.t. TSSF. Then, for any polynomial $t(n)$, $\mathcal{IND}_{rt}^{t(n)} \subsetneq \mathcal{SS}_r^{t(n)} \subsetneq \mathcal{IND}_{rr}^{t(n)}$.*

We omit the proof on account of space constraints. We note that the theorem can be similarly shown as a proof in [16].

3.2   Sufficient Condition for the Equivalence

In this subsection, we consider how properties of RSSF affect on the security of encryption schemes. We especially give a sufficient condition that semantic security and ciphertext indistinguishability for multiple messages become equivalent.

Theorem 3. *Let $t(n)$ be a polynomial. Suppose that $\langle (G, M, E, D), \{R_n\} \rangle \in \mathcal{IND}_{rr}^{t(n)}$. If $\{R_n\}$ is $t(n)$-semi-random, then $\langle (G, M, E, D), \{R_n\} \rangle \in \mathcal{IND}_{rt}^{t(n)}$.*

Theorem 4. *Let $t(n)$ be a polynomial. Suppose that $\langle (G, M, E, D), \{R_n\} \rangle \in \mathcal{IND}_{rr}^{t(n)}$. If $\{R_n\}$ is $t(n)$-samplable, then $\langle (G, M, E, D), \{R_n\} \rangle \in \mathcal{SS}_r^{t(n)}$.*

We omit the proofs for the above two theorems on account of space constraints. We note that the theorem can be similarly shown as a proof in [16].

Corollary 1. *Let $t(n)$ be a polynomial. Suppose that $\{R_n\}$ is $t(n)$-semi-random or $t(n)$-samplable. Then $\langle (G, M, E, D), \{R_n\} \rangle \in \mathcal{IND}_{rr}^{t(n)}$ if and only if $\langle (G, M, E, D), \{R_n\} \rangle \in \mathcal{SS}_r^{t(n)}$.*

Although we have a better sufficient condition for the equivalence between semantic security and ciphertext indistinguishability, the condition is not necessary for the equivalence.

Theorem 5. *Let $t(n)$ be a polynomial. Suppose that there exists a public-key encryption scheme that is semantically secure w.r.t. TSSF. There exists an encryption scheme (G, M, E, D) such that $\langle (G, M, E, D), \{R_n\} \rangle \in \mathcal{IND}_{rt}^{t(n)}$ and $\{R_n\}$ is not $t(n)$-semi-random.*

Proof. Suppose that $\langle (G, M, E, D), \{T_n\} \rangle \in \mathcal{IND}_{rt}^{t(n)}$, where $\{T_n\}$ is $q(n)$-TSSF. Then there exists an encryption scheme (G, M, E', D') such that $\langle (G, M, E', D'), \{T'_n\} \rangle \in \mathcal{IND}_{rt}^{t(n)}$, where $\{T'_n\}$ is $(q(n)+1)$-TSSF, $E'_e(\alpha; r) = E_e(\alpha; r_1)$, $D'_d(\beta) = D_d(\beta)$, $r = r_1 r_2$ and $|r_2| = 1$. We consider a RSSF $\{R_n\} = (\{0, 1\}^{q(n)} 1)^{t(n)}$. It is easy to see that $\langle (G, M, E', D'), \{R_n\} \rangle \in \mathcal{IND}_{rt}^{t(n)}$, because the last bit of random supplementary bit is not used in encrypting.

On the other hand, it is easy to see that $\{R_n\}$ and $\{T'_n\}$ are distinguishable. In other words, $\{R_n\}$ is not $t(n)$-semi-random.   □

3.3   Multiplicity

It is easy to see that the parameter of RSSF is available as a measure of compatibility between RSSFs and encryption schemes. The following theorem says that, for any pair of RSSF and encryption scheme, there may exist limitation on the numbers of messages which are encrypted with the same key and without losing security.

Theorem 6. *Let $t(\cdot)$ and $t'(\cdot)$ be polynomials. Suppose that there exists a public-key encryption scheme that is semantically secure w.r.t. TSSF. If $t(n) < t'(n)$ then $\mathcal{IND}_{rr}^{t'(n)} \subsetneq \mathcal{IND}_{rr}^{t(n)}$, $\mathcal{IND}_{rt}^{t'(n)} \subsetneq \mathcal{IND}_{rt}^{t(n)}$, and $\mathcal{SS}_{r}^{t'(n)} \subsetneq \mathcal{SS}_{r}^{t(n)}$.*

Proof. Let g be a pseudorandom generator which, given a seed s of length $q(n)$, outputs a string of length $t(n)q(n)$. We consider two RSSFs $R_n = \{g(s) : s \in \{0,1\}^{q(n)}\}$ and $R_n' = \{(g(s), g_l(s)) : s \in \{0,1\}^{q(n)}\}$, where $g_l(s)$ denotes the suffix of $g(s)$ of length $q(n)$. Let $\{T_n\}$ be $q(n)$-TSSF. Suppose that $\langle(G, M, E, D), \{T_n\}\rangle \in \mathcal{IND}_{rt}^{t(n)}$. It is easy to see that $\langle(G, M, E, D), \{R_n\}\rangle \in \mathcal{IND}_{rt}^{t(n)}$, which implies that $\langle(G, M, E, D), \{R_n\}\rangle \in \mathcal{SS}_{r}^{t(n)}$ and $\langle(G, M, E, D), \{R_n\}\rangle \in \mathcal{IND}_{rr}^{t(n)}$. It is also easy to see that $\langle(G, M, E, D), \{R_n'\}\rangle \notin \mathcal{IND}_{rt}^{t(n)+1}$ and $\langle(G, M, E, D), \{R_n'\}\rangle \notin \mathcal{IND}_{rr}^{t(n)+1}$, because encryptions of $x_1, \ldots, x_{t(n)}, x_{t(n)}$ and $y_1, \ldots, y_{t(n)}, y_{t(n)+1}$ are distinguishable. We consider a function f such that $f(x_1, \ldots, x_{t(n)}, x_{t(n)+1}) = 1$ if and only if $x_{t(n)} = x_{t(n)+1}$. Then $\langle(G, M, E, D), \{R_n'\}\rangle \notin \mathcal{SS}_{r}^{t(n)+1}$.

It is easy to see that $\mathcal{IND}_{rr}^{t'(n)} \subseteq \mathcal{IND}_{rr}^{t(n)}$, $\mathcal{IND}_{rt}^{t'(n)} \subseteq \mathcal{IND}_{rt}^{t(n)}$, and $\mathcal{SS}_{r}^{t'(n)} \subseteq \mathcal{SS}_{r}^{t(n)}$. This completes the proof. $\square$

4   Application

In [25], it is shown that the ElGamal encryption scheme [10] is semantically secure on condition that the decision Diffie-Hellman (DDH) problem is intractable. Let $\mathcal{G}$ be a group of some odd prime order q. Roughly speaking, the DDH problem is one to distinguish the uniform distribution on $\{(g, g^a, g^b, g^{ab}) : g \in \mathcal{G}, a, b \in \mathbb{Z}_q\} \subset \mathcal{G}^4$ from the uniform distribution on $\mathcal{G}^4$ (see, e.g., [5,7,19]). In this section, we consider the compatibility between the ElGamal encryption scheme and linear congruential sequences.

Let us give a simple description of the ElGamal encryption scheme $\mathbf{EG} = (G_{eg}, M_{eg}, E_{eg}, D_{eg})$. Key generation algorithm G_{eg} chooses an n-bit prime number p such that $p = 2q + 1$ and q is a prime number. Let $\mathcal{G}_p$ be the unique non-trivial subgroup of $\mathbb{Z}_p^*$. G_{eg} also chooses uniformly and randomly a generator $g \in \mathcal{G}_p$ and $x \in \mathbb{Z}_q$. G_{eg} finally outputs $((p, g, g^x), x)$. Message space M_{eg} is set to be $\mathcal{G}_p$. (Although, in the definition of encryption scheme, message space depends only on the security parameter, we use prime-dependent message space without loss of generality.) Encryption algorithm E_{eg}, given an encryption key (p, g, y), a message m and a random input r, outputs (g^r, my^r). We note that group operation is carried using the value p. Decryption algorithm D_{eg}, given a decryption key x and ciphertext (c_1, c_2), outputs $c_2/(c_1)^x$.

Let us consider the prime-indexed RSSF $\{R_p\}$ which corresponds to linear congruential sequences, where $R_p = \{(r, f_p(r), \ldots, f_p^{t(n)-1}(r)) : r \in \mathbb{Z}_q\}$ and f_p is a function of the form $f_p(r) = ar + b \bmod q$.

Now we are ready to consider the security of the ElGamal encryption scheme w.r.t. linear congruential sequence for random inputs. First, we restate some trivial statements using our terminology.

Proposition 1. *Suppose that the DDH problem is intractable. If the parameter a for linear congruential sequence is public, then $\langle \mathbf{EG}, \{R_p\} \rangle \in \mathcal{SS}_r^1$ and $\langle \mathbf{EG}, \{R_p\} \rangle \notin \mathcal{SS}_r^k$ for any $k \geq 2$.*

The above proposition seems to say that the linear congruential sequence is useless at all for the ElGamal encryption scheme. However, we do not have to publicize the parameter of the linear congruential sequence.

Proposition 2. *Suppose that the DDH problem is intractable. If the parameter of the linear congruential sequence is not public but randomly and uniformly distributed, then $\langle \mathbf{EG}, \{R_p\} \rangle \in \mathcal{SS}_r^2$.*

We do not know whether or not $\langle \mathbf{EG}, \{R_p\} \rangle \in \mathcal{SS}_r^3$ on the same assumption. So, we consider a bit stronger assumption. Let $\mathcal{L}_k = \{(gh, g^a h, \ldots, g^{a^k} h) : g, h \in \mathcal{G}_p, a \in \mathbb{Z}_q\} \subset (\mathcal{G}_p)^{k+1}$. We call the problem to distinguish the uniform distribution on $\mathcal{L}_k$ from the uniform distribution on $(\mathcal{G}_p)^{k+1}$ *decision k-skew-power series* (k-DSPS) problem. If $h = 1$ then the k-DSPS problem is reducible to the DDH problem. It seems that the k-DSPS problem is somewhat artificial. However, it is just a subproblem of a natural problem. We note that $\mathcal{G}_p$ is a commutative ring w.r.t. two operators $\oplus_g$ and $\otimes_g$, where $g^a \oplus_g g^b = g^{a+b}$ and $g^a \otimes_g g^b = g^{ab}$. The DDH problem is considered as the equivalence problem between $\alpha \otimes_g \beta$ and γ, where $\alpha, \beta, \gamma \in \mathcal{G}_p$. Similarly, the (computational) Diffie-Hellman problem is considered as the evaluating problem for $\alpha \otimes_g \beta$, where $\alpha, \beta \in \mathcal{G}_p$. Naturally, we can define *expression* on $\mathcal{G}_p$ using the additive operator $\oplus_g$ and the multiplicative operator $\otimes_g$. So, the equivalence problem for two expressions on $\mathcal{G}_p$ is more general than the DDH problem. It is easy to see that the k-DSPS problem is also a subproblem of the equivalence problem for two expressions on $\mathcal{G}_p$. We note that if both of two expressions on $\mathcal{G}_p$ do not include any multiplicative operator, the subproblem is easily solved.

Theorem 7. *Suppose that the k-DSPS problem is intractable, where k is a constant. If the parameter of the linear congruential sequence is not public but randomly and uniformly distributed, then $\langle \mathbf{EG}, \{R_p\} \rangle \in \mathcal{SS}_r^{k+1}$.*

Proof. The ciphertext skew-indistinguishability w.r.t. LCG follows directly from the assumption. Using Theorem 2, we get the assertion. □

We consider a bit stronger assumption that $z(n)$-DSPS problem is intractable for any polynomial $z(\cdot)$ and name it *DSPS assumption*. Then we get the following.

Corollary 2. *Under the DSPS assumption,* $\langle \mathbf{EG}, \{R_p\} \rangle \in \mathcal{SS}_r^{v(n)}$ *for any polynomial* $v(\cdot)$*.*

We note that in the case of the DSS in [2] the secret key can be detected by solving some simultaneous linear equations. However, in the case of the ElGamal encryption scheme w.r.t. LCG, such equations do not appear in ciphertext. Thus, the techniques in [2] do not seem to be applicable to the case of the ElGamal encryption scheme w.r.t. LCG.

5   Concluding Remarks

We have extended the framework proposed in [16] where we can uniformly and comprehensively discuss security notions of public-key encryption schemes even for the case where some cryptographically weak pseudorandom generator is used as random nonce generator to encrypt plaintext messages. We have also shown some separation results between security notions for multiple messages and given a sufficient condition for the equivalence between the security notions. Obtained results give us a clear sight for designing sequence generators for random inputs to public-key encryption schemes. We have shown that the LCG is available to random inputs to the ElGamal encryption schemes on some similar assumption with the DDH assumption, although the LCG itself is cryptographically weak [6,17,24]. However, reliability of the assumption may be controversial, thought it is weaker than a natural assumption where the equivalence problem for two expressions on $\mathcal{G}_p$ is intractable.

References

1. M. Bellare, A. Desai, D. Pointcheval, and P. Rogaway. Relations among notions of security for public-key encryption schemes. In H. Krawczyk, editor, *Advances in Cryptology — CRYPTO'98*, volume 1462 of *Lecture Notes in Computer Science*, pages 26–45. Springer-Verlag, 1998.
2. M. Bellare, S. Goldwasser, and D. Micciancio. Pseudo-random number generation within cryptographic algorithms: The DSS case. In B. S. Kaliski Jr., editor, *Advances in Cryptology — CRYPTO'97*, volume 1294 of *Lecture Notes in Computer Science*, pages 277–291. Springer-Verlag, 1997.
3. M. Bellare and A. Sahai. Non-malleable encryption: Equivalence between two notions, and an indistinguishability-based characterization. In M. Wiener, editor, *Advances in Cryptology — CRYPTO'99*, volume 1666 of *Lecture Notes in Computer Science*, pages 519–536. Springer-Verlag, 1999.
4. M. Blum and S. Micali. How to generate cryptographically strong sequences of pseudo-random bits. *SIAM Journal on Computing*, 13(4):850–864, 1984.
5. D. Boneh. The decision Diffie-Hellman problem. In J. P. Buhler, editor, *Proceedings of the 3rd International Symposium on Algorithmic Number Theory (ANTS-3)*, volume 1423 of *Lecture Notes in Computer Science*, pages 48–63. Springer-Verlag, 1998.
6. J. Boyar. Inferring sequences produced by pseudo-random number generators. *Journal of the Association for Computing Machinery*, 36(1):129–141, 1989.

7. W. Diffie and M. E. Hellman. New directions in cryptography. *IEEE Transactions on Information Theory*, IT-22(6):644–654, 1976.
8. D. Dolev, C. Dwork, and M. Naor. Non-malleable cryptography. In *Proceedings of the 23rd Annual ACM Symposium on Theory of Computing*, pages 542–552. ACM Press, 1991.
9. D. Dolev, C. Dwork, and M. Naor. Non-malleable cryptography. *SIAM Journal on Computing*, 30(2):391–437, 2000.
10. T. ElGamal. A public key cryptosystem and a signature scheme based on discrete logarithms. *IEEE Transactions on Information Theory*, IT-31(4):469–472, 1985.
11. O. Goldreich. *Foundation of Cryptography (Fragment of a Book – Version 2.03)*, 1998.
12. O. Goldreich. *Modern Cryptography, Probabilistic Proofs and Pseudorandomness*, volume 17 of *Algorithms and Combinatorics*. Springer-Verlag, 1999.
13. O. Goldreich. *Foundations of Cryptography: Basic Tools*. Cambridge University Press, 2001.
14. S. Goldwasser and S. Micali. Probabilistic encryption. *Journal of Computer and System Sciences*, 28(2):270–299, 1984.
15. T. Koshiba. A theory of randomness for public key cryptosystems: The ElGamal cryptosystem case. *IEICE Transactions on Fundamentals of Electronics, Communications and Computer Sciences*, E83-A(4):614–619, 2000.
16. T. Koshiba. A new aspect for security notions: Secure randomness in public-key encryption schemes. In K. Kim, editor, *Proceeding of the 4th International Workshop on Practice and Theory in Public Key Cryptography (PKC2001)*, volume 1992 of *Lecture Notes in Computer Science*, pages 87–103. Springer-Verlag, 2001.
17. H. Krawczyk. How to predict congruential generators. *Journal of Algorithms*, 13(4):527–545, 1992.
18. M. Luby. *Pseudorandomness and Cryptographic Applications*. Princeton Univ. Press, 1996.
19. U. M. Maurer and S. Wolf. Diffie-Hellman protocol. *Designs, Codes and Cryptography*, 19(2-3):147–171, 2000.
20. S. Micali, C. Rackoff, and B. Sloan. The notion of security for probabilistic cryptosystems. *SIAM Journal on Computing*, 17(2):412–426, 1988.
21. M. Naor and M. Yung. Public-key cryptosystems provably secure against chosen ciphertext attacks. In *Proceedings of the 22nd Annual ACM Symposium on Theory of Computing*, pages 427–437. ACM Press, 1990.
22. C. Rackoff and D. R. Simon. Non-interactive zero-knowledge proof of knowledge and chosen ciphertext attack. In J. Feigenbaum, editor, *Advances in Cryptology — CRYPTO'91*, volume 576 of *Lecture Notes in Computer Science*, pages 433–444. Springer-Verlag, 1992.
23. T. Saito, T. Koshiba, and A. Yamamura. The decision Diffie-Hellman assumption and the quadratic residuosity assumption. *IEICE Transactions on Fundamentals of Electronics, Communications and Computer Sciences*, E84-A(1):165–171, 2001.
24. J. Stern. Secret linear congruential generators are not cryptographically secure. In *Proceedings of the 28th Annual IEEE Symposium on Foundations of Computer Science*, pages 421–426. IEEE Computer Society Press, 1987.
25. Y. Tsiounis and M. Yung. On the security of ElGamal based encryption. In H. Imai and Y. Zheng, editors, *Proceedings of the 1st International Workshop on Practice and Theory in Public Key Cryptography (PKC'98)*, volume 1431 of *Lecture Notes in Computer Science*, pages 117–134. Springer-Verlag, 1998.

26. A. C. Yao. Theory and applications of trapdoor functions. In *Proceedings of the 23rd Annual IEEE Symposium on Foundations of Computer Science*, pages 80–91. IEEE Computer Society Press, 1982.

Multi-recipient Public-Key Encryption
with Shortened Ciphertext

Kaoru Kurosawa

Department of Computer and Information Sciences, Ibaraki University,
4-12-1 Nakanarusawa, Hitachi, Ibaraki, 316-8511, Japan
Tel/Fax. +81-294-38-5135
kurosawa@cis.ibaraki.ac.jp

Abstract. In the trivial n-recipient public-key encryption scheme, a ciphertext is a concatenation of independently encrypted messages for n recipients. In this paper, we say that an n-recipient scheme has a "*shortened ciphertext*" property if the length of the ciphertext is almost a half (or less) of the trivial scheme and the security is still almost the same as the underlying single-recipient scheme. We first present (multi-plaintext, multi-recipient) schemes with the "*shortened ciphertext*" property for ElGamal scheme and Cramer-Shoup scheme. We next show (single-plaintext, multi-recipient) hybrid encryption schemes with the "*shortened ciphertext*" property.

1 Introduction

1.1 Background

Suppose that there are n recipients. Let pk_i be the public key of recipient i for $1 \leq i \leq n$. The security of a public-key encryption scheme in the multi-recipient setting is different from the single-recipient setting. For example, if e is the common public exponent in RSA, then e encryptions of the same plaintext M under different moduli lead to an easy recovery of M. Further results by Hastad [11] and Coppersmith [7,8] proved that even the time-stamp variants can be successfully attacked with e ciphertexts.

In the trivial n-recipient public-key encryption scheme, a ciphertext is just a concatenation of independently encrypted messages for n recipients using a single-recipient public-key encryption algorithm $\mathcal{E}$. That is, $\mathcal{E}_{pk_1}(M_1)\|\cdots \|\mathcal{E}_{pk_n}(M_n)$, where $\|$ denotes concatenation. In general, this trivial scheme is not secure in the sense of invertibility even if $\mathcal{E}$ is secure in the same sense, as shown in the above RSA example.

Recently, Bellare et al. [2] and Baudron et al. [1] independently proved that the trivial n-recipient scheme is secure in the sense of indistinguishability [10] if $\mathcal{E}$ is secure in the same sense, where indistinguishability is a stronger security notion than invertibility.

However, their nice results [2,1] still do not capture the essence of the multi-recipient setting:

D. Naccache and P. Paillier (Eds.): PKC 2002, LNCS 2274, pp. 48–63, 2002.

(1) The length of the ciphertext of the trivial n-recipient scheme is n times larger than that of the underlying single-recipient scheme.

(2) Consider a single-recipient hybrid encryption scheme which encrypts a long message M using a pseudorandom generator G and sends the seed r of G using a public-encryption scheme. That is,

$$C = M \oplus G(r) \| \mathcal{E}_{pk}(r), \tag{1}$$

where $\|$ denotes concatenation. A natural extension of the hybrid scheme to an n-recipient scheme will be that

$$M \oplus G(r) \| \mathcal{E}_{pk_1}(r) \| \cdots \| \mathcal{E}_{pk_n}(r). \tag{2}$$

Their results [2,1] only imply that the latter part $\mathcal{E}_{pk_1}(r) \| \cdots \| \mathcal{E}_{pk_n}(r)$ is secure in the sense of indistinguishability if the single-recipient part $\mathcal{E}_{pk}(r)$ is secure in the same sense.

1.2   Our Contribution

In this paper, we consider n-recipient public-key encryption schemes such that the length of the ciphertext is almost a half (or less) of the trivial n-recipient scheme and the security is still almost the same as the underlying single-recipient scheme. We say that such a scheme has a *"shortened ciphertext"* property.

1. We first give the definitions of our model and the security.
2. We next present (*multi*-plaintext, multi-recipient) schemes with the *"shortened ciphertext"* property for ElGamal scheme and Cramer-Shoup scheme and prove their security.
3. We also prove that the above mentioned (*single*-plaintext, multi-recipient) scheme of eq.(2) is secure in the sense of indistinguishability against chosen plaintext attack if the underlying single-recipient public-key scheme is secure in the same sense.
4. We finally present how to construct a (single-plaintext, multi-recipient) scheme secure against chosen *ciphertext* attack with the "shortened ciphertext" property. The underlying single-recipient public-key scheme needs to be secure in the sense of indistinguishability against chosen ciphertext attack. (For example, we can use Rabin-SAEP or RSA-SAEP$^+$ [4] as the underlying single-recipient scheme.)

Cramer-Shoup scheme is a practical public-key encryption scheme which is secure in the sense of indistinguishability against chosen-ciphertext attack under the decision Diffie-Hellman (DDH) assumption in the standard model [9]. The basic Cramer-Shoup scheme uses universal one-way hash functions (UOH) [9, Sec.3]. Bellare et al. derived the concrete security of the basic Cramer-Shoup scheme by assuming the concrete security of UOH [2]. On the other hand, Cramer and Shoup also presented a hash-free variant which does not use UOH [9, Sec.5.3].

We derive the concrete security of the hash-free variant of Cramer-Shoup scheme. It is of independent interest because it truly depends only on the DDH assumption, but not UOH. We then present a (multi-plaintext, multi-recipient) hash-free Cramer-Shoup scheme that has the *"shortened ciphertext"* property.

One further advantage of our multi-recipient schemes (in the discrete log setting) is that the encryption operation can be significantly faster than if the encryption operations were performed separately for each recipient.

Finally, in all of our multi-recipient schemes, the decryption algorithm is the same as the single-recipient one. Therefore, no extra cost is required for each recipient.

1.3 Related Works

The "broadcast" problem has been addressed by other authors in the context of traitor-tracing [6,12,5,13]. The traitor-tracing schemes such that [12,5,13] can have even shorter ciphertexts than our schemes, but with the tradeoff that a small coalition of recipients can break the traitor-tracing aspect of the scheme, i.e., construct a new private key that does not identify anyone in the coalition. In our schemes, no coalition can do this since each private key uniquely identifies the recipient.

Bellare and Rogaway [3] proved that the single recipient hybrid encryption scheme shown in eq.(1) is secure in the sense of indistinguishability against chosen plaintext under the random oracle moel if $\mathcal{E}_{pk}$ is a trapdoor oneway permutation. They also proved that the following scheme secure in the sense of indistinguishability against chosen ciphertext under the random oracle moel.

$$C = \mathcal{E}_{pk}(r)||M \oplus G(r)||H(M||r),$$

where H is a hash function. Before that, Zheng and Seberry [16] proposed a scheme such that

$$C = \mathcal{E}_{pk}(r)||(G(r) \oplus (M||H(M))).$$

2   Single-Recipient Encryption Scheme

A single-recipient public-key encryption scheme $\mathcal{PE} = (\mathcal{K}, \mathcal{E}, \mathcal{D})$ consists of three algorithms. The key generation algorithm $\mathcal{K}$ outputs (pk, sk) on input some global information I, where pk is a public key and sk is the secret key; we write $(pk, sk) \overset{R}{\leftarrow} \mathcal{K}(I)$. The encryption algorithm $\mathcal{E}$ outputs a ciphertext C on input the public key pk and a plaintext M; we write $C \overset{R}{\leftarrow} \mathcal{E}_{pk}(M)$. The decryption algorithm $\mathcal{D}$ outputs M or *reject* on input the secret key sk and a ciphertext C; we write $x \leftarrow \mathcal{D}_{sk}(C)$, where $x = M$ or *reject*. We require that $\mathcal{D}_{sk}(\mathcal{E}_{pk}(M)) = M$ for each plaintext M.

An adversary B runs in two stages. In "find" stage, it takes a public key pk and outputs two equal length messages M_0 and M_1 together with some state information *state*. In "guess" stage, it gets a challenge ciphertext $C_b \overset{R}{\leftarrow} \mathcal{E}_{pk}(M_b)$ from the encryption oracle $\mathcal{E}_{pk}$, where b is a randomly chosen bit. B finally outputs a bit $\tilde{b}$. The advantage of B is measured by the probability $\Pr(\tilde{b} = b)$.

Formally, the security of $\mathcal{PE}$ in the sense of indistinguishability against chosen-plaintext attack is defined as follows.

Definition 2.1. *For $b = 0$ and 1, define the experiment as follows.*

$$(pk_1, sk_1) \overset{R}{\leftarrow} K(I), (M_0, M_1, state) \overset{R}{\leftarrow} B(find, pk),$$
$$C_b \overset{R}{\leftarrow} \mathcal{E}_{pk}(M_b), \tilde{b} \overset{R}{\leftarrow} B(guess, C_b, state).$$

Let

$$\mathrm{Adv}^{s\text{-}cpa}_{\mathcal{PE}, I}(B) \overset{\mathrm{def}}{=} \Pr(\tilde{b} = 0 \mid b = 0) - \Pr(\tilde{b} = 0 \mid b = 1)$$
$$\mathrm{Adv}^{s\text{-}cpa}_{\mathcal{PE}, I}(t) \overset{\mathrm{def}}{=} \max_B \mathrm{Adv}^{s\text{-}cpa}_{\mathcal{PE}, I}(B),$$

where the maximum is over all B with time-complexity t.

(In the superscript, s- denotes "single recipient".)

Definition 2.2. *We say that $\mathcal{PE}$ is secure against chosen-plaintext attack if $\mathrm{Adv}^{s\text{-}cpa}_{\mathcal{PE}, I}(t)$ is negligible for polynomially bounded t, where the complexity is measured as a function of a security parameter.*

It is easy to see that

$$\Pr(\tilde{b} = b) = \frac{1}{2} + \frac{1}{2}\mathrm{Adv}^{s\text{-}cpa}_{\mathcal{PE}, I}(B) \tag{3}$$

The security against chosen-ciphertext attack is defined similarly except for that the adversary B gets the decryption oracle $\mathcal{D}_{sk}$ and is allowed to query any ciphertext C at most q_d times, where it must be that $C \neq C_b$ in the guess stage. We denote the advantages by $\mathrm{Adv}^{s\text{-}cca}_{\mathcal{PE}, I}(B)$ and $\mathrm{Adv}^{s\text{-}cca}_{\mathcal{PE}, I}(t, q_d)$, respectively.

3   Multi-recipient Encryption Scheme

Suppose that there are n recipients. Let $N \overset{\mathrm{def}}{=} \{1, \cdots, n\}$. We define (*single*-plaintext, multi-recipient) public-key encryption schemes and (*multi*-plaintext, multi-recipient) public-key encryption schemes as follows.

- In a (*single*-plaintext, multi-recipient) public-key encryption scheme, a sender sends the same plaintext M secretly to a subset of recipients $S \subseteq N$ by broadcasting a ciphertext C_S.
- In a (*multi*-plaintext, multi-recipient) public-key encryption scheme, a sender sends an independent plaintext M_i secretly to each recipient $i \in S$ by broadcasting a ciphertext C_S.

3.1 "Shortened Ciphertext" Property

A multi-recipient public-key encryption scheme is naturally constructed from a single-recipient public-key encryption scheme $\mathcal{PE} = (\mathcal{K}, \mathcal{E}, \mathcal{D})$ as follows. The key generation algorithm runs $\mathcal{K}(I)$ n times independently. A ciphertext C_N is

$$C_N = \mathcal{E}_{pk_1}(M_1) || \cdots || \mathcal{E}_{pk_n}(M_n),$$

where $||$ denotes concatenation. We call this scheme the *trivial multi-recipient* scheme.

Bellare et al. [2] proved that the trivial multi-recipient scheme is secure in the sense of indistinguishability if $\mathcal{PE}$ is secure in the same sense. Baudron et al. [1] proved the same result independently. However, the length of the ciphertext of the trivial multi-recipient scheme is n times larger than that of the single-recipient scheme.

In this paper, we consider multi-recipient public-key encryption schemes such that (1) the length of the ciphertext is almost a half (or less) of the trivial multi-recipient scheme and (2) the security is still almost the same as the underlying single-recipient scheme. We say that such a scheme has a *"shortened ciphertext"* property.

3.2 Our Model

For a single-recipient public-key encryption scheme $\mathcal{PE} = (\mathcal{K}, \mathcal{E}, \mathcal{D})$, we define a (multi-plaintext, multi-recipient) public-key encryption scheme $\mathcal{PE}^n = (\mathcal{K}^n, \mathcal{E}^n, TAKE)$ as follows.

- The key generation algorithm $\mathcal{K}^n$ outputs $\underline{pk} \overset{\text{def}}{=} (pk_1, \cdots, pk_n)$ and $\underline{sk} \overset{\text{def}}{=} (sk_1, \cdots, sk_n)$ on input some global information I, where (pk_i, sk_i) is a pair of encryption/decryption keys of recipient i.
- For $S = \{1_1, \cdots i_s\}$, let M_{i_j} be a plaintext for recipient $i_j \in S$. Let $\underline{M}_S \overset{\text{def}}{=} (M_{i_1}, \cdots, M_{i_s})$. Then the encryption algorithm $\mathcal{E}^n$ computes a ciphertext C_S for $\underline{M}_S$ on input $\underline{pk}$, S and $\underline{M}_S$; we write $C_S \overset{R}{\leftarrow} \mathcal{E}^n_{\underline{pk}}(S, \underline{M}_S)$.
- $TAKE$ is a hash function that takes a part of a ciphertext as follows. For $T \subset S \subseteq N$, it outputs C_T on input T, S and C_S. We write $C_T \leftarrow TAKE_T(C_S)$. Especially, for $i \in S$, we write $C_i \leftarrow TAKE_i(C_S)$. We require that $\mathcal{D}_{sk_i}(TAKE_i(C_S)) = M_i$ for all $i \in S$ and any M_i.

A (single-plaintext, multi-recipient) public-key encryption scheme is defined similarly.

Remark 3.1. In our multi-recipient schemes, the decryption algorithm is the same as the single-recipient scheme. Therefore, no extra cost is required for each recipient.

3.3 Security

We generalize the definition of security for the multi-recipient setting given by Bellare et al. [2] to (multi-plaintext,multi-recipient) schemes as follows.

We consider an experiment as follows. At the beginning, a challenge bit b is randomly chosen and fixed. An adversary B is provided with the encryption oracle $\mathcal{E}_{\underline{pk}}^n$ and it is allowed to query $(S, \underline{M}_S^0, \underline{M}_S^1)$ at most q_e times. $\mathcal{E}_{\underline{pk}}^r$ returns a ciphertext $\mathcal{E}_{\underline{pk}}^n(S, \underline{M}_S^b)$. (Since b is fixed at the beginning, the same b is used across all the queries.) B finally outputs a bit $\tilde{b}$. We require that $|M_{i_j}^0| = |M_{i_j}^1|$ for all $i_j \in S$, where $\underline{M}_S^0 = (M_{i_1}^0, \cdots, M_{i_s}^0)$ and $\underline{M}_S^1 = (M_{i_1}^1, \cdots, M_{i_s}^1)$.

Each time, B can choose $(S, \underline{M}_S^0, \underline{M}_S^1)$ arbitrarily, where S as well as $(\underline{M}_S^0, \underline{M}_S^1)$ may be related to his other queries to $\mathcal{E}_{\underline{pk}}^n$. Then the security of $\mathcal{PE}^n$ against chosen-plaintext attack is defined as follows.

Definition 3.1. *For $b = 0$ and 1, define the experiment as follows.*

$$(\underline{pk}, \underline{sk}) \overset{R}{\leftarrow} K^n(I), \ \tilde{b} \leftarrow B^{\mathcal{E}_{\underline{pk}}^n}(I, \underline{pk}).$$

Let

$$\mathrm{Adv}_{\mathcal{PE}^n, I}^{n\text{-}cpa}(B) \overset{\mathrm{def}}{=} \Pr(\tilde{b} = 0 \mid b = 0) - \Pr(\tilde{b} = 0 \mid b = 1)$$

$$\mathrm{Adv}_{\mathcal{PE}^n, I}^{n\text{-}cpa}(t, q_e) \overset{\mathrm{def}}{=} \max_B \mathrm{Adv}_{\mathcal{PE}^n, I}^{n\text{-}cpa}(B),$$

where the maximum is over all B with time-complexity t.

In the superscript, n- denotes "n recipients".

Definition 3.2. *We say that $\mathcal{PE}^n$ is secure against chosen-plaintext attack if $\mathrm{Adv}_{\mathcal{PE}^n, I}^{n\text{-}cpa}(t)$ is negligible for polynomially bounded t, where the complexity is measured as a function of a security parameter.*

The security against chosen-ciphertext attack is defined similarly except for that the adversary B gets n decryption oracles $\mathcal{D}_{sk_1}, \cdots, \mathcal{D}_{sk_n}$. It is allowed to query any ciphertext C to any decryption oracle $\mathcal{D}_{sk_i}$ at most q_d times for each i, where it must be that $C \neq TAKE_i(C_S)$ for any output C_S of the encryption oracle $\mathcal{E}_{\underline{xpk}}$. We denote the advantages by $\mathrm{Adv}_{\mathcal{PE}^n, I}^{n\text{-}cca}(B)$ and $\mathrm{Adv}_{\mathcal{PE}^n, I}^{n\text{-}cca}(t, q_e, q_d)$, respectively.

The security of (single-plaintext, multi-recipient) schemes is defined similarly. For simplicity, the same notation as above will be used.

Remark 3.2. In the definition of Bellare et al. [2], (i) $|S| = 1$ and there are n encryption oracles $\mathcal{E}_{pk_1}, \cdots, \mathcal{E}_{pk_n}$. (ii) B is allowed to query at most q_e times to each $\mathcal{E}_{pk_i}$. It is easy to see that our definition is more general if we ignore (ii).

3.4   Sufficient Condition

We say that an adversary is type 0 if $q_e = 1$ and his query to $\mathcal{E}_{pk}^n$ is $(N, \underline{M}_N^0, \underline{M}_N^1)$. That is, we consider an adversary which runs in two stages, the find stage and the guess stage, as in the single-recipient case.

Definition 3.3. *Let* $\mathrm{AdvTO}_{\mathcal{PE}^n, I}^{n\text{-}cpa}(t)$ *be the* $\max_B \mathrm{Adv}_{\mathcal{PE}^n, I}^{n\text{-}cpa}(B)$, *where the maximum is over all type* 0 *adversaries* B *with time-complexity* t. *Define* $\mathrm{AdvTO}_{\mathcal{PE}^n, I}^{n\text{-}cca}(t, q_d)$ *similarly.*

The next lemma shows that $\mathcal{PE}^n$ is secure if $\mathrm{AdvTO}_{\mathcal{PE}^n, I}^{n\text{-}x}(t)$ is negligible, where $x = cpa$ or cca. Therefore, we do not have to evaluate $\mathrm{Adv}_{\mathcal{PE}^n, I}^{n\text{-}x}(t, q_e)$ directly.

Let T_n denote the time to compute a ciphertext $C_N = \mathcal{E}_{pk}^n(N, \underline{M}_N)$.

Lemma 3.1. *In an n-recipient broadcast/multicast public-key encryption scheme* $\mathcal{PE}^n$,

$$\mathrm{Adv}_{\mathcal{PE}^n, I}^{n\text{-}cpa}(t, q_e) \leq q_e \cdot \mathrm{AdvTO}_{\mathcal{PE}^n, I}^{n\text{-}cpa}(t'),$$
$$\mathrm{Adv}_{\mathcal{PE}^n, I}^{n\text{-}cca}(t, q_e, q_d) \leq q_e \cdot \mathrm{AdvTO}_{\mathcal{PE}^n, I}^{n\text{-}cca}(t', q_d),$$

where $t' = t + O(q_e T_n)$.

A proof is given in Appendix.

4   Multi-recipient "ElGamal" Encryption Scheme

In this section, we show a (multi-plaintext, multi-recipient) ElGamal scheme which has the "*shortened ciphertext*" property. Let $\mathcal{G}$ be a group with a prime order p and let g be a generator of $\mathcal{G}$. Let $I = (p, g)$ be the global information.

Let $T^{\exp}$ denote the time needed to perform an exponentiation in $\mathcal{G}$.

4.1   ElGamal Scheme and DDH Problem

Informally, the decision Diffie-Hellman (DDH) problem is stated as follows. Given g^x, g^y, g^z, decide if $z = xy \bmod p$ with nonnegligible probability. Formally, let

$$DH \overset{\mathrm{def}}{=} \{(g^x, g^y, g^{xy}) \mid x \in Z_p, y \in Z_p\}$$
$$RA \overset{\mathrm{def}}{=} \{(g^x, g^y, g^z) \mid x \in Z_p, y \in Z_p, z \in Z_p\}.$$

Let D be a distinguisher which outputs 0 or 1. Define

$$\mathrm{Adv}_{p,g}^{ddh}(D) \overset{\mathrm{def}}{=} \Pr[D(X) = 0 | X \in DH] - \Pr[D(X) = 0 | X \in RA],$$
$$\mathrm{Adv}_{p,g}^{ddh}(t) \overset{\mathrm{def}}{=} \max_D \mathrm{Adv}_{p,g}(D),$$

where the maximum is over all D with "time-complexity" t. The DDH assumption is that $\mathrm{Adv}_{p,g}^{ddh}(t)$ is negligible.

ElGamal encryption scheme $\mathcal{EG} = (\mathcal{K}, \mathcal{E}, \mathcal{D})$ is as follows.

$$\mathcal{K}(I) : sk = x, pk = X(\leftarrow g^x), \text{ where } x \stackrel{R}{\leftarrow} Z_p.$$
$$\mathcal{E}_{I,X}(M) : (Y, W) = (g^r, M \cdot X^r), \text{ where } r \stackrel{R}{\leftarrow} Z_p.$$
$$\mathcal{D}_{I,x}(Y, W) : M \leftarrow W \cdot Y^{-x}.$$

It is well known that ElGamal scheme is secure in the sense of indistinguishability against chosen plaintext attack under the DDH assumption.

4.2 Proposed Scheme

Now we present the proposed (multi-plaintext,multi-recipient) ElGamal scheme $\mathcal{EG}^n = (\mathcal{K}^n, \mathcal{E}^n, TAKE)$. The key generation algorithm $\mathcal{K}^n(I)$ runs $\mathcal{K}(I)$ n times independently. Let x_i be the secret key and $X_i(= g^{x_i})$ be the public-key of recipient i.

For $S = \{1_1, \cdots i_s\}$, let M_{i_j} be a plaintext for recipient $i_j \in S$. Then a ciphertext for S is

$$C_S = (g^r, M_{i_1} X_{i_1}^r, \ldots, M_{i_s} X_{i_s}^r),$$

where $r \stackrel{R}{\leftarrow} Z_p$. $TAKE_i$ is defined as $(g^r, M_i X_i^r) \leftarrow TAKE_i(C_S)$. For $T \subset S \subseteq N$, $C_T \leftarrow TAKE_T(C_S)$ is defined naturally.

We will show that our scheme has the *"shortened ciphertext"* property. First, in the trivial multi-recipient scheme, a ciphertext is

$$C_S^{trivial} = (g^{r_{i_1}}, M_{i_1} X_1^{r_{i_1}}) || \cdots || (g^{r_{i_s}}, M_s X_s^{r_{i_s}}).$$

Therefore, in our scheme, the size of the ciphertext is almost a half of that of the trivial multi-recipient scheme. We next prove that our scheme is still secure. More precisely, we prove that our scheme is secure in the sense of indistinguishability against chosen plaintext attack under the DDH assumption.

Lemma 4.1. *In the proposed (multi-plaintext,multi-recipient) ElGamal encryption scheme,*

$$\text{AdvTO}_{\mathcal{EG}^n(p,g)}^{n\text{-}cpa}(t) \leq 2 \cdot \text{Adv}_{p,g}^{ddh}(t') + \frac{1}{p}, \tag{4}$$

where $t' = t + O(n \cdot T^{exp})$.

A proof is given in Appendix. From lemma 4.1 and lemma 3.1, we obtain the following theorem.

Theorem 4.1. *In the proposed (multi-plaintext,multi-recipient) ElGamal encryption scheme,*

$$\text{Adv}_{\mathcal{EG}^n(p,g)}^{n\text{-}cpa}(t, q_e) \leq q_e(2 \cdot \text{Adv}_{p,g}^{ddh}(t') + \frac{1}{p}), \tag{5}$$

where $t' = t + O(q_e n \cdot T^{exp})$.

The concrete security of the trivial multi-recipient ElGamal encryption scheme derived by Bellare et al. [2] satisfies the same equation as eq.(4). Hence, the coefficient q_e in eq.(5) can be considered as the cost for the "*shortened ciphertext*" property.

4.3   S/MIME CMS

S/MIME CMS (IETF RFC 2630) is a (single-plainext, multi-recipient) scheme such that
$$C_S = (g^r, Wrap(X_{i_1}^r, K), ..., Wrap(X_{i_s}^r, K)),$$

where K is a content-encryption key to be transported, $Wrap$ is a symmetric key-wrapping operation.

The Wrap operation takes the role of the multiplication in the basic ElGamal scheme. Therefore, Theorem 4.1 shows that this scheme is secure if Wrap is secure enough.

5   Multi-recipient "Cramer-Shoup" Encryption Scheme

In this section, we first show the concrete security of the hash-free variant of Cramer-Shoup scheme. We next present a (multi-plaintext,multi-recipient) hash-free Cramer-Shoup scheme which has the "*shortened ciphertext*" property.

Let $\mathcal{G}$ be a group with a prime order p and let g_1 be a generator of $\mathcal{G}$. Let $I = (p, g_1)$ be the global information.

5.1   Concrete Security of the Hash-Free Cramer-Shoup Scheme

Bellare et al. derived the concrete security of the basic Cramer-Shoup scheme [9, Sec.3] by assuming the security of universal one-way hash functions (UOH) [2]. In this subsection, we derive the concrete security of the hash-free variant of Cramer-Shoup scheme, which does not need to assume UOH.

The hash-free variant of Cramer-Shoup scheme $\mathcal{CS} = (\mathcal{K}, \mathcal{E}, \mathcal{D})$ is as follows [9, Sec.5.3]. Let F be a polynomial time computable injection from G^3 to $(Z_p^*)^k$ for some k. Let (pk, sk) be

$$sk : z, x_1, x_2, (y_{11}, y_{12}), \cdots, (y_{k1}, y_{k2}),$$
where each element is randomly taken from Z_p.
$$pk : g_2, h(= g_1^z), c(= g_1^{x_1} g_2^{x_2}), d_1(= g_1^{y_{11}} g_2^{y_{12}}), \cdots, d_k(= g_1^{y_{k1}} g_2^{y_{k2}}),$$
where g_2 is randomly chosen from G.

For a plaintext M, let a ciphertext (u_1, u_2, e, v) be

$$u_1 = g_1^r, u_2 = g_2^r, e = h^r M, v = (cd_1^{\alpha_1} \cdots d_k^{\alpha_k})^r,$$

where $r \xleftarrow{R} Z_p$ and $(\alpha_1, \cdots, \alpha_k) = F(u_1, u_2, e)$.

On input (u_1, u_2, c, v), the decryption algorithm $\mathcal{D}_{sk}$ first computes $F(u_1, u_2, e)$ $= (\alpha_1, \cdots, \alpha_k)$. Next if

$$v = u_1^{x_1 + \alpha_1 y_{11} + \cdots + \alpha_k y_{k1}} u_2^{x_2 + \alpha_1 y_{12} + \cdots + \alpha_k y_{k2}}, \tag{6}$$

Then $\mathcal{D}_{sk}$ outputs

$$M \leftarrow e/u_1^z. \tag{7}$$

Otherwise, $\mathcal{D}_{sk}$ outputs *reject*. Let

$$\epsilon \stackrel{\text{def}}{=} \left(1 - \frac{1}{p}\right)\frac{q_d}{p} + \frac{1}{p}.$$

Theorem 5.1. *In the hash-free Cramer-Shoup scheme,*

$$\mathrm{Adv}^{s\text{-}cca}_{\mathcal{CS},(p,g_1)}(t, q_d) \leq 2 \cdot \mathrm{Adv}^{ddh}_{p,g_1}(t') + 3\epsilon, \tag{8}$$

where $t' = t + O(q_d \cdot T^{exp})$.

A proof will be given in the final paper.

5.2   Proposed Scheme

Now the proposed (multi-plaintext,multi-recipient) hash-free Cramer-Shoup scheme $\mathcal{CS}^n = (\mathcal{K}^n, \mathcal{E}^n, TAKE)$ is described as follows. The key generation algorithm $\mathcal{K}^n(I)$ runs $\mathcal{K}(I)$ n times independently with a restriction such that g_2 is common for all pk_i, where $pk_i = (g_2, h_i, c_i, d_{1i}, \cdots, d_{ki})$. That is, the encryption keys pk_i are not independent of each other while the secret keys sk_i are independently chosen. This is possible because w is not a part of sk_i, where $g_2 = g_1^w$.

For $S = \{1_1, \cdots i_s\}$, let M_i be a plaintext for recipient $i \in S$. Then a ciphertext for S is

$$C_S = (u_1, u_2, e_{i_1}, v_{i_1}, \cdots, e_{i_n}, v_{i_n})$$

such that $u_1 = g_1^r, u_2 = g_2^r$ and $e_i = h_i^r M_i$, $v_i = (c_i d_{1i}^{\alpha_{1i}} \cdots d_{ki}^{\alpha_{ki}})^r$, where $r \stackrel{R}{\leftarrow} Z_p$ and $(\alpha_{1i}, \cdots, \alpha_{ki}) = F(u_1, u_2, e_i)$. $TAKE_i$ is defined as $(u_1, u_2, e_i, v_i) \leftarrow TAKE_i(C_S)$. $C_S \leftarrow TAKE_S(C_N)$ is defined naturally.

Note that the size of the ciphertext of our scheme is almost a half of the trivial multi-recipient scheme. We next prove that our scheme is still secure. More precisely, we prove that our scheme is secure in the sense of indistinguishability against chosen ciphertext attack under the DDH assumption.

Lemma 5.1. *In the proposed (multi-plaintext,multi-recipient) Cramer-Shoup scheme,*

$$\mathrm{AdvTO}^{n\text{-}cca}_{\mathcal{CS}^n,(p,g_1)}(t, q_d) \leq 2 \cdot \mathrm{Adv}^{ddh}_{p,g_1}(t') + 3n\epsilon, \tag{9}$$

where $t' = t + O(n \cdot q_d \cdot T^{exp})$.

The proof is similar to that of Theorem 5.1. From lemma 5.1 and lemma 3.1, we obtain the following theorem.

Theorem 5.2. *In the proposed (multi-plaintext,multi-recipient) Cramer-Shoup scheme,*

$$\text{Adv}_{CS^n,(p,g_1)}^{n\text{-}cca}(t, q_d) \le q_e(2 \cdot \text{Adv}_{p,g_1}^{ddh}(t') + 3n\epsilon), \tag{10}$$

where $t' = t + O(n \cdot q_d \cdot T^{exp}) + O(q_e n T^{exp})$.

Comparing with the concrte security of the trivial multi-recipient (basic) Cramer-Shoup scheme given by Bellare et al. [2], we can see that our scheme takes no extra cost fot the *"shortened ciphertext"* property except negligible factors.

6   Multi-recipient Hybrid Encryption Scheme

In this section, we first prove that the (single-plaintext,multi-recipient) hybrid encryption scheme mentioned in Sec.1.1 is secure against chosen plaintext attack if the underlying single-recipient public-key scheme is secure in the sense of indistinguishability.

We next present a (single-plaintext,multi-recipient) scheme secure against chosen ciphertext attack with the *"shortened ciphertext"* property. The underlying single-recipient public-key scheme needs to be secure in the sense of indistinguishability against chosen ciphertext attack. In this sheme, we can use Rabin-SAEP or RSA-SAEP$^+$ [4] as the underlying single-recipient scheme, for example.

6.1   IND-CPA Hybrid Scheme

For a single-recipient public-key encryption scheme $\mathcal{PE} = (\mathcal{K}, \mathcal{E}, \mathcal{D})$, define a single-recipient *hybrid* encryption scheme $\mathcal{H} = (\mathcal{K}_H, \mathcal{E}_H, \mathcal{D}_H)$ as follows. The key generation algorithm is $\mathcal{K}_H = \mathcal{K}$. For a plaintext M, a ciphertext is

$$C = \mathcal{E}_{pk}(r)||M \oplus G(r),$$

where pk is a public key, r is a random element and G is a pseudorandom generator.

We next define an (single-plaintext,multi-recipient) scheme $\mathcal{H}^n = (\mathcal{K}_H^n, \mathcal{E}_H^n, TAKE)$ for $\mathcal{H}$ as follows. The key generation algorithm $\mathcal{K}_H^n(I)$ runs $\mathcal{K}_H(I)$ n times independently, where I is some global information. Let (pk_i, sk_i) be the pair of public/secret keys of recipient i.

Let M be a plaintext for $S = \{1_1, \cdots i_s\}$. Then a ciphertext for S is

$$C_S = \mathcal{E}_{pk_{i_1}}(r)|| \cdots ||\mathcal{E}_{pk_{i_s}}(r)||M \oplus G(r),$$

where $r \xleftarrow{R} Z_p$. $TAKE_i$ is defined as $\mathcal{E}_{pk_i}(r)||M \oplus G(r) \leftarrow TAKE_i(C_S)$. For $T \subset S \subseteq N$, $C_T \leftarrow TAKE_T(C_S)$ is defined naturally.

It is clear that the size of C_S is less than a half of the trivial scheme if $|M| > |\mathcal{E}_{pk_i}(r)|$. We will prove that $\mathcal{H}^n$ is secure against chosen plaintext attack if $\mathcal{PE}$ is secure in the same sense.

Consider that G is a random oracle. Suppose that an adversary makes at most q_G queries to the G-oracle. Let r be l-bits long. Let $\mathcal{PE}^n$ be the trivial multi-recipient scheme for $\mathcal{PE}$.

Then we first show that $\mathcal{H}^n$ is secure if $\mathcal{PE}^n$ is secure against type 0 adversaries.

Lemma 6.1. *In the proposed (single-plaintext,multi-recipient) scheme $\mathcal{H}^n$,*

$$\mathrm{AdvTO}^{n\text{-}cpa}_{\mathcal{H}^n,I}(t) \leq \mathrm{AdvTO}^{n\text{-}cpa}_{\mathcal{PE}^n,I}(t') + \frac{q_G}{2^{l-3}}, \tag{11}$$

where $t' = t + O(q_G) + O(n)$.

A proof will be given in the final paper. For $\mathcal{PE}^n$, the result of Bellare et al. implies that [2]

$$\mathrm{AdvTO}^{n\text{-}cpa}_{\mathcal{PE}^n,I}(t) \leq n \cdot \mathrm{Adv}^{cpa}_{\mathcal{PE},I}(t')$$

where $t' = t + O(\log(n))$. Therefore, from lemma 3.1, we obtain the following theorem.

Theorem 6.1. *In the proposed (single-plaintext,multi-recipient) scheme $\mathcal{H}^n$,*

$$\mathrm{Adv}^{n\text{-}cpa}_{\mathcal{H}^n,I}(t,q_e) \leq q_e(n \cdot \mathrm{Adv}^{cpa}_{\mathcal{PE},I}(t') + \frac{q_G}{2^{l-3}}), \tag{12}$$

where $t' = t + O(q_G) + O(n) + O(q_e T_n)$, where T_n denotes the time to compute a ciphertext C_N.

6.2 IND-CCA Hybrid Scheme

For a single-recipient public-encryption scheme $\mathcal{PE} = (\mathcal{K}, \mathcal{E}, \mathcal{D})$, define a single-recipient hybrid encryption scheme $\mathcal{HY} = (\mathcal{K}_Y, \mathcal{E}_Y, \mathcal{D}_Y)$ as follows. The key generation algorithm is $\mathcal{K}_Y = \mathcal{K}$. For a plaintext M, a ciphertext is $C = c_1||c_2||c_3$ with

$$c_1 = M \oplus G(r), \quad c_2 = H(r||M), \quad c_3 = \mathcal{E}_{pk}(r),$$

where pk is a public key, r is a random element, H is a hash function and G is a pseudorandom generator. The decryption algorithm $\mathcal{D}_Y$ is defined as

$$\mathcal{D}_{Y\,sk}(c_1||c_2||c_3) = \begin{cases} reject & \text{if } \mathcal{D}_{sk}(c_3) = reject \text{ or } c_2 \neq H(\hat{r}||c_1 \ominus G(\hat{r})) \\ c_1 \oplus G(\hat{r}) & otherwise, \end{cases}$$

where sk is a secret key and $\hat{r} = \mathcal{D}_{sk}(c_3)$.

Now we define an (single-plaintext,multi-recipient) scheme $\mathcal{HY}^n = (\mathcal{K}^n_Y, \mathcal{E}^n_Y, TAKE)$ for $\mathcal{HY} = (\mathcal{K}_Y, \mathcal{E}_Y, \mathcal{D}_Y)$ as follows. The key generation algorithm $\mathcal{K}^n_Y(I)$ runs $\mathcal{K}_Y(I)$ n times independently, where I is some global information. Let (pk_i, sk_i) be the pair of public/secret keys of recipient i.

Let M be a plaintext for $S = \{1_1, \cdots i_s\}$. Then a ciphertext for S is

$$C_S = c_1 || c_2 || \mathcal{E}_{pk_{i_1}}(r) || \cdots || \mathcal{E}_{pk_{i_s}}(r),$$

where $r \overset{R}{\leftarrow} Z_p$. $TAKE_i$ is defined as $c_1 || c_2 || \mathcal{E}_{pk_i}(r) \leftarrow TAKE_i(C_S)$. For $T \subset S \subseteq N$, $C_T \leftarrow TAKE_T(C_S)$ is defined naturally.

It is clear that the size of C_S is less than a half of the trivial scheme if $|c_1| + |c_2| > |\mathcal{E}_{pk_i}(r)|$. We will prove that $\mathcal{HY}^n$ is secure against chosen ciphertext attack if $\mathcal{PE}$ is secure in the same sense.

Let $\mathcal{PE}^n$ be the trivial multi-recipient scheme for $\mathcal{PE}$. We consider that G and H are random oracles. Suppose that an adversary makes at most q_G queries to the G-oracle, at most q_H queries to the H-oracle and at most q_d queries to each decryption oracle $\mathcal{D}_{sk_i}$. Suppose that r is l-bits long, M is k-bits long, $r || M$ is m-bits long and $H(r || M)$ be h bits long. Let

$$\sigma \overset{def}{=} n q_d \left(\frac{1}{2^{h-2}} + \frac{1}{2^{k-1}} \right) + 5 \frac{q_G + q_H}{2^{l-2}}.$$

Then

Lemma 6.2. *In the proposed (single-plaintext,multi-recipient) scheme* $\mathcal{HY}^n$,

$$\texttt{AdvTO}^{n-cca}_{\mathcal{HY}^n, I}(t, q_d) \leq 2\texttt{AdvTO}^{n-cca}_{\mathcal{PE}^n, I}(t', q_d) + \sigma,$$

where $t' = t + O(q_d q_H) + O(q_G) + O(n)$.

A proof will be given in the final paper. Similarly to Theorem 6.1, we finally have the following Theorem.

Theorem 6.2. *In the proposed (single-plaintext,multi-recipient) scheme* $\mathcal{HY}^n$,

$$\texttt{Adv}^{n-cca}_{\mathcal{HY}^n, I}(t, q_e, q_d) \leq q_e (2n \cdot \texttt{Adv}^{cca}_{\mathcal{PE}, I}(t', q_d) + \sigma),$$

where $t' = t + O(q_d q_H) + O(q_G) + O(n) + O(q_e T_n)$, *where* T_n *denotes the time to compute* C_N.

6.3   Improvement on Multi-recipient ElGamal and Cramer-Shoup

In our (multi-plaintext,multi-recipient) ElGamal encryption scheme, suppose that $M = M_{i_1} = \cdots = M_{i_s}$. In this case, let a ciphertext be

$$\bar{C} = (Mg^r, X^r_{i_1}, \cdots, X^r_{i_s}).$$

This scheme is better than our scheme of Sec.4.2 because M is multiplied once. The security is proved similarly. Further, we can consider a hybrid scheme such that

$$\bar{C}' = (Kg^r, X^r_{i_1}, \cdots, X^r_{i_s}) || G(K) \oplus M.$$

We can improve our multi-recipient Cramer-Shoup scheme similarly.

Acknowledgement

The author thanks Dr. Burt Kaliski for providing many comments, who shepherded the rewriting of the paper.

References

1. O.Baudron, D.Pointcheval and J.Stern: "Extended Notions of Security for Multicast Public Key Cryptosystems", ICALP '2000 (2000)
2. M.Bellare, A.Boldyreva and S.Micali: "Public-key encryption in a multi-recipient setting: Security proofs and improvements", Advances in Cryptology - Eurocrypt'2000 Proceedings, Lecture Notes in Computer Science Vol.1807, Springer Verlag, pp.259–274 (2000)
3. M.Bellare and P.Rogaway: "Random oracles are practical: A paradigm for designing efficient protocols", Proc. of the 1st CCS, pp.62–73, ACM Press, New York, 1993.
   (http://www-cse.ucsd.edu/users/mihir/crypto2k)
4. D.Boneh: "Simplified OAEP for the RSA and Rabin Functions", Advances in Cryptology - Crypto'2001 Proceedings, Lecture Notes in Computer Science Vol.2139, Springer Verlag, pp.275–291 (2001)
5. D. Boneh and M. Franklin: "An efficient public key traitor tracing scheme", Advances in Cryptology - Crypto'99 Proceedings, Lecture Notes in Computer Science Vol.1666, Springer Verlag, pp.338-353 (1999)
6. B. Chor, A. Fiat, and M. Naor, B. Pinkas: "Tracing traitors", IEEE Trans. on IT, vol.46, no.3, pages 893–910 (2000).
7. D.Coppersmith: "Finding a small root of a univariate modular equation", Advances in Cryptology - Eurocrypt'96 Proceedings, Lecture Notes in Computer Science Vol.1070, Springer Verlag, pp.155-165 (1996)
8. D.Coppersmith: "Small solutions to polynomial equations, and low exponent RSA vulnerabilities", Journal of Cryptology, 10, pp.233-260 (1997)
9. R.Cramer and V.Shoup: "A practical public key cryptosystem provably secure against adaptive chosen ciphertext attack", Advances in Cryptology - Crypto'98 Proceedings, Lecture Notes in Computer Science Vol.1462, Springer Verlag, pp.13–25 (1998)
10. S.Goldwasser and S.Micali : "Probabilistic encryption", Journal Computer and System Sciences, vol.28, pp.270–299 (1984).
11. J.Hastad : "Solving simultaneous modular equations of low degree", SIAM Journal of Computing, vol.17, pp.336–341 (1988).
12. K. Kurosawa and Y. Desmedt: Optimum traitor tracing and asymmetric schemes with arbiter. *Advances in Cryptology – Eurocrypt'98, Lecture Notes in Computer Science #1403, Springer Verlag* (1999) 145–157
13. K.Kurosawa and T.Yoshida: "Linear code implies public-key traitor tracing", PKC'02 (this proceedings)
14. M.Naor and O.Reingold : "Number theoretic constructions of efficient pseudorandom functions", FOCS'97, pp.458–467 (1997).
15. M.Stadler: "Publicly verifiable secret sharing", Advances in Cryptology - Eurocrypt'96 Proceedings, Lecture Notes in Computer Science Vol.1070, Springer Verlag, pp.190–199 (1996)
16. Y.Zheng amd J.Seberry: "Practical approaches to attaining security against adaptively chosen ciphertext attacks", Advances in Cryptology - Crypto'92 Proceedings, Lecture Notes in Computer Science Vol.740, Springer Verlag, pp.292–304 (1992)

A   Proof of Lemma 3.1

We show a proof for (multi-plaintext, multi-recipient) schemes against chosen-plaintext attack. The proofs for the other cases are similar. Let B be an adversary which has time-complexity t and makes at most q_e queries. We will design an type 0 adversary D_B with time-complexity at most t'.

Similar to [2], we consider a hybrid experiment with a parameter l such that $0 \le l \le q_e$ as follows.

Experiment-l: Let the i-th query of B be $(S, \underline{M}_S^0, \underline{M}_S^1)$. If $i \le l$, then $\mathcal{E}_{pk}$ returns $\mathcal{E}_{pk}(S, \underline{M}_S^1)$. Otherwise, it returns $\mathcal{E}_{pk}(S, \underline{M}_S^0)$.

Let
$$p_l \stackrel{\text{def}}{=} \Pr[\tilde{b} = 0 \text{ in Experiment-}l].$$
Then it is easy to see that
$$\mathrm{Adv}_{\mathcal{PE}^n, I}^{n\text{-cpa}}(B) = p_0 - p_{q_e}.$$

Next our D_B works as follows. On input $(I, \underline{pk})$, D_B chooses l randomly such that $1 \le l \le q_e$. It runs B by giving $(I, \underline{pk})$ to B. Let the i-th query of B be $(S, \underline{M}_S^0, \underline{M}_S^1)$.

1. If $i < l$, then D_B returns $C_S^1 \stackrel{R}{\leftarrow} \mathcal{E}_{pk}(S, \underline{M}_S^1)$.
2. If $i > l$, then D_B returns $C_S^0 \stackrel{R}{\leftarrow} \mathcal{E}_{pk}(S, \underline{M}_S^0)$.
3. If $i = l$, then D_B queries $(N, \underline{M}_N^0, \underline{M}_N^1)$ to his encryption oracles, where $\underline{M}_S^0$ and $\underline{M}_S^1$ are naturally embedded in $\underline{M}_N^0$ and $\underline{M}_N^1$, respectively. The oracle returns $C_N^b \stackrel{R}{\leftarrow} \mathcal{E}_{pk}(N, \underline{M}_N^b)$ to D_B. D_B finally gives $C_S^b = TAKE_S(C_N^b)$ to B.

Suppose that B outputs $\tilde{b}$ finally. Then D_B outputs $\tilde{b}$.

Now we can see that
$$\Pr(\tilde{b} = 0 \mid b = 0) = (p_0 + \cdots p_{q_e-1})/q_e$$
$$\Pr(\tilde{b} = 0 \mid b = 1) = (p_1 + \cdots p_{q_e})/q_e$$

because l is randomly chosen. Therefore,
$$\mathrm{Adv}_{\mathcal{PE}^n, I}^{n\text{-cpa}}(D_B) = (p_0 - p_{q_e})/q_e = \mathrm{Adv}_{\mathcal{PE}^n, I}^{n\text{-cpa}}(B)/q_e.$$

Hence
$$\mathrm{Adv}_{\mathcal{PE}^n, I}^{n\text{-cpa}}(B) = q_e \cdot \mathrm{Adv}_{\mathcal{PE}^n, I}^{n\text{-cpa}}(D_B).$$

By taking the maximum, we obtain that
$$\mathrm{Adv}_{\mathcal{PE}^n, I}^{n\text{-cpa}}(t, q_e) \le q_e \cdot \mathrm{AdvTO}_{\mathcal{PE}^n, I}^{n\text{-cpa}}(t').$$

Finally, the overhead of D_B is to pick the random number l and execute some conditional statements. It is $O(q_e \cdot T_n)$.

B   Proof of Lemma 4.1

By extending the result of Stadler [15, in the proof of Proposition 1] and Naor and Reingold [14, lemma 3.2], Bellare et al. proved the following proposition [2].

Proposition B.1. *[2] There is a probabilistic algorithm R such that on input g^a, g^b, g^c, R outputs $g^{b'}, g^{c'}$, where b' is random and*

$$c' = \begin{cases} ab' \bmod p & \text{if } c = ab \bmod p \\ random & \text{if } c \neq ab \bmod p \end{cases}$$

R runs in $O(T^{exp})$ time.

Now we show a proof of lemma 4.1. Let B be a type 0 adversary attacking the proposed scheme with time-complexity at most t. We will design an adversary D_B for the DDH problem, where D_B has time complexity at most t'.

Let the input to D_B be g^r, g^x, g^z. D_B runs R of Proposition B.1 n times independently on input (g^r, g^x, g^z). Then R outputs $X_1 = g^{x_1}, \cdots, X_n = g^{x_n}$ and $Z_1 = g^{z_1}, \cdots, Z_n = g^{z_n}$, where $x_1, \cdots, x_n$ are random and

$$z_i = \begin{cases} rx_i \bmod p & \text{if } z = rx \bmod p \\ random & \text{if } z \neq rx \bmod p \end{cases}$$

D_B gives $X_1, \cdots, X_n$ to B as n public keys and runs B. Suppose that B queries $(M_{0,1}, \ldots, M_{0,n})$ and $(M_{1,1}, \ldots, M_{1,n})$ in the find stage. Then D_B chooses a random bit b and gives $\tilde{C} = (g^r, M_{b,1} \cdot Z_1, \cdots, M_{b,n} \cdot Z_n)$ to B as a challenge ciphertext. Suppose that B outputs $\tilde{b}$ in the guess stage. Finally, D_B outputs $b \oplus \tilde{b}$.

First suppose that $(g^r, g^x, g^z) \in DH$. Then $\tilde{C}$ is a legal ciphertext. Therefore, as shown in eq.(3), we have

$$\Pr(D_B \text{ outputs } 0) = \Pr(\tilde{b} = b) = \frac{1}{2} + \frac{1}{2}\text{Adv}^{n\text{-cpa}}_{\mathcal{EG}^n,(p,g)}(B). \tag{13}$$

Next suppose that $(g^r, g^x, g^z) \in RA$. If $z \neq rx$, then $Z_1, \cdots, Z_n$ are random and $\Pr(\tilde{b} = b) = 1/2$. Hence, we have

$$\Pr(D_B \text{ outputs } 0) = \Pr(\tilde{b} = b)$$
$$\leq \frac{1}{2}(1 - \frac{1}{p}) + \frac{1}{p} = \frac{1}{2} + \frac{1}{2p} \tag{14}$$

From eq.(13) and eq.(14), we have

$$\text{Adv}^{ddh}_{p,g}(D_B) \geq \frac{1}{2}\text{Adv}^{n\text{-cpa}}_{\mathcal{EG}^n,(p,g)}(B) - \frac{1}{2p}$$

$$\text{Adv}^{n\text{-cpa}}_{\mathcal{EG}^n,(p,g)}(B) \leq 2\text{Adv}^{ddh}_{p,g}(D_B) + \frac{1}{p}$$

By taking the maximum, we have

$$\text{AdvTO}^{n\text{-cpa}}_{\mathcal{EG}^n,(p,g)}(t) \leq 2 \cdot \text{Adv}^{ddh}_{p,g}(t') + \frac{1}{p}.$$

It is easy to see that $t' = t + O(n \cdot T^{exp})$.

Efficient and Unconditionally Secure Digital Signatures and a Security Analysis of a Multireceiver Authentication Code

Goichiro Hanaoka[1], Junji Shikata[1], Yuliang Zheng[2], and Hideki Imai[1]

[1] Information & Systems, Institute of Industrial Science, University of Tokyo
4-6-1 Komaba, Meguro-ku, Tokyo 153-8508, Japan.
{hanaoka,shikata}@imailab.iis.u-tokyo.ac.jp, imai@iis.u-tokyo.ac.jp
[2] Department of Software and Information Systems, UNC Charlotte
9201, University City Blvd, Charlotte, NC 28223, USA
yzheng@uncc.edu

Abstract. Digital signatures whose security does not rely on any unproven computational assumption have recently received considerable attention. While these unconditionally secure digital signatures provide a foundation for long term integrity and non-repudiation of data, currently known schemes generally require a far greater amount of memory space for the storage of users' secret information than a traditional digital signature. The focus of this paper is on methods for reducing memory requirements of unconditionally secure digital signatures. A major contribution of this paper is to propose two novel unconditionally secure digital signature schemes that have significantly shortened secret information for users. As a specific example, with a typical parameter setting the required memory size for a user is reduced to approximately $\frac{1}{10}$ of that in previously known schemes. Another contribution of the paper is to demonstrate an attack on a multireceiver authentication code proposed by Safavi-Naini and Wang, and present a method to fix the problem of the code.

1 Introduction

Digital signatures represent one of the most widely used security technologies for ensuring unforgeability and non-repudiation of digital data. While some data only require the assurance of integrity for a relatively short period of time, say up to two years, there are many cases where it is necessary for signed documents to be regarded as legally valid for a much longer period of time. Some of the examples of data that require long-term integrity include court records, long-term leases and contracts.

In August 1999, a team of cryptography researchers from around the world completed the factorization of an 512-bit RSA composite with the use of the Number Field Sieve method [3]. With the rapid advancement in the speed of computers, one can safely predict that factoring even larger composites may become feasible at some point of time in future. We also note that innovative

D. Naccache and P. Paillier (Eds.): PKC 2002, LNCS 2274, pp. 64–79, 2002.

factoring algorithms may emerge, dramatically changing the landscape of public key cryptosystems whose security hinges on the presumed hardness of certain number theoretic problems. In yet another significant development, the past few years have witnessed significant progress in quantum computers. These computers, if built, will have the capacity to improve profoundly known algorithms for factoring and solving discrete logarithms [16,1], whereby challenging the long term security of all digital signature schemes based on number-theoretic problems.

The above discussions show clearly that there is a need to devise digital signature schemes that provide assurance of long term integrity. A possible solution to this problem is digital signature schemes whose security does not rely on any unproven assumption. The present authors have recently proposed the first unconditionally secure digital signature schemes (with transferability) [9]. An interesting and very useful property of these signature schemes is that they admit transferability, allowing the recipient of a signature to transfer it to another recipient without fearing that the security of the signature might be compromised. However, these signature schemes do have a disadvantage, namely the size of a user's secret information is very large. This disadvantage may pose a serious problem in practice, especially when a user's secret information need to be stored in such devices as smart cards.

A major contribution of this work is to propose two novel unconditionally secure digital signature schemes that require significantly less amount of memory for each user's secret information. As an example, consider an organization that has 100,000 users. With the new signature schemes, the required memory size for each user is reduced to approximately $\frac{1}{10}$ of that required by previously known schemes. Another contribution of this paper is to present an attack on a multireceiver authentication code proposed by Safavi-Naini and Wang, which is followed by a method to fix that problem. Safavi-Naini and Wang's multireceiver authentication code is related to one of our new unconditionally secure digital signature schemes. More specifically, one of our approaches succeeds in reducing the required memory size for a user's secret information by unifying secret data for both signing and verification.

1.1   Related Work

Unconditionally secure authentication codes. There have been attempts to modify unconditionally secure authentication codes [7,17] with the aim of enhancing the codes with added security properties. An obvious approach is to transform an unconditionally secure authentication code into an unconditionally secure digital signature. To achieve this, however, one faces two insurmountable technical hurdles. The first hurdle lies in authentication codes, especially the conventional Cartesian ones, which do not provide the function of non-repudiation, simply because a receiver can easily forge a sender's message and vice versa. The second hurdle is that the receiver is always designated, which means that a signature cannot be verified by another party without having the shared key.

An extension to authentication codes is called, *authentication codes with arbitration* or A^2-codes [18,19,10,8]. These codes involve a trusted third party called an arbiter. The arbiter help resolve disputes at times when a receiver forges a sender's message or the sender claims that the message has been forged by the receiver. A^2-codes have been further improved to have a less trustworthy arbiter as one of the requirements. These improved codes are called, A^3-codes [2,5,8]. A property common to both codes is that the receiver of an authenticated message has to be designated. Therefore, in a signature system where the receiver is not designated, both A^2-codes and A^3-codes cannot be used as digital signatures.

Another extension made to authentication codes, *multireceiver authentication codes* (MRA) [6,13,8], have been extensively studied in the literature. In a MRA scheme, a broadcast message can be verified by any one of the receivers. Earlier MRA schemes required the sender himself to be designated. In order to ease the requirement of the designated sender, several variations of *MRA with dynamic sender* or DMRA have been proposed [13,14,15]. Among these schemes, we especially looked into Safavi-Naini and Wang's DMRA [13,15] which we thought has an interesting construction. In their scheme, a user's secret information for generating authenticated messages and that for verifying them is the same. Which means that, their scheme requires significantly less amount of memory size compared to other DMRAs. Further, in one of our new schemes, with this application, the required memory size for a user's secret information of our schemes can be reduced as well.

It is important to note that these schemes make sense only in the case of broadcasting. If MRA or DMRA is used for point-to-point authentication, then the sender can easily generate a fraudulent message, which is accepted by the receiver and not by other participants. The situation is made complex due to a reason that the same fraudulent message may had been generated by the receiver himself. A further problem associated to this situation is that, MRA nor DMRA provide transferability. In particular, if an authenticated message is transferred from one verifier to another, the second verifier can forge a message that appears to be perfectly valid and may naturally transfer it to the next verifier. For these reasons, neither MRA nor DMRA satisfies the non-repudiation requirement of digital signature.

Unconditionally secure digital signatures. Chaum and Roijakkers [4] originally made the attempt to construct an unconditionally secure signature scheme using cryptographic protocols. However, their basic scheme was impractical, as it only signed a single bit message. Furthermore, their level of security of a signature decreased as the signature moved from one verifier to another. In practice, it is important for a signature scheme to have *transferability*, i.e., its security is not compromised when a signature is transferred among users. By applying A^3-codes, Johansson [8] proposed an improved version of Chaum-Roijakkers scheme, but Johansson did not address transferability of signature scheme.

Pfitzmann and Waidner proposed another version of unconditionally secure signature schemes [11,12]. However, their unconditional security was limited for signers. Recently, the present authors proposed an unconditionally secure digital signature which addresses all known required properties including transferability [9]. However, that signature scheme (the HSZI-AC00 scheme, for short) requires a large amount of memory, which could be a problem in certain applications, e.g. smart card based systems.

1.2   Main Results

In this paper, we first present an attack on Safavi-Naini and Wang's DMRA [15]. More specifically, in their scheme, by observing a valid signature of an honest signer, a coalition of adversaries can make an impersonation attack with non-negligible probability. We also show a simple method to fix that problem.

Next, we show two novel unconditionally secure digital signature schemes that admit transferability. Both these schemes significantly reduce the required memory size for a user's secret information. In the first one, *symmetric construction*, the required memory size for a user's secret information is significantly reduced by unifying secret information for signing and that for verification. However, the required memory size for a signature is slightly increased compared to the HSZI-AC00 scheme. The basic idea behind unifying secret information for signing and verification in the symmetric construction is partially based on the idea from the fixed version of Safavi-Naini and Wang's DMRA. In the second construction, *asymmetric construction*, the required memory size is reduced without increasing the required memory size for a signature. More precisely, this scheme is optimal in terms of the required memory size for a signature as well as in the HSZI-AC00 scheme. As an example for 100,000 users with appropriate security parameter settings, the required memory size for a user is reduced to $\frac{1}{10}$ of that required in the previous method.

The organization of the remaining part of this paper is as follows: In Section 2, we give a brief review of Safavi-Naini and Wang's multireceiver authentication code, and demonstrate an attack on it. We also show a method to fix the problem. In Section 3, new unconditionally secure digital signature schemes are presented. Lastly, Section 4 presents a comparison between the proposed schemes with the previous method.

2   An Analysis of Safavi-Naini and Wang's DMRA

In general, DMRA is an authentication code where any entity in a system can generate and verify an authenticated message. In this section, we give a brief review of Safavi-Naini and Wang's multireceiver authentication codes with dynamic senders (the SW-DMRA, for short) [13,15]. As already mentioned, in this scheme, secret information for generating an authenticated message and that for verifying is the same. Primarily due to this property, the required memory size for a user's secret information in the SW-DMRA could be decreased to be significantly smaller to that of other DMRAs. However, the SW-DMRA is insecure when used as in [15]. In this section, we also demonstrate an attack on the SW-DMRA, and present a method to fix that problem. This attack is easy to perform and indeed, very effective. In this attack, by observing a valid authenticated message, colluders can forge any user's valid authenticated message with probability 1.

U_j accepts the broadcasted message if $f_i(U_j) = f_j(U_i)$.

2.1   Implementation of Safavi-Naini and Wang's DMRA

In this subsection, the construction of the SW-DMRA is shown in more detail. This scheme was originally presented in [13] and was then improved and simplified in [15]. Here, we show the improved version. The model of DMRA follows [15].

Let F_q be the finite field with q elements and $\mathcal{S}$ the set of source states. We assume $\mathcal{S} = F_q$ and that each user's identity U_i is represented as distinct number on F_q, and ω is the maximum number of colluders in the system. The construction of the SW-DMRA is as follows.

Safavi-Naini and Wang's DMRA [15]

1. **Key distribution:** The TA chooses uniformly at random two symmetric polynomials $F_0(x, y)$ and $F_1(x, y)$ over F_q with two variables x and y of degree less than $\omega + 1$.[1] For each U_i $(i = 1, \cdots, n)$, the TA privately sends a pair of polynomial $\{F_0(x, U_i), F_1(x, U_i)\}$ to U_i. This constitutes the secret information of U_i.
2. **Broadcast:** If U_i wants to authenticate a source state $s \in F_q$, U_i calculates the polynomial $a_i(x) := F_0(x, U_i) + sF_1(x, U_i)$ and broadcasts $(s, a_i(x))$ with his identity to other users.
3. **Verification:** U_j can verify the authenticity of $(s, a_i(x))$ by first calculating the polynomial $b_j(x) := F_0(x, U_j) + sF_1(x, U_j)$ and then accepting $(s, a_i(x))$ as authentic and being sent from U_i if $b_j(U_i) = a_i(U_j)$.

2.2   Performance

As shown in above, in this scheme, U_i's secret information $\{F_0(x, U_i), F_1(x, U_i)\}$ is utilized for both generating and verifying authenticated message. Namely, for each user, the whole distributed secret information is used whether he is a sender or a recipient. Hence, the required memory size for a user's secret information can be reduced to significantly small value. More precisely, this scheme is optimal in terms of the required memory size for a user's secret information due to lower

---

[1] It is important to note that the meaning of the parameter ω in this paper is different from that of w used in [15]. The authors of [15] describe "no $w-1$ subset of users can perform impersonation and/or substitution attack on any other pair of users" ([15], page 161, Def. 5.1) and "Then TA randomly chooses two symmetric polynomials of degree less than w with coefficients in $GF(q)$" ([15], page 163). Thus, we can see that ω in this paper is equivalent to $w - 1$ in [15]. We also note that our definition of ω is in line with relevant papers by other researchers, including [6,8].

bound on it [15]. In addition, this scheme is also optimal in terms of the required memory size for an authenticated message [15]. For the details, see Theorem 5.2 in [15].

Although the authors of [15] claimed that the probability of succeeding for a collusion of up to ω users in performing all known attacks is at most $\frac{1}{q}$, however, the above scheme is insecure. The details regarding the security of this scheme is shown in [15]. In the next section, we demonstrate an attack on the above DMRA.

Here, we further point out the transferability of DMRAs. Generally in DM-RAs as already mentioned, messages are transmitted over a broadcast channel, and in this particular situation, transferability is not required. However, for a digital signature (for point-to-point communication), transferability is a property that cannot be neglected. That is, a signature system must allow users to pass signatures among users without compromising the integrity of them. Generally speaking, DMRAs (and MRAs) do not fulfill this requirement. As an example to this, we show the vulnerability of the above DMRA where it allows users to pass authenticated messages among users without a broadcast channel.

Suppose that, U_{i_0} generates $(s, a_{i_0}(x))$ and sends it to U_{i_1}. Then, an adversary can modify the authenticated message as $(s, a'_{i_0}(x))$, such that $a'_{i_0}(U_{i_1}) = a_{i_0}(U_{i_1})$ and $a'_{i_0}(U_{i_2}) \neq a_{i_0}(U_{i_2})$ for a certain user U_{i_2}. On receiving $(s, a'_{i_0}(x))$, U_{i_1} accepts it as valid since $a'_{i_0}(U_{i_1}) = b_{i_1}(U_{i_0})$. However, when U_{i_1} further transfers $(s, a'_{i_0}(x))$ to U_{i_2}, U_{i_2} does not accept it since $a'_{i_0}(U_{i_2}) \neq b_{i_2}(U_{i_0})$, and U_{i_1} will be suspected to have forged it. We call this type of attack *transfer with a trap* following to [9]. For this reason, DMRA (and MRA) cannot be used as a digital signature.

In the remaining part of this section, we show an attack on the SW-DMRA, and also present a method to fix that problem. This attack is easy to perform and indeed, very effective. In this attack, by observing a valid authenticated message, ω colluders can forge any user's valid authenticated message with probability 1.

2.3   Attack on Safavi-Naini and Wang's DMRA

Let $\mathcal{W} = \{U_1, \cdots, U_\omega\}$ be the set of the colluders. These colluders can forge any user's authenticated message as described. When $U_0 (\notin \mathcal{W})$ transmits a valid authenticated message $(s, a_0(x))$, the colluders interrupt it and use it for forgery of another user's authenticated message. On observing $(s, a_0(x))$, the colluders generate authenticated messages $(s, a_1(x)), (s, a_2(x)), \cdots, (s, a_\omega(x))$. Letting

$$F_l(x, y) := (1, x, x^2, \cdots, x^\omega) A_l \begin{pmatrix} 1 \\ y \\ y^2 \\ \vdots \\ y^\omega \end{pmatrix}, \quad l = 0, 1,$$

where A_l $(l = 0, 1)$ are $(\omega+1) \times (\omega+1)$ symmetric matrices over F_q, the colluders now have a matrix D, where

$$D := (A_0 + sA_1) \begin{pmatrix} 1 & 1 & \cdots & 1 \\ U_0 & U_1 & \cdots & U_\omega \\ U_0{}^2 & U_1{}^2 & \cdots & U_\omega{}^2 \\ \vdots & \vdots & \cdots & \vdots \\ U_0{}^\omega & U_1{}^\omega & \cdots & U_\omega{}^\omega \end{pmatrix}.$$

Then, by using D, $A_0 + sA_1$ can be easily obtained as follows:

$$A_0 + sA_1 = D \begin{pmatrix} 1 & 1 & \cdots & 1 \\ U_0 & U_1 & \cdots & U_\omega \\ U_0{}^2 & U_1{}^2 & \cdots & U_\omega{}^2 \\ \vdots & \vdots & \cdots & \vdots \\ U_0{}^\omega & U_1{}^\omega & \cdots & U_\omega{}^\omega \end{pmatrix}^{-1}.$$

If the colluders $\mathcal{W}$ want to forge an authenticated message of a user U_j, where $U_j \notin \mathcal{W} \cup \{U_0\}$, $\mathcal{W}$ calculate

$$a'_j(x) = (1, U_j, U_j^2, \cdots, U_j^\omega)(A_0 + sA_1),$$

and broadcast $(s, a'_j(x))$ as an authenticated message of U_j for the source state s. Since $(s, a'_j(x))$ is exactly equal to U_j's valid authentication message for source state s, the colluders succeed in impersonation (or entity substitution) for U_j (with probability 1).

2.4   Method to Fix the Problem

An essential problem in the SW-DMRA is that $A_0 + sA_1$ can be calculated by using both ω colluders' secret information and an authenticated message generated by an honest user. In order to avoid calculating $A_0 + sA_1$, the rank of $A_0 + sA_1$ must be larger than ω. This implies that the degree of x and y in $F_0(x, y)$ and $F_1(x, y)$ must be at least $\omega + 1$. Letting the degree of x and y in $F_0(x, y)$ and $F_1(x, y)$ be at least $\omega + 1$, the colluders cannot succeed in the above attack with non-negligible probability. (See also the footnote that appeared earlier in this paper regarding the small but subtle difference between the definition of ω in this paper and that of w in [15].) It should be noted that both the required memory size for a user's secret information and that for an authenticated message are increased by this modification. The authors of [15] claimed that their original scheme is optimal in terms of memory sizes for a user's secret information and an authenticated message, however, the fixed version is not. Optimal construction of DMRA in terms of memory sizes for both a user's secret information and an authenticated message is an interesting open problem. We further point out that schemes in [14] and [9] are optimal only for memory sizes for an authenticated message.

3 Two Novel Methods for Constructing Efficient and Unconditionally Secure Digital Signatures

In this section, we show two constructions of unconditionally secure digital signature schemes, which are called *symmetric construction* and *asymmetric construction*, respectively. In these schemes, though the flexibility of parameter settings is partially lost, the required memory sizes are reduced considerably compared to the previous method. More precisely, in our proposed schemes, the number of signatures users can generate is determined to be only one, while in HSZI-AC00 scheme [9], it can be pre-determined flexibly.

3.1 Model

In this subsection, a model of unconditionally secure signature schemes is shown. This model basically follows as in [9] with a restriction of the number of signatures that users can generate.

We assume that there is a trusted authority, denoted by TA, and n users $\mathcal{U} = \{U_1, U_2, \cdots, U_n\}$. For each user $U_i \in \mathcal{U}$ ($1 \leq i \leq n$), for convenience we use the same symbol U_i to denote the identity of the user. The TA produces secret information on behalf of a user. Once being given the secret information, a user can generate and/or verify signatures by using his own secret information, respectively. A more formal definition is given below:

Definition 1. A scheme Π is an *One-Time Identity-based Signature Scheme for Unconditional Security in a Group (One-Time ISSUSG)* if it is constructed as follows:

1. **Notation:** Π consists of (TA, $\mathcal{U}$, $\mathcal{M}, \mathcal{E}, \mathcal{A}, \mathbf{Sig}, \mathbf{Ver}$), where
   - TA is a trusted authority,
   - $\mathcal{U}$ is a finite set of users (to be precise, users' unique names),
   - $\mathcal{M}$ is a finite set of possible messages,
   - $\mathcal{E}$ is a finite set of possible users' secret information,
   - $\mathcal{A}$ is a finite set of possible signatures,
   - $\mathbf{Sig} : \mathcal{E} \times \mathcal{M} \longrightarrow \mathcal{A}$ is a signing-algorithm,
   - $\mathbf{Ver} : \mathcal{M} \times \mathcal{A} \times \mathcal{E} \times \mathcal{U} \longrightarrow \{accept, reject\}$ is a verification-algorithm.
2. **Key Pair Generation and Distribution by TA:** For each user $U_i \in \mathcal{U}$, the TA chooses a secret information $e_i \in \mathcal{E}$, and transmits e_i to U_i via a secure channel. After delivering these secret information, the TA may erases e_i from his memory. And each user keeps his secret information secret.
3. **Signature Generation:** For a message $m \in \mathcal{M}$, a user U_i generates a signature $\alpha = \mathbf{Sig}(e_i, m) \in \mathcal{A}$ by using the secret information in conjunction with the signing-algorithm. The pair (m, α) is regarded as a signed message of U_i. After (m, α) is sent by U_i, no user is allowed to generate another signature. Namely, in this scheme only one signature is allowed to be generated, but any user can potentially become a signer.

4. Signature Verification: On receiving (m, α) from U_i, a user U_j checks whether α is valid by using his secret information e_j. More precisely, U_j accepts (m, α) as a valid, signed message from U_i if $\mathbf{Ver}(m, \alpha, e_j, U_i) = accept$.

The main difference between the above definition and the previous one in [9] is that the above model does not allow flexible pre-determination of the number of signatures per user. Hence, this model is called *One-Time* ISSUSG.

For a more formalized discussion for the security of a signature scheme in our model, we define the probability of success of various types of attacks. We consider three broad types of attacks: *impersonation*, *substitution* and *transfer with a trap*. In impersonation, adversaries try to forge a user's signature without seeing the user's valid signature. Note that the adversaries are allowed to observe another user's signature. In substitution, adversaries try to forge a user's signature for a message after seeing the user's valid signature for another message. In transfer with a trap, adversaries try to modify a valid signature to be accepted only by specific verifiers. Description of these attacks are given in [9].

To formally define the probabilities of success in the above three attacks, some notations must be introduced in ahead. Let $\mathcal{W} := \{W \subset \mathcal{U}| \ |W| \leq \omega\}$, where ω is maximum number of colluders among users. Each element of $\mathcal{W}$ represents a group of possibly colluding users. Let $e_W = \{e_{k_1}, \cdots, e_{k_j}\}$, where $W = \{U_{k_1}, \cdots, U_{k_j}\}$ ($j \leq \omega$), be the set of secret information for a $W \in \mathcal{W}$.

Definition 2. The success probabilities of impersonation, substitution and transfer with a trap attacks, denoted by P_I, P_S and P_T respectively, are formally defined as follows:

1) Success probability of impersonation: for $W \in \mathcal{W}$ and $U_i, U_j \in \mathcal{U}$ with $U_i, U_j \notin W$, we define $P_I(U_i, U_j, W)$ as

$$P_I(U_i, U_j, W) := \max_{e_W} \max_{1 \leq k \leq n, k \neq i} \max_{(m, \alpha)} \max_{(m', \alpha')}$$
$$\Pr(U_j \text{ accepts } (m', \alpha') \text{ as valid from } U_i | e_W, (m, \alpha)),$$

where (m, α) is a valid signed message generated by a user U_k ($1 \leq k \leq n$, $k \neq i$) for a message m, and (m, α) runs over $\mathcal{M} \times \mathcal{A}$. Then, P_I is given as $P_I := \max_{\{U_i, U_j, W\}} \Pr(U_i, U_j, W)$, where $W \in \mathcal{W}$ and $U_i, U_j \in \mathcal{U}$ with $U_i, U_j \notin W$.

2) Success probability of substitution: for $W \in \mathcal{W}$ and $U_i, U_j \in \mathcal{U}$ with $U_i, U_j \notin W$, we define $P_S(U_i, U_j, W)$ as

$$P_S(U_i, U_j, W) := \max_{e_W} \max_{(m, \alpha)} \max_{(m', \alpha')}$$
$$\Pr(U_j \text{ accepts } (m', \alpha') \text{ as valid from } U_i | e_W, (m, \alpha)),$$

where (m, α) is a valid signed message generated by U_i for a message m, and (m', α') runs over $\mathcal{M} \times \mathcal{A}$ such that $m' \neq m$. Then, P_S is given as $P_S := \max_{\{U_i, U_j, W\}} \Pr(U_i, U_j, W)$, where $W \in \mathcal{W}$ and $U_i, U_j \in \mathcal{U}$ with $U_i, U_j \notin W$.

3) Success probability of transfer with a trap: for $W \in \mathcal{W}$ and $U_i, U_j \in \mathcal{U}$ with $U_j \notin W$ we define $P_T(U_i, U_j, W)$ as

$$P_T(U_i, U_j, W) := \max_{e_W} \max_{(m,\alpha)} \max_{(m,\alpha')}$$
$$\Pr(U_j \text{ accepts } (m, \alpha') \text{ as valid from } U_i | e_W, (m, \alpha)),$$

where (m, α) is a valid signed message generated by U_i, and α' is taken such that $\alpha \neq \alpha'$. Then, P_T is given as $P_T := \max_{\{U_i, U_j, W\}} \Pr(U_i, U_j, W)$, where $W \in \mathcal{W}$ and $U_i, U_j \in \mathcal{U}$ with $U_j \notin W$.

The concept of (n, ω, p_1, p_2)-secure One-Time ISSUSG signature scheme can now be defined, where both p_1 and p_2 are security parameters whose meanings will be made precise in the following definition.

Definition 3. Let Π be a One-Time ISSUSG with n users. Then, Π is (n, ω, p_1, p_2)-secure if the following conditions are satisfied: as long as there exist at most ω colluders, the following inequalities hold:

$$\max\{P_I, \ P_S\} \leq p_1, \quad P_T \leq p_2.$$

3.2 Symmetric Construction

In this subsection, we show an implementation in One-Time ISSUSG, called the *symmetric construction*. In this construction, the required memory size for a user's secret information is reduced partially based on the fixed version of the SW-DMRA. Namely, we introduce symmetric functions for unifying the secret information for signing and for verifying. However, it should be noted that it is not trivial to implement, since the SW-DMRA does not fulfill the transferability property. The essential reason behind why the SW-DMRA does not provide transferability is that, for U_i's authenticated message $(s_i, a_i(x))$, any entity can calculate $a_i(U_j)$ and find another function $a_i'(x)$ such that $a_i'(x) \neq a_i(x)$ and $a_i'(U_j) = a_i(U_j)$. This is hard to solve since U_j must be public. We show a solution to this problem in the following.

Symmetric Construction

1. **Key Generation and Distribution by TA:** Let F_{q_0} be the finite field with q_0 elements such that $q_0 \geq n(\omega + 1)q$, where q is a security parameter of the system. We assume that the size of q_0 is almost the same as $n(\omega + 1)q$. Then, the TA divides F_{q_0} into n disjoint subsets $\mathcal{U}_1, \cdots, \mathcal{U}_n$, such that $|\mathcal{U}_i| = (\omega+1)q$ for any i, and $\mathcal{U}_i \cap \mathcal{U}_j = \phi$ if $i \neq j$. Here, $\mathcal{U}_i$ ($1 \leq i \leq n$) are made public for all users. For each user U_i ($1 \leq i \leq n$), the TA picks uniformly at random, a number u_i from $\mathcal{U}_i$, respectively, and chooses uniformly at random two symmetric polynomials $F_0(x, y), F_1(x, y)$ over F_{q_0} with two variables x and y of degree at most $\omega + 1$. Moreover, we assume a message m is an element in F_{q_0} as well. For each user U_i ($1 \leq i \leq n$), the TA computes his secret

information $e_i := \{F_0(x, u_i), F_1(x, u_i), u_i\}$. Then, the TA sends e_i to U_i over a secure channel. Once the secret information has been delivered, there is now no need for the TA to keep the user's secret information.

2. **Signature Generation:** For a message $m \in F_{q_0}$, U_i generates a signature by $\alpha := \{a_{i,m}(x), u_i\}$ using his secret information, where $a_{i,m}(x) := F_0(x, u_i) + mF_1(x, u_i)$. Then, (m, α) is sent by U_i with his identity U_i.

3. **Signature Verification:** On receiving U_i's signature (m, α), user U_j checks whether α is valid or not, by the use of his secret information e_j. Specifically, U_j accepts (m, α) as being a valid message-signature pair from U_i if $(F_0(x, u_j) + mF_1(x, u_j))|_{x=u_i} = a_{i,m}(x)|_{x=u_j}$ and $u_i \in \mathcal{U}_i$.

Theorem 1. *The above scheme results in an $(n, \omega, \frac{1}{q_0}, \frac{1}{q})$-secure One-Time IS-SUSG scheme.*

Proof: See Appendix.

Theorem 2. *The required memory size in the above construction is given as follows:*

$$|\mathcal{A}| = (\omega + 1)qq_0^{\omega+2} \quad \text{(size of signature)}$$
$$|\mathcal{E}| = (\omega + 1)qq_0^{2\omega+4} \quad \text{(size of secret information)}.$$

Although in this scheme the required memory size of a signature is slightly increased compared to the HSZI-AC00 scheme [9], that of each user's secret information is significantly reduced. Comparison with the previous method is shown in the following section.

3.3   Asymmetric Construction

In the symmetric construction, though the required memory size of a user's secret information has significantly been reduced, the required memory size of a signature increased compared to the previous method. In this subsection, we show other methods for reducing the required memory size of a user's secret information without increasing the required memory size for a signature. One of the proposed schemes in this subsection is optimal, especially in terms of memory size for a signature. Such schemes are called *asymmetric constructions* since the secret information for signing and that for verification is different.

Asymmetric Construction

1. **Key Pair Generation and Distribution by TA:** Let F_q be the finite field with q elements such that $q \geq n$. The TA picks n elements $v_1, v_2, \dots, v_n$ uniformly at random in F_q^ω for users $U_1, U_2, \dots, U_n$ respectively, and chooses two polynomials uniformly at random, $G_0(x, y_1, \dots, y_\omega)$ and $G_1(x, y_1, \dots, y_\omega)$, over F_q with $\omega + 1$ variables $x, y_1, \cdots, y_\omega$, in which the degree of x is at most $\omega + 1$ and that of every y_i is at most 1. Moreover, we assume that each

user's identity U_i and a message m are elements of F_q. For each user U_i ($1 \le i \le n$), the TA computes U_i's secret information $e_i := \{G_0(U_i, y_1 \ldots, y_\omega), G_1(U_i, y_1, \ldots, y_\omega), G_0(x, v_i), G_1(x, v_i), v_i\}$. The TA then sends e_i to U_i over a secure channel. Once all the keys are delivered, there is no need for the TA to keep the user's secret information.

2. **Signature Generation:** For a message $m \in F_q$, U_i generates a signature by $\alpha = G_0(U_i, y_1, \ldots, y_\omega) + m G_1(U_i, y_1, \ldots, y_\omega)$ using $G_0(U_i, y_1, \ldots, y_\omega)$ and $G_1(U_i, y_1, \ldots, y_\omega)$. Then, (m, α) is sent by U_i with his identity U_i.

3. **Signature Verification:** On receiving (m, α) from U_i, user U_j checks whether α is valid by the use of his secret information. More specifically, U_j accepts (m, α) as being a valid message-signature pair from U_i if $(G_0(x, v_i) + m G_1(x, v_i))|_{x=U_i} = \alpha|_{(y_1, \ldots, y_\omega) = (v_{1,j}, \ldots, v_{\omega,j})}$.

Theorem 3. *The above scheme results in an $(n, \omega, (\frac{2}{q} - \frac{1}{q^2}), \frac{1}{q})$-secure One-Time ISSUSG scheme.*

Similarly to Theorem 1, the proof of Theorem 3 can be given. The above scheme can be slightly modified, resulting in another $(n, \omega, \frac{1}{q}, \frac{1}{q})$-secure One-Time ISSUSG scheme.

Theorem 4. *In the above construction, the following modification also produces an $(n, \omega, \frac{1}{q}, \frac{1}{q})$-secure One-Time ISSUSG scheme: Instead of choosing randomly, the TA may choose n elements $v_1, \ldots, v_n \in F_q^\omega$, for users' secret information, such that for any $\omega + 1$ vectors*

$$v_{i_1} = (v_{1,i_1}, \ldots, v_{\omega,i_1}), \ldots, v_{i_{\omega+1}} = (v_{1,i_{\omega+1}}, \ldots, v_{\omega,i_{\omega+1}}),$$

the $\omega + 1$ new vectors $(1, v_{1,i_1}, \ldots, v_{\omega,i_1}), \ldots, (1, v_{1,i_{\omega+1}}, \ldots, v_{\omega,i_{\omega+1}})$ are linearly independent.

Though the proposed $(n, \omega, \frac{1}{q}, \frac{1}{q})$-secure One-Time ISSUSG scheme is more secure than the proposed $(n, \omega, \frac{2}{q} - \frac{1}{q^2}, \frac{1}{q})$-secure One-Time ISSUSG scheme in terms of impersonation or substitution, it requires more complicated transactions for generating each user's secret information.

Theorem 5. *The required memory size in the above constructions is given as follows:*

$$|\mathcal{A}| = q^{\omega+1} \qquad \text{(size of signature)}$$
$$|\mathcal{E}| = q^{5\omega+6} \qquad \text{(size of a user's secret information)}.$$

Corollary 1. *The construction proposed in Theorem 4 is optimal in terms of the memory size of a signature.*

The proof follows as from [15]. Since the model of One-Time ISSUSG is regarded as a restricted version of that of MRA, lower bounds on required memory sizes for MRA can also be applied to One-Time ISSUSG. The required memory size for the above construction matches the lower bound on a signature presented in Theorem 5.2 in [15].

Table 1. The required memory sizes of each user's secret information, in the proposed symmetric construction ($(n, \omega, \frac{1}{q_0}, \frac{1}{q})$-secure One-Time ISSUSG), asymmetric construction ($(n, \omega, \frac{1}{q}, \frac{1}{q})$-secure One-Time ISSUSG) and the HSZI-AC00 scheme ($(n, \omega, 1, \frac{1}{q}, \frac{1}{q})$-secure ISSUSG [9]), assuming that $|q| = 160$ bits and ω is determined appropriately for each n.

	$n = 1,000$	$n = 10,000$	$n = 100,000$	$n = 1,000,000$
	$\omega = 500$	$\omega = 2,000$	$\omega = 10,000$	$\omega = 50,000$
Symmetric construction	22Kbyte	91Kbyte	464Kbyte	2,393Kbyte
Asymmetric construction	49Kbyte	196Kbyte	977Kbyte	4,883Kbyte
HSZI-AC00 scheme [9]	69Kbyte	508Kbyte	4,493Kbyte	41,993Kbyte

4   Comparison

In this section, we compare the proposed schemes with the previous method [9]. In the HSZI-AC00 scheme [9], the number of signatures that each user can generate can be pre-determined in a flexible manner. In order to compare the proposed One-Time ISSUSG schemes with the HSZI-AC00 scheme, we set the number of signatures that a user can generate to be one in the previous method. The following proposition shows the required memory sizes for the HSZI-AC00 scheme for this parameter setting.

Proposition 1 ([9]). *Letting the number of users be n and the maximum number of colluders ω, then the required memory sizes for the HSZI-AC00 scheme ($(n, \omega, 1, \frac{1}{q}, \frac{1}{q})$-secure ISSUSG [9][2]) are:*

$$|\mathcal{A}| = q^{\omega+1} \qquad \text{(size of signature)}$$
$$|\mathcal{E}| = q^{2n+3\omega+2} \qquad \text{(size of a user's secret information)},$$

assuming that each user is allowed to generate at most 1 signature, the probability of succeeding the impersonation and substitution is at most $\frac{1}{q}$ and that the probability of succeeding transfer with a trap is at most $\frac{1}{q}$.

As shown in the Table 1, the required memory size of each user's secret information is significantly reduced in the proposed schemes. In the symmetric construction, though the required memory size of a signature increases, that of each user's secret information is considerably reduced. As an example, for 100,000 users with appropriate security parameter settings, the required memory size for a user's secret information is reduced to 10.3% of that required in the HSZI-AC00 scheme. In the asymmetric construction, the reduction of

---

[2] It has now been found that $(n, \omega, \psi, \frac{1}{q}, \frac{1}{q-1})$-secure ISSUSG in [9] is in fact, $(n, \omega, \psi, \frac{1}{q}, \frac{1}{q})$-secure ISSUSG (see the security definition in [9]). Therefore, we have $(n, \omega, 1, \frac{1}{q}, \frac{1}{q-1})$-secure ISSUSG in [9] to be described as $(n, \omega, 1, \frac{1}{q}, \frac{1}{q})$-secure ISSUSG. Details on security of these schemes can be obtained from the present authors.

Table 2. The required memory sizes of a signature, in the proposed symmetric construction $((n, \omega, \frac{1}{q_0}, \frac{1}{q})$-secure One-Time ISSUSG), asymmetric construction $((n, \omega, \frac{1}{q}, \frac{1}{q})$-secure One-Time ISSUSG) and the HSZI-AC00 scheme $((n, \omega, 1, \frac{1}{q}, \frac{1}{q})$-secure ISSUSG [9]), assuming that $|q| = 160$ bits and ω is determined appropriately for each n.

	$n = 1,000$	$n = 10,000$	$n = 100,000$	$n = 1,000,000$
	$\omega = 500$	$\omega = 2,000$	$\omega = 10,000$	$\omega = 50,000$
Symmetric construction	12Kbyte	46Kbyte	233Kbyte	1,197Kbyte
Asymmetric construction	10Kbyte	40Kbyte	196Kbyte	977Kbyte
HSZI-AC00 scheme [9]	10Kbyte	40Kbyte	196Kbyte	977Kbyte

the required memory size of each user's secret information is less than that in the symmetric construction. However, the required memory of a signature is less than that of the symmetric construction. More precisely, the proposed asymmetric construction is optimal in terms of the required memory size of a signature, reminiscent to the HSZI-AC00 scheme. Table 2 shows the required memory sizes for a signature in the proposed schemes and that in the HSZI-AC00 scheme.

References

1. D. Boneh and R. J. Lipton, "Quantum cryptanalysis of hidden linear functions," Proc. of CRYPTO'95, LNCS 963, Springer-Verlag, pp.424-437, 1995.
2. E. F. Brickell and D. R. Stinson, "Authentication codes with multiple arbiters," Proc. of Eurocrypt'88, LNCS 330, Springer-Verlag, pp.51-55, 1988.
3. S. Cavallar, B. Dodson, A. K. Lenstra, et al., "Factorization of a 512-bit RSA modulus," Proc. of Eurocrypt'00, LNCS 1807, Springer-Verlag, pp.1-18, 2000.
4. D. Chaum and S. Roijakkers, "Unconditionally secure digital signatures,' Proc. of CRYPTO'90, LNCS 537, Springer-Verlag, pp.206-215, 1990.
5. Y. Desmedt and M. Yung, "Arbitrated unconditionally secure authentication can be unconditionally protected against arbiter's attack," Proc. of CRYPTO'90, LNCS 537, Springer-Verlag, pp.177-188, 1990.
6. Y. Desmedt, Y. Frankel and M. Yung, "Multi-receiver/Multi-sender network security: efficient authenticated multicast/feedback," Proc. of IEEE Infocom'92, pp.2045-2054, 1992.
7. E. N. Gilbert, F. J. MacWilliams and N. J. A. Sloane, "Codes which detect deception," Bell System Technical Journal, 53, pp.405-425, 1974.
8. T. Johansson, "Further results on asymmetric authentication schemes," Information and Computation, 151, pp.100-133, 1999.
9. G. Hanaoka, J. Shikata, Y. Zheng and H. Imai, "Unconditionally secure digital signature schemes admitting transferability," Proc. of Asiacrypt2000, LNCS 1976, Springer-Verlag, pp.130-142, 2000.
10. K. Kurosawa, "New bound on authentication code with arbitration," Proc. of CRYPTO'94, LNCS 839, Springer-Verlag, pp.140-149, 1994.
11. B. Pfitzmann and M. Waidner "Fail-stop signatures and their application," Proc. of Securicom 91, 9th Worldwide Congress on Computer and Communications Security and Protection, pp.145-160, 1991.

12. T. P. Pedersen and B. Pfitzmann, "Fail-stop signatures," SIAM J. on Comp., 26, no.2, pp.291-330, 1997.
13. R. Safavi-Naini and H. Wang, "New results on multi-receiver authentication codes," Proc. of Eurocrypt'98, LNCS 1403, pp.527-541, 1998.
14. R. Safavi-Naini and H. Wang, "Broadcast authentication in group communication," Proc. of Asiacrypt'99, LNCS 1716, Springer-Verlag, pp.399-411, 1999.
15. R. Safavi-Naini and H. Wang, "Multireceiver authentication codes: models, bounds, constructions and extensions," Information and Computation, 151, pp.148-172, 1999.
16. P. W. Shor, "Polynomial-time algorithms for prime factorization and discrete logarithms on a quantum computer," SIAM J. Comp., 26, no.5, pp.1484-1509, 1997.
17. G. J. Simmons, "Authentication theory/coding theory," Proc. of CRYPTO'84, LNCS 196, Springer-Verlag, pp.411-431, 1984.
18. G. J. Simmons, "Message authentication with arbitration of transmitter/receiver disputes," Proc. of Eurocrypt'87, Springer-Verlag, pp.151-165, 1987.
19. G. J. Simmons, "A Cartesian construction for unconditionally secure authentication codes that permit arbitration," Journal of Cryptology, 2, pp.77-104, 1990.

Appendix: Proof of Theorem 1

Assume that after seeing a signed message (m_{i_0}, α) published by U_{i_0}, the colluders $U_1, \cdots, U_\omega$ want to generate (m_{i_1}, α'), such that $m_{i_1} = m_{i_0}$ and the user U_{i_2} will accept it as a valid signed message of the user U_{i_1}, i.e. α consists of $\{u'_{i_1}, a'_{i_1, m_{i_1}}(x)\}$ such that $a'_{i_1, m_{i_1}}(u_{i_2}) = F_0(u'_{i_1}, u_{i_2}) + m_{i_0} F_1(u'_{i_1}, u_{i_2})$ and $u'_{i_1} \in \mathcal{U}_{i_1}$. Letting

$$F_l(x, y) = (1, x, x^2, \cdots, x^{\omega+1}) A_l \begin{pmatrix} 1 \\ y \\ y^2 \\ \vdots \\ y^{\omega+1} \end{pmatrix}, \quad l = 0, 1,$$

where A_l $(l = 0, 1)$ are $(\omega+2) \times (\omega+2)$ symmetric matrices over F_{q_0}, the colluders have a $(\omega + 2) \times (\omega + 1)$ matrix D, where

$$D := (A_0 + m_{i_0} A_1) \begin{pmatrix} 1 & 1 & \cdots & 1 \\ U_{i_0} & U_1 & \cdots & U_\omega \\ U_{i_0}^2 & U_1^2 & \cdots & U_\omega^2 \\ \vdots & \vdots & \cdots & \vdots \\ U_{i_0}^{\omega+1} & U_1^{\omega+1} & \cdots & U_\omega^{\omega+1} \end{pmatrix}.$$

From Lemma 2.1 in [13], there exist q_0 different matrices X such that

$$D = X \begin{pmatrix} 1 & 1 & \cdots & 1 \\ U_{i_0} & U_1 & \cdots & U_\omega \\ U_{i_0}^2 & U_1^2 & \cdots & U_\omega^2 \\ \vdots & \vdots & \cdots & \vdots \\ U_{i_0}^{\omega+1} & U_1^{\omega+1} & \cdots & U_\omega^{\omega+1} \end{pmatrix}.$$

This implies that there are q_0 different values for $A_0 + m_{i_0} A_1$.

In order for the colluders to succeed the attack, they need to find a pair of u'_{i_1} and $a'_{i_1, m_{i_1}}(x)$ such that

$$a'_{i_1, m_{i_1}}(u_{i_2}) = (1, u'_{i_1}, \cdots, u'^{\omega+1}_{i_1})(A_0 + m_{i_0} A_1) \begin{pmatrix} 1 \\ u_{i_2} \\ u_{i_2}^2 \\ \vdots \\ u_{i_2}^{\omega+1} \end{pmatrix}$$

and $u'_{i_1} \in \mathcal{U}_{i_1}$. Letting d be $(1, u'_{i_1}, \cdots, u'^{\omega+1}_{i_1})(A_0 + m_{i_0} A_1) \begin{pmatrix} 1 \\ u_{i_2} \\ u_{i_2}^2 \\ \vdots \\ u_{i_2}^{\omega+1} \end{pmatrix}$, q_0 dif-

ferent matrices for $A_0 + m_{i_0} A_1$ result in q_0 different values for d. This indicates that the probability of succeeding to find $a'_{i_1, m_{i_1}}(x)$, such that $a'_{i_1, m_{i_1}}(u_{i_2}) = d$, does not exceed $\frac{1}{q_0}$, i.e. $P_I = \frac{1}{q_0}$. Similarly, we can prove $P_S \le \frac{1}{q_0}$ and $P_T = \frac{1}{q}$.

Here, we briefly show the proof for $P_T = \frac{1}{q}$. Assume that after seeing a signed message (m_{i_0}, α) published by U_{i_0}, the colluders $U_1, \cdots, U_\omega$ want to generate (m_{i_0}, α'), such that $\alpha' \ne \alpha$ and the user U_{i_1} will accept it as a valid signed message of the user U_{i_0}. Let α be $\{u_{i_0}, a_{i_0, m_{i_0}}(x)\}$ as described in Section 3.2. Since $a_{i_0, m_{i_0}}(x)$ is a polynomial with a variable x of degree at most $\omega + 1$, $a'_{i_0, m_{i_0}}(x)$ $(a'_{i_0, m_{i_0}}(x) \ne a_{i_0, m_{i_0}}(x))$ has at most $\omega + 1$ pairs of $\{c, a'_{i_0, m_{i_0}}(c)\}$, such that $c \in F_{q_0}$ and $a'_{i_0, m_{i_0}}(c) = a_{i_0, m_{i_0}}(c)$, where $a'_{i_0, m_{i_0}}(x)$ is a polynomial with a variable x of degree at most $\omega + 1$. Hence, the best strategy for succeeding transfer with a trap is as follows: The colluders choose uniformly at random $\omega + 1$ distinct numbers $u_{i_1}^{(1)}, \cdots, u_{i_1}^{(\omega+1)}$ from $\mathcal{U}_{i_1}$ and generate $a'_{i_0, m_{i_0}}(x)$ $(a'_{i_0, m_{i_0}}(x) \ne a_{i_0, m_{i_0}}(x))$ such that $a'_{i_0, m_{i_0}}(u_{i_1}^{(1)}) = a_{i_0, m_{i_0}}(u_{i_1}^{(1)})$, $a'_{i_0, m_{i_0}}(u_{i_1}^{(2)}) = a_{i_0, m_{i_0}}(u_{i_1}^{(2)})$, $\cdots$, $a'_{i_0, m_{i_0}}(u_{i_1}^{(\omega+1)}) = a_{i_0, m_{i_0}}(u_{i_1}^{(\omega+1)})$. Then, the colluders send $\alpha' = \{u_{i_0}, a'_{i_0, m_{i_0}}(x)\}$ to U_{i_1}. The attack is successful if and only if $u_{i_1} \in \{u_{i_1}^{(1)}, u_{i_1}^{(2)}, \cdots, u_{i_1}^{(\omega+1)}\}$. Hence, $P_T = \frac{\omega+1}{(\omega+1)q} = \frac{1}{q}$.

Formal Proofs for the Security of Signcryption

Joonsang Baek[1], Ron Steinfeld[1], and Yuliang Zheng[2]

[1] School of Network Computing, Monash University,
McMahons Road, Frankston, VIC 3199, Australia
{joonsang.baek,ron.steinfeld}@infotech.monash.edu.au
[2] Dept. Software and Info. Systems,
UNC Charlotte, NC 28223, USA
yzheng@uncc.edu

Abstract. Signcryption is a public key or asymmetric cryptographic method that provides simultaneously both message confidentiality and unforgeability at a lower computational and communication overhead. In this paper, we propose a sound security model for signcryption that admits rigorous formal proofs for the confidentiality and unforgeablity of signcryption. A conclusion that comes out naturally from this work is that, as an asymmetric encryption scheme, signcryption is secure against adaptive chosen ciphertext attack in the random oracle model relative to, quite interestingly, the Gap Diffie-Hellman problem, and as a digital signature scheme, signcryption is existentially unforgeable against adaptive chosen message attack in the random oracle model relative to the discrete logarithm problem.

1 Introduction

1.1 Motivation for Research

To achieve message confidentiality and authenticity, there have been a great number of proposals of cryptographic building blocks both in the symmetric and asymmetric settings. Furthermore, ever since provable security with respect to strong attack models was regarded as important for proposals of new schemes, intensive efforts have been made in this line of research. In the early stage, Zheng and Seberry [26] proposed several practical asymmetric encryption schemes secure against adaptive chosen ciphertext attack, where the adversary is allowed to make queries to a decryption oracle to learn any information about a target ciphertext with the only restriction that the target ciphertext itself cannot be queried to the decryption oracle. Afterwards, schemes with security proofs against such an attack in the reductionist style (in other words, proofs of reduction from attacking the asymmetric encryption schemes to solving a computationally hard problems) under the heuristic assumption called random oracle model [6], were followed [5] [10] [17]. Moreover, the asymmetric encryption scheme with security proof without such an assumption was also proposed [7] and received great attention. For provable security of digital signature schemes,

D. Naccache and P. Paillier (Eds.): PKC 2002, LNCS 2274, pp. 80–98, 2002.

slight modifications of the schemes in [8] and [19] were proved [18] [15] to be existentially unforgeable against adaptive chosen message attack [12] in the random oracle model.

There has been growing interest in the integration of message confidentiality with authenticity. In the symmetric setting, some heuristic methods to support confidentiality and authenticity at the same time for transmitted data were considered in the internet standards such as IPSec [13] and SSL [9], and recently, these methods have been analyzed in [4] and [14]. In the asymmetric setting, Zheng [23] proposed a scheme called 'signcryption' which simultaneously and efficiently provides message confidentiality and unforgeability. Due to the potential of signcryption, especially in applications that demand high speed and low communication overhead, it is important to research into *rigorous security proofs in the reductionist style* for signcryption schemes.

The aim of this paper is to propose a precise security model for signcryption and provide rigorous proofs based on the proposed model. As a result of this work, we conclude that signcryption does meet strong security requirements with respect to message confidentiality and unforgeability under known cryptographic assumptions.

1.2   Related Work

At PKC '98, Tsiounis and Yung [22] studied a variant of a strengthened ElGamal encryption scheme originally proposed in [26], where Schnorr signature is used to provide non-malleability for the ElGamal encryption. However, the security goal of their scheme is to provide confidentiality and consequently, strong authentication for message origin is not supported in their scheme. The same scheme was also analyzed by Schnorr and Jakobsson [20] under both the generic and the random oracle models.

At ISW 2000, Steinfeld and Zheng [21] proposed the first signcryption scheme whose security is based on integer factorization. They provided a formal security model and security proof for the unforgeability of the proposed scheme. However, they left open a formal proof of the confidentiality of their scheme.

In a separate development, various researchers have made some interesting observations in the symmetric setting. At Asiacrypt 2000, Bellare and Namprepre [4] proposed formal security models for the compositions of symmetric encryption and message authentication. They concluded that only 'Encrypt-then-MAC (EtM)' composition is *generically* secure against chosen ciphertext attack and existentially unforgeable against chosen message attack. Krawczyk [14] considered the same problem while examining how to build secure channels over insecure networks. He showed that 'MAC-then-Encrypt (MtE)' composition was secure too under the assumption that the encryption method employed was either a secure CBC mode or a stream cipher that XORs the data with a random pad.

Very recently [1] (and independently of our work), in [1] it has been shown that earlier results in [4] and [14] can be extended to the asymmetric setting. Although security notions of [1] bear some similarities to ours, the generic analysis given in that paper does not appear to be applicable in deriving our security results for signcryption, primarily due to the special structure of signcryption.

1.3   Differences between Our Model and Previous Models

To address the significant difference between security implication of the compositions of encryption and authentication in the symmetric setting and that in the asymmetric setting, we consider the confidentiality of the 'Encrypt-then-MAC (EtM)' and 'Encrypt-and-MAC (EaM)' compositions in the symmetric setting, and the security of the corresponding *simple* asymmetric versions, namely, 'Encrypt-then-Sign (SimpleEtS)' and 'Encrypt-and-Sign (SimpleEaS)', defined in the natural way, with the signer's public key being appended. As was independently observed in [1], it is not hard to see that while the symmetric composition EtM is secure against chosen ciphertext attack (indeed, EtM is generically secure as shown in [4]), the simple asymmetric version SimpleEtS is *completely insecure against adaptive chosen ciphertext attack*, even if the underlying encryption scheme is secure against adaptive chosen ciphertext attack. The reason is that in the asymmetric versions, a ciphertext in the composed scheme contains an additional component (not present in the symmetric versions), namely the *sender's signature public key*. The fact that this component is easily malleable implies the insecurity of the asymmetric version SimpleEtS under adaptive chosen ciphertext attack.

As an example, let us assume that Alice encrypts and signs her message m following the SimpleEtS composition. That is, she encrypts the message m using an asymmetric encryption algorithm $\mathcal{E}_{pk_B}(\cdot)$ and computes $c = \mathcal{E}_{pk_B}(m)$. Then she signs on c using her digital signature algorithm $\mathcal{S}_{sk_A}(\cdot)$ to produce $\sigma = \mathcal{S}_{sk_A}(c)$. Now the ciphertext C is (c, σ). However, an adversary Eve now generates her own public and private key pair (pk_E, sk_E) and signs on c obtained by eavesdropping the ciphertext C en route from Alice to Bob. Namely, she can produce $C' = (c, \mathcal{S}_{sk_E}(c))$ where $\mathcal{S}_{sk_E}(\cdot)$ is Eve's digital signature algorithm. Then she hands in her public key pk_E (which may be contained in Eve's digital certificate) to Bob. Now notice that C' which is different from C is always verified as being valid using Eve's public key pk_E. Thus Bob decrypts C' into m. Hence Eve succeeds in her chosen ciphertext attack on the SimpleEtS scheme even if the underlying asymmetric encryption scheme is strong, say, secure against adaptive chosen ciphertext attack.

1.4   Signcryption: A *Variant* of Encrypt-and-Sign (EaS)

The most attractive feature of signcryption is its efficiency. To achieve this goal, signcryption can be viewed as an instantiation of the *Encrypt-and-Sign (EaS)* paradigm. Besides efficiency gains, however, signcryption has some important security-related improvements on the (insecure) SimpleEtS and SimpleEaS compositions. That is, signcryption seems to 'fix', intuitively, the following two problems with the confidentiality of those simple compositions. The first problem is with the malleability of SimpleEtS discussed above in the asymmetric setting.

The second problem (which has pointed out in [4] and [14] for the scheme EaM in the symmetric setting), is that the EaS composition cannot be *generically* secure because the signature part can reveal some information about the plaintext message, and this may be true even though the underlying signature scheme is unforgeable. However, the result in [4] and [14] does not mean that every EaS composition is insecure. Rather one should read it as that security of cryptographic schemes employing EaS ought to be analyzed on a case by case basis.

1.5   Our Contributions

As mentioned earlier, signcryption has features which intuitively fix the above mentioned confidentiality problems of the SimpleEtS and SimpleEaS compositions. A main contribution of this paper is to provide a *rigorous proof that this intuition is indeed correct*, under known cryptographic assumptions in the random oracle model for the underlying hash functions. More specifically, we define a strong security notion that is similar to the well known 'IND-CCA2' [3] notion for standard public-key encryption schemes, and prove the confidentiality of Zheng's original signcryption schemes in the security notion. Our notion for confidentiality is even stronger than the direct adaptation of 'IND-CCA2' to the setting of signcryption, since we allow the attacker to query the signcryption oracle, as well as the unsigncryption oracle. We also prove the unforgeability of signcryption in a strong sense, namely existential unforgeability against adaptive chosen message attack.

2   Preliminaries

2.1   The Gap Diffie-Hellman Problem

At PKC 2001, Okamoto and Pointcheval proposed a new class of computational problems, called gap problems [16]. A gap problem is dual of inverting and decisional problems . More precisely, this problem is to solve an inverting problem with the help of an oracle for a decisional problem. In this paper, we only recall the Gap Diffie-Hellman (GDH) problem, among the various gap problems discussed in [16], on which the confidentiality of signcryption is based.

Definition 1 (The Gap Diffie-Hellman Problem). Let A_{gdh} be an adversary for the GDH Problem. Consider a following experimental algorithm that takes a security parameter $k \in \mathbb{N}$. A_{gdh}'s job is to compute the Diffie-Hellman key $g^{xy} \bmod p$ of $g^x \bmod p$ and $g^y \bmod p$ with the help of Decisional Diffie-Hellman (DDH) oracle $DDH_g(\cdot, \cdot, \cdot)$. Note that this DDH oracle tests whether a given tuple is a Diffie-Hellman tuple (DH-tuple) or not. For example, if (X, Y, Z) is a DH-tuple, $DDH_g(X, Y, Z) = 1$. Otherwise, it returns 0.

Experiment **GDHExp$_{\text{GDH}, A_{gdh}}^{\text{invert}}(k)$**
    Choose primes (p, q) such that $|p| = k$ and $q|(p-1)$
    Choose $g \in (\mathbb{Z}/p\mathbb{Z})^*$ such that $\text{Ord}(g) = q$

$$x \leftarrow_R \mathbb{Z}/q\mathbb{Z}; \; X \leftarrow g^x \bmod p$$
$$y \leftarrow_R \mathbb{Z}/q\mathbb{Z}; \; Y \leftarrow g^y \bmod p$$
$$g^{xy} \bmod p \leftarrow A_{gdh}^{DDH_g(\cdot,\cdot,\cdot)}(k, g, X, Y)$$
$$\mathbf{return} \; g^{xy} \bmod p$$

Now let $\mathbf{Succ}^{\text{invert}}_{\text{GDH},A_{gdh}}(k) \stackrel{\text{def}}{=} \Pr[\mathbf{GDHExp}^{\text{invert}}_{\text{GDH},A_{gdh}}(k) = g^{xy} \bmod p]$. Then define an advantage function of A_c as follows.

$$\mathbf{Adv}^{\text{invert}}_{\text{GDH}}(k, t, q_{ddh}) \stackrel{\text{def}}{=} \max_{A_{gdh}}\{\mathbf{Succ}^{\text{invert}}_{\text{GDH},A_{gdh}}(k)\},$$

where the maximum is taken by all A_{gdh} with execution time t and making q_{ddh} queries to the DDH oracle. We say the GDH problem is secure if $\mathbf{Adv}^{\text{invert}}_{\text{GDH}}(k, t, q_{ddh})$ is a negligible function in k[1] for any adversary A_{gdh} with polynomial time bound in k and whose queries are polynomial in k.

2.2   Description of the Original Signcryption Scheme (SDSS1-Type)

Note that the signcryption scheme described in this section is the one derived from the shorthand digital signature scheme (SDSS1) (named by the author of [23]) which is a variant of ElGamal based signature schemes. Another signcryption scheme derived from SDSS2 can be described and analyzed in a very similar manner presented in this paper. So we only consider the SDSS1-type signcryption scheme. Note also that the hash functions used in the signcryption scheme are assumed to be random oracles [6] in this paper. And the *bind* information, which is hashed in the signcryption process, contains such information as Alice and Bob's public keys. We remark that κ, which is a Diffie-Hellman key, is directly provided as input to random oracle H without being hashed by the random oracle G in our description. Since hashing Diffie-Hellman key in signcryption is allowed to be done quite flexibly as noted in [23] and [24], we do not regard this as a major modification of the scheme.

Definition 2. Let $\text{SC} = (\mathcal{COM}, \mathcal{K}_A, \mathcal{K}_B, \mathcal{SC}, \mathcal{USC})$ be a signcryption scheme. Let $k \in \mathbb{N}$ be a security parameter. Suppose that $\text{H} : \{0,1\}^* \rightarrow \mathbb{Z}/q\mathbb{Z}$ and $\text{G} : \{0,1\}^* \rightarrow \{0,1\}^l$ are random oracles. Note that l is a security parameter, i.e. key length, for a symmetric encryption scheme described below. Let $\text{E}_\alpha(\cdot)$ denote a symmetric encryption function under some key α and $\text{D}_\alpha(\cdot)$ denote a decryption function of the symmetric encryption. (We assume that there is a one-to-one correspondence between l and k. We also assume that $\text{D}_\alpha(\cdot)$ is one-to-one over some ciphertext space $\mathcal{C}$ for all α. (This implies that the symmetric encryption is deterministic.)) Also, note that $|\cdot|$ indicates the number of bits in the binary representation of an integer.

---

[1] We say a probability function $f : \mathbb{N} \rightarrow \mathbb{R}_{[0,1]}$ is negligible in k if, for all $c > 0$, there exists $k_0 \in \mathbb{N}$ such that $f(k) \leq \frac{1}{k^c}$ whenever $k \geq k_0$. Here, $\mathbb{R}_{[0,1]} = \{x \in \mathbb{R} \mid 0 \leq x \leq 1\}$.

Signcryption SC

Common parameter generation $\mathcal{COM}(k)$
    Choose prime p such that $|p| = k$
    Choose prime $q|(p-1)$ such that $q > 2^{l_q(k)}$
    where $l_q(k) \in \mathsf{N}$ for some function l_q
    Choose $g \in (\mathbb{Z}/p\mathbb{Z})^*$ such that $\mathrm{Ord}(g) = q$
    $cp_{sc} \leftarrow (p, q, g)$
    `return` cp_{sc}
Alice's key generation $\mathcal{K}_A(k, cp_{sc})$
    $x_A \leftarrow_R \mathbb{Z}/q\mathbb{Z}; \; y_A \leftarrow g^{x_A} \bmod p$
    `return` (y_A, x_A)
Bob's key generation $\mathcal{K}_B(k, cp_{sc})$
    $x_B \leftarrow_R \mathbb{Z}/q\mathbb{Z}; \; y_B \leftarrow g^{x_B} \bmod p$
    `return` (y_B, x_B)
Signcryption $\mathcal{SC}^{\mathsf{G},\mathsf{H}}_{x_A, y_B}(m)$ by Alice the Sender
    $x \leftarrow_R \mathbb{Z}/q\mathbb{Z}; \; \kappa \leftarrow y_B^x \bmod p; \; \tau \leftarrow \mathsf{G}(\kappa)$
    Get $y_A(= g^{x_A} \bmod p); \; bind \leftarrow y_A \| y_B$
    $c \leftarrow \mathsf{E}_\tau(m); \; r \leftarrow \mathsf{H}(m \| bind \| \kappa); \; s \leftarrow x/(r + x_A) \bmod q$
    $C \leftarrow (c, r, s)$
    `return` C
Unsigncryption $\mathcal{USC}^{\mathsf{G},\mathsf{H}}_{y_A, x_B}(C)$ by Bob the Recipient
    Parse C as (c, r, s); Check whether $r, s \in \mathbb{Z}/q\mathbb{Z}$ and $c \in \mathcal{C}$
    `if` (c, r, s) is not in correct spaces
        `return` "reject"
    `else`
        $\omega \leftarrow (y_A g^r)^s \bmod p; \; \kappa \leftarrow \omega^{x_B} \bmod p; \; \tau \leftarrow \mathsf{G}(\kappa)$
        $m \leftarrow \mathsf{D}_\tau(c)$
        Get $y_B(= g^{x_B} \bmod p); \; bind \leftarrow y_A \| y_B$
        `if` $\mathsf{H}(m \| bind \| \kappa) = r$ `return` m
        `else return` "reject"

---

3 Security Notions for Signcryption Scheme

3.1 Security Notions for Confidentiality of Signcryption

Taking into account all the aspects of confidentiality issues discussed in the first section, we now explain in detail a confidentiality attack model for signcryption, which we call the *Flexible Unsigncryption Oracle (FUO)*-model. In this model, the adversary Eve's goal is to break the confidentiality of messages between Alice and Bob. Eve is given Alice's public key pk_A and Bob's public key pk_B, and has access to Alice's signcryption oracle (with Bob as recipient), as well as a *flexible* unsigncryption oracle, which on input a signcrypted text C, returns output after performing unsigncryption under sender's public key $pk_{A'}$ chosen by Eve at her will (Eve may choose sender's public key as Alice's public key

pk_A, say, $pk_{A'} = pk_A$.) and Bob's private key sk_B. In other words, the flexible unsigncryption oracle is not constrained to be executed only under pk_A and sk_B – Alice's public key can be replaced by the public key generated by Eve. Accordingly, the FUO-model gives Eve the full chosen-ciphertext power with the ability to choose the sender's public key as well as the signcrypted text.

Note, however, that in the FUO-model for signcryption Eve also has access to Alice's signcryption oracle. This can be useful to Eve because Alice's private key, which is involved in the signcryption process, can be exploited to achieve Eve's goal, namely to decrypt signcrypted texts from Alice to Bob. This is an important difference between the FUO attack model for signcryption and the standard chosen-ciphertext attack model for traditional asymmetric encryption schemes (where the attacker can simulate the encryption oracle by himself).

Using the notion of indistinguishability of encryption (also known as semantic security) [11], we now formalize the concept of security against adaptive chosen ciphertext attack for signcryption with respect to the FUO-model. We say a signcryption scheme is secure in the sense of indistinguishability (abbreviated by 'ind'), if there is no polynomial-time adversary that can learn any information about the plaintext from the signcrypted text except for its length. Following a commonly accepted practice, we denote by FUO-IND-CCA2 the security of signcryption against adaptive chosen ciphertext attack with respect to the FUO-model under the indistinguishability notion.

Definition 3 (FUO-IND-CCA2). Let $\mathsf{SC} = (\mathcal{COM}, \mathcal{K}_A, \mathcal{K}_B, \mathcal{SC}, \mathcal{USC})$ be a signcryption scheme. Let A_c be an adversary that conducts adaptive chosen ciphertext attack. A_c is composed of a find-stage algorithm A_1 and a guess-stage algorithm A_2 and has access to random oracles, the signcryption oracle which performs signcryption under the fixed keys x_A and y_B and the flexible unsigncryption oracle. A_c's job is to correctly guess the bit b after making a number of queries to its oracles with restriction that A_2 is not allowed to query the target signcrypted text C to the unsigncryption oracle $\mathcal{USC}^{\mathsf{G,H}}_{y_A, x_B}(\cdot)$ in which the flexible unsigncryption oracle $\mathcal{USC}^{\mathsf{G,H}}_{x_B}(\cdot)$ executes unsigncryption under Alice's public key y_A and Bob's private key x_B. Note that in describing our attack model, the unsigncryption oracle is denoted by $\mathcal{USC}^{\mathsf{G,H}}_{x_B}(\cdot)$, namely, there is no specified sender's public key in the subscript. This is chosen intentionally to highlight that the sender's public key is given more *flexibly* to the unsigncryption oracle (or the recipient). (However, it is important to note that A_c is *allowed* to make the query C to the unsigncryption oracle $\mathcal{USC}^{\mathsf{G,H}}_{y_{A'}, x_B}(\cdot)$ where the flexible unsigncryption oracle $\mathcal{USC}^{\mathsf{G,H}}_{x_B}(\cdot)$ performs unsigncryption under the public key $y_{A'}$ which is arbitrarily chosen by A_c and is different from y_A.) Let $k \in \mathbb{N}$ be a security parameter and s be state information. A specification for the experimental algorithm is as follows.

Experiment $\mathbf{Cca2Exp}^{\text{fuo}-\text{ind}-\text{cca2}}_{\mathsf{SC}, A_c}(k)$
    $cp_{sc} \leftarrow \mathcal{COM}(k)$
    Pick $\mathsf{G} : \{0,1\}^* \to \{0,1\}^l$ at random
    Pick $\mathsf{H} : \{0,1\}^* \to \mathbb{Z}/q\mathbb{Z}$ at random

$(y_A, x_A) \leftarrow_R \mathcal{K}_A(k, cp_{sc})$

$(y_B, x_B) \leftarrow_R \mathcal{K}_B(k, cp_{sc})$

$(m_0, m_1, s) \leftarrow A_1^{\mathsf{G},\mathsf{H},\mathcal{SC}_{x_A,y_B}^{\mathsf{G},\mathsf{H}}(\cdot),\mathcal{USC}_{x_B}^{\mathsf{G},\mathsf{H}}(\cdot)}(k, \mathsf{find}, y_A, y_B)$

$b \leftarrow_R \{0,1\}; C \leftarrow \mathcal{SC}_{x_A,y_B}^{\mathsf{G},\mathsf{H}}(m_b)$

$b' \leftarrow A_2^{\mathsf{G},\mathsf{H},\mathcal{SC}_{x_A,y_B}^{\mathsf{G},\mathsf{H}}(\cdot),\ \mathcal{USC}_{x_B}^{\mathsf{G},\mathsf{H}}(\cdot)}(k, \mathsf{guess}, C, y_A, y_B, s)$

if $b' = b$ and C was never queried to $\mathcal{USC}_{y_A,x_B}^{\mathsf{G},\mathsf{H}}(\cdot)$

return 1

else return 0

Now let $\mathbf{Succ}_{SC,A_c}^{fuo-ind-cca2}(k) \overset{\text{def}}{=} 2\Pr[\mathbf{Cca2Exp}_{SC,A_c}^{fuo-ind-cca2}(k) = 1] - 1$. Then an advantage function of FUO-IND-CCA2 is defined as follows.

$$\mathbf{Adv}_{SC}^{fuo-ind-cca2}(k, t, q_g, q_h, q_{sc}, q_{usc}) \overset{\text{def}}{=} \max_{A_c}\{\mathbf{Succ}_{SC,A_c}^{fuo-ind-cca2}(k)\},$$

where the maximum is taken over all A_c with execution time t. Note that q_{sc} is the number of queries to the signcryption oracle and q_{usc} is the number of queries to the unsigncryption oracle, respectively. Also, note that q_g and q_h are the number of queries to the random oracles G and H, respectively. We say SC is FUO-IND-CCA2 secure if $\mathbf{Adv}_{SC}^{fuo-ind-cca2}(k, t, q_g, q_h, q_{sc}, q_{usc})$ is a negligible function in k for any adversary A_c with polynomial time bound in k and whose queries are polynomial in k.

Now we recall the definition of security against chosen plaintext attack for the symmetric encryption [2] used in the signcryption under the notion of indistinguishability.

Definition 4 (IND-CPA for Symmetric Encryption). Let $SC^{\mathrm{SYM}} = (\mathsf{K}, \mathsf{E}, \mathsf{D})$ be a symmetric encryption scheme. Let A_p' be an adversary for IND-CPA. A_p' is composed of a find-stage algorithm A_1' and a **guess**-stage algorithm A_2'. Let $l \in \mathbb{N}$ be a security parameter and s be state information. A specification for the experimental algorithm is as follows.

Experiment $\mathbf{CpaExp}_{SC^{\mathrm{SYM}},A_p'}^{ind-cpa}(l)$

$\kappa \leftarrow_R \mathsf{K}(l)$

$(m_0, m_1, s) \leftarrow A_1'^{\mathsf{E}_\kappa(\cdot)}(l, \mathsf{find})$

$b \leftarrow_R \{0,1\}; c \leftarrow \mathsf{E}_\kappa(m_b)$

$b' \leftarrow A_2'^{\mathsf{E}_\kappa(\cdot)}(l, \mathsf{guess}, m_0, m_1, c, s)$

if $b' = b$ return 1 else return 0

Now let $\mathbf{Succ}_{SC^{\mathrm{SYM}},A_p'}^{ind-cpa}(l) \overset{\text{def}}{=} 2\Pr[\mathbf{CpaExp}_{SC^{\mathrm{SYM}},A_p'}^{ind-cpa}(l) = 1] - 1$. Then an advantage function of IND-CPA for symmetric encryption is defined as follows.

$$\mathbf{Adv}_{SC^{\mathrm{SYM}}}^{ind-cpa}(l, t, q_e) \overset{\text{def}}{=} \max_{A_p'}\{\mathbf{Succ}_{SC^{\mathrm{SYM}},A_p'}^{ind-cpa}(l)\},$$

where the maximum is taken over all A_p' with execution time t and q_e denotes the number of queries to the encryption oracle, made by A_p' during the attack.

We say $\mathsf{SC}^{\mathrm{SYM}}$ is IND-CPA secure if $\mathbf{Adv}_{\mathsf{SC}}^{\mathrm{ind-cpa}}(l, t, q_e)$ is a negligible function in l for any adversary A'_p whose time complexity is polynomial in l.

3.2   Security Notion for Unforgeability of Signcryption

Following the security notion for unforgeability of signcryption formalized in [21], we define unforgeability of the signcryption scheme SC. Since signcryption offers non-repudiation for the sender Alice, it is essential that even the receiver Bob cannot impersonate Alice and forge valid signcrypted texts from Alice to himself. To ensure that our proof of unforgeability covers this aspect, we allow the forger in our attack model to have access to Bob's private key as well as the corresponding public key. A formal definition is as follows.

Definition 5. An experiment of forgery for SC is realized by the following procedure that takes as input a security parameter $k = |p| \in \mathbb{N}$.

Experiment $\mathbf{ForgeExp}_{\mathsf{SC},F}^{\mathrm{cma}}(k)$

    $cp_{sc} \leftarrow \mathcal{COM}(k)$
    Pick $\mathsf{G} : \{0,1\}^* \to \{0,1\}^l$ at random
    Pick $\mathsf{H} : \{0,1\}^* \to \mathbb{Z}/q\mathbb{Z}$ at random
    $(y_A, x_A) \leftarrow_R \mathcal{K}_A(k, cp_{sc})$
    $(y_B, x_B) \leftarrow_R \mathcal{K}_B(k, cp_{sc})$
    if $F^{\mathsf{G},\mathsf{H},\mathcal{SC}_{x_A,y_B}^{\mathsf{G},\mathsf{H}}(\cdot)}(y_A, y_B, x_B)$ outputs (m, C) such that
    (1) $\mathcal{USC}_{y_A,x_B}^{\mathsf{G},\mathsf{H}}(C) = m$ and
    (2) m was never queried to $\mathcal{SC}_{x_A,y_B}^{\mathsf{G},\mathsf{H}}(\cdot)$
    return 1 else return 0

Now let $\mathbf{Succ}_{\mathsf{SC},F}^{\mathrm{cma}}(k) \overset{\mathrm{def}}{=} \Pr[\mathbf{ForgeExp}_{\mathsf{SC},F}^{\mathrm{cma}}(k) = 1]$. Then an advantage function of F can be defined as follows.

$$\mathbf{Adv}_{\mathsf{SC}}^{\mathrm{cma}}(k, t, q_g, q_h, q_s) \overset{\mathrm{def}}{=} \max_F \{\mathbf{Succ}_{\mathsf{SC},F}^{\mathrm{cma}}(k)\},$$

where the maximum is taken over all F with execution time t and at most q_g, q_h and q_{sc} queries to the random oracles G, H and the signcryption oracle $\mathcal{SC}$, respectively, made by F. We say SC is existentially unforgeable against adaptive chosen message attack if $\mathbf{Adv}_{\mathsf{SC}}^{\mathrm{cma}}(k, t, q_g, q_h, q_{sc})$ is a negligible function in k for any forger F whose time complexity is polynomial in k (Also, its queries are polynomial in k).

4   Security Reductions

4.1   Confidentiality of Signcryption

In this section, we provide a proof of a security reduction that signcryption is FUO-IND-CCA2 secure in the random oracle model, relative to the GDH problem. We show that an adversary A_{gdh} using an adaptive chosen ciphertext attacker A_c as a subroutine can solve the GDH problem. We assume that A_c is given the signcryption oracle and the flexible unsigncryption oracle described in the previous section. Note that the confidentiality of signcryption against adaptive chosen ciphertext is relative to the GDH problem. This is because, with the help of DDH oracle, the signcryption and unsigncryption oracles are successfully simulated. Now we state the results as a following theorem.

Theorem 1. *If the GDH problem is hard and the symmetric encryption scheme* $\mathsf{SC}^{\mathrm{SYM}}$ *in signcryption* SC *is IND-CPA secure, then* SC *is FUO-IND-CCA2 secure in the random oracle model. Concretely,*

$$\mathbf{Adv}_{\mathsf{SC}}^{\mathrm{fuo-ind-cca2}}(k, t, q_g, q_h, q_{sc}, q_{usc})$$

$$\leq 4\mathbf{Adv}_{\mathsf{GDH}}^{\mathrm{invert}}(k, t_1, q_{ddh}) + \mathbf{Adv}_{\mathsf{SC}^{\mathrm{SYM}}}^{\mathrm{ind-cpa}}(l, t_2, 0) + \frac{q_{sc}(q_g + q_h + 1) + q_{usc}}{2^{l_q(k)-1}}$$

where k and l denote the security parameters, t denotes execution time for FUO-IND-CCA2 adversaries, q_{sc} and q_{usc} denote the number of queries to the signcryption and the unsigncryption oracles, respectively. Here, $t_1 = O(t + time_g + time_h + time_{sc} + time_{usc})$ and $t_2 = O(t_1)$, where $time_g(= O(q_g^2 + 1))$, $time_h(= O(q_h^2 + 1))$, $time_{sc}(= O(k^3))$ and $time_{usc}(= O(k^3 + q_{usc})(q_g + q_h + time_d))$ denote the simulation time for the random oracles G and H, the signcryption and the unsigncryption oracles, respectively. Here, $time_d$ is simulation time for the symmetric decryption function D. Also, q_{ddh} denotes the number of queries to DDH oracle made by the adversary for the GDH problem and satisfies $q_{ddh} = O(q_g + q_h + q_{usc})$.

Proof 1. Suppose that $k(= |p|)$ is a security parameter. Let p and q be primes such that $q|(p-1)$ and g be element of order q. Let $X = g^x \bmod p$ and $Y = g^{x_B} \bmod p$. Now we construct an adversary A_{gdh} that given (k, p, q, g, X, Y), computes the Diffie-Hellman key $\kappa^* \stackrel{\mathrm{def}}{=} X^{x_B} \bmod p$ with the help of a Decisional Diffie-Hellman (DDH) oracle $DDH_g(\cdot, \cdot, \cdot)$, using FUO-IND-CCA2 adversary A_c. By definition, A_c consists of a find-stage algorithm A_1 and a guess-stage algorithm A_2.

Beginning of the Simulation. At the beginning of the simulation, A_{gdh} chooses a random string α^* for $\mathsf{G}(\kappa^*)$. (Note that A_{gdh} does not know the Diffie-Hellman key κ^* at this stage.) Then, A_{gdh} chooses random strings r^* and s^* from $\mathbb{Z}/q\mathbb{Z}$ and sets $(Xg^{-r^*s^*})^{\frac{1}{s^*}} \bmod p$ as Alice's public key y_A. Also A_{gdh} sets $y_B = Y$.

Simulation of Guess Stage and End of the Simulation. When A_1 outputs two plaintexts m_0 and m_1 after asking queries to the random oracles and signcryption/unsigncryption oracles during the find-stage, A_{gdh} chooses $b \in \{0, 1\}$ at random, computes $c^* = \mathsf{E}_{\alpha^*}(m_b)$. Then it answers A_1 with (c^*, r^*, s^*). When A_2 outputs a bit b' as its guess after asking queries to the random oracles and signcryption/unsigncryption oracles during the guess-stage, A_{gdh} returns κ^* which is a guess for the Diffie-Hellman key $X^{x_B} \bmod p$ and is a preimage of α^*.

Simulation of the Random Oracles. If A_1 or A_2 makes a query κ to its random oracle G, A_{gdh} runs a random simulator G-sim specified below and forwards the answers to A_1 or A_2. Note that two types of "query-answer" lists L_1^G and L_2^G are maintained for the simulation of the random oracle G, i.e., $L^G = L_1^G \cup L_2^G$. The list L_1^G consists of simple input/output entries for G of the form (κ_i, τ_i), where $i \in \mathbb{N}$. But the list L_2^G consists of special input/output entries for G which are of the form $\omega_i||(?, \tau_i)$ and implicitly represents the input/output relation $G(\omega_i^{x_B} \mod p) = \tau_i$, although the input $\omega_i^{x_B}$ is not explicitly stored and hence is denoted by '?'. New entries are added to L_2^G by either signcryption or unsigncryption oracle simulators, which will be specified.

Meanwhile, if A_1 or A_2 makes a query μ to the random oracle H, A_{gdh} runs another random oracle simulator H-sim and answers A_1 or A_2 with the output of H-sim taking μ as input.

Similarly to G-sim, the simulator H-sim also makes use of two input/output lists L_1^H and L_2^H. The list L_1^H consists of simple input/output entries for H of the form (μ_i, r_i). The list L_2^H consists of special input/output entries for H which are of the form $\omega_i||(m_i||bind_i||?, \tau_i)$ and implicitly represents the input/output relation $H(m_i||bind_i||\kappa_i) = \tau_i$, where $\kappa_i = \omega_i^{x_B} \mod p$ is not explicitly stored and hence is denoted by '?'. New entries are also added to L_2^H by either signcryption or unsigncryption oracle simulators. Now we provide complete specifications for G-sim and H-sim.

G-sim(L^G, κ)
   if $DDH_g(X, y_B, \kappa){=}1$
      then **return** $NULL$
   else if $DDH_g(\omega_i, y_B, \kappa){=}1$
      for some $\omega_i||(?, \tau_i) \in L_2^G$
      then **return** τ_i
   else if $\kappa = \kappa_i$ for some
      $(\kappa_i, \tau_i) \in L_1^G$ then **return** τ_i
   else $\tau_i \leftarrow_R \{0, 1\}^l$
      then **return** τ_i;
      $\kappa_i \leftarrow \kappa$; Put (κ_i, τ_i) into L_1^G

H-sim(L^H, μ)
   Parse μ as $m||bind||\kappa$,
      where κ is the rightmost k
      bits of μ
   if $DDH_g(X, y_B, \kappa) = 1$
      then **return** $NULL$
   else if $DDH_g(\omega_i, y_B, \kappa) = 1$
   and $m||bind = m_i||bind_i$ for some
      $\omega_i||(m_i||bind_i||?), r_i) \in L_2^H$
      then **return** r_i
   else if $\mu = \mu_i$ for some
      $(\mu_i, r_i) \in L_1^H$ then **return** r_i
   else $r_i \leftarrow \mathbb{Z}/q\mathbb{Z}$ then **return** r_i;
      $\mu_i \leftarrow \mu$; Put (μ_i, r_i) into L_1^H

Simulation of the Signcryption Oracle. When A_1 or A_2 makes a query m to its signcryption oracle $\mathcal{SC}$, A_{gdh} runs a signcryption oracle simulator $\mathcal{SC}$-sim, gets a result from $\mathcal{SC}$-sim and forwards a answer to A_1 or A_2. A specification for $\mathcal{SC}$-sim is given as follows.

$\mathcal{SC}$-sim$(L_2^G, L_2^H, y_A, y_B, m)$
   $\tau \leftarrow_R \{0, 1\}^l$; $c \leftarrow \mathsf{E}_\tau(m)$
   $r \leftarrow_R \mathbb{Z}/q\mathbb{Z}$; $s \leftarrow_R \mathbb{Z}/q\mathbb{Z}$
   $\omega \leftarrow (y_A g^r)^s \mod p$

$bind^* \leftarrow y_A || y_B$
$\omega_i \leftarrow \omega; \tau_i \leftarrow \tau; m_i \leftarrow m; r_i \leftarrow r$
Put $\omega_i || (?, \tau_i)$ into L_2^G
Put $(m_i || bind^* || ?, r_i)$ into L_2^H
$C \leftarrow (c, r, s)$
return C

Simulation of the Unsigncryption Oracle. When A_1 or A_2 makes a query $C, \bar{y_A}$ (the flexible public key chosen by the A_c) to its unsigncryption oracle USC, A_{gdh} runs a unsigncryption oracle simulator USC-sim, gets a result from the USC-sim and forwards a answer to A_1 or A_2. The following is a complete specification of USC-sim.

USC-sim$(L^G, L^H, X, \bar{y_A}, y_B, C)$
    Parse C as (c, r, s)
    $\omega \leftarrow (\bar{y_A} g^r)^s \bmod p$
    if $\omega = X$ return $NULL$
    $bind \leftarrow \bar{y_A} || y_B$
    if there exists $(\kappa_i, \tau_i) \in L_1^G$ such that $DDH_g(\omega, y_B, \kappa_i) = 1$ or
    there exists $\omega_i || (?, \tau_i) \in L_2^G$ such that $\omega = \omega_i$
        then $\tau' \leftarrow \tau_i$
    else
        $\tau' \leftarrow_R \{0, 1\}^l; \omega_i \leftarrow \omega; \tau_i \leftarrow \tau';$ Put $\omega_i || (?, \tau_i)$ into L_2^G
    $m \leftarrow D_{\tau'}(c)$
    if there exists $(\mu_i, r_i) \in L_1^H$ such that $DDH_g(\omega, y_B, \kappa_i) = 1$,
    where $\mu_i = m_i || bind_i || \kappa_i$ and κ_i denotes k rightmost bits of μ_i
    or there exists $\omega_i || (m_i || bind_i || ?, r_i) \in L_2^H$ such that $\omega = \omega_i$,
    $m = m_i$ and $bind = bind_i$ for some r_i
        then $r' \leftarrow r_i$
    else
        $\omega_i \leftarrow \omega; m_i \leftarrow m; bind_i \leftarrow bind$
        $r' \leftarrow_R \mathbb{Z}/q\mathbb{Z}; r_i \leftarrow r';$ Put $\omega_i || (m_i || bind_i || ?, r_i)$ into L_2^H
    if $r = r'$ then return m
    else return $NULL$

Putting It All Together. A complete specification of the adversary A_{gdh} is described as follows. Let s be state information.

Adversary $A_{gdh}(k, p, q, g, X, Y)$
    $r^* \leftarrow_R \mathbb{Z}/q\mathbb{Z}; s^* \leftarrow_R \mathbb{Z}/q\mathbb{Z}$
    $y_A \leftarrow (Xg^{-r^* s^*})^{\frac{1}{s^*}} \bmod p; y_B \leftarrow Y; \alpha^* \leftarrow_R \{0, 1\}^l; bind^* \leftarrow y_A || y_B$
    Run $A_1(k, \text{find}, y_A, y_B)$, using G-sim, H-sim, SC-sim and USC-sim
    to simulate answers to queries made by A_1 to its oracles
        if A_1 queries κ to G such that G-sim$(\kappa) = NULL$
            abort and return κ
        if A_1 queries μ to H such that H-sim$(\mu) = NULL$

abort and return κ, where κ is the k rightmost bits of μ
$A_1(k, \mathsf{find}, y_A, y_B)$ outputs (m_0, m_1, s)
$b \leftarrow_R \{0, 1\}$; $c^* \leftarrow \mathsf{E}_{\alpha^*}(m_b)$; $C^* \leftarrow (c^*, r^*, s^*)$
Run $A_2(k, \mathsf{guess}, m_0, m_1, C^*, y_A, y_B, s)$, using G-sim, H-sim,
$\mathcal{SC}$-sim and $\mathcal{USC}$-sim to simulate answers to
queries made by A_1 to its oracles
  if A_2 queries κ to G such that G-sim$(\kappa) = NULL$
   abort and return κ
  if A_2 queries μ to H such that H-sim$(\mu) = NULL$
   abort and return κ, where κ is the k rightmost bits of μ
$A_2(k, \mathsf{guess}, m_0, m_1, C^*, y_A, y_B, s)$ outputs b'
return κ^*

Analysis. Now we analyze our simulation. We consider A_c's execution in both the real attack experiment (*real*) and the GDH attack experiment (*sim*). Below, we define an event called Bad, which causes the joint distribution of A_c's view to differ in experiment *sim* from the distribution of A_c's view in experiment *real*.

For all outcomes of experiment *real* except those in the event Bad, A_c's view is distributed identically in experiments *real* and *sim*. Hence, outcomes in the complementary event ¬Bad of *real* have the same probability in experiment *sim*, and in particular:

$$\Pr[A_c \text{ wins} \wedge \neg\mathsf{Bad}]_{sim} = \Pr[A_c \text{ wins} \wedge \neg\mathsf{Bad}]_{real}$$
$$\geq \Pr[A_c \text{ wins}]_{real} - \Pr[\mathsf{Bad}]_{real}$$
$$\geq \frac{1}{2} + \frac{1}{2}\mathbf{Succ}_{SC,A_c}^{\text{fuo}-\text{ind}-\text{cca2}}(k) - \Pr[\mathsf{Bad}]_{real} \qquad (1)$$

Now we define an event GDHBrk in the experiment *sim* as follows:

- GDHBrk: A_c asks the Diffie-Hellman key $\kappa^* = X^{x_B} \bmod p$ to G-sim or A_c asks μ^* to H-sim such that κ^*, where κ^* is the k rightmost bits of μ^*.

Observe that if GDHBrk occurs then A_{gdh} will return the correct solution κ^* to the GDH instance that it is trying to compute. Hence, splitting $\Pr[A_c \text{ wins} \wedge \neg\mathsf{Bad}]_{sim} = \Pr[A_c \text{ wins} \wedge \neg\mathsf{Bad} \wedge \mathsf{GDHBrk}]_{sim} + \Pr[A_c \text{ wins} \wedge \neg\mathsf{Bad} \wedge \neg\mathsf{GDHBrk}]_{sim} \leq \mathbf{Succ}_{GDH,A_{gdh}}^{\text{invert}}(k) + \Pr[A_c \text{ wins} \wedge \neg\mathsf{Bad} \wedge \neg\mathsf{GDHBrk}]_{sim}$, and substituting in (1) we get:

$$\mathbf{Succ}_{GDH,A_{gdh}}^{\text{invert}}(k) + \Pr[A_c \text{ wins} \wedge \neg\mathsf{Bad} \wedge \neg\mathsf{GDHBrk}]_{sim} \geq$$
$$\frac{1}{2} + \frac{1}{2}\mathbf{Succ}_{SC,A_c}^{\text{fuo}-\text{ind}-\text{cca2}}(k) - \Pr[\mathsf{Bad}]_{real}. \qquad (2)$$

Since $\Pr[\mathsf{Bad}]_{real} = \Pr[\mathsf{Bad} \wedge (\neg\mathsf{GDHBrk} \vee \mathsf{GDHBrk})]_{real} \leq \Pr[\mathsf{Bad} \wedge \neg\mathsf{GDHBrk}]_{real} + \Pr[\mathsf{GDHBrk}]_{real} \leq \Pr[\mathsf{Bad} \wedge \neg\mathsf{GDHBrk}]_{real} + \mathbf{Succ}_{GDH,A_{gdh}}^{\text{invert}}(k)$, we have

$$2\mathbf{Succ}_{GDH,A_{gdh}}^{\text{invert}}(k) + \Pr[A_c \text{ wins} \wedge \neg\mathsf{Bad} \wedge \neg\mathsf{GDHBrk}]_{sim} \geq$$
$$\frac{1}{2} + \frac{1}{2}\mathbf{Succ}_{SC,A_c}^{\text{fuo}-\text{ind}-\text{cca2}}(k) - \Pr[\mathsf{Bad} \wedge \neg\mathsf{GDHBrk}]_{real}. \qquad (3)$$

In the remaining part of the proof we upper bound two terms in (3) as follows:

$$\Pr[\mathsf{Bad} \wedge \neg\mathsf{GDHBrk}]_{real} \leq \frac{q_{sc}(q_g + q_h + 1) + q_{usc}}{2^{l_q(k)}} \tag{4}$$

and

$$\Pr[A_c \text{ wins} \wedge \neg\mathsf{Bad} \wedge \neg\mathsf{GDHBrk}]_{sim} \leq \frac{1}{2} + \frac{1}{2}\mathbf{Adv}_{\mathsf{SC}^{\mathsf{SYM}}}^{\mathrm{ind-cpa}}(l, t_2, 0) \tag{5}$$

The advantage bound claim of the theorem follows upon substitution of (4) and (5) in (3), and taking maximums over all GDH adversaries with the appropriate resource parameters. The running time counts can be readily checked. Hence it remains to establish the bounds (4) and (5), which will be done below.

First, to establish (4), we upper bound the probability $\Pr[\mathsf{Bad} \wedge \neg\mathsf{GDHBrk}]_{real}$ of outcomes when the view of A_c during the real attack differs from its view during the simulation. It is easy to see that the inputs to A_c are identically distributed in both *real* and *sim*. But errors can occur in simulating answers to A_c's queries to its oracles G, H, $\mathcal{SC}$ and $\mathcal{USC}$. Accordingly, we split Bad $\wedge$ $\neg\mathsf{GDHBrk} = \mathsf{GBad} \vee \mathsf{HBad} \vee \mathsf{USCBad} \vee \mathsf{SCBad}$ into a union of bad outcomes in simulating each of the oracles. We bound each as follows and then add up the bounds using the union bound.

Signcryption Oracle Simulation Error. Notice that the signcryption oracle simulator chooses r and s independently and uniformly in $\mathbb{Z}/q\mathbb{Z}$ and τ independently and uniformly in $\{0,1\}^l$ and, then (defining $\omega = (y_A g^r)^s \bmod p$ and $\kappa = \omega^{x_B} \bmod p$) forces the following input-output pairs for the random oracles G and H: $\mathsf{G}(\kappa) = \tau$ and $\mathsf{H}(m||bind(= y_A||y_B)||\kappa) = r$. Due to randomness of the random oracles, this results in the same signcryptext distribution in *sim* as in *real*, if the images of H and G at the above points have not already been fixed due to earlier queries. But outcomes in *real* when the input to H or G has already been fixed cause a simulation error in *sim*.

Let $(\tilde{c}, \tilde{r}, \tilde{s})$ denote an output of the real signcryption oracle for each single query $\tilde{m}$. Namely, $(\tilde{c}, \tilde{r}, \tilde{s}) = (\mathsf{E}_{\tilde{\tau}}(\tilde{m}), \mathsf{H}(\tilde{m}||bind||y_B^{\tilde{x}} \bmod p), \tilde{x}/(\tilde{r} + x_A) \bmod q)$, where $\tilde{\tau} = \mathsf{G}(y_B^{\tilde{x}} \bmod p)$. Now we define the following events.

- E: $y_B^{\tilde{x}} \bmod p \in [L^{\mathsf{G}}]_{in} \cup [L^{\mathsf{H}}]_{in'} \cup \{\kappa^*(= y_B^x \bmod p)\}$.

Here, $[L^{\mathsf{G}}]_{in}$ is a set of all the inputs to the random oracle G, which exists in the list L^{G}. Also, $[L^{\mathsf{H}}]_{in'}$ is a set of all rightmost k bits of the inputs which exists in the list L^{H}. Thanks to uniform distribution of $y_B^{\tilde{x}} \bmod p$ in the group, we have $\Pr[E]_{real} \leq \frac{q_g + q_h + 1}{2^{l_q(k)}}$ for each signcryption oracle query.

Since there are up to q_{sc} signcryption queries, the total probability of outcomes in *real* leading to signcryption oracle simulation error is bounded as:

$$\Pr[\mathsf{SCBad}] \leq q_{sc}\left(\frac{q_g + q_h + 1}{2^{l_q(k)}}\right). \tag{6}$$

H-*Simulation Error.* The only event which can cause an error in simulating the random oracle H is the GDHBrk. Since HBad $\subseteq \neg\mathsf{GDHBrk}$, we have $\Pr[\mathsf{HBad}] = 0$.

G-*Simulation Error.* Thanks to the fixed-input DDH oracle available to A_{gdh}, the random oracle G is perfectly simulated for any query, hence we have we have $\Pr[\mathsf{GBad}] = 0$.

Unsigncryption Oracle Simulation Error. Let USCBad be an event that unsign-cryption simulation error occurs during the execution of A_c. Then we will bound USCBad $\wedge$ ¬SCBad. Note that (USCBad $\wedge$ ¬SCBad) $\subseteq$ ¬SCBad and (USCBad $\wedge$ ¬SCBad) $\subseteq$ ¬GDHBrk since USCBad $\subseteq$ ¬GDHBrk. Note also that the event USCBad $\wedge$ ¬SCBad is specified as follows.

- USCBad $\wedge$ ¬SCBad: A_c queries signcryptext $(y_{bad}, c_{bad}, r_{bad}, s_{bad})$ to the un-signcryption oracle $\mathcal{USC}$ such that
  (U.1) $\omega_{bad} = X$, where $\omega_{bad} = (y_{bad}g^{r_{bad}})^{s_{bad}} \bmod p$ and
  (U.2) $\kappa^*(= X^{x_B} \bmod p) \notin L_{in}^{\mathsf{G}} \cup L_{in'}^{\mathsf{H}}$ and
  (U.3) $r_{bad} = \mathsf{H}(m_{bad}||y_{bad}||y_B||\kappa^*)$ and
  (U.4) $m_{bad}||y_{bad}||y_B||\kappa^* \neq m_b||y_A||y_B||\kappa^*$

We remark that if (U.1) does not occur then there is no difference between $\mathcal{USC}$ and $\mathcal{USC}$-sim. Also (U.2) must hold, otherwise SCBad or GDHBrk happens. (U.3) must occur or else both $\mathcal{USC}$ and $\mathcal{USC}$-sim reject (namely, there is no difference between $\mathcal{USC}$ and $\mathcal{USC}$-sim). Finally, we establish (U.4) in the following claim.

Claim 1: $m_{bad}||y_{bad}||y_B||\kappa^* \neq m_b||y_A||y_B||\kappa^*$, i.e. the query to H by the unsigncryption oracle during unsigncryption of $(y_{bad}, c_{bad}, r_{bad}, s_{bad})$ is not the one used to create r^* in the challenge signcryptext (y_A, c^*, r^*, s^*).

proof: Suppose the contrary, i.e. that $m_{bad}||y_{bad}||y_B||\kappa = m_b||y_A||y_B||\kappa$. Then we have: (C.1) $y_{bad} = y_A$ and (C.2) $m_{bad} = \mathsf{D}_{\alpha^*}(c_{bad}) = \mathsf{D}_{\alpha^*}(c^*) = m_b$, and (C.3) $r_{bad} = r^*$ using (U.3) above. From (C.2) and the assumption that $\mathsf{D}_\alpha(\cdot)$ is one-to-one for any key α, we have (C.4) $c_{bad} = c^*$. Finally, since $\omega_{bad} = (y_{bad}g^{r_{bad}})^{s_{bad}} \bmod p = X = (y_Ag^{r^*})^{s^*} \bmod p$, then using (C.1) and (C.4) and the fact that $y_Ag^{r^*} \in\ <g>$ has order q (since $\mathrm{Ord}(g) = q$ is prime), we conclude that $s_{bad} = s^* \bmod q$ and since $(y_{bad}, c_{bad}, r_{bad}, s_{bad})$ was accepted, $s_{bad} \in \mathbb{Z}/q\mathbb{Z}$ so (C.5) $s_{bad} = s$. Combining (C.1), (C.3), (C.4), and (C.5), we arrive at the conclusion that $(y_{bad}, c_{bad}, r_{bad}, s_{bad})$ is equal to the challenge sign-cryptext, which is impossible since A_c is not allowed to query the challenge. □

For each signcryptext $(y_{bad}, c_{bad}, r_{bad}, s_{bad})$ queried to USC, $\Pr[(U.3)|(U.1) \wedge (U.2) \wedge (U.4)]_{real} = \frac{1}{2^{l_q(k)}}$ because $\mathsf{H}(\mu_{bad})$ is uniformly distributed in $\mathbb{Z}/q\mathbb{Z}$ and independent of r_{bad}, where $\mu_{bad} \stackrel{\mathrm{def}}{=} m_{bad}||y_{bad}||y_B||\kappa^*$, hence $\Pr[(U.1) \wedge (U.2) \wedge (U.3) \wedge (U.4)]_{real} \leq \frac{1}{2^{l_q(k)}}$.

Since A_c makes up to q_{usc} queries to $\mathcal{USC}$ we obtain

$$\Pr[\mathsf{USCBad} \wedge \neg\mathsf{SCBad}]_{real} \leq \frac{q_{usc}}{2^{l_q(k)}}. \tag{7}$$

Adding up (6) and (7) we obtain the desired bound (4).

To complete the proof it remains to deduce the second bound (5) on the probability $\Pr[A_c \text{ wins} \wedge \neg\mathsf{Bad} \wedge \neg\mathsf{GDHBrk}]_{sim}$. We do this by constructing an adversary A_p' against the IND-CPA of the symmetric encryption scheme $\mathsf{SC}^{\mathrm{SYM}}$

used in the signcryption scheme, and show that its probability of winning the 'IND-CPA' experiment sim' is at least $\Pr[A_c \text{ wins} \wedge \neg\mathsf{Bad} \wedge \neg\mathsf{GDHBrk}]_{sim'}$.

Now we construct the adversary $A_p' = (A_1', A_2')$ using A_{gdh} (which in turn makes use of the adversary A_c to achieve its goal). Let s' be state information. Now a specification follows.

Adversary $A_1'(l, \mathsf{find})$
    Find k corresponding to l
    $r^* \leftarrow_R \mathbb{Z}/q\mathbb{Z}; \; s^* \leftarrow_R \mathbb{Z}/q\mathbb{Z}; \; x \leftarrow_R \mathbb{Z}/q\mathbb{Z}; \; X \leftarrow g^x \bmod p$
    $y_A \leftarrow (Xg^{-r^*s^*})^{\frac{1}{s^*}} \bmod p; \; x_B \leftarrow_R \mathbb{Z}/q\mathbb{Z}; \; y_B \leftarrow g^{x_B} \bmod p$
    Run $A_1(k, \mathsf{find}, y_A, y_B)$, using G-sim, H-sim, $\mathcal{SC}$-sim and $\mathcal{USC}$-sim
    to simulate answers to queries made by A_1 to its oracles
        if A_1 queries κ to G such that G-sim$(\kappa) = NULL$
            abort and return κ
        if A_1 queries μ to H such that H-sim$(\mu) = NULL$
            abort and return κ where κ is the k rightmost bits of μ
    $A_1(k, \mathsf{find}, y_A, y_B)$ outputs (m_0, m_1, s)
    $s' \leftarrow s \, |k||r^*||s^*||y_A||y_B||L^\mathsf{G}||L^\mathsf{H}$
    return (m_0, m_1, s')

Outside the view of A_p', a random bit $b \in \{0, 1\}$ and a random key $\alpha \in \{0, 1\}^l$ are chosen and $c^* = \mathsf{E}_\alpha(m_b)$ is computed. Then (m_0, m_1, c^*, s') is provided as an input to A_2'.

Adversary $A_2'(l, \mathsf{guess}, m_0, m_1, c, s')$
    Retrieve $s||k||r^*||s^*||y_A||y_B||L^\mathsf{G}||L^\mathsf{H}$ from s'
    $C^* \leftarrow c^*||r^*||s^*$
    Run $A_2(k, \mathsf{guess}, m_0, m_1, C^*, y_A, y_B, C^*, s)$, using G-sim, H-sim,
    $\mathcal{SC}$-sim and $\mathcal{USC}$-sim to simulate answers to
    queries made by A_2 to its oracles
        if A_2 queries κ to G such that G-sim$(\kappa) = NULL$
            abort and return κ
        if A_2 queries μ to H such that H-sim$(\mu) = NULL$
            abort and return κ where κ is the k rightmost bits of μ
    $A_2(k, \mathsf{guess}, (m_0, m_1), C^*, y_A, y_B, s)$ outputs b'
    return b'

Now observe the following properties of A_p': (P.1) A_p' makes no queries to its symmetric encryption oracle. (P.2) If event A_c wins $\wedge \neg\mathsf{Bad} \wedge \neg\mathsf{GDHBrk}$ occurs, then A_c's view is identical in both sim and sim' (P.3) If A_c wins $\wedge\neg\mathsf{Bad} \wedge \neg\mathsf{GDHBrk}$ occurs in sim' then A_p' wins.

Combining (P.1), (P.2) and (P.3) we get the desired bound $\Pr[A_c \text{ wins} \wedge \neg\mathsf{Bad} \wedge \neg\mathsf{SDHBrk}]_{sim} \leq \frac{1}{2} + \frac{1}{2}\mathbf{Succ}^{\mathrm{ind-cpa}}_{\mathsf{SC}^{\mathrm{SYM}}, A_p'}(l) \leq \frac{1}{2} + \frac{1}{2}\mathbf{Adv}^{\mathrm{ind-cpa}}_{\mathsf{SC}^{\mathrm{SYM}}}(l, t_2, 0)$, which establishes (5) and completes the proof. $\qquad\square$

4.2   Unforgeability of Signcryption

In this section, we state our results on unforgeability of signcryption. Due to lack of space, all the proofs for showing signcryption SC is existentially unforgeable against adaptive chosen message attack [12] are omitted in this version of the paper. The basic idea of proofs is to use the ID reduction technique [15].

Theorem 2. *If the signcryption scheme* SC *is forged with* q_s, q_g *and* q_h *queries to the signcryption oracle* SC *and the random oracles* G *and* H, *respectively, within execution time* t, *then the discrete logarithm of the sender's public key* $y_A = g^{x_A} \bmod p$ *can be found with the following bound.*

$$\mathbf{Adv}_{\mathsf{SC}}^{\mathrm{cma}}(k, t, q_g, q_h, q_{sc}) \leq 2q_h \big(\mathbf{Adv}_{\mathsf{DLP}}^{\mathrm{search}}(k, t^*)\big)^{\frac{1}{2}} + \frac{1}{2^{l_q(k)}}$$

where execution time $t^* = O(t + time_{sc} + time_v + time_c)$. *Note that* $time_{sc}$ *is the simulation time of* q_{sc} *signcryptexts* $time_v$ *and* $time_c$ *and denote the time for verification in* IDSC *which is an identification scheme derived from* SC *and the calculation time of* $x_A \bmod q$, *respectively.*

5   Conclusions

We have proved the confidentiality of Zheng's original signcryption scheme with respect to a strong well-defined security notion similar to the well known 'IND-CCA2' notion defined for standard public-key encryption schemes. Our confidentiality notion is even stronger than the direct adaptation of 'IND-CCA2' to the setting of signcryption, since we allow the attacker to query the signcryption oracle, as well as the unsigncryption oracle. We have also proved the unforgeability of signcryption in a strong sense, namely existential unforgeability against adaptive chosen message attack. Currently we are working on strengthening our confidentiality result even further by allowing the attacker to have 'flexible access' to the signcryption oracle, i.e., the ability to specify an arbitrary recipient's public key in signcryption queries. We will call this new model *Flexible Signcryption Oracle (FSO)*-model. We are also working on extending results presented in this paper to prove the security of various other signcryption schemes proposed in [21] and [25]. We leave technical details for the on-going work to future papers.

Acknowledgement

The authors would like to thank anonymous referees for their helpful comments. The first two authors would also like to thank Dr Jan Newmarch from Monash University for his support and encouragement.

References

1. J. An : *Authenticated Encryption in the Public-Key Setting: Security Notions and Analyses*, available at http://eprint.iacr.org/.

2. M. Bellare, A. Desai, E. Jokipii and P. Rogaway: *A Concrete Security Treament of Symmetric Encryption*, Proceedings of FOCS '97, IEEE Computer Society Press, 1997, pages 394–403.
3. M. Bellare, A. Desai, D. Pointcheval and P. Rogaway: *Relations Among Notions of Security for Public-Key Encryption Schemes*, Advances in Cryptology - Proceedings of CRYPTO '98, Vol. 1462 of LNCS, Springer-Verlag 1998, pages 26–45.
4. M. Bellare and C. Namprepre: *Authenticated Encryption: Relations among notions and analysis of the generic composition paradigm*, Advances in Cryptology - Proceedings of ASIACRYPT 2000, Vol. 1976 of LNCS, Springer-Verlag 2000, pages 531–545.
5. M. Bellare and P. Rogaway: *Optimal asymmetric encryption*, Advances in Cryptology -Proceedings of Eurocrypt '94, Vol. 950 of LNCS, Springer-Verlag 1994, pages 92–111.
6. M. Bellare and P. Rogaway: *Random Oracles are Practical: A Paradigm for Designing Efficient Protocols*, Proceedings of First ACM Conference on Computer and Communications Security 1993, pages 62–73.
7. R. Cramer and V. Shoup: *A Practical Public Key Cryptosystem Provably Secure against Adaptive Chosen Ciphertext Attack*, Advances in Cryptology - Proceedings of CRYPTO '98, Vol. 1462 of LNCS, Springer-Verlag 1998, pages 13–25.
8. T. ElGamal: *A Public Key Cryptosystem and a Signature Scheme Based on Discrete Logarithms*, IEEE Trans. Information Theory, 31, 1985, pages 469–472.
9. A. Frier, P. Karlton and P. Kocher: *The SSL 3.0 Protocol*, Netscape Communications Corp., 1996, available at http://home.netscape.com/eng/ssl3/ssl.toc.html.
10. E. Fujisaki and T. Okamoto: *How to Enhance the Security of Public-Key Encryption at Minimum Cost*, Proceedings of Public Key Cryptography '99 (PKC '99), Vol. 1666 of LNCS, Springer-Verlag 1999, pages 53–68.
11. S. Goldwasser and S. Micali: *Probabilistic Encryption*, Journal of Computer and System Sciences, Vol. 28, 1984, pages 270–299.
12. S. Goldwasser, S. Micali and R. Rivest: *A Digital Signature Scheme Secure Against Adaptive Chosen-Message Attacks*, SIAM Journal on Computing, 17, 2, 1988, pages 281–308.
13. S. Kent and R. Atkinson: *IP Encapsulating Security Payload (ESP)*, RFC 2406, 1998.
14. H. Krawczyk: *The Order Of Encryption And Authentication For Protecting Communications (Or: How Secure Is SSL?)*, Advances in Cryptology - Proceedings of CRYPTO 2001, Vol. 2139 of LNCS, Springer-Verlag 2001, pages 310–331.
15. K. Ohta and T. Okamoto: *On Concrete Security Treatment of Signatures Derived from Identification*, Advances in Cryptology - Proceedings of CRYPTO '98, Vol. 1462 of LNCS, Springer-Verlag 1998, pages 354–369.
16. T. Okamoto and D. Pointcheval: *The Gap-Problems: A New Class of Problems for the Security of Cryptographic Schemes*, Proceedings of Public Key Cryptography 2001 (PKC 2001), Vol. 1992 of LNCS, Springer-Verlag 2001, pages 104–118.
17. D. Pointcheval: *Chosen-Ciphertext Security for Any One-Way Cryptosystem*, Proceedings of Public Key Cryptography 2000 (PKC 2000), Vol. 1751 of LNCS, Springer-Verlag 2000, pages 129–146.
18. D. Pointcheval and J. Stern: *Security Arguments for Digital Signatures and Blind Signatures*, Jornal of Cryptology, Vol. 13-Number 3, Springer-Verlag 2000, pages 361-396.

19. C. P. Schnorr: *Efficient Identification and Signatures for Smart Cards*, Advances in Cryptology - Proceedings of CRYPTO '89, Vol. 435 of LNCS, Springer-Verlag 1990, pages 235–251.
20. C. P. Schnorr and M. Jakobsson: *Security of Signed ElGamal Encryption* , Advances in Cryptology - Proceedings of ASIACRYPT 2000, Vol. 1976 of LNCS, Springer-Verlag 2000, pages 73–89.
21. R. Steinfeld and Y. Zheng: *A Signcryption Scheme Based on Integer Factorization*, Proceedings of Information Security Workshop 2000 (ISW2000), Vol. 1975 of LNCS, Springer-Verlag 2000, pages 308–322.
22. Y. Tsiounis and M. Yung: *On the Security of ElGamal-Based Encryption*, Proceedings of Public Key Cryptography '98 (PKC '98), Vol. 1431 of LNCS, Springer-Verlag 1998, pages 117–134.
23. Y. Zheng: *Digital Signcryption or How to Achieve Cost (Signature & Encryption)* ≪ *Cost (Signature) + Cost (Encryption)*, Advances in Cryptology - Proceedings CRYPTO '97, Vol. 1294 of LNCS, Springer-Verlag 1997, pages 165–179.
24. Y. Zheng: *Digital Signcryption or How to Achieve Cost (Signature & Encryption)* ≪ *Cost (Signature) + Cost (Encryption)*, full version, available at http://www.pscit.monash.edu.au/ yuliang/pubs/.
25. Y. Zheng: *Identification, Signature and Signcryption Using High Order Residues Modulo an RSA Composite*, Proceedings of Public Key Cryptography 2001 (PKC 2001), Vol. 1992 of LNCS, Springer-Verlag 2001, pages 48–63.
26. Y. Zheng and J. Seberry: *Immunizing public key cryptosystems against chosen ciphertext attacks*, the Special Issue on Secure Communications, IEEE Journal on Selected Areas in Communications, Vol. 11, No. 5, 1993, pages 715–724.

A Provably Secure Restrictive
Partially Blind Signature Scheme

Greg Maitland and Colin Boyd

Information Security Research Centre
Queensland University of Technology
Brisbane, Australia.
{g.maitland,c.boyd}@qut.edu.au

Abstract. The concept of partially blind signatures was first introduced by Abe and Fujisaki. Subsequently, in work by Abe and Okamoto, a provably secure construction was proposed along with a formalised definition for partially blind schemes. The construction was based on a witness indistinguishable protocol described by Cramer et al. and utilises a blind Schnorr signature scheme.

This paper investigates incorporating the restrictive property proposed by Brands into a partially blind signature scheme. The proposed scheme follows the construction proposed by Abe and Okamoto and makes use of Brands' restrictive blind signature scheme.

1 Introduction

Blind signature schemes were first introduced by Chaum [9] and allow a recipient to acquire a signature on a message m without revealing anything about the message to the signer. One of the first applications for blind signatures was in the area of electronic cash. However, the complete lack of control over the message being signed makes tasks such as including expiry information in the blind signature difficult. The signer cannot rely on the recipient to include any specific information in the blindly signed message. The typical solution to this difficulty has been to associate different signing keys with different classes of messages. This is undesirable as it leads to a proliferation of signing keys and a potential verifier must have access to all possible active certified keys.

In the context of electronic cash schemes based around the use of blind signatures, the specific problems arise because of the need to expire coins as well as the need to clearly nominate the denominational value of each coin. Practical schemes must allow exact payments and therefore usually accommodate coins of varying denominations. In addition, blindly issued coins require the bank to maintain a database of previously spent coins in order to detect double-spending. Without any extra measures, the size of the database would increase indefinitely over time and this would reduce the cost-effective and efficient operation of the database. In order to contain the size of the database, 'old' spent coins need to be removed after an appropriate amount of time. Thus, a coin must have an expiry date after which it is no longer acceptable in a payment transaction.

D. Naccache and P. Paillier (Eds.): PKC 2002, LNCS 2274, pp. 99–114, 2002.
© Springer-Verlag Berlin Heidelberg 2002

A partially blind signature scheme allows a signer to produce a blind signature on a message for a recipient and the signature explicitly includes common agreed information which remains clearly visible despite the blinding process. Abe and Fujisaki [2] first introduced the concept in response to the need for the signer to regain some control over the signatures produced by a blind signature scheme. When used in electronic cash scheme design, the common agreed information allows expiry date and denominational information to be included in the blind signature while requiring that the verifier has access to only a single certified public key.

Early papers on the construction of partially blind signatures [1,13] based around Schnorr, DSS and Nyberg-Rueppel schemes concentrated on withstanding parallel algebraic attacks [?]. More recently, Abe and Okamoto [3] described a provably secure partially blind signature based on a witness indistinguishable protocol using blinded Schnorr signatures [15] as a building block.

However, the previously published partially blind signatures lack the restrictive property. Restrictive blind signature schemes were proposed by Brands [5] and allow a recipient to receive a blind signature on a message not known to the signer but the choice of message is restricted and must conform to certain rules. In practical applications such as Brands' cash [5,6], the signer is assured that the recipient's identity is embedded in some sense in the resulting blind signature.

While Brands' cash has received wide attention for its ability to detect and reveal the identity of double-spenders, it also possesses another property – transfer-resistance. That is, the spender of a coin must have access to the private key of the customer who withdrew the coin in order to spend it. This discourages the transfer of coins from one user to another as the withdrawing user must reveal private key information if another user is to spend the coin. Transfer-resistance is a useful tool in discouraging illegal activities such as money laundering and blackmail.

Main Contribution: Since Brands' cash remains an important building block in several cash schemes [7,4,14], it is relevant to consider ways of incorporating the property of partial blindness into Brands' restrictive blind signature scheme. Pointcheval [16] and Abe-Okamoto [3] have constructed security arguments for blind signatures based on witness indistinguishable protocols. Using the techniques proposed by Abe and Okamoto [3], we utilise a witness indistinguishable protocol to create a restrictive partially blind signature scheme with provable security. In the process, we introduce a multiplicative variant of the blind Schnorr signature, which to the authors' knowledge has not previously been published. We also utilise multiplicative (rather than additive) secret sharing in the construction of the witness indistinguishable protocol.

Organisation of the Paper: Section 2 describes the basic definitions associated with partially blind signatures while section 3 reviews both Schnorr [17] and Chaum-Pedersen [8] protocols in connection with the Cramer et al. construction for witness indistinguishable protocols. Section 4 discusses blinding operations for both the Schnorr and Chaum-Pedersen protocols. A restrictive partially blind signature is presented in section 5 and its security is discussed in section 6.

2 Definitions

We follow the definitions provided by Abe and Okamoto [3] which have been adapted for partially blind signatures from the security definitions of Juels, Luby, and Ostrovsky [12].

In the context of partially blind signatures, the signer and the user are assumed to agree on a piece of common information, denoted by info. It may happen that info is decided by the signer; in other situations, info may just be sent from the user to the signer. This negotiation is considered to be done outside of the signature scheme. Abe and Okamoto [3] formalize this notion by introducing a function Ag which is defined outside of the scheme. Function Ag is a polynomial-time deterministic algorithm that takes two arbitrary strings $info_s$, and $info_u$, that belong to the signer and the user, respectively, and outputs info. To compute Ag, the signer and the user will exchange $info_s$ and $info_u$ with each other. If the signer is allowed to control the selection of info, then Ag is defined such that it depends only on $info_s$. In this case, the user does not need to send $info_u$.

Definition 1 (Partially Blind Signature Scheme). *A partially blind signature scheme is a four-tuple* $(\mathcal{G}, \mathcal{S}, \mathcal{U}, \mathcal{V})$.

- $\mathcal{G}$ *is a probabilistic polynomial-time algorithm, that takes security parameter k and outputs a public and secret key pair (pk, sk).*
- $\mathcal{S}$ *and $\mathcal{U}$ are a pair of probabilistic interactive Turing machines each of which has a public input tape, a private input tape, a private random tape, a private work tape, a private output tape, a public output tape, and input and output communication tapes. The random tape and the input tapes are read-only, and the output tapes are write-only. The private work tape is read-write. The public input tape of $\mathcal{U}$ contains pk generated by $\mathcal{G}(1^k)$, the description of Ag, and $info_u$. The public input tape of $\mathcal{S}$ contains the description of Ag and $info_s$. The private input tape of $\mathcal{S}$ contains sk, and that for $\mathcal{U}$ contains a message msg. The lengths of $info_s$, $info_u$, and msg are polynomial in k. $\mathcal{S}$ and $\mathcal{U}$ engage in the signature issuing protocol and stop in polynomial-time. When they stop, the public output tape of $\mathcal{S}$ contains either completed or not-completed. If it is completed, then its private output tape contains common information info. Similarly, the private output tape of $\mathcal{U}$ contains either $\perp$ or $(info, msg, sig)$.*
- $\mathcal{V}$ *is a (probabilistic) polynomial-time algorithm. $\mathcal{V}$ takes $(pk, info, msg, sig)$ and outputs either accept or reject.*

Definition 2 (Completeness). *If $\mathcal{S}$ and $\mathcal{U}$ follow the signature issuing protocol, the signature scheme is complete if, for every constant $c > 0$, there exists a* *bound k_0 such that $\mathcal{S}$ outputs completed and* info $= Ag(\mathsf{info}_s, \mathsf{info}_u)$ *on its proper tapes, and $\mathcal{U}$ outputs* (info, msg, sig) *that satisfies*

$$\mathcal{V}(pk, \mathsf{info}, msg, sig) = accept$$

with probability at least $1 - 1/k^c$ for $k > k_0$. The probability is taken over the coin flips of $\mathcal{G}$, $\mathcal{S}$ and $\mathcal{U}$.

A message-signature tuple (info, msg, sig) is considered valid with regard to pk if it leads $\mathcal{V}$ to accept. We define the partial blindness property as follows.

Definition 3 (Partial Blindness). *Let $\mathcal{U}_0$ and $\mathcal{U}_1$ be two honest users that follow the signature issuing protocol. Let $\mathcal{S}^*$ play the following game in the presence of an independent umpire.*

1. *$(pk, sk) \leftarrow \mathcal{G}(1^k)$.*
2. *$(msg_0, msg_1, \mathsf{info}_{u_0}, \mathsf{info}_{u_1}, Ag) \leftarrow \mathcal{S}^*(1^k, pk, sk)$.*
3. *The umpire sets up the input tapes of $\mathcal{U}_0$, $\mathcal{U}_1$ as follows:*
   - *The umpire selects $b \in_R \{0, 1\}$ and places msg_b and msg_{1-b} on the private input tapes of $\mathcal{U}_0$ and $\mathcal{U}_1$, respectively. b is not disclosed to $\mathcal{S}^*$.*
   - *Place info_{u_0} and info_{u_1} on the public input tapes of $\mathcal{U}_0$ and $\mathcal{U}_1$ respectively. Also place pk and Ag on their public input tapes.*
   - *Randomly select the contents of the private random tapes.*
4. *$\mathcal{S}^*$ engages in the signature issuing protocol with $\mathcal{U}_0$ and $\mathcal{U}_1$ in a parallel and arbitrarily interleaved fashion. If either signature issuing protocol fails to complete, the game is aborted.*
5. *Let $\mathcal{U}_0$ and $\mathcal{U}_1$ output $(\mathsf{info}_0, msg_b, sig_b)$ and $(\mathsf{info}_1, msg_{1-b}, sig_{1-b})$, respectively, on their private tapes. If $\mathsf{info}_0 \neq \mathsf{info}_1$ holds, then the umpire provides $\mathcal{S}^*$ with the no additional information. That is, the umpire gives $\perp$ to $\mathcal{S}^*$. If $\mathsf{info}_0 = \mathsf{info}_1$ holds, then the umpire provides $\mathcal{S}^*$ with the additional inputs $\{sig_b, sig_{1-b}\}$ ordered according to the corresponding messages $\{msg_0, msg_1\}$.*
6. *$\mathcal{S}^*$ outputs $b' \in \{0, 1\}$. The signer $\mathcal{S}^*$ wins the game if $b' = b$.*

A signature scheme is partially blind if, for every constant $c > 0$, there exists a bound k_0 such that for all probabilistic polynomial-time algorithm $\mathcal{S}^*$, $\mathcal{S}^*$ outputs $b' = b$ with probability at most $1/2 + 1/k^c$ for $k > k_0$. The probability is taken over the coin flips of $\mathcal{G}$, $\mathcal{U}_0$, $\mathcal{U}_1$, and $\mathcal{S}^*$.

Definition 4 (Unforgeability). *Let $\mathcal{S}$ be an honest signer that follow the signature issuing protocol. Let $\mathcal{U}^*$ play the following game in the presence of an independent umpire.*

1. *$(pk, sk) \leftarrow \mathcal{G}(1^n)$.*
2. *$Ag \leftarrow \mathcal{U}^*(pk)$.*
3. *The umpire places sk, Ag and a randomly taken info_s on the proper input tapes of $\mathcal{S}$.*

4. $\mathcal{U}^*$ engages in the signature issuing protocol with $\mathcal{S}$ in a concurrent and interleaving way. For each info, let ℓ_{info} be the number of executions of the signature issuing protocol where $\mathcal{S}$ outputs completed and info is on its output tapes. (For info that has never appeared on the private output tape of $\mathcal{S}$, define $\ell_{\text{info}} = 0$.)

5. $\mathcal{U}^*$ outputs a single piece of common information, info, and $\ell_{\text{info}} + 1$ signatures $(msg_1, sig_1), \ldots, (msg_{\ell_{\text{info}} + 1}, sig_{\ell_{\text{info}} + 1})$.

A partially blind signature scheme is unforgeable if, for any probabilistic polynomial-time algorithm $\mathcal{U}^*$ that plays the above game, the probability that the output of $\mathcal{U}^*$ satisfies

$$\mathcal{V}(pk, \text{info}, msg_j, sig_j) = accept$$

for all $j = 1, \ldots, \ell_{\text{info}} + 1$ is at most $1/k^c$ where $k > k_0$ for some bound k_0 and some constant $c > 0$. The probability is taken over the coin flips of $\mathcal{G}$, $\mathcal{S}$, and $\mathcal{U}^*$.

The following definition of a restrictive blind signature is due to Brands [6].

Definition 5 (Restrictiveness). Let msg be message such that the receiver-knows a representation $(a_1, \ldots, a_k)$ of msg with respect to a generator-tuple $(g_1, \ldots, g_k)$ at the start of a blind signature protocol. Let $(b_1, \ldots, b_k)$ be the representation the receiver knows of the blinded number msg' of msg after the protocol has finished. If there exist two functions I_1 and I_2 such that

$$I_1(a, \ldots, a_k) = I_2(b_1, \ldots, b_k),$$

regardless of msg and the blinding transformations applied by the receiver, then the protocol is called a restrictive blind signature protocol. The functions I_1 and I_2 are called blinding-invariant functions of the protocol with respect to $(g_1, \ldots, g_k)$.

3 Witness Indistinguishable Protocols

The Okamoto-Schnorr identification protocol is a well known example of a witness indistinguishable protocol. Informally, a proof of knowledge is witness indistinguishable if the verifier cannot tell which witness the prover is using even if the verifier knows all possible witnesses [11]. Pointcheval [16] has presented security arguments for the blind Okamoto-Schnorr signature scheme. The witness indistinguishable property is necessary in order to prove security. Abe-Okamoto [3] have constructed security arguments for a partially blind signature scheme based on a witness indistinguishable protocol. We also seek to use a witness indistinguishable protocol as the basis for a provably secure scheme.

Cramer, Damgård, and Schoenmakers [10] presented a method for constructing witness indistinguishable protocols by combining suitable three-move proofs of knowledge with a compliant secret sharing scheme. In particular, the proofs of knowledge must possess the *special soundness* and *special honest verifier zero-knowledge* properties. A proof of knowledge has special soundness if, given two transcripts of the protocol which share a common commitment, a witness can be computed in polynomial time. A protocol is *honest verifier zero-knowledge* if there is a simulator which produces conversations that are indistinguishable from real conversations between the honest prover and the honest verifier. *Special honest verifier zero-knowledge* requires that there is a procedure that can take any challenge as input and produce a conversation indistinguishable from the space of all conversations between the honest prover and honest verifier that involve this challenge.

As an example of the construction, Cramer, Damgård, and Schoenmakers [10] presented a proof of knowledge of d out of n secrets using Schnorr's protocol as the basic proof of knowledge and a 'matrix' method for the secret sharing scheme. It is this scheme (with $d = 1$ and $n = 2$) that Abe and Okamoto [3] use to construct a provably secure partially blind signature scheme. Note that the secret sharing scheme is reduced to a simple additive scheme where both shares sum to give the secret.

While Cramer, Damgård, and Schoenmakers [10] concentrate on a construction which utilises several instances of the same proof of knowledge, they note that it is also possible to combine instances of different proofs of knowledge. In this paper, we will combine a Schnorr proof of knowledge of a discrete log [17] with a Chaum-Pedersen proof of equivalence of discrete logs [8]. With this in mind, we now review both the Schnorr and Chaum-Pedersen schemes with particular focus on the special soundness and special honest verifier zero-knowledge properties.

3.1   Schnorr's Proof of Knowledge of a Discrete Log

Let two primes p and q be given such that q divides $p - 1$ and let $g \in \mathbb{Z}_p^*$ be an element of order q. The group generated by g is denoted by G_q. The private key is $x \in \mathbb{Z}_q^*$ and the public key is (p, q, g, y) where $y = g^x$. The underlying identification protocol is as follows:

- The prover chooses $r \in_R \mathbb{Z}_q$ at random and computes $a = g^r$. The commitment value, a, is sent to the verifier.
- The verifier chooses a random challenge $c \in_R \mathbb{Z}_q$ and sends it to the prover.
- The prover sends back the response $s = r + cx \bmod q$.
- The verifier accepts the proof if and only if $a = g^s y^{-c}$.

Special Soundness: Let (c, s) and (c', s') be two signatures that are derived from the same commitment a. Then, the witness x can be found by observing that

$$a = g^s y^{-c} = g^{s'} y^{-c'} \text{ which implies that}$$
$$y = g^{\frac{s - s'}{c - c'}} = g^x \text{ and so}$$
$$x = \frac{s - s'}{c - c'} \bmod q.$$

Special Honest Verifier Zero-knowledge: A simulator can generate transcripts of the Schnorr protocol as follows:

- Select $c', s' \in_R \mathbb{Z}_q^*$
- Calculate $a' = g^{s'} y^{-c'}$

The transcript (a', c', s') satisfies $a' = g^{s'} y^{-c'}$ by construction and is statistically indistinguishable from actual protocol transcripts.

3.2   Chaum-Pedersen Signature

We review the Chaum-Pedersen [8] protocol and properties. Let two primes p and q be given such that q divides $p - 1$ and let $g \in \mathbb{Z}_p^*$ be an element of order q. The group generated by g is denoted by G_q. The private key is $x \in \mathbb{Z}_q^*$ and the public key is (p, q, g, y) where $y = g^x$. The underlying identification protocol (utilising a message m) is as follows:

- The prover chooses $r \in_R \mathbb{Z}_q$ at random and computes $(z, a, b) = (m^x, g^r, m^r)$. The tuple (z, a, b) is sent to the verifier.
- The verifier chooses a random challenge $c \in_R \mathbb{Z}_q$ and sends it to the prover.
- The prover sends back the response $s = r + cx \bmod q$.
- The verifier accepts the proof if and only if $a = g^s y^{-c}$ and $b = m^s z^{-c}$.

Special Soundness: Let (z, c, s) and (z, c', s') be two signatures that are derived from the same commitment a. Then, the witness x can be found by observing that

$$a = g^s y^{-c} = g^{s'} y^{-c'} \text{ which implies that}$$
$$y = g^{\frac{s - s'}{c - c'}} = g^x \text{ and so}$$
$$x = \frac{s - s'}{c - c'} \bmod q$$

Special Honest Verifier Zero-knowledge: A simulator can generate transcripts of the Chaum-Pedersen protocol involving a message m as follows:

- Select $z', c', s' \in_R \mathbb{Z}_q^*$
- Calculate $a' = g^{s'} y^{-c'}$
- Calculate $b' = (m)^{s'} (z')^{-c'}$

The transcript (z', a', b', c', s') satisfies $a' = g^{s'} y^{-c'}$ and $b' = (m)^{s'} (z')^{-c'}$ by construction and is statistically indistinguishable from actual protocol transcripts.

4   Blinding Techniques

In this section, we review the blinding techniques which may be applied to the Schnorr [17] and Chaum-Pedersen [8] protocols. As detailed below, the standard blinding of the challenge for the Chaum-Pedersen protocol is multiplicative in nature. The usual blind Schnorr protocol [15] uses an additive blinding of the challenge. Since our aim is to combine these two types of proof of knowledge to form a witness indistinguishable protocol which we can subsequently blind, we need blinding operations which are consistently either additive or multiplicative. To this end, the blinding of the Schnorr protocol outlined below uses a multiplicative (rather than the more usual additive) blinding of the challenge.

4.1   Brands' Restrictive Blind Signature

The restrictive blind signature scheme described in this section is derived from the Chaum-Pedersen scheme [8] described in section 3.2 and is Brands' original restrictive blind signature scheme [5,6].

Let g be a generator of a cyclic group G of order q. Let $y = g^x$ be the public key of the signer, and m a message from the receiver. The signer is supposed to sign m by forming $z = m^x$ and providing a signed proof that $\log_g y = \log_m z$. The Chaum-Pedersen protocol can be diverted to form a restrictive blind signature in the following fashion.

- The signer generates a random number $r \in_R \mathbb{Z}_q$, and sends $z = m^x$, $a = g^r$ and $b = m^r$ to the receiver.
- The receiver generates at random numbers $\alpha, \beta \in_R \mathbb{Z}_q$ and computes

$$m' = m^\alpha g^\beta \text{ and}$$
$$z' = z^\alpha y^\beta.$$

The receiver also chooses $u, v \in_R \mathbb{Z}_q$ and computes a' and b' as follows:

$$a' = a^u g^v \text{ and}$$
$$b' = a^{u\beta} b^{u\alpha} (m')^v$$

The receiver then computes $c' = \mathcal{H}(m' \parallel z' \parallel a' \parallel b')$ and sends $c = c'/u$ mod q to the signer.
- The signer responds with $s = r + cx \mod q$.
- The receiver accepts if and only if $a = g^s y^{-c}$ and $b = m^s z^{-c}$.
- If the receiver accepts, compute $s' = us + v \mod q$.

(z', c', s') is a valid signature on m' satisfying

$$c' = \mathcal{H}\left(m' \parallel z' \parallel g^{s'} y^{-c'} \parallel (m')^{s'} (z')^{-c'} \right).$$

Thus, the receiver has a signature on a message m' where $m' = m^\alpha g^\beta$ and (α, β) are values chosen by the receiver.

Correctness

$$g^{s'}y^{-c'} = g^{us+v}y^{-cu} = (g^s y^{-c})^u g^v = a^u g^v = a'$$

$$(m')^{s'}(z')^{-c'} = (m')^{us+v}(z')^{-cu} = (m')^v(m')^{us}(z')^{-cu}$$

$$= (m')^v((m')^s(z')^{-c})^u$$

$$= (m')^v((m^\alpha g^\beta)^s(z^\alpha y^\beta)^{-c})^u$$

$$= (m')^v((m^{s\alpha}g^{s\beta})(m^{-c\alpha}y^{-c\beta}))^u$$

$$= (m')^v((m^{s\alpha}z^{-c\alpha})(g^{s\beta}y^{-c\beta}))^u$$

$$= (m')^v((m^s z^{-c})^\alpha(g^s y^{-c})^\beta)^u$$

$$= (m')^v(b^\alpha a^\beta)^u$$

$$= a^{u\beta}b^{u\alpha}(m')^v$$

$$= b'$$

Blindness: Let (m, r, z, a, b, c, s) be *any* of the views of the protocol as seen by the signer. Therefore, $a = g^s y^{-c}$, $b = m^s z^{-c}$ and $s = r + cx$. Let (z', c', s') be a valid signature on a message m' obtained by the receiver. Choose the unique blinding factors

$$u = c'/c \mod q$$

$$v = s' - us \mod q$$

and determine a representation $m' = m^\alpha g^\beta$. (While finding a representation is difficult, we only need to exploit the existence of such representations. In fact, there are q representations of m'.) Note that the fact that $z = m^x$ and $z' = m'^x$ has been established by the interactive proof provided by the signer during blind signature formation and the fact that the blind signature is valid. Therefore, $z' = (m')^x = (m^\alpha g^\beta)^x = z^\alpha y^\beta$.

By setting $a' = a^u g^v$ and $b' = a^{u\beta}b^{u\alpha}(m')^v$, we find that

$$g^{s'}y^{-c'} = g^{v+su}y^{-cu} = g^v(g^s y^{-c})^u = g^v a^u = a'$$

$$(m')^{s'}(z')^{-c'} = (m')^{v+su}(z')^{-cu} = (m')^v((m')^s(z')^{-c})^u$$

$$= (m')^v\left((m^\alpha g^\beta)^s(z^\alpha y^\beta)^{-c}\right)^u$$

$$= (m')^v\left((m^s z^{-c})^\alpha(g^s y^{-c})^\beta\right)^u$$

$$= (m')^v(b^\alpha a^\beta)^u$$

$$= (m')^v b^{u\alpha}a^{u\beta}$$

$$= b'$$

Hence, there exist blinding factors that could have been used to transform any view into the particular signature (z', c', s') on m'. Therefore, the signer's view is statistically independent of the receiver's signature (z', c', s') on m'.

Restrictiveness: The restrictive nature of the protocol is captured by the following assumption.

Assumption 1 (Restrictiveness). *The recipient obtains a signature on a message that can only be of the form $m' = m^\alpha g^\beta$ with α and β randomly chosen by the recipient. In addition, in the particular case where $\beta = 0$, if there exists a representation (μ_1, μ_2) of m with respect to bases g_1 and g_2 such that $m = g_1^{\mu_1} g_2^{\mu_2}$ and if there exists a representation (μ'_1, μ'_2) of m' with respect to bases g_1 and g_2 such that $m' = g_1^{\mu'_1} g_2^{\mu'_2}$, then the relation $I_1(\mu_1, \mu_2) = \mu_1/\mu_2 = \mu'_1/\mu'_2 = I_2(\mu'_1, \mu'_2)$ holds.*

4.2   Schnorr Blind Signature Scheme – Multiplicative Variant

As discussed previously, we seek a blind variant of the Schnorr [17] protocol which uses multiplicative (rather than the standard additive operation) to blind the challenge. This can be accomplished with the following protocol.

- The signer generates a random number $r \in_R \mathbb{Z}_q$, and sends $a = g^r$ to the receiver.
- The receiver chooses blinding factors $u, v \in_R \mathbb{Z}_q$ and computes a' as follows:

$$a' = a^u g^v$$

  The receiver then computes $c' = \mathcal{H}(m \parallel a')$ and sends $c = c'/u \mod q$ to the signer.
- The signer responds with $s = r + cx \mod q$.
- The receiver accepts if and only if $a = g^s y^{-c}$.
- If the receiver accepts, compute $s' = us + v \mod q$.

(c', s') is a valid signature on m satisfying $c' = \mathcal{H}\left(m \parallel g^{s'} y^{-c'}\right)$.

Correctness

$$g^{s'} y^{-c'} = g^{us+v} y^{-cu} = (g^s y^{-c})^u g^v = a^u g^v = a'$$

Blindness: Let (r, a, c, s) be *any* of the views of the protocol as seen by the signer. Therefore, $a = g^s y^c$ and $s = r + cx$. Let (c', s') be a valid signature on a message m obtained by the receiver. By choosing blinding factors

$$u = c'/c$$
$$v = s' - su (= s' - sc'/c = \frac{cs' - c's}{c})$$
$$a' = a^u g^v$$

we find that

$$g^{s'} y^{c'} = g^{v+su} y^{cu} = g^v (g^s y^c)^u = a^u g^v = a'.$$

Hence, there exist blinding factors that could have been used to transform any view into the particular signature (c', s') on m. Therefore, the signer's view is statistically independent of the receiver's signature (c', s') on m.

5   A Restrictive Partially Blind Signature Scheme

The construction of Cramer et al. [10] for proving knowledge of d out of n secrets uses a homogeneous collection of proofs of knowledge. However, Cramer et al. [10] note that it is possible to combine different proofs of knowledge. We mix Schnorr [17] and Chaum-Pedersen [8] proofs of knowledge in the particular case when $d = 1$ and $n = 2$. That is, the prover demonstrates knowledge of either the private key related to a Schnorr public key or knowledge of the private key related to a Chaum-Pedersen public key. As discussed in section 3, the Schnorr and Chaum-Pedersen proofs of knowledge met the requirements (special soundness and special honest verifier zero-knowledge) for the construction of a witness indistinguishable protocol as described by Cramer et al. [10].

The protocol is converted into a blind signature issuing protocol by applying the blinding operations previously described for both the Schnorr and Chaum-Pedersen protocols. In order to achieve partial blindness, we apply the same adaptation used by Abe and Okamoto [3] and use a specialised hash function to map the agreed common information, info, into the public key of the Schnorr proof of knowledge. As a result, no one can know the private key associated with the Schnorr public key. A signer who knows the private key associated with the Chaum-Pedersen protocol can complete the blind issuing protocol as it is only necessary to demonstrate knowledge of one of the two private keys. Since the blinding operations do not alter the public keys, the association between info and Schnorr public key remains visible in spite of any blinding operations.

The restrictive property of the resulting scheme follows from the application of the same blinding operations used in Brands' original restrictive blind signature [5,6].

The setup for the scheme is as follows. Let two primes p and q be given such that q divides $p - 1$ and let $g \in \mathbb{Z}_p^*$ be an element of order q. The group generated by g is denoted by G_q. Choose a key pair (x_1, y_1) for the Chaum-Pedersen proof of knowledge. That is, let $x_1 \in_R \mathbb{Z}_q$ be a private key associated with the corresponding public key $y_1 = g^{x_1}$. Let $\mathcal{H} : \{0,1\}^* \to \mathbb{Z}_q$ be a public hash function.

The common information, info, is placed in the Schnorr public key y_2 by setting $y_2 = \mathcal{F}(\text{info})$, where $\mathcal{F} : \{0,1\}^* \to G_q$ is a public hash function which maps arbitrary strings into elements in G_q. Abe and Okamoto [3] show two deterministic constructions for $\mathcal{F}$. The signer then signs with private key x_1 which is associated with y_1. Since the resulting signature is bound to both public keys, y_1 and y_2, the common information info is also bound to the signature. This adaptation preserves witness indistinguishability which is needed for the proof of security. It is assumed that the signer $\mathcal{S}$ and the recipient $\mathcal{R}$ have previously agreed on the common information info. The full signature issuing protocol is shown in fig. 1. Note that additional group membership tests have been omitted for the sake of clarity.

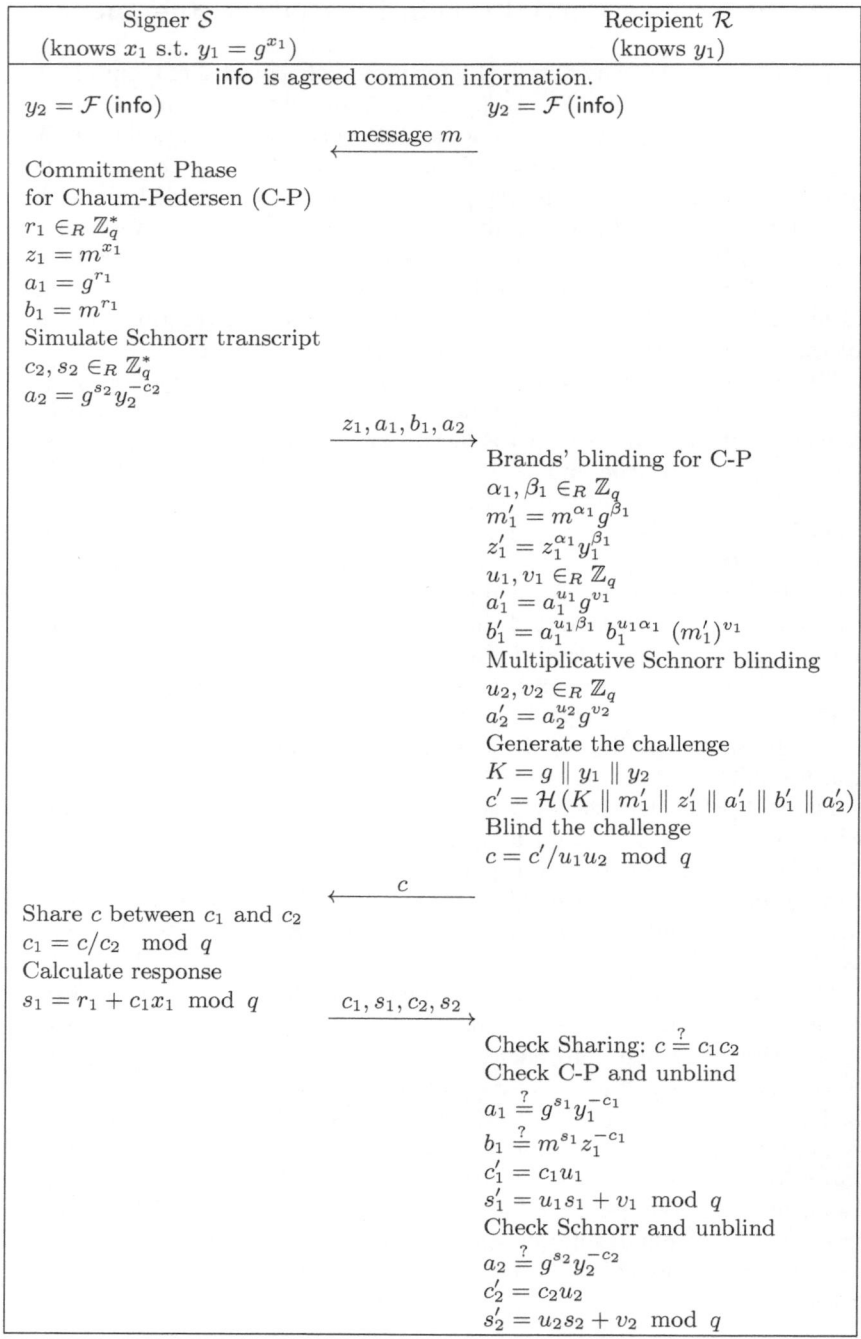

Fig. 1. Restrictive Partially Blind Signature on a message $m_1' \in G_q$

The resulting signature on a message m_1' derived from the base message m and with common information info is a tuple

$$(z_1', c_1', s_1', c_2', s_2').$$

The signature is valid if it satisfies

$$c_1' \cdot c_2' = \mathcal{H}\left(K \parallel m_1' \parallel z_1' \parallel g^{s_1'} y_1^{-c_1'} \parallel (m_1')^{s_1'} (z_1')^{-c_1'} \parallel g^{s_2'} \mathcal{F}(\text{info})^{-c_2'}\right) \quad \bmod q$$

where $K = g \parallel y_1 \parallel \mathcal{F}(\text{info})$.

Correctness

$$c' = u_1 u_2 c = u_1 u_2 c_1 c_2 = (u_1 c_1)(c_2 u_2) = c_1' c_2'$$

$$g^{s_1'} y_1^{-c_1'} = g^{u_1 s_1 + v_1} y_1^{-c_1 u_1} = (g^{s_1} y_1^{-c_1})^{u_1} g^{v_1} = a_1{}^{u_1} g^{v_1} = c_1'$$

$$(m_1')^{s_1'} (z_1')^{-c_1'} = (m_1')^{u_1 s_1 + v_1} (z_1')^{-c_1 u_1} = \left((m_1')^{s_1} (z_1')^{-c_1}\right)^{u_1} (m_-')^{v_1}$$

$$= \left((m^{\alpha_1} g^{\beta_1})^{s_1} (z_1^{\alpha_1} y_1^{\beta_1})^{-c_1}\right)^{u_1} (m_1')^{v_1}$$

$$= \left((m^{s_1} z_1^{-c_1})^{\alpha_1} (g^{s_1} y_1^{-c_1})^{\beta}\right)^{u_1} (m_1')^{v_1}$$

$$= a_1{}^{u_1 \beta_1} b_1{}^{u_1 \alpha_1} (m_1')^{v_1} = b_1'$$

$$g^{s_2'} y_2^{-c_2'} = g^{u_2 s_2 + v_2} y_2^{-c_2 u_2} = (g^{s_2} y_2^{-c_2})^{u_2} g^{v_2} = a_2{}^{u_2} g^{v_2} = a_2'$$

Restrictiveness: As previously noted, since the blinding operations for the Chaum-Pedersen protocol are the same as those used for Brands' restrictive blind signature [5,6], the restrictive nature of our protocol follows from the properties attributed to Brands' restrictive blind signature [5,6].

6   Security

This section discusses the security of the scheme under the assumption of the intractability of the discrete logarithm problem and ideal randomness of hash functions $\mathcal{H}$ and $\mathcal{F}$.

Lemma 1. *The proposed scheme is partially blind.*

Proof. When $\mathcal{S}^*$ is given $\bot$ in step 5 of the game defined in definition 3, $\mathcal{S}^*$ determines b with a probability $\frac{1}{2}$ (the same probability as randomly guessing b).

Suppose that in in step 5, $\text{info}_1 = \text{info}_0$. Let $(c_1', s_1', c_2', s_2', m_1')$ be one of the signatures subsequently given to $\mathcal{S}^*$. Let $(r_1, z_1, a_1, b_1, c_1, s_1, a_2, c_2, s_2, \text{info}, m)$ be data appearing in the view of $\mathcal{S}^*$ during one of the executions of the signature issuing protocol at step 4 of definition 3. It is sufficient to show that there exists a tuple of random blinding factors $(\alpha_1, \beta_1, u_1, v_1, u_2, v_2)$ that maps

$$(r_1, z_1, a_1, b_1, c_1, s_1, a_2, c_2, s_2, m) \mapsto (c'_1, s'_1, c'_2, s'_2, m'_1).$$

Choose the unique blinding factors

$$u_1 = c'_1/c_1 \mod q$$
$$v_1 = s'_1 - u_1 s_1 \mod q$$
$$u_2 = c'_2/c_2 \mod q$$
$$v_2 = s'_2 - u_2 s_2 \mod q$$

and determine a representation $m'_1 = m^{\alpha_1} g^{\beta_1}$ (which is known to exist).

The fact that $z_1 = m^{x_1}$ and $z'_1 = m'^{x_1}_1$ has been established by the interactive proof provided by the signer during blind signature formation and the fact that the blind signature is valid. Therefore, $z'_1 = (m'_1)^{x_1} = (m^{\alpha_1} g^{\beta_1})^{x_1} = z_1^{\alpha_1} y_1^{\beta_1}$. Since $a_1 = g^{s_1} y_1^{-c_1}$ and $a_2 = g^{s_2} y_2^{-c_2}$, we find that

$$c'_1 c'_2 = \mathcal{H}\left(K \parallel m'_1 \parallel z'_1 \parallel g^{s_1} y_1^{-c'_1} \parallel (m'_1)^{s'_1}(z'_1)^{-c'_1} \parallel g^{s_2} y_2^{-c'_2}\right)$$

$$= \mathcal{H}\left(K \parallel m'_1 \parallel z'_1 \parallel g^{v_1+u_1 s_1} y_1^{-u_1 c_1} \parallel (m'_1)^{v_1+u_1 s_1}(z'_1)^{-u_1 c_1} \parallel g^{v_2+u_2 s_2} y_2^{-u_2 c_2}\right)$$

$$= \mathcal{H}\left(K \parallel m'_1 \parallel z'_1 \parallel a_1^{u_1} g^{v_1} \parallel a_1^{u_1 \beta_1} b_1^{u_1 \alpha_1}(m')^{v_1} \parallel a_2^{u_2} g^{v_2}\right)$$

$$= \mathcal{H}\left(K \parallel m'_1 \parallel z'_1 \parallel a'_1 \parallel b'_1 \parallel a'_2\right)$$

where $a'_1 = a_1^{u_1} g^{v_1}$, $b'_1 = a_1^{u_1 \beta_1} b_1^{u_1 \alpha_1}(m')^{v_1}$, and $a'_2 = a_2^{u_2} g^{v_2}$.

Thus blinding factors always exist which lead to the same relation defined in the signature issuing protocol. Therefore, even an infinitely powerful $\mathcal{S}^*$ succeeds in determining b with probability $\frac{1}{2}$.   □

Lemma 2. *The proposed scheme is unforgeable if $\ell_{\mathsf{info}} < poly(\log n)$ for all* info.

Due to space considerations, a proof of this lemma is omitted. The security argument given by Abe and Okamoto [3] is acknowledged as being more generic than the particular application detailed by Abe and Okamoto [3]. The proof of our lemma follows the same general construction.

7   Conclusions

The blinding of the Schnorr protocol utilised by our scheme uses multiplicative blinding for the challenge rather than the more usual additive method. As a result, the consequent witness indistinguishable protocol uses a novel multiplicative sharing scheme in its construction.

We have shown a particular construction of a restrictive partially blind signature scheme based on a witness indistinguishable protocol which combines both the Schnorr and Chaum-Pedersen signature schemes. The provable security of the construction has been considered in terms of the formal definitions proposed by Abe and Okamoto [3]. The scheme uses Brands' restrictive blind signature [5,6] as a building block and is suitable for inclusion in cash schemes which currently utilise Brands' restrictive blind signature. The partially blind property aids in the practical deployment of these cash schemes as it allows for the easy implementation of coin expiration dates and multiple coin denominations.

Acknowledgments

We would like to thank the anonymous referees for their insightful observations and suggestions. This research is part of an ARC SPIRT project undertaken jointly by Queensland University of Technology and Telstra (Australia).

References

1. Masayuki Abe and Jan Camenisch. Partially blind signature schemes. In *Symposium on Cryptography and Information Security*. IEICE, January 1997.
2. Masayuki Abe and Eiichiro Fujisaki. How to date blind signatures. In Kwangjo Kim and Tsutomu Matsumoto, editors, *International Conference on the Theory and Application of Cryptology and Information Security (ASIACRYPT'96)*, volume 1163 of *Lecture Notes in Computer Science*, pages 244–251. Springer-Verlag, November 1996.
3. Masayuki Abe and Tatsuaki Okamoto. Provably secure partially blind signatures. In Mihir Bellare, editor, *Advances in Cryptology—CRYPTO 2000*, volume 1880 of *Lecture Notes in Computer Science*, pages 271–286. Springer-Verlag, 20–24 August 2000.
4. C. Boyd, E. Foo, and C. Pavlovski. Efficient electronic cash using batch signatures. In J. Pieprzyk, R. Safavi-Naini, and J. Seberry, editors, *Australasian Conference on Information Security and Privacy (ACISP'99)*, volume 1587 of *Lecture Notes in Computer Science*, pages 244–257. Springer-Verlag, 1999.
5. Stefan Brands. An efficient off-line electronic cash system based on the representation problem. Technical Report CS-R9323, Centrum voor Wiskunde en Informatica (CWI), March 1993.
6. Stefan Brands. Untraceable off-line cash in wallets with observers. In Douglas R. Stinson, editor, *Advances in Cryptology—CRYPTO '93*, volume 773 of *Lecture Notes in Computer Science*, pages 302–318. Springer-Verlag, 22–26 August 1993.
7. A. Chan, Y. Frankel, and Y. Tsiounis. Easy come — easy go divisible cash. In Kaisa Nyberg, editor, *Advances in Cryptology—EUROCRYPT 98*, volume 1403 of *Lecture Notes in Computer Science*, pages 561–576. Springer-Verlag, 1998.
8. D. Chaum and T. Pryds Pedersen. Wallet databases with observers. In Ernest F. Brickell, editor, *Advances in Cryptology—CRYPTO '92*, volume 740 of *Lecture Notes in Computer Science*, pages 89–105. Springer-Verlag, 1993, 16–20 August 1992.
9. David Chaum. Blind signatures for untraceable payments. In David Chaum, Ronald L. Rivest, and Alan T. Sherman, editors, *Advances in Cryptology: Proceedings of Crypto 82*, pages 199–203. Plenum Press, New York and London, 1983, 23–25 August 1982.

10. Ronald J. F. Cramer, Ivan B. Damgård, and L. A. M. Schoenmakers. Proofs of partial knowledge and simplified design of witness hiding protocols. In *116*, page 18. Centrum voor Wiskunde en Informatica (CWI), ISSN 0169-118X, February 28 1994. AA (Department of Algorithmics and Architecture).
11. U. Feige and A. Shamir. Witness indistinguishable and witness hiding protocols. In Baruch Awerbuch, editor, *Proceedings of the 22nd Annual ACM Symposium on the Theory of Computing*, pages 416–426, Baltimore, MY, May 1990. ACM Press.
12. A. Juels, M. Luby, and R. Ostrovsky. Security of blind digital signatures. In Burton S. Kaliski Jr., editor, *Advances in Cryptology—CRYPTO '97*, volume 1294 of *Lecture Notes in Computer Science*, pages 150–164. Springer-Verlag, 17–21 August 1997.
13. Shingo MIYAZAKI, Masayuki ABE, and Kouichi SAKURAI. Partially blind signature schemes for the dss and for a discrete log. based message recovery signature. In *Korea-Japan Joint Workshop on Information Security and Cryptology*, pages 217–226, 1997.
14. DaeHun Nyang and JooSeok Song. Preventing double-spent coins from revealing user's whole secret. In J.S. Song, editor, *Second International Conference on Information Security and Cryptology (ICISC'99)*, volume 1787 of *Lecture Notes in Computer Science*, pages 13–20. Springer-Verlag, 1999.
15. T. Okamoto. Provably secure and practical identification schemes and corresponding signature schemes. In Ernest F. Brickell, editor, *Advances in Cryptology—CRYPTO '92*, volume 740 of *Lecture Notes in Computer Science*, pages 31–53. Springer-Verlag, 1993, 16–20 August 1992.
16. D. Pointcheval. Strengthened security for blind signatures. In Kaisa Nyberg, editor, *Advances in Cryptology—EUROCRYPT 98*, volume 1403 of *Lecture Notes in Computer Science*, pages 391–403. Springer-Verlag, 1998.
17. C. P. Schnorr. Efficient signature generation by smart cards. *Journal of Cryptology*, 4(3):161–174, 1991.
18. L. A. M. Schoenmakers. An efficient electronic payment system withstanding parallel attacks. Technical Report CS-R9522, CWI - Centrum voor Wiskunde en Informatica, March 31, 1995.

$M + 1$-st Price Auction
Using Homomorphic Encryption

Masayuki Abe and Koutarou Suzuki

NTT Information Sharing Platform Laboratories
1-1 Hikari-no-oka, Yokosuka, Kanagawa, 239-0847 Japan
{abe,koutarou}@isl.ntt.co.jp

Abstract. This paper provides a $M + 1$-st price auction scheme using homomorphic encryption and the mix and match technique; it offers secrecy of bidding price and public verifiability. Our scheme has low round communication complexity: 1 round from each bidder to auctioneer in bidding and $\log p$ rounds from auctioneer to trusted authority in opening when prices are selected from p prefixed choices.

1   Introduction

The $M + 1$-st price auction is a type of sealed-bid auction for selling M units of a single kind of goods, and is famous as the Vickrey auction in the case of $M = 1$. In this auction, the $M + 1$-st (highest) price is the winning price, M bidders who bid higher prices than the winning price are winning bidders, and each winning bidder buys one unit of the goods at the $M + 1$-st winning price. The $M + 1$-st price auction is celebrated in economics or game theory for having *incentive compatibility*, that is, the *dominant strategy* (optimal strategy) for each bidder is to bid honestly his own true value [Vic61]. Because the true value is assumed to be issued, keeping the bidding prices secret is more significant than is true in the usual highest price auction, where most bidding prices are not the bidder's honest price.

This paper proposes an $M + 1$-st price auction that enjoys auction secrecy and public verifiability; it uses a homomorphic encryption and the mix and match technique from [JJ00]. Our scheme has low round communication complexity: 1 round from each bidder to one auctioneer in bidding and $\log p$ rounds from the auctioneer to trusted authority in opening, where p is the number of prices. The usual M-th highest price auction scheme can be created with slight modification.

In contrast to the many papers on first price sealed-bid auctions, as shown in Section 1.1, there are few papers on $M + 1$-st price auctions. Harkavy, Tygar and Kikuchi proposed a Vickrey auction, where the bidding price is represented by polynomials that are shared by auctioneers [HTK98]. In their scheme, each bidder must communicate with plural auctioneers to bid. Naor, Pinkas and Sumner realized sealed-bid auctions by combining Yao's secure computation with oblivious transfer [NPS99]. Their scheme can compute any circuit, and so can realize various types of auctions, e.g., $M + 1$-st price auction. Though their scheme is

D. Naccache and P. Paillier (Eds.): PKC 2002, LNCS 2274, pp. 115–124, 2002.

versatile and efficient, the cut-and-choose technique is needed to achieve verifiability, so the atomic protocol must be executed k times, where k is the security parameter of cut-and-choose, and each bidder must communicate with not only the auctioneer but also the auction issuer to bid. Kikuchi proposed an $M + 1$-st price auction, where the bidding price is represented by the degree of a polynomial shared by auctioneers [Kik01]. In his scheme, a large number of auctioneers is required (the number of auctioneers must be more than the number p of prices), and each bidder must communicate with these auctioneers not only to bid but also to determine the winning price and bidders.

In comparison to these schemes, our scheme has only one auctioneer and much simpler communication: each bidder sends his bid to just the auctioneer to bid and the auctioneer communicates with the trusted authority using $\log p$ rounds to open the bids. Thus our scheme is easy to implement.

Section 2 explains the $M + 1$-st price auction and requirements. In section 3, we introduce our $M + 1$-st price auction and discuss its security and efficiency. Section 4 concludes the paper.

1.1   Related Work

There are many papers on first price sealed-bid auctions, but few on $M + 1$-st price auctions. Kikuchi, Harkavy and Tygar presented an anonymous sealed-bid auction that uses an encrypted vector to represent bidding price [KHT98]. Kudo used a time server to realize sealed-bid auctions [Kud98]. Cachin proposed a sealed-bid auction using homomorphic encryption and an oblivious third party [Cac99]; its complexity is a polynomial of the logarithm of the number of possible prices. Sakurai and Miyazaki proposed a sealed-bid auction in which a bid is represented by the bidder's undeniable signature of his bidding price [SM99]. Sako proposed a sealed-bid auction in which a bid is represented by an encrypted message with a public key that corresponds to his bidding price [Sak00]. Stubblebine and Syverson proposed an open-bid auction scheme that uses a hash chain technique[SS99]. Kobayashi, Morita and Suzuki proposed a sealed-bid auction that uses only hash chains [SKM00,KMSH01]. Omote and Miyaji proposed a sealed-bid auction with $\log p$ efficiency, however, it leaks some information [OM00]. Baudron and Stern proposed a sealed-bid auction based on circuit evaluation using homomorphic encryption [BS01]. Chida, Kobayashi and Morita proposed a sealed-bid auction with $\log p$ round complexity [CKM01].

2 $M + 1$-st Price Auction

2.1   Auction Rules

The sealed-bid auction is a type of auction in which bids are kept secret during the bidding phase. In the bidding phase, each bidder sends his sealed bidding price. In the opening phase, the auctioneer opens the sealed bids and determines the winning price and winning bidders according to a predetermined rule. In the case of an $M + 1$-st price auction, the $M + 1$-st (highest) price is the winning price and bidders who bid higher than the winning price are winning bidders. The $M + 1$-st price auction is used for selling M units of a single kind of goods. If $M = 1$, it is equivalent to the well-known Vickrey auction.

- *Bidding* : The auctioneer shows M units of a single kind of goods for auction, e.g., M Swiss watches, and calls the bidders to bid their price for the item. Each bidder then decides his price, seals his price, e.g., by envelope, and puts his sealed price into the auctioneer's ballot box.
- *Opening* : After all bidders have cast their sealed prices, the auctioneer opens his ballot box. He reveals each sealed price, determines winning price, the $M + 1$-st (highest) price, and finds the wining bidders who bid higher than the winning price. Each winning bidder buys one unit of the goods at the $M + 1$-st winning price. (If more than M bidders bid at the same highest price, the auction fails.)

The $M + 1$-st price auction is celebrated in economics or game theory for having *incentive compatibility*, that is, the *dominant strategy* (optimal strategy) for each bidder is to bid honestly his own true value [Vic61]. The reason is that for each bidder his bidding price does not affect the winning price (in contrast with the usual highest price auction where higher bidding price yields higher winning price). Accordingly, the bidder finds that it is optimal to bid as high as he is willing to go.

2.2   Requirements

To achieve a fair auction, the $M + 1$-st price auction must satisfy two requirements: secrecy and public verifiability.

First, only the winning price and bidders should be revealed. If the auctioneer can know the M-th bidding price (that is the lowest price of bidding prices of M winning bidders) before opening, he can tell a collusive bidder to bid at slightly cheaper price than the M-th bidding price, and can maximize the winning price to gain more money. Even if a bidder (or an auctioneer) can know the bidding prices of other bidders after opening, he can collect information about the bidding strategy or finances of the other bidders, and can utilize it to cheat at the next auction. Because of incentive compatibility, the bidding price is the bidder's honest price for the goods. It follows that information on bidding prices has more significance than is true in the usual highest price auction, where bidding price is not the bidder's honest price.

- *Secrecy* : The information revealed is the $M + 1$-st winning price and the wining bidders. All other bidding prices must be kept secret, even from the auctioneer.

Due to the secrecy requirement, only the results of the auction can be known. Accordingly, it is necessary to convince all bidders that anyone can verify the correctness of the results of the auction.

– *Public verifiability* : Anyone must be able to verify the correctness of the auction.

3   Proposed $M + 1$-st Price Auction

3.1   Underlying Idea

We can construct our $M + 1$-st price auction by using probabilistic public key encryption $E(m)$ that provides indistinguishability, *homomorphic property*, and *randomizability*. The homomorphic property means that $E(a)E(b) = E(ab)$, and the randomizability means that one can compute a randomized ciphertext $E'(m)$ only from the original ciphertext $E(m)$, i.e. without knowing either the decryption key or the plaintext. For instance, ElGamal encryption or Paillier encryption [Pai99] have the properties desired, so our auction scheme can be built based on these encryption schemes.

One important technical issue is how to represent and encrypt the bidding prices so that the succeeding tasks are done easily. In this work, we assume that the possible bidding prices consist of p prices labelled $1, \ldots, p$. The correspondence between the label and real price is determined beforehand. A sealed bid, say b, which represents price j $(1 \leq j \leq p)$ is a vector of ciphertexts

$$b(j) = (\underbrace{E(z), ..., E(z)}_{j}, \underbrace{E(1), ..., E(1)}_{p-j})$$

where $E(1)$ and $E(z)$ denote encryption of 1 and common public element z $(\neq 1)$, respectively. Each encryption must be done independently so that they are indistinguishable from each other. The encryption is done using a public key generated and maintained by the authorities in the threshold manner.

Now, bidder B_i $(1 \leq i \leq b)$ posts $b_i(p_i) = (b_{1,i}, \ldots, b_{p,i})$ as his bidding price p_i. Consider the component-wise product of all bids;

$$\prod_i b_i(p_i) = (\prod_i b_{1,i}, \ldots, \prod_i b_{p,i}).$$

Observe that, due to the homomorphic property, the j-th component of this vector has the form

$$c_j = \prod_i b_{j,i} = E(z^{n(j)})$$

where $n(j) = \#\{i \mid j \leq p_i\}$ is the number of bidders whose bidding price is equal to or higher than j. Notice that $n(j)$ monotonically falls as j increases. Let us assume that the auctioneers can test whether $n(j) \leq M$ holds or not without gaining any further information such as $n(j)$ itself. By repeating this test, they can find the winning $M + 1$-st bidding price, say p_{win}, that satisfies $n(p_{win}) \geq M + 1$ and $n(p_{win} + 1) \leq M$. The auctioneers then determine the wining bidders by opening all bids at the price $p_{win} + 1$, i.e., decrypt $b_{p_{win}+1,i}$ $(1 \leq i \leq b)$ and find winning bidders B_i with $D(b_{p_{win}+1,i}) = z$.

To examine whether $n(j) \le M$ or not without revealing any further information, we use the mix and match technique that allows us to determine whether the decryption $D(c)$ of ciphertext c belongs to a specified set S of some plaintexts. By homomorphicity and randomizability of encryption E, we can apply mix and match to accumulated bid c_j.

To provide public verifiability, each bidder must prove that his bid $\boldsymbol{b}(j)$ is valid, i.e. it suits the form described above, in zero-knowledge manner. This seems, however, difficult to do efficiently. To overcome this difficulty, we develop a technique that involves taking the "differential" and "integral" of a vector of homomorphic ciphertexts. Each bidder B_i posts the "differential" $\Delta\boldsymbol{b}(j)$ of $\boldsymbol{b}(j)$

$$\Delta\boldsymbol{b}(j) = (\underbrace{E(1), ..., E(1)}_{j-1}, E(z), \underbrace{E(1), ..., E(1)}_{p-j})$$

that contains $p-1$ $E(1)$'s and one $E(z)$ as j-th component (note that the "differential" of Heaviside's step function is Dirac's delta function). He then proves the correctness of his bid (this can be done efficiently by using the homomorphicity). To recover $\boldsymbol{b}(j)$, the auctioneers take the "integral" of $\Delta\boldsymbol{b}(j)$

$$\boldsymbol{b}(j)_p = \Delta\boldsymbol{b}(j)_p, \boldsymbol{b}(j)_{p-1} = \Delta\boldsymbol{b}(j)_{p-1}\boldsymbol{b}(j)_p, \ldots, \boldsymbol{b}(j)_1 = \Delta\boldsymbol{b}(j)_1\boldsymbol{b}(j)_2$$

where $\boldsymbol{b}(j)_i$ and $\Delta\boldsymbol{b}(j)_i$ denote the i-th components of vectors $\boldsymbol{b}(j)$ and $\Delta\boldsymbol{b}(j)$ respectively.

3.2   Building Blocks

We summarize the cryptographic tools used in our auction. We denote a ciphertext of ElGamal encryption with public key $g, y = g^x$ by $E(m) = (G = g^r, M = my^r)$.

We use the proof of equality of logarithms [CP92] and the proof of OR of statements [CDS94]. By using the proofs, we have the following verifiable encryption, decryption, powering, mix [Abe99], and mix and match [JJ00] processes.

- *Verifiable encryption* : We can prove that ciphertext $E(m) = (G = g^r, M = my^r)$ is an encryption of m without revealing the secret random r by proving $\log_g G = \log_y M/m$.
- *Verifiable decryption* : We can prove that plaintext $m = M/G^x$ is the decryption of $E(m) = (G, M)$ without revealing the secret key x by proving $\log_G M/m = \log_g y$.
- *Verifiable powering* : We can prove that ciphertext $E'(m^r) = (G' = G^r, M' = M^r)$ is a power of $E(m) = (G, M)$ without revealing the secret random r by proving $\log_G G' = \log_M M'$.
- *Verifiable mix* [Abe99] : The publicly verifiable mix randomizes and permutes its input ciphertexts without revealing the randomization and the permutation to hide the correspondence between inputs and outputs; a proof of the correctness of the mixing can be given.

First, we construct a publicly verifiable 2-input mix that randomizes and permutes two inputs in a publicly verifiable manner. We can prove that ciphertext $E'(m) = (G' = Gg^r, M' = My^r)$ is a randomization of $E(m) = (G, M)$ without revealing the secret random r by proving $\log_g G'/G = \log_y M'/M$. By combining this with the OR proof, we can prove that the 2-input mix randomizes and swaps OR randomizes and does not swap two inputs. We then can construct a publicly verifiable n-input mix by combining $n \log_2 n - n + 1$ 2-input mixes based on Waksman's permutation network.

- *Mix and match* [JJ00] : By using the mix and match one can examine whether the decryption $D(c)$ of ciphertext c belongs to a specific set $S = \{p_1, p_2, \ldots, p_n\}$ of plaintexts.
  First, we construct n ciphertexts $c_i = c/E(p_i)$ $(0 \le i \le n)$. We then take the power $c_i^{r_i}$ of them using a secret random factor r_i, mix them, and decrypt the mixed n ciphertexts in a publicly verifiable manner. If there exists one plaintext 1, we are convinced that $c \in S$. If there exists no plaintext 1, we are convinced that $c \notin S$.

3.3 Protocol

There are bidders $B_1, \cdots, B_b$, auctioneer A, and trusted authority T. Auctioneer A plays the role of a bulletin board. Trusted authority T generates a secret key and a public key in the preparation phase. In the opening phase, it receives ciphertexts from auctioneer and performs mix and match and decrypts them. If desired, the trusted authority can be built in a distributed way to make it trustful in a threshold sense.

- *Preparation* : Trusted authority T generates a secret key and a public key for ElGamal encryption E, and publishes the public key.
  Auctioneer A publishes a price list $P = \{1, 2, \cdots, p\}$ for the auction and a generator z of the cyclic group used for encryption.
- *Bidding* : In the bidding phase, each bidder B_i $(1 \le i \le b)$ decides his bidding price $p_i \in P$ and computes encrypted vector

$$\Delta b_{j,i} = \begin{cases} E(z) & \text{if } j = p_i \\ E(1) & \text{if } j \ne p_i \end{cases} \quad (1 \le j \le p)$$

and constructs the proofs of

$$\text{``}\Delta b_{1,i} \cdots \Delta b_{p,i} = E(z)\text{''} \text{ and } \text{``}\Delta b_{j,i} = E(1) \text{ OR } \Delta b_{j,i} = E(z)\text{''}.$$

He then publishes the encrypted vector and the proofs.
- *Opening* : In the opening phase, auctioneer A publicly takes "integral"

$$b_{p,i} = \Delta b_{p,i}, b_{p-1,i} = \Delta b_{p-1,i} b_{p,i}, \ldots, b_{1,i} = \Delta b_{1,i} b_{2,i} \quad (1 \le i \le b)$$

and "superimposition"

$$c_j = b_{j,1} \cdots b_{j,b} \quad (1 \le j \le p).$$

From the homomorphic property, we have the encrypted vector

$$c_j = E(z^{n(j)}) \quad (1 \le j \le p)$$

where $n(j) = \#\{i \mid j \le p_i\}$. By applying the mix and match technique [JJ00] to c_j, we can examine whether $n(j) \le M$ or not, i.e., we can examine whether $D(c_j) \in \{1, z, z^2, \dots, z^M\}$ or not. To determine winning $M + 1$-st bidding price, i.e., price p_{win} s.t. $n(p_{win}) \ge M + 1$ and $n(p_{win} + 1) \le M$, we perform a binary search using the examination by mix and match; auctioneer A sends c_j to trusted authority T for $\lceil \log p \rceil$ rounds, and trusted authority T performs mix and match.

To determine winning bidders, we decrypt $b_{p_{win}+1,i}$ $(1 \le i \le b)$ and find winning bidders B_i with $D(b_{p_{win}+1,i}) = z$. Thus auctioneer A sends $b_{p_{win}+1,i}$ $(1 \le i \le b)$ to trusted authority T, and trusted authority T, who decrypts them.

Finally, auctioneer A publishes the winning price and the winning bidders.

Notice that we can also create the usual M-th price auction with some slight modification.

3.4   Security

We discuss the security of our auction. First, we consider the case where all bidders are honest and all input bids are independently and privately made. Against passively deviating auctioneers, our scheme leaks no information and achieves auction secrecy, since the underlying encryption scheme is indistinguishable and the building blocks, mix and mix and match, are secure. Against actively deviating auctioneers, all steps of our scheme except the bidding step are robust, i.e., an adversary can not manipulate the messages without detection, since all steps are publicly verifiable.

Now, we consider malicious bidders. In such a case, we are not sure whether the bids are still independent or not. Indeed, in the bidding step, the malicious bidder can bid at any price relative to the bidding price of other bidder. He can construct a bidding vector of any price by shifting and randomizing the components of another bidder's bidding vector. Fortunately, we can avoid such an attack by encrypting the whole bidding vector and its poof using non-malleable, publicly verifiable, threshold encryption scheme, e.g., Shoup and Gennaro's encryption [SG98]. After all bidders publish their encrypted bids, the auctioneers threshold decrypt them and check the proof, and continue the protocol. Since each bid is encrypted in a non-malleable manner, the malicious bidder can not create a dishonest bid by modifying the bid of another bidder.

Finally, notice that of course our protocol does not improve on the security offered by the original $M + 1$-st price auction. For instance, consider that $M + 1$ malicious bidders can fault the protocol by bidding at the highest price p and making $M + 1$ winning bidders. Note, however, that the original $M + 1$-st price auction also fails. Accordingly, this attack is against the original concept of the $M + 1$-st price auction, not our protocol. Thus preventing this kind of attack exceeds the scope of this paper.

3.5   Efficiency

We discuss communication and computational complexity of our auction and compare it to the $M + 1$-st price auction described in [Kik01].

Table 1. The communication complexity of our scheme.

	pattern	round	volume
Bidding (per one bidder)	$B_i \to A$	1	$O(p)$
Determining $M + 1$-st price	$A \to T$	$\lceil \log p \rceil$	$O(M + 1)$
Determining winning bidders	$A \to T$	1	$O(b)$

Table 2. The computational complexity of our scheme.

	computational complexity
Bidder (per one bidder)	p encryptions and $p + 1$ proofs
Auctioneer	$2bp$ ciphertext multiplications
Mixing	$\lceil \log p \rceil$ times $M + 1$ input mixings
Decrypting	$\lceil \log p \rceil (M + 1) + b$ decryptions

Table 1 shows the communication pattern and the number of rounds and volume per communication round in our scheme when there are b bidders bid and there are p potential bidding prices. Since only 1 communication round from a bidder to the auctioneer is required in the bidding phase, our scheme achieves the "bid and go" concept. Only $\lceil \log p \rceil$ rounds of communication are required in the opening phase, since we can use binary searching by virtue of the mix and match technique.

In [Kik01], the number of auctioneers must be more than the number p of prices, and each bidder must communicate with these auctioneers not only to bid but also to determine the winning price and bidders. In comparison with these schemes, our scheme has only one auctioneer and the communications in our scheme is quite simple.

Table 2 shows the computational complexity of our scheme. The complexity of each bidder is proportional to p, so it might be heavy for a large price range. The complexity of the auctioneer is proportional to bp, and this dominates the cost of the whole protocol. The complexity of mixing is proportional to $\lceil \log p \rceil$, and the complexity of one $M + 1$ input mix is proportional to $M \log M$ [Abe99,AH01]. The complexity of decryption is proportional to b, so it might be heavy for a large number of bidders.

In [Kik01], the number of auctioneers must exceed the number p of prices, and the complexity of each auctioneer is $O(bp)$. In our scheme, the factor dominating the complexity is the complexity of the auctioneer ($O(bp)$) so our scheme is more efficient than [Kik01].

4   Conclusion

We have introduced an $M + 1$-st price sealed-bid auction scheme that offers bidding price secrecy and public verifiability; it uses homomorphic encryption. The scheme has low round communication complexity: 1 round from each bidder to auctioneer in bidding and $\log p$ rounds from auctioneer to decryptor in opening.

We can also construct an $M + 1$-st price auction by using Paillier encryption [Pai99] instead of ElGamal encryption. The complexity of our auction, and almost all existing auction schemes, is proportional to the number p of prices. Accordingly, one important goal is to make the complexity proportional to the size $\log p$ of prices.

References

Abe99.   M. Abe, "Mix-Networks on Permutation Networks", *Proceedings of ASI-ACRYPT '99*, pp. 317–324, (1999).

AH01.   M. Abe and F. Hoshino, "Remarks on Mix-network based on Permutation Network", *Proceedings of PKC 2001*, pp. 317–324, (2001).

BS01.   O. Baudron and J. Stern, "Non-interactive Private Auctions", *Proceedings of Financial Cryptography 2001*, , (2001).

Cac99.   C. Cachin, "Efficient Private Bidding and Auctions with an Oblivious Third Party", *Proceedings of 6th ACM Conference on Computer and Communications Security*, pp. 120–127, (1999).

CDS94.   R. Cramer, I. Damgård and B. Schoenmakers, "Proofs of Partial Knowledge and Simplified Design of Witness Hiding Protocol", *Proceedings of CRYPTO '94*, pp. 174–187, (1994).

CKM01.   K. Chida, K. Kobayashi and H. Morita, "Efficient Sealed-bid Auctions for Massive Numbers of Bidders with Lump Comparison", *Proceedings of ISC '01*, , (2001).

CP92.   D. L. Chaum and T. P. Pedersen, "Wallet Databases with Observers", *Proceedings of CRYPTO '92*, pp. 89–105, (1992).

HTK98.   M. Harkavy, J. D. Tygar and H. Kikuchi, "Electronic Auctions with Private Bids", *Proceedings of Third USENIX Workshop on Electronic Commerce*, pp. 61–74, (1998).

JJ00.   M. Jakobsson and A. Juels, "Mix and Match: Secure Function Evaluation via Ciphertexts", *Proceedings of ASIACRYPT 2000*, pp. 162–177, (2000).

Kik01.   H. Kikuchi, "(M+1)st-Price Auction Protocol", *Proceedings of Financial Cryptography 2001*, , (2001).

KHT98.   H. Kikuchi, M. Harkavy and J. D. Tygar, "Multi-round Anonymous Auction Protocols", *Proceedings of first IEEE Workshop on Dependable and Real-Time E-Commerce Systems*, pp. 62–69, (1998).

KMSH01.   K. Kobayashi, H. Morita, K. Suzuki and M. Hakuta, "Efficient Sealed-bid Auction by using One-way Functions", *IEICE Trans. Fundamentals*, , (Jan. 2001).

Kud98.   M. Kudo, "Secure Electronic Sealed-Bid Auction Protocol with Public Key Cryptography", *IEICE Trans. Fundamentals, vol. E81-A, no. 1*, pp. 20–27, (Jan. 1998).

NPS99.   M. Naor, B. Pinkas and R. Sumner, "Privacy Preserving Auctions and Mechanism Design", *Proceedings of ACM conference on E-commerce*, pp. 129–139, (1999).

OM00.   K. Omote and A. Myaji, "An Anonymous Auction Protocol with a Single Non-trusted Center Using Binary Trees", *Proceedings of ISW2000*, pp. 108–120, (2000).

Pai99.   P. Paillier, "Public-Key Cryptosystems Based on Composite Degree Residuosity Classes", *Proceedings of EUROCRYPT '99*, pp. 223–238, (1999).

Sak00.   K. Sako, "Universally verifiable auction protocol which hides losing bids", *Proceedings of Public Key Cryptography 2000*, pp. 35–39, (2000).

SG98.   V. Shoup and R. Gennaro, "Securing Threshold Cryptosystems against Chosen Ciphertext Attack", *Proceedings of EUROCRYPT '98*, pp. 1–16, (1998).

SKM00.   K. Suzuki, K. Kobayashi and H. Morita, "Efficient Sealed-Bid Auction using Hash Chain", *Proceedings of ICISC 2000*, LNCS 2015, (2000).

SM99.   K. Sakurai and S. Miyazaki, "A bulletin-board based digital auction scheme with bidding down strategy", *Proceedings of 1999 International Workshop on Cryptographic Techniques and E-Commerce*, pp. 180–187, (1999).

SS99.   S. G. Stubblebine and P. F. Syverson, "Fair On-line Auctions Without Special Trusted Parties", *Proceedings of Financial Cryptography 99*, , (1999).

Vic61.   W. Vickrey, "Counterspeculation, Auctions, and Competitive Sealed Tenders", *Journal of Finance*, pp. 8–37, (Mar. 1961).

Client/Server Tradeoffs for Online Elections

Ivan Damgård and Mads Jurik

Aarhus University, Dept. of Computer Science, **BRICS**[*]

Abstract. We present various trade offs for voting schemes which, compared to known solutions, allow voters to do less work at the expense of
more work done by the tallying servers running the election. One such
scheme produces ballots of essentially minimal size while keeping the
work load on the tally servers on a practical level. Another type of trade
off leads to a voting scheme that remains secure, even if an adversary can
monitor all client machines used by voters to participate. This comes at
the price of introducing an additional party who is trusted to carry out
registration of voters correctly.

1 Introduction

Voting schemes is one of the most important examples of advanced cryptographic
protocols with immediate potential for practical applications. The most important goals for such protocols are

- Privacy: only the final result is made public, no additional information about
  votes will leak
- Robustness: the result correcly reflects all submitted and well-formed ballots,
  even if some voters and/or possibly some of the entities running the election
  cheat.
- Verifiability: after the election, the result can be verified by anyone.

Other properties may be considered as well, such as receipt-freeness, i.e, voters
are not able to prove after the fact that they voted for a particular candidate,
thereby discouraging vote-buying or coercing.

Various fundamentally different approaches to voting are known in the literature: one may use blind signatures and anonymous channels[6], where the
channels can be implemented using MIX nets (see [2,1] for instance) or based
some physical assumption. Another approach is to use several servers to count
the votes and have voters verifiably secret share votes among the servers [8,7].
Finally, one may use homomorphic encryption, where a voter simply publishes
an encryption of his vote. Encryptions can be combined into an encryption of
the result, and finally a number of decryption servers can cooperate to decrypt
the result [4], assuming the private key needed for this is secret-shared among
them.

---

[*] Basic Research in Computer Science,
 Centre of the Danish National Research Foundation.

D. Naccache and P. Paillier (Eds.): PKC 2002, LNCS 2274, pp. 125–140, 2002.

Since anonymous channels are quite difficult to implement in practice and verifiable secret sharing requires communication between a voter and all servers, the third method seems the most practical, and this paper deals only with variants of this approach.

In the following, we let L be the number of candidates, M the number of voters, w the number of decryption servers, and k the security parameter for the cryptosystem used. We assume for simplicity that each voter can vote for one candidate. In [4], a solution was given that may be based on any homomorphic threshold encryption scheme if the scheme comes with certain associated efficient protocols. One example of this is El Gamal encryption. The ballot size in this scheme is $O(\log M + b)$ where b is the block size that the encryption scheme is set up to handle. The scheme was designed for the case of $L = 2$, and the generalization to general L given in [4] has complexity exponential in L for the decryption of the final result. Even for $L = 2$, an exhaustive search over all possible election results is required to compute the final result. Therefore, this scheme does not scale well to large elections with many candidates.

In [5,3], solutions were given using a variant of the approach from [4], but based on Paillier's cryptosystem. These are the first solutions that scale reasonably well to large elections, still the most efficient of these protocols produce ballots of size $O((\log L)max(k, L \log M))$. As long as $k > L \log M$, this is logarithmic in L, but for larger values of L and M it becomes linear in L, and each voter has to do $\Omega(\log L)$ exponentiations using a modulus of length $L \log M$ bits. In a real application, one must assume that voters typically have only rather limited computing power available, so that the computation and communication needed for each voter is a rather critical parameter. On the other hand, decryption servers can be expected to be high-end machines connected by high-speed networks.

Thus for a large scale election, it is reasonable to consider the possibility of moving work away from voters at the expense of increased load on the servers. The central issue here is how much we can expect to reduce the size of ballots, since both communication and computational complexity for the voter is directly linked to this parameter. A moments reflection will show that there is no fundamental reason why the size of a ballot should depend on M or be linear in L. Of course, a ballot must be at least $\log L$ bits long, since otherwise we cannot distinguish between the L candidates. Also, it would be unreasonable to expect the encryption to be secure if the size of an encryption (a ballot) did not increase with the security parameter k. Thus a ballot size of $O(k + \log L)$ bits would be essentially optimal. In principle, this is easy to achieve: each voter V_i publishes an encryption of v_i (the id of the candidate he votes for), and the decryption servers use generic multiparty computation [13] to produce securely the result. This is always possible because the encryptions and the decryption key which is shared among the servers together determine the result and could be used to compute it efficiently if they were public. Such a solution, however, would be much too inefficient to have any practical value. It would increase the complexity for the servers by a factor corresponding to at least the size of a Boolean circuit computing the decryption.

In this paper, we present a solution that achieves ballot size $O(k + \log L)$ bits and where each server needs to broadcast $O(ML(k + L \log M))$ bits. Most of this work can be done in a preprocessing phase, and only $O(M(k + L \log M))$ bits need to be sent while the election is running. We assume the random oracle model and that a static adversary corrupts less than $w/2$ servers and any number of voters. Then the protocol can be proved to be private, robust and verifiable, based on semantic security of Paillier's public key system and the strong RSA assumption. We also present a variant with somewhat larger voter load, where the ballot size is $\log L(k + L)$ bits. This is still less than previous Paillier-based solutions, the communication per server is $O(M \log M(k + L \log M))$ bits. Also here, preprocessing is possible, leading to the same on-line cost as before. This variants can be proved secure in the random oracle model in the same sense as the previous variant, but assuming only semantic security of Paillier's public key system. Both variants can be executed in constant-round. None of the variants are receipt-free as they stand, but under an appropriate physical assumption, they can be made receipt-free using the techniques of [14].

Previous solutions based on the same assumption require each server to read each voters encrypted vote, process this, and broadcast a single piece of data. This amounts to communication that is linear in M, like in the systems we propose here. Thus the extra cost for servers in our solution is that more rounds of interaction are required and that the amount of communication is increased by a factor of L or $\log M$.

The main new technique we use is to have voters work with a cryptosystem with block size $max(k, \log L)$. The servers then securely transform this to encryptions in a related cryptosystem with block size $max(k, L \log M)$, and compute the result using this second system. On top of this, we borrow some techniques from [9].

We note that optimal ballot size can also be achieved using the approach mentioned above based on anonymous channels, where the channels can be implemented using a MIX network. This is because the MIX net hides the origin of a ballot, therefore all ballots can decrypted after mixing and vote counting becomes trivial. For some MIX implementations we get communication complexity for the servers comparable to what we achieve here. However, all known efficient implementations of MIX networks are based on El Gamal encryption, so that the alternative of basing the protocol on Paillier encryption is not available under the MIX approach. Moreover, and perhaps more importantly, it seems to be inherent in the MIX approach that MIX servers do their work sequentially, i.e., each MIX server can only act after the previous one has completed (part of) its work. By contrast, the threshold cryptography approach we use allows servers to complete the protocol in a constant number of rounds. Finally, using a MIX net, it is not clear that one can push most of the server work into a preprocessing phase, as we do here.

The final tradeoff we present is of a completely different type, that relates more to practical security of elections: one of the worst potential weaknesses of electronic voting in practice is that voters are likely to be non-expert computer users, and most likely will use their own machines, home PCs, to cast votes, say over the Internet. Whereas tools such as SSL plus signed applets can be used to give reasonable assurance that the client software used for this is genuine, it is very difficult (some would say impossible) to make sure that the user's machine is not infected by a virus that would monitor key strokes etc., and later transmit these to an adversary who could then easily find out who the voter voted for. By contrast, it seems like a more reasonable assumption that for instance a high-security server placed at some neutral site is not corrupted.

Motivated by this, we propose a solution with the following properties: privacy for the voter is ensured, even if his machine is completely monitored by an adversary, who can follow key strokes, screen image, mouse events, etc. Correctness of the result is ensured, assuming that a particular trusted party, who takes part in registering voters, behaves correctly (cheating will not allow him to break the privacy, however). Whereas this party can in principle be held accountable and can be caught if he cheats, such verification is rather cumbersome. Hence, in practice, this solution trades trust in client machines against some amount of trust in a designated party. We note that a natural candidate for such a player often exists anyway in traditional manual voting schemes, and so in fact no "new" trust is needed - we discuss this in more detail later.

The basic idea of this solution is quite general. It can be combined with our first tradeoff without significant loss of efficiency, but can also be applied to a very simple multicandiate election protocol, that can be based on Paillier encryption or on El-Gamal, and requires the servers to do only L decryptions.

2   The Minimal Vote System

In this section we introduce a scheme in which ballots are of essentially minimal size. This requires that a transformation of the votes are performed by the tally servers to a larger representation of the vote. From the transformed vote the result of the election can be found using the homomorphic properties as usual ([5], [4]).

2.1   Needed Properties

In the reduction of the voter load we need a pair of public-key cryptosystems CS_1 and CS_2 with their respective encryption and decryption functions E_1, E_2, D_1, D_2 . An encryption of m in CS_i under public key pk using random input r will be denoted $E_i(pk, m, r)$, but we will suppress the public keys from the notation as they are kept fixed at all times once generated. We will also often suppress r from the notation for simplicity. N_1 and N_2 will denote the size of the plaintext space for CS_1 and CS_2. The 2 cryptosystems should satisfy:

- **Semantically secure**: Both CS_1 and CS_2 are semantically secure.

- CS_2 **is a threshold system**: The private key in CS_2 can be shared among w decryption servers, such that any minority of servers have no information on the key, whereas any majority of servers can cooperate to decrypt a ciphertext while revealing no information other than the plaintext.
- CS_2 **is homomorphic**: There exists an efficiently computable operation denoted $\otimes$ that when applied to two ciphertexts yield an encryption of the sum of the two plaintexts, that is, we have: $E_2(m_1 \bmod N_2) \otimes E_2(m_2 \bmod N_2) = E_2(m_1 + m_2 \bmod N_2)$. Furthermore, given $\alpha \in Z_{N_2}, E_2(m)$ it is easy to compute an encryption $E_2(\alpha m \bmod N_2)$.
- CS_2 **supports MPC multiplication**: There exists an interactive protocol, denoted MPC multiplication, that the decryption servers can execute on input two encryptions. The protocol produces securely a random encryption containing the product of the corresponding plaintexts, in other words, we can produce $E_2(m_1 m_2 \bmod N_2, r_3)$ from $E_2(m_1 \bmod N_2, r_1)$ and $E_2(m_2 \bmod N_2, r_2)$ without revealing information about m_1 or m_2.
- **Interval proofs**: There exists a zero-knowledge proof of knowledge (that can be made non-interactive in the random oracle model) such that having produced $E_i(m)$, a player can prove in zero-knowledge that m is in some given interval I. For optimal efficiency we will need that the length of the proof corresponds to a constant number of encryptions. For the special case of $I = 0..N_i$ ($i = 1, 2$), this just amounts to proving that you know the plaintext corresponding to a given ciphertext.
- **Transformable**: There exists a number $B \leq N_1$ such given an encryption $E_1(m, r)$ where it is guaranteed that $m \leq B$, there is an interactive protocol for the decryption severs producing as output $E_2(m, r)$, without revealing any extra information.
- **Random value generation**: The decryption servers can cooperate to generate an encryption $E_2(R)$ where R is a random value unknown to all servers.
- **Vote size**: $L \leq B \leq N_1$ so that votes for different candidates can be distinguished and encryptions be transformed.
- **Election size**: Let $j = \lceil \log_2 M \rceil$. We need that $(2^j)^L < N_2$ to ensure that we do not get a overflow when the final result is computed.
- **Factorization of N_2**: All prime factors of N_2 are super-polynomially large in the security parameter.

We do not want to give the impression this set-up is more general that it really is. We know only one efficient example of systems with the above properties, this example is described below. But we stick to above abstract description to shield the reader from unnecessary details, and to emphasize what the essential properties are that we use.

Example 1. We present a pair of cryptosystems that satisfy the above requirements. This is based on the Damgård-Jurik generalization of Paillier's cryptosystem presented in [5]. A short definition of the basic scheme without going into details about threshold decryption (which can be found in [5]):

DJ (n,s):

- **Public Key**: (n, s), where $n = pq$, p, q primes.
- **Private Key**: d, where $d = 0 \bmod \lambda$ ($\lambda = \mathrm{lcm}(p - 1, q - 1)$) and $d = 1 \bmod n^s$.
- **Plaintext space**: $\mathcal{Z}_{n^s}$
- **Ciphertext space**: $\mathcal{Z}^*_{n^{s+1}}$
- **Encryption**: $E(m) = (n + 1)^m r^{n^s} \bmod n^{s+1}$, where $r \in \mathcal{Z}^*_n$ is random.
- **Decryption**: $L(c^d \bmod n^{s+1})$, where $L(x) = \frac{x-1}{n}$.

Given a n we can choose $CS_1 = DJ(n, s)$ and $CS_2 = DJ(n, s')$ where $s \leq s'$. To satisfy the semantic security condition we need the *decisional composite residuosity assumption* (DCRA), which was introduced by Paillier in [15]:

Conjecture 1. Let A be any probabilistic polynomial time algorithm, and assume A gets n, x as input. Here n has k bits, and is chosen as described above, and x is either random in $Z^*_{n^2}$ or it is a random n'th power in $Z^*_{n^2}$. A outputs a bit b. Let $p_0(A, k)$ be the probability that $b = 1$ if x is random in $Z^*_{n^2}$ and $p_1(A, k)$ the probability that $b = 1$ if x is a random n'th power. Then $| p_0(A, k) - p_1(A, k) |$ is negligible in k.

Given the conjecture and the transformation shown below, we have all the properties satisfied:

- Semantically secure: Under the DCRA both CS_1 and CS_2 are semantically secure.
- CS_2 Homomorphic: The Damgård-Jurik cryptosystem is homomorphic, where the $\otimes$ operation is multiplication modulo $n^{s'}$. Also we have $E(m)^\alpha \bmod n^{s'+1} = E(\alpha m \bmod n^{s'})$.
- CS_2 supports MPC multiplication: An efficient protocol is shown in [9], requiring each server to broadcast a constant number of encryptions.
- Interval proofs: The proof construction in Appendix A constructs the required proof using communication equivalent to a constant number of encryptions.
- Random value generation: The decryption servers do the following: each server $0 < i \leq w$ chooses at random $R_i \in Z_{N^2}$. The values $E_2(R_i)$ are published followed by zero-knowledge proofs that R_i is known by server i. These proofs can be done using the Multiparty Σ-protocol technique from section 6 of [9] allowing the zero-knowledge proofs to be done concurrently in a non malleable way.
  We then form $E_2(R) = E_2(R_1) \otimes ... \otimes E_2(R_w)$. Thus R is random and unknown to all servers.
- Transformable: An encryption in CS_1 can be transformed to encryption in CS_2 by using the method described below. This method requires that the bound B on the input message satisfies $\log(B) \leq \log(N_1) - k_1 - \log(w) - 2$, where k_1 is a secondary security parameter ($k_1 = 128$ for instance).
- Vote size: we need $L \leq B$ which as mentioned above means $\log(L) \leq \log(N_1) - k_1 - \log(w) - 2$. For most realistic values of k, k_1, L, w this will be satisfied even with $s = 1$, but otherwise s can always be increased.

- Election size: $M^L < N_2 = n^{s'}$ can be satisfied by choosing s' large enough.
- Factorization of N_2: we have $N_2 = n^{s'} = (pq)^{s'}$ and p, q must of course be large to have any security at all.

We now show how to transform the ciphertext $E_1(m)$ from CS_1 to CS_2, where it is known that $0 \leq m \leq B$. Our transformation will work if $\log(B) \leq \log(N_1) - k_1 - \log(w) - 2$.

The crucial observation is that a ciphertext $E_1(m)$ in CS_1 can always be regarded as a ciphertext in CS_2, simply by thinking of it as a number modulo $n^{s'+1}$. It is not hard to see that as a CS_2 encryption, it is an encryption of a number $m' \in Z_{n^{s'}}$ with $m' = m \bmod n^s$. This is not good enough since we want $m = m' \bmod n^{s'}$. All we know is that $m' = m + tn^s \bmod n^{s'}$ for some t we cannot directly compute. To get around this, we mask m with some random bits so that we can find t by decryption, as detailed below.

The masking can be done in 2 ways:

- **Trusted Third Party**: A trusted third party generates a random value R of size $log(B) + k_1$. The 3rd party reveals the value $E_2(R)$.
- **MPC approach**: The servers each generate a value R_i of length $log(B) + k_1$ bits, reveal $E_2(R_i)$ and prove they have done so using an interval proof. This should be done using the Multiparty Σ-protocol technique of [9]. All encryptions with correct proofs are combined using the homomorphic property to get (I is the set of servers which supplied a correct proof):

$$E_2(R) = \Pi_{i \in I} E(R_i) = E(\Sigma_{i \in I} R_i)$$

This means that R is at most $w2^{log(B)+k_1}$.

Note that the condition on B and R ensures that $m + R < N_1$.

1. We consider the encryption $e = E_1(m)$ as a ciphertext e in CS_2. As noted above, this will be the encryption $E_2(m + tn^s \bmod n^{s'}, r)$ for unknown t and r.
2. Now let $e' = e \otimes E_2(R)$.
3. The servers decrypt e' to get a message $m + R + tn^s \bmod n^{s'}$. Since we have $m + R < N_1$, we can find $m + R$ and t just by integer division. And if at least one server has chosen its R_i at random, information on m will be statistically hidden from the servers, since R is at least k_1 bits longer than m.
4. We now set $e'' = e \otimes E_2(-tn^s, 1)$. Due to the homomorphic properties this is equal to $E_2(m)$.

2.2 Preparation

The preparation phase requires the generation of the 2 cryptosystems with key distribution for threshold decryption in CS_2. We also need a publicly known polynomial of degree $L - 1$ which satisfies the equation:

$$f(i) = M^i \bmod N_2 \qquad \forall i : 0 \leq i < L$$

By assumption N_2 has only very large prime factors. Hence any difference of form $i - j$ where $0 \le i, j < L$ is invertible modulo N_2 and this is sufficient to ensure that f can be constructed using standard Lagrange interpolation.

The next and last part of the preparation has to be done once for each election. For each voter, the severs generate a random encryption $E_2(R)$ as described earlier. Then we execute $L - 2$ MPC multiplications to get encryptions $E_2(R^j)$ for $j = 1, ..., L - 1$.

2.3 Voting

The voter generates a vote for candidate i by making an encryption $E_1(i)$ and an interval proof that it is the encryption of a value in the interval $\{0, ..., L - 1\}$.

2.4 Transformation

When the servers receive the vote as a ciphertext in CS_1 they have to transform it into a corresponding vote in CS_2, that can be added together to give a meaningful result. This is done by transforming $E_1(i)$ to $E_2(M^i)$. This has to be done for each vote and can be done in the following way:

1. We transform $E_1(i)$ into $E_2(i)$.
2. The servers decrypt $E_2(i) \otimes E_2(R)$ to get $z = i + R$. It follows that $i^j = (z - R)^j$, and this can be rewritten using the standard binomial expansion. The result is that $i^j = \alpha_0 + \alpha_1 R + ... + \alpha_j R^j$ for publicly known values $\alpha_0, ..., \alpha_j$. Hence encryptions $E_2(i^j)$ can be computed without interaction from the encryptions $E_2(R^j)$ from the preparation phase, using the homomorphic property. From these encryptions, we can, using the polynomial f computed in the preparation, construct an encryption $E_2(f(i))$, still with no further interaction. The result of this satisfies $E_2(f(i) \bmod N_2, r) = E_2(M^i \bmod N_2, r)$

2.5 Calculating Result

Now we can combine all the transformed votes using the homomorphic property of CS_2 and decrypt the result. This will give a value of the form:

$$\sum v_i M^i \qquad \forall i : 0 \le v_i < M$$

Since M is the number of voters an overflow of $v_i \bmod M$ cannot have occurred and since $M^L < N_2$ we get that the number of votes on the i'th candidate will be v_i.

2.6 Complexity

From the voters point of view the computational (modular multiplications) and communicational complexity (bits) of this protocol will be $O(log(L) + k)$. This is within a constant of the smallest possible.

The decryption servers' work depends on the cryptosystems used, and can only really be compared in the number of usages of the primitives: transformations (from CS_1 to CS_2), decryptions, MPC multiplications, and random value generations.

In the preparation, we generate M random values and do $M(L-2)$ MPC Multiplications. During election we do M transformations from CS_1 to CS_2 and M decryptions, plus 1 to get the result. To calculate the powers of R in the preprocessing, $\mathcal{O}(L)$ rounds of communication are needed. Constant round solutions can also be devised using techniques from [16], but the total communication will be larger. The protocol for the election itself is constant round.

3 An Alternative System

Here we look at an alternative scheme that requires more work for the voter, but the work required by the tallying servers can be reduced compared to the previous scheme for some parameter values.

3.1 Needed Properties

In this trade off scheme we also need a pair of cryptosystems CS_1 and CS_2 with properties as described earlier, except for two changes:

- **Zero-knowledge proofs**: Interval proofs are not needed for this scheme. Instead we need that a player can generate an encryption $E_1(v)$ and prove in zero-knowledge that $v \in \{2^0, ..., 2^{L-1}\}$. For the example of Paillier based encryption, a protocol for this purpose is given in [5].
- **Vote Size**: In this scheme, we need $2^L \le B \le N_1$ instead of $\log_2 L \le B$.

3.2 Preparation

The cryptosystems must be set up as for the previous scheme.

In preparation of each election a pair of values have to be generated for each voter (recall that we defined j to be minimal, such that $2^j > M$):

- An encryption of some random R: $E_2(R \bmod N_2)$.
- The inverse of R raised to the j'th power: $E_2(R^{-j} \bmod N_2)$.

These values are generated before the election so that the result of the election is more efficiently computed when the votes start to arrive. The values can be generated with one of these 2 methods:

- **Trusted third party**: The trusted third party generates the 2 encryptions.
- $O(\log(j))$ **MPC multiplications**: The servers cooperate on generating a random encryption $E_2(R)$. Using the inversion method from [16] the value

$E_2(R^{-1})$ is generated [1]. Then the servers use the MPC multiplication $O(log(j))$ times to get $E_2(R^{-j})$.

3.3 Voting

The voter generates a vote for candidate i by setting $v = 2^i$, making $E_1(v)$ and a proof that it is the encryption of a message from the set $\{2^0, ..., 2^{L-1}\}$.

3.4 Transformation

The goal of the transformation is to compute $E_2((v)^j)$ from $E_1(v)$ and can be done as follows:

1. The encryption of the vote v is transformed to $e = E_2(v)$ in CS_2
2. The servers perform a MPC multiplication of $e = E_2(v)$ and $E_2(R)$ to get $e' = E_2(vR \bmod N_2)$
3. The servers decrypt e' to get $vR \bmod N_2$ which reveals no information of v since R is chosen at random (note that by assumption on N_2, both v and R are prime to N_2 except with negligible probability).
4. The servers raises vR to the j'th power in public and make an encryption of this, $e'' = E_2((vR)^j \bmod N_2, 1)$ (we use a default value of 1 for the random input to encryption, no randomness is needed here).
5. The servers make a MPC multiplication of e'' and $E_2(R^{-j} \bmod N_2)$ to get the transformed encryption of the vote

$$E_2(v^j \bmod N_2, r) = E_2((2^j)^i \bmod N_2, r).$$

3.5 Calculating Result

To calculate the result the transformed votes are combined using the homomorphic property of CS_2, and the resulting ciphertext is decrypted. The plaintext from the decryption will have the form:

$$\sum v_i(2^j)^i \qquad \forall i : 0 \leq v_i < 2^j$$

Since $2^j > M$, where M is the number of voters an overflow cannot have occurred for a single candidate and the whole election cannot have caused a overflow since $(2^j)^L < N_2$. The number of votes on the i'th candidate is v_i.

---

[1] This is done by generating another encryption of a random value R' in the same way as the first. Then compute the MPC multiplication of the 2 and decrypt it to get $RR' \bmod N_2$. This is inverted and encrypted again. Then this is MPC multiplied with $E_2(R')$ again to get $E_2((RR')^{-1}R' \bmod N_2) = E_2(R^{-1} \bmod N_2)$

3.6   Complexity

The communication needed from the voter is now $O(L + k)$, plus the size of the proof of correctness for the encryption (which in the Damgård-Jurik scheme will have size $O(log(L))$ encryptions using the techniques from [5]).

If a trusted third party is used then there is no precomputation for the tally servers, but otherwise they have to generate the pair of values: to generate the inverses we need 1 random value generation, 2 MPC multiplications and 1 decryption, and for calculating the j'th power we need at most $2\log_2(M)$ multiplications which means that we use a total of $M(\log_2(M)+2)$ MPC multiplications and M decryptions and random values.

For the election itself, the number of transformations we need from CS_1 to CS_2 is M. In the protocol we use a decryption when raising each vote to the j'th power, so we need $M + 1$ decryptions. And finally we need a total of $2M$ MPC multiplications.

The preparation can be done in $O(log(M))$ rounds, while the protocol after preparation is constant round.

In comparison with the first scheme, we see that the voters do more work here, and the complexity of the election after preparation is comparable, but slightly lower in the first scheme. The main difference is that the complexity of the preparation is $O(ML)$ MPC multiplications in the first scheme and $O(M \log M)$ in the second. Another difference is that the first scheme requires ML encryptions to be stored between preparation and election, while the second scheme requires only $2M$ encryptions.

Thus the second scheme may have an advantage if $\log M$ is less than L. Even for large scale elections, this may well happen, since even if $10^6 \leq M \leq 10^9$ $\log M$ is only between 20 and 30.

4   Protecting Clients against Hackers

How can a voter be protected against a curious person that has full access to his computer during an election? In this section we look at a way to trade trust in the security of the client computer against trust in a third party. We first describe the basic idea on a high level and then give two ways to implement the idea.

We assume that we have a trusted party T (we discuss later in which sense he has to be trusted). T will for each voter choose a random permutation π permuting the set $0, 1, ..., L-1$. He then privately (and possibly by non-electronic means) sends a list containing, for each candidate number i, the candidate's name and $\pi(i)$. When using his own (or any) client machine to cast his vote, the voter decides on a candidate - say candidate number i, finds his name on the list, and tells the client software that he votes for candidate $\pi(i)$. The client software could simply present a list of numbers from 0 to L_1 to choose from, without any corresponding names. The client software sends an encryption of $\pi(i)$ to the tally servers.

At the same time as π is generated, T also sends to the tally servers an encryption of π. Using this encryption, the servers can transform the encryption of $\pi(i)$ into an encryption of i, and the election result can then computed using the homomorphic properties as usual.

As for security of this, consider first correctness: as we have described the system, we clearly have to trust that T encrypts for the servers the correct permutation for each voter. If not, the result will be incorrect. Note, however, that T cannot decrypt the encryption of $\pi(i)$ sent from the client machine, so it cannot manipulate the permutation and be certain to favor a particular candidate. If T was suspected of foul play against a particular voter, the information held by the voter could be verified against the encryption of π, and then cheating would always be caught. But since this is a rather cumbersome procedure, it is unlikely to happen very often, and so some amount of trust has to be invested in T.

As for privacy, clearly an attacker monitoring the client machine gets no information on who the voter voted for, by the random choice of π. Furthermore, even if T pools its information with a minority of the severs, they cannot break the privacy of the voter unless they break the encryption. A breach of privacy would require both that T is corrupt and that it participates in an attack where client machines are infected.

In practice, who might play the role of T? As an example, in many countries, there is an authority which, prior to elections and referendums, sends by private paper mail a card to every eligible voter, and this card must be used when casting a vote. Such an authority could naturally play the role of T, and simply print the information about π on the card sent out. In other countries voters must contact a government office to get registered, in this case the permutation could be generated on the fly and the information handed directly to the voter.

For the first implementation of this idea we use a cryptosystem CS with encryption and decryption functions E, D and plaintext space of size N.

4.1   Needed Properties

Here we need less assumptions because we do not need to transform the votes between different cryptosystems.

- CS **is homomorphic**: as defined earlier
- CS **supports MPC multiplication**: as defined earlier
- **Zero-Knowledge proofs**: we need that a player can generate an encryption $E(v)$ and prove in zero-knowledge that $v \in \{M^0, ..., M^{L-1}\}$. For the example of Paillier based encryption, a protocol for this purpose is given in [5].
- **Election size**: To ensure that the final result is correct we need $M^L < N$.
- **Factorization of** N: We assume that N has only very large prime factors so that factoring N is infeasible.

4.2   Preparation

T picks a random permutation π for each voter and gives the $\pi(i)$ values to the voter as described above. Then T generates a polynomial of degree $L - 1$ for each of the voters with the property that

$$f(M^i) = M^{\pi^{-1}(i)} \bmod N \quad \forall i : 0 \leq i < L$$

If doing this by Lagrange interpolation fails, this can only be because some number less than N was found to be non-invertible modulo N, which implies N can be factored. Since this was assumed infeasible, the construction fails with negligible probability. The L coefficients of the polynomial are then encrypted to produce encryptions $c_0, ..., c_{L-1}$ and these are given to the tallying servers.

The tally servers for each voter generates a random encryption $E(R)$ and compute encryptions of the powers $E(R^2), ..., E(R^{L_1})$.

4.3 Voting

To make a vote for candidate i the voter gives $\pi(i)$ to the client machine who makes an encryption $E(M^{\pi(i)})$ and appends a zero-knowledge that one of $M^0, ..., M^{L-1}$ was encrypted.

4.4 Transformation

We need to transform the vote $E(M^{\pi(i)})$. First we use the encryptions of powers of R from the preparation to compute encryptions $E(M^{2\pi(i)}), ..., E(M^{(L-1)\pi(i)})$. This is done the same way as in the minimal vote scheme and requires only one decryption and local computation. From this and $c_0, ..., c_{L-1}$, the servers can clearly use the homomorphic property and $O(L)$ MPC multiplication to make an encryption $E(f(M^{\pi(i)}))$. If T participates, it can be done much more efficiently: since T knows the coefficients of f, he can produce $E(f(M^{\pi(i)}))$ from $E((M^{2\pi(i)}), ..., E(M^{(L-1)\pi(i)})$ by only local computation, and prove in zero-knowledge to the servers that this was correctly done. The proof is straightforward to construct using techniques from [9][2].

We then have

$$E(f(M^{\pi(i)})) = E(M^{\pi^{-1}(\pi(i))}) = E(M^i)$$

which is what we wanted.

4.5 Combination

The result can then be found using the homomorphic addition of the transformed votes to get a number of the form:

$$\sum v_i M^i \qquad \forall i : 0 \leq v_i < M$$

since M is the number of voters and $M^L < N$ an overflow cannot have occurred and the number of votes on the i'th candidate will be v_i.

---

[2] In [9], a zero-knowledge protocol was given by which a player can prove that a committed constant was correctly "multiplied into" a given encryption, and this is exactly what we need here

4.6   Complexity

Since we don't have any reduction in the size of the cryptosystem the voters the communication and computational complexities are $O(L \log M + k)$ plus the size of the proof that the vote has the right form.

For the tallying servers the complexity of both preparation and election is comparable to the minimal scheme in case T participates also in the election. Otherwise we will need $O(ML)$ MPC multiplications during the election itself.

4.7   Combination with Minimal Votes

Since the scheme we just presented is similar to the minimal vote scheme it is straightforward to combine the two. This only adds the cost of transforming the vote from CS_1 to CS_2. The polynomial must now have the form

$$f(i) = M^{\pi^{-1}(i)} \bmod N$$

and the voter send an encryption of form $E_1(\pi(i))$ as his encrypted vote.

4.8   An Alternative Implementation

A very simple way to implement multicandidate elections from homomorphic encryption is as follows: the voter produces encryptions $e_1, ..., e_L$, where $e_i = E(1)$ if he votes for candidate i and all other encryptions contain 0. He proves in zero-knowledge that each e_j encrypts 0 or 1, and opens $e_1 \otimes ... \otimes e_L$ to reveal 1, in order to prove he voted for one candidate. The tally servers can then combine all 0/1 votes for each candidate separately using the homomorphic property and decrypt. This method places a quite large workload on voters, but on the other hand it can be based on El-Gamal encryption as well as on Paillier, and it is the only known way in which elections with large L can be efficiently based on El-Gamal encryption (the method from[4] is exponential in L).

It is straightforward to apply the client protection method to this voting scheme: the trusted party T generates and communicates a permutation to each voter as described above. Then to encrypt a permutation π for the tally servers, T will generate an $L \times L$ permutation matrix M_π representing π^{-1} in the standard way and publish encryptions of each entry in M_π. We let $E(M_\pi)$ denote this (ordered) set of encryptions. The voter will now send a set of encryptions where $e_1, ..., e_L$, where $e_{\pi(i)} = E(1)$. Since T knows the entries of M_π, he can by only local computations and using the homomorphic property produce random encryptions $e'_1, ..., e'_L$ such that $e_i = E(1)$ and all the others contain 0. This is done by applying M_π to the vector of encryptions and multiplying by random encryptions of 0. Since $E(M_\pi)$ was made public, he can then prove in zero-knowledge to the servers that this was correctly done using techniques from [9]. Finally the computation of the final result can be completed as above.

References

1. Abe: *Universally verifiable MIX net with verification work independent of the number of MIX centers*; proceedings of EuroCrypt 98, Springer Verlag LNCS.
2. Ohkubo and Abe: *A Length-Invariant Hybrid Mix* Proceedings of Asiacrypt 00, Springer Verlag LNCS.
3. Baudron, Fouque, Pointcheval, Poupard and Stern: *Practical Multi-Candidate Election Scheme*, manuscript, May 2000.
4. R.Cramer, R.Gennaro, B.Schoenmakers: *A Secure and Optimally Efficient Multi-Authority Election Scheme*, Proceedings of EuroCrypt 97, Springer Verlag LNCS series, pp. 103-118.
5. Damgård and Jurik: *A Generalisation, a Simplification and some Applications of Paillier's Probabilistic Public-Key System*, Proc. of Public Key Cryptography 2001, Springer Verlag LNCS series.
6. A. Fujioka, T. Okamoto & K. Otha: *A practical secret voting scheme for large scale elections.*, Advances in Cryptology - Auscrypt '92, pp. 244-251.
7. B. Schoenmakers: *A simple publicly verifiable secret sharing scheme and its application to electronic voting*, Advances in Cryptology - Crypto '99, vol. 1666 of LNCS, pp. 148-164.
8. R. Cramer, M. Franklin, B. Schoenmakers & M. Yung: *Multi-authority secret ballot elections with linear work*, Advances in Cryptology - Eurocrypt '96, vol. 1070 of LNCS, pp. 72-83.
9. R. Cramer, I. Damgård and J. Nielsen:*Multiparty Computation from Threshold Homomorphic Encryption*, Proceedings of EuroCrypt 2001, Springer Verlag LNCS series 2045, pp.280-300.
10. Boudot: *Efficient Proof that a Comitted Number Lies in an Interval*, Proc. of EuroCrypt 2000, Springer Verlag LNCS series 1807.
11. Damgård and Fujisaki: *An Integer Commitment Scheme based on Groups with Hidden Order*, Manuscript, 2001, available from the Eprint archive.
12. Fujisaki and Okamoto: *Statistical Zero-Knowledg Protocols to prove Modular Polynomial Relations*, proc. of Crypto 97, Springer Verlag LNCS series 1294.
13. Oded Goldreich, Silvio Micali, and Avi Wigderson: *How to play any mental game or a completeness theorem for protocols with honest majority*, in *Proceedings of the Nineteenth Annual ACM Symposium on Theory of Computing*, pages 218–229, New York City, 25–27 May 1987.
14. M.Hirt and K.Sako: *Efficient Receipt-Free Voting based on Homomorphic Encryption*, Proceedings of EuroCrypt 2000, Springer Verlag LNCS series, pp. 539-556.
15. P.Pallier: *Public-Key Cryptosystems based on Composite Degree Residue Classes*, Proceedings of EuroCrypt 99, Springer Verlag LNCS series, pp. 223-238.
16. J. Bar-Ilan, and D. Beaver: *Non-Cryptographic Fault-Tolerant Computing in a Constant Number of Rounds*, Proceedings of the ACM Symposium on Principles of Distributed Computation, 1989, pp. 201-209.

A   Interval Proofs for Paillier Encryptions

Given a Paillier encryption $E(m, r)$ (computed modulo N^2), we sketch here an efficient method to prove in zero-knowledge that m is in some given interval I. In [5] a protocol for this purpose is given. However, there one needs to supply an encryption of every bit in the binary expansion of m. We want a more efficient method, where only a constant number of encryptions need to be sent. In the following, *opening an encryption* $E(m, r)$ means revealing m, r. However, for simplicity, we will suppress r in the notation in most cases.

In [10] Baudot gives an efficient method for proving that a committed number lies in a given interval. The protocol requires sending only a constant number of commitments and is zero-knowledge in the random oracle model that we also use here. It assumes that the number has been committed to using a commitment scheme with some specific properties. The scheme proposed by Fujisaki and Okamoto [12] will suffice, assuming the strong RSA assumption. See [10] for a short description of the commitment scheme and associated protocols. It should be noted that there are some technical problems with the proof of soundness for the associated protocols given in [12], but these problems have recently been fixed in [11]. The modulus N used for Paillier encryption can also serve as part of the public key for the commitment scheme in Baudot's protocol. In addition, we need two elements $g, h \in Z_N^*$ of large order, such that g is in the group generated by h. The prover must not know the discrete logarithm of g base h or vice versa. We assume that g, h are generated as part of the procedure that sets up N and shares the private key among the decryption servers. A commitment to m in this scheme using random input r is $Com(m, r) = g^m h^r \mod N$. We will often just write $Com(m)$ for simplicity.

Now, the basic idea is the following: given $E(m)$, the prover provides a commitment $Com(m)$, proves that the commitment contains the same number as the encryption, and then uses Baudot's protocol to prove that $m \in I$. The only missing link here is how to show that the same number m is contained in encryption and commitment. This can be done as follows:

1. Let T be the maximal bit-length of m (based on the interval I). The prover chooses at random u, an integer of length $m + 2k_1$ where k_1 is the secondary security parameter. He sends $a = E(u), b = Com(u)$ to the verifier.
2. The verifier chooses a k-bit challenge e.
3. The prover opens the encryption $a \cdot E(m)^e \mod n^2$ and the commitment $b \cdot Com(m)^e \mod N$, to reveal in both cases the number $z = u + em$. The verifier checks that the openings were correct.

This protocol can be made non-interactive in the standard way using a hash function and the Fiat-Shamir heuristic. It is then also statistically zero-knowledge in the random oracle model.

What we have done is to combine two already known protocols for proving knowledge of the contents of an encryption, respectively a commitment. Then, when we prove soundness of this protocol using a standard rewinding argument, the fact that we use the same challenge e and the same response z is both cases will ensure the prover must know one single value that is inside both the encryption and the commitment. Indeed, if the prover for given a, b could answer two different challenges e, e' by numbers z, z', then this common value would be $(z - z')/(e - e')$. The strong RSA assumption is used here, to show that $e - e'$ must divide $z - z'$, except with negligible probability. Details are deferred to the final version of the paper.

Self-tallying Elections and Perfect Ballot Secrecy

Aggelos Kiayias[1] and Moti Yung[2]

[1] Graduate Center, CUNY, NY USA,
akiayias@gc.cuny.edu
[2] CertCo, NY USA
moti@cs.columbia.edu

Abstract. Strong voter privacy, although an important property of an election scheme, is usually compromised in election protocol design in favor of other (desirable) properties. In this work we introduce a new election paradigm with strong voter privacy as its primary objective. Our paradigm is built around three useful properties of voting schemes we define: (1) *Perfect Ballot Secrecy*, ensures that knowledge about the partial tally of the ballots of any set of voters is *only* computable by the coalition of all the remaining voters (this property captures strong voter privacy as understood in real world elections). (2) *Self-tallying*, suggests that the post-ballot-casting phase is an open procedure that can be performed by any interested (casual) third party. Finally, (3) *Dispute-freeness*, suggests that disputes between active parties are prevented altogether, which is an important efficient integrity component.
We investigate conditions for the properties to exist, and their implications. We present a novel voting scheme which is the first system that is dispute-free, self-tallying and supports perfect ballot secrecy. Previously, any scheme which supports (or can be modified to support) perfect ballot secrecy suffers from at least one of the following two deficiencies: it involves voter-to-voter interactions and/or lacks fault tolerance (one faulty participant would fail the election). In contrast, our design paradigm obviates the need for voter-to-voter interaction (due to its dispute-freeness and publicly verifiable messages), and in addition our paradigm suggests a novel "corrective fault tolerant" mechanism. This mechanism neutralizes faults occurring before and after ballot casting, while self-tallying prevents further faults. Additionally, the mechanism is secrecy-preserving and "adaptive" in the sense that its cost is proportional to the number of faulty participants. As a result, our protocol is more efficient and robust than previous schemes that operate (or can be modified to operate) in the perfect ballot secrecy setting.

1 Introduction

One of the most challenging cryptographic protocol problems is electronic voting. We can distinguish two major settings for this problem: The first one based on homomorphic encryption was introduced in [CF85] (see also [BY86,Ben87]). The second one, based on anonymous channels (usually implemented through mix-nets, e.g. [OKST97,Jak99]), was introduced in [Cha81]; for a related approach

D. Naccache and P. Paillier (Eds.): PKC 2002, LNCS 2274, pp. 141–158, 2002.
© Springer-Verlag Berlin Heidelberg 2002

based on blind signatures see [Cha88,FOO92,Sak94]. Election protocols is a very active area of research which has progressively produced various tools for privacy and fault tolerance (e.g., [DLM82,Mer83,Yao82,Cha88,B89,PIK94,SK94,SK95], [BT94,CFSY96,CGS97,Abe99,Sch99]). There are, in fact, two notable sub-cases for the basic problem: (1) small scale (boardroom) elections, where the protocol is essentially run by the voters; (2) large scale (country wide) elections, where tally (or mix) authorities are involved. Typically, the first case allows for better privacy, while the second case implies the necessity of robustness where a voter misbehavior cannot disrupt the election.

Previous small scale voting-schemes, satisfy voter privacy in a strong way (e.g. small scale cases in [DLM82,Mer83,Yao82,Cha88,PW92]). However these schemes are very sensitive to failures, have high time/communication complexity requirements and/or require voter-to-voter private interaction (therefore are subject to costly disputes). On the other hand, large scale schemes rely on the assumption that (a subset of) the authorities do not try to violate the privacy of the voter by assuming some conditions. Examples of such conditions are: "at least one of the authorities remains honest (in mix-net based voting schemes, e.g. [Abe99])," or "at most t authorities collude against the voters but not more (distributed government schemes e.g. [BY86,CFSY96,CGS97])." The dependency of voter privacy on the authorities not colluding in such (large scale) schemes, was noted in [Bra99]. While the above achievements are remarkable, nevertheless, there is much more to wish for with respect to voter privacy in conjunction with efficiency, smooth operation and availability of election results.

Our main goal in this work is to investigate a new paradigm where the strong voter privacy of small-scale elections is possible, but to achieve it with increased efficiency and reliability (i.e., avoiding voter-to-voter interaction and tolerating faulty participants). The new paradigm will be able to combine strong voter privacy with the advantages of the bulletin board paradigm by separating a pre-processing step and an actual ballot casting step, while still implementing all communications via the bulletin board. Our contribution can be summarized as follows:

(1) On a Conceptual/Definitional Level
We introduce the concepts of Self-Tallying, Perfect Ballot Secrecy and Dispute-Freeness: A self-tallying voting-scheme, allows any casual third party to perform the tally computation and in general the post-ballot-casting phase (which becomes independent of any active participant's behavior and of any fault). Consequently, there are no authorities or voters involved in the post-election phase that becomes an *open procedure*. Furthermore, the ballots' availability implies that the counting can be split arbitrarily into chunks amongst a group of third-party talliers (without revealing any partial information about the votes) something that results in a speed-up of the tallying process. Perfect Ballot Secrecy (PBS) ensures that knowledge of the partial tally of the ballots of any set of voters (beyond what is known trivially) is only accessible to the coalition of the remaining voters (as secrecy is perceived in real world elections). Self-tallying and Perfect Ballot

Secrecy are both highly desired properties of election systems. As we will show, these properties are not consistent with traditional robustness of the large scale election schemes (started in [CF85] and followed by much of the homomorphic-encryption based work since then [BY86,Ben87,SK94,CFSY96,CGS97,Sch99], [FPS00,DJ00,KMO01]). Thus, we need a novel notion of fault tolerance which we suggest here: Corrective Fault Tolerance. It involves the honest users correcting faults which are publicly detectable due to Dispute-Freeness: a voting-scheme that is dispute-free has built-in prevention mechanisms that eliminate disputes between the active participants; in essence, any third party should be able to check whether an active participant follows the protocol. Such publicly verifiable scheme has a "public" audit trail which contributes to the reliability cf the voting protocol (whereas, a typical small scale election lacks such reliability). Note that a dispute-free scheme cannot employ PKI or private channels between the participants.

(2) On a Protocol Design Level
We present a boardroom voting scheme which has a number of advantages compared to previous such voting schemes, both in efficiency and voter privacy. It is rooted in our new design paradigm which attempts to preserve as much reliability as possible, while employing homomorphic-encryption in the PBS setting. A key step in our design (that distinguishes it from past work) is that the voter does not select the randomness to be used in its ballot but rather it is generated distributively in a preprocessing stage ahead of ballot-casting. Our scheme is dispute-free, self-tallying and supports perfect ballot secrecy in the most efficient way: if all voters participate, the complexity of the post-ballot-casting phase is essentially optimal, requiring a total of at most $3n$ operations, where n is the number of ballots. Note that perfect ballot secrecy is achieved without voter-to-voter interaction. Our scheme can be viewed as optimizing the "all-honest" case (this design is known as the optimistic approach in the distributed computing literature). The protocol employs *corrective fault tolerance*, in the case of faulty disruption by participants. In such a fault tolerant scheme, the usual robustness properties of large scale schemes are replaced, since the latter are incompatible with perfect ballot secrecy. After ballot casting, no further faults are possible due to the employment of the notion of self-tallying. If PBS is not a prime objective our scheme can be readily transformed to a dispute-free, self-tallying, multi-authority based scheme that is more suitable for large scale elections.

Our voting paradigm allows batching many elections run among the same set of voters (boardroom setting) in such a way so that the online cost for the voter is essentially optimal (merely that of ballot-casting: constant in the number of participants). Additionally our paradigm allows the post-ballot-casting phase to be parallelized arbitrarily, breaking the tallying task into smaller tasks which can be assigned to casual third-party talliers that can work on problem instances independently. The combination of partial counts by talliers can be done in a straightforward manner without the voters and without loss of security. In contrast, if we adopt a typical homomorphic-encryption based scheme to the case where "all voters are talliers" [BY86,Ben87,SK94,CFSY96,CGS97,Sch99], then, these schemes imply a post-ballot-casting involvement of the voters who must act as talliers, before the result can be announced. This is true also for the recent Paillier-based [Pai99] election schemes in [FPS00,DJ00].

2   Requirements for Voting Schemes

A voting-scheme needs to fulfill a variety of requirements to become useful. A brief presentation of requirements follows:

Privacy. Ensures the secrecy of the contents of ballots. Usually, in large scale elections, privacy is achieved by trusting some servers/ authorities. In small scale elections, privacy is achieved typically by intensive voter-to-voter communications.

Universal-Verifiability. Ensures that any party, including a casual observer, can be convinced that all valid votes have been included in the final tally.

Robustness. Ensures that the system can tolerate a certain number of faulty participants. Strong robustness implies that each voter is dealt with independently (which is the most suitable notion for large scale voting). This is shown to be impossible when all voters are also talliers (i.e., in a small scale election). As a result, in this work we consider a more relaxed form of robustness, a notion which we call **corrective fault tolerance**. Under this concept, fault tolerance is achieved through actions of the honest participants.

We note that the combination of universal-verifiability and robustness (which is seemingly contradicting) is a contribution of the fundamental work of Benaloh et al. [CF85,Ben87], to which the notion of enhanced privacy (via distributed talliers) was added in [BY86].

Receipt-Freeness. The voter cannot provide a receipt that reveals in which way he/she voted [BT94]. This was further developed in [SK95,Oka97,HS00] and it is a typical requirement in a country-wide elections to political offices.

Fairness. No partial-tally is revealed to anyone before the end of the election procedure [FOO92].

We introduce three additional desired properties for election schemes:

Dispute-Freeness. The fact that participants follow the protocol at any phase can be publicly verified by any casual third party. This property extends universal verifiability from the tallying phase to any part of the election protocol. A dispute-free voting scheme does not involve bilateral zero-knowledge proofs and dispute resolution mechanisms. In a dispute-free protocol the active **detection** of misbehaving is substituted with built-in **prevention** mechanisms which add integrity.

Self-Tallying. The post-ballot-casting phase can be performed by any interested (casual) third party. This property can be viewed as another strengthening of universal verifiability, in a different direction though. We note that self-tallying is a property inconsistent with the anonymous channel approach to elections, since in the post-ballot-casting phase a mix-network or some other mechanism between the active participants needs to be executed. Note also that a self-tallying scheme needs to cope with fairness explicitly, since the last voter to cast the last ballot may have access to the election results before choosing her vote. Nevertheless this can be dealt with effortlessly, as we will show, by having the authority that manages the deadline of the election cast a final "dummy vote" (in a publicly verifiable manner). Until this final vote, any partial tally is just a random value.

Perfect Ballot Secrecy. Ensures that knowledge of the partial tally of the ballots of a set of voters (beyond what is known and computed trivially by merely having the final tally) is *only* accessible to the coalition of *all* remaining voters. This property strengthens the privacy property and makes it independent of servers' behavior. Such high level of secrecy is a natural notion pertaining to elections and has appeared before in the context of non-robust procedures involving voter-to-voter communications in [Cha88].

2.1   Mutual Disjointness of Properties

We next point out that self-tallying and certain perfect ballot secrecy implementations are not consistent with strong robustness as the following propositions reveal. (The propositions are stated without a formal model, but can be instantiated formally as well; we avoid lengthy formalities since this subsection is merely a motivation for our design paradigm).

Proposition 1. *A self-tallying scheme cannot be robust and support privacy at the same time.*

To see this, assume that there is a scheme that is self-tallying and robust at the same time. Suppose that $n - 1$ of n registered voters actually show up in the election. By the definition of the properties if the scheme is self-tallying and robust it should be possible for any third party (e.g., the timing authority) to compute the partial tally of the $n - 1$ votes. In the case that all voters vote, this third party may perform the computation that can be performed when only $n-1$ voters show up therefore revealing the vote of the excluded voter, in violation of privacy.

Candidates for Perfect Ballot Secrecy (PBS) are voting-schemes based on distributing the power of talliers, where it is possible for the voters to simulate the computation of the distributed government. Alternative schemes involve using an anonymous channel that is implemented in such a way that no assumed trusted parties are employed, i.e. voter communication implements the anonymous channel (schemes where specific authorities are trusted not to collude, e.g.

[NSS91], are automatically excluded). Here we concentrate on the first approach as it appears to be more natural for obtaining efficient constructions in the PBS setting. Robustness in such schemes is usually based on some threshold secret-sharing mechanism (of messages or private keys), that produces shares among a set of authorities (this set, in fact, coincides with the set of voters in the PBS setting). In these schemes any set of t authorities may uncover the contents of any cast ballot. If the voters play the role of the authorities to achieve PBS, it is clear that the threshold t should be n, otherwise the PBS property is not satisfied. Obviously, setting the threshold to n implies lack of fault-tolerance. As a result we can conclude:

Proposition 2. *A voting-scheme with robustness based on secret sharing (of values or keys) cannot satisfy Perfect Ballot Secrecy.*

3   The Voting Scheme: Basic Steps and Mechanisms

The participants in the protocol are n voters denoted by $V_1, \ldots, V_n$ and the bulletin board authority. Each voter has a unique identification string denoted by $I(V_j)$. Identification strings are publicly known.

3.1   The Bulletin Board

A bulletin board is used for all necessary communication between the parties interacting in the voting scheme [CF85]. The bulletin board is a public-broadcast channel with memory. Any party (even third-parties) can read information from the bulletin board. Writing on the bulletin board by the active parties is done in the form of appending data in a specially designed area for each party. Erasing from the bulletin board is not possible, and appending is verified so that any third party can be sure of the communication transcript. In the sequel, the phrase "party X publishes value Y" means that X appends Y to the portion of the bulletin board that belongs to X. The bulletin board authority (server) participates in the protocol to alleviate the computational cost of the participants and administer the election. Server-based ciphertext processing helps in reducing the computations of the parties, whenever trusted. All computation performed by this authority will be publicly verifiable (e.g., by repeating the computation whenever not trusted). The bulletin board authority is also responsible for administering the election, namely, it performs actions such as starting and terminating the election, and maintaining a registry of the eligible voters that should gain access to the bulletin board.

3.2   Initialization

Let $\mathcal{G}_k$ be a family of groups, such that finding discrete logarithms in groups of $\mathcal{G}_k$ is hard (there is no probabilistic polynomial-time algorithm that finds discrete logarithms with non-negligible probability in k). For example, if p, q are large primes with $q \mid p - 1$, then the unique subgroup G of $\mathbf{Z}_p^*$ of size q, is an element of $\mathcal{G}_k$ where k is the number of bits of p, q. Let Gen be a probabilistic polynomial-time algorithm that given 1^k generates the description of a group $G \in \mathcal{G}_k$, and three random elements from G, f, g, h (with relative discrete logs unknown); this can be also be produced distributively, see [GJKR99]. We will denote the order of G by q. Arithmetic in the exponents is in $\mathbf{Z}_q$.

We assume that all parties, either observe Gen and its output, or are using a suitable cryptographic protocol for it. Therefore, all parties obtain the elements g, f, h. Every voter V_j selects a random value $\alpha_j \in \mathbf{Z}_q$ and publishes $h_j := h^{\alpha_j}$ (the voter's personal generator for G).

3.3 Preprocessing: The Pre-voting Stage

Each voter V_i, selects n random values $s_{i,j} \in \mathbf{Z}_q$, $j = 1, \ldots, n$, such that $\sum_{j=1}^n s_{i,j} = 0$. As we will see, this method will randomize the actual ballots while keeping global consistency; we note that such a technique is typical in various settings, e.g. in re-randomization of individual keys in proactive protocols [OY91]. V_i then, publishes the pairs $\langle R_{i,j}, R'_{i,j} \rangle$, s.t. $R_{i,j} := g^{s_{i,j}}$ and $R'_{i,j} := h_j^{s_{i,j}}$. V_i should prove to any third party that $\log_g R_{i,j} = \log_{h_j} R'_{i,j}$. Using a proof of knowledge introduced in [CP93], this is possible as described in figure 1. Note that this protocol is proven to be zero-knowledge only in the case of a honest verifier (see e.g. [CGS97]), but this is sufficient in our setting.

Prover (V_i)		Verifier
publishes $\langle R_{i,j}, R'_{i,j} \rangle$		
$w \in_R \mathbf{Z}_q$		
$a := g^w, b := h_j^w$	$\xrightarrow{a,b}$	
	$\xleftarrow{c}$	$c \in_R \mathbf{Z}_q$
$r := w + s_{i,j}c$	$\xrightarrow{r}$	$g^r \overset{?}{=} a(R_{i,j})^c$
		$h_j^r \overset{?}{=} b(R'_{i,j})^c$

Fig. 1. Proving that $\log_g R_{i,j} = \log_{h_j} R'_{i,j}$

The well-known Fiat-Shamir heuristics [FS87] can be used to make the proof non-interactive and ensure that the challenge c is chosen "honestly": if $\mathcal{H}$ is a cryptographically strong hash function (thought of as a random oracle), then c is defined as $\mathcal{H}(I(V_i), R_{i,j}, R'_{i,j}, a, b)$. Consequently V_i publishes $\langle R_{i,j}, R'_{i,j}, a, b, r \rangle$; the verifier computes c using the hash function and checks the two equalities as in the figure. This method ensures that the challenge c is chosen at random (under the assumption that $\mathcal{H}$ is a random oracle hash). When c is chosen using a random oracle hash we will denote the sequence $\langle a, b, r \rangle$ defined as above for the values $R_{i,j}, R'_{i,j}$ and bases g, h_j by PKEQDL$[x : (R_{i,j} = g^x) \wedge (R'_{i,j} = h_j^x)]$. Such proofs will be used in other parts of our voting scheme to ensure that the participants are following the protocol.

Theorem 1. *At any time, after the completion of the pre-voting stage,*
(i) Any third-party can verify that $\log_g R_{i,j} = \log_{h_j} R'_{i,j}$, for any i, j.
(ii) Any third-party can verify that $\sum_{j=1}^n s_{i,j} = 0$, for any i.
(iii) If at least one voter chose the $s_{i,j}$ values at random, then the values $t_j :=$
$\sum_{i=1}^n s_{i,j}$ are random elements of $\mathbf{Z}_q$ with the property $\sum_{j=1}^n t_j = 0$.

Proof. (i) is achieved using the non-interactive version of the proof of knowledge described in figure 1. (ii) can be easily checked by multiplying $R_{i,j}$: it should hold that $\prod_{j=1}^n R_{i,j} = 1$ for all $i = 1, \ldots, n$. For item (iii), just note that, $\sum_{j=1}^n t_j = \sum_{j=1}^n \sum_{i=1}^n s_{i,j} = \sum_{i=1}^n \sum_{j=1}^n s_{i,j} = \sum_{i=1}^n 0 = 0$. Since each t_j contains a value from each voter V_i, if at least one voter chose the $s_{i,j}$ values at random, this is enough to randomize all t_j values.   □

The bulletin board authority for each $j = 1, \ldots, n$ computes the product $R'_j := \prod_{i=1}^n R'_{i,j}$ and publishes it on the board. The contents of the bulletin board after the end of the preprocessing are shown in figure 2 (note that in the left hand table, each row when its values are multiplied together the result is the value 1).

$R_{i,j}$:

V_1 :	$g^{s_{1,1}}$	$\ldots$	$g^{s_{1,n}}$	$= 1$
V_2 :	$g^{s_{2,1}}$	$\ldots$	$g^{s_{2,n}}$	$= 1$
$\vdots$	$\vdots$	$\ldots$	$\vdots$	$\vdots$
V_n :	$g^{s_{n,1}}$	$\ldots$	$g^{s_{n,n}}$	$= 1$
	g^{t_1}	$\ldots$	g^{t_n}	$= 1$

$R'_{i,j}$:

V_1 :	$h_1^{s_{1,1}}$	$\ldots$	$h_n^{s_{1,n}}$
V_2 :	$h_1^{s_{2,1}}$	$\ldots$	$h_n^{s_{2,n}}$
$\vdots$	$\vdots$	$\ldots$	$\vdots$
V_n :	$h_1^{s_{n,1}}$	$\ldots$	$h_n^{s_{n,n}}$
	$R'_1 = h_1^{t_1}$	$\ldots$	$R'_n = h_n^{t_n}$

Fig. 2. The contents of the Bulletin Board after the preprocessing phase

3.4   Ballot-Casting

Voter V_j reads R'_j from the bulletin board and raises it to α_j^{-1} in order to obtain $h^{s_{1,j}+\cdots+s_{n,j}} = h^{t_j}$. For now, we will assume that votes are either 1 or -1 (yes/no). We note that this is done only for the sake of the exposition as it is possible to modify our protocol in a *direct* and *efficient* manner to support voting between c candidates, or support "0-voting" i.e. abstaining from the formation of the election result (see section 3.7). V_j selects a $v_j \in \{1, -1\}$ at his choice, and publishes the ballot $B_j := h^{t_j} f^{v_j}$.

It is imperative that V_j convinces any third party that he followed the protocol i.e. that the random portion of B_j has been produced by the application of V_j's secret value α_j^{-1} on R'_j (note that the value R'_j is publicly accessible). This can be done as described in figure 3. We note here that one significant difference from previous similar proofs of ballot validity (as those in [CFSY96,CGS97]) is that the value t_j is not known to the voter, and the proof has to rely on the voter (prover) knowing the secret "Diffie-Hellman-key-exchange"-like value α_j.

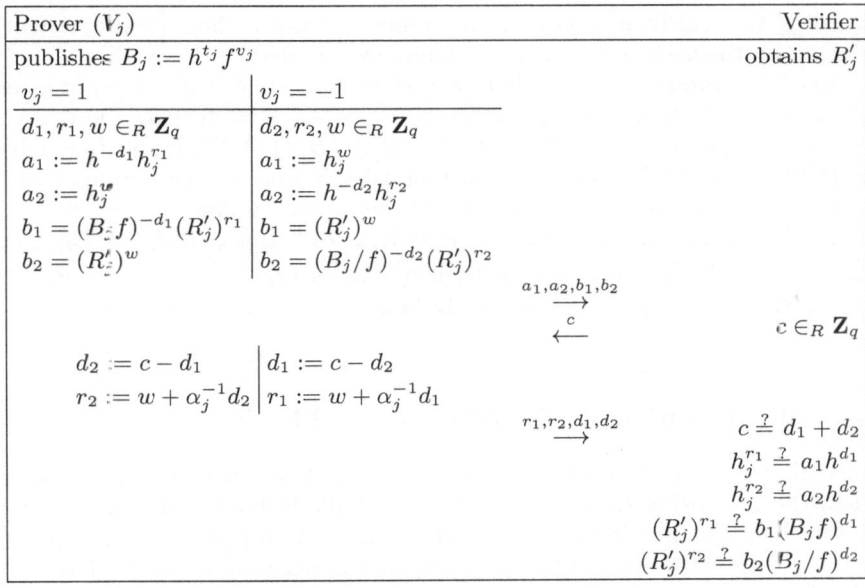

Fig. 3. Proving that $(\log_{R'_j} B_j f = \log_{h_j} h) \vee (\log_{R'_j} B_j/f = \log_{h_j} h)$

More formally, the protocol of figure 3, is a proof of knowledge in the sense of [CDS94,DDPY94] as it satisfies completeness and special soundness; additionally it is special honest verifier zero knowledge. As before, using the Fiat-Shamir heuristics [FS90] we can make the above protocol non-interactive using random oracle hashing, by choosing $c = \mathcal{H}(I(V_j), B_j, R'_j, a_1, a_2, b_1, b_2)$.

Theorem 2. *The protocol of figure 3 satisfies the following:*
(i) It is a proof of knowledge for the relation

$$(\log_{R'_j} B_j f = \log_{h_j} h) \vee (\log_{R'_j} B_j/f = \log_{h_j} h)$$

(ii) It is Special Honest Verifier Zero Knowledge.
(iii) It ensures that the ballot B_j is formed properly.

Proof. (i) The witness for the relation is the value α_j^{-1} (the secret value of V_j). Completeness can be shown in a straightforward manner.

Regarding special soundness: Given some R'_j, B_j, suppose we have two accepting conversations with the same first move: $(a_1, a_2, b_1, b_2, c, r_1, r_2, d_1, d_2)$ and $(a_1, a_2, b_1, b_2, c', r'_1, r'_2, d'_1, d'_2)$, with $c \neq c'$. For special soundness the goal is to show that a witness can be constructed in polynomial-time. It is easy to check that either $\frac{r_1 - r'_1}{d_1 - d'_1}$ or $\frac{r_2 - r'_2}{d_2 - d'_2}$ is a witness for the relation. At least one of these values is defined since if both $d_1 = d'_1$ and $d_2 = d'_2$ it holds that $c = c'$ (assumed false). Note that a cheating prover can convince the verifier without using a witness by guessing the challenge c sent by the verifier and computing a_1, a_2, b_1, b_2

according to c (instead of prior to receiving c). Such a cheating prover will be detected by the verifier with overwhelming probability $1 - 1/q$.

(ii) The protocol is special honest verifier zero knowledge, because given a random c, if we choose at random r_1, r_2, d_1, d_2 s.t. $c = d_1 + d_2$ the conversation $(h_j^{r_1} h^{-d_1}, h_j^{r_2} h^{-d_2}, (R_j')^{r_1}(B_j f)^{-d_1}, (R_j')^{r_2}(B_j/f)^{-d_2}, c, r_1, r_2, d_1, d_2)$ is an accepting conversation that it is indistinguishable from the accepting conversations generated by the honest prover and the honest verifier.

(iii) From the relation $(\log_{R_j'} B_j f = \log_{h_j} h) \vee (\log_{R_j'} B_j/f = \log_{h_j} h)$, if we denote by x the value $\log_{h_j} h$ then it follows that either $B_j = (R_j')^x f$ or $B_j = (R_j')^x/f$ is true which is exactly how V_j is supposed to form the ballot B_j. $\square$

3.5   Administrating and Terminating the Election

The bulletin board authority is responsible for the administration of the election. When the pre-voting stage is completed the bulletin board authority signs the bulletin board and announces the start of the election process. It is imperative that the bulletin board authority prevents reading of the cast ballots as the election progresses in order to ensure fairness. This is because the last voter to cast a ballot is able to compute the election result before choosing his/her vote and casting the final ballot. Fairness can be ensured as follows: the bulletin board authority participates in the pre-voting stage acting as one of the voters, say voter i_0. The bulletin board authority does not cast a ballot; instead when the deadline of the election process is reached it publishes $B_{i_0} := (R_{i_0}')^{\alpha_{i_0}^{-1}} = h^{t_{i_0}}$ together with the non-interactive proof of knowledge PKEQDL$[x : (h = h_{i_0}^x) \wedge (B_{i_0} = (R_{i_0}')^x)]$ (see section 3.3) that ensures that the correct value is published — note that this amounts to a publicly verifiable 0-vote. The bulletin board authority also signs the contents of the bulletin board, thus officially terminating the election process and prohibiting the deposition of any other ballots.

Given the way the voters' ballots are formed and theorem 1(iii), it is easy to see that:

Proposition 3. *The administration of the election by the Bulletin Board Authority as described above ensures fairness.*

3.6   The Final Stage: Self-tallying and Corrective Fault-Tolerance

All voters participate: Self-tallying
If all voters participate in the election, then computing the final tally can be done by any (casual) third party in optimal time: $n - 1$ multiplications in G and an exhaustive search of $2n$ steps, worst-case. Since $\sum_{j=1}^n t_j = 0$ (see theorem 1,iii) it holds that the tally $T := \prod_{j=1}^n B_j = f^{\sum_{j=1}^n v_j}$ (note that v_{i_0} the "vote" cast by the bulletin board authority is equal to 0). Because $T \in \{f^{-n+1}, \ldots, f^{n-1}\}$ it can be inverted by a brute-force algorithm that will check all the possible values.

By a baby-step giant-step method the inversion can be made in $\mathcal{O}(\sqrt{n})$ group operations.

Corrective fault tolerance

In order to achieve corrective fault-tolerance, when some voters stop participating at some phase of the protocol, the remaining active voters must react to reveal the shares that were intended for them. Here we deal with two cases: (i) when some registered voters do not participate in the pre-voting stage, and (ii) when some voters do not cast a ballot before the deadline of the election. We note here that corrective fault-tolerance is not intended to capture all fault possibilities of the active participants, and there can be catastrophic cases for which the protocol must restart (with the faulty participants deactivated) for example when some of the voters that cast a ballot do not participate in the corrective phase. Note though, that whenever the majority is honest there is a way to prevent a restart of the protocol by Byzantine agreement procedures — an issue which is beyond the scope of this paper. Nevertheless, our protocol is intended for the small scale boardroom model, where malicious failures (where members of the board misbehave publicly) are not typical, and also in this case, a restart of the protocol is not prohibitive.

Nevertheless, as we will see in section 4.1, corrective fault tolerance does provide significant increased of robustness, when compared to all previous election schemes in the Perfect Ballot Secrecy setting. Next we outline the two procedures which constitute corrective fault tolerance.

(i) Some registered voters do not participate in preprocessing. The method presented here is also useful when some voters that participated in the preprocessing phase prefer not to vote. This is important in the batched version of the self-tallying scheme (see section 4.2). Denote the set of voters whose shares should be cancelled by S, and the set of remaining voters by $\overline{S}$.

The corrective phase is as follows: each voter V_k, $k \in \overline{S}$, publishes $R_k'' :=$ $h_k^{\sum_{j \in S} s_{k,j}}$, together with the non-interactive proof of knowledge PKEQDL$[x :$ $(h_k^x = R_k'') \wedge (g^x = \prod_{j \in S} R_{k,j})]$ (see section 3.3). The bulletin board authority modifies the R_k' values (that were computed at the end of the preprocessing phase) as follows:

$$\forall k \in \overline{S} \quad R_k' := R_k' R_k'' / \prod_{i \in S} R_{i,k}'$$

Then, the protocol proceeds normally with ballot-casting (section 3.4). It is easy to see that the values $t_k := \log_{h_k} R_k'$ for $k \in \overline{S}$ satisfy the properties of the t-values in theorem 1(iii): $\sum_{k \in \overline{S}} t_k = 0$ and $\{t_k\}_{k \in \overline{S}}$ are random elements of $\mathbf{Z}_q$ provided that at least one voter V_k, $k \in \overline{S}$ chose the shares $s_{k,j}$ at random.

(ii) Some voters do not cast a ballot. Denote the set of voters that did not cast a ballot by S', and the set of remaining voters by $\overline{S'}$. Each voter V_k, $k \in \overline{S'}$, publishes $e_k := \sum_{j \in S'} s_{k,j}$ and $\Phi_k := (\prod_{j \in S'} R_{j,k}')^{\alpha_k^{-1}}$.

The value e_k can be universally verified by checking that $g^{e_k} = \prod_{j \in S'} R_{k,j}$ for all $k \in \overline{S'}$. The correctness of the value Φ_k can be universally verified by having the voter V_k publish the non-interactive proof of knowledge $\mathrm{PKEQDL}[x : (h = h_k^x) \wedge (\Phi_k = (\prod_{j \in S'} R'_{j,k})^x)]$ (see section 3.3). After the completion of the corrective round the tally computation can be performed by any third party as follows: $T := \prod_{k \in \overline{S'}} B_k h^{e_k} (\Phi_k)^{-1}$. It is easy to see that $T \in \{f^{|\overline{S'}|}, \ldots, f^{-|\overline{S'}|}\}$; inverting T is done in a brute-force manner as before.

We note here that these two corrective phases, are not exclusive and both can be implemented in a single execution of a protocol.

3.7   Multi-way Elections

There are many standard ways to extend our voting scheme from yes/no voting to 1-out-of-c voting for c candidates (for a constant c) in an efficient manner[1]. We describe one such possibility following ideas from Cramer, Gennaro and Schoenmakers [CGS97]. The resulting scheme has the same complexity in all respects, with the exception that the proof of validity of the ballot is increased by the factor c, and the exhaustive search at the tallying phase requires searching in the augmented possible tally value space.

Instead of f, in the initialization stage the values $f_1, \ldots, f_c \in G$ are given for use by all participants (where the $\log_h f_\ell$ is not known to any party). V_j casts a vote $v_j \in \{1, \ldots, c\}$ by publishing the ballot $h^{t_j} f_{v_j}$. The proof of ballot validity is modified as shown in figure 4.

Theorem 3. *The protocol of figure 4 satisfies the following:*
(i) It is a proof of knowledge for the relation $\vee_{\ell=1}^{c} (\log_{R'_j} B_j / f_\ell = \log_{h_j} h)$.
(ii) It is Special Honest Verifier Zero Knowledge.
(iii) It ensures that the ballot B_j is formed properly.

The election protocol is otherwise exactly the same to the yes/no case. In the final stage the product $T_1 \ldots T_c$ is revealed where $T_\ell \in \{f_\ell^0, \ldots, f_\ell^{n-1}\}$. Revealing the tallies, requires a total of n^{c-1} search steps in the worst case. By using a baby-step giant-step method it is possible to reduce the time needed to $\mathcal{O}(\sqrt{n}^{c-1})$ group operations (see also [CGS97]) . We would like to further note that the searching task can be arbitrarily partitioned among many processors in a distributed environment.

4   The Voting Scheme

Stage 1. All participants run the initialization as described in section 3.2. Voters register with the bulletin board authority that checks their eligibility, and gain access to the bulletin board.

---

[1] To go beyond constant c one needs either to use another method than homomorphic-based encryption, or base the scheme on sharing Paillier's cryptosystem [Pai99] as in [BFPPS01] which we can employ as well, at the expense of losing some of our scheme's properties.

Prover (V_j)	Verifier
publishes $B_j := h^{t_j} f_{v_j}$	obtains R'_j
for $\ell \in \{1, \ldots, c\} - \{v_j\}$	
$d_\ell, r_\ell \in_R \mathbf{Z}_q, r_{v_j}, w \in_R \mathbf{Z}_q$	
$a_\ell = h^{-d_\ell} h_j^{r_\ell}$	
$a_{v_j} = h_j^w$	
$b_\ell = (B_j/f_\ell)^{-d_\ell} (R'_j)^{r_\ell}$	
$b_{v_j} = (R'_j)^w$	
$\qquad\qquad\qquad \xrightarrow{\{a_\ell\}_\ell, \{b_\ell\}_\ell}$	
$\qquad\qquad\qquad \xleftarrow{\quad c \quad}$	$c \in_R \mathbf{Z}_q$
$d_{v_j} := c - (\sum_{\ell \neq v_j} d_\ell)$	
$r_{v_j} := w + \alpha_j^{-1} d_{v_j}$	
$\qquad\qquad\qquad \xrightarrow{\{r_\ell\}_\ell, \{d_\ell\}_\ell}$	$c \stackrel{?}{=} \sum_\ell d_\ell$
	for $\ell = 1, \ldots, c,$
	$h_j^{r_\ell} \stackrel{?}{=} a_\ell h^{d_\ell}$
	$(R'_j)^{r_\ell} \stackrel{?}{=} b_\ell (B_j/f_\ell)^{d_\ell}$

Fig. 4. Multi-way Elections: Proving that $\vee_{\ell=1}^c (\log_{R'_j} B_j/f_\ell = \log_{h_j} h)$

Stage 2. The voters together with the bulletin board authority execute the pre-processing stage of section 3.3. At the end of the preprocessing stage, if some registered voters failed to participate the corrective step of section 3.3(i) is employed. Subsequently the bulletin board authority signs the bulletin board and officially starts the election.

Stage 3. Voters publish their ballots as described in section 3.4 in the designated space for them in the bulletin board. Note that this process is not anonymous and as a result double-voting is eliminated. When the deadline for the election is reached the bulletin board casts the "final vote" and thus opens the election results (see section 3.5).

Stage 4. If all voters who received shares in the preprocessing phase cast a ballot, the election tally is recoverable by any third party as described in section 3.6 (self-tallying). If not all voters participated the corrective fault tolerance round of section 3.6(ii) is employed.

Complexity. Stage 1 requires $\mathcal{O}(1)$ computation and communication by all participants. In stage 2, each voter spends $\mathcal{O}(n)$ for computing and communicating the preprocessing shares. In stage 3, the voter computes the ballot and the proof of validity that needs $\mathcal{O}(1)$ computation and $\mathcal{O}(1)$ communication. Stage 4, if all voters that received shares at stage 2 cast a ballot, requires $n-1$ multiplications and a brute-force step that takes $2n$ steps worst-case, which can be reduced to $\mathcal{O}(\sqrt{n})$. The corrective rounds of sections 3.6 have the following complexity: if

b voters stop participating, each active voter needs to perform $b - 1$ operations and to publish the resulting corrective value that requires $\mathcal{O}(1)$ communication.

Assuming the existence of an homomorphic encryption with an associated discrete log problem which is secure and a random oracle hash, it holds that:

Theorem 4. *The described protocol is a voting-scheme that satisfies privacy, fairness, universal-verifiability, corrective fault-tolerance, dispute-freeness, self-tallying and perfect ballot secrecy.*

4.1 Comments on PBS Voting and Dispute-Freeness

In a voting-scheme with perfect-ballot secrecy, the actual vote of a participant can only be revealed if all the remaining voters collude against him. In our case Perfect Ballot Secrecy is ensured computationally. Our voting scheme can be modified so that Perfect Ballot Secrecy is information theoretic however the resulting scheme will not be dispute-free anymore.

Other voting schemes based on homomorphic encryption can be modified so that they achieve Perfect Ballot Secrecy. Usually the computational/ communication cost is substantial. The general idea is to make the set of authorities coincides with the set of voters and to set the threshold to n (for schemes that are based on secret sharing). This choice disables the robustness property as seen in proposition 2. Note that mix-net based schemes are not necessarily excluded from the PBS setting (since it may be possible for the voters to simulate the mix-net), but the homomorphic encryption setting seems to be more natural as a base for PBS. In any case, a mix-net PBS scheme would face similar robustness problems since *all* voters would need to be active in the mixing phase in order to ensure perfect ballot secrecy.

Let us discuss the notion of dispute-freeness and its importance in the PBS homomorphic-encryption setting. The schemes of [CFSY96] and [CGS97] include phases that are not publicly verifiable and therefore they are not dispute-free: the first uses private channels between voters and authorities whereas the second includes a key-generation phase between authorities that is not publicly-verifiable (note that we do not claim that lack of dispute-freeness is necessarily inherent in these schemes). Since in PBS voting the voters play the role of the authorities this can lead to voters accusing other voters of invalidity of actions, which is certainly not desirable. For this reason we will focus our discussion of PBS schemes (and in general of voting without authorities) on schemes that are dispute-free i.e. [Sch99] and our voting scheme.

The [Sch99]-scheme can be transformed to the PBS setting: choosing the threshold t to be n and letting the voters play the role of the talliers. The complexity of the voter then becomes $\mathcal{O}(n^2)$ before ballot casting and all voters have to be active in the post ballot casting stage spending $\mathcal{O}(n)$ computation. Due to the fact that *all* voters need to be active in the tallying phase, the scheme is not robust (as it is the case for all schemes that base fault-tolerance on secret-sharing, in the PBS setting, see proposition 2). Note though that it is possible to achieve some form of corrective fault-tolerance by adding additional rounds of communication and computation, but this amounts to implementing our own corrective steps (which become more complex when put on top of the [Sch99]-scheme rather than as used in our scheme).

The complexity of our voting scheme is substantially better than the PBS-version of the [Sch99] scheme. In our case in the pre-voting stage, each voter needs computation and communication $\mathcal{O}(n)$. Tallying is optimal as it takes $3n$ steps, without the participation of the voters. Corrective fault tolerance costs $\mathcal{O}(b)$ group operations for a participant, where b is the number of faults.

As we pointed out before, most homomorphic encryption based election schemes can be readily modified into the PBS setting. With no exception this will force all voters to be active in the post-ballot-casting phase and in fact each voter will have to perform an $\mathcal{O}(n)$ computation at this stage. If one of the voters fails to participate in the post-ballot-casting phase the entire election fails. This is much too late in the process to allow such failures. In contrast, our election scheme optimizes this setting: if all voters participate in the election there is no need for them to participate in the post-ballot-casting phase at all. Moreover if some voters do not participate in the voting phase the election does not necessarily fail since we have shown a set of corrective measures that can be executed. This delicate fault tolerance distinction is an important achievement of our scheme. Performance-wise, what our active corrective fault tolerance requires from active voters is not $\mathcal{O}(n)$ but $\mathcal{O}(b)$ work for b absent voters, namely work proportional to the absentees and not to the whole voter population (what the distributed computing literature calls "adaptive fault tolerance").

4.2   Batched Boardroom PBS-Elections

Batching a series of elections is one of the ways to maximize the gain from our voting scheme.

Phase 1. All board members execute the pre-voting stage for several elections in the beginning of a time-period. The work of each participant for each of the elections is linear in the total members of the board. The output of this stage will be kept for later use.

Phase 2. If all members of the board are going to vote in a particular election, the election is held directly as in sections 3.4 and 3.6. If not all members of the board are "present" in the election (something that is known in advance) the values R_j' are properly modified so that the self-tallying property is preserved as described in section 3.6(i). If some voters fail to cast a ballot the corrective phase of section 3.6(ii) is executed.

The complexity of the batched protocol is as follows: The pre-voting stage can be executed off-line ahead of time preparing for coming L elections. It requires $\mathcal{O}(Ln)$ computation for each board member and $\mathcal{O}(Ln^2)$ storage space in total. Each election itself requires $\mathcal{O}(1)$ per participant and then any passive third party can compute the final tally with $n - 1$ multiplications and a worst-case of $2n$ steps in the brute-force stage. The corrective phase requires linear (in the number of absentees) computations from any active participant. Thus, we get:

Theorem 5. *The described batched election protocol is a voting-scheme that satisfies privacy, fairness, universal-verifiability, corrective fault-tolerance, dispute-freeness, self-tallying, perfect ballot secrecy where the on-line cost is that of ballot-casting: constant in the number of participants.*

4.3   Adapting to Large Scale: The Non-PBS Version

If Perfect Ballot Secrecy is not an objective our scheme can be readily modified to an authority-based self-tallying election scheme that is more suitable for the large scale setting. In the modified scheme the voter needs to be active only in the registration phase and the ballot-casting phase.

Stage 1. As in the PBS-scheme, where the set of participants includes a number of authorities $A_1, \ldots, A_m$.

Stage 2. Only the authorities are active in the preprocessing phase, with each A_i issuing the values $s_{i,1}, \ldots, s_{i,n}$ as described in section 3.3.

Stage 3. Identical to the ballot-casting stage as described in the PBS-version.

Stage 4. If all voters who received shares in the preprocessing phase cast a ballot, the election tally is recoverable by any third party as described in section 3.6 (self-tallying). If not all voters participate, corrective fault tolerance has the authorities publishing the shares of the voters that did not cast a ballot.

The computation/communication for each authority is linear in n, whereas the ballot-casting stage remains of constant time for each voter. It is easy to see that:

Theorem 6. *The described protocol is a voting-scheme that satisfies privacy (assuming not all authorities collude), fairness, universal-verifiability, corrective fault-tolerance, dispute-freeness, and self-tallying.*

References

Abe99.   Masayuki Abe, *Mix-Networks on Permutation Networks*, ASIACRYPT 1999.

BFPPS01.   Olivier Baudron, Pierre-Alain Fouque, David Pointcheval, Guillaume Poupard and Jacques Stern, *Practical Multi-Candidate Election system*, In the Proceedings of PODC 2001.

Ben87.   Josh Benaloh, *Verifiable Secret-Ballot Elections*, PhD Thesis, Yale University, 1987.

BY86.   Josh Benaloh and Moti Yung, *Distributing the Power of a Government to Enhance the Privacy of Voters*, PODC 1986.

BT94.   Josh Benaloh and Dwight Tuinstra, *Receipt-Free Secret-Ballot Elections*,
           STOC 1994.
B89.   Colin Boyd, *A New Multiple Key Cipher and an Improved Voting Scheme*,
           EUROCRYPT 1989.
Bra99.   Stefan Brands, *Rethinking Privacy*, Ph.D. thesis, pages 230-231.
Cha81.   David Chaum, *Untraceable Electronic Mail, Return Addresses, and Digital
           Pseudonyms*, Communications of the ACM 24(2): 84-88, 1981.
Cha88.   David Chaum, *Elections with Unconditionally-Secret Ballots and Disrup-
           tion Equivalent to Breaking RSA* EUROCRYPT 1988.
CP93.   David Chaum and Torben P. Pedersen, *Wallet Databases with Observers*,
           CRYPTO 1992.
CF85.   Josh D. Cohen (Benaloh) and Michael J. Fischer, *A Robust and Verifiable
           Cryptographically Secure Election Scheme*, FOCS 1985.
CGS97.   Ronald Cramer, Rosario Gennaro and Berry Schoenmakers. *A Secure
           and Optimally Efficient Multi-Authority Election Scheme*, EUROCRYPT
           1997.
CDS94.   Ronald Cramer, Ivan Damgård and Berry Schoenmakers, *Proofs of Partial
           Knowledge and Simplified Design of Witness Hiding Protocols*. CRYPTO
           1994.
CFSY96.   Ronald Cramer, Matthew K. Franklin, Berry Schoenmakers and Moti
           Yung, *Multi-Autority Secret-Ballot Elections with Linear Work*, EURO-
           CRYPT 1996.
DJ00.   Ivan Damgård and Mats Jurik, *A Generalisation, a Simplification and
           Some Applications of Paillier's Probabilistic Public-Key System*, Public
           Key Cryptography 2001, pp. 119-136.
DLM82.   Richard A. DeMillo, Nancy A. Lynch, Michael Merritt, *Cryptographic
           Protocols*, STOC 1982: pp. 383-400.
DDPY94.   Alfredo De Santis, Giovanni Di Crescenzo, Giuseppe Persiano, Moti Yung,
           On Monotone Formula Closure of SZK, FOCS 1994.
FS90.   Uriel Feige and Adi Shamir, *Witness Indistinguishable and Witness Hiding
           Protocols*, STOC 1990.
FS87.   Amos Fiat and Adi Shamir, *How to Prove Yourself: Practical Solutions
           to Identification and Signature Problems*, CRYPTO 1986.
FPS00.   Pierre-Alain Fouque, Guillaume Poupard and Jacques Stern, *Sharing De-
           cryption in the Context of Voting or Lotteries*, In the Proceedings of Fi-
           nancial Cryptography 2000.
FOO92.   Atsushi Fujioka, Tatsuaki Okamoto and Kazuo Ohta: *A Practical Secret
           Voting Scheme for Large Scale Elections*, ASIACRYPT 1992.
GJKR99.   Rosario Gennaro, Stanislaw Jarecki, Hugo Krawczyk and Tal Rabin, *Se-
           cure Distributed Key Generation for Discrete-Log Based Cryptosystems*
           EUROCRYPT 1999.
HS00.   Martin Hirt and Kazue Sako, *Efficient Receipt-Free Voting Based on Ho-
           momorphic Encryption*, EUROCRYPT 2000.
Jak99.   Markus Jakobsson, *Flash Mixing*, Principles of Distributed Computing
           (PODC), 1999.
KMO01.   Jonathan Katz, Steven Myers, and Rafail Ostrovsky, *Cryptographic Coun-
           ters and Applications to Electronic Voting*, EUROCRYPT 2001.
Mer83.   Michael Merrit, *Cryptographic Protocols*, Ph.D. Thesis, Georgia Institute
           of Technology 1983.
NSS91.   Hannu Nurmi, Arto Salomaa, and Lila Santean, *Secret Ballot Elections in
           Computer Networks.*, Computers & Security 36, 10 (1991), 553-560.

OKST97.   Wakaha Ogata, Kaoru Kurosawa, Kazue Sako and Kazunori Takatani, *Fault tolerant anonymous channel*, In the Proceedings of ICICS '97, LNCS No. 1334, pp. 440–444, 1997.

Oka97.   Tatsuaki Okamoto, *Receipt-Free Electronic Voting Schemes for Large Scale Elections*, Workshop on Security Protocols, 1997.

OY91.   R. Ostrovsky and M. Yung, *How to withstand mobile virus attacks*, ACM Symposium on Principles of Distributed Computing (PODC), 1991, pp. 51-61.

Pai99.   Pascal Paillier, *Public-Key Cryptosystems Based on Composite Degree Residuosity Classes*, EUROCRYPT 1999.

PIK94.   Choonsik Park, Kazutomo Itoh and Kaoru Kurosawa, *Efficient Anonymous Channel and All/Nothing Election Scheme*, EUROCRYPT 1993.

PW92.   Birgit Pfitzmann and Michael Waidner, *Unconditionally Untraceable and Fault-tolerant Broadcast and Secret Ballot Election*, Hildesheimer Informatik-Berichte, Institut für Informatik, Universität Hildesheim, 1992.

Sak94.   Kazue Sako, *Electronic Voting Schemes, Allowing Open Objection to the Tally*, In the Transactions of the Institue of Electronics, Information, and Communication Engineers, volume E77-A, n. 1, pp. 24-30, 1994.

SK94.   Kazue Sako and Joe Kilian, *Secure Voting Using Partially Compatible Homomorphisms*, CRYPTO 1994.

SK95.   Kazue Sako and Joe Kilian, *Receipt-Free Mix-Type Voting Scheme - A Practical Solution to the Implementation of a Voting Booth*, EUROCRYPT 1995.

Sch99.   Berry Schoenmakers, *A Simple Publicly Verifiable Secret Sharing Scheme and its Applications to Electronic Voting*, CRYPTO 1999.

Yao82.   Andrew C. Yao, *Protocols for Secure Computations*, Proc. 23 rd IEEE Symp. on Foundations of Computer Science, Chicago, IL (Nov. 1982), 160–164. 17.

Efficient 1-Out-n Oblivious Transfer Schemes*

Wen-Guey Tzeng

Department of Computer and Information Science
National Chiao Tung University
Hsinchu, Taiwan 30050
tzeng@cis.nctu.edu.tw

Abstract. In this paper we propose an efficient (string) OT_n^1 scheme for any $n \geq 2$. We build our OT_n^1 scheme from fundamental cryptographic techniques directly. It achieves optimal efficiency in terms of the number of rounds and the total number of exchanged messages for the case that the receiver's choice is unconditionally secure. The computation time of our OT_n^1 scheme is very efficient, too. The receiver need compute 2 modular exponentiations only no matter how large n is, and the sender need compute $2n$ modular exponentiations. The distinct feature of our scheme is that the system-wide parameters are independent of n and *universally usable*, that is, all possible receivers and senders use the same parameters and need no trapdoors specific to each of them. For our OT_n^1 scheme, the privacy of the receiver's choice is unconditionally secure and the secrecy of the un-chosen secrets is based on hardness of the decisional Diffie-Hellman problem.

We extend our OT_n^1 scheme to distributed oblivious transfer schemes. Our distributed OT_n^1 scheme takes full advantage of the research results of secret sharing and is conceptually simple. It achieves better security than Naor and Pinkas's scheme does in many aspects. For example, our scheme is secure against collusion of the receiver R and t-1 servers and it need not restrict R to contact at most t servers, which is difficult to enforce.

For applications, we present a method of transforming any single-database PIR protocol into a symmetric PIR protocol with only one extra unit of communication cost.

1 Introduction

Rabin [33] proposes the concept of the two-party oblivious transfer (OT) scheme in the cryptographic scenario. It has many flavors, such as, original oblivious transfer (OT), 1-out-2 oblivious transfer (OT_2^1) and 1-out-n oblivious transfer (OT_n^1). For OT, the sender S has only one secret m and would like to have the receiver R to obtain m with probability 0.5. On the other hand, R does not want S to know whether it gets m or not. For OT_2^1, S has two secrets m_1 and m_2 and would like to give R one of them at R's choice. Again, R does not want S to

* Research supported in part by National Science Council grant 90-2213-C09-145 and MOE Excellence grant 90-E-FA04-1-4, Taiwan, ROC.

know which secret it chooses. OT_n^1 is a natural extension of OT_2^1 to the case of n secrets, in which S has n secrets $m_1, m_2, \ldots, m_n$ and is willing to disclose exactly one of them to R at R's choice. OT_n^1 is also known as "all-or-nothing disclosure of secrets (ANDOS)" in which R is not allowed to gain combined information of the secrets, such as, their exclusive-or. Essentially, all these flavors are equivalent in the information theoretic sense [10,13,16]. Oblivious transfer is a fundamental primitive for cryptography and secure distributed computation [24,26] and has many applications, such as, private information retrieval (PIR), fair electronic contract signing, oblivious secure computation, etc [6,15,22].

A general approach for constructing an OT_n^1 scheme is that we first construct a basis OT_2^1 scheme and then build the OT_n^1 scheme by (explicitly or implicitly) invoking the basis OT_2^1 scheme for many runs, typically, n or $\log_2 n$ runs [10,12,28]. Another approach is to build an OT_n^1 scheme from basic techniques directly [31,32,34,36]

In this paper we propose an efficient OT_n^1 scheme for any $n \geq 2$. We build our OT_n^1 scheme from fundamental cryptographic techniques directly. It achieves optimal efficiency in the number of rounds and the total number of exchanged messages for the case that R's choice is unconditionally secure. The computation time of our OT_n^1 scheme is very efficient. R need compute 2 modular exponentiations only no matter how large n is, and S need compute $2n$ modular exponentiations. By the speedup techniques [25], S's computation time can be much reduced. The distinct feature of our scheme is that the system-wide parameters are independent of n and *universally usable*, that is, all possible receivers and senders use the same parameters and need no trapdoors (eg. factorization of $N = pq$) specific to each of them. For our OT_n^1 scheme, the privacy of R's choice α is unconditionally secure and the secrecy of the un-chosen secrets m_i, $i \neq \alpha$, is based on hardness of the decisional Diffie-Hellman problem. Our OT_n^1 scheme can be parallelized to construct an OT_n^k scheme, in which R can get k secrets among n secrets at its choice.

We can combine our OT_n^1 scheme with any secret sharing scheme to form an efficient distributed OT_n^1 scheme [30]. In this setting, there are p servers. Each server holds partial information about the secrets m_i's. If R contacts t (the threshold) or more servers, it can compute m_α of its choice; otherwise, it cannot get any information about the secrets. Our threshold OT_n^1 scheme takes full advantage of the research results of secret sharing and is conceptually simple. In particular, we can construct access-structure distributed OT_n^1 scheme (Γ-OT_n^k).

For applications, we present a method of transforming any single-database PIR protocol into a symmetric PIR (SPIR) protocol with only one extra unit of communication cost. As SPIR is equivalent to OT_n^1, this transformation provides a reduction from PIR to OT_n^1 with almost no extra communication cost. In particular, any computational PIR [27], in which the receiver's choice is computationally private, with efficient communication complexity can be transformed to an OT_n^1 scheme (with R's choice is computationally secure) with almost the same efficiency for communication complexity. Some communication-efficient single-database PIR schemes have been proposed [14,27].

1.1   Previous Work and Comparison

Oblivious transfer has been studied in various flavors and security models extensively (cf. [2,5,8,10,12,18,22,28,32,34,36]). In particular, bit OT_2^1 (where m_1 and m_2 are only one bit) attracts much attention from researchers since it is the basis oblivious transfer scheme to which string OT_2^1 and OT_n^1 schemes are reduced. Most previous oblivious transfer schemes are based on hardness of factoring or quadratic residuosity problems.

The reduction approach is studied in [9,10,12,16,28]. For example, a k-bit string OT_2^1 scheme can be achieved by invoking βk runs of a bit OT_2^1 scheme for some β, $2 \leq \beta \leq 18$, [9,10,12]. In [28], a string OT_n^1 scheme is constructed by invoking $\log_2 n$ runs of a string OT_2^1 scheme.

The generic construction is studied in [1,22,32,34,36,31]. Stern [36] proposes a general construction for OT_n^1 based on the public-key encryption scheme that has some specific properties. The privacy of the receiver's choice of the scheme is computationally secure. The scheme takes $O(\sqrt{\log_2 n})$ rounds if better efficiency for exchanged messages is desired.

Recently, Naor and Pinkas [31] proposes a two-round OT_n^1 scheme that is computationally efficient in amortized analysis, that is, one modular exponentiation per invocation. In comparison, their scheme is indeed more efficient than ours in computation when the scheme is invoked many times. But, the system parameter of their scheme is $O(n)$, while ours is a constant. Furthermore, our protocol can be extended to threshold oblivious transfer easily and used to transfer any PIR protocol into a SPIR protocol without increasing communication complexity. Aiello, etc. [1] proposes a general methodology for constructing a two-round OT_n^1 scheme based on the homomorphic property of a public-key encryption scheme. But, no specific construction is given. Furthermore, in their construction, each receiver need a pair of public and private keys.

Distributed oblivious transfer has been studied in various contents under variant models, such as function evaluation [4] and private information retrieval [23]. Naor and Pinkas [30] identify the important attributes of distributed oblivious transfer. They propose a threshold OT_2^1 scheme such that R and the involved servers need do polynomial evaluation only. For comparison, in our distributed version the receiver and each server need one invocation of our OT_n^1 scheme. Nevertheless, their scheme is only for threshold OT_2^1, not threshold OT_n^1, and comes with cost of privacy and simplicity. For example, a coalition of less than t servers can compute R's choice. One scheme (based on sparse polynomials) is not secure against collusion of R and a single server. Some schemes cannot prevent R from learning linear combination of secrets. Furthermore R cannot contact more than t servers; otherwise, the scheme is not secure. On the contrary, in our scheme R's choice is unconditionally secure against any coalition of the servers.

In some sense, our schemes fall in the category of non-interactive oblivious transfer [5,35], in which R selects a public key and S performs non-interactive oblivious transfer using R's public key. The schemes in [35] are based on the quadratic residuosity assumption. Each R uses a specific Blum integer N that is re-usable by the R. The privacy of R's choice is computationally secure and the privacy of the un-chosen secret is unconditionally secure. The bit OT_2^1 scheme is extended to the bit OT_n^1 scheme. The k-bit string OT_2^1 scheme invokes k runs of the bit OT_2^1 scheme. The number (size) of exchanged messages is not as efficient as ours. For example, if k is close to the security parameter, our k-bit string OT_2^1 scheme exchanges $O(k)$ bits and that of [35] exchanges $O(k^2)$ bits.

Transforming any PIR scheme to a symmetric PIR scheme has been studied in [20,28]. Naor and Pinkas [28] show such a reduction using one call to the base PIR scheme and $\log_2 n$ calls to an OT_2^1 scheme. Crescenzo, etc [20] show a reduction using communication $poly(k)$ times of that of the base PIR scheme, where k is the security parameter. In comparison, our reduction uses only one extra communication cost.

2   1-Out-n Oblivious Transfer

Let $m_1, m_2, \ldots, m_n$ be the secrets of S. We assume that S is honest, that is, it won't send secrets that are not the same as claimed ones, either in content or in order. An OT_n^1 scheme should meet the following requirements:

1. Correctness: if both R and S follow the protocol, R gets m_α after executing the protocol with S, where α is its choice.
2. Receiver's privacy: after executing the protocol with R, S shall not get information about R's choice α.
3. Sender's privacy: after executing the protocol with S, R gets no information about other m_i's or their combinations, $i \neq \alpha$,

We first present a basic scheme that is secure against the curious (passive) receiver and then modify it to be secure against the active receiver.

2.1 OT_n^1 against the Passive Receiver

Let g and h be two generators in G_q of an order-q group, where q is prime. Let $x \in_R X$ denote that x is chosen uniformly and independently from the set X. We assume that the decisional Diffie-Hellman (DDH) problem over G_q is hard. That is, it is not possible to distinguish the following two distribution ensembles with a non-negligible advantage in polynomial time:

- $D = \{D_{G_q}\} = \{(g, g^a, g^b, g^{ab})\}_{G_q}$, where $g \in_R G_q \backslash \{1\}$ and $a, b \in_R Z_q$;
- $R = \{R_{G_q}\} = \{(g, g^a, g^b, g^c)\}_{G_q}$, where $g \in_R G_q \backslash \{1\}$ and $a, b, c \in_R Z_q$.

For simplicity, we omit the security parameter $size(q)$ in the later arguments. Note that the DDH assumption is stronger than the discrete logarithm assumption. Typically, G_q is the set of quadratic residues of Z_p^*, where $p = 2q + 1$ is also prime. Any element in $G_q \backslash \{1\}$ is a generator of G_q.

The system-wide parameters are (g, h, G_q), which can be used by all possible senders and receivers. Assume that the discrete logarithm $\log_g h$ is unknown to all. As long as $\log_g h$ is not revealed, g and h can be used repeatedly. Our OT_n^1 scheme is as follows. Wlog, we assume that the secrets m_i's are all in G_q.

OT_n^1 scheme:

- S's input: $m_1, m_2, \ldots, m_n \in G_q$; R's choice: α, $1 \le \alpha \le n$;
1. R sends $y = g^r h^\alpha$, $r \in_R Z_q$.
2. S sends $c_i = (g^{k_i}, m_i(y/h^i)^{k_i})$, $k_i \in_R Z_q$, $1 \le i \le n$;
3. By $c_\alpha = (a, b)$, R computes $m_\alpha = b/a^r$.

Correctness. Since $c_\alpha = (a, b) = (g^{k_\alpha}, m_\alpha(y/h^\alpha)^{k_\alpha})$, we have

$$b/a^r = m_\alpha(y/h^\alpha)^{k_\alpha}/(g^{k_\alpha})^r = m_\alpha(g^r h^\alpha/h^\alpha)^{k_\alpha}/(g^{k_\alpha})^r = m_\alpha.$$

Efficiency. The scheme takes only two rounds. This is optimal since at least R has to choose α and let S know, and S has to respond to R's request. R sends one message y to S and S sends n messages c_i, $1 \le i \le n$, to R. This is also optimal (within a constant factor of 2) by the argument for the lower bound $\Omega(n)$ of communication cost of the single-database PIR when R's choice is unconditionally secure [15].

For computation, R need do 2 modular exponentiations for y and m_α. Straightforwardly, S need do $2n$ modular exponentiations for c_i, $1 \le i \le n$. We can reduce the computation by using the fast exponentiation methods. Let $l = \lfloor \log_2 q \rfloor$. S can pre-compute g^{2^j} and h^{-2^j}, $1 \le j \le l$. When y is received, S computes y^{2^j}, $1 \le j \le l$. Then, S chooses k_i, $1 \le i \le n$, and computes c_i by multiplying appropriate g^{2^j}, h^{-2^j}, and y^{2^j}, $1 \le j \le l$.

Security. The above OT_n^1 scheme has the properties that the choice α of R is unconditionally secure and R gets no information about any other m_i, $i \ne \alpha$, if the DDH problem is hard.

Theorem 1. *For the OT_n^1 scheme, the choice α of R is unconditionally secure.*

Proof. For any α', there is r' that satisfies $y = g^{r'} h^{\alpha'}$. Therefore, S cannot get any information about R's α even if it has unlimited computing power.   □

Theorem 2. *For the OT_n^1 scheme, if R follows the protocol, it gets no information about m_i, $1 \le i \ne \alpha \le n$, assuming that the DDH problem is hard. That is, all c_i's, $1 \le i \ne \alpha \le n$, are computationally indistinguishable from a random $z = (g, h, a, b)$, $g, h \in_R G_q \backslash \{1\}$, $a, b \in_R G_q$, even if R knows the r and α in $y = g^r h^\alpha$.*

Proof. Since the DDH assumption is stronger than the DL assumption, R cannot compute two different pairs of (r, α) and (r', α') that both satisfy $y = g^r h^\alpha = g^{r'} h^{\alpha'}$. Otherwise, R computes $\log_g h = (r' - r)/(\alpha - \alpha')$. Therefore, R cannot get two secrets.

We show that c_i, $i \ne \alpha$, looks random assuming that the DDH problem is hard. Formally, we define the random variable of c_i as

$$C_i = (g, h, g^{k_i}, m_i(g^r h^{\alpha-i})^{k_i})$$

where $k_i \in_R Z_q$, $g, h \in_R G_q \backslash \{1\}$. Note that we treat g and h as random variables in C_i. Let $Z = (r_1, r_2, r_3, r_4)$, where $r_1, r_2 \in_R G_q \backslash \{1\}$ and $r_3, r_4 \in_R G_q$. We show that if C_i and Z are computationally distinguishable by distinguisher $\mathcal{A}$, D and R of the DDH problem are computationally distinguishable by the following $\mathcal{A}'$, which uses $\mathcal{A}$ as a procedure:

- Input: (g, u, v, w); (which is either from R or D)
1. If $u = 1$ then output 1;
2. Randomly select $r \in Z_q$;
3. If $\mathcal{A}(g, u, v, m_i v^r w^{\alpha-i}) = 1$ then output 1 else output 0.

We can see that if $(g, u, v, w) = (g, g^a, g^b, g^{ab})$ is from D and $a \neq 0$,

$$(g, u, v, m_i v^r w^{\alpha-i}) = (g, h, g^b, m_i(g^r h^{\alpha-i})^b)$$

has the right form for C_i, where $h = u$. If $(g, u, v, w) = (g, g^a, g^b, g^c)$ is from R and $a \neq 0$,

$$(g, u, v, m_i v^r w^{\alpha-i}) = (g, h, g^b, m_i g^{br+c(\alpha-i)})$$

is uniformly distributed over $G_q \backslash \{1\} \times G_q \backslash \{1\} \times G_q \times G_q$, which is Z. Therefore, if $\mathcal{A}$ distinguishes C_i and Z with a non-negligible advantage ϵ, $\mathcal{A}'$ distinguishes R and D with an advantage $\epsilon \cdot (1 - 1/q) + 1/q$, where $1/q$ is the offset probability in Step 1. □

2.2   Without System-Wide Parameters

We can remove the requirement of using system-wide parameters (g, h, G_q). Now, S first chooses g, h and G_q, and sends them to R, that is, the following step is added to the scheme.

> 0. S chooses (g, h, G_q) and sends them to R, where $g, h \in_R G_q \backslash \{1\}$.

When R receives (g, h, G_q), it need check that q is prime, $g \neq 1$ and $h \neq 1$. Otherwise, if S chooses a non-prime q and g and h of small orders, it can get information about R's choice. Even if S knows $\log_g h$, R's choice α is still unconditionally secure.

2.3 OT_n^1 against the Active Receiver

R may compute y of some special form such that it can compute combined information of the secrets. We don't know whether such y exists. To prevent this attack, we can require R to send a non-interactive zero-knowledge proof of knowledge of r and α that satisfy $y = g^r h^\alpha$, denoted by NI-ZKIP(g, h, y). The new step 1 of the OT_n^1 scheme becomes:

> $1'$. R sends $y = g^r h^\alpha$ and $\beta = $ NI-ZKIP(g, h, y), where $r \in_R Z_q$.

In this case, S should check validity of NI-ZKIP(g, h, y) in Step 2. If the check fails, S aborts the protocol. In fact, this modification results in a very secure OT_n^1 scheme. We shall discuss this in Section 7.

We can apply the technique in [31] so that the protocol is secure against the active R under the random oracle model, in which a one-way hash function is assumed to be a random function. Let H be a one-way hash function. We modify the steps 2 and 3 as:

2' S sends $c_i = (g^{k_i}, m_i \oplus H((y/h^i)^{k_i}, i))$, $k_i \in_R Z_q$, $1 \le i \le n$;

3' By $c_\alpha = (a, b)$, R computes $m_\alpha = b \oplus H(a^r, \alpha)$.

Theorem 3. *The sender's privacy of the OT_n^1 scheme, consisting of steps 1', 2' and 3', is secure against the active receiver under the random oracle model.*

Proof. In the random oracle model, the receiver has to know the whole information $(y/h^i)^{k_i}$ in order to get $H((y/h^i)^{k_i}, i)$. Nevertheless, computing computing k_i from g^{k_i} is to solve the discrete logarithm problem, which is computationally hard. □

3 k-Out-n Oblivious Transfer

We can have k parallel runs of the OT_n^1 scheme to obtain an efficient OT_n^k scheme, which takes only two rounds.

OT_n^k scheme:

- S's input: $m_1, m_2, \ldots, m_n$; R's choice: $\alpha_1, \alpha_2, \ldots, \alpha_k$, where $1 \le \alpha_i \le n$, $1 \le i \le k$;
1. R sends $y_l = g^{r_l} h^{\alpha_l}$, $r_l \in_R Z_q$, $1 \le l \le k$.
2. S sends $c_{i,l} = (g^{k_{i,l}}, m_i(y_l/h^i)^{k_{i,l}})$, $k_{i,l} \in_R Z_q$, $1 \le l \le k$, $1 \le i \le n$;
3. By $c_{\alpha_l, l} = (a, b)$, R computes $m_{\alpha_l} = b/a^{r_l}$. $1 \le l \le k$.

We can show that the OT_n^k scheme has the same correctness and security properties as those of the OT_n^1 scheme.

4 Threshold Oblivious Transfer

For a threshold t-out-of-p OT_n^1 (or (t, p)-OT_n^1) scheme, there are three types of parties: one sender S, p servers $S_1, S_2, \ldots, S_p$, and one receiver R. S has n secrets $m_1, m_2, \ldots, m_n$. It computes shares $m_{i,j}$, $1 \le j \le p$, of m_i, $1 \le i \le n$, and distributed shares $m_{i,j}$, $1 \le i \le n$, to server S_j, $1 \le j \le p$. Then, R chooses α, $1 \le \alpha \le n$, and contacts with any t or more servers to get information about the shares. We assume a mechanism, such as the broadcast channel, for ensuring that R contacts severs with the same request. By the received information, R should be able to compute m_α and no others.

By [30], a (t, p)-OT_n^1 scheme should meet the following requirements:

1. Correctness: if R and servers follow the protocol and R receives information from t or more servers, R can compute one m_α, where α is its choice.

2. Sender's privacy: even if R receives information from t or more servers, it gains no information about any other m_i, $1 \leq i \neq \alpha \leq n$. Furthermore, if R receives information from less than t servers, it gains no information about any m_i, $1 \leq i \leq n$.
3. Receiver's privacy: there is a threshold t', $t' \geq 1$, such that no coalition of less than t' servers can gain any information about the choice α of R. The threshold t' should be as large as possible.
4. Security against receiver-server collusion: after R gets m_α, there is a threshold t'', $1 \leq t'' \leq t$, such that no coalition of less than t'' servers and R can gain any information about any other m_i, $1 \leq i \neq \alpha \leq n$. The threshold t'' should be as close to t as possible.

By the OT_n^1 scheme in Section 2, we can easily construct a threshold (t, p)-OT_n^1 scheme. Our scheme can make use of any threshold secret sharing scheme. Our (t, p)-OT_n^1 scheme achieves $t' = \infty$ and $t'' = t$. Both are optimal.

We construct our (t, p)-OT_n^1 scheme using the standard (t, p)-secret-sharing scheme. Let m_i be shared by the servers via polynomial $f_i(x)$ of degree t-1 such that $f_i(0) = m_i$, $1 \leq i \leq n$. Each server S_j, $1 \leq j \leq p$, holds the shares $m_{i,j} = f_i(j)$, $1 \leq i \leq n$. By contacting t servers, R can compute t shares of $m_{\alpha,j}$'s and construct m_α, where α is R's choice. Our (t, p)-OT_n^1 scheme is as follows.

$(\mathbf{t}, \mathbf{p}) - \mathbf{OT_n^1}$ scheme:

– S_j's input: $m_{1,j}, m_{2,j}, \ldots, m_{n,j}$; R's choice: α, $1 \leq \alpha \leq n$;
1. R sends $y = g^r h^\alpha$ to t different servers $S_{j_1}, S_{j_2}, \ldots, S_{j_t}$, $r \in Z_q$;
2. Each S_{j_l}, $1 \leq l \leq t$, sends $c_{i,j_l} = (g^{k_{i,j_l}}, m_{i,j_l}(y/h^i)^{k_{i,j_l}})$, $1 \leq i \leq n$, to R;
3. By $c_{\alpha,j_l} = (a_{j_l}, b_{j_l})$, R computes shares $m_{\alpha,j_l} = b_{j_l}/a_{j_l}^r$, $1 \leq l \leq t$. Then, R interpolates these t shares to get

$$m_\alpha = \sum_{l=1}^{t} m_{\alpha,j_l} \left(\prod_{1 \leq d \neq l \leq t} \frac{j_d}{j_d - j_l} \right)$$

by Lagrange's interpolation method.

Correctness. If R contacts with t or more servers, it can compute t shares m_{α,j_l} of m_α, $1 \leq l \leq t$. Therefore, it can compute m_α as shown in the scheme.

Efficiency. The scheme takes only two rounds. This is optimal, again. R sends one message y to t servers and each contacted server S_j responds with n messages $c_{i,j}$, $1 \leq i \leq n$. For computation, R need do $t + 1$ modular exponentiations for y and t shares m_{α,j_l}, $1 \leq l \leq t$, and one Lagrange interpolation for m_α. Each contacted server S_j need do $2n$ modular exponentiations for $c_{i,j}$, $1 \leq i \leq n$.

Security. Our (t, p)-OT_n^1 scheme has the following security properties:

1. Sender's privacy: if R contacts with t or more servers, the privacy of m_i, $1 \leq i \neq \alpha \leq n$, is at least as strong as the hardness of the DDH problem. (The

proof is similar to that of Theorem 2.) Furthermore, if R gets information from less than t servers, R cannot compute information about any m_i, $1 \le i \le n$. This is guaranteed by the polynomial secret sharing scheme we use.

2. Receiver's privacy is unconditionally secure. Since for any α', there is r' that satisfies $y = g^{r'}h^{\alpha'}$. Even if the servers have unlimited computing power, they cannot compute R's choice α.

3. It is secure against collusion of R and t-1 servers $S_{r_1}, S_{r_2}, \ldots, S_{r_{t-1}}$, assuming the hardness of the DDH problem. Since for R and $S_{r_l}, 1 \le l \le t-1$, the privacy of shares $m_{i,j}$, $i \ne \alpha$, $j \ne r_1, r_2, \ldots, r_{t-1}$, is at least as strong as the hardness of the DDH problem, R and these t-1 servers cannot compute any information about other secrets m_i, $1 \le i \ne \alpha \le n$.

4.1 (t, p)-OT_n^k Scheme

We can extend the (t,p)-OT_n^1 scheme to a (t,p)-OT_n^k scheme easily. This is done by executing k parallel runs of the (t,p)-OT_n^1 scheme, similar to the OT_n^k scheme in Section 4.

4.2 (p, p)-OT_n^1 Scheme

For (p,p)-OT_n^1, we can use $m_i = m_{i,1}m_{i,2}\cdots m_{i,p}$ to share m_i. Then, R can compute $m_\alpha = (b_1 b_2 \cdots b_p)/(a_1 a_2 \cdots a_p)^r$. It need do $2p-1$ modular multiplications and one modular exponentiations.

4.3 Verifiable (t, p)-OT_n^k Scheme

We can combine Feldman's or Peterson's verifiable secret sharing scheme and our OT_n^k scheme to form a verifiable (t,p)-OT_n^k scheme. In this case, the sender S, who has all m_i's, publishes the verification values for m_i's. Typically, the verification values for the shares of m_i are $g^{a_0}, g^{a_1}, \ldots, g^{a_{t-1}}$, where m_i is shared via a degree-$(t$-1$)$ polynomial $f_i(x) = m_i + a_1 x + a_2 x^2 + \cdots + a_{t-1}x^{t-1}$. After computing m_{α,j_l}, $1 \le l \le t$, R can verify these shares using the verification values published by S.

5 Access-Structure Oblivious Transfer

Let $\Gamma = \{\gamma_1, \gamma_2, \ldots, \gamma_z\}$ be a monotonic access structure over p servers $S_1, S_2, \ldots, S_p$. Each $\gamma_i = \{S_{i_1}, S_{i_2}, \ldots, S_{i_l}\}$ is an authorized set of servers such that all servers in γ_i together can construct the shared secret. Assume that n messages $m_1, m_2, \ldots, m_n$ are shared according to Γ by some secret sharing scheme $\mathcal{S}$ such that $\mathcal{S}(\gamma) = (m_1, m_2, \ldots, m_n)$ if and only if $\gamma \in \Gamma$, where $\mathcal{S}(\gamma)$ means that $\mathcal{S}$ computes shared secrets from shares of the servers in γ.

We define Γ-OT_n^1 such that R can get the secret m_α from the servers in an authorized set $\gamma \in \Gamma$, where α is R's choice. The requirements for a satisfactory Γ-OT_n^1 are the same as those for the threshold OT_n^1 schemes in Section 4.

We can combine our OT_n^1 scheme and a general secret sharing scheme $\mathcal{S}$ to form a Γ-OT_n^1 scheme as follows.

1. Let S_j obtain a share $m_{i,j}$ of m_i by the secret sharing scheme S, $1 \leq i \leq n$.
2. Let γ be an authorized set that R contacts its servers to obtain m_α. When R contacts $S_j \in \gamma$ with $y = g^r h^\alpha$, S_j responds with $c_{i,j} = (g^{k_{i,j}}, m_{i,j}(y/h^i)^{k_{i,j}})$, $1 \leq i \leq n$.
3. R computes $m_{\alpha,j}$ for each $S_j \in \gamma$ and applies $S(\gamma)$ to compute m_α.

The above $\Gamma\text{-}OT_n^1$ scheme meets the requirements. This can be proved by the same arguments for the threshold oblivious transfer schemes in Section 4. We omit them here.

6   Applications

Efficient string OT_n^1 schemes can improve practical efficiency of the schemes in which oblivious transfer is used. One primary application is for private information retrieval (PIR), in which the user (U) wants to query one data block from a database, but U does not want the database manager (DBM) to know which data block he is interested in [15]. The regular PIR does not restrict U to obtain only one data block of the database. We consider the symmetric PIR (SPIR), in which DBM does not want to release more than one data block [23]. Assume that the database has n data blocks m_i's, each is in G_q. The following steps achieve SPIR. U wants to obtain m_α.

1. U sends $y = g^r h^\alpha$ to DBM;
2. DBM computes $c_i = (g^{k_i}, m_i(y/h^i)^{k_i})$, $1 \leq i \leq n$;
3. Now, DBM treats c_i's as its data blocks. DBM and U perform a regular PIR protocol so that U obtains c_α.
4. U computes $m_\alpha = b/a^r$, where $c_\alpha = (a, b)$.

This method transforms any single-database PIR scheme into a single-database SPIR scheme with only an extra unit of communication cost in step 1. If U's choice α of the base PIR scheme in Step 3 is computationally private, the transformed SPIR scheme's user privacy is computationally secure. On the other hand, if the base PIR scheme is unconditionally secure, the user's choice of the transformed SPIR is unconditionally private.

The transformed SPIR scheme uses at most one more round than that of the base PIR scheme. The reason is that the fist step may be combined with the first step of the base PIR in step 3.

Theorem 4. *If there exists a single-database PIR scheme with computation complexity $t(n)$, communication complexity $c(n)$ and round complexity $r(n)$, there exists an OT_n^1 scheme with computation complexity $t(n) +$ (2n modular exponentiations), communication complexity $c(n) + 1$ and round complexity $r(n) + 1$, but with the additional assumption of hardness of the DDH problem.*

7   Further Security

Naor and Pinkas [28] give a very formal definition for security of OT_n^1 oblivious transfer:

1. Receiver's privacy – indistinguishability: S's views of R's different choices α and α', $\alpha \neq \alpha'$, are computationally indistinguishable.
2. Sender's privacy – compared with Ideal Model: The Ideal Model is that there is a trusted third party (TTP) that gets S's secrets $m_1, m_2, \ldots, m_n$ and R's choice α and gives m_α to R. Sender's secrecy is that for every probabilistic poly-time substitute R' for R, there is a corresponding R'' in the Ideal Model such that the outputs of R' and R'' are computationally indistinguishable.

The modified OT_n^1 scheme, consisting of Steps 1', 2 and 3, in Section 2.3 meets both requirements.

Theorem 5. *The modified OT_n^1 scheme, consisting of Steps 1', 2 and 3, in Section 2.3 meets both the requirements of Receiver's privacy and Sender's privacy above.*

Proof. Since R's choice is unconditionally secure, the scheme meets the requirement of Receiver's privacy.

For each probabilistic polynomial-time adversary R', substituting for R, in the real run, we can construct a corresponding R'' (in the Ideal Model) whose output is computationally indistinguishable from that of R' as follows. R'' uses R' as a *re-settable* subroutine. When R' sends y and $\beta = \text{NI-ZKIP}(g, h, y)$ to S, R'' simulates R' to get α in a re-settable way with an overwhelming probability. If β is not legal or the simulation fails to produce α, TTP outputs $\perp$ (*abort*). The probability of TTP outputting $\perp$ is almost equal to that of S outputting $\perp$. After obtaining α, R'' sends α to TTP and gets m_α. R'' sets $c_\alpha = (g^k, m_\alpha(y/h^\alpha)^k)$ and $c_i = (a_i, b_i)$ for $1 \leq i \neq \alpha \leq n$, $a_i, b_i \in_R G_q$, and outputs the simulation result of R' on $c_1, c_2, \ldots, c_n$. The output of R'' is computationally indistinguishable from that of R'. If there is a claim that R' gets information about $m_{\alpha'}$, $\alpha' \neq \alpha$. We can use R' to solve the DDH problem by manipulating its input c_i's, which is similar to the proof of Theorem 2. Therefore, the scheme meets the requirement of Sender's privacy. $\square$

8   Conclusion

We have presented an efficient (string) OT_n^1 scheme and extended it to construct threshold, access-structure and verifiable OT_n^k schemes for any $n \geq 2$ and $1 \leq k \leq n$. We also present its application on private information retrieval. It is interesting to find more applications of this construction.

References

1. B. Aiello, Y. Ishai, O. Reingold, "Priced oblivious transfer: how to sell digital goods," *In Proceedings of Advances in Cryptology - Eurocrypt 01*, Lecture Notes in Computer Science 2045, pp.119-135, Springer-Verlag, 2001.

2. D. Beaver, "How to break a 'secure' oblivious transfer protocols," *In Proceedings of Advances in Cryptology - Eurocrypt 92*, Lecture Notes in Computer Science 658, pp.285-196, Springer-Verlag, 1993.
3. D. Beaver, "Equivocable oblivious transfer," *In Proceedings of Advances in Cryptology - Eurocrypt 96*, Lecture Notes in Computer Science 1070, pp.119-130, Springer-Verlag, 1996.
4. D. Beaver, J. Feigenbaum, J. Kilian,P. Rogaway, "Locally random reductions: improvements and applications," *Journal of Cryptology* 10(1), pp.17-36, 1997.
5. M. Bellare, S. Micali, "Non-interactive oblivious transfer," *In Proceedings of Advances in Cryptology - Crypto 89*, Lecture Notes in Computer Science 435, pp.547-557, Springer-Verlag, 1990.
6. M. Ben-Or, S. Goldwasser, A. Wigderson, "Completeness theorems for non-cryptographic fault-tolerant distributed computation", *In Proceedings of the 20th ACM Symposium on the Theory of Computing*, pp.1-10, 1988.
7. R. Berger, R. Peralta, T. Tedrick, "A provably secure oblivious transfer protocol," *In Proceedings of Advances in Cryptology - Eurocrypt 84*, Lecture Notes in Computer Science 209, pp.379-386, Springer-Verlag, 1985.
8. B. den Boer, "Oblivious transfer protecting secrecy," *In Proceedings of Advances in Cryptology - Eurocrypt 90*, Lecture Notes in Computer Science 473, pp.31-45, Springer-Verlag, 1991.
9. G. Brassard, C. Crépeau, "Oblivious transfers and privacy amplification," *In Proceedings of Advances in Cryptology - Eurocrypt 97*, Lecture Notes in Computer Science 1233, pp.334-346, Springer-Verlag, 1997.
10. G. Brassard, C. Crépeau, J.-M. Robert, "Information theoretic reduction among disclosure problems," *In Proceedings of the 27th IEEE Symposium on Foundations of Computer Science*, pp.168-173, 1986.
11. G. Brassard, C. Crépeau, J.-M. Robert, "All-or-nothing disclosure of secrets," *In Proceedings of Advances in Cryptology - Crypto 86*, Lecture Notes in Computer Science 263, pp.234-238, Springer-Verlag, 1987.
12. G. Brassard, C. Crépeau, M. Santha, "Oblivious transfer and intersecting codes," *IEEE Transactions on Information Theory* 42(6), pp.1769-1780, 1996.
13. C. Cachin, "On the foundations of oblivious transfer," *In Proceedings of Advances in Cryptology - Eurocrypt 98*, Lecture Notes in Computer Science 1403, pp.361-374, Springer-Verlag, 1998.
14. C. Cachin, S.Micali, M. Stadler, "Computationally private informational retrieval with polylogarithmic communication," *In Proceedings of Advances in Cryptology - Eurocrypt 99*, Lecture Notes in Computer Science 1592, pp.402-414, Springer-Verlag, 1999.
15. B. Chor, O. Goldreich, E. Kushilevitz, M. Sudan, "Private information retrieval," *Journal of the ACM* 45(6), pp.965-982, 1998.
16. C. Crépeau, "Equivalence between two flavors of oblivious transfers," *In Proceedings of Advances in Cryptology - Crypto 87*, Lecture Notes in Computer Science 293, pp.350-354, Springer-Verlag, 1988.
17. C. Crépeau, "Verifiable disclosure of secrets and application", *In Proceedings of Advances in Cryptology - Eurocrypt 89*, Lecture Notes in Computer Science 434, pp.150-154, Springer-Verlag, 1990.
18. C. Crépeau, J. van de Graff, A. Tapp, "Committed oblivious transfer and private multi-party computations," *In Proceedings of Advances in Cryptology - Crypto 95*, Lecture Notes in Computer Science 963, pp.110-123, Springer-Verlag, 1995.

19. C. Crépeau, J. Kilian, "Achieving oblivious transfer using weakened security assumptions," *In Proceedings of the 29th IEEE Symposium on Foundations of Computer Science*, pp.42-52, 1988.
20. G.Di Crescenzo, T. Malkin, R. Ostrovsky, "Single database private information retrieval implies oblivious transfer," *In Proceedings of Advances in Cryptology - Eurocrypt 00*, Lecture Notes in Computer Science , pp.122-138, Springer-Verlag, 2000.
21. T. ElGamal, "A public-key cryptosystem and a signature scheme based on discrete logarithms," *IEEE Transactions on Information Theory* 31(4), pp.469-472, 1985.
22. S. Even, O. Goldreich, A. Lempel, "A randomized protocol for signing contracts," *Communications of the ACM* 28, pp.637-647, 1985.
23. Y. Gertner, Y. Ishai, E. Kushilevitz, T. Malkin, "Protecting data privacy in private data retrieval schemes," *In Proceedings of the 30th ACM Symposium on Theory of Computing*, pp.151-160, 1998.
24. O. Goldreich, R. Vainish, "How to solve any protocol problem: an efficient improvement," *In Proceedings of Advances in Cryptology - Crypto 87*, Lecture Notes in Computer Science 293, pp.73-86, Springer-Verlag, 1988.
25. D.M. Gordon, "A survey of fast exponentiation methods", *Journal of Algorithms* 27(1), pp.129-146, 1998.
26. J. Kilian, "Founding cryptography on oblivious transfer," *In Proceedings of the 20th ACM Symposium on Theory of Computing*, pp.20-31, 1988.
27. E. Kushilevitz, R. Ostrovsky, "Replication is not needed: single database, computationally-private informational retrieval," *In Proceedings of the 38th IEEE Symposium on Foundations of Computer Science*, pp.364-373, 1997.
28. M. Naor, B. Pinkas, "Oblivious transfer and polynomial evaluation," *In Proceedings of the 31st ACM Symposium on Theory of Computing*, pp.145-254, 1999.
29. M. Naor, B. Pinkas, "Oblivious transfer with adaptive queries," *In Proceedings of Advances in Cryptology - Crypto 99*, Lecture Notes in Computer Science 1666, pp.573-590, Springer-Verlag, 1999.
30. M. Naor, B. Pinkas, "Distributed oblivious transfer," *In Proceedings of Advances in Cryptology - Asiacrypt 00*, Lecture Notes in Computer Science 1976, pp.205-219, Springer-Verlag, 2000.
31. M. Naor, B. Pinkas, "Efficient oblivious transfer protocols," *In Proceedings of 12th Annual Symposium on Discrete Algorithms (SODA)* , pp.448-457, 2001.
32. V. Niemi, A.Renvall, "Cryptographic protocols and voting," *In Result and Trends in Theoretical Computer Science*, Lecture Notes in Computer Science 812, pp.307-316, 1994.
33. M. Rabin, "How to exchange secrets by oblivious transfer," Technical Report TR-81, Aiken Computation Laboratory, Harvard University, 1981.
34. A. Salomaa, L. Santean, "Secret selling of secrets with several buyers," *In the 42nd EATCS Bulletin*, pp.178-186, 1990.
35. A. De Santis, G. Persiano, "Public-randomness in public-key cryptography," *In Proceedings of Advances in Cryptology - Eurocrypt 90*, Lecture Notes in Computer Science 473, pp.46-62, Springer-Verlag, 1991.
36. J.P. Stern, "A new and efficient all-or-nothing disclosure of secrets protocol," *In Proceedings of Advances in Cryptology - Asiacrypt 98*, Lecture Notes in Computer Science 1514, pp.357-371, Springer-Verlag, 1998.

Linear Code Implies Public-Key Traitor Tracing

Kaoru Kurosawa[1] and Takuya Yoshida[2]

[1] Department of Computer and Information Sciences,
Ibaraki University, Japan
kurosawa@cis.ibaraki.ac.jp
[2] Department of Communications and Integrated Systems,
Tokyo Institute of Technology, Japan
takuya@crypt.ss.titech.ac.jp

Abstract. In this paper, we first show that three public-key (k, n)-traceability schemes can be derived from an $[n, u, d]$-linear code $\mathcal{C}$ such that $d \geq 2k + 1$. The previous schemes are obtained as special cases. This observation gives a more freedom and a new insight to this field. For example, we show that Boneh-Franklin scheme is equivalent to a slight modification of the corrected Kurosawa-Desmedt scheme. This means that BF scheme is redundant or overdesigned because the modified KD scheme is much simpler. It is also shown that the corrected KD scheme is the best among them.

1 Introduction

In such applications as pay TV, CD-ROM distribution and online databases, data should only be available to authorized users. To prevent unauthorized users from accessing data, the data supplier will encrypt data and provide only the authorized users with personal keys to decrypt it. However, some authorized users (*traitors*) may create a pirate decoder.

A (k, n)-traceability scheme is a scheme in which at least one traitor is detected from a confiscated pirate decoder if there are at most k traitors among n authorized users. Chor, Fiat and Naor [4] introduced the first (k, n)-traceability scheme. Their scheme is, however, non-constructive. Stinson and Wei showed some explicit constructions by using combinatorial designs [10]. In the above two schemes, a private-key encryption scheme is used to encrypt a session key.

On the other hand, the first public-key (k, n)-traceability scheme was shown by Kurosawa and Desmedt [6, Sec.5]. That is, anyone can broadcast encrypted data to authorized users. Although Shamir's $(k + 1, n)$-threshold secret sharing scheme was used in their original scheme, we should use Shamir's $(2k - 1, n)$-threshold secret sharing scheme to avoid a linear attack given by [10]. We call such a corrected scheme the corrected KD scheme.

After that, Boneh and Franklin presented another public-key (k,n)-traceability scheme [2]. Only the above two schemes are known as public-key (k,n)-traceability schemes currently.

In this paper, we first show that three public-key (k, n)-traceability schemes can be derived from an $[n, u, d]$-linear code $\mathcal{C}$ such that $d \geq 2k + 1$. We call

D. Naccache and P. Paillier (Eds.): PKC 2002, LNCS 2274, pp. 172–187, 2002.

them linear coded KD scheme (LC-KD scheme), linear coded BF scheme (LC-BF scheme) and linear coded KD' scheme (LC-KD' scheme), respectively. The previous schemes are obtained as special cases. This observation gives a more freedom and a new insight to the study of this field.

For example, we show that Boneh-Franklin scheme (BF scheme) is equivalent to a slight modification of the corrected KD scheme. (We call it modified KD scheme. It will be given in Sec.5.3.) This means that BF scheme is redundant or overdesigned because modified KD scheme is much simpler. Indeed, BF scheme must use a public code matrix Γ and $2k$ additional secret random numbers $\beta_1, \cdots, \beta_{2k}$ which modified KD scheme does not require. More generally, we prove the equivalence between LC-BF scheme and LC-KD' scheme.

We also show that LC-KD scheme is better than LC-KD' scheme from a view point of key generation. This implies that the corrected KD scheme is better than modified KD scheme from a view point of key generation. Since modified KD scheme is better than BF scheme as shown above, we see that the corrected KD scheme is the best among them.

We finally prove the secrecy and the black box traceability of LC-KD scheme under the decision Deffie-Hellman assumption. Those of LC-KD' scheme and LC-BF scheme are proved similarly. The tracing algorithm of BF scheme for any pirate decoder is obtained as a special case. (It is not written clearly in the original paper [2]. It is not written at all in their latest version [3].)

Generalized Scheme	Original Scheme
LC-KD scheme	corrected KD scheme
LC-KD' scheme	modified KD scheme
LC-BF scheme	BF scheme

2   Preliminaries

2.1   Notation

An $[n, u, d]$-linear code is a linear code of length n, dimension u and the minimum Hamming distance d.

Let $q > n$ be a prime. Let G_q be a group of prime order q. Let $g \in G_q$ be a generator of G_q. For example, G_q is a subgroup of Z_p^* of order q, where $q \mid p - 1$. Alternatively, we can use an elliptic curve over a finite field.

· denotes the inner product of two vectors over $GF(q)$.

2.2   DDH Assumption

The decision Diffie-Hellman assumption (DDH) assumption says that no polynomial statistical test can distinguish with non negligible advantage between the two distributions $\mathbf{D} = (g, g^r, y, y^r)$ and $\mathbf{R} = (g, g^r, y, v)$, where g, y, v are chosen at random from G_q and r is chosen at random in Z_q.

2.3   Model of Traitor Tracing

In the model of traceability schemes, there are a data supplier T, a set of n authorized users and a pirate user. Some authorized users are malicious and they are called *traitors*. The traitors create a pirate key e_p. The pirate key is used in a pirate decoder.

Suppose that there are at most k traitors. Then a (k, n)-traceability scheme is a scheme such that at least one traitor is detected from a confiscated pirate decoder. A (k, n)-traceability scheme has four components.

Key Generation: The key generation algorithm $\mathcal{K}$ is a probabilistic polynomial time algorithm that outputs $(e_T, e_1, \cdots, e_n)$ on input 1^l, where l is the security parameter. e_T is the broadcast encryption key of the data supplier T and e_i is the personal decryption key of authorized user i.

T runs $\mathcal{K}$ and sends e_i to authorized user i secretly.

Encryption: The encryption algorithm $\mathcal{E}$ is a probabilistic polynomial time algorithm that takes an encryption key e_T and a session key s to return a header h; we write

$$h \xleftarrow{R} e_T(s).$$

The data m is encrypted by using a secure symmetric encryption function E with the session key s as $E_s(m)$. Finally, T broadcasts $(h, E_s(m))$.

Decryption: Then decryption algorithm $\mathcal{D}$ is a deterministic algorithm that takes the personal decryption key e_i and a header h to return the session key s; we write

$$s \leftarrow e_i(h).$$

Each authorized user i can recover s from h by using his personal key e_i and then decrypt $E_s(m)$ to obtain the data m.

Tracing: T can detect at least one traitor from a pirate key e_p by using a tracing algorithm. We have *black box* traceability if the pirate decoder can only be used as an oracle. That is, the tracing algorithm cannot examine the pirate key e_p. For black box tracing, we shall assume that the pirate decoder is resettable to its initial state, as in [5].

In what follows, a session key s is chosen from G_q.

3   Previous Public-Key (k, n) Traceability Schemes

3.1   Corrected Kurosawa-Desmedt Scheme

Key Generation: The data supplier T chooses a uniformly random polynomial $f(x) = a_0 + a_1 x + \cdots + a_{2k-1} x^{2k-1}$ over $GF(q)$. Then T gives to each authorized user i the personal decryption key $e_i = f(i)$, where $i = 1, 2, \ldots, n$. He next publishes g and $y_0 = g^{a_0}, y_1 = g^{a_1}, \ldots, y_{2k-1} = g^{a_{2k-1}}$ as the public key.

Encryption: For a session key $s \in G_q$, T computes a header as $h = (g^r, sy_0^r, y_1^r, \ldots, y_{2k-1}^r)$, where r is a random number. T broadcasts h.

Decryption: Each user i computes s from h as follows by using $f(i)$.

$$s = U/(g^r)^{f(i)}, \quad \text{where } U = sy_0^r \prod_{j=1}^{2k-1} (y_j^r)^{i^j}.$$

3.2   Boneh-Franklin Scheme

BF scheme makes use of a public code matrix Γ defined as follows. Consider the following $(n - 2k) \times n$ matrix G:

$$G = \begin{pmatrix} 1 & 1 & 1 & \cdots & 1 \\ 1 & 2 & 3 & \cdots & n \\ 1^2 & 2^2 & 3^2 & \cdots & n^2 \\ \vdots & \vdots & \vdots & \ddots & \vdots \\ 1^{n-2k-1} & 2^{n-2k-1} & 3^{n-2k-1} & \cdots & n^{n-2k-1} \end{pmatrix} \pmod{q}$$

Let $w_1, \ldots, w_{2k}$ be a basis of the linear space of vectors satisfying

$$G\mathbf{x} = 0 \bmod q. \tag{1}$$

Viewing these $2k$ vectors as the columns of a matrix, we obtain an $n \times 2k$ matrix Γ:

$$\Gamma = \begin{pmatrix} | & | & | & & | \\ w_1 & w_2 & w_3 & \cdots & w_{2k} \\ | & | & | & & | \end{pmatrix}$$

Define the code as the set of rows of the matrix Γ. Hence, it consists of n codewords each of length $2k$.

Key Generation: For $i = 1, \ldots, 2k$, the data supplier chooses a random $a_i \in Z_q$ and compute $y_i = g^{a_i}$. Then T computes $z = \prod_{i=1}^{2k} y_i^{\beta_i}$ for random $\beta_1, \ldots, \beta_{2k} \in Z_q$ and publishes $z, y_1, \ldots, y_{2k}$ as the public key. The personal decryption key of user i is computed as

$$\theta_i = (\sum_{j=1}^{2k} a_j\beta_j)/(\sum_{j=1}^{2k} a_j\gamma_j) \pmod{q},$$

where $\gamma^{(i)} = (\gamma_1, \ldots, \gamma_{2k}) \in \Gamma$ is the i'th codeword of Γ.

Encryption: For a session key $s \in G_q$, T computes a header as $h = (sz^r, y_1^r, \ldots, y_{2k}^r)$, where r is a random number. T broadcasts h.

Decryption: Each user i computes s from h as follows by using θ_i.

$$s = sz^r/U^{\theta_i}, \quad \text{where } U = \prod_{j=1}^{2k} (y_j^r)^{\gamma_j}.$$

Remark 3.1. In the key generation, $a_1, \cdots, a_{2k}$ must be chosen so that $\sum_{j=1}^{2k} a_j \gamma_j \neq 0 \pmod{q}$ for $i = 1, \cdots, n$. This was overlooked in [2].

4   Linear Code Implies Public-Key Traitor Tracing

This section shows that if there exists an $[n, u, d]$-linear code $\mathcal{C}$ such that $d \geq 2k + 1$, then three public-key (k, n)-traceability schemes are derived. We call them linear coded KD scheme (LC-KD scheme), linear coded BF scheme (LC-BF scheme) and linear coded KD' scheme (LC-KD' scheme), respectively. The corrected KD scheme and the original BF scheme are obtained as special cases.

Let H be a parity check matrix of an $[n, u, d]$-linear code over $GF(q)$ such that $d \geq 2k + 1$. Any $2k$ columns of H are linearly independent because $d \geq 2k + 1$. This property plays a central role in the proof of traceability of our schemes.

We assume that H is publicly known. Note that H is an $(n - u) \times n$ matrix over $GF(q)$. Let the ith column of H be $\mathbf{b}_i = (b_{1,i}, b_{2,i}, \cdots, b_{n-u,i})^T$.

4.1   LC-KD Scheme

Assume that the first row of H is $(1, \cdots, 1)$.

Key Generation: The data supplier T chooses $(a_1, \cdots, a_{n-u})$ uniformly at random Let $(e_1, \cdots, e_n) = (a_1, \cdots, a_{n-u})H$. T gives e_i to authorized user i as the personal decryption key for $i = 1, 2, \ldots, n$. He next publishes $y_1 = g^{a_1}, y_2 = g^{a_2}, \ldots, y_{n-u} = g^{a_{n-u}}$ as the public key.

Encryption: For a session key $s \in G_q$, T computes a header as $h = (g^r, s y_1^r, y_2^r, \ldots, y_{n-u}^r)$, where r is a random number. T broadcasts h.

Decryption: Each user i computes s from h as follows by using e_i.

$$s = U/(g^r)^{e_i}, \text{ where } U = s y_1^r \prod_{j=2}^{n-u} (y_j^r)^{i^j}. \tag{2}$$

The tracing algorithm will be given in Sec.7.

4.2   LC-BF Scheme

Key Generation: The data supplier T chooses $(a_1, \cdots, a_{n-u})$ uniformly at random in such a way that $(a_1, \cdots, a_{n-u}) \cdot \mathbf{b}_i \neq 0$ for $i = 1, \cdots, n$. The personal decryption key of user i is computed as

$$\theta_i = (a_1, \ldots, a_{n-u}) \cdot (\beta_1, \ldots, \beta_{n-u})/(a_1, \ldots, a_{n-u}) \cdot \mathbf{b}_i. \tag{3}$$

Next let $y_i = g^{a_i}$. Then T computes $z = \prod_{i=1}^{n-u} y_i^{\beta_i}$ for random $\beta_1, \ldots, \beta_{n-u} \in Z_q$ and publishes $z, y_1, \ldots, y_{n-u}$ as the public key.

Encryption: For a session key $s \in G_q$, T computes a header as $h = (sz^r, y_1^r, \ldots, y_{n-u}^r)$, where r is a random number. T broadcasts h.

Decryption: Each user i computes s from h as follows by using θ_i.

$$s = sz^r/U^{\theta_i}, \text{ where } U = \prod_{j=1}^{n-u} (y_j^r)^{b_{j,i}}. \tag{4}$$

4.3   LC-KD' Scheme

This is a slight modification of LC-KD scheme.

Key Generation: The data supplier T chooses $(a_1, \cdots, a_{n-u})$ uniformly at random in such a way that $(a_1, \cdots, a_{n-u}) \cdot \mathbf{b}_i \neq 0$ for $i = 1, \cdots, n$. Let $(e_1, \cdots, e_n) = (a_1, \cdots, a_{n-u})H$. (Note that $e_i \neq 0$ for $i = 1, \cdots, n$.) T gives e_i to authorized user i as the personal decryption key for $i = 1, 2, \ldots, n$. He next publishes $y_1 = g^{a_1}, y_2 = g^{a_2}, \ldots, y_{n-u} = g^{a_{n-u}}$ as the public key.

Encryption: For a session key $s \in G_q$, T computes a header as $h = (sg^r, y_1^r, y_2^r, \ldots, y_{n-u}^r)$, where r is a random number. T broadcasts h.

Decryption: Each user i computes s from h as follows.

$$s = sg^r/U^{1/e_i}, \text{ where } U = \prod_{j=1}^{n-u} (y_j^r)^{b_{j,i}}. \tag{5}$$

Remark 4.1. In h, s is multiplied to g^r in LC-KD' scheme while it is multiplied to y_1^r in LC-KD scheme.

5   Relationship with the Original Schemes

5.1   Corrected KD Scheme

Let $\mathcal{C}$ be an $[n, n - 2k, d]$-Reed Solomon code over $GF(q)$, where $d = 2k + 1$. Then it is clear that the corrected KD scheme is obtained from LC-KD scheme as a special case.

5.2   BF Scheme

In BF scheme, note that G (shown in Sec.3.2) is a generator matrix of an $[n, n - 2k, d]$ Reed-Solomon code over $GF(q)$. Further we see that $G \cdot \Gamma = \mathcal{O}$ from eq.(1). Hence Γ^T is a parity check matrix of the Reed-Solomon code $\mathcal{C}$. This implies that the original BF scheme is obtained from LC-BF scheme as a special case.

5.3   Modified KD Scheme

In LC-KD' scheme, let $\mathcal{C}$ be an $[n, n - 2k, d]$-Reed Solomon code over $GF(q)$, where $d = 2k + 1$. Then the following scheme is obtained. We call it modified KD scheme because it is a slight modification of the corrected KD scheme.

Key Generation: The data supplier T chooses a uniformly random polynomial $f(x) = a_0 + a_1 x + \cdots + a_{2k-1} x^{2k-1}$ over $GF(q)$ such that $f(i) \neq 0$ for $i = 1, \cdots, n$. Then T gives $f(i)$ to authorized user i as the personal decryption key for $i = 1, 2, \ldots, n$. He next publishes $y_0 = g^{a_0}, y_1 = g^{a_1}, \ldots, y_{2k-1} = g^{a_{2k-1}}$.

Encryption: For a session key $s \in G_q$, T computes a header as $h = (sg^r, y_0^r, y_1^r, \ldots, y_{2k-1}^r)$, where r is a random number. T broadcasts h.

Decryption: Each user i computes s from h as follows by using $f(i)$.

$$s = sg^r / U^{1/f(i)}, \text{ where } U = \prod_{j=0}^{2k-1} (y_j^r)^{i^j}. \qquad (6)$$

Remark 5.1. In h, s is multiplied to g^r in modified KD scheme while it is multiplied to y_1^r in the corrected KD scheme.

6   Equivalence

6.1   LC-BF Scheme = LC-KD' Scheme

LC-BF scheme is more complicated than LC-KD' scheme because it uses secret random numbers $\beta_1, \cdots, \beta_{n-u}$ which LC-KD' scheme does not use. Nevertheless, we show that they are equivalent. This means that LC-BF scheme is redundant or overdesigned.

Public-key equivalence: In the key generation of LC-BF scheme, let

$$c = \sum_{i=1}^{n-u} a_i \beta_i.$$

For any fixed $(a_1, \cdots, a_{n-u})$, it is easy to see that $\Pr(c \neq 0) = 1 - (1/q)$. Therefore, we assume that $c \neq 0$ in what follows.

The public key of LC-BF scheme is $pk = (z, y_1, \ldots, y_{n-u})$. First since q is a prime and $z \in G_q$, z is a generator of G_q. Next note that

$$z = \prod_{i=1}^{n-u} y_i^{\beta_i} = \prod_{i=1}^{n-u} g^{a_i \beta_i} = z^c.$$

Let $a_i' = a_i/c$. Then we have

$$y_i = g^{a_i} = z^{a_i/c} = z^{a_i'}.$$

Now it is clear that $(a_1, \cdots, a_{n-u}) \cdot \mathbf{b}_i \neq 0$ if and only if $(a'_1, \cdots, a'_{n-u}) \cdot \mathbf{b}_i \neq 0$, where $i = 1, \cdots, n$. Therefore, the public key pk of LC-BF scheme is equivalent to that of LC-KD' scheme.

Header equivalence: Clear.

Decryption equivalence: In LC-BF scheme, from eq.(3), we obtain that

$$1/\theta_i = (a_1, \ldots, a_{n-u}) \cdot \mathbf{b}_i/c = (a'_1, \cdots, a'_{n-u})\mathbf{b}_i.$$

On the other hand, in LC-KD' scheme,

$$e_i = (a_1, \ldots, a_{n-u}) \cdot \mathbf{b}_i.$$

Therefore, $1/\theta_i$ of LC-BF scheme is equivalent to e_i of LC-KD' scheme.

Secrecy equivalence: The same public key and the same header are used in both schemes. Therefore, the secrecy of LC-BF scheme against outside enemies is equivalent to that of LC-KD' scheme.

Traceability equivalence: Suppose that there exists a pirate decoder M_0 for LC-BF scheme which is not (black box) traceable. Then we show that there exists a pirate decoder M_1 for LC-KD' scheme which is not (black box) traceable. Let k traitors be $i_1, \cdots, i_k$ in both schemes.

Consider LC-KD' scheme in which a public key is $pk = (g, y_1, \cdots, y_{n-u})$ and the private key of user i is e_i. From the above equivalence, the same pk is used and the private key of user i is $\theta_i = 1/e_i$ in LC-BF scheme.

From our assumption, there exists an algorithm B which creates an untraceable pirate decoder M_0 from pk and $\theta_{i_1}, \cdots, \theta_{i_k}$ for LC-BF scheme.

Now in LC-KD' scheme, our traitors first create M_0 by running B on input pk and $1/e_{i_1}, \cdots, 1/e_{i_k}$. They then use M_0 as their pirate decoder M_1.

Finally it is easy to show that if there is a tracing algorithm which detects some traitor from M_1, then M_0 is also traceable. This contradicts our assumption. Hence, M_1 is not traceable.

The converse part is proved similarly.

Now we have proved the following theorem.

Theorem 6.1. *LC-BF scheme is equivalent to LC-KD' scheme.*

6.2   BF Scheme = Modified KD Scheme

From Theorem 6.1, we have the following equivalence.

Corollary 6.1. *BF scheme is equivalent to modified KD scheme.*

However, BF scheme is more complicated than the modified KD scheme because it must use a public code matrix Γ and $2k$ additional secret random numbers $\beta_1, \cdots, \beta_{2k}$. This means that BF scheme is redundant or overdesigned.

6.3   Comparison

We compare three schemes, LC-KD scheme, LC-BF scheme and LC-KD' scheme. We have seen that LC-BF scheme is equivalent to LC-KD' scheme, and hence redundant.

Now in LC-KD' scheme, $a_1, \cdots, a_{n-u}$ must be chosen in such a way that $e_i \neq 0$ for $i = 1, \cdots, n$, which LC-KD scheme does not require. This check is very inefficient if n is large. Therefore. LC-KD scheme is better than LC-KD' scheme from a view point of key generation.

Similarly, the corrected KD scheme is better than modified KD scheme from a view point of key generation. Further, modified KD scheme is better than BF scheme as shown in Sec.6.2. As a conclusion, we see that the corrected KD scheme is the best among them.

7   Secrecy and Traceability

In this section, we prove the secrecy and the traceability of LC-KD scheme, LC-KD' scheme and LC-BF scheme.

Note that any $2k$ columns of H are linearly independent because $d \geq 2k + 1$.

7.1   Secrecy of LC-KD Scheme

Theorem 7.1. *LC-KD scheme is indistinguishably secure against chosen plaintext attack under the DDH assumption.*

Proof. Similarly to the proof of [6, Theorem 14], we can show that the secrecy of LC-KD scheme is reduced to that of ElGamal encryption scheme. It is well known that ElGamal encryption scheme is indistinguishably secure against chosen plaintext attack under the DDH assumption. The details will be given in the final paper.

7.2   Black Box Tracing Algorithm for LC-KD Scheme

Let BAD be the set of at most k traitors who created a confiscated pirate decoder. Let A be a subset of at most k users. We first describe a procedure TEST which checks whether $A \cap BAD \neq \emptyset$.

Suppose that $(e_T, e_1, \cdots, e_n)$ is being used as the key. For a random encryption key $e'_T = (a'_1, \cdots, a'_{n-m})$, let the corresponding private decryption keys be $(e'_1, \cdots, e'_n) = (a'_1, \cdots, a'_{n-u})H$. We say that e'_T matches with A if $e'_i = e_i$ for all $i \in A$.

TEST(A)
Step 1. T chooses e'_T which matches A randomly. (We can do this because any $2k$ columns of H are linearly independent.) He chooses a random session key s' and computes an *illegal* header $h' \overset{R}{\leftarrow} e'_T(s')$.

Step 2. T gives h' to the pirate decoder. Let the output of the pirate decoder be s_A.

Output:

$$TEST(A) = \begin{cases} 1 & \text{if } s_A = s' \\ 0 & \text{otherwise} \end{cases}$$

We next describe a procedure $TEST2(A, m)$ which runs $TEST(A)$ m times independently, where m is a sufficiently large positive integer.

TEST2(A, m)
Set *counter* $:= 0$. For $i = 1, 2, \ldots, m$, do
Step 1. Run $TEST(A)$ randomly.
Step 2. Let *counter* $:= counter + TEST(A)$. Reset the pirate decoder.
Output: $TEST2(A, m)$, the final value of *counter*.

We say that a set of users A is *marked* if $TEST2(A, m) = m$. We now present our tracing algorithm.

Black box tracing algorithm
Find a marked set $A = \{i_1, i_2, \ldots, i_k\}$ by exhaustive search. Suppose that $i_1 < i_2 < \cdots < i_k$. For $j = 1, 2, \ldots, k$, do:
Step 1. Let $B := A \setminus \{i_1, i_2, \ldots, i_j\}$. Run $TEST2(B, m)$.
Step 2. Let $m_j = TEST2(B, m)$.
Output: i_j such that $m_{j-1} - m_j$ is the maximum. (If there are more than one such j, choose one of them arbitrarily.) User i_j is a traitor.

Remark 7.1. By testing all the permutations on $\{i_1, i_2, \ldots, i_k\}$ (instead of $i_1 < i_2 < \cdots < i_k$), we can detect all traitors who are active in A. All active traitors are found by applying this process to all marked sets A.

7.3   Validity of Our Tracing Algorithm

We can show the validity of our tracing algorithm by using the following three *test conditions*.

(1) If $A \supseteq BAD$, then $\Pr(TEST(A) = 1)$ is overwhelming.

(2) If $A \cap BAD = \emptyset$, then $\Pr(TEST(A) = 1)$ is negligible.

(3) If $A \cap BAD \neq \emptyset$ and $A \setminus BAD \neq \emptyset$, then for any $i \in A \setminus BAD$,

$$|\Pr(TEST(A) = 1) - \Pr(TEST(A \setminus \{i\}) = 1)|$$

is negligible.

Theorem 7.2. *If the above three conditions are satisfied, then our black box tracing algorithm succeeds with overwhelming probability. That is user i_j is a traitor.*

Proof. If $A \supseteq BAD$, then $TEST2(A, m) = m$ with overwhelming probability from (1). Therefore, there exists at least one marked A. On the other hand, from (2), if $A \cap BAD = \emptyset$, then $TEST2(A, m) \ll m$. This means that if A is marked, then $A \cap BAD \neq \emptyset$.

Now suppose that A is marked. Let $m_0 = m$. It is easy to see that $m_k = 0$. If $m_{j-1} - m_j$ is the maximum, then $m_{j-1} - m_j \geq m/k$. On the other hand, if $j \in A \setminus BAD$, then $m_{j-1} - m_j \ll m/k$ from (3). Therefore, if $m_{j-1} - m_j$ is the maximum, then $i_j \in BAD$.

We finally show that LC-KD scheme satisfies the above three test conditions under the DDH assumption. We assume that a pirate decoder decrypts valid headers with overwhelming probability.

Theorem 7.3 (Test Condition (1)). *In LC-KD scheme, if $A \supseteq BAD$, then* $\Pr(TEST(A) = 1)$ *is overwhelming under the DDH assumption.*

Theorem 7.4 (Test Condition (2)). *In LC-KD scheme, if $A \cap BAD = \emptyset$, then* $\Pr(TEST(A) = 1)$ *is negligible under the DDH assumption.*

Theorem 7.5 (Test Condition (3)). *In LC-KD scheme, if $A \cap BAD \neq \emptyset$ and $A \setminus BAD \neq \emptyset$, then for any $i \in A \setminus BAD$,*

$$|\Pr(TEST(A) = 1) - \Pr(TEST(A \setminus \{i\}) = 1)|$$

is negligible under the DDH assumption.

The proofs will be given in Appendix.

7.4   Secrecy and Traceability of LC-KD' Scheme

The secrecy and the traceability of LC-KD' Scheme are proved similarly.

Theorem 7.6. *LC-KD' scheme is indistinguishably secure against chosen plaintext attack under the DDH assumption.*

Theorem 7.7 (Test Condition (1)). *In LC-KD' scheme, if $A \supseteq BAD$, then* $\Pr(TEST(A) = 1)$ *is overwhelming under the DDH assumption.*

Theorem 7.8 (Test Condition (2)). *In LC-KD' scheme, if $A \cap BAD = \emptyset$, then* $\Pr(TEST(A) = 1)$ *is negligible under the DDH assumption.*

Theorem 7.9 (Test Condition (3)). *In LC-KD' scheme, if $A \cap BAD \neq \emptyset$ and $A \setminus BAD \neq \emptyset$, then for any $i \in A \setminus BAD$,*

$$|\Pr(TEST(A) = 1) - \Pr(TEST(A \setminus \{i\}) = 1)|$$

is negligible under the DDH assumption.

We show the proof of Theorem 7.8 in Appendix. The other theorems are proved similarly to those of LC-KD scheme.

7.5   Secrecy and Traceability of LC-BF Scheme

The secrecy and the traceability of LC-BF Scheme are equivalent to those of LC-KD' scheme as shown in Sec.6.1.

References

1. M. Bellare, A. Boldyreva and S. Micali, "Public-key encryption in a multi-user setting: Security proofs and improvements," *Proceedings of EUROCRYPT 2000*, LNCS 1807, Springer Verlag, pp.259–274, 2000.
2. D. Boneh and M. Franklin, "An efficient public key traitor tracing scheme (Extended Abstract)," *Proceedings of CRYPTO '99*, LNCS 1666, Springer Verlag, pp.338–353, 1999.
3. D. Boneh and M. Franklin, "An efficient public key traitor tracing scheme *(full-version of [2])*," http://crypto.stanford.edu/~dabo/, 2001.
4. B. Chor, A. Fiat, and M. Naor, "Tracing traitors," *Proceedings of CRYPTO '94*, LNCS 839, Springer Verlag, pages 257–270, 1994.
5. B. Chor, A. Fiat, and M. Naor, B. Pinkas, "Tracing traitors," *IEEE Transactions on Information Theory*, Vol.46, No.3, pp.893–910, 2000.
6. K. Kurosawa and Y. Desmedt, "Optimum traitor tracing and asymmetric schemes with arbiter," *Proceedings of EUROCRYPT '98*, LNCS 1403, Springer Verlag, pp.145–157, 1999.
7. M. Naor and O. Reingold, "Number theoretic constructions of efficient pseudo-random functions," *Proceedings of 38th IEEE Symposium on Foundations of Computer Science*, pp.458–467, 1997.
8. M. Stadler, "Publicly verifiable secret sharing," *Proceedings of EUROCRYPT '96*, LNCS 1070, Springer Verlag, pp.190–199, 1996.
9. D. Stinson and R. Wei, "Combinatorial properties and constructions of traceability schemes and frameproof codes," *SIAM Journal on Discrete Mathematics*, Vol.11, No.1, pp.41–53, 1998.
10. D. Stinson and R. Wei, "Key preassigned traceability schemes for broadcast encryption," *Proceedings of SAC'98*, LNCS 1556, Springer Verlag, pp.144–156, 1998.

A   Proof of Theorem 7.3

By extending the result of Stadler [8, in the proof of Proposition 1] and Naor and Reingold [7, lemma 3.2], Bellare et al. proved the following proposition [1].

Proposition A.1. *[1] There is a probabilistic algorithm* Σ *such that on input* g^a, g^b, g^c, Σ *outputs* $g^{b'}, g^{c'}$, *where* b' *is random and*

$$c' = \begin{cases} ab' \bmod p & \text{if } c = ab \bmod p \\ random & \text{if } c \neq ab \bmod p \end{cases}$$

Σ *runs in* $\mathcal{O}(T^{exp})$ *time, where* T^{exp} *is the time needed to perform an exponentiation.*

Now we show that

$$p_0 = |\Pr(P \text{ decrypts valid headers correctly}) - \Pr(TEST(A) = 1)|$$

is negligible for any pirate decoder P.

Suppose that $p_0 \geq \epsilon$ for some nonnegligible probability ϵ. Then we show that there exists a probabilistic polynomial time Turing machine M which can distinguish $\mathbf{D} = (g, g^a, y, y^a)$ and $\mathbf{R} = (g, g^a, y, v)$ with nonnegligible probability, where g, y, v are chosen at random from G_q and a is chosen at random in Z_q.

From our assumption, there is an algorithm B which creates a pirate decoder such that $p_0 \geq \epsilon$ from a public key $pk = (g, y_1, \cdots, y_{2k})$ and the private keys of BAD.

Now on input $d = (g, g'y, y')$, M works as follows.

1. Choose e_i at random for each $i \in A$ and let $e_i' = e_i$ for each $i \in A$.
2. Let $OUT = \{i_1, i_2, \ldots, i_k\}$ be a k-subset of users such that $OUT \cap A = \emptyset$.
3. For $j = 1, 2, \ldots, k$, M runs Σ of Proposition A.1 k times independently on input $d = (g, g', y, y')$. Let the output of Σ be $g^{e_{i_j}}, (g')^{e_{i_j}'}$.
4. Compute $g^{a_1}, g^{a_2}, \ldots, g^{a_{n-u}}$ from $\{g^{e_i} \mid i \in OUT \cup A\}$, where

$$(e_1, \cdots, e_n) = (a_1, \cdots, a_{n-u})H.$$

Each a_i is written as a linear combination of $\{e_i \mid i \in A \cup BAD\}$ because any $2k$ columns of H are linearly independent and $|A \cup BAD| \leq 2k$. Therefore, we can do this.

5. Compute $(g')^{a_1'}, (g')^{a_2'}, \ldots, (g')^{a_{n-u}'}$ from $\{(g')^{e_i'} \mid i \in OUT \cup A\}$, where

$$(e_1', \cdots, e_n') = (a_1', \cdots, a_{n-u}')H.$$

6. Select a random session key s' and compute h' as follows.

$$h' = (g', s'(g')^{a_1'}, (g')^{a_2'}, \ldots, (g')^{a_{n-u}'}).$$

7. Create a pirate decoder P by running B on input a public key $(g, g^{a_1}, g^{a_2}, \ldots, g^{a_{n-u}})$ and the private keys of BAD, $\{e_i \mid i \in BAD\}$.
8. Give h' to the pirate decoder P. Let the output of P be s_A.
9. Finally M outputs 1 if $s_A = s'$ or 0 otherwise.

For $OUT = \{i_1, i_2, \ldots, i_k\}$, it holds that

$$e_{i_j}' = \begin{cases} e_{i_j} \bmod p & \text{if } d \leftarrow \mathbf{D} \\ \text{random} & \text{if } d \leftarrow \mathbf{R}. \end{cases}$$

from Proposition A.1. Therefore, if d is chosen from $\mathbf{D}$, h' is a legal header. On the other hand, if d is chosen from $\mathbf{R}$, h' is an illegal header used in $TEST(A)$. Hence, we have

$$|\Pr(M(d) = 1 \mid d \in \mathbf{D}) - \Pr(M_k(d) = 1 \mid d \in \mathbf{R})|$$
$$= p_0$$
$$\geq \epsilon.$$

from our assumption.

This means that M can distinguish $\mathbf{D}$ and $\mathbf{R}$ with nonnegligible probability.

B   Proof of Theorem 7.4

Suppose that $\Pr(TEST(A) = 1) \geq \epsilon$ for some nonnegligible probability ϵ. Then we show that there exists a probabilistic polynomial time Turing machine M which can distinguish $\mathbf{D} = (g, g^a, y, y^a)$ and $\mathbf{R} = (g, g^a, y, v)$ with nonnegligible probability, where g, y, v are chosen at random from G_q and a is chosen at random in Z_q.

From our assumption, there is an algorithm B which creates a pirate decoder P such that $\Pr(TEST(A) = 1) \geq \epsilon$ from a public key $pk = (g, y_1, \cdots, y_{2k})$ and the private keys of BAD.

Now on input $d = (g, g', y, y')$, M works as follows.

1. Choose $a_2', \ldots, a_{n-u}'$ at random. Let a_1' be such that $g^{a_1'} = y$.
2. Select a random session key s' and compute h' as follows.

$$h' = (g', s'y', y^{a_2'}, y^{a_3'}, \ldots, y^{a_{n-u}'}).$$

3. Compute $g^{e_1'}, g^{e_2'}, \ldots, g^{e_n'}$ from $g^{a_1'}, g^{a_2'}, \ldots, g^{a_{n-u}'}$, where

$$(e_1', \cdots, e_n') = (a_1', \cdots, a_{n-u}')H.$$

4. Choose e_i at random for each $i \in BAD$. Let $g^{e_i} = g^{e_i'}$ for each $i \in A$.
5. From $\{g^{e_i} \mid i \in A \cup BAD\}$, compute $g^{a_1}, g^{a_2}, \ldots, g^{a_{n-u}}$, where

$$(e_1, \ldots, e_n) = (a_1, \cdots, a_{n-u}) \cdot H$$

Each a_i is written as a linear combination of $\{e_i \mid i \in A \cup BAD\}$ because any $2k$ columns of H are linearly independent and $|A \cup BAD| \leq 2k$. Therefore, we can do this.

6. Create a pirate decoder P by running B on input a public key $(g, g^{a_1}, g^{a_2}, \ldots, g^{a_{n-u}})$ and the private keys of BAD, $\{e_i \mid i \in BAD\}$. Give h' to the pirate decoder P. Let the output of P be s_A.
7. Finally M outputs 1 if $s_A = s'$ or 0 otherwise.

Then we obtain that

$$|\Pr(M(d) = 1 \mid d \leftarrow \mathbf{D}) - \Pr(M(d) = 1 \mid d \leftarrow \mathbf{R})|$$
$$= |\Pr(s_A = s' \mid d \leftarrow \mathbf{D}) - \Pr(s_A = s' \mid d \leftarrow \mathbf{R})|$$

First we see that $\Pr(s' = s \mid d \leftarrow \mathbf{R})$ is negligible because y' is random. Next it is easy to see that if d is chosen from $\mathbf{D}$, then h' is a testing header used in $TEST(A)$. Therefore,

$$\Pr(s_A = s' \mid d \leftarrow \mathbf{D}) = Pr(TEST(A) = 1) \geq \epsilon$$

from our assumption.

This means that M can distinguishes $\mathbf{D}$ and $\mathbf{R}$ with nonnegligible probability.

C   Proof of Theorem 7.5

Suppose that

$$|\Pr(TEST(A) = 1) - \Pr(TEST(A \setminus \{\tilde{i}\}) = 1)| \geq \epsilon$$

for some nonnegligible probability ϵ. Then we show that there exists a probabilistic polynomial time Turing machine M which can distinguish $\mathbf{D} = (g, g^r, y, y^r)$ and $\mathbf{R} = (g, g^r, y, v)$ with nonnegligible probability, where g, y, v are chosen at random from G_q and r is chosen at random from Z_q.

From our assumption, there is an algorithm B which creates a pirate decoder P such that

$$|\Pr(TEST(A) = 1) - \Pr(TEST(A \setminus \{\tilde{i}\}) = 1)| \geq \epsilon$$

from a public key $pk = (g, y_1, \ldots, y_{n-u})$ and the private keys of BAD.

Now on input $d = (g, g', y, y')$, M works as follows.

1. Choose e_i for each $i \in BAD \cup (A \setminus \{\tilde{i}\})$. Let $e_{\tilde{i}}$ be such that $g^{e_{\tilde{i}}} = y$.
2. Compute $g^{a_1}, g^{a_2}, \ldots, g^{a_{n-u}}$ from $\{g^{e_i} \mid i \in BAD \cup A\}$, where

$$(e_1, \cdots, e_n) = (a_1, \cdots, a_{n-u})H.$$

3. Create a pirate decoder P by running B on input a public key $(g, g^{a_1}, g^{a_2}, \ldots, g^{a_{n-u}})$ and the private keys of BAD, $\{e_i \mid i \in BAD\}$.
4. Next let $e_i' = e_i$ for each $i \in A \setminus \{\tilde{i}\}$ and $e_{\tilde{i}}'$ be such that $y^{e_{\tilde{i}}'} = y'$.
5. Compute $y^{a_1'}, y^{a_2'}, \ldots, y^{a_{n-u}'}$ from $\{y^{e_i'} \mid i \in BAD \cup A\}$, where

$$(e_1', \cdots, e_n') = (a_1', \cdots, a_{n-u}')H.$$

6. Select a random session key s' and compute h' as follows.

$$h' = (g', s'y^{a_1'}, y^{a_2'}, \ldots, y^{a_{n-u}'}).$$

Give h' to the pirate decoder P. Let the output of P be s_A.
7. Finally M outputs 1 if $s_A = s'$ or 0 otherwise.

It is easy to see that if d is chosen from $\mathbf{D}$, then h' is an illegal header used in $TEST(A)$. On the other hand, if d is chosen from $\mathbf{R}$, then h' is an illegal header used in $TEST(A \setminus \{\tilde{i}\})$.

Therefore,

$$\begin{aligned}
|\Pr(M(d) = 1 \mid d \leftarrow \mathbf{D}) &- \Pr(M(d) = 1 \mid d \leftarrow \mathbf{R})| \\
&= \left|\Pr(TEST(A) = 1) - \Pr(TEST(A \setminus \{\tilde{i}\}) = 1)\right| \\
&\geq \epsilon
\end{aligned}$$

from our assumption.

This means that M can distinguish $\mathbf{D}$ and $\mathbf{R}$ with nonnegligible probability.

D   Proof of Theorem 7.8

Suppose that $\Pr(TEST(A) = 1) \geq \epsilon$ for some nonnegligible probability ϵ. Then we show that there exists a probabilistic polynomial time Turing machine M which can distinguish $\mathbf{D} = (g, g^a, y, y^a)$ and $\mathbf{R} = (g, g^a, y, v)$ with nonnegligible probability, where g, y, v are chosen at random from G_q and a is chosen at random in Z_q.

From our assumption, there is an algorithm B which creates a pirate decoder such that $\Pr(TEST(A) = 1) \geq \epsilon$ from a public key $pk = (g, y_1, \cdots, y_{2k})$ and the private keys of BAD.

Now on input $d = (g, g', y, y')$, M works as follows.

1. Choose e_i at random for each $i \in BAD$.
2. For each $i \in A$, choose t_i at random and compute y^{t_i}. Define e_i as $g^{e_i} = y^{t_i}$.
3. From $\{g^{e_i} \mid i \in A \cup BAD\}$, compute $g^{a_1}, g^{a_2}, \ldots, g^{a_{n-u}}$, where

$$(e_1, \ldots, e_n) = (a_1, \cdots, a_{n-u}) \cdot H.$$

4. Create a pirate decoder P by running B on input a public key $(g, g^{a_1}, g^{a_2}, \ldots, g^{a_{n-u}})$ and the private keys of BAD, $\{e_i \mid i \in BAD\}$.
5. For each $i \in A$, compute $\beta_i = (y')^{t_i}$. For each $i \in BAD$, choose a random element β_i.
6. Suppose that $y' = y^r$. Define e'_i as $\beta_i = g^{re'_i}$ for each $i \in (A \cup BAD)$.
7. From $\{\beta_i \mid i \in A \cup BAD\}$, compute $g^{ra'_1}, g^{ra'_2}, \ldots, g^{ra'_{n-u}}$, where $\beta_i = g^{re'_i}$ and

$$(e'_1, \ldots, e'_n) = (a'_1, \cdots, a'_{n-u}) \cdot H.$$

8. Select a random session key s' and compute h' as follows.

$$h' = (s'g', g^{ra'_1}, g^{ra'_2}, \ldots, g^{ra'_{n-u}}).$$

Give h' to the pirate decoder P. Let the output of P be s_A.

9. Finally M outputs 1 if $s_A = s'$ or 0 otherwise.

Then we obtain that

$$|\Pr(M(d) = 1 \mid d \leftarrow \mathbf{D}) - \Pr(M(d) = 1 \mid d \leftarrow \mathbf{R})|$$
$$= |\Pr(s_A = s' \mid d \leftarrow \mathbf{D}) - \Pr(s_A = s' \mid d \leftarrow \mathbf{R})|$$

First we see that $\Pr(s' = s \mid d \leftarrow \mathbf{R})$ is negligible because g' is random.

Next we will show that if d is chosen from $\mathbf{D}$, then h' is an illegal header used in $TEST(A)$. In this case, $y' = y^r$ and $g' = g^r$ for some r. We need to show that $e'_i = e_i$ for each $i \in A$. Assume that $y = g^x$. Then

1. $e_i = xt_i$ since $y^{t_i} = g^{e_i}$.
2. On the other hand,

$$g^{re'_i} = \beta_i = (y')^{t_i} = y^{rt_i} = g^{xrt_i}.$$

Therefore, $e'_i = xt_i$.

Hence, $e'_i = e_i$. Therefore, h' is an illegal header used in $TEST(A)$. Consequently,

$$\Pr(s_A = s' \mid d \leftarrow \mathbf{D}) = Pr(TEST(A) = 1) \geq \epsilon$$

from our assumption.

This means that M can distinguishes $\mathbf{D}$ and $\mathbf{R}$ with nonnegligible probability.

Design and Security Analysis
of Anonymous Group Identification Protocols

Chan H. Lee[1], Xiaotie Deng[1], and Huafei Zhu[2]

[1] Department of Computer Science,
City University of Hong Kong
{cschlee, csdeng}@cityu.edu.hk
[2] Zhejiang Univ. Zhejiang-Inst-Information Science and Engineering,
Department of Information and Electronics Engineering,
Hangzhou 310027 Peoples R. China
zhuhf@isee.zju.edu.cn

Abstract. Two provably secure group identification schemes are presented in this report: 1) we extend De Santis, Crescenzo and Persiano's (SCP) anonymous group identification scheme to the discrete logarithm based case; then we provide a 3-move anonymous group identification scheme, which is more efficient than that presented in [SCPM, CDS], with the help of this basic scheme; 2) we also extend the original De Santis, Crescenzo and Persiano anonymous group identification scheme to the general case where each user holds public key which is chosen by herself independently. The communication cost for one round execution of the protocol is $2mk$, where k is bit length of public key n and m is the number of users in the group.

1 Introduction

Anonymous group identification scheme is a method that allows a member of a group, say Alice convinces a verifier, say Bob that she is a member of the group without revealing any information about her identity in the group. A full and general solution to the problem of anonymous group identification has been presented in [SCPM] based on the closure properties of statistical zero knowledge languages under monotone logic formula composition. Later, Cramer, Damgard and Schoenmakers suggest a new general approach for proofs of partial knowledge independently [CDS]. The structure of an anonymous group identification protocol based on the techniques presented in [SCPM] (or [CDS], if we restrict CDS's scheme to the discrete logarithm based case), can be stated as follows [CM]: Let p be a large prime and G be a cyclic sub-group of Z_p^* with order q. Let g be a generator of G. The system public key is (p, q, g) available to all group users. Each user U_i in the group chooses $x_i \in z_q$ at random and computes $y_i := g^{x_i} \bmod p$. The public key is y_i and the secret key is x_i. The set $S := \{y_1, \cdots, y_m\}$ contains the information of all legal users. A prover, say Alice wants to prove her knowledge of y_i to a verifier, say Bob without revealing any information of the index i. To authenticate membership of the group anonymously

D. Naccache and P. Paillier (Eds.): PKC 2002, LNCS 2274, pp. 188–198, 2002.

(without loss of generality, we assume the prover knows the secret information of y_1), the protocol is performed as follows:

- The prover computes $t_1 = g^{r_1}$, $t_2 = g^{s_2}y_2^{c_2}$, $\cdots$, $t_m = g^{s_m}y_m^{c_m}$, where $r_1 \in z_q$, $s_2, \cdots, s_m \in z_q$ and $c_2, \cdots, c_m \in z_q$ are chosen uniformly at random. Then she sends $t_1, t_2, \cdots, t_m$ to the verifier.
- The verifier chooses $b \in z_q$ uniformly at random and send it to the prover.
- The prover computes $c_1 = b \oplus c_2 \oplus \cdots \oplus c_m$, $s_1 = (r_1 - x_1 c_1) \bmod q$, then sends $(s_1, s_2, \cdots, s_m)$ and $(c_1, c_2, \cdots, c_m)$ to the verifier.
- The verifier tests whether $b = c_1 \oplus c_2 \oplus \cdots \oplus c_m$ and $t_1 = g^{s_1}y_1^{c_1}$, $\cdots$, $t_m = g^{s_m}y_m^{c_m}$. If all conditions are valid then the verifier accepts. Otherwise it rejects.

It is clear that the computational complexity is about $2m$-exponent computations for the prover (or the verifier) while the communication costs is about $3mn$-bit, with probability $1/2^n$ rejecting an unqualified group user, where m is the number of users, n is the bit length of the security parameter p ($p = 2q + 1$, p, q are two large primes).

Since the anonymity property often constrains the communication to heavily depend on the number of users in the group, communication cost is one of the most important measures for efficiency considerations. Motivated by the communication efficiency consideration, De Santis, Crescenzo and Persiano have developed elegant protocols minimizing the communication involved in the schemes. The proof of security is based on the difficulty of factoring problem. We sketch their basic protocol below (see [SCP] for more details):

- Initialization: Let n be a security parameter, uniformly choosing n-bit primes $p \equiv q \equiv 3 \bmod 4$ and setting $x = pq$.
- For $i = 1, \cdots, m$, uniformly choosing $w_i \in Z_x^*$ and computing $y_i = w_i^2$ $\bmod x$; Setting $pk_i = (x, y_i)$ and $sk_i = w_i$ to user U_i;

To show the membership of the group anonymously, one round of protocol is performed as follows.

- The prover chooses $r \in Z_x^*$ and $c_1, \cdots, c_m \in \{0, 1\}$ uniformly at random, then sends $u = r^2 y_1^{c_1} \cdots y_m^{c_m} \bmod x$ to the verifier;
- The verifier chooses a bit $b \in \{0, 1\}$ uniformly at random and sends it to the prover.
- If $b = c_1 \oplus \cdots \oplus c_m$, the prover sets $d_j = c_j$, for $j = 1, \cdots, m$ and $s = r$; If $b \neq c_1 \oplus \cdots \oplus c_m$, then sets $s = rw_i^{1-2d_i}$ and $d_i = 1 - c_i$. Finally the prover sends $(s, d_1, \cdots, d_m)$ to the verifier.
- The verifier checks whether $b = d_1 \oplus \cdots \oplus d_m$ and $u = s^2 y_1^{d_1} \cdots y_m^{d_m}$ $\bmod x$. If the both conditions hold, the verifier outputs *Accept*; else it outputs *Reject*;

It is clear that one round execution of the protocol rejects an un-qualified user with probability $1/2$. The computational cost is $(\frac{m}{2} + 1)$ modular multiplications (modular x), on average while the communication cost is $(m + 2n)$-bit. If the protocol runs n times, then the total computation cost is $(m+2)n$ modular multiplications (modular p, we use the same measurement of modular multiplication) and the communication cost is $(m+2n)n$-bit, where m is the number of users in the group and n is bit length of private key p ($|p|=|q|=n$, and $|x|=2n$).

1.1   A Simple Modification of SPC's Scheme

Since the original SPC's scheme is multiple-round identification protocol. It is desired if one is able to provide a standard 3-move scheme. A natural modification of multiple-round SPC's scheme to a 3-move anonymous identification protocol can be stated as follows.

- The prover chooses $r \in Z_x^*$ and $c_1, \cdots, c_m \in z_q$ uniformly at random, then sends $u = r^2 y_1{}^{c_1} \cdots y_m{}^{c_m} \bmod x$ to the verifier;
- The verifier chooses $b \in z_q$ uniformly at random and sends it to the prover.
- If $b = c_1 \oplus \cdots \oplus c_m$, setting $d_j = c_j$, for $j = 1, \cdots, m$ and $s = r$; If $b \neq c_1 \oplus \cdots \oplus c_m$, setting $d_j = c_j$ $(j \neq i)$, $d_i = c_1 \oplus \cdots c_{i-1} \oplus b \oplus \cdots \oplus c_m$ and $s = rw_i^{c_i - d_i}$. Finally the prover sends $(s, d_1, \cdots, d_m)$ to the verifier.
- The verifier checks whether $b = d_1 \oplus \cdots \oplus d_m$ and $u = s^2 y_1{}^{d_1} \cdots y_m{}^{d_m} \bmod x$. If the both conditions hold, it outputs *Accept*; else it outputs *Reject*;

Notice that any honest prover has to compute the value $w_i^{c_i - d_i} \bmod x$ if $b \neq c_1 \oplus \cdots \oplus c_m$ (this event happens with overwhelming probability). It follows that the computational cost of the prover is $(m+1)$ exponential computation modular x. Equivalently, it needs $3(m+1)n$ modular multiplications (modular p), according to the well known square and multiply algorithm for modular exponentiation that requires, on average, $1.5n$ modular multiplications for an n-bit exponent. And the communication cost of this protocol is about $2(m+1)n$-bit.

1.2   Our Works

We are interested in the construction of a standard 3-round anonymous identification scheme (for example, a protocol is more efficient than the above simple modification of SCP's scheme). Our solution is follows: we first extend De Santis, Crescenzo and Persiano's (SCP) anonymous group identification scheme to the discrete logarithm based case; then we provide a 3-move anonymous group identification scheme, which is more efficient than that presented in [SCPM, CDS], with the help of this basic scheme. The computational cost of our 3-move scheme is $(m+1)$-exponent computations for a prover (or a verifier) and the communication cost is $(m+2)n$-bit, with probability $1/2^n$ rejecting an unqualified group member, where m is the number of users, n is the bit length of the security parameter p ($p = 2q + 1$, p, q are two large primes).

We remark that to achieve the same security level as our 3-move identification scheme (with probability $1/2^n$ rejecting an unqualified group member), the original SCP's should be run n times independently. It follows that the total communication cost of running n times of the original SCP's anonymous identification scheme is $(m+2n)n$-bit while our 3-move protocol is $(m+2)n$-bit.

We point out that the computation cost of our 3-move protocol is $(m + 1)$-exponent computations for a prover (or a verifier), that is, it needs $1.5(m + 1)n$ modular p multiplication computation. However the computation cost of running n times of the original SCP's anonymous identification scheme is $(m + 2)n$ modular multiplications (modular p, we use the same measurement of modular operation). It is clear that the computation complexity of our 3-move scheme costs slightly more than that of running n times of the original SCP's scheme. We believe that the computational inefficiency of our 3-move scheme is inevitable since the prover of the original SCP's scheme is required to reply a single bit challenge and hereby the exponential computation is NOT needed. This is the key difference between a one bit challenge scheme and n-bit challenge scheme.

We realize that the computation and communication complexity of the above mentioned protocols grow linearly with number of the member of the group. The growth could make anonymous authentication protocol impractical for very large dynamic groups. It is interesting problem if one is able to develop a new anonymous authentication protocol such that the computational and communication complexity to identify the membership of a user in a given group is constant, that is, both communication and computation complexity are independent on the number of users in the group, e.g., notable works of Boneh and Franklin [BF]. This is our further research topic.

2   Notions and Definitions

In this section, we introduce some useful notations presented in [SCP], then we provide security definition on anonymous group identification protocols.

Probabilistic algorithms. The notation $x \leftarrow$ S denotes the random process of selecting element x from set S with uniform probability over S. The notation $y \leftarrow$ A(x), where A is an probabilistic algorithm, denotes the random process of obtaining y when running algorithm A on input x. A probability space will be denoted by $\{R_1; \cdots; R_m : v\}$, where v denotes the value that the random value can assume, and $R_1, \cdots, R_m$ is a sequence of random processes generating value v. By $\text{Prob}[R_1; \cdots; R_m : E]$ we denote the probability of event E, after execution of the random processes $R_1, \cdots, R_n$.

Interactive protocols. If A and B are two interactive probabilistic polynomial Turing machines, by pair (A, B) we denote an interactive protocol. By $\text{TR}_{(A,B)}(x)$ we denote a set of transcripts of the interaction between A and B with common input x. The notation $t \leftarrow (A(y), B)(x)$ denotes the transcript t has been generated through an execution of the protocol (A, B), where x is a common input to A and B, and y is A's private input. For any $t \in \text{TR}_{(A,B)}(x)$, by $\text{OUT}_C(t)$ we denote the output of C, where $C \in \{A, B\}$. We will say B ACCEPT if $\text{OUT}_B(t)=$ACCEPT.

An anonymous identification scheme consists of two phases: initial phase and identification phase. Each user holds with a pair of public and private key at the end of execution of the initial protocol. In identification phase, a user tries to convince the verifier of some statement which certifies her knowledge of secret key received in the initial phase. By INIT, we denote a initial protocol and by (P, V), we denote two-party protocol, where P is proof algorithm executed by A and V is a verification algorithm executed by the verifier B. With the help of these notations, we are able to present two equivalent security definitions which may be convenient for us to prove the security aspects of the proposed schemes.

Definition 1. It is convenient for us to define the security of an anonymous group identification scheme in the case that each user in the group shares common system public keys and one round execution of the protocol rejects an un-qualified user with probability $1/2$. An anonymous identification scheme $\{INIT, (P, V)\}$ is secure if it satisfies:

- Correctness: For each user $U_i \in S$, $\text{Prob}[(sk_1, \cdots, sk_m, pk) \leftarrow INIT(1^n); t \leftarrow (P(sk_i), V)(pk) : OUT_V(t) = ACCEPT] = 1$;
- Soundness: For any user $U_i \notin S$ and any probabilistic polynomial time algorithm, the advantage:P': $\text{Prob}[(sk_1, \cdots, sk_m, pk) \leftarrow INIT(1^n); t \leftarrow (P'(\phi), V)(pk) : OUT_V(t) = ACCEPT] - 1/2$ is negligible, where $P'(\phi)$ indicates the input of private key is empty string;
- Anonymity: For any user $U_i, U_j \in S$ and any probabilistic polynomial time algorithm V', the probability space Π_1 and Π_2 are equal, where $\Pi_1 = [(sk_1, \cdots, sk_m, pk) \leftarrow INIT(1^n); t \leftarrow (P(sk_i), V')(pk) : t]$ and $\Pi_2 = [(sk_1, \cdots, sk_m, pk) \leftarrow INIT(1^n); t \leftarrow (P(sk_j), V')(pk) : t]$.

Remark: There are several equivalent security definitions of a group identification scheme. We sketch the two notions, which are useful to define security aspects of a group identification scheme in different settings.

Definition 2. It is convenient for us to define the security in the case that each user in the group shares common system public keys and one round execution of the protocol is enough to authenticate her membership of the given group. We say an anonymous identification scheme $\{INIT, (P, V)\}$ is secure if it satisfies:

- Correctness: For each user $U_i \in S$, $\text{Prob}[(sk_1, \cdots, sk_m, pk) \leftarrow INIT(1^n); t \leftarrow (P(sk_i), V)(pk) : OUT_V(t) = ACCEPT] = 1$;
- Soundness: For any user $U_i \notin S$ and any probabilistic polynomial time algorithm, the advantage of P': $\text{Prob}[(sk_1, \cdots, sk_m, pk) \leftarrow INIT(1^n); t \leftarrow (P'(\phi), V)(pk) : OUT_V(t) = ACCEPT]$ is negligible, where $P'(\phi)$ indicates the input of private key is empty string;
- Anonymity: For any user $U_i, U_j \in S$ and any probabilistic polynomial time algorithm V', the probability space Π_1 and Π_2 are equal, where $\Pi_1 = [(sk_1, \cdots, sk_m, pk) \leftarrow INIT(1^n); t \leftarrow (P(sk_i), V')(pk):t]$ and $\Pi_2 = [(sk_1, \cdots, sk_m, pk) \leftarrow INIT(1^n); t \leftarrow (P(sk_j), V')(pk) : t]$.

Definition 3. It is convenient for us to define the security of an anonymous group identification scheme in the case that each user in the group holds with different public key and one round execution of the protocol rejects an un-qualified user with probability $1/2$. We say an anonymous identification scheme $\{INIT, (P, V)\}$ is secure if it satisfies:

- Correctness: For each user $U_i \in S$, $\text{Prob}[(pk_1, \cdots, pk_m, sk_i) \leftarrow INIT(1^n); t \leftarrow (P(sk_i), V)(pk_1, \cdots, pk_m) : OUT_V(t) = ACCEPT] = 1$;
- Soundness: For any user $U_i \notin S$, for any probabilistic polynomial time algorithm P': $\text{Prob}[(pk_1, \cdots, pk_m) \leftarrow INIT(1^n); t \leftarrow (P'(\phi), V) (pk_1, \cdots, pk_m) : OUT_V(t) = ACCEPT] - 1/2$ is negligible, where $P'(\phi)$ indicates the input of private key is empty string;
- Anonymity: For arbitrary two different legitimate users $U_i, U_j \in S$ and any probabilistic polynomial time algorithm V', the probability space Π_1 and Π_2 are equal, where $\Pi_1 = [(pk_1, \cdots, pk_m, sk_i) \leftarrow INIT(1^n); t \leftarrow (P(sk_i), V') (pk_1, \cdots, pk_m) : t]$ and $\Pi_2 = [(pk_1, \cdots, pk_m, sk_j) \leftarrow INIT(1^n); t \leftarrow (P(sk_j), V') (pk_1, \cdots, pk_m) : t]$.

Since a zero-knowledge proof system achieves un-linkability (i.e., separate identification transcripts can not be shown have been made by a single individual [SPH]). It is desirable if the anonymous identification scheme shares zero-knowledge property. The notion of zero knowledge proof was introduced by Goldwasser, Micali and Rackoff [GMR]. We sketch some useful notions below: Let R be a relationship over a language L. Let $x \in L$ and $w(x) := \{w : (x, w) \in R\}$ be a witness set such that the membership can be tested in polynomial time. A proof system (P, V) is called perfect zero-knowledge if for any probabilistic polynomial time Turing machine V', there exists a simulator $S_{V'}$ such that:

- $S_{V'}$ outputs $\perp$ with probability at most $1/2$;
- And that conditioned on not outputting $\perp$, the simulator's output is distributed as the verifier's view in a real interaction with the prover.

A weak notion is called an honest verifier zero-knowledge: there is a simulator S that on input x produces conversations that are indistinguishable from the real conversations with input x between the honest prover and the honest verifier. Hence an honest verifier zero-knowledge protocol also implies the unlinkability in the sense of the computational indistinguishablity.

3   Basic Anonymous Identification Scheme

We first extend De Santis, Crescenzo and Persiano's (SCP) anonymous group identification scheme to the discrete logarithm based case.

3.1   Descriptions

Let p, q be two large primes such that $p - 1 = 2q$. Let G be a cyclic sub-group of Z_p^* with order q. Let g be a generator of G. The system public key is (p, q, g) available to all group users. Each user U_i in the group chooses $x_i \in z_q$ at random and computes $y_i := g^{x_i} \bmod p$. The public key is y_i and the secret key is x_i. The set $S := \{y_1, \cdots, y_m\}$ contains all users. A prover, say Alice wants to prove her knowledge of y_i to a verifier, say Bob without revealing any information of the index i. One round of the protocol can be executed as follows:

- Alice chooses $r \in z_q$ and $c_i \in \{0, 1\}$ uniformly at random then sends the value $u := g^r \, y_1^{c_1} \cdots y_m^{c_m}$ to Bob.
- Bob chooses a bit $b \in \{0, 1\}$ uniformly at random and then sends it to Alice.
- Alice checks the validation whether $b = c_1 \oplus \cdots \oplus c_m$. If the equation is satisfied, then Alice sends $(r, c_1, \cdots, c_m)$ to Bob. Otherwise, Alice sets $c_j \leftarrow c_j$ and $c_i \leftarrow (1 - c_i)$ and $r \leftarrow (r + (2c_i - 1)x_i) \bmod q$ and then sends $(r, c_1, \cdots, c_m)$ to Bob.
- Bob checks the validation of the two conditions $b = c_1 \oplus \cdots \oplus c_m$ and $u := g^r \, y_1^{c_1} \cdots y_m^{c_m}$. If both conditions hold, he accepts; Otherwise he rejects.

The communication cost is $(m + 2n)$-bit, and the computation cost is 1-exponent computation plus $m/2$ multiplications over G for one round execution of the protocol. If the protocol runs n times then the computation cost is about $\frac{1}{2}(m + 3n)n$ modular multiplications (modular p) according to the well known square and multiply algorithm for modular exponentiation requires, on average $1.5n$ modular multiplications for an n-bit exponent.

3.2   Security Analysis

Since the protocol needs multiple-round interactions between the honest prover and the honest verifier, we want to show that the protocol is secure according to the definition 1.

Correctness. Correctness can be easily verified according to the definition 1.

Soundness. Suppose there exists unqualified user $U' \notin S$ and a probabilistic polynomial time proof algorithm P' with non-negligible advantage to make the honest verifier accept, then there exists a polynomial time algorithm P^* solves the discrete logarithm problem with non-negligible probability.

Proof. We need to show an algorithm that takes (g, y) as input and produces the $\mathrm{DL}_g(y)$ as output (given access to a subroutine that breaks the protocol). Now we are given an random element $y \in G$, the adversary (running U' and P' together) chooses a set of random elements $r_1, \cdots, r_m \in z_q$ and compute $y_i = y^{r_i}$. Then it chooses a random element $r \in Z_q$ and computes $u := g^r y_1^{c_1} \cdots y_m^{c_m}$. By assumption there is a probabilistic polynomial time proof algorithm P' with non-negligible advantage to make the honest verifier accept, it follows P' is able to output $(u; r'; (c'_1, \cdots, c'_m)) \leftarrow P'(u; r; (c_1, \cdots, c_m))$ with non-negligible probability such that $c_1 \oplus \cdots \oplus c_m \neq c'_1 \oplus \cdots \oplus c'_m$ and $u := g^r \, y_1^{c_1} \cdots y_m^{c_m} = g^{r'} y_1^{c'_1} \cdots y_m^{c'_m}$. Denote $d_i = c'_i - c_i$ $(1 \leq i \leq m)$. Hence with non-negligible probability, the adversary obtains the equation: $g^{r-r'} = y_1^{d_1} \cdots y_m^{d_m}$. It follows that

$r - r' = (r_1 d_1 + \cdots r_m d_m) \mathrm{DLog}(y) \bmod q$. Hence the adversary is able to compute the discrete logarithm of any randomly given element y with non-negligible probability. We arrive at the contradiction of the hardness assumption of the discrete logarithm problem.

Anonymity. Anonymity follows from the fact that the distribution of the variable $r \leftarrow (r + (2c_i - 1)x_i) \bmod q$ over z_q (of the user U_i) and the distribution of the variable $r' \leftarrow (r' + (2c_j - 1)x_j) \bmod q$ over z_q (of the user U_j) are uniformly distributed if r and r' are chosen uniformly at random from z_q.

Perfect zero-knowledge. This basic scheme shares zero-knowledge property. We want to show that for any probabilistic polynomial time Turing machine V', there exists a simulator $S_{V'}$ such that: 1) $S_{V'}$ outputs $\perp$ with probability at most $1/2$; 2) Conditioned on not outputting $\perp$, the simulator's output is distributed as the verifier's view in a real interaction with the prover. The simulator $S_{V'}$ can be constructed as follows:

- Setting the random tape of V': Let $poly(\cdot)$ be a polynomial bound running time of V'. The simulator $S_{V'}$ starts by uniformly selecting a random string $Random \in \{0,1\}^{poly(|q|)}$, to be used as the contents of the random tape of V';
- Simulating the first step of the prover: The simulator selects $b' \in \{0,1\}$, $r \in z_q$ and $c_i \in \{0,1\}$ uniformly at random such that $b' = c_1 \oplus \cdots \oplus c_m$, and computes the value $u := g^r y_1^{c_1} \cdots y_m^{c_m}$;
- Simulating the verifier's first step: The simulator initiates an execution of V' by placing x on V''s common input tape, $Random$ on its random tape and b' on its incoming message tape. After polynomial number of steps of V', the simulator can read the outgoing message b;
- Simulating the prover's second step: If $b' = b$, then the simulator halts with output $(u, b, r, c_1, \cdots, c_m)$;
- Failure of the simulator: Otherwise, the simulator halts with output $\perp$.

Using the hypothesis that V' is polynomial time, it follows that so is the simulator. It is left to show that $S_{V'}$ outputs $\perp$ with probability at most $1/2$ and that conditioned on not outputting $\perp$, the simulator's output is distributed as the verifier's view in a real interaction with the prover.

Notice that regardless of the value of b', the distribution of the message that $S_{V'}$ sends at the first move is the same as the distribution of the messages that the honest prover sends. And the random string $Random$ on its random tape chosen by the simulator is uniformly distributed. The fact implies that V's reply in the move 2 is independent of the value of b'. Consequently, $S_{V'}$ outputs $\perp$ with probability at most $1/2$.

We denote by $\mu(u, b, r, c_1, \cdots, c_m)$ the distribution of the transcripts between the honest prover and the V' while $\nu(u, b, r, c_1, \cdots, c_m)$ be the distribution of simulator $S_{V'}$'s distribution. Since for every fixed u and $Random$, the value b of the output of V' is uniquely determined and the simulation of the prover first step conditioned on not outputting $\perp$ is same as that of the honest prover, it follows the distribution of the simulator's output is identical to that of the verifier's view in a real interaction with the honest prover.

3.3   A Variations of Basic Anonymous Identification Scheme

We now are able to provide a variation of this basic scheme. The key generation scheme is the same as that in the basic scheme presented in the above section. To identify the membership of the group (without loss of generality, we assume that the prover knows the secret information of y_1), the protocol is performed as follows:

- The prover chooses $s, d_1, c_2, \cdots, c_m \in z_q$ uniformly at random, and computes $u = g^s y_1^{d_1} y_2^{c_2} \cdots y_m^{c_m}$ and then sends u to the verifier.
- The verifier chooses $b \in z_q$ uniformly at random and sends it to the prover.
- The prover computs $c_1 = b \oplus c_2 \cdots \oplus c_m$, and $r = s + (d_1 - c_1)x_1 \bmod q$. Then sends $(r, c_1, c_2, \cdots, c_m)$ to the verifier.
- If both conditions $b = c_1 \oplus c_2 \cdots \oplus c_m$ and $u = g^r y_1^{c_1} y_2^{c_2} \cdots y_m^{c_m}$ are satisfied, it accepts, Otherwise, it rejects.

3.4   Security Analysis

The proof of correctness, soundness and anonymity are the same as that presented in the basic scheme. To show the protocol is the honest verifier zero-knowledge proof system, we choose $b \in z_q$ at random, then we choose $c_1, \cdots, c_m \in z_q$ such that $b = c_1 \oplus c_2 \cdots \oplus c_m$. Finally we choose $r \in z_q$ uniformly at random and compute $u = g^s y_1^{d_1} y_2^{c_2} \cdots y_m^{c_m}$. The conversation is $(u, b, r, c_1, \cdots, c_m)$. Since b, r and $c_1, \cdots, c_m \in z_q$ are chosen uniformly at random, it follows the simulated conversation is indistinguishable from the real conversation.

The computational complexity is $(m+1)$-exponent computations for a prover (or a verifier), that is the total computation complexity is $1.5(m+1)n$ modular multiplications (modular p). And the communication cost is $(m+2)n$-bit, with the probability $1/2^n$ rejecting an unqualified group member. The facts imply that our 3-move scheme is more efficient than that presented in [SCPM, CDS].

4   Anonymous Group Identification Protocol with Independent Modular

In this section, we extend the original De Santis, Crescenzo and Persiano anonymous group identification scheme to the general case where each user holds public key which is chosen by herself independently. The communication cost for one round execution of the protocol is $2mk$, where k is bit length of public key n and m is the number of users in the group.

Let S be a set of elements $\{n_1, n_2, \cdots, n_m\}$. Each n_i is a product of two primes, P_i and Q_i such that $P_i \equiv Q_i \equiv 3 \bmod 4$ (Any integer n_i with this property is called Blum integer). A prover, say Alice wants to prove to a verifier, say

Bob that she knows the factors of some $n_j \in S$ without revealing any information of the index j. One round of the protocol can be executed as follows:

- Alice selects m elements $x_i \in Z_{n_i}^*$ at random, squares them to get $a_i = x_i^2 \bmod n_i$ ($a_i \neq a_j$ if $i \neq j$), then sends a_i to Bob ($i = 1, 2, \cdots m$);
- Bob randomly chooses a bit $b \in \{-1, 1\}$ and sends it to Alice.
- Alice sends Bob m square roots $z_1, z_2, \cdots, z_m$ of $a_1, a_2, \cdots, a_m$ such that $(\frac{z_1}{n_1})(\frac{z_2}{n_2}) \cdots (\frac{z_m}{n_m}) = b$, where $(\frac{z}{n})$ is Jacobi symbol and $(z_1, z_2, \cdots, z_m)$ is either $(x_1, \cdots, x_{i-1}, x_i, \cdots, x_m)$ or $(x_1, \cdots x_{i-1}, y_i, \cdots, x_m)$.
- Bob checks validation of $z_i^2 \equiv a_i \bmod n_i$ ($i = 1, 2, \cdots, m$) and $(\frac{z_1}{N_1})(\frac{z_2}{N_2}) \cdots (\frac{z_m}{N_m}) = b$. If both tests passed, he accepts, otherwise he rejects.

Security analysis. To show the protocol is secure, the following result is needed, which can be found in [BSMP]:

- Fact 1: If a is a quadratic residue modulo n, where $P \equiv Q \equiv 3 \bmod 4$, then a has four square roots modulo N, denoted by $x, -x, y, -y$;
- Fact 2: If $x^2 = y^2 \bmod N$ and if $x \neq \pm y \bmod N$, where $P \equiv Q \equiv 3 \bmod 4$ and $N = PQ$, then $(\frac{x}{n}) = (\frac{-x}{n})$ and $(\frac{x}{n}) = -(\frac{y}{n})$.

Correctness. If Alice knows two factors of $n_i \in S$, then she can always make Bob accept.

   Proof. Alice computes $(\frac{x_1}{n_1})(\frac{x_2}{n_2}) \cdots (\frac{x_m}{n_m})$ and compares it with b. If it is equal then sends $x_1, x_2, \cdots, x_m$ to Bob. Otherwise, Alice replaces x_i by y_i such that $x_i^2 \equiv y_i^2 \equiv a_i \bmod n_i$ and $(\frac{x_i}{n_i}) = -(\frac{y_i}{n_i})$, then she sends $x_1, \cdots, y_i, \cdots, x_m$ to Bob. This is true if Alice knows two prime factors of $n_i \in S$. Hence Alice can always make Bob accept.

Soundness. Suppose there exists unqualified user $U' \notin S$ and a probabilistic polynomial time proof algorithm P' with non-negligible advantage to make the honest verifier accept, then there exists a polynomial time algorithm P^* factoring the Blum integer with non-negligible probability.

   Proof. Given m legitimate users $n_1, \cdots, n_m$ in the group S, two factors of each n_i ($1 \leq i \leq m$) is not known by the U' since she is not a legitimate user in the group S. By protocol, U' must commit the values x_i ($x_i^2 \equiv a_i \bmod n_i$, $1 \leq i \leq m$) and then sends the commitments to the verifier at the first move. Since b is a random bit chosen by the verifier, by assumption P' is able to provide $(z_1, z_2, \cdots, z_m)$ which is pairs either $(x_1, \cdots, x_{i-1}, x_i, \cdots, x_m)$ or $(x_1, \cdots x_{i-1}, y_i, \cdots, x_m)$ for some i with non-negligible probability. The fact implies that there exists a polynomial time algorithm P^* (by running U' and P' together) factoring the Blum integer with non-negligible probability.

Anonymity. The distribution of transcript of any legitimate user is equal.

   Proof. Any legitimate user, say Alice sends Bob random sequence $a_1, \cdots, a_m$ at first. After she receives challenge bit b, Alice sends the correspondent square roots sequence $z_1, \cdots, z_m$ such that $(\frac{z_1}{n_1})(\frac{z_2}{n_2}) \cdots (\frac{z_m}{n_m}) = b$ to Bob. Notice that the distribution of $\{(\frac{z_1}{n_1}), (\frac{z_2}{n_2}), \cdots, (\frac{z_m}{n_m})\}$ is uniform over $\{1, -1\}^m$ if the distribution of random variant $(z_1, z_2, \cdots, z_m)$ is uniform. Hence the distribution of transcript of any legitimate user is uniform. It follows the protocol achieves anonymity property.

5   Conclusion

We have remarked that the computation and communication complexity of the above mentioned protocols grow linearly with number of the member of the group and the growth could make anonymous authentication protocol impractical for very large dynamic groups. It is desired if one is able to develop a new anonymous authentication protocol such that both computational and communication complexity to identify the membership of a user in a given group is constant, as notable works of Boneh and Franklin's. This is our further research topic.

Acknowledgements

Research is partially supported by research grants from City University (Project No. 7001023,7001232,7100133).

References

BF.   D. Boneh, and M. Franklin. Anonymous authentication with subset queries. In proceedings of the 6th ACM conference on Computer and Communications Security, pp. 113–119.

BP.   N. Braic and B. Pfitzmann. Collision free accumulators and fail-stop signature scheme without trees. Eurocrypt'97, 480-494, 1997.

BSMP. M. Blum, A. De Santis, S. Micali, and G. Persiano, Non-Interactive Zero Knowledge, SIAM Journal on Computing, vol. 19, n. 6, December 1991, pp. 1084-1118.

CDS.   R. Cramer, I. Damgaard, B. Schoenmakers: Proofs of Partial Knowledge and Simplified Design of Witness Hiding Protocols, Proceedings of CRYPTO '94, Santa Barbara Ca., Springer Verlag LNCS, vol. 839, pp. 174-187.

SPH.   S. Schechter, T. Parnell, A. Hartemink. Anonymous Authentication of Membership in Dynamic Group. Financial Cryptography'99. Springer-Verlag, 1999, 184-195.

SCP.   A. De Santis, and G. Di Crescenzo and G. Persiano. Commmunication-efficient Anonymous Group Identification. With An extended abstract appears in the Proc. of the Fifth ACM Conference on Computer and Communications Security. 1998, page 73-82.

SCPM. A. De Santis, G. Di Crescenzo, G. Persiano, and M. Yung, On Monotone Formula Closure of SZK, Proceedings of 35th IEEE Symposium on Foundations of Computer Science (FOCS '94), Santa Fe, New Mexico, USA, November 20-22, 1994, pp. 454-465.

On the Security of the Threshold Scheme Based on the Chinese Remainder Theorem

Michaël Quisquater*, Bart Preneel, and Joos Vandewalle

Katholieke Universiteit Leuven,
Department Electrical Engineering-ESAT, COSIC,
Kasteelpark Arenberg 10, B–3001 Heverlee, Belgium
michael.quisquater@esat.kuleuven.ac.be

Abstract. Threshold schemes enable a group of users to share a secret by providing each user with a share. The scheme has a threshold $t + 1$ if any subset with cardinality $t + 1$ of the shares enables the secret to be recovered.

In 1983, C. Asmuth and J. Bloom proposed such a scheme based on the Chinese remainder theorem. They derived a complex relation between the parameters of the scheme in order to satisfy some notion of security. However, at that time, the concept of security in cryptography had not yet been formalized.

In this paper, we revisit the security of this threshold scheme in the modern context of security. In particular, we prove that the scheme is asymptotically optimal both from an information theoretic and complexity theoretic viewpoint when the parameters satisfy a simplified relationship. We mainly present three theorems, the two first theorems strengthen the result of Asmuth and Bloom and place it in a precise context, while the latest theorem is an improvement of a result obtained by Goldreich *et al.*

1 Introduction

A threshold scheme enables a secret to be shared among a group of l members providing each member with a share. The scheme has a threshold $t + 1$ if any subset with cardinality $t+1$ out of the l shares enables the secret to be recovered. We will use the notation $(t + 1, l)$ to refer to such a scheme.

Ideally, in a $(t+1)$ threshold scheme, t shares should not give any information on the secret. We will discuss later how to express this information. In the 80*ies*, several algebraic constructions of $(t + 1, l)$ threshold schemes were proposed.

Shamir used the Lagrange polynomial interpolation. In the Shamir scheme [S79], the secret space is usually a field[1] and the secret consist of the constant term of a polynomial $p(x)$ of degree at most t if the threshold is $t+1$. The shares are $p(x_i)$, where the x_i's are public and belong to the secret space. Blakley

---

* F.W.O.-research fellow, sponsored by the Fund for Scientific Research – Flanders (Belgium).
[1] Note that this condition might be relaxed, see e.g [DF94].

D. Naccache and P. Paillier (Eds.): PKC 2002, LNCS 2274, pp. 199–210, 2002.

used projective spaces to construct such schemes [B79]. Karnin *et al.* consider variations on the previous schemes using coding theory [KGH83].

Mignotte [M82] and Asmuth and Bloom [AB83] used congruence classes and the Chinese remainder theorem to define $(t+1, l)$ threshold schemes. The public parameters are the co-prime and increasing numbers p_i's, $i = 0, \ldots, l$. First the secret $r_0 \stackrel{\triangle}{=} s$ is chosen from the secret space $\mathbb{Z}_{p_0}$. Then the values r_i's are randomly chosen in $\mathbb{Z}_{p_i}$ for $i = 1, \cdots, t$ if the threshold is $t+1$. Using the Chinese remainder theorem, $Y \in \mathbb{Z}_{\prod_{i=0}^{t} p_i}$ is computed such that $Y \equiv r_i \bmod p_i$ for $i = 0, \ldots, t$. The shares are $s_i = Y \bmod p_i$ for $i = 1, \ldots, l$. Note that Mignotte [M82] defined the secret as Y and dropped the space depending on p_0. The main advantage of the schemes [M82] and [AB83] over [S79] (and [B79]) is that the computational complexity of the reconstruction of the secret from $t + 1$ shares behaves as $\mathcal{O}(t + 1)$ while it behaves as $\mathcal{O}((t + 1) \cdot log^2(t + 1))$ for the Shamir scheme.

It is known that any set of t shares of a $(t + 1, l)$ Shamir scheme gives no information from an information theoretic and complexity theoretic viewpoint. The argument can be found in [S79], even if the concepts used are not the same. Also, the sizes of the share spaces and the secret space are equal. Therefore, the Shamir scheme is called ideal and perfect zero-knowledge (see the definitions 5 and 7 in section 2).

However, in the $(t + 1, l)$ threshold scheme based on the Chinese remainder theorem, the sizes of the share spaces and the secret space are not equal. In addition, few results are known about the information on the secret given by any set of t shares. In the scheme of Mignotte [M82], any share substantially decreases the entropy of the secret. Asmuth and Bloom [AB83] showed that the entropy of the secret decreases "not too much" when t shares are known provided that the parameters of the scheme satisfy a complex condition. The problem with this approach is that the notion of security is unclear, moreover the way one has to choose the parameters might led to schemes far from ideal schemes. Goldreich *et al.* [GRS00] show that any set of $t - 1$ shares gives no information on the secret using the zero-knowledge theory provided that the parameters on the system satisfy a natural condition (the primes p_i's have to be consecutive).

In this paper, we revisit the security of the threshold scheme based on the Chinese remainder theorem when the parameters are consecutive primes using modern concepts of security in cryptography [GB01]. We introduce the concept of an asymptotically perfect and an asymptotically ideal schemes which are natural relaxations of perfect and ideal schemes. We prove that the $(t + 1, l)$ threshold scheme based on the Chinese remainder theorem with consecutive primes is asymptotically ideal (and therefore asymptotically perfect) and perfect zero-knowledge. This means, in both cases, that t shares give no information on the secret. The two first theorems strengthen the result of Asmuth and Bloom [AB83], while the latest is an improvement of a result in [GRS00].

This paper is organized as follows. In section 2, we discuss basic definitions of threshold schemes, including the definition of an asymptotically perfect and an asymptotically ideal scheme. In section 3, we detail the threshold scheme to be studied. Section 4 describes the previous work on the security of Chinese remainder theorem based threshold schemes. In section 5, we find an upper bound on the loss of entropy of the secret generated by shares when the secret is uniformly selected. Using these result, we prove that the scheme is asymptotically perfect and asymptotically ideal when the secret is uniformly chosen and the parameters of the system satisfy a natural condition (the primes p_i's are consecutive). Finally, we prove that the scheme with consecutive primes is perfect zero-knowledge.

2   Theoretical Notions about Threshold Schemes

In this section, we present different definitions related to threshold schemes. Definitions 1, 3, 5, 7 are slight modifications of those presented in [DF94]. Definitions 2, 4, 6 are introduced in the current paper.

Let us first define a threshold scheme.

Definition 1. *Let $\mathcal{X}$ be a set of pairs of public and security parameters. A $(t+1, l)$ threshold scheme is a collection of pairs of algorithms $(Share_{(x,1^k)}, Combine_{(x,1^k)})$, where $(x, 1^k) \in \mathcal{X}$, such that:*

1. *$Share_{(x,1^k)}$ is a probabilistic polynomial time algorithm taking as input a secret s coming from the secret space $\mathcal{S}(x, 1^k) \subseteq \{0,1\}^k$ and producing as output a set of l shares s_i coming each from the share space $\mathcal{S}_i(x, 1^k)$, $i = 1, \ldots, l$.*
2. *$Combine_{(x,1^k)}$ is a polynomial time algorithm taking as input any set of $t+1$ shares out of the l and producing as output the unique secret s.*

Note that in this definition, no probability is associated to the secret space $\mathcal{S}(x, 1^k)$.

Next, we define the loss of entropy of the secret generated by the knowledge of a set shares. So far as the authors know this definition is new in the context of the threshold scheme. Note that this quantity is related to the average mutual information (see [G68]). The concept of loss of entropy of the secret will be used in the definition of perfect and asymptotically perfect schemes.

Definition 2. *Let $(Share_{(x,1^k)}, Combine_{(x,1^k)})$ be a $(t+1, l)$ threshold scheme. Let $P(x, 1^k)$ be the probability distribution on $\mathcal{S}(x, 1^k)$. Then, we define the loss of entropy of the secret generated by the knowledge of $\{s_i : i \in I\}$ by the values:*

$$\Delta_{(x,1^k)}(s_i : i \in I) = H(s \in \mathcal{S}(x, 1^k)) - H(s \in \mathcal{S}(x, 1^k)|s_i : i \in I)$$

where $H(\cdot)$ [2] is the entropy function.

---

[2]   The entropy of S selected from the alphabet $\mathcal{S}$ is defined as

$$H(S) = \sum_{s \in \mathcal{S}} P(S = s) \log(1/P(S = s)).$$

Remark 1. Note that while the average mutual information is always positive, the loss of entropy $\Delta(y) = H(S) - H(S|Y = y)$ may be negative. Consider the random variable $S \in \{-1, 0, 1\}$ such that $P(S = -1) = 7/8$, $P(S = 0) = 1/16$ and $P(S = 1) = 1/16$. Consider the random variable Y taking the value 1 if $S \geq 0$ and 0 otherwise, we have $P(S = -1|Y = 1) = 0$, $P(S = 0|Y = 1) = 1/2$ and $P(S = 1|Y = 1) = 1/2$. Therefore, $\Delta(1) = H(S) - H(S|Y = 1) = (7/8 \log(8/7) + 1/16 \log(16) + 1/16 \log(16)) - (1/2 \log(1/2) + 1/2 \log(1/2)) = 0.668 - 1 \approx -0.33$.

Let us introduce now a probability distribution $P(x, 1^k)$ on the secret space $\mathcal{S}(x, 1^k)$.

The following definition enables us to define the security of a threshold scheme from an information theoretic viewpoint. This definition depends on the set of probability distributions $P(x, 1^k)$.

Definition 3. *A threshold scheme $(t + 1, l)$ is called perfect with respect to the set of probability distributions $P(x, 1^k)$ on $\mathcal{S}(x, 1^k)$ if for all $(x, 1^k) \in \mathcal{X}$, it holds that:*

- *$H(s \in \mathcal{S}(x, 1^k)) \neq 0$ and,*
- *for all $I \subset \{1 \ldots l\}$ with $|I| \leq t$, we have*

$$\Delta_{(x,1^k)}(s_i : i \in I) = 0.$$

Let us introduce the asymptotic version of the previous definition. This relaxation will enable us to prove that the threshold scheme based on the Chinese remainder theorem is asymptotically perfect while it is not perfect in the strict sense.

Definition 4. *A threshold scheme $(t+1, l)$ is asymptotically perfect with respect to the set of probabilities $P(x, 1^k)$, if for all $\epsilon > 0$, there exists $k_0 \geq 0$ such that for all $(x, 1^k) \in \mathcal{X}$ with $k \geq k_0$, we have for all $I \subset \{1, \ldots, l\}$ with $|I| \leq t$,*

$$|\Delta_{(x,1^k)}(s_i : i \in I)| \leq \epsilon.$$

and $H(s \in \mathcal{S}(x, 1^k)) \neq 0$.

Remark 2. $|I|$ denotes the cardinality of the set I.

Remark 3. Note that it is essential to take the absolute value here, as Δ may be negative. However, if the distribution of the secret is uniform, one has $\Delta \geq 0$.

While security is an important factor, efficiency in terms of memory usage is also of great interest. This efficiency is measured by comparing the size of the share spaces to the size of the secret space. Indeed, the length of the elements depend on the size of these spaces if an optimal representation is used. The definition of an ideal scheme includes the property of security and efficiency.

Definition 5. *A threshold scheme* $(t + 1, l)$ *is ideal with respect to the set of probabilities* $P(x, 1^k)$ *if:*

- *it is perfect with respect to this set of probabilities and,*
- *if for all* $(x, 1^k) \in \mathcal{X}$, *we have*

$$|\mathcal{S}_i(x, 1^k)| = |\mathcal{S}(x, 1^k)| \quad \forall i = 1, \ldots, l.$$

Let us introduce the asymptotic version of the previous definition. This relaxation will enable us to prove that the threshold scheme based on the Chinese remainder theorem is asymptotically ideal even though it is not strictly ideal.

Definition 6. *A threshold scheme* $(t + 1, l)$ *is asymptotically ideal with respect to the set of probabilities* $P(x, 1^k)$ *if:*

- *it is asymptotically perfect with respect to this set of probabilities and,*
- *for all* $\epsilon > 0$, *there exists some* $k_0 \geq 0$ *such that for all* $(x, 1^k) \in \mathcal{X}$ *with* $k \geq k_0$, *we have for all* $i \in \{1, \ldots, l\}$,

$$|\mathcal{S}_i(x, 1^k)|/|\mathcal{S}(x, 1^k)| \leq 1 + \epsilon$$

When the shared key is associated to a public key, the entropy of the secret is zero. Therefore, we can not use the concept of perfect scheme to study the security of the schemes used in conjunction with public key cryptosystems. In order to solve this problem, Desmedt and Frankel [DF94] proposed to use the zero-knowledge theory. Working this way, it is possible to study the security of a threshold scheme even if the shared key is related to a public key.

Definition 7. *A threshold scheme* $(t + 1, l)$ *is perfect zero-knowledge if there exists a set of probabilistic polynomial time algorithms* $Simul(x, 1^k)$ *such that for all polynomial* $poly(\cdot)$, *there exists some* $k_0 \geq 0$ *such that for all* $(x, 1^k) \in \mathcal{X}$ *with* $k \geq k_0$, *we have for all* $s \in \mathcal{S}(x, 1^k)$ *and for all* $I \subset \{1, \ldots, l\}$ *with* $|I| \leq t$,

$$\sum_{s_I \in \mathcal{S}_I(x, 1^k)} |P(I_{|Share_{(x, 1^k)}(s)} = s_I) - P(Simul(x, 1^k) = s_I)| \leq 1/poly(k),$$

where s_I, $\mathcal{S}_I(x, 1^k)$, *and* $I_{|(s_1, \ldots, s_l)}$ *and represent respectively* $(s_{i_1}, \ldots, s_{i_j})$, $\mathcal{S}_{i_1}(x, 1^k) \times \ldots \times \mathcal{S}_{i_j}(x, 1^k)$ *and* $(s_{i_1}, \ldots, s_{i_j})$ *for* $I = \{i_1, \ldots, i_j\}$.

Note that this definition is independent of the probability distribution $P(x, 1^k)$ on $\mathcal{S}(x, 1^k)$.

In the next section, we present the threshold scheme whose security we study in the following sections.

3   Threshold Scheme Based on the CRT

Below, we describe two algorithms, corresponding to the sharing and reconstruction phases. of the threshold scheme based on the Chinese remainder theorem. We adopted the version present in [GRS00]. In the remainder of the text, $x \in_R S$ means that x is selected from S with an uniform probability.

Initialisation:
Let $t + 1 \leq l$ and consider the primes $p_0 < p_1 < p_2 < ... < p_l$.

Sharing:
To share a secret $r_0 \overset{\triangle}{=} s \in \mathbb{Z}_{p_0}$, the dealer:

1. chooses $r_1 \in_R \mathbb{Z}_{p_1}, ..., r_t \in_R \mathbb{Z}_{p_t}$;
2. determines $Y \in \mathbb{Z}_P$ where $P \overset{\triangle}{=} \prod_{i=0}^{t} p_i$ such that $Y \equiv r_i \mod p_i$ for $i = 0, 1, ..., t$;
3. computes the shares $s_i = Y \mod p_i$ for $i = 1, ..., l$.

This algorithm is denoted by $Share_{(t+1, p_0, ..., p_l, 1^{|p_0|})}(s) = (s_1, ..., s_l)$.

Reconstruction:
Given a set of $t + 1$ shares $\{s_i : i \in I\}$, the secret s is recovered as follow:

1. compute $X \in \mathbb{Z}_{\prod_{i \in I} p_i}$ such that $X \equiv s_i \mod p_i$ for $i \in I$, using the Chinese remainder theorem;
2. compute $s = X \mod p_0$.

This algorithm is denoted by $Comb_{(t+1, p_0, ..., p_l, 1^{|p_0|})}(s_i : i \in I) = s$.

Remark 4. $|p_i|$ denotes the number of bits of p_i.

Remark 5. There are many different versions of the threshold scheme based on the Chinese remainder in the literature. Mignotte [M82] and Asmuth and Bloom [AB83] used coprime numbers p_i's while Goldreich *et al.* [GRS00] focused only on prime numbers. Also, Mignotte [M82] defined the secret as Y in the sharing algorithm and dropped the space depending on p_0. This last version lead to a very insecure scheme.

4   Previous Work about the Security of the Threshold Scheme Based on the CRT

In [M82], they compute the equivalent of the loss on entropy of the secret generated by the knowlegde on shares (see definition 2 in section 2). Note that the security of this scheme is quite weak.

The scheme [AB83] is a modification of the scheme [M82] by considering the secret $Y \mod p_0$ instead of Y itself. In addition, they [AB83] request that the parameters of the system (the co-prime numbers p_i's) are increasing numbers and that

$$\prod_{i=1}^{t+1} p_i > p_0 \prod_{i=1}^{t} p_{l-i+1} \tag{1}$$

for a $(t + 1, l)$ threshold scheme such that the entropy of the secret decreases "not too much" when t shares are known. First, notice that the notion of security used is quite unclear. Note that at this time, modern security concepts were not yet build and therefore the notion of security of a threshold scheme did not make use of them. Also, this condition (1) might lead to schemes where the size of the shares are much more bigger that the size of the secret (if we choose p_0 very small) which we try to avoid. Finally, in practice, we have to generate co-prime numbers (usually primes numbers) and check whether the condition (1) is satisfied which is not very handy.

In [GRS00], Goldreich *et al.* advice to choose the primes (co-prime numbers are likely valid as well) as close as possible and prove that $t - 1$ shares (or less) give no information on the secret in the sens of the zero-knowledge theory for a $(t + 1, l)$ threshold scheme.

5   Security of a Threshold Scheme Based on the CRT

In the following Lemma, we compute an upper bound on the loss of entropy of the secret generated by the knowledge of shares when the secret is uniformly selected from the secret space. Recall that $x \in_R S$ means that x is selected from S with an uniform probability.

Lemma 1. *Let the secret* $s \in_R \mathbb{Z}_{p_0}$, *the shares* s_i $(i = 1, ..., l)$ *be generated by the algorithm* $Share_{(t+1, p_0, ..., p_l, 1^{|p_0|})}(s)$, *and* $I \subseteq \{1, ..., l\}$.
The loss of entropy of the secret $s \in_R \mathbb{Z}_{p_0}$ *generated by the knowledge of the shares* $\{s_i \in \mathbb{Z}_{p_i} : i \in I\}$ *satisfies the following relations:*

$$\Delta_{(t, p_0, ..., p_l)}(s_i : I) \leq \log\left((p_0(\lfloor (C(I) + 1)/p_0 \rfloor + 1)/C(I)\right) \qquad \textit{if } C(I) \neq 0,$$
$$= \log p_0 \qquad\qquad\qquad\qquad \textit{otherwise,}$$

where $C(I) = \lfloor \prod_{i=0}^{t} p_i / \prod_{v \in I} p_v \rfloor$.

Proof. Define $C^*(I) \triangleq \prod_{i=0}^{t} p_i / \prod_{v \in I} p_v$, $C(I) \triangleq \lfloor C^*(I) \rfloor$ and $P \triangleq \prod_{i=0}^{t} p_i$.

Consider the case $C(I) \neq 0$.

Let's prove that for all $s \in \mathbb{Z}_{p_0}$, $P(S = s | s_i : i \in I) \leq (\lfloor (C(I) + 1)/p_0 \rfloor + 1)/C(I)$.

Let $s \in \mathbb{Z}_{p_0}$. Denote with V, the set of possible values for $X \in \mathbb{Z}_P$ given the set $\{s_i : i \in I\}$.

In order to determine a lower bound B on the cardinality of V, we study the number of solutions $X \in \mathbb{Z}_P$ of the linear system $X \equiv s_i \bmod p_i$ for all $i \in I$. From the Chinese remainder theorem, it follows that the solutions of this system are $X_0 + r \cdot \prod_{i \in I} p_i$, where X_0 is the unique solution of the system in $\mathbb{Z}_{\prod_{i \in I} p_i}$ and $r \in [0, \ldots, C(I) - 1]$ or $[0, \ldots, C(I)]$ depending on the value of X_0. Therefore, $B = C(I)$.

Similarly, in order to determine an upper bound A on the number of elements $X \in V$ such that $X \bmod p_0$, we study the number of solutions $r \in [0, \ldots, C(I)]$ of the system $s \equiv X_0 + r \cdot \prod_{i \in I} p_i \bmod p_0$, or equivalently $r \equiv (s - X_0) \cdot (\prod_{i \in I} p_i)^{-1} \bmod p_0$. It follows that $A = \lfloor (C(I) + 1)/p_0 \rfloor + 1$.

Eventually, we have $P(S = s | s_i : i \in I) \leq A/B = (\lfloor (C(I)+1)/p_0 \rfloor + 1)/C(I)$. By definition

$$H(S|s_i : i \in I) \geq \log(C(I)/(\lfloor (C(I) + 1)/p_0 \rfloor + 1)).$$

Moreover, s is uniformly chosen in $\mathbb{Z}_{p_0}$, therefore $H(S) = \log(p_0)$. We find

$$\Delta_{(t,p_0,\ldots,p_l)}(s_i : I) \leq \log(p_0 \cdot (\lfloor (C(I) + 1)/p_0 \rfloor + 1)/C(I)).$$

The case $C(I) = 0$ is trivial since the set of shares $\{s_i : i \in I\}$ enables us to recover the secret exactly using the Chinese remainder theorem. Hence, it follows that $H(S|s_i : i \in I) = 0$.

$\square$

In the remainder of the text, we only consider threshold schemes with consecutive primes. We will refer to such threshold shemes using the notation $(Share_{(t+1,l,p_0,1^{|p_0|})}, Comb_{(t+1,l,p_0,1^{|p_0|})})$.

Using the previous Lemma, we can prove the asymptotical perfection of the scheme when the secret is uniformly chosen and the primes p_i's are consecutive. Remind that $|p_i|$ denotes the number of bits of p_i.

Theorem 1. *The $(t + 1, l)$ threshold scheme based on the Chinese remainder theorem with consecutive primes p_i's is asymptotically perfect with respect to the uniform probability on $\mathbb{Z}_{p_0}$.*

More formally, for all $\epsilon > 0$, there exists some $k_0 \geq 0$ such that for all threshold schemes $(Share_{(t+1,l,p_0,1^{|p_0|})}, Comb_{(t+1,l,p_0,1^{|p_0|})})$ with $|p_0| \geq k_0$ we have for all $I \subset \{1, \ldots, l\}$ with $|I| \leq t$,

$$|\Delta_{(t+1,l,p_0,1^{|p_0|})}(s_i : i \in I)| \leq \epsilon.$$

Proof. First, we have that $\Delta_{(t,p_0,\ldots,p_l)}(s_i : i \in I) \geq 0$ by the remark on the definition (2).

Define $C^*(I) \triangleq \prod_{i=0}^{t} p_i / \prod_{v \in I} p_v$ and $C(I) \triangleq \lfloor C^*(I) \rfloor$.

By hypothesis, the primes p_i's ($0 \leq i \leq l$) are consecutive. It follows that $p_{i+1} < p_i + p_i^{1/2+1/21}$ for p_i sufficiently large (see [R88], p. 193).

Consider the case $|I| = t$.

If $I = \{1, \ldots, t\}$, it follows from the Chinese remainder theorem that $\Delta_{(t,p_0,\ldots,p_l)}(s_i : i \in I) = 0$.

Assume $I \neq \{1, \ldots, t\}$. Because the primes p_i's are consecutive, it holds that $C(I) > 0$, for all sufficiently large prime p_0. Also, $C(I) = \lfloor p_0 \cdot \prod_{i=1}^{t} p_i / \prod_{i \in I} p_i \rfloor \leq \lfloor p_0 \cdot p_t/(p_t + 2) \rfloor$. Note that $\lfloor p_0 \cdot p_t/(p_t + 2) \rfloor < p_0 - 1$ if and only if $p_t/(p_t + 2) < (p_0 - 1)/p_0$. This last inequality is equivalent to $p_t < 2p_0 - 2$, which holds for p_0 sufficiently large because the primes p_i's are consecutive. Therefore $C(I) < p_0 - 1$, for all prime p_0 sufficiently large and for all $I \neq \{1, \ldots, t\}$ such that $|I| = t$.

We deduce that $p_0 \cdot (\lfloor (C(I)+1)/p_0 \rfloor + 1)/C(I) = p_0/C(I)$, for all sufficiently large prime p_0. Using Lemma 1, we have

$$\Delta_{(t,p_0,\ldots,p_l)}(s_i : I) \leq \log(p_0/C(I)). \tag{2}$$

Because the primes p_i's are consecutive, it holds that, for all sufficiently large p_0

$$p_0^{t+1}/(p_0^t + \sum_i a_i p_0^{b_i}) \leq C^*(I)$$

where $a_i \in \mathbb{R}^+$ and $0 < b_i < t$, for all i.

For all sufficiently large primes p_0 and for all $I \neq \{1, \ldots, t\}$ with $|I| = t$, it holds

$$p_0/C(I) \leq p_0/(C^*(I) - 1) \leq p_0(p_0^t + \sum_i a_i p_0^{b_i})/(p_0^{t+1} - (p_0^t + \sum_i a_i p_0^{b_i})).$$

Applying the logarithm operator and using (2), we get

$$\Delta_{(p_0, \ldots, p_l)}(s_i : i \in I) \leq \log(p_0(p_0^t + \sum_i a_i p_0^{b_i})/(p_0^{t+1} - (p_0^t + \sum_i a_i p_0^{b_i}))).$$

The upper bound converges to 0 when p_0 converges to infinity.

Consider the case $|I| < t$. It holds that $\Delta_{(p_0, \ldots, p_l)}(s_i : i \in I) \leq \log((C^*(I) + 2 + 2p_0)/(C^*(I) - 1))$. Note that $2 + 2p_0$ and -1 are negligible in front of $C^*(I)$. Therefore this upper bound converges to 0 when the prime p_0 converges to infinity. The result follows.   □

The next theorem tells us that the threshold scheme is moreover asymptotically ideal.

Theorem 2. *The $(t + 1, l)$ threshold scheme based on the Chinese remainder theorem with consecutive primes p_i's is asymptotically ideal with respect to the uniform probability on $\mathbb{Z}_{p_0}$.*

More formally,

- *$(Share_{(t+1,l,p_0,1^{|p_0|})}, Comb_{(t+1,l,p_0,1^{|p_0|})})$ is asymptotically perfect with respect to this probability distribution and,*
- *for all $\epsilon > 0$, there exists some $k_0 \geq 0$ such that for all p_0 with $|p_0| \geq k_0$ the consecutive primes p_i's satisfy $p_i/p_0 \leq 1 + \epsilon$ for $i = 0, \ldots, l$.*

Proof. The first part comes from the previous theorem.

Let us prove the second part. The primes p_i's ($0 \leq i \leq l$) are consecutive, it follows that $p_{i+1} < p_i + p_i^{1/2+1/21}$ for p_i's sufficiently large (see [R88], p. 193). This means that for all $j \geq 0$, $p_j < p_0 + f(p_0)$ where $f(p_0)/p_0 \geq 0$ converges to 0 if p_0 converges to infinity. The result follows.   □

Eventually, we prove that this scheme is perfect zero-knowledge when the secret is uniformly selected and the primes p_i's are consecutive. Goldreich *et al.* [GRS00] proved that for the $(t + 1, l)$ threshold scheme with consecutive primes p_i's, $t - 1$ shares give no information on the secret from a complexity theoretic viewpoint. By improving the last part of their proof, we are able to prove that in fact t shares give no information on the secret.

Theorem 3. *The threshold scheme $(t+1, l)$ based on the Chinese remainder theorem with consecutive primes p_i's is perfect zero-knowledge.*

More formally, there exists a set of polynomial algorithms, denoted by $Sim_{(t+1,l,p_0,1^{|p_0|})}$, such that for all polynomials $p(\cdot)$, there exists some $k_0 \geq 0$ such that for all threshold schemes $(Share_{(t+1,l,p_0,1^{|p_0|})}, Comb_{(t+1,l,p_0,1^{|p_0|})})$ and $|p_0| \geq k_0$, we have

for all $s \in \mathbb{Z}_{p_0}$ and for all $I \subset \{1, \ldots, l\}$ such that $|I| \leq t$,

$$\frac{1}{2} \sum_{s_I \in \mathbb{Z}_{p_I}} |P(I_{|Share_{(t+1,l,p_0,1^{|p_0|})}}(s) = s_I) - P(Sim_{(t+1,l,p_0,1^{|p_0|})} = s_I)| \leq \frac{1}{p(|p_0|)},$$

where $I_{|(s_1,\ldots,s_l)}$, $\mathbb{Z}_{p_I}$ and s_I represent respectively $(s_{i_1}, \ldots, s_{i_j})$, $\mathbb{Z}_{p_{i_1}} \times \cdots \times \mathbb{Z}_{p_{i_j}}$ and $(s_{i_1}, \ldots, s_{i_j})$ for $I = \{i_1, \ldots, i_j\}$.

Proof. Define $K \triangleq \prod_{i=1}^{t} p_i$, $M(I) \triangleq \prod_{i \in I} p_i$. The notation $[x]_y$ indicates the minimum positive representant of $x \bmod y$.

First, note that $I_{|Share_{(t+1,l,p_0,1^{|p_0|})}}(s) = ([Y(s)]_{p_i} : i \in I)$, where $Y(s) \in \mathbb{Z}_{p_0 \cdot K}$ is the random variable computed according to the sharing phase on the secret $s \in \mathbb{Z}_{p_0}$.

We claim that $Sim_{(t+1,l,p_0,1^{|p_0|})} = ([Y(s')]_{p_i} : i \in I)$, where $Y(s') \in \mathbb{Z}_{p_0 \cdot K}$ is the random variable computed according to the sharing phase on the value $s' \in \mathbb{Z}_{p_0}$ chosen at random.

Therefore, we have to prove that for all polynomial $p(\cdot)$, there exists a $k_0 \geq 0$ such that for all p_0 with $|p_0| \geq k_0$, we have,

for all $s \in \mathbb{Z}_{p_0}$ and for all $I \subset \{1, \ldots, l\}$ with $|I| \leq t$,

$$\frac{1}{2} \sum_{s_I \in \mathbb{Z}_{p_I}} |P([Y(s)]_{p_i} = s_i : i \in I) - P([Y(s')]_{p_i} = s_i : i \in I)| \leq \frac{1}{p(|p_0|)}.$$

Let $I \subset \{1, ..., l\}$ such that $|I| \leq t$.

By the Chinese remainder theorem, there is a bijection between $\mathbb{Z}_{M(I)}$ and $\prod_{i \in I} \mathbb{Z}_{p_i}$.

Therefore, the left hand side of the previous inequality is equivalent to:

$$\frac{1}{2} \sum_{z=0}^{M(I)-1} |P([Y(s)]_{M(I)} = z) - P([Y(s')]_{M(I)} = z)|. \tag{3}$$

Note that

$$|P([Y(s)]_{M(I)} = z) - P([Y(s')]_{M(I)} = z)| \leq$$

$$|P([Y(s)]_{M(I)} = z) - P(U_{M(I)} = z)| + |P([Y(s')]_{M(I)} = z) - P(U_{M(I)} = z)|,$$

where $U_{M(I)}$ is a uniform random variable on $\mathbb{Z}_{M(I)}$.

Let us find an upper bound on the first term of the right hand side of the inequality.

Because of the bijection between $\prod_{i=0}^{t} \mathbb{Z}_{p_i}$ and $\mathbb{Z}_{p_0 K}$, $Y(s) = s + r \cdot p_0$ with $r \in_R \mathbb{Z}_K$. Note that r is the only random element in this expression. The addition of s and the multiplication by p_0 together induce a permutation of the elements of $\mathbb{Z}_{M(I)}$. Therefore,

$$\sum_{z=0}^{M(I)-1} |P([Y(s)]_{M(I)} = z) - P(U_{M(I)} = z)| =$$

$$\sum_{z=0}^{M(I)-1} |P([r]_{M(I)} = z) - P(U_{M(I)} = z)| \tag{4}$$

Splitting the sum into two parts, we get

$$(4) = \sum_{z=0}^{[K]_{M(I)}-1} |P([r]_{M(I)} = z) - P(U_{M(I)} = z)|$$
$$+ \sum_{z=[K]_{M(I)}}^{M(I)-1} |P([r]_{M(I)} = z) - P(U_{M(I)} = z)|$$

Note that if $0 \le z \le [K]_{M(I)} - 1$,

$$P([r]_{M(I)} = z) = (((K - [K]_{M(I)})/M(I)) + 1)/K,$$

and if $[K]_{M(I)} \le z \le M(I) - 1$,

$$P([r]_{M(I)} = z) = (K - [K]_{M(I)})/M(I)K.$$

Also,

$$P(U_{M(I)} = z) = 1/M(I).$$

Therefore,

$$(4) = 2\left([K]_{M(I)}/K - [K]^2_{M(I)}/M(I)K\right). \tag{5}$$

Because, the primes are consecutives, $p_{i+1} < p_i + p_i^{1/2+1/21}$. It follows that $M(I) < p_0^{|I|} + \sum_i a_i p_0^{b_i}$, where $a_i \in \mathbb{R}_0^+$ and $b_i < |I|$, for all i.
If $|I| < t$, for all p_0 large enough, we have

$$M(I) < p_0^{|I|} + \sum_i a_i p_0^{b_i} < p_0^t < K.$$

Therefore,

$$(3) \le 2M(I)/K \le 2(p_0^{|I|} + \sum_i a_i p_0^{b_i})/p_0^t. \tag{6}$$

If $|I| = t$, $M(I) > K$ because the primes increase.
Therefore,

$$(3) \le 2(M(I) - K)/K \le 2(p_0^t + \sum_i a_i p_0^{b_i} - p_0^t)/p_0^t. \tag{7}$$

In both cases, the upper bound behaves as the inverse of an exponential in $|p_0|$, where $|p_0|$ denotes the number of bits of p_0. Also, both bounds depend neither on s nor on I. Therefore, (3) is bounded by the maximum of the bounds (6) and (7) over all $I \subset \{1, \ldots, l\}$ with $|I| \le t$. The result follows. $\qquad \square$

6 Conclusions

In this paper, we analyzed the security of a threshold scheme based on the Chinese remainder theorem in the context of theoretical cryptography. We have introduced the definition of an asymptotically perfect and asymptotically ideal schemes that are natural relaxations of perfect and ideal schemes. We have proved that the scheme based on the CRT is asymptotically ideal and perfect zero-knowledge if the parameters of the system satisfy a natural condition. Those properties imply that any set of t shares of a $(t + 1, l)$ threshold scheme based on the Chinese remainder theorem gives no information on the secret.

Acknowledgements

The authors would like to thank Philippe Delsarte and Jacques Stern for their interest in this work and for their valuable suggestions. Also, they would like to thank Madhu Sudan for answering some questions. We are also grateful to the anonymous referees for their valuable remarks. Michael Quisquater is a F.W.O.-research fellow, sponsored by the Fund for Scientific Research – Flanders (Belgium).

References

AB83.   Asmuth, C., Bloom, J.: A modular approach to key safeguarding. *IEEE Trans. inform. Theory*, 1983, **IT-29**, pp. 208–210.

B79.   Blakley, G.R.: Safeguarding cryptographic keys. *AFIPS Conf. Proc.*, 1979, **48**, pp. 313–317.

DF94.   Desmedt, Y., Frankel, Y.: Homomorphic zero-knowledge threshold schemes over any finite abelian group. *SIAM J. discr. math.*, 1994, **7**, pp. 667–679.

G68.   Gallager, R.G.: Information Theory and Reliable Communication. Willey, 1968.

GB01.   Goldwasser S., Bellare M.: Lectures Notes on Cryptography. 1996–2001. http://www-cse.ucsd.edu/users/mihir/papers/gb.html.

GRS00. Goldreich, O., Ron, D., Sudan, M.: Chinese remainder with errors. *IEEE Trans. Inform. Theory*, 2000, **IT-46**, pp. 1330–1338.

KGH83. Karnin, E.D., Greene, J.W., Hellman, M.E.: On secret sharing systems. *IEEE Trans. Inform. Theory*, 1983, **IT-29**, pp. 35–41.

M82.   Mignotte, M.: How to share a secret. Advances in Cryptology – Eurocrypt'82, LNCS, 1983, **149**, Springer-Verlag, pp. 371–375.

R88.   Ribenboim, P.: The Book of Prime Number Records. Springer-Verlag, 1988.

S79.   Shamir, A.: How to share a secret. *Commun. ACM* 1979, **22**, pp. 612–613.

SV88.   Stinson, D.R., Vanstone S.A. *SIAM J. discr. math.*, 1988, **1**, pp. 230–236.

Solving Underdefined Systems
of Multivariate Quadratic Equations

Nicolas Courtois[1], Louis Goubin[1], Willi Meier[2], and Jean-Daniel Tacier[2]

[1] CP8 Crypto Lab, SchlumbergerSema
36-38 rue de la Princesse, BP45
F-78430 Louveciennes Cedex, France
{NCourtois, LGoubin}@slb.com
[2] FH Aargau, CH-5210 Windisch
{meierw,jd.tacier}@fh-aargau.ch

Abstract. The security of several recent digital signature schemes is based on the difficulty of solving large systems of quadratic multivariate polynomial equations over a finite field $\mathbf{F}$. This problem, sometimes called MQ, is known to be NP-hard. When the number m of equations is equal to the number n of variables, and if $n < 15$, Gröbner base algorithms have been applied to solve MQ. In the overdefined case $n \ll m$, the techniques of relinearization and XL, due to A. Shamir et. al., have shown to be successful for solving MQ. In signature schemes, we usually have $n \gg m$. For example signature schemes Flash and Sflash submitted to Nessie call for primitives or the UOV scheme published at Eurocrypt 1999. Little is known about the security of such underdefined systems.
In this paper, three new and different methods are presented for solving underdefined multivariate systems of quadratic equations. As already shown at Eurocrypt 1999, the problem MQ becomes polynomial when $n \geq m(m+1)$ for fields $\mathbf{F}$ of characteristic 2. We show that for any field, for about $n \geq 2^{m/7}(m+1)$, exponential but quite small in practice, the problem becomes polynomial in n.
When $n \to m$ the complexity of all our 3 algorithms tends to q^m. However for practical instances of cryptosystems with $n \approx \mathcal{O}(m)$, we show how to achieve complexities significantly lower than exhaustive search. For example we are able break Unbalanced Oil and Vinegar signature schemes for some "bad" choices of the parameters (but not for the parameters proposed in [4]).

1 Introduction

Since the 1970's many digital signature schemes have been proposed and the best are probably those based on factoring or discrete logarithms in well chosen groups. However in many specific applications the classical standardized schemes are either too slow, or give signatures that are too long. In order to fill the gap, several new digital signature schemes based on multivariate polynomials have been studied recently J. Patarin et. al. hoping to do better. These signature schemes can be very efficient in smart card implementations and are among the

D. Naccache and P. Paillier (Eds.): PKC 2002, LNCS 2274, pp. 211–227, 2002.
© Springer-Verlag Berlin Heidelberg 2002

shortest signature schemes ever known [10]. They differ in the type of trapdoor structure embedded into the public polynomials, see [4] for a particular example of such a scheme and for an overview of various other schemes. Several of these schemes were broken soon after being proposed, for others the security is an open problem.

Most multivariate schemes rely on the problem of solving systems of multivariate polynomial modular equations over a small finite field $\mathbf{F}$. The general problem is called MQ and is known to be NP-complete, even for $q = 2$, cf. [3]. In practice, the public key will be a system of m quadratic polynomials $G_i(x_1, ..., x_n)$, $i = 1, ..., m$, with n variables x_j, $j = 1, ..., n$ over a finite field $\mathbf{F}$ of (small) order q, where m and n are (large enough) integers. Messages are represented as elements of the vector space $\mathbf{F}^m$, whereas signatures are elements of $\mathbf{F}^n$. An element x is a signature of a message y if the public polynomials evaluated at x give the correct components of y, i.e., if $G_i(x_1, ..., x_n) = y_i$ for $i = 1, ..., m$. The trapdoor information enables a legitimate signer to find a solution x of the system for a given message y.

Several multivariate signature schemes use MQ systems of m quadratic equations in n variables with $n \gg m$. For example cryptosystems Flash and Sflash submitted to Nessie call for primitives [9] or the Unbalanced Oil and Vinegar scheme (UOV) [4].

As opposed to the case $m \gg n$, where useful methods for solving MQ are known (see [6], [1]), only one result seems to be known for finding a solution if $n \gg m$: In the massively underdefined case $n \geq m(m + 1)$, a polynomial algorithm for solving MQ is given in [4], provided the field $\mathbf{F}$ has characteristic 2.

In this paper, three different methods are developed for solving MQ in the underdefined case $n \gg m$ (algorithms A, B and C). We also generalize the known algorithm from [4] that solves in polynomial time massively underdefined systems of equations over fields of characteristic 2. We show that it can be extended to odd characteristics. The present version works for roughly about $n \geq 2^{m/7}(m + 1)$, exponential but in practice not so big.

The three algorithms A, B and C can also be applied for practical systems when $n = \mathcal{O}(m)$. Depending on the choice of m, n and q, one or the other of the algorithms as presented turns out to be more efficient, and no one outperforms the others in general. Their complexity remain exponential, but each of the 3 algorithms enables solving MQ with a complexity significantly lower than exhaustive search for some practical parameter sets.

The three algorithms apply different but well known principles: The birthday paradox, a linearization technique, and reduced representations of quadratic forms. These principles are used however in a novel way. By studying and comparing the efficiency of different algorithms for the same problem, we attempt to get a better understanding of the difficulty of MQ. As a cryptographic application, we obtain new criteria for the security parameters of general multivariate signature schemes. The security of schemes like Flash and Sflash is not affected by the results of this paper. However our algorithms can be used to break Unbalanced Oil and Vinegar signature schemes for some "bad" choices of the parameters (but not for the parameters proposed in [4]). Note that no attack was previously known for these parameters. This shows that the choice of the parameters for Unbalanced Oil and Vinegar must be made carefully.

In section 2 the problem MQ is described. In section 3, algorithms A, B and C for solving MQ in the underdefined case $n \gg m$ are presented, and their efficiency is studied. Section 4 presents efficient algorithms for solving massively underdefined MQ systems. In section 5, our methods are applied to the cryptanalysis of practical multivariate signature schemes. In Appendix A, a result on which algorithm C is based upon is derived.

2   The Problem MQ

Let $\mathbf{F}$ be a finite field of order q. Consider a (random) system of m simultaneous equations in n variables over $\mathbf{F}$,

$$G_\ell(x_1, x_2, ..., x_n) = y_\ell, \quad \ell = 1, ..., m,$$

where the G_ℓ are (not necessarily homogeneous) polynomials of degree two, i.e., G_ℓ is of the form

$$G_\ell(x_1, ..., x_n) = \sum_{i=1}^{n} \sum_{j \geq i}^{n} \alpha_{ij\ell} x_i x_j + \sum_{k=1}^{n} \gamma_{k\ell} x_k, \quad \ell = 1, ..., m.$$

Hereby the coefficients of the polynomials as well as the components of the vectors $x = (x_1, x_2, ..., x_n)$ and $y = (y_1, y_2, ..., y_m)$ are elements in $\mathbf{F}$. Depending on the parameters m and n, several algorithms have been developed to solve MQ: If $m = n < 15$, Gröbner bases algorithms can be applied to solve MQ (see [2] for one of the most efficient variants amongst such algorithms). In the overdefined case $m \gg n$, the methods of relinearization and XL have shown to be useful (see [6] and [1]). In particular, in the overdefined case $m = \varepsilon n^2$, the XL algorithm is expected to be polynomial. In the massively underdefined case $n \geq m(m + 1)$, a polynomial algorithm has been developed in [4] to solve MQ in case $\mathbf{F}$ has characteristic 2.

3   Solving MQ for Underdefined Systems of Equations

Suppose a given system of quadratic equations is underdefined, i.e., $n \gg m$. Several algorithms are presented in this section for solving MQ faster than by exhaustive search when $n \gg m$. Our goal is to find one among about q^{n-m} expected solutions.

The complexity of our algorithms will be compared to the complexity of exhaustive search that is about $\mathcal{O}(q^m)$. Thus a natural choice for an elementary operation is a numeric evaluation of all m quadratic polynomials G_ℓ for a single set of values of $x_1, ..., x_n$. If we want otherwise measure the complexity in terms of numbers of operations in $GF(q)$, the complexity should be multiplied by about $m \cdot n^2$.

3.1   Algorithms for Solving MQ over Any Finite Field

Algorithm A. Choose k variables out of n and k' equations out of m. Write each equation G_ℓ, $\ell = 1, ..., k'$, in the following form:

$$g_\ell(x_1, .., x_k) + \sum_{i=1}^{k} x_i \cdot \left(\sum_{j=k+1}^{n} \beta_{\ell i j} x_j \right) + g'_\ell(x_{k+1}, ..., x_n) = y_\ell$$

where g_ℓ, $g_{\ell'}$ are multivariate quadratic polynomials. Our aim is to remove the part of G_ℓ where $x_1, ..., x_k$ and $x_{k+1}, ..., x_n$ are mixed. For each G_ℓ this is done by imposing k linear relations on the variables $x_{k+1}, ..., x_n$ by

$$\sum_{j=k+1}^{n} \beta_{\ell i j} x_j = c_{\ell i}, \quad i = 1, ..., k,$$

where the constants $c_{\ell i}$ are elements in $\mathbf{F}$. Let $k = \min(m/2, \lfloor \sqrt{n/2 - \sqrt{n/2}} \rfloor)$, and let $k' = 2k$. Then $k' \leq m$, and we have

$$kk' \leq 2(\sqrt{n/2 - \sqrt{n/2}})^2 \leq n - 2\sqrt{n/2} \leq n - 2k,$$

(i.e., $2k^2 \leq n - 2k$ is satisfied). Therefore $n - k - kk' \geq k$. Thus imposing kk' linear constraints on the $n - k$ variables $x_{k+1}, ..., x_n$, we can still express them by $\bar{k} \geq k$ independent new variables $x'_1, ..., x'_{\bar{k}}$. Restricting to the equations G_ℓ, $\ell = 1, ..., 2k$, the system to solve becomes

$$g'_\ell(x_1, ..., x_k) + h_\ell(x'_1, ..., x'_{\bar{k}}) = y_\ell, \quad \ell = 1, ..., 2k.$$

where g'_ℓ differs from g_ℓ by linear summands in $x_1, ..., x_k$. This system can be solved in about q^k rather than q^{2k} trials: Generate the set of vectors obtained by evaluating g'_ℓ, $\ell = 1, ..., 2k$, in all q^k arguments. Similarly generate a set of q^k result vectors for $y_\ell - h_\ell$, $\ell = 1, ..., 2k$. By the birthday paradox, with some probability the sets have an element in common (see e.g. [8], p. 53). Once this partial system is solved, with probability q^{2k-m} the remaining $m - 2k$ equations will be satisfied too. Otherwise repeat the whole attack as described, with a different choice of subsets of k variables and of k' equations.

Thereby some polynomial overhead arises by imposing each time a new set of kk' linear constraints on a different set of $n - k$ variables. However this can be mostly avoided if n is slightly larger than m: Suppose that k, m and n besides $2k^2 \leq n - 2k$ also satisfy $2k^2 > m - 2k$. The latter inequality guarantees that the search space is still large enough if only the constants $c_{\ell i}$ change in each trial, but the subsets of variables and equations are chosen only once, so that the linear constraints (except the constants) remain the same. This means that in a parameterized expression describing the new variables $x'_1, ..., x'_{\bar{k}}$, only the constants change. Hence in substituting these variables in the quadratic expressions G_ℓ each time, only the linear parts need to be changed. Thus if $2k^2 > m - 2k$ we have:

Complexity of Algorithm A: $\mathcal{O}(q^{m-k})$, where $k = \min(m/2, \lfloor\sqrt{n/2 - \sqrt{n/2}}\rfloor)$. Hence the complexity of algorithm A for increasing n tends to $\mathcal{O}(q^{m/2})$.

Example: Let $n = 40$. Then $k = 4$ satisfies $2k^2 \le n - 2k$. As this holds by equality, $m = 39$ is the largest number of equations so that also $2k^2 > m - 2k$ is satisfied. Suppose furthermore that $q = 16$, $m = 20$. Then the complexity of algorithm A is of order 2^{64} instead of 2^{80} operations.

Algorithm B. This algorithm uses linearization to reduce the search complexity for solving MQ. Let k be an integer to be specified. In an initial step chose $m - k$ of the quadratic equations to eliminate the quadratic terms $x_i x_j$, $1 \le i, j \le k$. Hereby these terms are simply regarded as linear variables. The aim is to get k selected equations in which the variables $x_1, ..., x_k$ occur only linearly. This is possible if

$$k(k + 1)/2 \le m - k.$$

Hence

$$k \approx \lfloor\sqrt{2m + 2} - 1.5\rfloor,$$

which is at most $m/2$ for $m \ge 2$. After the initial step, which is done only once, the algorithm proceeds as follows:

1. Choose random values in **F** for the variables $x_{k+1}, ..., x_n$.
2. Substitute these values in the k selected quadratic equations to get a system of k linear equations in $x_1, ..., x_k$.
3. Solve this system of k linear equations.
4. Go back to 1. as long as the values for $x_1, ..., x_n$ thus determined do not satisfy the other $m - k$ quadratic equations.

Step 3 is of complexity $\mathcal{O}(k^3) = \mathcal{O}(m^{3/2})$. However this is not measured by numbers of numeric evaluations of systems of quadratic polynomials but by simple operations like addition and multiplication in the field **F**. To estimate the complexity of algorithm B, first note that in step 2, a number of $n - k$ values are substituted in k quadratic equations of n variables. This also includes a step of formally simplifying these equations, whose complexity can be reduced by only varying $m - k$ out of $n - k$ variables in step 1 in each trial, and leaving the other variables constant throughout the search. Thus the complexity of step 2 is growing with $k(m - k)^2$. The complexity of the formal step may be some multiple of the unit complexity and can dominate the complexity of step 3. Let $K = \max(C_2, C_3)$, where C_2 and C_3 measure the complexity of steps 2 and 3, respectively. Then we get

Complexity of Algorithm B: $K \cdot q^{m-k}$, where $k = \lfloor\sqrt{2m + 2} - 1.5\rfloor$, and where the factor K grows polynomially in k or $m - k$, respectively, and is not explicitly quantified.

Remark: There are possibilities to combine the principles applied in algorithms A and B, leading to algorithms with lower complexity of the exponential part compared to each of algorithms A and B, but at the cost of an increased polynomial overhead. Depending on the variant to be specified of such a combined algorithm, and depending on m, n and q, this algorithm may be more efficient than algorithms A and B alone.

3.2   An Algorithm for Solving MQ over Fields of Characteristic 2

In this section, a general method for simplifying underdefined systems of multivariate quadratic equations over fields of characteristic 2 is described. Combined with a relinearization or XL algorithms [6,1] it gives another algorithm to solve MQ in case $n \gg m$.

Preliminaries. Let $\mathbf{F}$ denote the field $GF(2^s)$. Then a quadratic form Q with n variables over $\mathbf{F}$ is a homogeneous polynomial in these variables of total degree two. Two quadratic forms Q_1 and Q_2 are equivalent if Q_1 can be transformed into Q_2 by means of a nonsingular linear transformation of the variables. A quadratic form Q with n variables is nondegenerate if it is not equivalent to a quadratic form with fewer than n variables. A linear form f over $\mathbf{F}$ with n variables is a linear expression $\sum_{i=1}^{n} a_i x_i$, where the coefficients a_i as well as the variables x_i are in $\mathbf{F}$. In later use, $\underline{f}$ will denote an element of $\mathbf{F}^n$, i.e., a column vector with components $a_i \in \mathbf{F}$, whereas the linear form f will denote the scalar product of $\underline{f}$ with $\underline{x} \in \mathbf{F}^n$. A nondegenerate quadratic form over $\mathbf{F}$ can be transformed in a sum of $\lfloor \frac{n}{2} \rfloor$ products of pairs of linear forms $f_{2i-1} f_{2i}$, $i=1,...,\lfloor \frac{n}{2} \rfloor$ plus at most two square terms. More precisely for n odd, $Q(\underline{x})$ can be transformed in:

$$f_1 f_2 + f_3 f_4 + \cdots + f_{n-2} f_{n-1} + f_n^2$$

and for n even in one of the two following forms:

$$f_1 f_2 + f_3 f_4 + \cdots + f_{n-1} f_n$$
$$f_1 f_2 + f_3 f_4 + \cdots + f_{n-1} f_n + f_{n-1}^2 + a f_n^2$$

In the last formula, a stands for an element whose trace over $\mathbf{F}$ has value 1. A constructive proof is given in ([7], p.286). The reduction of $Q(\underline{x})$, as described in [7] requires $O(n^3)$ operations in $GF(2^s)$. The derivation of this fact is straightforward but lengthy.

Simplifying underdefined systems of quadratic equations with more unknowns than equations.   Suppose t is a positive integer and $n \geq (t + 1)m$. Then we show that it is possible to adaptively fix $t \cdot m$ linear relations between the unknowns, so that by eliminating unknowns using these relations, we get a simpler system of m equations with m unknowns, where a few equations simultaneously have become linear in the remaining m variables.

By a linear relation between the unknowns we mean a relation $\sum_{i=1}^{n} a_i x_i = b$, where a_i, $i = 1, ..., n$ and b are elements of $\mathbf{F}$. The equations that have thus become linear can be used to eliminate further unknowns so that we get a simplified system with less unknowns and equations. If in a later step for solving this system it turns out that there exists no solution, we assign different values b to the relations.

The following Lemma is derived from results in [7] and states two basic facts on quadratic forms that will be useful later. Similar facts also hold for any polynomial of degree two.

Lemma 1. *Let $Q(\underline{x})$ be a nondegenerate quadratic form with n variables over $\mathbf{F}$. Suppose Q is written in reduced representation, $Q = f_1 f_2 + f_3 f_4 + ...$, where the f_i's, $i = 1, ..., n$ denote appropriate linear forms. Then*

a) *the coefficient vectors $\underline{f}_i$, $i = 1, ..., n$, are linearly independent over $\mathbf{F}$*
b) *Q has $\lfloor \frac{n}{2} \rfloor$ product terms, and at most $\lfloor \frac{n}{2} \rfloor + 1$ linear relations in $x_1, ..., x_n$ need to be fixed in order that Q becomes linear in the remaining variables*

The next result gives a simple lower bound for the number of equations that can be made linear (depending on t) by fixing linear relations.

Proposition 1. *Let a system of m polynomial equations of degree two with n unknowns be given. Denote $u = \lfloor \log_2(t+1) \rfloor$. Suppose $n \geq (t+1)m$ and that $m \geq u - 1$. Then a number $\nu \leq t \cdot m$ of linear relations between the unknowns can be fixed so that at least $u - 1$ equations become linear in the remaining $n - \nu \geq m$ unknowns.*

Proof: As stated in Lemma 1, b), the polynomial G_1 can be made linear by fixing at most $\lfloor \frac{n}{2} \rfloor + 1$ linear relations. Using the linear relations thus fixed, $\lfloor \frac{n}{2} \rfloor + 1$ unknowns can be eliminated. Iterating this procedure from G_2 onwards, we can fix further linear forms and eliminate unknowns, while the number R of remaining unknowns is at least m. Suppose $t + 1$ is a power of 2, i.e $t + 1 = 2^u$. The general case can be easily reduced to this case. Thus check whether $R \geq m$ holds if the above procedure has been iterated $u - 1$ times: $R \geq 2^u m - (2^{u-1}m + 1) - (2^{u-2}m + 1) - ... - (2m + 1) = 2m - (u - 1) \geq m$, by assumption.

As $u - 1$ variables can be eliminated using the linear equations, Proposition 1 can immediately be used to (slightly) reduce the search for a solution of MQ: The complexity of this search is approximately $q^{m-\log_2(n/m)}$ instead of q^m. We show that depending on t one can generally do better than indicated in Proposition 1. In fact, for very large t, i.e., for $t \geq m$, solving systems of m polynomial equations of degree two with $n \geq (t+1)m$ unknowns over $\mathbf{F} = GF(2^s)$ has been shown to be easy (cf. [4]). Our method does work for general t, but to get specific results, we focus here on small values of t, as these are of main interest for our cryptographic applications.

The idea is to successively fix linear relations so that the number of product terms decreases *simultaneously* in two polynomials G_i. This can be applied to derive the following result (see Appendix A):

Theorem 1. *Let $G_i(x_1, x_2, ..., x_n) = y_i$, $i = 1, ..., m$, denote a system of m polynomial equations of degree two in n unknowns over **F**, where $m > 10$ is even, and $n \geq (t+1)m$. Then $t \cdot m$ linear relations between the unknowns can be fixed to get a system of m equations with m variables so that*

- *if $t = 2$, G_1 is linear, and G_2 in reduced representation is the sum of at most one product of linear forms, a square of a linear form, and linear terms.*
- *if $t = 3$, G_1 and G_2 are linear, and G_3 in reduced representation is the sum of about $\frac{2m}{9} + 2$ products of linear forms, a square of a linear form, and linear terms.*

Remarks: A similar result also holds for an odd number m of equations. Moreover $m > 10$ is just chosen to assure that certain steps in the proof are not void. The complexity of the procedure to get the modified system of m equations with m unknowns in Theorem 1 is of order $\mathcal{O}(n^3)$. By a similar technique, for larger t some more equations can be made linear, e,g, if $t = 8$, about 5 equations can be made simultaneously linear. The method equally applies if the number of variables is a not an integer multiple of the number of equations. Moreover it is possible to improve on Theorem 1, as is shown in Appendix A. Theorem 1 immediately shows that the complexity of solving MQ in case $n \geq 4m$ is at most of order $\mathcal{O}(q^{m-2})$ (without any polynomial overhead). However solving MQ can be significantly improved if Theorem 1 is combined with the methods of relinearization and XL as introduced in [6] and [1] for solving overdefined systems of multivariate quadratic equations.

In [1], the efficiency of relinearization is investigated, and another algorithm for the same purpose, XL (for extended relinearization), is introduced and discussed. Suppose the given system has m equations with n variables, $m > n$, such that $m = \varepsilon n^2$ for $0.1 < \varepsilon \leq 1/2$. Then in [1] it is stated that the algorithm XL is expected to succeed with work factor

$$WF \approx \frac{n^{(\omega \lceil \frac{1}{\sqrt{\varepsilon}} \rceil)}}{(\lceil \frac{1}{\sqrt{\varepsilon}} \rceil)!}, \tag{1}$$

where $2 \leq \omega < 3$ is the exponent of gaussian reduction.

This bound only holds asymptotically in the number of variables n. Therefore in [1] experimental results for various concrete values of m and n are given. In particular, an experiment with 11 equations (over $GF(2^7)$) and 9 variables is reported. In order to solve such a system, the XL algorithm leads to 3543 linear equations in the same number of variables. Thus the complexity of XL to solve a system of quadratic equations with $m = 11$ equations and $n = 9$ variables is of the order 2^{35}, which is much larger than the work factor given by (1). The complexity drops however, if $m - n$ is larger: In ([1], Table 1) results of an experimental analysis of relinearization are given. For our purpose, we quote that solving $m = 12$ equations with $n = 8$ variables leads to a linear system of only 336 equations with 324 variables. The complexity of solving this system is of the order 2^{25}, i.e. it is close to the asymptotic work factor in (1) evaluated for $n = 8$. We now proceed to solve MQ:

Algorithm C. Let $n = t \cdot m$, $t \geq 2$.

1. Suitably fix linear relations between the variables with the simultaneous condition that
   i) two (or three) equations become linear (Theorem 1)
   ii) the simplified system of equations gets sufficiently overdefined for XL to become efficient.
2. Apply XL to solve the simplified system of quadratic equations.

The complexity of algorithm C depends on the complexity of XL. To obtain precise estimates of the complexity of algorithm C, we restrict to cases as mentioned, where the exact complexity of XL (or of relinearization) has been determined experimentally. This is applied in the following examples.

Example 1. Let $t \geq 3$, $m = 16$, and $q = 2^s$. Then apply the techniques used to prove Theorem 1 to the initial system of equations, to get a system of m equations with m variables, where the first two equations are linear and the third equation is a sum of at most 4 products of linear forms, a square of a linear form, and linear terms. Thus we need 5 relations to be fixed in order to eliminate the product terms and the square, so that the third equation also becomes linear. Use these relations and the three linear equations to get a system of 13 equations with 8 unknowns. Apply the result in [1] on relinearization, as quoted, to solve a system of 12 (or 13) equations with 8 variables, so that we get an upper bound for the total complexity of the order of $2^{5s} \cdot 2^{25} = 2^{5s+25}$. Using a refinement of Theorem 1 as sketched in Appendix A, and using the approximation (1), we may even arrive at a complexity of 2^{4s+26}. Thus the complexity of solving MQ for $m = 16$ and $n \geq 64$, is of an order between 2^{4s+26} and 2^{5s+25}.

Example 2: Let $t \geq 2$, $m = 16$, and $q = 2^s$. By similar arguments as in Example 1 we estimate the complexity of algorithm C to solve MQ to be of an order between 2^{4s+28} and 2^{5s+26}.

The complexities as determined in the above examples are the product of the complexity of a (partial) search and the complexity of the XL algorithm, i.e., of solving (large) linear systems of equations. This complexity is measured in numbers of $GF(q)$-operations rather than in numbers of evaluations of m quadratic polynomials in n variables. Therefore the estimates as given in Examples 1 and 2 may be viewed as upper bounds for the complexity of algorithm C.

3.3   Comparing Efficiency of the Algorithms

Our results show that the problem MQ, even in the underdefined case $n \gg m$, remains exponential in general, as long as $n < m^2$. For different regions of a three dimensional space in q, m and n, one or the other of the algorithms we have presented for solving MQ will be more efficient. To illustrate this point, let, e.g., $m = 16$. Then if n is only slightly larger than m, we expect that algorithm B will outperform other algorithms for solving MQ. However, if n is getting larger, algorithm A will be more efficient than algorithm B. In the case that the order of $\mathbf{F}$ is a power of 2, $q = 2^s$, compare algorithm A with algorithm C: Let, e.g., $n = 48$. Then for algorithm A, $k = 4$ is a suitable value and thus the complexity of algorithm A is of order 2^{12s}. On the other hand the complexity of algorithm C is upper bounded by 2^{5s+26} (see Example 2). Thus this method outperforms algorithm A as soon as $s \geq 4$, e.g., if $s = 4$ the complexities are 2^{46} for algorithm C, compared to 2^{48} for algorithm A, and if $s = 8$ they are 2^{66} compared to 2^{96}. This is due to the fact that the complexity of algorithm A is dominated by a search part and the polynomial overhead can be practically ignored, whereas the complexity of algorithm C is the product of the complexities of a small search and a larger polynomial part.

4 Solving MQ for Massively Underdefined Systems of Equations

In the massively underdefined case $n \geq m(m+1)$, a polynomial algorithm was developed in [4] to solve MQ in case $\mathbf{F}$ has characteristic 2, leaving the case of odd characteristic open. In this section, we extend these results to odd characteristics and solve a random underdefined MQ in polynomial time[1] as soon as:

$$\begin{cases} n \geq m(m+1) & \text{if } \mathbf{F} \text{ has characteristic 2;} \\ n \geq \text{roughly } 2^{\frac{m}{7}}(m+1) & \text{if } \mathbf{F} \text{ has an odd characteristic.} \end{cases}$$

Let $(\mathcal{S})$ be the following system:

$$(\mathcal{S}) \quad \begin{cases} \displaystyle\sum_{1 \leq i \leq j \leq n} a_{ij1} x_i x_j + \sum_{1 \leq i \leq n} b_{i1} x_i + \delta_1 = 0 \\ \quad\vdots \\ \displaystyle\sum_{1 \leq i \leq j \leq n} a_{ijm} x_i x_j + \sum_{1 \leq i \leq n} b_{im} x_i + \delta_m = 0 \end{cases}$$

The main idea of the algorithm consists in using a change of variables such as:

$$\begin{cases} x_1 = \alpha_{1,1} y_1 + \alpha_{2,1} y_2 + \ldots + \alpha_{t,1} y_t + \alpha_{t+1,1} y_{t+1} + \ldots + \alpha_{n,1} y_n \\ \quad\vdots \\ x_n = \alpha_{1,n} y_1 + \alpha_{2,n} y_2 + \ldots + \alpha_{t,n} y_t + \alpha_{t+1,n} y_{t+1} + \ldots + \alpha_{n,n} y_n \end{cases}$$

whose $\alpha_{i,j}$ coefficients (for $1 \leq i \leq t$, $1 \leq j \leq n$) are found step by step, in order that the resulting system $(\mathcal{S}')$ (written with respect to these new variables y_1, ..., y_n) is easy to solve.

- We begin by choosing randomly $\alpha_{1,1}$, ..., $\alpha_{1,n}$.
- We then compute $\alpha_{2,1}$, ..., $\alpha_{2,n}$ such that $(\mathcal{S}')$ contains no $y_1 y_2$ terms. This condition leads to a system of m linear equations in the n unknowns $\alpha_{2,j}$ $(1 \leq j \leq n)$:

$$\sum_{1 \leq i \leq j \leq n} a_{ijk} \alpha_{1,i} \alpha_{2,j} = 0 \qquad (1 \leq k \leq m).$$

---

[1] In time polynomial in the size of the initial system that can be exponential.

– We then compute $\alpha_{3,1}$, ..., $\alpha_{3,n}$ such that $(\mathcal{S}')$ contains neither $y_1 y_3$ terms, nor $y_2 y_3$ terms. This condition is equivalent to the following system of $2m$ linear equations in the n unknowns $\alpha_{3,j}$ $(1 \le j \le n)$:

$$\begin{cases} \sum_{1 \le i \le j \le n} a_{ijk} \alpha_{1,i} \alpha_{3,j} = 0 & (1 \le k \le m) \\ \sum_{1 \le i \le j \le n} a_{ijk} \alpha_{2,i} \alpha_{3,j} = 0 & (1 \le k \le m) \end{cases}$$

– ...

– Finally. we compute $\alpha_{t,1}$, ..., $\alpha_{t,n}$ such that $(\mathcal{S}')$ contains neither $y_1 y_t$ terms, nor $y_2 y_t$ terms, ..., nor $y_{t-1} y_t$ terms. This condition gives the following system of $(t-1)m$ linear equations in the n unknowns $\alpha_{t,j}$ $(1 \le j \le n)$:

$$\begin{cases} \sum_{1 \le i \le j \le n} a_{ijk} \alpha_{1,i} \alpha_{t,j} = 0 & (1 \le k \le m) \\ \quad \vdots \\ \sum_{1 \le i \le j \le n} a_{ijk} \alpha_{t-1,i} \alpha_{t,j} = 0 & (1 \le k \le m) \end{cases}$$

In general, all these linear equations provide at least one solution (found by Gaussian reductions). In particular, the last system of $m(t-1)$ equations and n unknowns generally gives a solution, as soon as $n > m(t-1)$.

Moreover, the t vectors $\begin{pmatrix} \alpha_{1,1} \\ \vdots \\ \alpha_{1,n} \end{pmatrix}$, ..., $\begin{pmatrix} \alpha_{t,1} \\ \vdots \\ \alpha_{t,n} \end{pmatrix}$ are very likely to be linearly independent for a random system $(\mathcal{S})$. The remaining $\alpha_{i,j}$ constants (i.e. those with $t+1 \le i \le n$ and $1 \le j \le n$) are randomly chosen, so as to obtain a bijective change of variables. By rewriting the system $(\mathcal{S})$ with respect to these new variables y_i, we have the following system:

$$(\mathcal{S}') \quad \begin{cases} \sum_{i=1}^{t} \beta_{i,1} y_i^2 + \sum_{i=1}^{t} y_i L_{i,1}(y_{t+1}, ..., y_n) + Q_1(y_{t+1}, ..., y_n) = 0 \\ \quad \vdots \\ \sum_{i=1}^{t} \beta_{i,m} y_i^2 + \sum_{i=1}^{t} y_i L_{i,m}(y_{t+1}, ..., y_n) + Q_m(y_{t+1}, ..., y_n) = 0 \end{cases}$$

where each $L_{i,j}$ is an affine function and each Q_i is a quadratic function. Then we compute y_{t+1}, ..., y_n such that:

$$\forall i, \ 1 \le i \le t, \ \forall j, \ 1 \le j \le m, \ L_{i,j}(y_{t+1}, ..., y_n) = 0.$$

This is possible because we have to solve a linear system of mt equations and $n-t$ unknowns, which generally provides at least one solution, as long as $n \ge (m+1)t$. We pick one of these solutions. It remains to solve the following system of m

equations in the t unknowns $y_1, ..., y_t$:

$$(\mathcal{S}'') \quad \begin{cases} \sum\limits_{i=1}^{t} \beta_{i1} y_i^2 = \lambda_1 \\ \quad\vdots \\ \sum\limits_{i=1}^{t} \beta_{im} y_i^2 = \lambda_m \end{cases}$$

where $\lambda_k = -Q_k(y_{t+1}, ..., y_n)$ $(1 \leq k \leq m)$. We call this problem the MQ^2 problem with t variables and m equations. We have two cases:

4.1   When F Has Characteristic 2 and $n \geq m(m+1)$

In this case, it is enough to have $t = m$ or slightly bigger and MQ^2 is easy. Then the system $(\mathcal{S}'')$ gives the y_i^2 by Gaussian reduction and since $z \mapsto z^2$ is a bijection on any field of characteristic 2, we will then find y_i from the y_i^2.

Our algorithm works for $n \geq (m+1)t = m(m+1)$ as claimed.

4.2   When the Characteristic of F Is Odd and $n = \mathcal{O}(m^2)$

This case is still not completely solved when $n \geq m(m+1)$. In what follows we show an algorithm in which n grows exponentially in m, but very slowly. More precisely when $n \geq$ about $2^{\frac{m}{7}} m(m+1)$, then the system will be solved in polynomial time in n. In practice for many systems with $n = \mathcal{O}(m^2)$ we will also have $n \geq$ about $2^{\frac{m}{7}} m(m+1)$ and our algorithm will solve these cases.

The starting point is the exponential algorithm already mentioned in [4]. In order to solve the MQ^2 problem with $t = \mathcal{O}(m)$ we fix all with the exception of about m variables. The resulting system is linear in the y_i^2, and is then solved by gaussian elimination. For each resulting solution obtained for y_i^2, the probability that it is indeed a square in $\mathbf{F}$ is $1/2$. The probability that all the y_i^2 are squares is 2^{-m} and therefore we need to repeat the attack 2^m times. For this there must be at least about $\log_q(2^m) = \frac{m}{\log_2 q}$ additional variables. Therefore, the algorithm solves the MQ^2 problem in time 2^m when $t \geq m + \frac{m}{\log_2(q)}$.

Certainly, the exponential algorithm is efficient for $m \leq 40$. Now we will improve it. We will show a reduction from the MQ^2 problem with t variables and m equations to the MQ^2 problem with $\frac{t}{40+40/\log_2 q}$ variables and $m - 40$ equations. For this we do the following:

1. We assume that the available computing power is greater than 2^{40} operations.
2. First we ignore most of the variables except the $40 + 40/\log_2 q$ variables $y_1, \cdots y_{40+40/\log_2 q}$.
3. With a multiple of 2^{40} operations we find a nonzero solution to the first 40 equations, provided that the contribution of the other variables is zero.
4. The remaining variables are divided in groups of at least $40 + 40/\log_2 q$ variables.

5. For each group of variables, in about 2^{40} operations, we find a nonzero solution, such that their contribution to the first 40 equations is zero.
6. Now we have found a solution $y_1, \ldots y_{40+40/\log_2 q}, \ldots, y_t$ such that the first 40 equations are satisfied.
7. This solution to the first 40 equations, gives in fact many solutions: for example if we have a nonzero solution, $y_{1+40+40/\log_2 q}, \ldots y_{2 \cdot (40+40/\log_2 q)}$ such that their contribution to the first 40 equations is zero, such is also the case for the values
$$z y_{1+40+40/\log_2 q}, \ldots z y_{2 \cdot (40+40/\log_2 q)} \text{ and for any value of } z.$$
8. For each group starting from the second, we can add a new variable z_i, $i = 1.. \frac{t}{40+40/\log_2 q} - 1$ as described in 7.
9. Whatever are the values of the z_i, the first 40 equations are satisfied.
10. Now we have another MQ^2 system: with $m - 40$ equations and with $\frac{t}{40+40/\log_2 q} - 1$ variables z_i, such that if it is satisfied, the whole original system is satisfied.

The reduction from MQ^2 with (t, m) to the problem with $\left(\frac{t}{40+40/\log_2 q}, m - 40 \right)$ can be iterated. Therefore, we see that we can solve MQ^2 for any m as long as

$$t \geq (40 + 40/\log_2 q)^{m/40}$$

The complexity of the algorithm is about $2^{40} \cdot t$, which is essentially linear in t: for each group of $(40 + 40/\log_2 q)$ variables we solve a small MQ^2 in 2^{40}, remaining parts can be neglected. Moreover, if $t > (40 + 40/\log_2 q)^{m/40}$, we ignore the remaining variables and the complexity will be only $2^{40} (40 + 40/\log_2 q)^{m/40}$.

Conclusion for odd characteristic. Now we combine our result for MQ^2 with the reduction from MQ to MQ^2 that works for $n \geq (m+1)t = m(m+1)$ described in 4.

Therefore, a massively underdefined system MQ with

$$n \geq (40 + 40/\log_2 q)^{m/40} (m + 1)$$

can be solved in time about

$$2^{40} (40 + 40/\log_2 q)^{m/40}.$$

In practice we have usually $\log_2 q > 4$ and therefore:

$$n \geq (50)^{m/40}(m + 1) \geq 2^{m/7}(m + 1)$$

Example 1: Let $q \approx 2^8$, $m = 40$. The exhaustive search for such MQ is in 2^{320}, whatever is n. Now, if there is enough variables, $n > 1845$, our new algorithm gives about 2^{46} instead of 2^{320}.

Example 2: Let $q = 127$, $m = 80$. The exhaustive search for such MQ is in 2^{559}, whatever is n. Now, if there is enough variables, $n > 136000$, our new algorithm gives about 2^{51} instead of 2^{559}.

5   Application: Cryptanalysis of Certain Multivariate Signature Schemes

For several recent signature schemes, the public key consists of a system of m quadratic equations in n variables and where $n \gg m$ (cf. e.g., [4], [9]). For these systems, signatures can be forged if this system of quadratic equations can be solved. Therefore as an immediate cryptographic application, our results lead to new criteria for the choice of the security parameters of such systems.

Due to the parameters chosen for the signature schemes Quartz, Flash and Sflash submitted to Nessie call for primitives, the security of these schemes is not affected by our results. However for some "bad" choices of the parameters, the Unbalanced Oil and Vinegar signature scheme (cf. [4]) can be broken. Note however that the UOV scheme is not broken for the parameters proposed in [4]. We give below two examples of such "bad" choices for the parameters:

Let $\mathbf{F} = GF(2^4)$, and let $m = 16$ be the number of public equations. Furthermore let either $n = 48$ or $n = 64$. Then $q = 2^s = 16$, and t in the notation of subsection 3.2 is either 2 or 3. The public key is given in terms of a set of elements in $\mathbf{F}$, describing the coefficients of the public system of quadratic equations. The length of the public key is 9 Kbytes for $t = 2$ and 16 Kbytes for $t = 3$. The number $m = 16$ of equations has been chosen to defeat Gröbner bases algorithms to solve MQ, and $q^{16} = 2^{64}$ has been chosen in order to prevent from an exhaustive search. Moreover $t \geq 2$ was chosen to escape from an attack as given in [5] and [4], which exploits the trapdoor in Oil and Vinegar signature schemes, and which does hold for $n \approx m$.

Our attack does not rely on the fact that a trapdoor is hidden in the construction of the public polynomials. Rather we directly apply algorithms A and C to show that the complexity of solving MQ with these parameters is significantly lower than 2^{64} trials for exhaustive search. Interestingly, for the chosen parameter sizes the complexities of the two algorithms come quite close. Let $n = 48$. Then the complexity of algorithm A is of order 2^{48} whereas the complexity of algorithm C is about 2^{46} (see subsection 3.3).

If $n = 64$, $k = 5$ satisfies $2k^2 \geq n - 2k$ and is thus a suitable parameter for algorithm A. Hence the complexity of algorithm A is 2^{44}. The complexity of algorithm C for $n = 64$ is upper bounded by a value between 2^{42} and 2^{45}. If for $m = 16$ and $n = 48$ one wants to increase the security at the cost of a moderate increase of the size of the public key, one could choose a larger subfield, say $q = 2^6$ instead of 2^4. Then algorithm A has complexity 2^{66} but the complexity of algorithm C is at most 2^{56}. Hence the security increase is insufficient. As a consequence of our algorithms, for a multivariate signature scheme with $n = t \cdot m$, $t \geq 2$, the number m has to be 24 or larger. This shows that the choice of the parameters for Unbalanced Oil and Vinegar must be made carefully.

References

1. N. Courtois, A. Klimov, J. Patarin, A. Shamir, *Efficient Algorithms for Solving Overdefined Systems of Multivariate Polynomial Equations*, Advances in Cryptology – EUROCRYPT'2000, Proceedings, B. Preneel (Ed.), Lecture Notes in Computer Science, Springer Verlag, vol. 1807, pp. 392 - 407.
2. J.-Ch. Faugère, *A new efficient algorithm for computing Gröbner bases* (F_4), Journal of Pure and Applied Algebra 139 (1999), pp. 61-88. See www.elsevier.com/locate/jpaa.
3. M. R. Garey, D. S. Johnson, *Computers and Intractability, A Guide to the Theory of NP-completeness*, W. H. Freeman and Company, New York, 1979.
4. A. Kipnis, J. Patarin, L. Goubin, *Unbalanced Oil and Vinegar Signature Schemes*, Advances in Cryptology – EUROCRYPT'99, Proceedings, J. Stern (Ed.), Lecture Notes in Computer Science, Springer Verlag, vol. 1592, pp. 206 - 222.
5. A. Kipnis, A. Shamir, *Cryptanalysis of the Oil and Vinegar Signature Scheme*, Advances in Cryptology – CRYPTO'98, Proceedings, H. Krawczyk (Ed.), Lecture Notes in Computer Science, Springer Verlag, vol. 1462, pp. 257 - 266.
6. A. Kipnis, A. Shamir, *Cryptanalysis of the HFE Public Key Cryptosystem by Relinearization*, Advances in Cryptology – CRYPTO'99, Proceedings, M. Wiener (Ed.), Lecture Notes in Computer Science, Springer Verlag, vol. 1666, pp. 19 - 30.
7. R. Lidl, R. Niederreiter, *Finite fields, Encyclopedia of mathematics and its applications*, vol. 20, 1997.
8. A.J. Menezes, P.C. van Oorschot, S.A. Vanstone, *Handbook of applied cryptography*, CRC Press, 1996.
9. J. Patarin, N. Courtois, L. Goubin, *FLASH, a Fast Multivariate Signature Algorithm*, in Progress in Cryptology–CT-RSA 2001, D. Nacchache, ed , vol 2020, Springer Lecture Notes in Computer Science, pp. 298-307.
10. J. Patarin, L. Goubin, N. Courtois, *Quartz, 128-bit long digital signatures*, Cryptographers' Track RSA Conference 2001, San Francisco 8-12 Avril 2001, LNCS2020, Springer-Verlag. Also published in Proceedings of the First Open NESSIE Workshop, 13-14 November 2000, Leuven, Belgium.

Appendix A: Deriving Theorem 1

In order to derive Theorem 1, a few preparatory steps are explained. For simultaneously reducing the number of product terms in two polynomials G_i, first ignore linear and constant parts and concentrate on homogeneous (degree two) parts. Let $n > 2$ be even (the case n odd is similar) and let $Q_1 = f_1 f_2 + f_3 f_4 + ... + q_1$ and $Q_2 = g_1 g_2 + g_3 g_4 + ... + q_2$ be reduced representations of the homogeneous parts of G_1 and G_2 (which are assumed to be nondegenerate). Depending on the case, q_i, $i = 1, 2$, is an abbreviation for 0 or $f_{n-1}^2 + a' f_n^2$ (or for $g_{n-1}^2 + a'' g_n^2$ respectively) for some $a', a'' \in \mathbf{F}$.

Restrict first to reducing the number of product terms in Q_1 and Q_2, and deal with squares of linear terms later. To start with, both Q_1 and Q_2 have $\frac{n}{2}$ product terms.

Consider, e.g., the relation imposed by setting $f_1 = b$, $b \in \mathbf{F}$ arbitrary. This relation is applied to every polynomial G_i and obviously reduces the number of product terms in Q_1 by one, as $Q_1 = f_3 f_4 + ... + b f_2 + q_1$. For iterating our procedure in later steps, we need to see the explicit effect this linear relation has on Q_2. Recall (cf. Lemma 1, a)) that the coefficient vectors $\underline{g}_i$ of g_i, $i = 1, ..., n$, are a basis in $\mathbf{F}^n$. Therefore the coefficient vector $\underline{f}_1$ can be written (use Gaussian elimination) as a linear combination $\underline{f}_1 = \sum_{i=1}^{n} \alpha_i \underline{g}_i$ for suitable $\alpha_i \in \mathbf{F}$, $i = 1, ..., n$, where not all α_i's are 0. Thus we get the identity of linear forms $\sum_{i=1}^{n} \alpha_i g_i = f_1$. Suppose, e.g., that $\alpha_1 \neq 0$. Use the relation $\sum_{i=1}^{n} \alpha_i g_i = f_1 = b$ to express g_1 as $g_1 = \sum_{i=2}^{n} \alpha_i' g_i + b'$, where $\alpha_i' = \frac{\alpha_i}{\alpha_1}$, $i = 1, ..., n$ and $b' = \frac{b}{\alpha_1}$. Thus substituting g_1 in Q_2 we get

$$Q_2 = (\sum_{i=2}^{n} \alpha_i' g_i + b')g_2 + g_3 g_4 + ... + g_{n-1} g_n + q_2 = (g_3 + \alpha_4' g_2)(g_4 + \alpha_3' g_2) + \quad (2)$$

$$+ ... + (g_{n-1} + \alpha_n' g_2)(g_n + \alpha_{n-1}' g_2) + (\alpha_2' + \alpha_3' \alpha_4' + ... \alpha_{n-1}' \alpha_n')g_2^2 + b' g_2 + q_2,$$

where the last expression has $\frac{n}{2} - 1$ products of $n - 2$ linear forms g_j', $j = 3, ..., n$ (we still focus only on product terms and not on squares). Note that using (2) the simultaneous reduction of product terms in Q_1 and Q_2 with a given linear relation can be carried out efficiently. After eliminating one variable x_i using the relation $f_1 = b$, Q_1 has $n - 1$ variables and $\frac{n}{2} - 1$ product terms and is now of the form (renaming f_i' by f_i) $Q_1 = f_3 f_4 + ... + f_{n-1} f_n +$ linear terms + squares of linear terms, and similarly for Q_2.

To simultaneously eliminate further product terms in Q_1 and Q_2, consider the system of $n - 1$ linear equations with unknowns $\alpha_i, \beta_j \in \mathbf{F}$, $i, j = 3, ..., n$,

$$\sum_{i=3}^{n} \alpha_i \underline{f}_i + \sum_{j=3}^{n} \beta_j \underline{g}_j = 0, \quad (3)$$

We still have $2(n-2)$ unknowns, and thus many solutions, from which we choose a nontrivial one. Furthermore, the $\underline{f}_i$'s, as well as the $\underline{g}_i$'s, can be assumed to be linearly independent. Hence not all α_i's and not all β_j's are 0.

Then both sides of the identity of linear forms $\sum_{i=3}^{n} \alpha_i f_i = \sum_{j=3}^{n} \beta_j g_j$ are of the form $\sum_{i=1}^{n} a_i x_i$ for suitable $a_i \in \mathbf{F}$, $i = 1, ..., n$. So let $\sum_{i=1}^{n} a_i x_i = b$, $b \in \mathbf{F}$ arbitrary, be the relation to be fixed. Then we can eliminate one product term in Q_1 and one in Q_2 as before, and in the same time eliminate one further variable x_i. This procedure can be repeated while the linear system (3) has a nontrivial solution. After we have fixed r relations, $n - 2r$ linear forms remain involved in products in each of Q_1 and Q_2, and the number of variables after elimination has decreased to $n - r$. Therefore system (3) has a solution as long as $(n - 2r) + (n - 2r) > n - r$. This simplifies to $r < \frac{n}{3}$. As soon as $r + 1 > \frac{n}{3}$ for some $r > 0$, consider, e.g., polynomials G_1 and G_3 and simultaneously eliminate product terms in G_1 and G_3 and so on.

Finally fix linear forms occurring in squares. As squaring is a linear bijective operation in characteristic 2, sums of squares simplify to a single square of a linear relation and we need only fix one linear relation in each polynomial G_i in which we have eliminated product terms.

Proof of Theorem 1 (Sketch): The proof proceeds in three steps. (In subsequent equalities between integers and fractions, either floors or ceilings should be taken. These operations depend on divisibility properties of n and can be ignored as far as their effects cancel out in book-keeping of terms.) Let Q_1, Q_2 and Q_3 denote the homogeneous parts of the polynomials G_1, G_2 and G_3.

Step 1: Simultaneously eliminate product terms in Q_1 and Q_2 by fixing appropriate linear relations between the variables as described. We can eliminate $r+1$ products, where the condition $r < \frac{n}{3}$ holds. Thus $r + 1 = \frac{n}{3}$, and in each of Q_1 and Q_2 there remain $\frac{n}{2} - \frac{n}{3} = \frac{n}{6}$ product terms with $\frac{n}{3}$ linear forms as factors involved. Moreover, using the fixed linear relations, eliminate $\frac{n}{3}$ unknowns in all polynomials G_i. Thus all G_i's are polynomials of $n - \frac{n}{3} = \frac{2n}{3}$ variables and for $i > 2$, G_i has at most $\frac{n}{3}$ product terms with at most $\frac{2n}{3}$ linear forms as factors.

In a similar way, in Steps 2 and 3 the numbers of product terms in Q_i, $i = 1, 2, 3$, are further reduced: In Step 2, product terms in Q_1 and Q_3 are simultaneously eliminated, whereas Step 3 deals with simultaneously eliminating product terms in Q_2 and Q_3. Book-keeping of the number of remaining nonlinear summands in the Q_i's leads to the simplified system of m equations in m variables as stated in Theorem 1. Details are omitted here due to space limitation.

A refinement. In all three steps of the proof of Theorem 1, a number $r + 1$ is computed, which is the number of products that can simultaneously be eliminated in reduced representations of two quadratic forms. The number r has been limited by the condition that the sum of the numbers of linear forms occurring in products in both quadratic forms exceeds the number of components of the coefficient vectors of the linear forms. This was to assure that a linear system of equations similar to (3) has nontrivial solutions. However, with a probability $p > 0$, these coefficient vectors are linearly dependent even if not enough of them are available to satisfy the above condition. It can be shown that this probability is about 0.63. By trying Step 1 a few times, each time choosing different linear relations to be fixed, one can increase this probability to close to 1. This applies also to the other steps and allows to eliminate a few more nonlinear terms than stated in Theorem 1.

Selective Forgery of RSA Signatures
with Fixed-Pattern Padding

Arjen K. Lenstra[1] and Igor E. Shparlinski[2]

[1] Citibank, N.A. and Technical University Eindhoven
1 North Gate Road Mendham, NJ 07945-3104, USA
arjen.lenstra@citicorp.com
[2] Department of Computing, Macquarie University
Sydney, NSW 2109, Australia
igor@comp.mq.edu.au

Abstract. We present a practical selective forgery attack against RSA signatures with fixed-pattern padding shorter than two thirds of the modulus length. Our result extends the practical existential forgery of such RSA signatures that was presented at Crypto 2001. For an n-bit modulus the heuristic asymptotic runtime of our forgery is comparable to the time required to factor a modulus of only $\frac{9}{64}n$ bits. Thus, the security provided by short fixed-pattern padding is negligible compared to the security it is supposed to provide.

1 Introduction

Let N be an RSA modulus, and let n denote its bit length. At Crypto 2001 two attacks were presented against RSA signatures with a fixed-pattern padding shorter than $2n/3$: a practical existential forgery attack that runs in time polynomial in n and a selective forgery attack with unspecified non-polynomial runtime [2], see also [5,6,10] for several previously known results. The attack of [2] can, however, not be guaranteed to work for all selected messages. In this paper we extend the selective forgery attack by presenting a modification that works for all selected messages. It can be shown to have heuristic asymptotic expected runtime

$$e^{(1+o(1))(\log N)^{1/3}(\log\log N)^{2/3}}$$

for $N \to \infty$, where log denotes the natural logarithm. Our modified attack works well in practice. This is illustrated by a successful selective forgery attack against a 1024-bit RSA modulus.

Despite a series of increasingly effective attacks, fixed padding RSA signatures remain adopted by several standards. For more details and additional references see [2]. Although the attacks do not extend to random padding, they can be dangerous if the padding is obtained by applying a 'weak' hash-function to the message.

Let d and e satisfy $ed \equiv 1 \mod \varphi(N)$, where $\varphi(N)$ is the Euler function. The value of d is *private* while N and e are *public*. We assume that the residue ring of integers modulo N is represented by the elements $\mathbf{Z}_N = \{0, 1, \ldots, N-1\}$.

D. Naccache and P. Paillier (Eds.): PKC 2002, LNCS 2274, pp. 228–236, 2002.

A fixed-pattern padding scheme works by concatenating each ℓ-bit message with the same $(n - \ell)$-bit padding. The resulting padded message, which is an element of $\mathbf{Z}_N$, is then signed by computing its d-th power modulo N. It has been shown in [2] that for $\ell > n/3$ the attacker can generate in deterministic polynomial time four interrelated ℓ-bit messages so that valid signatures on three of them can be used to generate a valid signature on the remaining one. This is an existential chosen message attack because there is no control over the message for which the signature is forged. It was shown in [2] that the attack succeeds for 1024-bit RSA moduli.

It has also been described in [2] how the attack can be modified into a selective forgery attack, i.e., an attack where the message whose signature is forged is selected in advance. However, this modification has not been analyzed in detail. For example, neither the general strategy nor the precise runtime have been described, although it is mentioned that it no longer runs in polynomial time. Actually, the selective forgery from [2] works only occasionally. For most selected messages it will not be successful. In this paper we present some considerations which help to facilitate a selective forgery attack. As a result our selective forgery attack may be expected to work for all selected messages. Our analysis includes an optimal choice of parameters and a heuristic estimate of the asymptotic runtime. The runtime is subexponential, but it is much lower than a brute force factorization attack via the number field sieve. Furthermore, we present an example of a successful selective forgery attack against an unfactored 1024-bit RSA modulus.

In Section 2 we review the attacks from [2] and present some additional observations concerning them. In Section 3 we present our alternative approach to the selective forgery attack and analyze its runtime. In Section 4 an example of a successful selective forgery attack is presented. For ease of reference the notation from [2] is maintained as much as possible.

2   Idea of the Attack

For an ℓ-bit message m the fixed-pattern padding is denoted by $R(m) \in \mathbf{Z}_N$. The signature $s(m)$ is defined as

$$s(m) = R(m)^d \bmod N. \tag{1}$$

Following [2], we define

$$R(m) = \omega \cdot m + a \tag{2}$$

where ω and a are the fixed multiplicative and additive redundancies, respectively. Given a fixed $(n - \ell)$-bit padding Π, left-padding $\Pi|m$ is obtained using $\omega = 1, a = 2^{\ell}\Pi$ and right-padding $m|\Pi$ using $\omega = 2^{n-\ell}, a = \Pi$. Note that in the former case Π and in the latter case m should be small enough to make sure that $R(m) \in \mathbf{Z}_N$.

Let $m_1, \ldots, m_4$ be four distinct ℓ-bit messages such that

$$R(m_1) \cdot R(m_2) \equiv R(m_3) \cdot R(m_4) \bmod N. \tag{3}$$

With (1) it follows that

$$s(m_3) = \frac{s(m_1) \cdot s(m_2)}{s(m_4)} \mod N$$

unless the inversion modulo N of $s(m_4)$ fails. The latter possibility is ignored from now on, since it would lead to a factor of N. In any case, if equation (3) is satisfied, then the signature $s(m_3)$ of m_3 can be computed given signatures $s(m_1), s(m_2)$, and $s(m_4)$ of m_1, m_2, and m_4, respectively.

With $P = a/\omega \mod N$ and (2) congruence (3) is equivalent to

$$P(m_3 + m_4 - m_1 - m_2) \equiv m_1 m_2 - m_3 m_4 \mod N.$$

With

$$t = m_3, \quad x = m_1 - m_3, \quad y = m_2 - m_3, \quad z = m_3 + m_4 - m_1 - m_2 \qquad (4)$$

this becomes

$$Pz \equiv xy - tz \mod N. \qquad (5)$$

For an existential forgery attack, integers t, x, y, z satisfying (5) are constructed so that the corresponding $m_1, \ldots, m_4$ are at most ℓ bits long. We describe the construction from [2] in slightly more detail than can be found in [2]. Let $\frac{P_i}{Q_i}$ denote the i-th continued fraction convergent to P/N. Then

$$\left| \frac{P}{N} - \frac{P_i}{Q_i} \right| \leq \frac{1}{Q_i Q_{i+1}}.$$

There is an integer j such that $Q_j < N^{1/3} \leq Q_{j+1}$. Let $u = |PQ_j - NP_j|$. Then

$$0 < u \leq N/Q_{j+1} < N^{2/3} \quad \text{and} \quad Pz \equiv u \mod N$$

for an integer z with $|z| < N^{1/3}$, namely either $z = Q_j$ or $z = -Q_j$.

Given z, an integer y is selected with $N^{1/3} \leq y \leq 2N^{1/3}$ and $\gcd(y, z) = 1$. It follows that t can be found such that $0 \leq t < y$ and

$$tz \equiv -u \mod y.$$

With

$$x = (u + tz)/y \leq u/y + z \leq 2N^{1/3}$$

and $Pz \equiv u \mod N$, the integers $t, x, y, z \leq 2N^{1/3}$ satisfy congruence (5), as desired. From $|z| < N^{1/3}$ and $y \geq N^{1/3}$ it follows that $y + z > 0$, so that $x + t = (u + t(y + z))/y > 0$ since $u > 0$. Therefore, the messages

$$m_1 = x + t, \quad m_2 = y + t, \quad m_3 = t, \quad m_4 = x + y + z + t$$

(cf. (4)) are positive and about ℓ bits long, assuming that $\ell \approx n/3$. Clearly, this attack runs in polynomial time.

For a selective forgery attack, congruence (5) is rewritten as

$$(P + m_3)z \equiv xy \bmod N. \tag{6}$$

Given m_3, integers x, y, z satisfying (6) are sought such that the corresponding m_1, m_2, m_4 are no more than ℓ bits long. In [2] it is suggested to compute the continued fraction expansion of $(P + m_3)/N$, resulting in z, u with $|z| < N^{1/3}$ and $0 < u < N^{2/3}$ such that

$$(P + m_3)z \equiv u \bmod N \tag{7}$$

and to write u as the product xy of two integers x and y of about the same size. Since z and u are almost certainly unique (over a random choice of the message m_3 and the value P that follows from the padding) this attack fails if u cannot be factored in the prescribed way. Indeed, it follows from [7, Theorem 21] that with overwhelming probability a randomly selected integer u does not have a divisor in the range $[u^{1/2-\eta(u)}, u^{1/2+\eta(u)}]$ for any function $\eta(u) \to 0$. It is also useful to recall that for any fixed $0 < \delta \leq 1/2$ the density of the integers u having a prime divisor exceeding $u^{1-\delta}$ is positive. More precisely the density is $-\log(1 - \delta)$, see [3]. Thus, for almost all messages m_3 the resulting u simply does not split into two factors of about the same size. This point is not mentioned in [2], and neither is it explained how one should go about factoring u. In Section 3 we address both these problems.

3   Improvements

As usual $L_M(\alpha, \gamma)$ denotes any quantity of the form

$$\exp((\gamma + o(1))(\ln M)^\alpha (\ln \ln M)^{1-\alpha})$$

for $M \to \infty$. Then factoring u in congruence (7) using the number field sieve takes about

$$L_{N^{2/3}}\left(1/3, (64/9)^{1/3}\right) = L_N\left(1/3, (128/27)^{1/3}\right)$$

see [9]. However, as noted in Section 2, the selective forgery attack fails if u cannot be factored as xy, with x and y of about the same order of magnitude.

We show that by allowing a little bit of 'slackness' and by working with marginally longer messages of size $O(N^{1/3+\varepsilon})$, one can efficiently produce a sequence of u-values based on a single message m_3. Moreover, this allows us to use the elliptic curve factoring method [11] to quickly search for a u with a large smooth part. Overall we obtain a considerable speedup of the approach that uses the number field sieve.

Fix a small positive ε and let $M = \lfloor N^{1/3} \rfloor$. For a random integer k with $0 < k < N^\varepsilon$ apply the continued fraction algorithm to $(P + m_3 - kM)/N$ to find v_k, w_k such that

$$0 \leq v_k \leq N^{1/3}, \qquad 0 \leq |w_k| \leq N^{2/3},$$

and
$$(P + m_3 - kM)v_k \equiv w_k \bmod N.$$
It follows that
$$(P + m_3)v_k \equiv w_k + kMv_k \bmod N.$$
Multiplying both sides by -1 if necessary, we obtain the congruence
$$(P + m_3)z_k \equiv u_k \bmod N$$
with $0 \leq |z_k| \leq N^{1/3}$ and $0 \leq u_k \leq 2N^{2/3+\varepsilon}$.

Analyzing the continued fraction algorithm we see that unless most of the fractions $(P+m_3-kM)/N$ admit abnormally good approximations, different values of k are likely to produce different pairs (v_k, w_k), and thus different (z_k, u_k). We remark that a fraction A/N has abnormally good approximations if and only if it has a very large partial quotient in its continued fraction expansion. On the other hand, one easily derives from [12, Theorem 5.10, Theorem 5.17, and (5.11)] that 'on average' over all $A \in \mathbf{Z}_N$ with $\gcd(A, N) = 1$, the largest quotient of A/N is $O(\log^2 N)$. This shows how the value u in (7) can be randomized, thereby solving one problem with the selective forgery attack proposed in [2]. It remains to analyze how many values u_k have to be generated before a 'good' one can be recognized quickly.

A positive integer is Y-smooth if all its prime factors are at most Y. Let $\Psi(X, Y)$ denote the total number of Y-smooth numbers up to X. The following estimate is a substantially relaxed and simplified version of (for example) [8, Corollary 1.3]: for a fixed arbitrary $\delta > 0$, $X \geq 10$, and $\alpha \leq (\log X)^{1-\delta}$,

$$\Psi(X, X^{1/\alpha}) = X\alpha^{-\alpha+o(\alpha)} \tag{8}$$

for $\alpha \to \infty$.

From the sequence of u_k values we are interested in those u_k that have a factor exceeding $0.5\sqrt{u_k}$ that is $N^{1/\alpha}$-smooth with

$$\alpha = c(\log N)^{1/3}(\log\log N)^{-1/3}, \tag{9}$$

for a constant c.

We remark that this choice of α optimizes (up to the value of the constant c which we choose later) the trade-off between the number of trials before a 'good' u_k is found and the complexity of finding an $N^{1/\alpha}$-smooth factor of such numbers using the elliptic curve factoring method [11].

Thus $\log\alpha = (1/3 + o(1))\log\log N$ for $N \to \infty$. According to (8) one may expect that there are

$$\Psi(N^{1/3}, N^{1/\alpha}) = \Psi(N^{1/3}, (N^{1/3})^{3/\alpha}) = N^{1/3}(\alpha/3)^{-\alpha/3+o(\alpha)}$$

integers $s \in [(N/2)^{1/3}, N^{1/3}]$ that are $N^{1/\alpha}$-smooth. Also, the number of primes $p \in [N^{1/3+\varepsilon}, 2N^{1/3+\varepsilon}]$ is proportional to $N^{1/3+\varepsilon}/\log N$. Thus, for such s and p, the number of products sp is

$$N^{2/3+\varepsilon}\alpha^{-\alpha/3+o(\alpha)}(\log N)^{-1}.$$

With (9) this becomes

$$N^{2/3+\varepsilon} L_N(1/3, -c/9).$$

It follows that we may expect that one among $L_N(1/3, c/9)$ numbers u_k has an $N^{1/\alpha}$-smooth part that exceeds $0.5\sqrt{u_k}$. Note that $L_N(1/3, c/9) < N^{\varepsilon}$ for any fixed $\varepsilon > 0$ and $N \to \infty$. Using the elliptic curve factoring method [11] the $N^{1/\alpha}$-smooth part of u_k can be found in heuristic expected time

$$L_{N^{1/\alpha}}\left(1/2, \sqrt{2}\right) = L_N\left(1/3, 2\sqrt{1/3c}\right).$$

Therefore the total complexity of finding a 'good' u_k is

$$L_N\left(1/3, c/9\right) L_N\left(1/3, 2\sqrt{1/3c}\right) = L_N\left(1/3, c/9 + 2\sqrt{1/3c}\right).$$

This is minimized for $c = 3$ giving $L_N(1/3, 1)$ for the total heuristic expected runtime. Note that $L_N(1/3, 1)$ is substantially faster than

$$L_N(1/3, (128/27)^{1/3}) \approx L_N(1/3, 1.68),$$

the runtime of the approach that attempts to use the number field sieve to factor u directly. The latter approach is not always successful because u may not split into two factors of about equal size.

Because

$$L_N(1/3, 1) = L_{N^{9/64}}\left(1/3, (64/9)^{1/3}\right) \tag{10}$$

one may be tempted to expect that our selective forgery attack against 1024-bit moduli is easier than factoring 150-bit moduli using the number field sieve. However, (10) is an asymptotic result, useful for understanding the asymptotic growth rate of the runtime of our method, not to obtain absolute runtimes. To illustrate this, implementations of the number field sieve factoring algorithm use very fast sieving-based smoothness tests. Using the elliptic curve factoring method as smoothness test instead leads to the same heuristic asymptotic runtime for the number field sieve, but doing so would make it much slower in practice. Our selective forgery attack is in theory based on the elliptic curve method, but uses in practice a combination of trial division and the elliptic curve method – much faster sieving based smoothness tests do not seem to apply.

Nevertheless, and as shown in Section 4, our method is very practical. On average it turns out that a selective forgery attack against 1024-bit moduli can be expected to be easier than factoring moduli of about 250 bits using the number field sieve. Factoring 250-bit moduli is currently considered to be a triviality. Consequently, obtaining a 1024-bit selective forgery is a simple matter too. This practical result was obtained using a moderately efficient implementation of the elliptic curve method. With more careful coding it should not be hard to improve upon the practical performance of our method.

4   Example

We present a selective forgery attack against $N = \text{RSA-1024}$, the as yet unfactored 1024-bit challenge modulus from RSA Laboratories:

$N = \text{RSA-1024}$

    = C05748BB FB5ACD7E 5A77DC03 D9EC7D8B B957C1B9 5D9B2060
       90D83FD1 B67433CE 83EAD737 6CCFD612 C72901F4 CE0A2E07
       E322D438 EA4F3464 7555D62D 04140E10 84E999BB 4CD5F947
       A7667400 9E231854 9FD102C5 F7596EDC 332A0DDE E3A35518
       6B9A046F 0F96A279 C1448A91 51549DC6 63DA8A6E 89CF8F51
       1BAED645 0DA2C1CB,

see http://www.rsa.com/rsalabs/challenges/factoring/numbers.html.
   With $\omega = 1$ and $a = 2^{1023} + 2^{365}$ and

$m_3 = $ 167148 0115C7FF 50D924CC 6DD0B4EE AA7C04FD E74073D7
       8D010BB2 8DB1B371 C8D2A0E1 EE09EA3E D721BCCE

(the hexadecimal representation of the first 103 digits of π) a search of a few hours on a 600 MHz PIII laptop using a commercially available implementation of the elliptic curve factoring method produced:

$R(m_1) = $ 80000000 00000000 00000000 00000000 00000000 00000000
          00000000 00000000 00000000 00000000 00000000 00000000
          00000000 00000000 00000000 00000000 00000000 00000000
          00000000 00000000 00002000 12CDBE43 3BF454BD CE9C1D5C
          6BEB3D7C DC937495 8CAB854E 56EE8476 F1FF524D 3C5E8E25
          5D60E809 04C3DDB8,

$R(m_2) = $ 80000000 00000000 00000000 00000000 00000000 00000000
          00000000 00000000 00000000 00000000 00000000 00000000
          00000000 00000000 00000000 00000000 00000000 00000000
          00000000 00000000 00002000 075BC9B1 A93BA55B DC35329E
          B66E4BC1 915568BA EEEDC419 E3114231 626E8C21 9DF736BE
          12312CF1 C92314A0,

$R(m_3) = $ 80000000 00000000 00000000 00000000 00000000 00000000
          00000000 00000000 00000000 00000000 00000000 00000000
          00000000 00000000 00000000 00000000 00000000 00000000
          00000000 00000000 00002000 00167148 0115C7FF 50D924CC
          6DD0B4EE AA7C04FD E74073D7 8D010BB2 8DB1B371 C8D2A0E1
          EE09EA3E D721BCCE,

$R(m_4) =$ 80000000 00000000 00000000 00000000 00000000 00000000
00000000 00000000 00000000 00000000 00000000 00000000
00000000 00000000 00000000 00000000 00000000 00000000
00000000 00000000 00002000 1AA5C13B 5A416F97 8EC675C4
A924CE38 3A44C314 C4DF7204 E5D5197F D2E1363B 98D81A66
5AF68931 6B749CB9.

Because $R(m_1), \ldots, R(m_4)$ satisfy (3), the signature $s(m_3)$ on the preselected message m_3 can be forged, as desired, if $s(m_1)$, $s(m_2)$, and $s(m_4)$ are known.

5 Conclusion

In this paper we have extended the existential forgery attack against short fixed-pattern padding RSA signatures from [2] to a practical selective forgery attack. Here 'short' means that the fixed-pattern padding is shorter than two thirds of the modulus length. The heuristic asymptotic runtime of our method was shown to be $L_N(1/3, 1)$. It thus provides an example where a runtime of $L_N(1/3, 1)$ is achieved using the elliptic curve factoring method. As noted in [1, Section 4.2], where an earlier example is given, this is rare, as such runtimes are usually associated with Coppersmith's discrete logarithm algorithm for finite fields of fixed small characteristic [4] and the number field sieve [9].

It remains an open question if short fixed-pattern padding RSA signatures can be selectively forged in polynomial time. Neither is it known if attacks exist against longer fixed-pattern padding RSA signatures. It is quite natural to try to build multiplicative relations including more than four signatures (which could be a way to attack longer paddings), however at the moment it is not clear how to approach this. Until these issues are settled, research into the practical malleability of fixed-pattern padding RSA signatures remains an interesting subject because it may shed new light on the properties of RSA, still the world's foremost public key system.

Acknowledgment

The authors thank Allan Steel for his assistance with the elliptic curve factoring method.

References

1. D. Boneh, R.J. Lipton, 'Algorithms for black-box fields and their application to cryptography' Proc. Crypto'96, Santa Barbara, Lect. Notes in Comp. Sci., vol 1109, Springer-Verlag, Berlin, 1996, 283–297.
2. E. Brier, C. Clavier, J.-S. Coron and D. Naccache, 'Cryptanalysis of RSA signatures with fixed-pattern padding', Proc. Crypto'01, Santa Barbara, Lect. Notes in Comp. Sci., vol. 2139, Springer-Verlag, Berlin, 2001, 433–439.

3. S.D. Chowla and J. Todd, 'The density of reducible integers', *Canad. J. Math.*, **1** (1949) 297–299.

4. D. Coppersmith, 'Fast evaluation of logarithms in fields of characteristic two', *IEEE Trans. Inform. Theory* **30** (1984) 587–594.

5. M. Girault and J.-F. Misarsky, 'Selective forgery of RSA signatures using redundancy', *Proc. Eurocrypt'97, Konstanz*, Lect. Notes in Comp. Sci., vol. 1233, Springer-Verlag, Berlin, 1997, 495–507.

6. M. Girault and J.-F. Misarsky, 'Cryptoanalysis of countermeasures proposed for repairing ISO 9796', *Proc. Eurocrypt'00, Bruges*, Lect. Notes in Comp. Sci., vol. 1807, Springer-Verlag, Berlin, 2000, 81–90.

7. R.R. Hall and G. Tenenbaum, *Divisors*, Cambridge Univ. Press, 1988.

8. A. Hildebrand and G. Tenenbaum, 'Integers without large prime factors', *J. de Théorie des Nombres de Bordeaux*, **5** (1993) 411–484.

9. A.K. Lenstra and H.W. Lenstra, Jr., (Editors), *The developments of the number field sieve*, Lect. Notes in Mathematics, vol. 1554, Springer-Verlag, Berlin, 1993.

10. J.-F. Misarsky, 'A multiplicative attack using LLL algorithm on RSA signatures with redundancy, ', *Proc. Crypto'97, Santa Barbara*, Lect. Notes in Comp. Sci., vol. 1294, Springer-Verlag, Berlin, 1997, 221–234.

11. H.W. Lenstra, Jr., 'Factoring integers with elliptic curves', *Ann. of Math.*, **126** (1987) 649–673.

12. H. Niederreiter, *Random number generation and Quasi–Monte Carlo methods*, SIAM Press, 1992.

New Chosen-Plaintext Attacks on the One-Wayness of the Modified McEliece PKC Proposed at Asiacrypt 2000

Kazukuni Kobara and Hideki Imai

Institute of Industrial Science, The University of Tokyo
4-6-1, Komaba, Meguro-ku, Tokyo, 153-8505 Japan
Tel: +81-3-5452-6232
FAX: +81-3-5452-6631
{kobara,imai}@iis.u-tokyo.ac.jp

Abstract. McEliece PKC (Public-Key Cryptosystem), whose security is based on the decoding problem, is one of a few alternatives for the current PKCs that are mostly based on either IFP (Integer Factoring Problem) or DLP (Discrete Logarithm Problem), which would be solved in polynomial-time after the emergence of quantum computers. It is known that the McEliece PKC with an appropriate conversion satisfies (in the random oracle model) the strongest security notion IND-CCA2 (IN-Distinguishability of encryption against adaptively Chosen-Ciphertext Attacks) under the assumption that breaking OW-CPA (One-Wayness against Chosen-Plaintext Attacks) of the underlying McEliece PKC, i.e. the McEliece PKC with no conversion, is infeasible. Breaking OW-CPA of it is still infeasible if an appropriate parameter, $n \geq 2048$ with optimum t and k, is chosen since the binary work factor to break it with the best CPA is around 2^{106} for $(n, k, t) = (2048, 1278, 70)$. The aim of the modification at Asiacrypt 2000 is to improve it of the next smaller parameter $n = 1024$ to a safe level 2^{88} from an almost dangerous level 2^{62}. If his idea works correctly, we can use the more compact system safely. In this paper, we carefully review the modification at Asiacrypt 2000, and then show that the one-wayness of it is vulnerable against our new CPAs.

1 Introduction

Since the concept of public-key cryptosystem (PKC) was introduced by Diffie and Hellman [5], many researchers have proposed numerous PKCs based on various problems, such as integer factoring, discrete logarithm, decoding a large linear code, knapsack, inverting polynomial equations, lattice and so on. While some of them are still alive, most of them were broken by cryptographers due to their intensive cryptanalysis. As a result, almost all of the current secure systems on the market employ only a small class of PKCs, such as RSA and elliptic curve cryptosystems, which are all based on either integer factoring problem (IFP) or discrete logarithm problem (DLP). This situation would cause a serious problem

D. Naccache and P. Paillier (Eds.): PKC 2002, LNCS 2274, pp. 237–251, 2002.

after someone discovers one practical algorithm which breaks both IFP and DLP in polynomial-time. Who can prove that such an algorithm will never be found? Actually, Shor has already found a (probabilistic) polynomial-time algorithm in [17], even though it requires a quantum computer that is impractical so far. In order to prepare for such unfortunate situations, we need to find another secure scheme relying on neither IFP nor DLP.

The McEliece PKC, proposed by R.J. McEliece in [15], is one of a few alternatives for the PKCs based on IFP or DLP. It is based on the decoding problem of a large linear code with no visible structure which is conjectured to be an NP-complete problem.[1] While several attacks [1,3,4,7,11,14,19] are known on the McEliece PKC, all of them can be prevented by either enlarging the parameter size or applying an appropriate conversion to it [10].

The McEliece PKC with an appropriate conversion in [10] satisfies (in the random oracle model [2]) the strongest security notion IND-CCA2 (INDistinguishability of encryption [6] against adaptively Chosen-Ciphertext Attacks) under the assumption that it is infeasible to break OW-CPA (One-Wayness against Chosen-Plaintext Attacks) of the underlying McEliece PKC. OW-CPA is said to be broken if one can recover the whole plaintext of an arbitrarily given ciphertext using neither partial knowledge on the plaintext nor decryption oracles. It is still infeasible to break OW-CPA of the McEliece PKC if an appropriate parameter, $n \geq 2048$ with optimum t and k, is chosen since the binary work factor to break it with the best CPA [4] is around 2^{106} for $(n, k, t) = (2048, 1278, 70)$.

At Asiacrypt 2000, a modification of the McEliece PKC was proposed by P. Loidreau. While his modification does not improve the immunity against attacks using decryption oracles, such as the malleability attack [8,19] and the reaction attack [7], or attacks using partial knowledge on the target plaintext, such as the related-message attack [3], the message-resend attack [3] and the known-partial-plaintext attack [9], it does not matter since all of them can be prevented with a conversion. The aim of his modification is to improve the binary work factor for breaking OW-CPA of the next smaller parameter $n = 1024$ to a safe level 2^{88} from an almost dangerous level 2^{62}. If his idea works correctly, we can use the more compact system safely.

In this paper, we carefully review the modification at Asiacrypt 2000 to see whether it truely improves OW-CPA or not. Then we show that it is vulnerable against our "new" CPAs on OW (even though the modification certainly enhances OW against "ever known" CPAs). Our attacks exploit only the modified structure of it and thus cannot be applied to the original (unmodified) McEliece. This means the OW-CPA of the the original (unmodified) McEliece PKC is still infeasible as long as an secure parameter is chosen.

This paper is organized as follows: in Section 2 and 3, we describe both the McEliece PKC and the ever known CPAs on OW of it, respectively. Then, in Section 4, we review the modified cryptosystem proposed by Loidreau [13].

---

[1] The complete decoding problem of an arbitrary linear code is proven to be NP-complete in [20].

Finally, in Section 5, we show our new CPAs which weaken the one-wayness of the modified cryptosystem.

2   McEliece Public-Key Cryptosystem

2.1   Cryptosystems

The McEliece PKC consists of the following key generation, encryption and decryption systems:

Key generation: One generates the following three matrices G,S,P:

  G: $k \times n$ generator matrix of a binary Goppa code that can correct up to t errors, and for which an efficient decoding algorithm $\Psi()$ is known. The parameter t is given by $\lfloor \frac{d_{min}-1}{2} \rfloor$ where d_{min} denotes the minimum Hamming distance of the code.

  S: $k \times k$ random binary non-singular matrix

  P: $n \times n$ random permutation matrix.

  Then, computes the $k \times n$ matrix $G' = SGP$.

  Secret key: (S, P) and $\Psi()$

  Public key: (G', t)

Encryption: The ciphertext c of a given message msg is calculated as follows:

$$c = msg \cdot G' \oplus z \tag{1}$$

  where msg a binary vector of length k, and z denotes a random binary error vector of length n having t 1's.

Decryption: First, one calculates cP^{-1} where

$$c \cdot P^{-1} = (msg \cdot S)G \oplus z \cdot P^{-1} \tag{2}$$

and P^{-1} denotes the inverse of P. Second, applies the decoding algorithm $\Psi()$ to cP^{-1}. Since the Hamming weight of $z \cdot P^{-1}$ is t, $\Psi()$ can correct it:

$$msg \cdot S = \Psi(c \cdot P^{-1}). \tag{3}$$

Now, the plaintext msg of c can be obtained by

$$msg = (msg \cdot S)S^{-1}. \tag{4}$$

2.2   Underlying Codes

As the underlying codes of the McEliece PKC, we recommend to employ Goppa codes but other codes, such as Reed-Solomon codes, BCH codes and so on. The difference between them is whether the weight distribution is determined by the public parameters n and k. While the Goppa codes have a variety of the weight distributions according to the underlying Goppa polynomials even if both n and k are fixed, both the Reed-Solomon codes and BCH codes have only the fixed weight distribution depending on both n and k. In other words, when both n and k are given from a public matrix G', one can know the underlying code G if codes like Reed-Solomon or BCH are used. Then once G is found, an adversary can reveal the permutation P between G and G' using the SSA(Support Splitting Algorithm) [16] that can reveal the permutation P between the codes having the same weight distribution. The other secret matrix S can be revealed using G and $G'P^{-1}$ with a simple linear algebra.

The next case we have to avoid is that the candidates for G is small enough to enumerate. In this case, the following attack is possible [14]. An adversary picks up a candidate for G and then sees whether it has the same weight distribution as G'. If it has, it is the correct G. The following processes to obtain both P and S are the same as the previous attack.

The former attack can be avoided using a Goppa code, and then the latter attack can be avoided using a Goppa code where the cardinality of the Goppa polynomials is too large to enumerate.

3   Known Chosen Plaintext Attacks on One-Wayness of McEliece PKC

Since the aim of the modification at Asiacrypt 2000 is to enhance the immunity against CPAs on OW, we focus on them. Note that the attack on the public key [14] can be avoided if one choose the underlying Goppa polynomial out of a large set enough to avoid the exhaustive search, and also the other attacks either abusing decryption oracles, such as the malleability attack [8,19] and the reaction attack [7], or abusing partial knowledge on the target plaintext, such as the related-message attack [3], the message-resend attack [3] and the known-partial-plaintext attack [9], can be avoided by applying an appropriate conversion in [10].

Only the following two attacks are known as the CPAs on OW of the McEliece PKC. They can be summarized as follows.

3.1   Generalized Information-Set-Decoding Attack

Let G'_k denote k independent columns picked out of G', and then let c_k and z_k denote the corresponding k coordinates of c and z, respectively. They have the following relationship

$$c_k = msg \cdot G'_k \oplus z_k. \tag{5}$$

If $z_k = 0$ and G'_k is non-singular, msg can be recovered [1] by

$$msg = (c_k \oplus z_k)G'^{-1}_k. \tag{6}$$

Even if $z_k \neq 0$, msg can be obtained by guessing z_k among small Hamming weights [11], i.e. $Hw(z_k) \leq j$ for small j. The correctness of the recovered plaintext msg is verifiable by checking whether the Hamming weight of

$$c \oplus msg \cdot G' = c \oplus c_k G'^{-1}_k \cdot G' \oplus z_k G'^{-1}_k \cdot G' \tag{7}$$

is t or not.

The corresponding algorithm is summarized as follows:

Algorithm 1 (GISD)

Input: a ciphertext c, a public key (G', t) and an attack parameter $j \in Z$.
Output: a plaintext msg.

1. Choose k independent columns out of G', and then calculate $\hat{G}'_k := G_k'^{-1}G'$. Let I denote the set of the indexes of the k chosen columns, and then J denote the set of the remaining columns.

2. Do the following until msg is found:
   2.1 Calculate $\hat{z} := c \oplus c_k\hat{G}'_k$. If $Hw(\hat{z}) = t$, output $msg := c_kG_k'^{-1}$.
   2.2 For i_1 from 1 to j do the following:
      i. For i_2 from 1 to $\binom{n}{i_1}$ do the following:
         A. Choose a new z'_k, such that $Hw(z'_k) = i_1$.
         B. If $Hw(\hat{z} \oplus z'_k\hat{G}'_k) = t$, output $msg := (c_k \oplus z'_k)G_k'^{-1}$.
   2.3 Replace one coordinate in I with a coordinate in J, and then renew the $\hat{G}'_k := G_k'^{-1}G'$ using Gaussian elimination.

We estimate the binary work factor of the above GISD attack as follows. In Step 1, $G_k'^{-1}G'$ is the $k \times n$ matrix where the chosen k columns make the identity matrix. It can be obtained by the Gaussian elimination with the work factor of

$$\sum_{i=1}^{k} \frac{(k-1)(n-i+1)}{4} = \frac{k(k-1)(2n+1-k)}{8} \tag{8}$$

bit operations. When one checks the Hamming weight in Step 2.1 and Step B, he/she does not need to calculate the whole n coordinates of $c \oplus c_k\hat{G}'_k$ in Step 2.1 and $\hat{z} \oplus z'_k\hat{G}'_k$ in Step B, respectively, since he/she can know whether their weight exceeds t or not with around $2t$ coordinates in J provided that wrong cases have the average weight of $n/2$. Thus the binary work factor for calculating the $2t$ coordinates of $c \oplus c_k\hat{G}'_k$ in Step 2.1 is $t \cdot k/2$, and that of $\hat{z} \oplus z'_k\hat{G}'_k$ in Step B is $t \cdot i_1$. Accordingly, the work factor for Step 2.2 is

$$V_j = \sum_{i_1=1}^{j} t \cdot i_1 \cdot \binom{k}{i_1}. \tag{9}$$

In Step 2.3, one needs to update $\hat{G}'_k = G_k'^{-1}G'$ whose binary work factor is

$$\frac{(k-1)(n-k)}{4}. \tag{10}$$

Since Step 2 is repeated around T_j times where:

$$T_j = \frac{\binom{n}{k}}{\sum_{i=0}^{j} \binom{t}{i}\binom{n-t}{k-i}}, \tag{11}$$

the total work factor is given by

$$W_j \approx \left\{ \frac{(k-1)(n-k)}{4} + \frac{t \cdot k}{2} + V_j \right\} \cdot T_j \qquad (12)$$

When n is given, designers of the cryptosystem can optimize both k and t to make (12) higher, and then attackers can optimize the attack parameter j to make it lower. For $n = 2^{10}$, $\min_j(\max_{k,t}(W_j)) \approx 2^{67}$, which can be achieved when $j = 1$, $t = 38$ to 40 and $k = n - m \cdot t = 644$ to 624, respectively. For $n = 2^{11}$, $\min_j(\max_{k,t}(W_j)) \approx 2^{113}$, which can be achieved when $j = 1$, $t = 63$ to 78 and $k = n - m \cdot t = 1355$ to 1190, respectively.

3.2   Finding-Low-Weight-Codeword Attack

This attack uses an algorithm which accepts both an arbitrary generator matrix and a positive integer w, and then finds out a codeword of weight w [18,4]. Since the codeword of weight t of the following $(k+1) \times n$ generator matrix

$$\begin{bmatrix} G' \\ c \end{bmatrix} \qquad (13)$$

is the error vector z where $c = msg \cdot G' \oplus z$, this algorithm can be used to recover msg from given c and G'.

This algorithm is summarized as follows:

Algorithm 2 (FLWC)

Input: a ciphertext c, a public key (G', t) and attack parameters $(p, \rho) \in Z \times Z$.
Output: a plaintext msg.

1. Choose $k+1$ independent columns from (13) and then apply Gaussian elimination to obtain a $(k+1) \times n$ matrix where chosen $k+1$ columns make the identity matrix. Let I denote a set of the indexes of the $k+1$ chosen coordinates, and J denote those of the remaining coordinates.
2. Do the following until a code word z of weight t is found:
   2.1 Split I in two subsets I_1 and I_2 at random where $|I_1| = \lfloor (k+1)/2 \rfloor$ and $|I_2| = \lceil (k+1)/2 \rceil$. The rows of the $(k+1) \times (n-k-1)$ matrix M corresponding to J are also split in two parts, a $(\lfloor (k+1)/2 \rfloor) \times (n-k-1)$ matrix M_1 and a $(\lceil (k+1)/2 \rceil) \times (n-k-1)$ matrix M_2 according to I_1 and I_2, respectively, i.e. if I_1 includes i-th coordinate, the i-th row of M is included in M_1.
   2.2 Select a ρ-element subset J_ρ of J at random.
   2.3 For i from 1 to $\binom{|I_1|}{p}$ do the following:
       i. Select a new set of p rows of the matrix M_1. Let $\mathcal{P}_{1,i}$ denote the set.
       ii. Sum up the chosen p rows of M_1 in Z_2. Let $\Lambda_{1,i|J_\rho}$ denote the chosen ρ coordinates of the result.
       iii. Store both $\mathcal{P}_{1,i}$ and $\Lambda_{1,i|J_\rho}$ in a hash table with 2^ρ entries using $\Lambda_{1,i|J_\rho}$ as an index.

2.4 For j from 1 to $\binom{|I_2|}{p}$ do the following:

    i. Select a new set of p rows of the matrix M_2. Let $\mathcal{P}_{2,j}$ denote the set.

    ii. Sum up the chosen p rows of M_2 in F_2. Let $\Lambda_{2,j|J_\rho}$ denote the chosen ρ coordinates of the result.

    iii. Store both $\mathcal{P}_{2,j}$ and $\Lambda_{2,j|J_\rho}$ in a hash table with 2^ρ entries using $\Lambda_{2,j|J_\rho}$ as an index.

2.5 Using the hash table, find all pairs of sets $(\mathcal{P}_{1,i}, \mathcal{P}_{2,j})$ such that $\Lambda_{1,i|J_\rho} = \Lambda_{2,j|J_\rho}$ and check whether $Hw(\Lambda_{1,i|J} \oplus \Lambda_{2,j|J}) = t - 2p$ where $\Lambda_{1,i|J}$ and $\Lambda_{2,j|J}$ denote the sums of the p rows of M_1 and M_2 corresponding to $\mathcal{P}_{1,i}$ and $\mathcal{P}_{2,j}$, respectively. If found, output the code word.

2.6 Replace one coordinate in I with a coordinate in J, and then make the chosen $k+1$ columns be the identity matrix using Gaussian elimination.

3. Apply the information-set decoding to $c \oplus z$, and then recover the corresponding message msg.

Under the assumption that each iteration is independent, one needs to repeat Step 2 around $T_{p,\rho}$ times where

$$T_{p,\rho} = \frac{\binom{k-2p}{\frac{k}{2}-p}\binom{2p}{p}\binom{-k+n+2p-t}{\rho}}{\binom{k}{\frac{k}{2}}\binom{-k+n}{\rho}} \cdot \frac{\binom{n-t}{k-2p}\binom{t}{2p}}{\binom{n}{k}}. \qquad (14)$$

In Step 2.1 to 2.4, one needs to compute both $\Lambda_{1,i|J_\rho}$ and $\Lambda_{2,j|J_\rho}$ for about $\binom{(k+1)/2}{p}$ combinations, respectively, whose binary work factor is around

$$\Omega_1(p,\rho) = p \cdot \rho \cdot \binom{(k+1)/2}{p}. \qquad (15)$$

In Step 2.5, around $\binom{(k+1)/2}{p}^2/2^\rho$ pairs of $(\mathcal{P}_{1,i}, \mathcal{P}_{2,j})$ satisfies $\Lambda_{1,i|J_\rho} \oplus \Lambda_{2,j|J_\rho} = 0$, and for each pair one needs to check the weight of $\Lambda_{1,i|J} \oplus \Lambda_{2,j|J}$. In the same way as Algorithm 1, one can know that $Hw(\Lambda_{1,i|J} \oplus \Lambda_{2,j|J}) \neq t - 2p$ by calculating the weight of around $2(t - 2p)$ coordinates in J. Thus the binary work factor for Step 2.5 is around

$$\Omega_2(p,\rho) = 2(t - 2p) \cdot p \cdot \frac{\binom{(k+1)/2}{p}^2}{2^\rho}. \qquad (16)$$

The binary work factor for updating the generator matrix in Step 2.6 is

$$\Omega_3(p,\rho) = \frac{k(n - k - 1)}{4}. \qquad (17)$$

Thus the total binary work factor is given by

$$W_{p,\rho} \approx (\Omega_1(p,\rho) + \Omega_2(p,\rho) + \Omega_3(p,\rho)) \cdot T_{p,\rho}. \qquad (18)$$

For $n = 2^{10}$, $\min_{p,\rho}(\max_{k,t}(W_{p,\rho})) \approx 2^{62}$, which can be achieved when $(p,\rho) = (2,19)$, $t = 36$ to 43 and $k = n - m \cdot t = 664$ to 594, respectively. For $n = 2^{11}$, $\min_{p,\rho}(\max_{k,t}(W_{p,\rho})) \approx 2^{106}$, which can be achieved when $(p,\rho) = (2,22)$, $t = 63$ to 79 and $k = n - m \cdot t = 1355$ to 1179, respectively.

4   Loidreau's Modification at Asiacrypt 2000

The aim of the modification at Asiacrypt 2000 [13] is to improve the difficulty of breaking OW-CPA without increasing n. It uses some linear transformation $f()$ such that $f(\mathcal{C}) = \mathcal{C}$ (C being the Goppa code of the PKC). Instead of choosing an error vector of small weight, it uses an error vector z' such that $f(z')$ has small weight. This way, the error vector itself can have higher Hamming weight, and it is harder to find it via the usual search methods.

In this section, we review the underlying principles and the modified cryptosystem more precisely.

4.1   Frobenius Automorphism Group of Goppa Codes

Let us consider the Goppa code $\Gamma(L, g)$ over F_{2^m} where $L = (\alpha_1, \cdots, \alpha_n)$ contains all the elements in F_{2^m}.

If all the coefficients of the Goppa polynomial g is in a subfield F_{2^s} of F_{2^m}, then the code $\Gamma(L, g)$ is invariant under the action of the Frobenius automorphism. That is, a Frobenius mapped word $\sigma(c)$ of a code word c of $\Gamma(L, g)$ is also a code word of $\Gamma(L, g)$:

$$\forall c = (c_{\alpha_1}, \cdots, c_{\alpha_n}) \in \Gamma(L, g), \qquad \sigma(c) = (c_{\sigma(\alpha_1)}, \cdots, c_{\sigma(\alpha_n)}) \in \Gamma(L, g) \quad (19)$$

where $\sigma : x \mapsto x^{2^s}$.

4.2   Orbits Generated by Frobenius Automorphism

The action of the Frobenius automorphism makes some orbits in the field. For simplicity, we consider the field extension $F_{2^{5s}}$ of F_{2^s}, and the corresponding Frobenius automorphism $\sigma : x \mapsto x^{2^s}$. The action of the Frobenius automorphism to $F_{2^{5s}}$ makes $N_5 = (2^{5s} - 2^s)/5$ orbits of size 5 and 2^s orbits of size 1. In other words, a word $\{z_{\alpha_1}, z_{\alpha_2}, \cdots, z_{\alpha_n}\}$ can be rewritten in the following form after reordering its labeling L:

$$z = \{Z_1, Z_2, \cdots, Z_{N_5}, Z_0\} \tag{20}$$

where $Z_i = \{z_{\alpha_j}, z_{\sigma(\alpha_j)}, z_{\sigma^2(\alpha_j)}, z_{\sigma^3(\alpha_j)}, z_{\sigma^4(\alpha_j)}\}$ for $i \in \{1, \cdots, N_5\}$ denotes an orbit of length 5 generated by α_j, and then Z_0 denotes a sub-vector of length 2^s corresponding to the 2^s orbits of length 1 generated by 2^s distinct elements in F_{2^s}.

For the reordered coordinate, the action of the Frobenius automorphism σ on a word z is given as follows:

$$\sigma(z) = \{\sigma(Z_1), \cdots, \sigma(Z_{N_5}), Z_0\} \tag{21}$$

where $\sigma(Z_i)$ is a left cyclic shift in Z_i, e.g. for $Z_{i_1} = \{1, 1, 1, 0, 0\}$ and $Z_{i_2} = \{1, 1, 0, 1, 0\}$, $\sigma^l(Z_{i_1})$ and $\sigma^l(Z_{i_2})$ for $l \in Z_5$ are listed as follows:

$$Z_{i_1} = \{1,1,1,0,0\}, \qquad\qquad Z_{i_2} = \{1,1,0,1,0\},$$
$$\sigma(Z_{i_1}) = \{1,1,0,0,1\}, \qquad\qquad \sigma(Z_{i_2}) = \{1,0,1,0,1\},$$
$$\sigma^2(Z_{i_1}) = \{1,0,0,1,1\}, \qquad\qquad \sigma^2(Z_{i_2}) = \{0,1,0,1,1\},$$
$$\sigma^3(Z_{i_1}) = \{0,0,1,1,1\}, \qquad\qquad \sigma^3(Z_{i_2}) = \{1,0,1,1,0\},$$
$$\sigma^4(Z_{i_1}) = \{0,1,1,1,0\}, \qquad\qquad \sigma^4(Z_{i_2}) = \{0,1,1,0,1\}. \quad (22)$$

4.3 t-Tower Decodable Vector

In the Loidreau's modified cryptosystem, t-tower decodable vectors are used instead of random error vectors of weight t.

The definition of a t-tower decodable vector is given as follows:

Definition 1 (t-Tower Decodable Vector) *t-tower decodable vector z' is a word of length n satisfying the following three conditions:*

Larger-weight: $Hw(z') > t$.
Reducibility: *There exists a linear combination $f()$ such that $Hw(z) \le t$ where*

$$z = f(z') = \sum_{i=0}^{m/s-1} b_i \cdot \sigma^i(z'), \qquad b_i \in F_2. \qquad (23)$$

Recoverability: *z' is uniquely recoverable from the above z.*

In [13], t-tower decodable vector z' is generated as follows:

Algorithm 3 (Generation of a t-Tower Decodable Vector)

Output: a t-tower decodable vector z'.

1. Set all the coordinates of z' to 0.
2. Choose randomly $p = \lfloor t/2 \rfloor$ orbits out of the N_5 orbits of length 5.
3. Flip 3 bits each at random in the chosen p orbits.

The following $f_1()$ or $f_2()$ where

$$z = f_1(z') = z' + \sigma(z') + \sigma^2(z'), \qquad (24)$$
$$z = f_2(z') = z' + \sigma^2(z') + \sigma^3(z') \qquad (25)$$

reduces the weight of z' within t since $\sigma^l(Z_{i_1})$ or $\sigma^l(Z_{i_2})$ in (22) cover all the patterns of a vector of length 5 and weight 3, and then they are transformed into the following patterns:

$$f_1(\sigma^l(Z_{i_1})) = \sigma^l(Z_{i_1} + \sigma(Z_{i_1}) + \sigma^2(Z_{i_1})) = \sigma^l(\{1,0,1,1,0\}),$$
$$f_1(\sigma^l(Z_{i_2})) = \sigma^l(Z_{i_2} + \sigma(Z_{i_2}) + \sigma^2(Z_{i_2})) = \sigma^l(\{0,0,1,0,0\}),$$
$$f_2(\sigma^l(Z_{i_1})) = \sigma^l(Z_{i_1} + \sigma^2(Z_{i_1}) + \sigma^3(Z_{i_1})) = \sigma^l(\{0,1,0,0,0\}),$$
$$f_2(\sigma^l(Z_{i_2})) = \sigma^l(Z_{i_2} + \sigma^2(Z_{i_2}) + \sigma^3(Z_{i_2})) = \sigma^l(\{0,0,1,1,1\}) \qquad (26)$$

where $\sigma^l()$ denotes a l-bit left cyclic shift. More formally, let p_1 and p_2 denote the number of $\sigma^l(Z_{i_1})$ for any l and $\sigma^l(Z_{i_2})$ for any l in z', respectively. Since $p_1 + p_2 = p = \lfloor t/2 \rfloor$ and

$$
\begin{aligned}
\min(f_1(z'), f_2(z')) &= \min(3p_1 + p_2, p_1 + 3p_2) \\
&= \min(2p_1 + \lfloor t/2 \rfloor, \lfloor t/2 \rfloor + 2p_2) \\
&\leq 2 \cdot \lfloor t/2 \rfloor \\
&\leq t,
\end{aligned} \tag{27}
$$

one can reduce the weight of z' within t using either $f_1()$ or $f_2()$.

Using the corrected vector z, one can uniquely recover the corresponding t-tower decodable vector z' since both $f_1()$ and $f_2()$ are one-to-one mappings.

4.4   Loidreau's Modified Cryptosystem

As we have seen in the previous subsections, Loidreau's modified cryptosystem [13] uses the field extension $F_{2^{5s}}$ of F_{2^s}, i.e. it employs a Goppa polynomial g (of degree t) over a subfield F_{2^s} of $F_{2^{5s}}$ to enable the Frobenius automorphism. It also employs a hiding polynomial g_1 over $F_{2^{5s}}$ of degree t_1 (which has no roots in L) to enlarge the cardinality of the underlying polynomial gg_1.

The cardinality of gg_1 is approximately given by $\{(2^{5s})^{t_1}/t_1\} \cdot \{(2^s)^t/t\}$ since the number of irreducible monic polynomials of degree x over F_{2^y} is around $(2^y)^x/x$ [12].

$\Gamma(L, gg_1)$ can be decoded using the decoding algorithm for $\Gamma(L, g)$ since $\Gamma(L, gg_1)$ is a subcode of $\Gamma(L, g)$. The plaintext size of $\Gamma(L, gg_1)$ is $k - t_1$. Both the key generation process and the encryption process are the same as the (unmodified) McEliece PKC except the following points:

- All the N_5 orbits of length 5 are open to the public as a part of a public key (but the order in each orbit is kept in secret). Note that the orbits can be opened without increasing the public key size by permuting orbits and then by permuting columns in each orbit as P. Since the units of orbits are the same as L, one can know them. While it reduces the cardinality of the permutations P, it still maintains a large amount (see Table 1 and 2, respectively).
- Both $f_1()$ and $f_2()$ are kept in secret (which is the same that the order in each orbit is kept in secret).
- t-tower decodable vectors z' are used as error vectors instead of random vectors of weight t.

The decryption process is described as follows:

Algorithm 4 (Decoding for the modified cryptosystem)

Input: a ciphertext c.
Output: a corresponding plaintext msg.
 1. Apply $f_1()$ and $f_2()$ to the given ciphertext c, respectively.

Table 1. Cardinalities of System Parameters

Cryptosystem	Permutations	Goppa polynomials	Error vectors	Orders in orbits
McEliece PKC [15]	$n!$	$\frac{(2^m)^t}{t}$	$\binom{n}{t}$	–
Loidreau's modified version [13]	$(5!)^{N_5} \cdot N_5!$	$\frac{(2^m)^{t_1}}{t_1} \cdot \frac{(2^s)^t}{t}$	$10^{\lfloor t/2 \rfloor} \cdot \binom{N_5}{\lfloor t/2 \rfloor}$	$(4!)^{N_5}$

2. Decode $f_1(c)$ and $f_2(c)$ using the decoding algorithm for $\Gamma(L, g)$. At least one of them can be corrected since the Hamming weight of the error vector of at least one of them is smaller than or equal to t.
3. Using the corrected error vector z, reconstruct the corresponding t-tower decodable vector z'.
4. Apply the information-set decoding to $c \oplus z'$, and then recover the corresponding message msg.

If both of $f_1(c)$ and $f_2(c)$ are corrected in Step 2, decrypt two messages and then discard one using the redundancy in the plaintexts. This means the modified cryptosystem requires a redundancy in a plaintext.

4.5 One-Wayness of Modified Cryptosystem against Ever Known Chosen-Plaintext Attacks

Since the Loidreau's modification enlarges the Hamming weight of the error vectors to $3\lfloor t/2 \rfloor$ from t, the binary work factors to break the one-wayness with the ever known CPAs, i.e. both the GISD and the FLWC attacks, are improved (see Table 3).

The Loidreau's modification employs new secrets $f_1()$ and $f_2()$ (or equivalently the order in each orbit). Also it reduces the cardinality of permutations P, Goppa polynomials gg_1 and error vectors z', respectively. If at least one of the cardinalities is small enough to enumerate, the cryptosystem will be broken by guessing it. Fortunately, all of them still preserve a sufficient amount enough to avoid exhaustive search for them (see Table 1 and 2).

5 Our New Chosen-Plaintext Attacks on the Modified Cryptosystem

In this section, we show our new chosen-plaintext attacks on the one-wayness of the Loidreau's modified cryptosystem.

Our attacks use the fact that 1's in a t-tower error vector z' is not uniformly distributed. (This means that our new attacks are not applicable to the (unmodified) McEliece PKC since 1's in its error vector is uniformly distributed.)

Table 2. Cardinalities of System Parameters for (n, k, t, t_1, s, N_5) = $(1024, 624, 40, 9, 2, 204)$

Cryptosystem	Permutations	Goppa polynomials	Error vectors	Orders in orbits
McEliece PKC [15]	2^{8769}	2^{375}	2^{240}	–
Loidreau's modified version [13]	2^{2685}	2^{162}	2^{157}	2^{935}

5.1   Attack I

This attack applies $f_1()$ and $f_2()$ to both the ciphertext and all the rows in the public generator matrix G', respectively. This gives

$$f_1(c) = msg \cdot f_1(G') + f_1(z') \quad \text{and} \tag{28}$$
$$f_2(c) = msg \cdot f_2(G') + f_2(z') \tag{29}$$

respectively [2]. One can view $f_1(G')$ and $f_2(G')$ as generator matrices, and do the usual search for $f_1(z')$ or $f_2(z')$.

Since either $f_1(z')$ or $f_2(z')$ has low weight and both GISD and FLWC are the generic decoding algorithms for an arbitrary linear code, msg of (28) and (29) can be decoded without knowing the algebraic structure of $f_1'(G')$ and $f_2'(G')$.

The corresponding algorithm is given as follows:

Algorithm 5 (Attack I)

Input: a ciphertext c, a public key (G', t) and attack parameters $(p, \rho) \in Z \times Z$.
Output: a plaintext msg.

1. Apply $f_1'()$ and $f_2'()$ to the given c and all the rows of G' respectively, and then obtain $f_1'(c)$, $f_1'(G')$, $f_2'(c)$ and $f_2'(G')$.
2. Execute the FLWC attack[3] on the pair of $f_1'(G')$ and $f_1'(c)$ and that of $f_2'(G')$ and $f_2'(c)$ respectively to find the code word of weight less than or equal to t. If found, it recovers msg.

For $t_1 = 9$, $\min_{p,\rho}(\max_{k',t}(W_j)) \approx 2^{61}$ that can be achieved when $(p, \rho) = (2, 19)$, $t = 38$ to 41 and $k' = n - m \cdot t - t_1 = 635$ to 605 respectively [4].

---

[2]   The Frobenius automorphism gives $f_1(c) = msg' \cdot G' \oplus f_1(z')$ for a certain msg'.
[3]   One can use the GISD attack, too.
[4]   This binary work factor is smaller than that of the (unmodified) McEliece PKC since the Loidreau's modification employs a subcode of $\Gamma(L, g)$, i.e. $k' = k - t_1$. Then t_1 should be chosen so that the cardinality of Goppa polynomials should be large enough to avoid collisions among users.

Table 3. Binary work factors to break OW-CPA for $(n, k, t, t_1, s_1, N_5) =$ $(1024, 624, 40, 9, 2, 204)$

Systems \ Attacks	Ever known attacks		Our new attacks	
	GISD[11]	FLWC[4]	Attack I	Attack II
McEliece PKC [15]	2^{67}	2^{62}	–	–
Loidreau's modified cryptosystem [13]	2^{94}	2^{88}	2^{61}	2^{42}

5.2   Attack II

For the error vector z' in the modified cryptosystem, it is proposed (roughly) to split the coordinates into N_5 orbits of five, then choose $p = \lfloor t/2 \rfloor$ such orbits, and in each of them to choose three positions for the non-zero bits. Under this strategy, one can again apply the usual search method, this time on orbits, rather than individual positions.

We found that it is not so difficult to choose $\lceil (k' - 2^s)/5 \rceil$ orbits of all zeros or almost all zeros out of the N_5 orbits. Note that $\lceil (k' - 2^s)/5 \rceil$ corresponds with more than or equal to k coordinates. Once such k coordinates are found, one can decrypt a given ciphertext using the information-set decoding.

The corresponding algorithm is given as follows:

Algorithm 6 (Attack II)

Input: a ciphertext c, a public key (G', t) and an attack parameter $j \in Z$.
Output: a plaintext msg.

1. Choose k' independent columns out of G' with which chosen $\lceil (k' - 2^s)/5 \rceil$ orbits of length 5 and 2^s orbits of length 1 correspond. Then calculate $\hat{G}'_{k'} := G'^{-1}_{k'} G'$. Let I denote a set of the indexes of the k' chosen columns, and then J denote a set of the remaining columns.
2. Do the following until msg is found:
   2.1 Calculate $\hat{z} := c \oplus c_{k'} \hat{G}'_{k'}$. If $Hw(\hat{z}) = 3 \lfloor t/2 \rfloor$, output $msg := c_{k'} G'^{-1}_{k'}$.
   2.2 For i_1 from 1 to j do the following:
      i. For i_2 from 1 to $\binom{\lceil (k' - 2^s)/5 \rceil}{i_1}$ do the following:
         A. Choose a new $z'_{k'}$ that contains i_1 non-zero orbits.
         B. If $Hw(\hat{z} \oplus z'_{k'} \hat{G}'_{k'}) = 3 \lfloor t/2 \rfloor$, output $msg := (c_{k'} \oplus z'_{k'}) G'^{-1}_{k'}$.
   2.3 Replace one orbit in I with a new orbit in J, and then renew the $\hat{G}'_{k'} := G'^{-1}_{k'} G'$ using Gaussian elimination.

This algorithm repeats Step 2 around T_j times where:

$$T_j = \frac{\binom{N_5}{\lceil (k' - 2^s)/5 \rceil}}{\sum_{i=0}^{j} \binom{\lfloor t/2 \rfloor}{i} \binom{N_5 - \lfloor t/2 \rfloor}{\lceil (k' - 2^s)/5 \rceil - i}}. \tag{30}$$

The binary work factors of Step 2.1, 2.2 and 2.3 are $t \cdot k'/2$, V_j and $5(k'-1)(n-k')/4$ respectively where

$$V_j = \sum_{i_1=1}^{j} t \cdot 3i_1 \cdot \binom{5}{3}^{i_1} \cdot \binom{\lceil (k'-2^s)/5 \rceil}{i_1}. \tag{31}$$

Thus the total work factor is given by

$$W_j \approx \left\{ \frac{5(k'-1)(n-k')}{4} + \frac{t \cdot k'}{2} + V_j \right\} \cdot T_j. \tag{32}$$

For $t_1 = 9$, $\min_j(\max_{k',t}(W_j)) \approx 2^{42}$ that can be achieved when $j = 1$, $t = 32$ to 50 and $k' = n - m \cdot t - t_1 = 693$ to 517, respectively.

6   Conclusion

The modified McEliece PKC proposed by Loidreau at Asiacrypt 2000 [13] employs interesting techniques using the Frobenius automorphism in Goppa codes. While it certainly improves the difficulty of breaking one-wayness against the "ever known" CPAs, it is vulnerable against our "new" CPAs, which exploit the modified structure, i.e. the biased 1's in a t-tower error vector. The binary work factor to break the one-wayness of the modified McEliece PKC with our new CPA is 2^{42}, which is feasible with currently available computational power.

Since our new attacks do not weaken the one-wayness of the (unmodified) McEliece PKC, it still satisfies OW-CPA for $n \geq 2048$ with optimum t and k. This means the (unmodified) McEliece PKC with an appropriate conversion still satisfies IND-CCA2.

Acknowledgments

The authors would like to thank anonymous referees for useful comments.

References

1. C. M. Adams and H. Meijer. "Security-Related Comments Regarding McEliece's Public-Key Cryptosystem". In *Proc. of CRYPTO '87, LNCS 293*, pages 224–228. Springer–Verlag, 1988.
2. M. Bellare and P. Rogaway. "Random Oracles are Practical: A Paradigm for Designing Efficient Protocols". In *Proc. of the First ACM CCCS*, pages 62–73, 1993.
3. T. Berson. "Failure of the McEliece Public-Key Cryptosystem Under Message-Resend and Related-Message Attack". In *Proc. of CRYPTO '97, LNCS 1294*, pages 213–220. Springer–Verlag, 1997.
4. A. Canteaut and N. Sendrier. "Cryptoanalysis of the Original McEliece Cryptosystem". In *Proc. of ASIACRYPT '98*, pages 187–199, 1998.

5. W. Diffie and M. Hellman. "New directions in cryptography". *IEEE Trans. IT*, 22(6):644–654, 1976.
6. S. Goldwasser and S. Micali. "Probabilistic encryption". *Journal of Computer and System Sciences*, pages 270–299, 1984.
7. C. Hall, I. Goldberg, and B. Schneier. "Reaction Attacks Against Several Public-Key Cryptosystems". In *Proc. of the 2nd International Conference on Information and Communications Security (ICICS'99), LNCS 1726*, pages 2–12, 1999.
8. K. Kobara and H. Imai. "Countermeasure against Reaction Attacks (in Japanese)". In *The 2000 Symposium on Cryptography and Information Security : A12*, January 2000.
9. K. Kobara and H. Imai. "Countermeasures against All the Known Attacks to the McEliece PKC". In *Proc. of 2000 International Symposium on Information Theory and Its Applications*, pages 661–664, November 2000.
10. K. Kobara and H. Imai. "Semantically Secure McEliece Public-Key Cryptosystems –Conversions for McEliece PKC–". In *Proc. of PKC '01, LNCS 1992*, pages 19–35. Springer–Verlag, 2001.
11. P. J. Lee and E. F. Brickell. "An Observation on the Security of McEliece's Public-Key Cryptosystem". In *Proc. of EUROCRYPT '88, LNCS 330*, pages 275–280. Springer–Verlag, 1988.
12. R. Lidl and H. Niederreiter. *"Finite Fields"*, page 13. *Cambridge University Press*, 1983.
13. P. Loidreau. "Strengthening McEliece Cryptosystem". In *Proc. of ASIACRYPT 2000*, pages 585–598. Springer–Verlag, 2000.
14. P. Loidreau and N. Sendrier. "Some weak keys in McEliece public-key cryptosystem". In *Proc. of IEEE International Symposium on Information Theory, ISIT '98*, page 382, 1998.
15. R. J. McEliece. "A Public-Key Cryptosystem Based on Algebraic Coding Theory". In *Deep Space Network Progress Report*, 1978.
16. N. Sendrier. "The Support Splitting Algorithm". *Rapport de recherche: ISSN0249-6399*, 1999.
17. P.W. Shor. "Polynomial-Time Algorithms for Prime Factorization and Discrete Logarithms on a Quantum Computer". *SIAM Journal on Computing*, 26(5):1484–1509, 1997.
18. J. Stern. "A method for finding codewords of small weight". In *Proc. of Coding Theory and Applications , LNCS 388*, pages 106–113. Springer–Verlag, 1989.
19. H. M. Sun. "Further Cryptanalysis of the McEliece Public-Key Cryptosystem". *IEEE Trans. on communication letters*, 4(1):18–19, 2000.
20. A. Vardy. "The Intractability of Computing the Minimum Distance of a Code". *IEEE Trans. on IT*, 43(6):1757–1766, 1997.

SPA-Based Adaptive Chosen-Ciphertext Attack on RSA Implementation

Roman Novak

Jozef Stefan Institute, Jamova 39, 1000 Ljubljana, Slovenia,
Roman.Novak@ijs.si

Abstract. We describe an adaptive chosen-ciphertext attack on a smart card implementation of the RSA decryption algorithm in the presence of side-channel information leakage. We studied the information leakage through power consumption variation. Simple power analysis (SPA) of the smart card that is widely used for secure Internet banking, Web access and remote access to corporate networks, revealed macro characteristics caused by improper implementation of Chinese remaindering. The findings can be used to eventually improve future implementations of fast RSA decryption.

1 Introduction

Smart card-based authentication and digital signature generation provide user identity for a broad range of business applications. The embedded microcontroller accompanied with cryptoprocessor and memory capabilities promises numerous security benefits. However, as security processor technology advances, new techniques are developed that compromise the benefits of its use. The research of new attack techniques contributes to improvement of future products while new protective measures pose new challenges to cryptoanalysts.

The implementation of a particular cryptographic algorithm often introduces new attack possibilities. Smart cards are prone to reverse engineering using chip testing equipment [1,2]. A well-known glitch attack introduces computation errors, which can be used very successfully to recover secrets by an adversary. For instance, a glitch attack against RSA [3] implementation based on the Chinese Remainder Theorem (CRT) could recover the private key using only one message and corresponding faulty signature [4,5]. Furthermore, the implementation often leaks additional side-channel information. Non-invasive attacks have been proposed based on timing information, a device's power consumption, and electromagnetic radiation [6,7]. Designers of cryptographic devices are very aware of attacks based on side-channel information leakage. Much attention has been given to preventing complex attacks while security holes remain and allow simple methods to succeed.

Simple Power Analysis (SPA) interprets a circuit's power consumption. More advanced techniques, like Differential Power Analysis (DPA) and Inferential Power Analysis (IPA), allow observation of the effects correlated to data values being manipulated [8,9]. Power analysis attacks have been known for a while

D. Naccache and P. Paillier (Eds.): PKC 2002, LNCS 2274, pp. 252–262, 2002.

and effective countermeasures exist that pose difficulties, even to a well funded and knowledgeable adversary [2]. On the other hand, it is difficult to address all weaknesses in implementing a cryptographic algorithm. The intent of this paper is to show a particular weakness of a smart-card-based RSA implementation. Little side-channel information is required to break this very common implementation.

We have applied SPA to a RSA-capable smart card. In particular, we have been testing a card that is used for secure Internet banking, Web access and remote access to corporate networks world-wide. The card provider is among leaders in the integration of strong authentication and electronic certification technology. The card embeds a cryptoprocessor dedicated to security. On the card, the DES, Triple-DES and RSA algorithms are implemented. Attention has been given to the RSA decryption operation.

Protective measures against power analysis attacks have been detected. However, the card's implementation of RSA decryption is based on the Chinese Remainder Theorem and leaks the information, which allows an adaptive chosen-ciphertext type of attack to reconstruct the private key.

The rest of the paper is structured as follows. Section 2 gives a short introduction on Simple Power Analysis. Section 3 defines a power trace, describes the data acquisition equipment and test parameters. Section 4 analyses a typical power consumption pattern during RSA decryption. SPA macro-characteristics are identified. Section 5 correlates power traces with a common RSA decryption algorithm based on the Chinese Remainder Theorem. The information leakage function is defined and its properties are studied. In Sect. 6 the adaptive chosen-ciphertext attack is described that makes use of the information leakage function. An RSA private key can be reconstructed by performing $t/2$ decryptions, where t is the bitlength of public modulus n. We conclude the paper by summarising our findings in Sect. 7.

2   Simple Power Analysis

Smart cards consist of logic gates, which are basically interconnected transistors. During operation, charges are applied to or removed from transistor gates. The sum of all charges can be measured through power consumption. Power analysis techniques are based on measurements of a circuit's power consumption. A similar approach may be used on electromagnetic radiation traces.

Several variations of power analysis have been developed [8,9]. The power consumption measurements of the smart card operations are interpreted directly in Simple Power Analysis (SPA). SPA can reveal instruction sequence and it can be used to reveal hidden data in algorithms in which the execution path depends on the data being processed. Conditional branching causes large SPA and sometimes timing characteristics. The method has been known for a while and fairly simple countermeasures exist [8].

The implementers of cryptographic algorithms are usually aware of SPA based attacks. They decide not to implement appropriate countermeasures only if they believe that a particular SPA characteristic could not threaten the overall security scheme.

3   Power Consumption Measurements

Power consumption measurements were obtained by measuring voltage variations across a resistor (25 ohm) that was inserted in series with the card ground
pin. In the following, a power trace refers to a set of power consumption measurements taken across a smart card operation.

The sampling speed was set at approximately 7.15 MSamples/s. 14-bit resolution was used. Measurements were taken asynchronously with the internal
processing of the card because the card uses the external clock signal only during communication with the reader. Otherwise, it uses an internally generated
randomised clock, which is considered to be, in combination with some other
countermeasures, one of the best countermeasures against power analysis attacks [2]. The internal clock is not available on the card's contacts.

One of the challenges of taking a measurement is to successfully trigger acquisition at the point of interest. A card actually performs a requested task after
communication has taken place between a reader and the card on the dedicated
line. The acquisition trigger point should be set with respect to the activities
on the communication line. A pre-settable low-to-high edge counter suffices for
triggering.

PC based data acquisition cards are available on the market at a price of
several thousand dollars. In order to evaluate the minimum resources needed to
perform simple power analysis we have decided to develop our own data acquisition equipment at minimum cost. Our hardware module has enough onboard
memory to store a power trace of 100 ms duration. The total cost of the module
was less than $100. However, the cost of the development was not negligible.

4   SPA Characteristics of RSA Decryption

In our case, power traces exhibit easily identifiable macro-characteristics of the
RSA decryption algorithm. A 512-bit modulus is used in the example. The length
of decryption varies with time. The average time needed by the card to complete
the operation is approximately 70 ms. Figure 1 shows typical power consumption
patterns during RSA decryption. After the first 3 ms of operation the trace
remains periodic for some time. Larger deviations in power consumption occur
approximately at the middle of the trace and in the last 3 ms of RSA decryption.

Large macro-features of the RSA decryption operation may be identified,
since the operations performed by different parts of a card's architecture vary
significantly. Selective use of the cryptoprocessor may cause such variations in
power consumption. We found a more detailed view of the same trace less infor-
mative. Further investigation using more sophisticated equipment showed that
the card uses an internal clock and that the frequency of the internal clock is
probably intentionally randomised.

Two periodic sequences, which consume more than 90% of the time, come from two exponentiations. Usually a RSA decryption implementation makes use of the Chinese Remainder Theorem, where two modular exponentiations with smaller moduli are performed instead of one. The number of areas with increased power consumption within each periodic sequence agrees with the number of squarings and multiplications in a repeated square-and-multiply binary exponentiation algorithm [10]. The number of squarings is one less than the bitlength of the exponent while the number of multiplications is equal to one less than the number of 1's in the exponent's binary representation. We could not differentiate multiplying from squaring with our power sampling equipment.

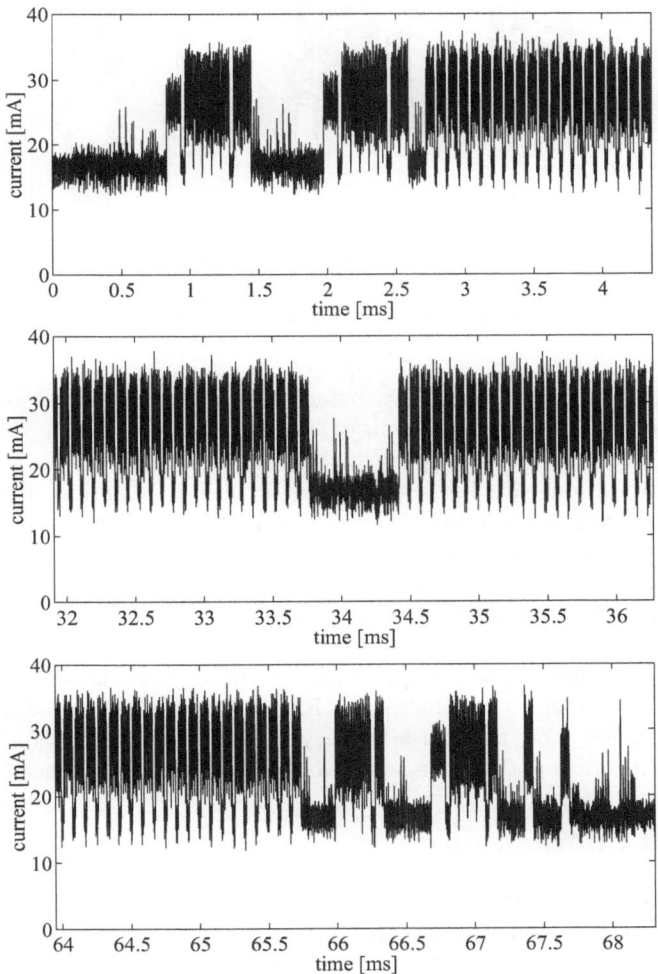

Fig. 1. Typical power consumption patterns during RSA decryption

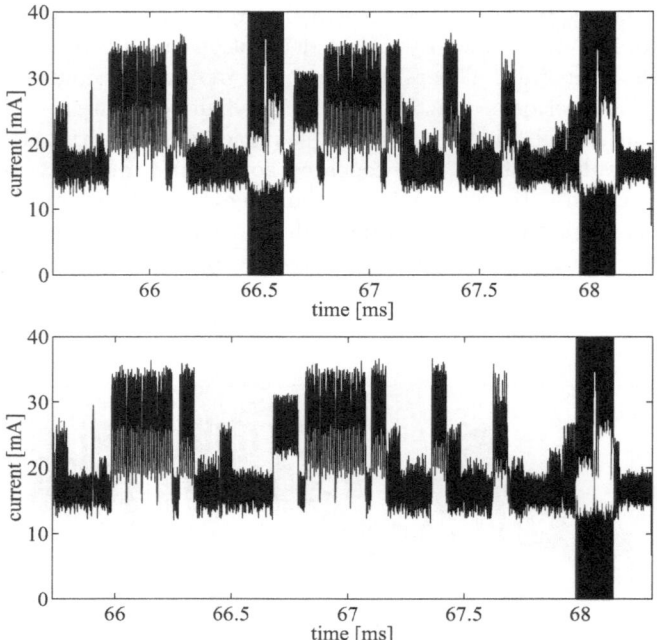

Fig. 2. Two types of power trace tails

The areas of larger consumption before and after exponentiations have to correspond to the required math steps of the algorithm outlined in the next section. The lengths of these areas appear to be randomised. We have not discovered any useful correlation with input ciphertext or output plaintext. However, the comparison between several power traces reveals a slight difference in the computation that follows both exponentiations. In Fig. 2, two similar patterns are highlighted on the upper trace while the first highlighted pattern is missing from the lower trace. We thought that a conditional branch in the RSA decryption might explain the optional pattern.

We identified these optional operations as the conditional add in Garner's version of CRT modular exponentiation. Figure 3 shows a detailed view of optional pattern. We show that an adversary can use the information about the algorithm's execution path in the adaptive chosen-ciphertext attack.

5   Leaked Information

Suppose p and q are distinct primes, and let modulus $n = pq$. Let e be an encryption exponent and d a decryption exponent, respectively. Pair (n, e) is publicly known while d is kept private. The RSA encryption computes $c = x^e \bmod n$ for some $x \in \mathbb{Z}_n$. The decryption also involves exponentiation in $\mathbb{Z}_n$ using the decryption exponent d, $x = c^d \bmod n$.

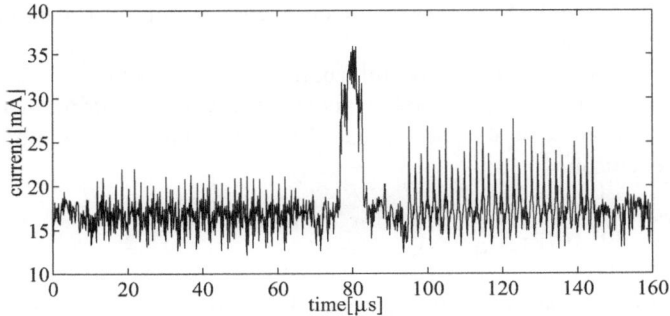

Fig. 3. Detailed view of optional pattern

When p and q are part of the private key, modular or mixed-radix representation of numbers can be used to improve the performance of RSA decryption. Each integer $x \in \mathbb{Z}_n$ can be uniquely represented by the numbers $x_p = x \bmod p$ and $x_q = x \bmod q$. RSA decryption can be performed using modular representation by two exponentiations, each considerably more efficient because the moduli are smaller. The modular representation of the value $c^d \bmod n$ can be computed as $c^d \bmod p$ and $c^d \bmod q$. In fact, as a consequence of Fermat's theorem, only $c^{d_{p-1}} \bmod p$ and $c^{d_{q-1}} \bmod q$ may be computed, where $d_{p-1} = d \bmod (p-1)$ and $d_{q-1} = d \bmod (q-1)$. The algorithm that solves simultaneous congruences in the Chinese Remainder Theorem (CRT) can do the conversion from a modular representation back to a standard radix representation. Gauss's algorithm for solving the associated system of linear congruences is not the best choice for large integers. Garner's algorithm has some computational advantages and is usually used for RSA decryption. Algorithm 1 outlines major steps of the RSA decryption algorithm using Garner's algorithm for CRT.

Algorithm 1. RSA decryption algorithm using Garner's algorithm for CRT
INPUT: ciphertext c, primes p and q, $p > q$, precomputed values $d_{p-1} = d \bmod (p-1)$, $d_{q-1} = d \bmod (q-1)$, $u = q^{-1} \bmod p$.
OUTPUT: plaintext x.

1. $x_p = c^{d_{p-1}} \bmod p$.
2. $x_q = c^{d_{q-1}} \bmod q$.
3. $t = x_p - x_q$.
4. If $t < 0$ then $t = t + p$.
5. $x = (((tu) \bmod p) q) + x_q$.

Step 4 needs additional explanation. The plaintext x is required to be from $\mathbb{Z}_n$. Because the difference in step 3 may be negative an additional conversion to least positive residue is required. The common way of doing that is to require prime p to be greater than prime q and to perform an addition in step 4.

Implementation of the above algorithm can produce the optional pattern in a power trace as a result of the conditional addition in step 4. The addition is also performed as the last operation in step 5, which explains the similar pattern at the end of the power trace.

We define function *diff* as the information leakage function (1). It returns 1 if the addition in step 4 is needed and 0 otherwise. Its argument is output plaintext x. The function can be evaluated only by analysing the power trace of the RSA decryption.

$$diff\,(x) = \begin{cases} 1 & x \bmod p - x \bmod q < 0 \\ 0 & \text{otherwise} \end{cases} , \quad p > q \ . \tag{1}$$

The information leakage function has the following properties that can be used in adaptive chosen-ciphertext attack by an adversary:

1. *diff* changes value from 0 to 1 only at multiples of prime p, $diff(kp-1) = 0$, $diff(kp) = 1$, $0 < k < q$.
2. The value of *diff* remains 1 for l consecutive values of argument x, where $0 < l < q$. l takes each value between 0 and q exactly once.

Proof (of the first property). One should note that, on increasing x, the difference $x \bmod p - x \bmod q$ may change its value only in multiples of primes p and q. Therefore, *diff* may change its value at the same values. Furthermore, $diff(kp) = 1$, $0 < k < q$, while $diff(mq) = 0$, $0 < m < p$, due to $kp \bmod q \neq 0$ and $mq \bmod p \neq 0$. Finally, because $diff(0) = 0$ and because the relation $p > q$ ensures at least one multiple of prime q between two multiples of prime p, *diff* must always change value from 0 to 1 at multiples of prime p. □

Proof (of the second property). The sequence of 1's cannot be longer than $q - 1$ because it is started at a multiple of prime p and terminated at a multiple of prime q. Suppose a sequence is terminated at kq. The sequence length is then $kq \bmod p$, which is one of two components of kq's modular representation. Because the other component is 0 and each number has a unique modular representation, two sequences cannot have the same length, which proves the second property. □

The number of cases for which $diff(x)$ equals each of two values can be computed using the above properties. Among n possible values for x, *diff* takes 1 in $(q-1)q/2$ cases and 0 in $pq - (q-1)q/2$ cases. Therefore, the probability to randomly pick a plaintext x where $diff(x) = 1$ is $(q-1)/(2p)$. In order to illustrate the properties of the information leakage function, Tab. 1 displays *diff* for $n = 35$, $p = 7$ and $q = 5$.

6   Key Reconstruction

The reconstruction of secret key d is possible by finding prime p. An adversary may start with plaintexts x_1 and x_2, such that $diff(x_1) = 0$ and $diff(x_2) = 1$. Then, using a binary search-like algorithm and SPA information, he finds the value x, where $diff(x - 1) = 0$ and $diff(x) = 1$. The value x is a multiple

Table 1. The information leakage function $diff$ for $n = 35$, $p = 7$ and $q = 5$

x	x_p	x_q	$diff(x)$	x	x_p	x_q	$diff(x)$	x	x_p	x_q	$diff(x)$
0	0	0	0	14	0	4	1	28	0	3	1
1	1	1	0	15	1	0	0	29	1	4	1
2	2	2	0	16	2	1	0	30	2	0	0
3	3	3	0	17	3	2	0	31	3	1	0
4	4	4	0	18	4	3	0	32	4	2	0
5	5	0	0	19	5	4	0	33	5	3	0
6	6	1	0	20	6	0	0	34	6	4	0
7	0	2	1	21	0	1	1				
8	1	3	1	22	1	2	1				
9	2	4	1	23	2	3	1				
10	3	0	0	24	3	4	1				
11	4	1	0	25	4	0	0				
12	5	2	0	26	5	1	0				
13	6	3	0	27	6	2	0				

of prime p that can be extracted by finding the greatest common divisor of x and modulus n. The adversary can control the output x of the RSA decryption by feeding the card with $x^e \bmod n$. The attack may be classified as SPA-based adaptive chosen-ciphertext attack. Algorithm 2 gives the steps that can be taken by the adversary to recover key material.

Algorithm 2. Reconstruction of prime p
INPUT: modulus n, public exponent e.
OUTPUT: prime p such that p divides n.

1. Repeat until computed $diff(x)$ equals 1:
    (a) Pick random number x, $0 \le x < n$.
    (b) $c = x^e \bmod n$.
    (c) Compute $diff(x)$ by analysing power trace while card decrypts c.
2. $m = x/2$, $l = 0$.
3. While $m \neq l$ do:
    (a) $c = m^e \bmod n$.
    (b) Compute $diff(m)$ by analysing power trace while card decrypts c.
    (c) If $diff(m) = 1$ then $x = m$; otherwise $l = m$.
    (d) $m = (l + x)/2$.
4. Compute $p = gcd(n, x)$.
5. Return(p).

The average number of repetitions needed in step 1 is determined by the probability $(q - 1)/(2p)$, computed in the previous section. The probability is usually high and only a few repetitions of step 1 is needed to pick x where

$diff(x) = 1$. At the end of step 3, variable x holds the value that is a multiple of prime p. l and x are lower and upper bounds of the search interval. On each repetition the interval is halved while $diff(l)$ remains 0 and $diff(x)$ remains 1. At $l = x - 1$ the first property of the information leakage function guarantees the upper bound x to be a multiple of prime p.

Primes p and q are in practice about the same bitlength, and sufficiently large to avoid the elliptic curve factoring algorithm [10]. For example, if a 1024-bit modulus n is to be used, then each of p and q should be about 512 bits in length. This can be used to speed up the restoration of prime p.

Suppose modulus n has a bitlength of t bits while primes p and q have a bitlength of $t/2$ bits, $2^{t/2-1} < p, q < 2^{t/2}$, and t is sufficiently large. The first sequence of 1's starts at p and ends at $2q - 1$, therefore $diff(2^{t/2}) = 1$. In that case, the first and fourth steps of the Alg. 2 are not needed, while the second step may be entered with $x = 2^{t/2}$. The modified algorithm requires only $t/2$ power traces.

Algorithm 3. Reconstruction of p when its bitlength is half bitlength of n
INPUT: modulus n with the bitlength t, public exponent e.
OUTPUT: prime p such that p divides n.

1. $x = 2^{t/2}$, $m = x/2$, $l = 0$.
2. While $m \neq l$ do:
   (a) $c = m^e \bmod n$.
   (b) Compute $diff(m)$ by analysing power trace while card decrypts c.
   (c) If $diff(m) = 1$ then $x = m$; otherwise $l = m$.
   (d) $m = (l + x)/2$.
3. Return(x).

Using Alg. 3 we managed to restore one of two secret primes and compute secret key d, which confirms our hypothesis about the implemented algorithm on our test card.

7   Conclusion

Power consumption is a well-known source of side-channel information leakage. Several techniques have been developed in the past to gather leaked information. SPA is the simplest among them. Efficient hardware and software based prevention measures exist. The implementers of cryptographic operations are usually aware of SPA based attacks. They decide not to implement appropriate countermeasures only if they believe that a particular SPA characteristic could not threaten the overall security scheme. This is not the practice to be followed.

We have reviewed a fast RSA decryption algorithm that is implemented on the smart card that embeds some state-of-the-art cryptographic solutions. Dedicated hardware for operations with very long integers may enable SPA to reveal macro steps of RSA decryption. When Garner's algorithm is used for conversion from modular representation back to a standard radix representation, improper implementation could leak the information about the modular representation of the plaintext. We have shown how an adversary could use very few bits of information in an adaptive chosen-ciphertext attack. The algorithm, given in the paper, requires $t/2$ decryptions, where t is the bitlength of the public modulus n. This kind of attack is possible only on open cards, which allow to make the choice of the input. Timing attack can be mounted under the same principles, however, the internally generated randomised clock and the additional software random delays require extraction of the SPA feature.

Proper implementation of Garner's algorithm should hide SPA characteristics that make factorisation of public modulus feasible. This can be achieved by balancing conditional operations with dummy operations, or even better, by changing the algorithm to use a constant execution path. Other protective measures should be reconsidered. We have shown that the cryptoprocessor carries an additional threat to security due to the easily detectable patterns of its use.

Every side-channel leakage must be considered with great care at the implementation phase of the algorithm. Even though countermeasures against sophisticated attacks exist, designs must be carefully checked against simple methods as well.

References

1. Anderson, R., Kuhn, M.G.: Tamper Resistance - a Cautionary Note. Proceedings of the Second USENIX Workshop on Electronic Commerce, Oakland, California, November 18–21, USENIX Association (1996) 1–11
2. Kömmerling, O., Kuhn, M.G.: Design Principles for Tamper-Resistant Smartcard Processors. Proceedings of the USENIX Workshop on Smartcard Technology - Smartcard'99, Chicago, Illinois, May 10–11, USENIX Association (1999) 9–20
3. Rivest, R.L., Shamir, A., Adleman L.: A Method for Obtaining Digital Signatures and Public-Key Cryptosystems. Communications of the ACM **21(2)** (1978) 120–126
4. Biham E., Shamir, A.: Differential Fault Analysis of Secret Key Cryptosystems. In: Kaliski, B.S. (ed.): Advances in Cryptology - Crypto'97. Lecture Notes in Computer Science, Vol. 1294. Springer-Verlag, Berlin Heidelberg New York (1997) 513–525
5. Bao, F., et al.: Breaking Public Key Cryptosystems in the Presence of Transient Faults. In: Christianson, B., et al. (eds.): Security Protocols. Lecture Notes in Computer Science, Vol. 1361. Springer-Verlag, Berlin Heidelberg New York (1997) 115–124
6. Kocher, P.: Timing Attacks on Implementation of Diffie-Hellman, RSA, DSS and Other Systems. In: Koblitz, N. (ed.): Advances in Cryptology - Crypto'96. Lecture Notes in Computer Science, Vol. 1109. Springer-Verlag, Berlin Heidelberg New York (1996) 104–113
7. Messerges, T.S., Dabbish, E.A., Sloan, R.H.: Investigation of Power Analysis Attacks on Smartcards. Proceedings of the USENIX Workshop on Smartcard Technology - Smartcard'99, Chicago, Illinois, May 10–11, USENIX Association (1999) 151–161

8. Kocher, P., Jaffe, J., Jun, B.: Differential Power Analysis. In: Wiener, M. (ed.): Advances in Cryptology - Crypto'99. Lecture Notes in Computer Science, Vol. 1666. Springer-Verlag, Berlin Heidelberg New York (1999) 388–397

9. Fahn, P.N., Pearson, P.K.: IPA: A New Class of Power Attacks. In: Koc, C.K., Paar, C. (eds.) Cryptographic Hardware and Embedded Systems - CHES'99. Lecture Notes in Computer Science, Vol. 1717. Springer-Verlag, Berlin Heidelberg New York (1999) 173–186

10. Menezes, A.J., van Oorschot, P.C., Vanstone, S.A.: Handbook of Applied Cryptography. CRC Press Series on Discrete Mathematics and Its Applications (1996)

A Combined Timing and Power Attack

Werner Schindler

Bundesamt für Sicherheit in der Informationstechnik (BSI)
Godesberger Allee 185-189, 53175 Bonn, Germany
Werner.Schindler@bsi.bund.de

Abstract. In [9]Walter and Thompson introduced a new side-channel attack on the secret exponents of modular exponentiations which uses techniques from timing attacks to exploit specific information gained by a power attack. Walter and Thompson assumed that the attacked device uses a particular table method combined with Montgomery's algorithm. In the present paper their attack is optimized and generalized. For 2-bit tables this leads to a reduction of the necessary sample size to 20 per cent. The original attack cannot be applied if 4-bit tables are used, a case of particular practical interest, whereas the optimized attack gets by with 500 measurements. The optimized version can straightforwardly be adapted to other table methods, other multiplication algorithms and inexact timings. Moreover, it is shown that the countermeasures proposed in [9] do not prevent the optimized attack if unsuitable parameters are chosen.

Keywords: Timing attack, power attack, Montgomery's algorithm.

1 Introduction

In the past half-decade side-channel attacks have attracted enormous attention as they have turned out to constitute serious threats for cryptosystems, especially if the cryptographic operations run on smart cards. Various types of timing attacks were introduced and optimized ([2], [1], [7], [8]), and a large number of papers were devoted to power attacks ([4] etc.). However, these timing attacks do not work if appropriate blinding techniques are used and various countermeasures against power attacks have been proposed. In [9] a new type of side-channel attack was introduced which uses techniques typical for timing attacks to exploit specific timing information stemming from a power attack (or, which made no difference in this context, from a radiation attack (cf. [3], for example)). In particular, this combined attack may be successful even if the attacked device could resist both, a "pure" timing attack (because blinding techniques are used) and a "pure" power attack (because appropriate countermeasures are employed). We optimize and, moreover, generalize this combined attack considerably.

As in [9], we attack the secret exponents of modular exponentiation (e.g., secret RSA exponents). We also assume that b-bit-tables (cf. [5], Alg. 14.82) and Montgomery's algorithm are used to carry out the modular exponentiations. (A b-bit table stores the powers of the basis up to the exponent $2^b - 1$.) We assume

D. Naccache and P. Paillier (Eds.): PKC 2002, LNCS 2274, pp. 263–279, 2002.

that the analysis of the power consumption enables the attacker to determine the times needed by the particular Montgomery multiplications (e.g., due to small peaks at the beginning of the modular multiplications), i.e. whether an extra reduction is necessary. As in [9] the focus of this paper is not the power measurement part but the guessing of the secret exponent.

The attacker uses a sample of modular exponentiations to guess the type of the particular Montgomery multiplications (squaring or a multiplication with a particular table entry) which in turn yields the secret exponent. In [9] for the most favourable parameter values a sample size of "less than 1000" turned out to be sufficient to recover a secret 384-bit exponent if a 2-bit table was used. For these parameters our optimized attack gets by with 200 samples. The original attack cannot be applied if 4-bit tables are used which is of particular practical interest. In contrast, even for non-optimal parameters our attack gets by with 500 samples to recover a 512-bit exponent, or a 1024-bit RSA exponent if the Chinese Remainder Theorem (CRT) is used, resp. Our approach can directly be adapted to other table methods and other modular multiplication algorithms. Even the times needed for the particular modular multiplications need not be determined exactly. Finally, we show that the countermeasures proposed in [9] do not prevent our attack if unsuitable parameters are used.

The paper is organized as follows: In Sect. 2 we recall the definition and basic facts concerning Montgomery's algorithm and table methods, and general assumptions are formulated. In Sect. 3 we explain the central ideas of our attack. The optimal decision strategy is derived in Sect. 7. The preliminary steps are discussed in Sects. 4-6. Experimental results are presented and discussed in Sect. 8. In Sect. 9 we compare the optimized attack with the original one. Sect. 10 considers generalizations of our attack under weaker assumptions. Then we propose effective countermeasures and conclude with final remarks.

2   General Assumptions

We assume that the attacked cryptographic device uses a b-bit table to compute $y^d(\mathrm{mod}\,M)$. Modular multiplications are calculated with Montgomery's algorithm (cf. [6]). We begin with some basic definitions.

Definition 1. As usually, for an integer b the term $b(\mathrm{mod}\ M)$ denotes the smallest nonnegative integer which is congruent to b modulo M. Further, $Z_M :=$ $\{0, 1, \ldots, M-1\}$, and for $x \in \mathbb{R}$ the term $\lceil x \rceil$ denotes the smallest integer $\geq x$.

The most elementary variant of Montgomery's algorithm transfers the modular multiplications to a modulus $R > M$ with $gcd(R, M) = 1$. Usually, R is a power of 2 whose exponent perfectly fits to the device's hardware architecture (cf. Remark 1(i)). Further, $R^{-1} \in Z_M$ denotes the multiplicative inverse of R in Z_M, i.e. $RR^{-1} \equiv 1 \pmod{M}$. The integer $M^* \in Z_R$ satisfies the integer equation $RR^{-1} - MM^* = 1$. For input $a', b' \in Z_M$ Montgomery's multiplication algorithm returns $\mathrm{MM}(a', b') := a'b'R^{-1}(\mathrm{mod}\,M)$.

Montgomery's algorithm

```
z:=a'b'
r:=(z(mod R)M*) (mod R)
s:=(z+rM)/R
if s≥M then s:=s-M
return s
```

In particular, $MM(aR(\mathrm{mod}\ M), bR(\mathrm{mod}\ M)) = abR(\mathrm{mod}\ M)$. The subtraction in line 4 is called *extra reduction*. For fixed values M and R the time for a Montgomery multiplication can only attain two different values, namely c_0 if no extra reduction has to be carried out and $c_0 + c_{\mathrm{ER}}$ else. Let $(d_{w-1}, \ldots, d_0)_2$ denote the binary representation of the secret exponent d where, as usually, d_{w-1} denotes its most significant bit. Therefrom we derive $\lceil w/b \rceil$ b-bit integers $D_{\lceil w/b \rceil - 1}, \ldots, D_0$ with $D_j := \sum_{k=0}^{b-1} d_{bj+k} 2^k$. Combining a b-bit table with Montgomery's algorithm gives Algorithm 1. First, the table entries $u_1, \ldots, u_{2^b - 1}$ are computed.

Algorithm 1

```
u_1:= MM(y, R^2(mod M))     (= yR (mod M))
for j:=2 to 2^(b-1) do   u_j:=MM(u_{j-1},u_1)
temp:=u_{D_{⌈w/b⌉-1}}
for i:=⌈w/b⌉-2 downto 0 do {
    for j:=1 to b do   temp:=MM(temp,temp)
    if (D_i>0) temp:=MM(temp,u_{D_i})
return MM(temp,1)          (=y^d(mod M))
```

The attacker analyzes the power consumption needed for the modular exponentiations $y_{(1)}{}^d(\mathrm{mod}\ M), \ldots, y_{(N)}{}^d(\mathrm{mod}\ M)$ for a given sample $y_{(1)}, \ldots, y_{(N)}$. The target of the attack is the secret exponent d. Next, we formulate the general assumptions. Note that our attack does also work under considerably weaker assumptions (cf. Sects. 10, 11). In particular, assumption e) may completely be dropped.

General Assumptions

a) The attacked device uses Algorithm 1 to compute $y^d(\mathrm{mod}\ M)$.
b) By observing the power consumption the attacker is able to determine the times needed by the particular Montgomery multiplications within Algorithm 1, i.e. he can decide whether an extra reduction is carried out.
c) The attacker has no knowledge about the base $y_{(k)}$ nor about the table entries $u_{1(k)}, \ldots, u_{2^b - 1(k)}$ $(1 \le k \le N)$.
d) Algorithm 1 uses the same secret exponent d for all modular exponentiations $y_{(1)}{}^d(\mathrm{mod}\ M), \ldots, y_{(N)}{}^d(\mathrm{mod}\ M)$
e) The attacker knows the ratios M/R and $(R^2(\mathrm{mod}\ M))/M$.

Remark 1. (i) Many implementations use a more efficient multiprecision variant of Montgomery's algorithm than listed above (cf. [5], Algorithm 14.36). Whether an extra reduction is necessary, however, merely depends on the parameters a', b', M and R but not on the chosen variant of Montgomery's algorithm or any hardware characteristics ([8], Remark 1). (The latter aspects, of course, influence the absolute values of the time constants c_0 and c_{ER}.)

(ii) Re: GA a): Our attack can easily be adapted to other table methods (cf. Sect. 10).

(iii) Re: GA c): This could be the consequence of a standard blinding technique which prevents "ordinary" timing attacks, namely the pre-multiplication of the base y with a register value v_a and a post-multiplication of $(yv_a)^d(\bmod M)$ with $v_b = v_a^{-d}(\bmod M)$. Before the next exponentiation both register values are updated via $v_a := v_a^2(\bmod M)$ and $v_b := v_b^2(\bmod M)$ (cf. [2], Sect. 10). Note that if the attacker knew the bases $y_{(1)}, y_{(2)}, \ldots$ a very small sample size would be sufficient to recover the secret key. In fact, the attacker could successively guess the b-bit blocks $D_{\lceil w/b \rceil - 1}, D_{\lceil w/b \rceil - 2}, \ldots$, compare the corresponding extra reduction / not extra reduction patterns with the observed ones and exclude wrong assumptions (cf. [9], Subsect. 3.3).

(iv) Re GA d): cf. Sect. 11.

(v) Re GA e): If the ratios M/R and $(R^2(\bmod M))/M$ are unknown they can be guessed efficiently (cf. Sect. 10).

3   The Central Ideas of Our Attack

In this section we sketch the fundamental ideas of our attack. Technical details will be treated in the following sections.

After the table entries $u_1, \ldots, u_{2^b-1}$ have been computed ("initialization phase") the "computation phase" begins. The "type" $T(i)$ of the ith Montgomery multiplication within the computation phase is determined by the secret exponent d. We distinguish between squarings (i.e., $T(i) = 'S'$) and multiplications of the temp value with table entry u_j (i.e. $T(i) = 'M_j'$). The attacker guesses the sequence $T(1), T(2), \ldots$. If all guessings are correct this in turn yields d besides its most significant block. The most significant block can be guessed in a similar manner or determined by exhaustive search.

The probability that a squaring requires an extra reduction equals $M/3R$ while it is linear in the ratio u_j/M if $T(i) = 'M_j'$ (cf. Sect. 4). If $T(i) = 'S'$ and if the sample size N is sufficiently large the ratio "# extra reductions in the ith Montgomery multiplication (counted over the whole sample) / N" should approximately equal $M/3R$. If $T(i) = 'M_j'$ the probability for an extra reduction depends on the particular base $y_{(k)}$, or more precisely, on the (unknown!) table entry $u_{j(k)}$. Our attack exploits the differences between these probabilities. The "source" of our attack is the initialization phase as the attacker knows the types of the $2^b - 1$ Montgomery multiplications. The observed extra reductions within the initialization phase are indicators for the magnitude of the ratios $u_{1(k)}/M, \ldots, u_{2^b-1(k)}/M$. To simplify further notation we introduce *er-values* $q_{j(k)}$ and set $\boldsymbol{q}'_{(k)} := (q'_{1(k)}, \ldots, q'_{2^b-1(k)})$ where $q'_{j(k)} := 1$ if the computation of the jth table entry, $u_{j(k)}$, requires an extra reduction for base $y_{(k)}$ and $q'_{j(k)} := 0$ else. Conditional to the observed *er-vector* $\boldsymbol{q}'_{(k)}$ the attacker first computes the joint conditional probability density for the vector $(u_{1(k)}/M, \ldots, u_{2^b-1(k)}/M) \in$

$[0,1)^{2^b-1}$, denoted by $g(u_{1(k)}/M, \dots, u_{2^b-1(k)}/M \mid \boldsymbol{q}'_{(k)})$. Different er-vectors $\boldsymbol{q}'_{(k)} \neq \boldsymbol{q}''_{(k)}$ yield different conditional densities $g(\cdot \mid \boldsymbol{q}'_{(k)}) \neq g(\cdot \mid \boldsymbol{q}''_{(k)})$.

To illustrate the essential ideas we consider the most elementary variant where the attacker estimates the types $T(1), T(2), \dots$ separately and independent from the others. (Since the extra reductions of subsequent Montgomery multiplications are not independent it yet may be reasonable to estimate the types of f consecutive Montgomery multiplications simultaneously, cf. Sects. 4,7,8.) Based on the observed er-values the attacker decides for that alternative $\theta \in \Theta := \{`S`, `M_1`, \dots, `M_{2^b-1}`\}$ which appears to be the most likely one (to be precised later). In a first step the attacker uses the conditional densities $g(\cdot \mid \boldsymbol{q}'_{(k)})$ from above to compute the conditional probabilities $p_{\theta'}(q_{i(k)} \mid \boldsymbol{q}'_{(k)})$ for all $k \leq N$ and each $\theta' \in \Theta$. (The index θ' means that the conditional probability holds under the hypothesis $T(i) = \theta'$.) Analogously as above, $q_{i(k)} := 1$ iff the ith Montgomery multiplication in the computation phase requires an extra reduction for base $y_{(k)}$.

The straight-forward approach, of course, was to decide for $\theta \in \Theta$ if the product $\prod_{k \leq N} p_{\theta'}(q_{i(k)} \mid \boldsymbol{q}'_{(k)})$ $(=$ joint conditional probability for $\left(q_{i(k)} \mid \boldsymbol{q}'_{(k)} \right)_{k \leq N}$ under the hypothesis $T(i) = \theta'$) is maximal for $\theta' = \theta$ (maximum likelihood estimator). Although already efficient the maximum likelihood decision strategy can still be improved by considering two further criteria. First, not all admissible hypotheses occur with the same probability. In fact, it is much more likely that a randomly chosen Montgomery multiplication within the computation phase is a squaring than a multiplication with any particular table entry. Loosely speaking, compared with $\prod_{k \leq N} p(`M_j`)(q_{i(k)} \mid \boldsymbol{q}'_{(k)})$ the term $\prod_{k \leq N} p(`S`)(q_{i(k)} \mid \boldsymbol{q}'_{(k)})$ gets some "bonus".

Unlike for the timing attacks in [2], [1], [7] and [8] a false estimator $\widetilde{\theta}$ does not imply that the subsequent estimators are worthless. Indeed, the correction of false estimators is possible after the types of all Montgomery multiplications have been guessed. In fact, squarings occur in subsequences whose lengths are multiples of b and each subsequence is followed by exactly one Montgomery multiplication with a table entry. An (isolated) erroneous estimator `M_j` instead of `S` (or vice versa) can thus easily be detected and localized ("local errors") whereas the detection, localization and correction of an erroneous estimator `M_j` instead of `M_t` requires much greater efforts ("global errors"). The optimal decision strategy takes the different kinds of possible estimation errors into account. Loosely speaking, it "prefers" local errors instead of global errors.

4   Conditional Probabilities

Recall that the attacker wants to estimate the types of the Montgomery multiplications in the computation phase on basis of the observed er-values $q'_{j(k)}$ and $q_{i(k)}$ within the initialization and computation phase, resp. In Sect. 4 we derive explicit formulas for the conditional probabilities mentioned in the previous section. We first introduce some further definitions.

Definition 2. *A realization of a random variable X is a value assumed by X. Further, $\mathcal{T} := \{`S`, `M_1`, \ldots, `M_{2^b-1}`\}$. Analogously to $q'_{(k)}$ the term $q_{i,\ldots,i+f-1(k)}$ abbreviates $(q_{i(k)}, \ldots, q_{i+f-1(k)})$. For $A \subseteq B$ the indicator function $1_A : B \to \mathbb{R}$ is defined by $1_A(x) := 1$ if $x \in A$ and $:= 0$ else.*

Lemma 1. (i) $\frac{\mathrm{MM}(a'b')}{M} = \left(\frac{a'}{M} \frac{b'}{M} \frac{M}{R} + \frac{a'b'M^*}{R} \pmod{R} \right) \pmod{1}$.

(ii) In particular, an extra reduction is necessary iff $\frac{\mathrm{MM}(a'b')}{M} < \frac{a'}{M} \frac{b'}{M} \frac{M}{R}$.

(iii) Let the random variables $V'_1, \ldots, V'_{2^b-1}$ and $V_1, V_2, \ldots$ be independent and equidistributed on $[0, 1)$ while $S'_0, \ldots, S'_{2^b-1}$ and $S_0, S_1, \ldots$ are defined recursively. In particular, S'_0 is $[0, 1)$-valued and

$$
S'_i := \begin{cases} \left(S'_0 (R^2 \pmod{M}/M)(M/R) + V'_1 \right) \pmod{1} & \text{for } i = 1 \\ \left(S'_{i-1} S'_1 M/R + V'_i \right) \pmod{1} & \text{for } 2 \le i \le 2^b - 1 \end{cases} \tag{1}
$$

Similarly, $S_0 := S'_r$ where r temporarily stands for the most significant b-bit block of d, i.e. $r = D_{\lceil w/b \rceil - 1}$. Further, for $i \ge 1$

$$
S_i := \begin{cases} \left(S^2_{i-1} M/R + V_i \right) \pmod{1} & \text{if } T(i) = `S` \\ \left(S_{i-1} S'_j M/R + V_i \right) \pmod{1} & \text{if } T(i) = `M_j` \end{cases} \tag{2}
$$

Analogously, let the $\{0,1\}$-valued random variables $W'_1, \ldots, W'_{2^b-1}$ and $W_1, W_2, \ldots$ be defined by

$$
W'_i := \begin{cases} 1_{S'_1 < S'_0 (R^2 (\bmod M)/M)(M/R)} & \text{for } i = 1 \\ 1_{S'_i < S'_{i-1} S'_1 M/R} & \text{for } 2 \le i \le 2^b - 1 \quad \text{and} \end{cases} \tag{3}
$$

$$
W_i := \begin{cases} 1_{S_i < S^2_{i-1} M/R} & \text{if } T(i) = `S` \\ 1_{S_i < S_{i-1} S'_j M/R} & \text{if } T(i) = `M_j` \end{cases} \tag{4}
$$

Then the random variables $S'_0, S'_1, \ldots, S'_{2^b-1}$ as well as $S_0, S_1, \ldots$ are independent. The random variables $S'_1, \ldots, S'_{2^b-1}, S_1, S_2 \ldots$ are independent and equidistributed on $[0, 1)$. Further, W_i and W_h are independent if $|i - h| > 1$.

Proof. Assertion (i) follows immediately from the definition of Montgomery's algorithm whereas (ii) is a consequence from (i) as the second summand of its right-hand side lies in $[0, 1)$. The assertions in (iii) concerning the random variables S'_i and S_i follow from the fact that the random variables $V'_1, V'_2, \ldots$ and $V_1, V_2, \ldots$ are independent and equidistributed on $[0, 1)$. The final assertion in (iii) follows from the definition of the random variables W_i.

Clearly, whether $\mathrm{MM}(a', b')$ requires an extra reduction depends deterministically on a' and b'. On the other hand, even small deviations in a' or b' usually cause "vast" deviations in the second summand of the right-hand side in Lemma 1(i). Recall that we neither know the base y nor the factors of any Montgomery multiplication. Assume for the moment that $a' := R^2 (\bmod M)$ and $y/M \in I_j$ (cf. the first line in Alg. 1) where $I_j := [j2^{-v}, (j+1)2^{-v})$ denotes a small interval (e.g. $v = 16$) and further, that the random variable B is equidistributed on the set $(Z_M/M) \cap I_j$. For realistic modulus size M the random variable $C := (a'BM^*)(\bmod R)/R$ should fulfil $\mathrm{Prob}(C \in I_i) \approx 2^{-v}$ for all $i \leq 2^v - 1$ while the sum $a'B/R + C$ should similarly be distributed as if both summands were independent (cf. the proof of Lemma A.3(iii) in [7]). In particular, the remainder of the sum (mod 1) then is "almost" equidistributed on $[0, 1)$. An extra reduction is necessary iff $(a'B/R + C)(\bmod 1) < a'B/R$. However, this is a formal analogon to the definitions of S_1' and W_1'. We can continue this analogy and derive the following mathematical model.

Mathematical Model. We interpret the components of the er-vector $q'_{(k)} = (q'_{1(k)}, \ldots, q'_{2^b-1(k)})$ as realizations of the random variables $W_1', \ldots, W_{2^b-1}'$ with $S_0' = y_{(k)}/M$. Similarly, we interpret $q_{1(k)}, q_{2(k)}, \ldots$ as realizations of $W_1, W_2, \ldots$.

Consequently, we have to study the stochastic processes $W_1', \ldots, W_{2^b-1}'$ and $W_1, W_2, \ldots$. As a first result, the probability for an extra reduction in the ith Montgomery multiplication equals

$$\mathrm{Prob}(W_i = 1) = \begin{cases} \frac{1}{3}\frac{M}{R} & \text{if } T(i) = \text{`}S\text{`} \\ \frac{u_j}{2M}\frac{M}{R} & \text{if } T(i) = \text{`}M_j\text{`}. \end{cases} \tag{5}$$

Remark 2. The random variables $W_1, W_2, \ldots$ are not independent but W_i and W_{i+1} are negative correlated. We point out that the random variables $W_1, W_2, \ldots$ are similarly defined as in [8] (cf. Theorem 2) or [7] (cf. Lemma 6.3). However, the requirements on the mathematical model are considerably higher than in [7] or [8] as we there were primarily interested in the variance of $W_1 + W_2 + \cdots$ to apply a version of the central limit theorem for dependent random variables which holds under relatively weak conditions. However, the experimental results (cf. Sect. 8) confirm the suitability of our mathematical model retrospectively. Lemma 2(ii) provides concrete formulas for the conditional probability densities $g(\cdot \mid q'_{(k)})$ mentioned in the previous section.

Lemma 2. *(i) For $1 \leq i \leq 2^b - 1$ and $w \in \{0, 1\}$ let $C'(i; w) := \{(s_0', \ldots, s_{2^b-1}') \in [0, 1)^{2^b} \mid w_i' = w\}$. Then $C'(i; 0) = [0, 1)^{2^b} \setminus C'(i; 1)$. In particular, $C'(1; 1) := \{(s_0', \ldots, s_{2^b-1}') \in [0, 1)^{2^b} \mid s_1' < s_0'(R^2(\bmod M))/R\}$ and further $C'(i; 1) := \{(s_0', \ldots, s_{2^b-1}') \in [0, 1)^{2^b} \mid s_i' < s_{i-1}'s_1'M/R\}$ for $i > 1$.*
(ii) Let the random variable S_0' be equidistributed on $[0, 1)$. The distribution of the random vector $(S_1', \ldots, S_{2^b-1}')$ conditional to $(W_1' = w_1', \ldots, W_{2^b-1}' = w_{2^b-1}')$ has the joint conditional probability density $g(s_1', \ldots, s_{2^b-1}' \mid w_1', \ldots, w_{2^b-1}') :=$

$$\frac{\int_0^1 1_{\bigcap_{i=1}^{2^b-1} C'(i; w_i')}(s_0', s_1', \ldots, s_{2^b-1}')\, ds_0'}{\int_{[0,1)^{2^b}} 1_{\bigcap_{i=1}^{2^b-1} C'(i; w_i')}(s_0', s_1', \ldots, s_{2^b-1}')\, ds_0' ds_1' \cdots ds_{2^b-1}'} \tag{6}$$

on $[0, 1)^{2^b-1}$.
(iii) For $w \in \{0, 1\}$ and $i \leq m \leq i + f - 1$ let $C_f(i, m; w, t) := \{(s_{i-1}, \ldots, s_{i+f-1})$

$\in [0,1)^{f+1} \mid w_m = w, T(m) = t\}$. Then $\mathcal{C}_f(i, m; 0, t) = [0,1)^{f+1} \setminus \mathcal{C}_f(i, m; 1, t)$. In particular, $\mathcal{C}_f(i, m; 1, `S`) = \{(s_{i-1}, \ldots, s_{i+f-1}) \in [0,1)^{f+1} \mid s_m < s_{m-1}^2 M/R\}$ and $\mathcal{C}_f(i, m; 1, `M_j`) = \{(s_{i-1}, \ldots, s_{i+f-1}) \in [0,1)^{f+1} \mid s_m < s_{m-1} s_j' M/R\}$.
(iv)

$$\text{Prob}(W_i = w_i, \ldots, W_{i+f-1} = w_{i+f-1} \mid W_1' = w_1', \ldots, W_{2^b-1}' = w_{2^b-1}') = \qquad (7)$$

$$\int_{[0,1)^{2^b+f}} g(s_1', \ldots, s_{2^b-1}' \mid w_1', \ldots, w_{2^b-1}') \cdot 1_{\bigcap_{m=i}^{i+f-1} \mathcal{C}_f(i,m;w_i,T(m))}(s_{i-1}, \ldots, s_{i+f-1}) \times$$

$$\times \qquad\qquad\qquad ds_1' \cdots ds_{2^b-1}' ds_{i-1} \cdots ds_{i+f-1}.$$

(v) If $S_0 = S_r'$ then

$$\text{Prob}(W_1 = 1 \mid W_1' = w_1', \ldots, W_{2^b-1}' = w_{2^b-1}') = \qquad (8)$$

$$\int_{[0,1)^{2^b-1}} g(s_1', \ldots, s_{2^b-1}' \mid w_1', \ldots, w_{2^b-1}') \cdot s_r'^2 \frac{M}{R} ds_1' \cdots ds_{2^b-1}'.$$

Proof. Assertions (i) and (iii) follow immediately from the definition of the random variables W_i' and W_i. Clearly, $\{(s_0', \ldots, s_{2^b-1}') \in [0,1)^{2^b} \mid W_1' = w_1', \ldots,$ $W_{2^b-1}' = w_{2^b-1}'\} = \bigcap_{i=1}^{2^b-1} C'(i, w_i')$. Equation (6) follows from the fact that the random variables $S_0', \ldots, S_{2^b-1}'$ are independent and equidistributed on $[0,1)$ and the definitions of conditional distributions and a marginal densities. As the random variables $S_{i-1}, \ldots, S_{i+f-1}$ are independent and equidistributed on $[0,1)$ assertion (iv) follows from the identity $\{(s_{i-1}, \ldots, s_{i+f-1}) \in [0,1)^{f+1} \mid W_i = w_i, \ldots, W_{i+f-1} = w_{i+f-1}'\} = \bigcap_{m=i}^{i+f-1} \mathcal{C}_f(i, m; w_m, T(m))$. The first Montgomery multiplication in the computation phase is a squaring. Hence $\text{Prob}(W_1 = 1) = \text{Prob}(S_r'^2 M/R + V_1 \geq 1) = S_r'^2 M/R$ which proves (v).

Example 1. Let $b = 2$, $f = 1$, $W_1' = W_3' = 1$ and $W_2' = 0$. Then the denominator of $g(s_1, s_2, s_3 \mid 1, 0, 1)$ equals

$$\int_0^1 \int_0^{s_0' \frac{R^2(\text{mod } M)}{M} \frac{M}{R}} \int_{s_1'^2 \frac{M}{R}}^1 \int_0^{s_1' s_2' \frac{M}{R}} 1 \, ds_3' ds_2' ds_1' ds_0' . \qquad (9)$$

The nominator of $g(s_1, s_2, s_3 \mid 1, 0, 1)$ is a weighted indicator function which, however, need not be evaluated explicitly. If $T(i) = `M_2`$ inserting this nominator in (7) gives

$$\text{Prob}(W_i = 1 \mid W_1' = 1, W_2' = 0, W_3' = 1) = \qquad (10)$$

$$\frac{\int_0^1 \int_0^{s_0' \frac{R^2(\text{mod } M)}{M} \frac{M}{R}} \int_{s_1'^2 \frac{M}{R}}^1 \int_0^{s_1' s_2' \frac{M}{R}} \int_0^1 \int_0^{s_{i-1} s_2' \frac{M}{R}} 1 \, ds_i ds_{i-1} ds_3' ds_2' ds_1' ds_0'}{\int_0^1 \int_0^{s_0' \frac{R^2(\text{mod } M)}{M} \frac{M}{R}} \int_{s_1'^2 \frac{M}{R}}^1 \int_0^{s_1' s_2' \frac{M}{R}} 1 \, ds_3' ds_2' ds_1' ds_0'}$$

The calculation of (10), or more generally, of (7) is elementary as it requires no more than the evaluation of 1-dimensional integrals of polynomials. If $T(i) = `S`$ then $\text{Prob}(W_i = 1 \mid W_1' = w_1', W_2' = w_2', W_3' = w_3') = M/3R$ for all w_1', w_2', w_3'.

Theorem 1. *Let* $\theta = (\omega_i, \ldots, \omega_{i+f-1}) \in \mathcal{T}^f$. *If* $T(i) = \omega_i, \ldots, T(i-f-1) = \omega_{i+f-1}$ *then* $p_\theta\left(\boldsymbol{q}_{i,\ldots,i+f-1(k)\,1\leq k\leq N} \mid \boldsymbol{q}'_{(k)\,1\leq k\leq N}\right)$ *denotes the conditional probability for the er-vector* $\boldsymbol{q}_{i,\ldots,i+f-1(k)\,1\leq k\leq N}$ *if* $\boldsymbol{q}'_{(k)\,1\leq k\leq N}$ *was observed in the initialization phase. In particular,*

$$p_\theta\left(\boldsymbol{q}_{i,\ldots,i+f-1(k)\,1\leq k\leq N} \mid \boldsymbol{q}'_{(k)\,1\leq k\leq N}\right) \approx \prod_{k=1}^{N} \int_{[0,1)^{2^b+f}} g(s'_1, \ldots, s'_{2^b-1} \mid q'_{1(k)}, \ldots, q'_{2^b-1(k)}) \times$$

$$\times\ 1_{\bigcap_{m=i}^{i+f-1} \mathcal{C}_f(i,m;w_i,\omega_m)}(s_{i-1}, \ldots, s_{i+f-1})\, ds'_1 \cdots ds'_{2^b-1} ds_{i-1} \cdots ds_{i+f-1}. \quad (11)$$

If $D_{\lceil w/b\rceil-1} = r$ *then*

$$\mathrm{Prob}\left((q_{1(k)})_{1\leq k\leq N} \mid \boldsymbol{q}'_{(k)\,1\leq k\leq N}\right) \approx \quad (12)$$

$$\prod_{k=1}^{N} \int_{[0,1)^{2^b-1}} g(s'_1, \ldots, s'_{2^b-1} \mid q'_{1(k)}, \ldots, q'_{2^b-1(k)}) {s'_r}^2 \frac{M}{R}\, ds'_1 \cdots ds'_{2^b-1}.$$

Proof. According to our mathematical model we interpret the observed er-vectors $\boldsymbol{q}'_{(k)}$ and $\boldsymbol{q}_{i,\ldots,i+f-1(k)}$ as realizations of random variables $W'_{1(k)}, \ldots, W'_{2^b-1(k)}$ and $W_{i(k)}, \ldots, W_{i+f-1(k)}$, resp., which correspond $T(i) = \omega_i, \ldots, T(i+f-1) = \omega_{i+f-1}$ (cf. Lemma 1(iii)). Theorem 1 is an immediate consequence of Lemma 2.

Remark 3. (i) In the proof of Theorem 1 we tacitly assumed that the values $y_{(1)}/M, \ldots, y_{(N)}/M \in [0,1)$ behave like realizations of independent and equidistributed random variables on $[0,1)$. This assumption surely is justified if the blinding technique described in Remark 1(iii) is applied or for RSA encryptions with (pseudo-)random padding (with or without blinding, resp.), for example.
(ii) Consider RSA-based signatures with fixed padding (i.e., integrity and information bytes ‖ fixed padding bytes ‖ hash value) for which no blinding is applied. Then the ratios $y_{(1)}/M, \ldots, y_{(N)}/M$ are almost constant ($\approx c'$). Consequently, the conditional probability $g(\cdot \mid \cdot)$ from Lemma 2(ii) does not fit to the changed situation. To obtain the needed analogon (which has to be inserted in (11) and (12)) the integrals $\int_0^1 \ldots ds'_0$ in (6) have to be replaced by integrals with respect to the Dirac measure with total mass on $c' \in [0,1)$. Equivalently, we may completely drop the integration with respect to s'_0, set $s'_0 := c'$ in $\mathcal{C}'(i;w)$ and project $\mathcal{C}'(i;w)$ onto the components $s'_1, \ldots, s'_{2^b-1}$. If the CRT is used $M = p_i$ for a particular prime factor of the RSA modulus. The (unknown) ratio M/R can be guessed as described in Sect. 10 and $c'(R^2(\mathrm{mod}\,M)/R)(M/R) \approx (q'_{1(1)} + \cdots q'_{1(N)})/N$. If the attacked device does not use the CRT the attack is trivial anyway as no blinding is applied (cf. Remark 1(iii)).
(iii) If the blinding technique from Remark 1(iii) is applied or if (pseudo-)random padding is used (cf. (i)) the attacker has to derive the needed timing information

from the power traces of single exponentiations (SPA). In the context of (ii) also DPA may be applied.

5   A Priori Distribution

Assume that the attacker wants to estimate $T(i), \ldots, T(i + f - 1)$ simultaneously ($f \geq 1$). Based on the observed er-vectors he decides for that alternative $\theta \in \Theta \subseteq \mathcal{T}^f$ which appears to be the most likely one. For a randomly chosen position i, however, not all $\theta \in \Theta$ occur with equal probability. Therefore, we derive a probability distribution η on Θ which at least approximates the exact probabilities. For simplicity, we assume $f \leq b + 1$.

Recall that squarings occur in subsequences whose lengths are multiples of b and are interrupted by single multiplications with table values. Hence the set of all admissible hypotheses Θ equals

$$\Theta = \theta_0 \cup \{\theta_{m,j} \mid 1 \leq m \leq f; 1 \leq j \leq 2^b - 1\} \qquad \text{for } f \leq b + 1 \qquad (13)$$

where $\theta_0 := (`S`, \ldots, `S`)$ means that $T(i) = `S`, \ldots T(i + f - 1) = `S`$. Analogously, $\theta_{m,j} := (`S`, \ldots, `S`, `M_j`, `S`, \ldots, `S`)$ means $T(i + m - 1) = `M_j`$ but $T(v) = `S`$ for $v \neq i + m - 1$).

First, let us derive an approximator $\eta_{m,j}$ of the (exact) probability that $(T(i), \ldots, T(i + f - 1)) = \theta_{m,j}$ for randomly chosen i. Without any knowledge about d it is reasonable to assume $\eta_{1,1} = \cdots = \eta_{f,2^b-1}$. In average, $2^{-b}(\lceil w/b \rceil - 1)$ many multiplications with the table entry u_j are carried out within the computation phase and thus (almost) as many blocks of f consecutive Montgomery multiplications of type $\theta_{m,j}$ exist. Further, in the computation phase about $(b + (2^b - 1)2^{-b})(\lceil w/b \rceil - 1)$ Montgomery multiplications are carried out in average. (The exact number depends on the concrete value of d.) Altogether, we hence set

$$\eta_{1,1} := \cdots = \eta_{f,2^b-1} := \frac{2^{-b}\left(\lceil w/b \rceil - 1\right)}{\left(b + (2^b - 1)2^{-b}\right)\left(\lceil w/b \rceil - 1\right)} = \frac{1}{b2^b + (2^b - 1)} \qquad \text{and}$$

$$\eta_0 := 1 - \frac{(2^b - 1)f}{b2^b + (2^b - 1)} = \frac{b2^b - (f-1)(2^b - 1)}{b2^b + (2^b - 1)}. \qquad (14)$$

6   Error Detection and Correction

After the attacker has guessed the types $T(1), T(2), \ldots$ of all Montgomery multiplications he therefrom determines an estimator $\widetilde{d}$ for d. Then he computes $y^{\widetilde{d}} \pmod M$ for a reference base y to check whether $\widetilde{d} = d$. Either $y^d \pmod M$ itself is known or the exponentiation of $y^{\widetilde{d}} \pmod M$ with the public exponent e (RSA) gives y if $\widetilde{d}$ is correct. (For RSA implementations using the CRT (cf. Sect. 10) M equals a particular prime factor p_i of the modulus $n = p_1 p_2$, and the attack yields an estimator $\widetilde{d}$ for $d(\bmod (p_i - 1))$. If $\widetilde{d}$ is correct, $\gcd(y^d(\bmod n) -$

$y^{\widetilde{d}}(\bmod n), p_1p_2) = p_i$ and $\gcd(y - y^{\widetilde{de}}(\bmod n), p_1p_2) = p_i$.) If $\widetilde{d}$ turns out to be wrong the attacker has to correct false estimators.

It seems to be inconsequent to consider error detection and error correction strategies before the decision strategy itself has been derived. However, it will turn out to be useful to classify the estimation errors first.

Example 2. Let $b = 4$ and let the correct type sequence be given by
. ..., 'S','M_3','S','S','S','S',   'M_{12}','S','S','S','S','M_1','S',... whereas a), b) and c) are possible estimation sequences

a) ..., 'S','M_3','S','S','S','M_{11}','M_{12}','S','S','S','S','M_1','S',...
b) ..., 'S','M_3','S','S','S','S',   'S',   'S','S','S','S','M_1','S',...
c) ..., 'S','M_3','S','S','S','S',   'M_{14}','S','S','S','S','M_1','S',...

The subsequences a), b) and c) contain exactly one false estimator. The error in a) ('M_{11}') can easily be located and corrected as the number of squarings between two multiplications with a table entry must be a multiple of $b = 4$. Similarly, as in b) nine squarings occur between 'M_3' and 'M_1' the fifth Montgomery multiplication cannot be a squaring. Its correction, however, is not as obvious as for a). For $f = 1$, i.e. if the attacker has guessed the types of all Montgomery multiplications separately, he first tries that alternative which appeared to be most likely one after 'S'. (For $f > 1$ the situation is similar.) For sequence c) it is even not obvious that an error ('M_{14}' instead of 'M_{12}') had occurred. It has to be searched exhaustively over all positions with type estimator $\neq$ 'S' (cf. Sect. 8). Of course, it is reasonable to start at those positions where the respective decisions have been "close".

Suggestively, we denote errors as in sequences a) and b) as *local errors*, or more precisely, as *local-a errors* and *local-b errors*, resp. Errors as in sequence c) are called *global errors*. The detection and localization of the local errors may be interpreted as a decoding problem. Therefore, we derive a $0-1$ sequence from the estimated type values by replacing 'S' by 0 and 'M_j' by 1. The code words are the $0-1$ sequences of the same length with isolated ones and subsequences of zeroes whose lengths are multiples of b. We decide for that code word with minimal Hamming distance. If the local errors occur "isolated" (as in Example 2) they can be localized separately, although their positions occasionally are not obvious. If the attacker has guessed $3b+1$ consecutive squarings, for example, then either the $(b + 1)^{th}$ or the $(2b + 1)^{th}$ estimator is wrong. Usually, especially for $b > 2$, also "neighboured" local errors can successfully be localized. Note, however, that this need not always be the case. For example, let $b = 2$ and assume that ..., 'S','S','S','S',... has been estimated instead of the correct subsequence ..., 'M_3', 'S', 'S', 'M_2',.... Then both local errors will not be detected. Especially for $b = 2$ the sample size N hence should be chosen sufficiently large (if possible!) that neighboured local errors are unlikely. The correction of local-b errors and the localization and correction of global errors has to be done simultaneously over all local-b error positions and all positions with estimator $\neq$ 'S', resp. The optimal decision strategy which will be derived in the next section considers the different error types. Roughly speaking, it clearly tries to avoid estimation errors but "favours" local errors instead of global errors.

7 The Optimal Decision Strategy

In the previous sections we have done the necessary preliminary work. Now we are going to put the pieces together to derive the optimal decision strategy to guess the types of f consecutive Montgomery multiplications simultaneously ($1 \leq f \leq b+1$). Therefore, we interpret the estimation of $T(i), \ldots, T(i+f-1)$ as a statistical decision problem.

Roughly speaking, in a statistical decision problem the statistician observes a sample $\omega \in \Omega$ which he interprets as a realization of a random variable X with unknown distribution p_θ. On basis of this observation he tries to estimate the parameter $\theta \in \Theta$ where Θ denotes the parameter space, i.e. the set of all admissible hypotheses (= possible parameters). Formally, a statistical decision problem is described by a 5-tupel $(\Theta, \Omega, s, \Delta, A)$ where A denotes the set of all possible alternatives the statistician can decide for, and Ω denotes the observation space. In our case the observations are the er-vectors $(\boldsymbol{q}'_{(k)}, \boldsymbol{q}_{i\ldots,i+f-1(k)})_{1 \leq k \leq N}$ and thus $\Omega = (\{0,1\}^{2^b-1+f})^N$. The parameter space Θ was defined in Sect. 5, and further $A := \Theta$. Applying a deterministic decision strategy $\tau \colon \Omega \to A$ means that the statistician decides for $\tau(\omega)$ upon observation ω. The loss function $s \colon \Theta \times A \to [0, \infty)$, quantifies the "damage" of a wrong decision, i.e. if the statistician decides for $\theta' \in A$ although $\theta \in \Theta$ was the correct parameter. For our attack potential errors must be "punished" by the loss function with regard to the effort which is necessary for their detection, localization and correction (cf. Sect. 8). Clearly, $s(\theta, \theta) = 0$ for all $\theta \in \Theta$ (correct decisions).

Optimal Decision Strategy. Let the a priori distribution η be defined as in Sect. 5. Let $\tau_{opt}((\boldsymbol{q}'_{(k)}, \boldsymbol{q}_{i,\ldots,i+f-1(k)})_{1 \leq k \leq N}) := \theta^*$ if the sum

$$\sum_{\theta \in \Theta} s(\theta, \theta') p_\theta \left((\boldsymbol{q}_{i,\ldots,i+f-1(k)} \mid \boldsymbol{q}'_{(k)})_{1 \leq k \leq N} \right) \eta(\theta) \tag{15}$$

is minimal for $\theta' = \theta^*$. Then τ_{opt} causes the minimal expected loss of all decision strategies. That is, τ_{opt} is optimal among all decision strategies which estimate $T(i), \ldots, T(i+f-1)$ simultaneously.

Proof. After reordering the sums the expected loss for a deterministic decision strategy τ equals $\sum_{\omega \in \{0,1\}^{2^b-1+f}} \sum_{\theta \in \Theta} s(\theta, \tau(\omega)) p_\theta(\omega) \eta(\theta)$. The optimal decision strategy minimizes the inner sum for each $\omega := (\boldsymbol{q}_{i,\ldots,i+f-1(k)}, \boldsymbol{q}'_{(k)})$. Further, $p_\theta \left((\boldsymbol{q}_{i,\ldots,i+f-1(k)}, \boldsymbol{q}'_{(k)})_{1 \leq k \leq N} \right) = p_\theta \left((\boldsymbol{q}_{i,\ldots,i+f-1(k)} \mid \boldsymbol{q}'_{(k)})_{1 \leq k \leq N} \right) \cdot \text{Prob} \left((\boldsymbol{q}'_{(k)})_{1 \leq k \leq n} \right)$. The last term is independent of θ which proves the assertion.

Remark 4. (i) The optimal decision strategy may not be unique. As Θ is finite it suffices to consider deterministic decision strategies.

(ii) The differentiation of the error types, i.e. using different $s(\cdot, \cdot)$-values for local-a, local-b and global errors, does not reduce the total number of errors but reduces the number of global errors at the expense of the local ones which are easier to detect, to localize and to correct.

(iii) The types $T(1), T(2), \ldots$ determine d besides its most significant b-bit block. The latter can be estimated using (12) (maximum likelihood estimator!).

8   Experimental Results

The er-values $q'_{1(k)}, \ldots, q'_{2^b-1(k)}$ and $q_{1(k)}, q_{2(k)}, \ldots$ depend on $y_{(k)}, d, M, R$ and b but not on implementation details (cf. Remark 1(i)). As GA b) further assumes that the attacker can determine the er-values exactly (cf. Sect. 10) Alg. 1 was emulated on a computer with pseudorandom moduli and pseudorandom bases $y_{(1)}, \ldots, y_{(N)}$. Program output was $q'_{1(k)}, \ldots, q'_{2^b-1(k)}$ and $q_{1(k)}, q_{2(k)}, \ldots$. In the first phase of the attack type estimators $\widetilde{T}(1), \widetilde{T}(2), \ldots$ for $T(1), T(2), \ldots$ were derived using the optimal decision strategy from Sect. 7. For $(b = 2, f = 1)$ we used the loss function values $s({}^\backprime S{}^\backprime, {}^\backprime M_j{}^\backprime) = 1$ (local-a error), $s({}^\backprime S{}^\backprime, {}^\backprime M_j{}^\backprime) = 1.5$ (local-b error) and $s({}^\backprime M_j{}^\backprime, {}^\backprime M_t{}^\backprime) = 4.0$ for $j \neq t$ (global error). For $(b = 4, f = 1)$ we defined $s({}^\backprime S{}^\backprime, {}^\backprime M_j{}^\backprime) := 1$, $s({}^\backprime S{}^\backprime, {}^\backprime M_j{}^\backprime) := 1.5$ and $s({}^\backprime M_j{}^\backprime, {}^\backprime M_t{}^\backprime) := 8.0$. For $f > 1$ we used the loss function $s_f((\omega_1, \ldots, \omega_f), (\omega'_1, \ldots, \omega'_f)) := \sum_{j=1}^{f} s(\omega_j, \omega'_j)$.

Table 1. Average number of errors per 100 type estimators

	local-a errors	local-b errors	global errors
$(b = 2, M'_r R \approx 0.99, \text{f=1}, N = 250)$	0.8	0.6	0.02
$(b = 2, M'_r R \approx 0.99, \text{f=3}, N = 200)$	0.4	0.3	0.05
$(b = 2, M'_r R \approx 0.7, \text{f=1}, N = 375)$	0.6	0.6	0.05
$(b = 2, M'_r R \approx 0.7, \text{f=3}, N = 300)$	0.4	0.4	0.06
$(b = 4, M'_r R \approx 0.7, \text{f=1}, N = 500)$	0.3	0.7	0.07
$(b = 4, M'_r R \approx 0.7, \text{f=1}, N = 550)$	0.2	0.5	0.05

In the second phase the local errors were localized which in particular enabled the immediate correction of the local-a errors. As described in Sect. 6 we interpreted the localization of the local errors as a decoding problem where we searched for the code word(s) with minimal Hamming distance. Clearly, the type estimation and the error correction are easiest for $b = 2$ as there exist the fewest alternatives. In contrast, the detection and localization of local errors is most difficult for $b = 2$ as the subsequences of consecutive squarings are shorter than for $b > 2$. For $b = 4$ and $w = 512$, for example, (e.g., 1024-bit RSA using the CRT; cf. Sect. 10) about 632 Montgomery multiplications are carried out in the computation phase. For ($b = 4$, $M/R \approx 0.7$, $f = 1$, $N = 500$) the attacker makes about 1.9 local-a, 4.4 local-b and 0.4 global errors in average. From the attacker's point of view the case $M/R \approx 0.99$ is the most favourable one. If $M/R \approx 0.5$ twice as many samples are needed to ensure similar success rates. For fixed parameters b, M/R, f and N the probabilities for wrong estimators do not depend on $w = \lceil log_2(d) \rceil$. The total number of errors (especially the global ones) hence increases linear in w. In particular, the necessary minimal sample size increases as $\log_2(M)$ increases.

Finally, the local-b errors and possible global errors have to be corrected. Therefore, the estimators which have been identified as local-b errors are replaced simultaneously by alternatives which had been ranked on positions 2 to 4 (behind the false estimator) in the type estimation phase, the most probable combinations of candidates first. If no global errors have been made this approach leads to a quick success. In fact, simulations using the parameters from Table 1 showed that for ($f = 1$, $b = 2$) and ($f = 1$, $b = 4$) the correct estimators usually are on rank 2, resp. nearly always on rank 2 or 3. In particular, for $b = 2$ the local-b errors sometimes can be corrected in the first attempt if no global errors have been made. If this procedure does not yield the searched exponent d the attacker presumably has made a global error. He then just repeats the steps from above, additionally changing one 'M_j'-estimator (= candidate for a global error), beginning at the position with the "closest" decision in the estimation phase. Provided that the local errors have been localized correctly this strategy can correct one global error. (The correction of more than one global error clearly is also possible but costly.)

Using the parameters from Table 1 for $w = 384$ (as in [9]) and ($b = 2$, $f = 1$) the attack was successful in about 90 per cent of the trials for both, $M/R \approx 0.99$ and $M/R \approx 0.7$. (To be precise, we did not actually carry out the final phase of the attack. To save computation time we resigned on checking the particular combinations of candidates by exponentiating a reference base y (cf. the first paragraph of Sect. 6). In fact, an attack was viewed as successful if our program could localize all local errors correctly and if at most one global error had been made (cf. the previous paragraph).) For ($b = 2$, $f = 3$) the success rate was 92 per cent. For ($b = 4$, $f = 1$) (with $N = 500$, resp. $N = 550$) and $w = 512$ about 93 per cent of the trials, resp. more than 95 per cent of the trials were successful. First simulations confirm that estimating $f > 1$ types simultaneously will also reduce the necessary sample size for $b = 4$.

9   A Brief Comparison with the Original Attack

In [9] Walter and Thompson treat exclusively the case $b = 2$. Based on $\sum_{k=1}^{N} q_{i(k)}$ they first decide whether $T(i) = 'S'$ or $T(i) \neq 'S'$. To distinguish between 'M_1', 'M_2' and 'M_3' they use the subset $A := \{y_{(k)} \mid q'_{2(k)} = 1\} \subset \{y_{(1)}, \ldots, y_{(N)}\}$ and, additionally, a subset $A_0 \subset A$. The number of extra reductions (counted over A or A_0, resp.) needed for the ith Montgomery multiplication is plotted for all i for which $T(i) \neq 'S'$ is assumed. In the most favourable case, i.e. for

$M/R \approx 0.99$, for sample size $N = 1000$ these numbers fall into three more or less separated subsets corresponding to 'M_1', 'M_2' and 'M_3', resp. (cf. [9], Figs. 2 and 3). (Implicitely, Walter and Thompson exploit that the random variables W_1', W_2' and W_3' are negative correlated.) Walter and Thompson assume that about 500 time measurements should also be sufficient (cf. [9], Sect. 4). Using the techniques from [9], however, this prognosis seems to be rather optimistic. First of all, there are no clear-cut decision rules but decisions are made by eye. Even for $N = 1000$ some global errors occur (cf. [9], Sect. 4) and for $N = 500$ the situation will be considerably less comfortable. Finally, as the random variables W_i' and W_j' are independent if $|i - j| > 1$ the original attack cannot be transferred to $b > 2$.

10   Weakening the Assumptions and Generalizations

The general assumptions GA a)-e) are fulfilled, for example, if an RSA implementation uses the standard blinding technique against timing attacks described in Remark 1(iii) but not the CRT. If the CRT is used, the ratios M/R and $(R^2(\mathrm{mod}\, M))/M$ are yet unknown. (Then M equals a particular prime factor p_i. As already pointed out in Sect. 6 it is sufficient to determine $d(\mathrm{mod}\, (p_1 - 1))$ or $d(\mathrm{mod}\, (p_2 - 1))$.) Let H temporarily denote the total number of Montgomery multiplications in the computation phase. As the least significant block D_0 of d is non-zero, $T(1) = \cdots = T(b) = T(H - b) = \cdots = T(H - 1) = 'S'$, and further, the second Montgomery multiplication in the initialization phase is a squaring, too. As the probability for an extra reduction in a squaring equals $M/3R$ the attacker uses these $(2b + 1)N$ squarings to estimate the ratio M/R. Similarly, from the first Montgomery multiplication in the initialization phase an estimator for $(R^2(\mathrm{mod}\, M))/M$ can be derived. Compared with the scenario from the preceding sections, i.e. that M/R and $(R^2(\mathrm{mod}\, M))/M$ are known, the additional estimation steps cause a lower success rate for equal sample size N. For example, using the parameter values from Table 1 the success rate for ($b = 2$, $M/R \approx 0.7$, $f = 1$, $N = 375$), resp. for ($b = 4$, $M/R \approx 0.7$, $f = 1$, $N = 500$), reduces from 90 to 83 per cent, resp. from 93 to 87 per cent.

Ga a) assumes that the attacked device uses a particular table method. However, our method can be transferred to other table methods (cf. [5], Sect. 14.83 and 14.85) in an obvious manner. Our attack can also be applied if another modular multiplication algorithm is used than Montgomery's (e.g. a simple shift-and-add algorithm) provided that the (random) time needed for a modular multiplication of a fixed factor with a random cofactor depends significantly on the fixed factor. Similarly as in Sect. 4 the attacker interprets the times needed by the multiplications in the initialization and the computation phase as realizations of suitably defined random variables $T_1', \ldots, T_{2^b-1}'$, resp., $T_1, T_2, \ldots$. If these random variables are continuously distributed (e.g. normally distributed, cf. [2]) the conditional probabilities $\mathrm{Prob}(W_i = w_i, \ldots, W_{i+f-1} = w_{i+f-1} \mid W_1' = w_1', \ldots, W_{2^b-1}' = w_{2^b-1}')$ from Sect. 4 correspond to conditional probability densities $f(T_i = t_i, \ldots, T_{i+f-1} = t_{i+f-1} \mid T_1' = t_1', \ldots, T_{2^b-1}' = t_{2^b-1}')$ where

$t'_1, \cdots, t'_{2^b-1}$ and $t_1, t_2, \ldots$ denote the times needed for the particular modular multiplications. (Recall that for Montgomery's algorithm $q_i \mapsto c + q_i\,c_{\mathrm{ER}}$ defines a bijection between the er-values and the running times.)

Moreover, the attacker may only be able to derive inexact values $\widetilde{t}'_j := t_j + t'_{\mathrm{Err};j}$ and $\widetilde{t}_i := t_i + t_{\mathrm{Err};i}$ from the power trace instead of t_j or t_i, resp., possibly a consequence of countermeasures against power attacks. The attacker then has to study the random variables $T'_1 + T'_{\mathrm{Err};1}, \ldots, T'_{2^b-1} + T'_{\mathrm{Err};2^b-1}$ and $T_1 + T_{\mathrm{Err};1}, T_2 + T_{\mathrm{Err};2}, \ldots$ instead of $T'_1, \ldots, T'_{2^b-1}$ and $T_1, T_2, \ldots$. The general approach yet remains unchanged.

11   Countermeasures

A standard blinding technique which prevents pure timing attacks is described in Remark 1(iii). However, it neither prevents the optimized nor the original attack from [9]. Walter and Thompson hence propose to apply another blinding technique which was also discussed in [2]. Namely, the base y shall not be exponentiated with the secret exponent d itself but with $d' := d + r\phi(M)$ where r is a non-negative pseudorandom integer which is renewed after each exponentiation and $\phi(\cdot)$ denotes the well-known Euler function. In fact, this violates assumption GA d) but does not necessarily prevent our attack.

Assume, for example, that for efficiency reasons $0 \le r < 2^4$. If d' has w' binary digits ($\lceil w'/b \rceil - 1)b$ many squarings are carried out within the computation phase. The number $\#(d')$ of multiplications with table entries and hence the total number of Montgomery multiplications, however, depend on d' rather than on w'. If two exponentiations require a different number of Montgomery multiplications the used exponents must be different. (Recall that the attacker knows the total number of Montgomery multiplications within the computation phase.) Consequently, the attacker divides the sample $y_{(1)}, \ldots, y_{(N)}$ into subsamples with respect to the number of Montgomery multiplications. Then he attacks each subsample separately as described in the previous sections. If there is a subsample which belongs to a unique exponent d' this attack will be successful.

The number $\#(d')$ may be viewed as a realization of a normally distributed random variable X with mean $(\lceil w'/b \rceil - 1)(1 - 2^{-b})$ and variance $(\lceil w'/b \rceil - 1)(1 - 2^{-b})2^{-b}$. If $513 \le w' < 516$ (e.g. for 1024-bit RSA using the CRT and $d' > 2^{512}$) and $b = 4$, for example, we have $\mathrm{Prob}(X = 120) \approx 0.145$, $\mathrm{Prob}(X = 119) = \mathrm{Prob}(X = 121) \approx 0.135$, $\mathrm{Prob}(X = 118) = \mathrm{Prob}(X = 122) \approx 0.114$, $\mathrm{Prob}(X = 117) = \mathrm{Prob}(X = 123) \approx 0.079$, $\mathrm{Prob}(X = 116) = \mathrm{Prob}(X = 124) \approx 0.051$ etc. Hence it is likely that at least one subsample belongs to a unique exponent d'. (In particular, note that for $d' = d$ not 512 but only 508 squarings are necessary.) Although the efficiency of our attack is reduced by factor 16 it is still practically feasible. To prevent the attack the range of the pseudorandom numbers should be chosen sufficiently large, e.g. $r \le 2^{16}$. Additionally, a lower bound for r may be chosen such that the number of squarings in the computation phase is constant for all admissible r's.

12   Final Remarks

Using suitable stochastical methods the efficieny of the original attack introduced by Walter and Thompson ([9]) was improved by factor 5 for 2-bit tables. Unlike the original attack the optimized attack works and is also practically feasible for $b > 2$. It can be adapted to other table methods, other modular multiplication algorithms and inexact timings in a straightforward manner. Finally, for unsuitable parameters the countermeasures proposed in [9] were shown to be insufficient.

References

1. J.-F. Dhem, F. Koeune, P.-A. Leroux, P.-A. Mestré, J.-J. Quisquater, J.-L. Willems: A Practical Implementation of the Timing Attack. In: J.-J. Quisquater and B. Schneier (eds.): Smart Card – Research and Applications. Lecture Notes in Computer Science **1820**, Berlin, Springer (2000), 175–191.
2. P. Kocher: Timing Attacks on Implementations of Diffie-Hellman, RSA, DSS and Other Systems. In: N. Koblitz (ed.): Advances in Cryptology – Crypto '96, Lecture Notes in Computer Science **1109**. Springer, Heidelberg (1996), 104–113.
3. K. Gandolfi, C. Mourtel, F. Olivier: Electromagnetic Analysis: Concrete Results. In: Ç.K. Koç, D. Naccache, C. Paar (eds.): Cryptographic Hardware and Embedded Systems — CHES 2001, Springer, Lecture Notes in Computer Science **2162**, Berlin (2001), 251–261.
4. P. Kocher, J. Jaffe, B. Jub: Differential Power Analysis. In: M. Wiener (ed.): Advances in Cryptology – Crypto '99. Lecture Notes in Computer Science **1666**, Berlin, Springer (1999), 388–397.
5. A.J. Menezes, P.C. van Oorschot, S.C. Vanstone: Handbook of Applied Cryptography, Boca Raton, CRC Press (1997).
6. P.L. Montgomery: Modular Multiplication without Trial Division, Math. Comp. **44**, no. 170, 519–521 (April 1985).
7. W. Schindler: Optimized Timing Attacks against Public Key Cryptosystems. To appear in Statistics & Decisions.
8. W. Schindler: A Timing Attack against RSA with the Chinese Remainder Theorem. In: Ç.K. Koç, C. Paar (eds.): Cryptographic Hardware and Embedded Systems — CHES 2000, Springer, Lecture Notes in Computer Science **1965**, Berlin (2000), 110–125.
9. C.D. Walter, S. Thompson: Distinguishing Exponent Digits by Observing Modular Subtractions. In: D. Naccache (ed.): Topics in Cryptology – CT-RSA 2001, Springer, Lecture Notes in Computer Science **2020**, Berlin (2000), 192–207.

A Fast Parallel Elliptic Curve Multiplication Resistant against Side Channel Attacks

Tetsuya Izu[1,*] and Tsuyoshi Takagi[2]

[1] Fujitsu Laboratories Ltd.,
4-1-1, Kamikodanaka, Nakahara-ku, Kawasaki, 211-8588, Japan
izu@flab.fujitsu.co.jp
[2] Technische Universität Darmstadt, Fachbereich Informatik,
Alexanderstr.10, D-64283 Darmstadt, Germany
ttakagi@cdc.informatik.tu-darmstadt.de

Abstract. This paper proposes a fast elliptic curve multiplication algorithm applicable for any types of curves over finite fields $\mathbb{F}_p$ (p a prime), based on [Mon87], together with criteria which make our algorithm resistant against the side channel attacks (SCA). The algorithm improves both on an addition chain and an addition formula in the scalar multiplication. Our addition chain requires no table look-up (or a very small number of pre-computed points) and a prominent property is that it can be implemented in parallel. The computing time for n-bit scalar multiplication is one ECDBL + $(n-1)$ ECADDs in the parallel case and $(n-1)$ ECDBLs + $(n-1)$ ECADDs in the single case. We also propose faster addition formulas which only use the x-coordinates of the points. By combination of our addition chain and addition formulas, we establish a faster scalar multiplication resistant against the SCA in both single and parallel computation. The improvement of our scalar multiplications over the previous method is about 37% for two processors and 5.7% for a single processor. Our scalar multiplication is suitable for the implementation on smart cards.

1 Introduction

In recent years, several elliptic-curve based cryptosystems (ECC) have been included in many standards [ANSI,IEEE,NIST,SEC,WAP]. The key length of ECC is currently chosen smaller than those of the RSA and the ElGamal-type cryptosystems. The small key size of ECC is suitable for implementing on low-power mobile devices like smart cards, mobile phones and PDAs (Personal Digital Assistants, such as Palm and Pocket PC). Let $E(K)$ be an elliptic curve over a finite field $K = \mathbb{F}_p$ (p a prime). The dominant computation of the encryption/decryption and the signature generation/verification of ECC is the scalar

---

* This work was done while the first author was staying at the Centre for Appllied Cryptographic Research (CACR), University of Waterloo and part of this work was done while the first author was visiting Fachbereich Informatik, Technische Universität Darmstadt.

D. Naccache and P. Paillier (Eds.): PKC 2002, LNCS 2274, pp. 280–296, 2002.
© Springer-Verlag Berlin Heidelberg 2002

multiplication $d * P$, where $P \in E(K)$ and d is an integer. It is usually computed by combining an adding $P + Q$ (ECADD) and a doubling $2 * P$ (ECDBL), where $P, Q \in E(K)$. Several algorithms have been proposed to enhance the running time of the scalar multiplication [Gor98,CMO98]. The choice of the coordinate system and the addition chain is the most important factor. A standard way in [IEEE] is to use the Jacobian coordinate system and the addition-subtraction chain. Some efficient addition chains use a table look-up method. It is useful for software implementation but not for smart cards because the cost of the memory spaces is expensive and an I/O interface to read the table is relatively slow.

This paper proposes a fast multiplication which is applicable for any type of elliptic curves over finite fields $K = \mathbb{F}_p$ (p a prime). The algorithm improves both the addition chain and the addition formula in the scalar multiplication. Our addition chain requires no table look-up (or a very small table) and a prominent property of our addition chain is that it can be implemented in parallel.[1] The latency of the scalar multiplication is the computation time of one ECDBL + $(n - 1)$ ECADDs. The improvement from the method in [IEEE] is the time of $(n - 2)$ ECDBLs $-(2n + 2)/3$ ECADDs. Moreover, our proposed addition chain computes the scalar multiplication after one ECDBL + $(n-1)$ ECADDs exactly, although the expected time of the binary method is only estimated on average.

The side channel attacks (SCA) allow an adversary to reveal the secret key in the cryptographic device by observing the side channel information such as the computing time and the power consumption [Koc96,KJJ99]. An adversary does not have to break the physical devise to obtain the secret key. It is a serious attack especially against mobile devices like smart cards. The simple power analysis (SPA) only uses a single observed information, while the differential power analysis (DPA) uses a lot of observed information together with statistic tools. There are two approaches to resist the SPA. The first one uses the indistinguishable addition and doubling in the scalar multiplication [CJ01]. In the case of prime fields, Hesse and Jacobi form elliptic curves achieve the indistinguishability by using the same formula for both an addition and a doubling [LS01,JQ01]. Because of the specialty of these curves, they are not compatible to the standardized curves in [ANSI,IEEE,SEC]. The second one uses the add-and-double-always method to mask the scalar dependency. The Coron's algorithm [Cor99] and the Montgomery form [OKS00] are in this category. To resist the DPA, some randomizations are needed [Cor99] and an SPA-resistant scheme can be converted to be a DPA-resistant scheme [Cor99,JT01]. The cost of the conversion is relatively cheap comparing with the scalar multiplication itself.

In this paper, we discuss a criteria, which makes our algorithms to be resistant against the SCA by comparing the Coron's algorithm. Moreover, We also propose addition formulas which only use the x-coordinates of the points. The computations of the ECADD and the ECDBL require $9M + 3S$ and $6M + 3S$, where M, S are the times for a multiplication and a squaring in the definition field $\mathbb{F}_p$. By combination of our addition chain and addition formulas, we estab-

---

[1] Recently, Smart proposed a fast implementation over a SIMD type processor, which allows to compute several operations in the definition field in parallel [Sma01].

lish a faster scalar multiplication algorithm resistant against the SCA in both single and parallel computations. The improvement of our scalar multiplication over the previously fastest method is about 37% for two processors and 5.7% for a single processor.

2   Elliptic Curves and Scalar Multiplications

In this paper we assume that $K = \mathbb{F}_p$ $(p > 3)$ be a finite field with p elements. Elliptic curves over K can be represented by the equation

$$E(K) := \{(x, y) \in K \times K | y^2 = x^3 + ax + b \ (a, b \in K, \ 4a^3 + 27b^2 \neq 0)\} \cup \mathcal{O}, \quad (1)$$

where $\mathcal{O}$ is the point of infinity. Every elliptic curve is isomorphic to a curve of this form, and we call it the Weierstrass form. An elliptic curve $E(K)$ has an additive group structure. Let $P_1 = (x_1, y_1), P_2 = (x_2, y_2)$ be two elements of $E(K)$ that are different from $\mathcal{O}$ and satisfy $P_2 \neq \pm P_1$. Then the sum $P_1 + P_2 = (x_3, y_3)$ is defined as follows:

$$x_3 = \lambda^2 - x_1 - x_2, \quad y_3 = \lambda(x_1 - x_3) - y_1, \quad (2)$$

where $\lambda = (y_2 - y_1)/(x_2 - x_1)$ for $P_1 \neq P_2$, and $\lambda = (3x_1^2 + a)/(2y_1)$ for $P_1 = P_2$. We call $P_1 + P_2 (P_1 \neq P_2)$ the elliptic curve addition (ECADD) and $P_1 + P_2 (P_1 = P_2)$, that is $2 * P_1$, the elliptic curve doubling (ECDBL). Let d be an integer and P be a point on the elliptic curve $E(K)$. The scalar multiplication is to compute the point $d * P$. There are three types of enhancements of the scalar multiplication. The first one is to represent the elliptic curve $E(K)$ with a different coordinate system, whose scalar multiplication is more efficient. For examples, a projective coordinate and a class of Jacobian coordinate has been studied [CMO98]. The second one is to use an efficient addition chain. The addition-subtraction chain is an example [MO90]. We can also apply the addition chains developed for the ElGamal cryptosystem over finite fields [Gor98]. The third one is to use a special type of curve such as the Montgomery form elliptic curve [OS00], or the Hesse form [JQ01,Sma01].

Coordinate System: There are several ways to represent a point on an elliptic curve. The costs of computing an ECADD and an ECDBL depend on the representation of the coordinate system. The detailed description of the coordinate systems is given in [CMO98]. The major coordinate systems are as follows: the affine coordinate system $(\mathcal{A})$, the projective coordinate system $(\mathcal{P})$, the Jacobian coordinate system $(\mathcal{J})$, the Chudonovsky coordinate system $(\mathcal{J}^C)$, and the modified Jacobian coordinate system $(\mathcal{J}^m)$. We summarize the costs in Table 1, where M, S, I denotes the computation time of a multiplication, a squaring, and an inverse in the definition field K, respectively. The speed of ECADD or ECDBL can be enhanced when the third coordinate is $Z = 1$ or the coefficient of the definition equation is $a = -3$.

Table 1. Computing times of an addition (ECADD) and a doubling (ECDBL)

Coordinate	ECADD		ECDBL	
System	$Z \neq 1$	$Z = 1$	$a \neq -3$	$a = -3$
$\mathcal{A}$	$2M + 1S + 1I$	—	$2M + 2S + 1I$	
$\mathcal{P}$	$12M + 2S$	$9M + 2S$	$7M + 5S$	$7M + 3S$
$\mathcal{J}$	$12M + 4S$	$8M + 3S$	$4M + 6S$	$4M + 4S$
$\mathcal{J}^C$	$11M + 3S$	$8M + 3S$	$5M + 6S$	$5M + 4S$
$\mathcal{J}^m$	$13M + 6S$	$9M + 5S$	$4M + 4S$	

Addition Chain: Let d be an n-bit integer and P be a point of the elliptic curve $E(K)$. A standard way for computing the scalar multiplication $d * P$ is to use the binary expression of $d = d_{n-1}2^{n-1} + d_{n-2}2^{n-2} + \ldots + d_1 2 + d_0$, where $d_{n-1} = 1$ and $d_i = 0, 1$ ($n = 0, 1, ..., n - 2$). Then Algorithm 1 and Algorithm 2 compute $d * P$ efficiently. We call these methods the binary methods (or the add-and-double methods). On average they require $(n-1)$ ECDBLs + $(n-1)/2$ ECADDs. Because computing the inverse $-P$ of P is essentially free, we can relax the binary coefficient to a signed binary $d_i = -1, 0, 1$ ($i = 0, 1, ..., n - 1$), which is called the addition-subtraction chain. The NAF offers a way to construct the addition-subtraction chain, which requires $(n-1)$ ECDBLs + $(n-1)/3$ ECADDs on average [IEEE].

```
INPUT d, P, (n)
OUTPUT d*P
 1: Q[0] = P                       1: Q[0] = P, Q[1] = 0
 2: for i=n-2 down to 0            2: for i=0 to n-1
 3:    Q[0] = ECDBL(Q[0])          3:    if d[i]==1
 4:    if d[i]==1                  4:       Q[1] = ECADD(Q[1],Q[0])
 5:       Q[0] = ECADD(Q[0],P)     5:    Q[0] = ECDBL(Q[0])
 6: return Q[0]                    6: return Q[1]
```

Algorithm 1 (leftside): Binary method from the most significant bit
Algorithm 2 (rightside): Binary method from the least significant bit

The other enhancement technique is to utilize pre-computed tables. The Brickell's method and the sliding windows methods are two of the standard algorithms [BSS99]. These algorithms have been developed for the efficient modular multiplications over finite fields. We can refer to the nice survey paper [Gor98]. In this paper we are interested in efficient algorithms without table look-up (or with a very small pre-computed table). Our goal is to propose an efficient algorithm that is suitable for smart cards, and the pre-computed table sometimes hinders to achieve the high efficiency because the memory spaces are expensive and an I/O interface to read the table is relatively slow.

Special Elliptic Curves: With a special class of elliptic curves, we can enhance the speed of a scalar multiplication. Okeya and Sakurai proposed to use the

Montgomery form [OS00]. The addition formula of the Montgomery form is much simpler than that of the Weierstrass form, and its scalar multiplication is also faster. However every Montgomery form cannot be generally converted to the Weierstrass form, because the order of the Montgomery form curves is always divisible by 4.

ECC has been standardized in several organizations like ANSI, IEEE, SEC, NIST, WAP. In all standards, the curves are defined by the Weierstrass form over $\mathbb{F}_p$ or $\mathbb{F}_{2^m}$, where p is a prime number or m is an integer. The example curves over $\mathbb{F}_p$ cannot be represented by the Montgomery form. Indeed, all curves in [NIST,ANSI] and all curves defined over a prime field with larger than 160-bit prime in [IEEE] are not compatible.

3   Side Channel Attacks to ECC

The side channel attacks (SCA) are serious attacks against mobile devices such as smart cards, mobile phones and PDAs. An adversary can obtain a secret key from a cryptographic device without breaking its physical protection. We can achieve the attack by analyzing side channel information, i.e., computing time, or power consumption of the devices. The timing attack (TA) and the power analysis attack are examples of the SCA [Koc96,KJJ99]. The simple power analysis (SPA) only uses a single observed information, and the differential power analysis (DPA) uses a lot of observed information together with statistic tools. As the TA can be regarded as a class of the SPA, we are only concerned with the SPA and the DPA in this paper.

Countermeasures against SPA: The binary methods of Algorithm 1 and 2 compute ECADDs when the bit of the secret key d is 1. Therefore we can easily detect the bit information of d by the SPA.

```
INPUT d, P, (n)
OUTPUT d*P
 1: Q[0] = P                    1: Q[0] = P, Q[1] = 0
 2: for i=n-2 down to 0         2: for i=0 to n-1
 3:    Q[0] = ECDBL(Q[0])       3:    Q[2] = ECADD(Q[0],Q[1])
 4:    Q[1] = ECADD(Q[0],P)     4:    Q[0] = ECDBL(Q[0])
 5:    Q[0] = Q[d[i]]           5:    Q[1] = Q[1+d[i]]
 6: return Q[0]                 6: return Q[1]
```

Algorithm 1' (leftside): Add-and-double-always method from the most significant bit (SPA-resistant)
Algorithm 2' (rightside): Add-and-double-always method from the least significant bit (SPA-resistant)

Coron proposed a simple countermeasure against the SPA by modifying the binary methods (Algorithm 1', 2') [Cor99]. These algorithms are referred as the add-and-double-always methods. In both algorithms, Step 3 and 4 compute both an ECDBL and an ECADD in every bits. Thus an adversary cannot guess the bit information of d by the SPA. A drawback of this method is their efficiency. Algorithm 1' requires $(n-1)$ ECADDs $+ (n-1)$ ECDBLs and Algorithm 2' requires n ECADDs $+ n$ ECDBLs.

Note that in Algorithm 1' and 2', there are no computational advantage even if we use the NAF because we have to compute both ECADD and ECDBL for each bit.

Möller proposed an SPA-resistant algorithm which is a combination of Algorithm 1' and the window method [Moe01]. However, his method requires extra table look-up (at least three elliptic curve points).

Another countermeasure is to establish the indistinguishability between an ECADD and an ECDBL. Joye, Quisquater and Smart proposed to use the Jacobi and Hesse form elliptic curves, which use the same mathematical formulas for both an ECADD and an ECDBL [JQ01,Sma01]. As we discussed above, a drawback of this approach is that the Jacobi and Hesse form are special types of elliptic curves and they cannot be used for the standard Weierstrass form.

SPA-Resistance to DPA-Resistance: Even if a scheme is SPA-resistant, it is not always DPA-resistant, because the DPA uses not only a simple power trace but also a statistic analysis, which has been captured by several executions of the SPA. Coron pointed out that some parameters of ECC must be randomized in order to be DPA-resistant [Cor99]. By the randomization we are able to enhance an SPA-resistant scheme to be DPA-resistant.

Coron also proposed three countermeasures, but Okeya and Sakurai showed the bias in his 1st and 2nd countermeasures. They asserted that Coron's 3rd method is secure against the DPA [OS00]. The key idea of Coron's 3rd countermeasure for the projective coordinate is as follows. Note that in the projective coordinate, we require 1 inversion and 2 multiplications in the definition fields to pull back from the projective point $(X_d : Y_d : Z_d)$ to the affine point (x_d, y_d). Let $P = (X : Y : Z)$ be a base point in a projective coordinate. Then $(X : Y : Z)$ equals to $(rX : rY : rZ)$ for all $r \in K$. If we randomize a base point with r before starting the scalar multiplication, the side information for the statistic analysis will be randomized. This countermeasure requires only three multiplications before the scalar multiplication, and no extra cost after the scalar multiplication.

The other enhancement method against the DPA was proposed by Joye-Tymen [JT01]. This countermeasure uses an isomorphism of an elliptic curve. The base point $P = (X : Y : Z)$ and the definition parameters a, b of an elliptic curve can be randomized in its isomorphic classes like $(r^2 X : r^3 Y : Z)$ and $r^4 a, r^6 b$, respectively. Let $(X'_d : Y'_d : Z'_d)$ be the point after computing the scalar multiplication. The point (x_d, y_d) is pulled back to the original curve by computing $r^{-2} X'_d$ and $r^{-3} Y'_s$. This method requires 3 squaring and 5 multiplications for the randomizing the point P, and 1 squaring, 3 multiplications, and 1 inversion for pulling back to the original curve. Joye-Tymen method can choose the Z-coordinate equal to 1 during the computation of the scalar multiplication and it improves the efficiency of the scalar multiplication in some cases.

4   Our Proposed Algorithm

We explain our proposed algorithm for the scalar multiplication in the following. The algorithm improved on the addition chain and the addition formula. Both improvements are based on the scalar multiplication by Montgomery [Mon87]. However, we firstly point out that the addition chain is applicable for not only Montgomery form curves but any type of curves. We enhance it to be suitable for implementation and study the security against the SPA compared with Coron's SPA-resistant algorithm (Algorithm 1'). We also establish the addition formulas, which only use the x-coordinate of the points, for the Weierstrass form curves.

4.1   Addition Chain

We describe our proposed addition chain in the following:

```
INPUT d, P, (n)
OUTPUT d*P
 1: Q[0] = P, Q[1] = 2*P
 2: for i=n-2 down to 0
 3:    Q[2] = ECDBL(Q[d[i]])
 4:    Q[1] = ECADD(Q[0],Q[1])
 5:    Q[0] = Q[2-d[i]]
 6:    Q[1] = Q[1+d[i]]
 7: return Q[0]
```

Algorithm 3: Our proposed addition chain (SPA resistant)

For each bit $d[i]$, we compute $Q[2] = \text{ECDBL } (Q[d[i]])$ in Step 3 and $Q[1] = \text{ECADD}(Q[0], Q[1])$ in Step 4. Then the values are assigned $Q[0] = Q[2], Q[1] = Q[1]$ if $d[i] = 0$ and $Q[0] = Q[1], Q[1] = Q[2]$ if $d[i] = 1$. We prove the correctness of our proposed algorithm in the following.

Theorem 1. *Algorithm 3, on input a point P and an integer $d > 2$, outputs the correct value of the scalar multiplication $d * P$.*

Proof. When we write $Q[0], Q[1]$, it means that $Q[0]$ in Step 5 and $Q[1]$ in Step 6 of Algorithm 3 in the following. The loop of Step 2 generates a sequence

$$(Q[0], Q[1])_{n-2}, (Q[0], Q[1])_{n-3}, ..., (Q[0], Q[1])_1, (Q[0], Q[1])_0, \qquad (3)$$

from the bit sequence $d[n-2], d[n-3], ..., d[1], d[0]$. At first we prove $Q[1] = Q[0] + P$ for each $(Q[0], Q[1])_i, i = 0, 1, .., n - 2$, by the induction for the number of the sequence. For $n = 2$ we have only one loop in Step 3 and we have two cases $d[0] = 0$ or 1. Then we obtain $Q[0] = 2 * P, Q[1] = 3 * P$ for $d[0] = 0$, and $Q[0] = 3 * P, Q[1] = 4 * P$ for $d[0] = 1$. The fact $Q[1] = Q[0] + P$ is correct for $n = 2$. Next, we assume that $Q[1] = Q[0] + P$ up to $n = k$. In this case we have $R[1] = R[0] + P$, where $(Q[0], Q[1])_1 = (R[0], R[1])$. For $n = k + 1$ we also have two cases $d[0] = 0$ or 1. Then we obtain $Q[0] = 2 * R[0], Q[1] = 2 * R[0] + P$ for

$d[0] = 0$, and $Q[0] = 2 * R[0] + P, Q[1] = 2 * R[0] + 2 * P$ for $d[0] = 1$. The fact $Q[1] = Q[0] + P$ is correct for $n = k + 1$. Thus we proved that $Q[1] = Q[0] + P$ for each $(Q[0], Q[1])_i, i = 0, 1, .., n - 2$.

Next, we prove that $Q[0]$ is equivalent to $Q[0]$ in Step 4 of Algorithm 1 ($Q[0]$ in Step 5 of Algorithm 2) for each loop of $d[i], (i = 0, 1, .., n - 2)$. In each loop of $d[i]$, for given $Q[0], Q[1]$, the new $Q[0]$ is computed as follows: ECDBL($Q[0]$) for $d[i] = 0$ and ECADD($Q[0], Q[1]$) $= Q[0] + (Q[0] + P) = 2 * Q[0] + P =$ ECADD(ECDBL($Q[0]$), P) for $d[i] = 1$. On the other hand, in each loop of $d[i]$ in Algorithm 1, for given $Q[0]$, the new $Q[0]$ is computed as follows: ECDBL($Q[0]$) for $d[i] = 0$ and ECADD(ECDBL($Q[0]$), P) for $d[i] = 1$. They are completely the same computations. Thus we can conclude that the output $d * P$ is correct.

Algorithm 3 requires one ECDBL in the initial Step 1, and $(n - 1)$ ECDBLs and $(n - 1)$ ECADDs in the loop. The computation time of the loop is same as that of Algorithm 1'.

Remark 1. Algorithm 3 does not depend on the representation of elliptic curves, and it is applicable to execute a modular exponentiation in any abelian group. Therefore the RSA cryptosystem, the DSA, the ElGamal cryptosystem can use our proposed algorithm.

Parallel Computation: First, note that ECADD and ECDBL of each loop of Algorithm 2' can be computed in parallel. Algorithm 2' then requires only n ECADDs with two processors. However, Algorithm 1' cannot be parallelized in this sense, because its loop is constructed from the most significant bit, and the output of ECADD requires the output of ECDBL in each loop. The addition chain of Algorithm 3 is also constructed from the most significant bit, but we can compute the loop of Algorithm 3 in parallel.

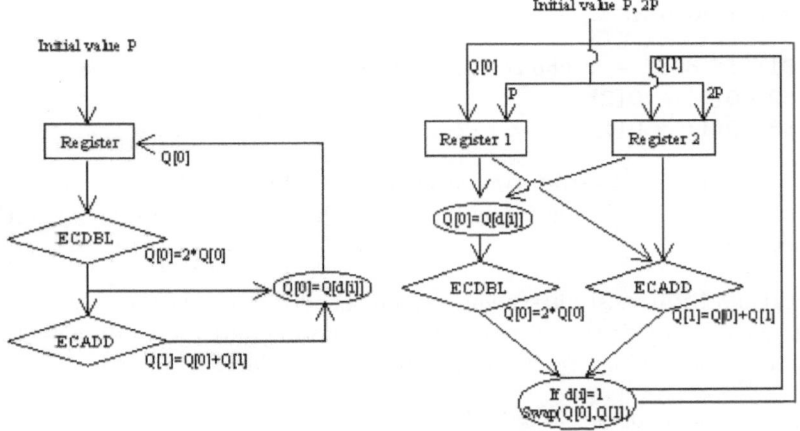

Fig. 1. Algorithm 1' (left), the parallel implementation of Algorithm 3 (right)

In the right side of Figure 1 we show an architecture of the parallel computation of the loop of Algorithm 3. It has two registers: Register 1 and Register 2, which are initially assigned $Q[0] = P$ and $Q[1] = 2 * P$, respectively. In Step 3, we choose the value $Q[d[i]]$ based on the bit information $d[i]$, then compute $\mathrm{ECDBL}(Q[d[i]])$ from $Q[d[i]]$. In Step 4, we compute $\mathrm{ECADD}(Q[0], Q[1])$ from the value $Q[0]$ in Register 1 and $Q[1]$ in Register 2. In both Step 3 and Step 4, they do not need the output from Step 3 nor Step 4, and they are excused independently. After finishing to compute both $\mathrm{ECDBL}(Q[d[i]])$ and $\mathrm{ECADD}(Q[0], Q[1])$, we assign the values in Register 1 and Register 2 based on the bit $d[i]$. If $d[i] = 0$, we assign the $\mathrm{ECDBL}(Q[d[i]])$ in Register 1 and the $\mathrm{ECADD}(Q[0], Q[1])$ in Register 2. If $d[i] = 1$, we swap the two variables, then we assign the $\mathrm{ECADD}(Q[0], Q[1])$ in Register 1 and the $\mathrm{ECDBL}(Q[d[i]])$ in Register 1.

In general the computation of an ECADD is slower than that of an ECDBL, so that the latency of the loop in Algorithm 3 depends on the running time of ECADDs. Thus the total running time of Algorithm 3 is one ECDBL and $(n-1)$ ECADDs, where n is the bit-length of d. Algorithm 1' always requires $(n-1)$ ECDBLs and $(n-1)$ ECADDs. The improvement of Algorithm 3 from Algorithm 1' is $(n-1)$ ECDBLs.

Security Consideration: We discuss the security of Algorithm 3 against the SCA. Algorithm 1' is commonly believed secure against the SPA [OS00]. The relation between Algorithm 1' and Algorithm 3 is as follows.

Theorem 2. *Algorithm 3 is as secure as Algorithm 1' against the SPA, if we use a computing architecture whose swapping power of two variables is negligible.*

Proof. The differences between Algorithm 1' and Algorithm 3 are Step 5 and Step 6 in Algorithm 3. In the steps, if $d[i] = 0$, we assign the $Q[0] = Q[2]$ and $Q[1] = Q[1]$, otherwise, we assign $Q[0] = Q[1]$ and $Q[1] = Q[2]$. We can modify the steps as follows:

```
S1: If d[i] = 1 then SWAP(Q[2],Q[1])
S2: Q[0] = Q[2]
S3: Q[1] = Q[1]
```

SWAP is a function to swap two variables. Only Step S1 depends on $d[i]$. If the power to execute SWAP is negligible, Algorithm 3 is as secure as Algorithm 1' against the SPA.

Next, an SPA-resistant scheme can be converted to a DPA-resistant scheme using Coron's 3rd or the Joye-Tymen's countermeasure as we discussed in the previous section. Thus, we have the following corollary.

Corollary 1. *Algorithm 3 with Coron's 3rd or Joye-Tymen's countermeasure is as secure as Algorithm 1' against the DPA, if we use a computing architecture whose swapping power of two variables is negligible.*

It is possible to implement the swapping of two variables in hardware using a few logic gates. Its power is usually negligible. In software we can implement it just to swap two pointer assignments. The swapping of the pointer assignments in software can be executed in several clocks, whose time or power trace is negligible. Therefore, our proposed method is secure against the DPA in many computing environments.

4-Parallel Computation: When a table of pre-computed points is allowed to be used, we can construct a scalar multiplication, which can be computed in parallel with more than two processors. There are several scalar multiplications using a pre-computed table [Gor98]. In this paper we are interested in a scalar multiplication with a very small table. The method that uses a very small table is proposed by Lim-Lee [LL94]. The simplest case of the Lim-Lee algorithm requires only one pre-computed value and its improvement over the binary method is $7/12$ on average. We review it in the following. Let $d = d_{n-1}2^{n-1} + d_{n-2}2^{n-2} + \ldots + d_1 2 + d_0$ be the binary representation of d with $d_{n-1} = 1$. Let $k = \lfloor n/2 \rfloor$. The exponent d is represented as

$$d = 2^k(f[k]2^k + f[k-1]2^{k-1} + \ldots + f[0]2^0) + (e[k]2^k + e[k-1]2^{k-1} + \ldots + e[0]2^0), \quad (4)$$

where $e[i] = d[i], f[i] = d[i+k]$ for $i = 0, 1, \ldots, k-1$, $f[k] = e[k] = 0$ for even n, and $f[k] = 1, e[k] = 0$ for odd n. Then we obtain $d*P = \sum_{i=0}^{k}(2^i)*(e[i]*P + f[i]*((2^k)*P))$, and $d*P$ can be computed like in the binary method. This method pre-computes the point $(2^k)*P$ and it is applied for only scalar exponentiations of the fixed based P. We modify the Lim-Lee method to be able to compute in parallel and to be secure against the SPA. The proposed algorithm carries 4 auxiliary variables $Q[0][0], Q[0][1], Q[1][0], Q[0][1]$, which are related with

$$Q[0][1] = Q[0][0] + P, Q[1][0] = Q[0][0] + 2^k*P, Q[1][1] = Q[0][0] + P + 2^k*P, \quad (5)$$

The proposed algorithm is as follows:

```
    INPUT d, P, (2^k)*P, (k, b (= n+1 mod 2))
    OUTPUT d*P
    1:  Q[0] = (2^k)*P, Q[1] = (2^k)*P + P
    2:  Q[0][0] = Q[e[k-b]]
    3:  Q[0][1] = Q[0][0] + P
    4:  Q[1][0] = Q[0][0] + (2^k)*P
    5:  Q[1][1] = Q[0][0] + P + (2^k)*P
    6:  for i = k-1-b down to 0
    7:      Q[f[i]+0][e[i]+0] = ECDBL(Q[f[i]][e[i]])
    8:      Q[f[i]+0][e[i]+1] = ECADD(Q[f[i]][e[i]],Q[f[i]+0][e[i]+1])
    9:      Q[f[i]+1][e[i]+0] = ECADD(Q[f[i]][e[i]],Q[f[i]+1][e[i]+0])
    10:     Q[f[i]+1][e[i]+1] = ECADD(Q[f[i]][e[i]],Q[f[i]+1][e[i]+1])
    11: return Q[0][0]
```

Algorithm 4: Our proposed addition chain II (SPA resistant)

Due to space limitations, we omit the proof of the correctness of Algorithm 4. When we compute from Step 7 to Step 10 in parallel, the latency of each loop is the time for computing ECADDs. The total number of loops is at most $n/2 - 1$, where n is the bit-length of d. Therefore Algorithm 4 can be computed at most $(n/2+3)$ ECADDs with 4 processors. It is about two times faster than Algorithm 3. Moreover, the security against the SPA can be discussed in the same way like Theorem 1 for Algorithm 3. If we use a computing architecture whose swapping powers of four variables are negligible, then Algorithm 4 is secure against the SPA. It is possible to apply Coron's 3rd or Joye-Tymen's countermeasure to make Algorithm 4 secure against the DPA.

4.2   Addition Formula

Let E be an elliptic curve defined by the standard Weierstrass form (1) and $P_1 = (x_1, y_1)$, $P_2 = (x_2, y_2)$, $P_3 = P_1 + P_2 = (x_3, y_3)$ be points on $E(K)$. Moreover, let $P_3' = P_1 - P_2 = (x_3', y_3')$. Then we obtain the following relations:

$$x_3 \cdot x_3' = \frac{(x_1 x_2 - a)^2 - 4b(x_1 + x_2)}{(x_1 - x_2)^2}, \quad x_3 + x_3' = \frac{2(x_1 + x_2)(x_1 x_2 + a) + 4b}{(x_1 - x_2)^2}. \quad (6)$$

On the other hand, letting $P_4 = 2 * P_1 = (x_4, y_4)$ leads to the relation

$$x_4 = \frac{(x_1^2 - a)^2 - 8bx_1}{4(x_1^3 + ax_1 + b)}. \quad (7)$$

Thus the x-coordinates of both P_3 and P_4 can be computed just form the x-coordinates of the points P_1, P_2, P_3'. We call this method the multiplicative (additive) x-coordinate-only method. The x-coordinate-only methods for a scalar multiplication were originally introduced by Montgomery [Mon87]. However, his main interest was to find a special form of elliptic curves on which the computing times are optimal. The additive method was not discussed in his paper.

When we use the x-coordinate-only methods, we need the difference of two points $P_3' = P_1 - P_2$. This may be a problem in general, but not in Algorithm 3. In each loop of Algorithm 3, the two points $(Q[0], Q[1])$ are simultaneously computed and they satisfy the equation $Q[1] - Q[0] = P$, where P is a base point of the scalar multiplication. Similarly, in each loop of Algorithm 4, the differences of the points for computing an ECADD are known by equation (5). Therefore, we can assume that the difference $P_2 - P_1$ for input values of ECADD(P_1, P_2) of Algorithm 3 (or Algorithm 4) are always known. On the contrary, in order to know that of Algorithm 2' we need extra computation. The x-coordinate-only methods for Algorithm 2' have no computational advantage.

When we apply the x-coordinate-only methods to Algorithm 3 (or Algorithm 4), the output is only the x-coordinate of $d * P$. This is enough for some cryptographic applications such as a key exchange scheme and an encryption/decryption scheme [SEC]. But other applications also require the y-coordinate of $d * P$ in the verification of a signature scheme [SEC]. However, the y-coordinate of $d * P$ is easily obtained in the following way: The final values of

$Q[0], Q[1]$ in Algorithm 3 (or Algorithm 4) are related by $Q[1] = Q[C] + P$. Let $P = (x_1, y_1), Q[0] = (x_2, y_2), Q[1] = (x_3, y_3)$. Here known values are x_1, y_1, x_2, x_3 and the target is y_2. Using a standard addition formula (2), we obtain the equation $y_2 = (2y_1)^{-1}(y_1^2 + x_2^3 + ax_2 + b - (x_1 - x_2)^2(x_1 + x_2 + x_3))$. This y-recovering technique was originally introduced by Agnew et al. for curves over $\mathbb{F}_{2^m}$ [AMV93]. The computing time for y-recovering is $16M + 4S + 1I$. [2]

In the implementation of the x-coordinate-only methods, the projective coordinate system offers a faster computation. In this system, equations (6) and (7) turn to be

$$\frac{X_3}{Z_3} = \frac{Z_3'}{X_3'} \frac{(X_1 X_2 - aZ_1 Z_2)^2 - 4bZ_1 Z_2(X_1 Z_2 + X_2 Z_1)}{(X_1 Z_2 - X_2 Z_1)^2}, \tag{8}$$

$$\frac{X_3}{Z_3} = \frac{2(X_1 Z_2 + X_2 Z_1)(X_1 X_2 + aZ_1 Z_2) + 4bZ_1^2 Z_2^2}{(X_1 Z_2 - X_2 Z_1)^2} - \frac{X_3'}{Z_3'}, \tag{9}$$

$$\frac{X_4}{Z_4} = \frac{(X_1^2 - aZ_1^2)^2 - 8bX_1 Z_1^3}{4(X_1 Z_1(X_1^2 + aZ_1^2) + bZ_1^4)}. \tag{10}$$

The computing times for (8),(9),(10) are $\text{ECADD}_m^{(x)} = 9M + 2S$, $\text{ECADD}_a^{(x)} = 10M + 2S$, $\text{ECDBL}^{(x)} = 6M + 3S$. If $Z_3' = 1$, the computing times deduce to $\text{ECADD}_{m(Z_3'=1)}^{(x)} = \text{ECADD}_{a(Z_3'=1)}^{(x)} = 8M + 2S$. The concrete algorithms to compute (8), (9), (10) are listed in the appendix.

5   Comparison

In this section, we compare the computing times of a scalar multiplication resistant against the SCA. As a result, we show that our proposed algorithm establishes a faster scalar multiplication. The improvement of our scalar multiplication over the previously fastest method is about 37% for two processors and 5.7% for a single processor.

Estimation: We compare the computing times of a scalar multiplication with Algorithm 1', 2', and 3 using different coordinate systems. All algorithms are assumed to be DPA-resistant using Coron's 3rd countermeasure or Joye-Tymen's countermeasure, which are described in Section 3. We estimate the total times to output a scalar multiplication $d * P = (x_d, y_d)$ on input d, $P = (x, y)$ and elliptic curve information (a, b, p). The times are given in terms of the numbers of the arithmetic in the definition field, i.e., the multiplication M, the squaring S, and the inverse I. Note that one inversion is always required in order to convert a point from the projective coordinates to the affine coordinates. In the estimation,

---

[2]   A similar discussion for y-recovering on Montgomery form is found in [OS01]. However, Algorithm 2 and Algorithm 4 in [OS01] doesn't output the expected values. The formulas for them must be $X_d^{rec} = 4By X_{d+1} Z_{d+1} Z_d X_d$, $Y_d^{rec} = Z_{d+1}^2 U^2 - X_{d+1}^2 V^2$, $Z_d^{rec} = 4By X_{d+1} Z_{d+1} Z_d^2$ and y-recovering needs only $13M + 1I$, which is faster than Algorithm 3 in [OS01].

we include the times for randomization by Coron's 3rd countermeasure or Joye-Tymen's countermeasure, and the times for recovering the y-coordinate in the x-coordinate-only method are also included. [3] In the estimation, we also give the estimated running time for a 160-bit scalar. The last numbers in the brackets are the estimation for $1S = 0.8M, 1I = 30M$ [OS01].

Single Case: In Table 2, we summarize the estimated running time using a single processor. Algorithm 3/Joye-Tymen with the x-coordinate-only methods is the fastest of all scalar multiplications ($2929.0M$). The previously fastest algorithm was Algorithm 1'/Joye-Tymen with the Jacobian coordinate system $\mathcal{J}$ ($3095.0M$). The improvement of the proposed algorithm over it is about 5.7%.

Table 2. Computing times of a scalar multiplication (a single processor)

	Addition formula	Computing Time	
		Total	$n = 160$
Algorithm 1'	$\mathcal{P}$	$(19n - 15)M + (7n - 7)S + 1I$	$3025M + 1113S + 1I$ $(3945.4M)$
/Coron 3rd	$\mathcal{J}$	$(16n - 10)M + (10n - 8)S + 1I$	$2550M + 1592S + 1I$ $(3853.6M)$
	$\mathcal{J}^{c}$	$(16n - 10)M + (9n - 7)S + 1I$	$2550M + 1433S + 1I$ $(3726.4M)$
	$\mathcal{J}^{m}$	$(17n - 10)M + (10n - 7)S + 1I$	$2710M + 1593S + 1I$ $(4014.4M)$
Algorithm 1'	$\mathcal{P}$	$(16n - 7)M + (7n - 4)S + 1I$	$2553M + 1116S + 1I$ $(3475.8M)$
/Joye-Tymen	$\mathcal{J}$	$(12n - 3)M + (9n - 5)S + 1I$	$1917M + 1435S + 1I$ $(3095.0M)$
	$\mathcal{J}^{c}$	$(13n - 4)M + (9n - 5)S + 1I$	$2076M + 1435S + 1I$ $(3254.0M)$
	$\mathcal{J}^{m}$	$(13n - 4)M + (9n - 5)S + 1I$	$2076M + 1435S + 1I$ $(3254.0M)$
Algorithm 2'	$\mathcal{P}$	$(19n + 4)M + 7nS + 1I$	$3085M + 1120S + 1I$ $(4011.0M)$
/Coron 3rd	$\mathcal{J}$	$(16n + 6)M + (10n + 2)S + 1I$	$2566M + 1602s + 1I$ $(3877.6M)$
	$\mathcal{J}^{c}$	$(16n + 16)M + (9n + 2)S + 1I$	$2566M + 1442S + 1I$ $(3749.6M)$
	$\mathcal{J}^{m}$	$(17n + 7)M + (10n + 3)S + 1I$	$2727M + 1603S + 1I$ $(4039.4M)$
Algorithm 2'	$\mathcal{P}$	$(19n + 9)M + (7n + 3)S + 1I$	$3049M + 1123S + 1I$ $(3977.4M)$
/Joye-Tymen	$\mathcal{J}$	$(16n + 9)M + (10n + 4)S + 1I$	$2569M + 1604S + 1I$ $(3882.2M)$
	$\mathcal{J}^{c}$	$(16n + 9)M + (9n + 4)S + 1I$	$2569M + 1444S + 1I$ $(3754.2M)$
	$\mathcal{J}^{m}$	$(13n + 9)M + (9n + 4)S + 1I$	$2089M + 1444S + 1I$ $(3274.2M)$
Algorithm 3	$\mathcal{P}$	$(19n - 8)M + (7n - 2)S + 1I$	$3032M + 1118S + 1I$ $(3956.4M)$
/Coron 3rd	$\mathcal{J}$	$(16n - 6)M + (10n - 2)S + 1I$	$2554M + 1598S + 1I$ $(3862.4M)$
	$\mathcal{J}^{c}$	$(16n - 5)M + (9n - 1)S + 1I$	$2555M + 1439S + 1I$ $(3736.2M)$
	$\mathcal{J}^{m}$	$(17n - 6)M + (10n - 3)S + 1I$	$2714M + 1597S + 1I$ $(4021.6M)$
	x (mul)	$\mathbf{(15n + 8)M + (5n + 2)S + 1I}$	$\mathbf{2408M + 802S + 1I}$ $\mathbf{(3079.6M)}$
	x (add)	$\mathbf{(16n + 7)M + (5n + 2)S + 1I}$	$\mathbf{2567M + 802S + 1I}$ $\mathbf{(3238.6M)}$
Algorithm 3	$\mathcal{P}$	$(19n - 4)M + 7nS + 1I$	$3036M + 1120S + 1I$ $(3962.0M)$
/Joye-Tymen	$\mathcal{J}$	$(16n - 4)M + (10n - 1)S + 1I$	$2556M + 1599S + 1I$ $(3865.2M)$
	$\mathcal{J}^{c}$	$(16n - 3)M + 9nM + 1I$	$2557M + 1440S + 1I$ $(3739.0M)$
	$\mathcal{J}^{m}$	$(17n - 5)M + (10n - 3)S + 1I$	$2715M + 1597S + 1I$ $(4022.6M)$
	x (mul)	$\mathbf{(14n + 15)M + (5n + 5)S + 1I}$	$\mathbf{2255M + 805S + 1I}$ $\mathbf{(2929.0M)}$
	x (add)	$\mathbf{(14n + 15)M + (5n + 5)S + 1I}$	$\mathbf{2255M + 805S + 1I}$ $\mathbf{(2929.0M)}$

---

[3] These algorithms may contain several inversions, but we can compute them by only one inversion and several multiplications instead. For example, we estimate two inversions $x^{-1}, y^{-1} \in \mathbb{F}_p$ as the cost for computing $z = (xy)^{-1}$, $x^{-1} = zy$ and $y^{-1} = zx$, that is, one inversion and three multiplications.

In order to demonstrate the efficiency of our algorithm, we implemented our proposed algorithm and the previously fastest algorithm on a Celeron 500 MHz using the LiDIA library [LiDIA]. It should be emphasized here that our implementation was not optimized for cryptographic purposes — it is only intended to provide a comparison. The improvement is about 10%. The results are as follows:

Table 3. Computing times on a Celeron 500 MHz using LiDIA (a single processor)

Previously fastest scheme	Algorithm 1'/Joye-Tymen ($\mathcal{J}$)	25.5 ms
Proposed scheme	Algorithm 3 /Joye-Tymen (x)	23.1 ms

Parallel Case: In Table 4, we summarize the estimated running time using two parallel processors. Algorithm 1' cannot be computed in parallel and Algorithm 2' has no computational advantage to use the x-coordinate-only methods. Therefore, the previously fastest algorithm was Algorithm 2'/Coron's 3rd with the Chudonovsky coordinate system $\mathcal{J}^C$ ($2181.6M$). Algorithm 3/Joye-Tymen with x-coordinate-only methods provides the fastest multiplication ($1593.4M$). The improvement of the proposed algorithm over it is about 37%.

Table 4. Computing times of a scalar multiplication (two parallel processors)

	Addition formula	Computing Time	
		Total	$n = 160$
Algorithm 2'	$\mathcal{P}$	$(12n+4)M + 2nS + 1I$	$1924M + 320S + 1I$ $\quad$ ($2210.0M$)
/Coron 3rd	$\mathcal{J}$	$(12n+6)M + (4n+2)S + 1I$	$1926M + 642S + 1I$ $\quad$ ($2469.6M$)
	$\mathcal{J}^C$	$(11n+6)M + (3n+2)S + 1I$	$1766M + 482S + 1I$ $\quad$ ($2181.6M$)
	$\mathcal{J}^m$	$(13n+7)M + (6n+3)S + 1I$	$2087M + 963S + 1I$ $\quad$ ($2887.4M$)
Algorithm 2'	$\mathcal{P}$	$(12n+9)M + (2n+3)S + 1I$	$1929M + 323S + 1I$ $\quad$ ($2217.4M$)
/Joye-Tymen	$\mathcal{J}$	$(12n+9)M + (4n+4)S + 1I$	$1929M + 644S + 1I$ $\quad$ ($2474.2M$)
	$\mathcal{J}^C$	$(11n+9)M + (3n+4)S + 1I$	$1769M + 484S + 1I$ $\quad$ ($2186.2M$)
	$\mathcal{J}^m$	$(13n+9)M + (6n+4)S + 1I$	$2089M + 964S + 1I$ $\quad$ ($2890.2M$)
Algorithm 3	$\mathcal{P}$	$(12n-1)M + (2n+3)S + 1I$	$1919M + 323S + 1I$ $\quad$ ($2207.4M$)
/Coron 3rd	$\mathcal{J}$	$(12n-2)M + (4n+4)S + 1I$	$1918M + 644S + 1I$ $\quad$ ($2463.2M$)
	$\mathcal{J}^C$	$11nM + (3n+5)S + 1I$	$1760M + 485S + 1I$ $\quad$ ($2178.0M$)
	$\mathcal{J}^m$	$(13n-2)M + (6n+1)S + 1I$	$2078M + 961S + 1I$ $\quad$ ($2876.8M$)
	x (mul)	$(9n+14)M + (2n+5)S + 1I$	$1454M + 325S + 1I$ $\quad$ ($1744.0M$)
	x (add)	$(10n+13)M + (2n+5)S + 1I$	$1613M + 325S + 1I$ $\quad$ ($1903.0M$)
Algorithm 3	$\mathcal{P}$	$(12n+3)M + (2n+5)S + 1I$	$1923M + 325S + 1I$ $\quad$ ($2213.0M$)
/Joye-Tymen	$\mathcal{J}$	$12nM + (4n+5)S + 1I$	$1920M + 645S + 1I$ $\quad$ ($2466.0M$)
	$\mathcal{J}^C$	$(11n+2)M + (3n+6)S + 1I$	$1762M + 486S + 1I$ $\quad$ ($2180.8M$)
	$\mathcal{J}^m$	$(13n-1)M + (6n+1)S + 1I$	$2079M + 961S + 1I$ $\quad$ ($2877.8M$)
	x (mul)	$(8n+21)M + (2n+8)S + 1I$	$1301M + 328S + 1I$ $\quad$ ($1593.4M$)
	x (add)	$(8n+21)M + (2n+8)S + 1I$	$1301M + 328S + 1I$ $\quad$ ($1593.4M$)

Acknowledgments

We would like to thank Edlyn Teske, Bodo Möller, and Evangelos Karatsiolis for their valuable comments, and the anonymous referees for their helpful comments.

References

AMV93. G.Agnew, R.Mullin and S.Vanstone, "An implementation of elliptic curve cryptosystems over $F_{2^{155}}$", *IEEE Journal on Selected Areas in Communications*, vol.11, pp.804-813, 1993.

ANSI. ANSI X9.62, Public Key Cryptography for the Financial Services Industry: The Elliptic Curve Digital Signature Algorithm (ECDSA), draft, 1998.

BSS99. I.Blake, G.Seroussi and N.Smart, *Elliptic Curves in Cryptography*, Cambridge University Press, 1999.

Cor99. J.Coron, "Resistance against differential power analysis for elliptic curve cryptosystems", *CHES'99*, LNCS 1717, pp.292-302, Springer-Verlag, 1999.

CMO98. H.Cohen, A.Miyaji and T.Ono, "Efficient elliptic curve exponentiation using mixed coordinates", *Asiacrypt'98*, LNCS 1514, pp.51-65, Springer-Verlag, 1998.

CJ01. C.Clavier and M.Joye, "Universal exponentiation algorithm – A first step towards provable SPA-resistance –", *CHES2001*, LNCS 2162, pp.300-308, Springer-Verlag, 2001.

Gor98. D.Gordon, "A survey of fast exponentiation methods", J. Algorithms, vol.27, pp.129-146, 1998.

IEEE. IEEE P1363, Standard Specifications for Public-Key Cryptography, 2000. Available from http://groupe.ieee.org/groups/1363/

JQ01. M. Joye and J. Quisquater, "Hessian elliptic curves and side-channel attacks", *CHES2001*, LNCS 2162, pp.402-410, Springer-Verlag, 2001.

JT01. M.Joye and C.Tymen, "Protections against differential analysis for elliptic curve cryptography", *CHES2001*, LNCS 2162, pp.377-390, Springer-Verlag, 2001.

Koc96. C.Kocher, "Timing attacks on Implementations of Diffie-Hellman, RSA, DSS, and other systems", *Crypto'96*, LNCS 1109, pp.104-113, Springer-Verlag, 1996.

KJJ99. C.Kocher, J.Jaffe and B.Jun, "Differential power analysis", *Crypto'99*, LNCS 1666, pp.388-397, Springer-Verlag, 1999.

LiDIA. LiDIA, A C++ Library For Computational Number Theory, Technische Universtät Darmstadt, http://www.informatik.tu-darmstadt.de/TI/LiDIA/

LS01. P.Liardet and N.Smart, "Preventing SPA/DPA in ECC systems using the Jacobi form", *CHES2001*, LNCS 2162, pp.391-401, Springer-Verlag, 2001.

LL94. C. Lim and P. Lee, "More flexible exponentiation with precomputation", *Crypto'94*, LNCS 839, p.95-107, Springer-Verlag, 1994.

Moe01. B.Möller, "Securing elliptic curve point multiplication against side-channel attacks", *ISC 2001*, LNCS 2200. p.324-334, Springer-Verlag, 2001.

Mon87. P.Montgomery, "Speeding the Pollard and elliptic curve methods for factorizations", *Math. of Comp*, vol.48, pp.243-264, 1987.

MO90. F. Morain and J. Olivos, "Speeding up the computation on an elliptic curve using addition-subtraction chains", Inform. Theory Appl. 24, pp.531-543, 2000.

NIST. National Institute of Standards and Technology, Recommended Elliptic Curves for Federal Government Use, in the appendix of FIPS 186-2, Available from http://csrc.nist.gov/publication/fips/fips186-2/fips186-2.pdf

OKS00. K.Okeya, H.Kurumatani and K.Sakurai, "Elliptic curves with the Montgomery form and their cryptographic applications", *PKC2000*, LNCS 1751, pp.446-465, Springer-Verlag, 2000.

OS00. K.Okeya and K.Sakurai, "Power analysis breaks elliptic curve cryptosystems even secure against the timing attack", *Indocrypt 2000*, LNCS 1977, pp.178-190, Springer-Verlag, 2000.

OS01. K.Okeya and K.Sakurai, "Efficient elliptic curve cryptosystems from a scalar multiplication algorithm with recovery of the y-coordinate on a Montgomery-form elliptic curve", *CHES2001*, LNCS 2162, pp.126-141, Springer-Verlag, 2001.

Sma01. N.Smart, "The Hessian form of an elliptic curve", *CHES2001*, LNCS 2162, pp.118-125, Springer-Verlag, 2001.

SEC. Standards for Efficient Cryptography Group (SECG), Specification of Standards for Efficient Cryptography. Available from http://www.secg.org

WAP. Wireless Application Protocol (WAP) Forum, Wireless Transport Layer Security (WTLS) Specification. Available from http://www.wapforum.org

Appendix

The appendix describes the formulas of $\texttt{ECDBL}^{(x)}$, $\texttt{ECADD}_m^{(x)}$, and $\texttt{ECADD}_a^{(x)}$, which are proposed in Section 5. In order to estimate the efficiency, we use three notations $\times, \cdot, *$ for the multiplication of the definition field K. The notation $\times$ is a standard multiplication in K. The notation $\cdot$ is executed in negligible time. The notation $*$ is also calculated in negligible time if we choose $Z_3' = 1$.

$$
\begin{aligned}
T_1 &\leftarrow X_1 \times X_2 \\
T_2 &\leftarrow Z_1 \times Z_2 \\
T_3 &\leftarrow X_1 \times Z_2 \\
T_4 &\leftarrow X_2 \times Z_1 \\
T_5 &\leftarrow a \times T_2 \ (= a Z_1 Z_2) \\
T_6 &\leftarrow T_1 - T_5 \ (= X_1 X_2 - a Z_1 Z_2) \\
T_7 &\leftarrow T_6^2 \ (= (X_1 X_2 - a Z_1 Z_2)^2) \\
T_8 &\leftarrow b \times T_2 \ (= b Z_1 Z_2) \\
T_9 &\leftarrow 4 \cdot T_8 \ (= 4 b Z_1 Z_2) \\
T_{10} &\leftarrow T_3 + T_4 \ (= X_1 Z_2 + X_2 Z_1) \\
T_{11} &\leftarrow T_9 \times T_{10} \ (= 4 b Z_1 Z_2 (X_1 Z_2 + X_2 Z_1)) \\
T_{12} &\leftarrow T_7 - T_{11} \ (= (X_1 X_2 - a Z_1 Z_2)^2 - 4 b Z_1 Z_2 (X_1 Z_2 + X_2 Z_1)) \\
X_3 &\leftarrow Z_3' * T_{12} \\
T_{13} &\leftarrow T_3 - T_4 \ (= X_1 Z_2 - X_2 Z_1) \\
T_{14} &\leftarrow T_{13}^2 \ (= (X_1 Z_2 - X_2 Z_1)^2) \\
Z_3 &\leftarrow X_3' \times T_{14}
\end{aligned}
$$

Formula 1. Computing $\texttt{ECADD}_m^{(x)}$ ($\cdot$ is negligible, $*$ is negligible if $Z_3' = 1$)

$$T_1 \leftarrow X_1 \times X_2$$
$$T_2 \leftarrow Z_1 \times Z_2$$
$$T_3 \leftarrow X_1 \times Z_2$$
$$T_4 \leftarrow X_2 \times Z_1$$
$$T_5 \leftarrow T_3 + T_4 \ (= X_1 Z_2 + X_2 Z_1)$$
$$T_6 \leftarrow a \times T_2 \ (= a Z_1 Z_2)$$
$$T_7 \leftarrow T_1 + T_6 \ (= X_1 X_2 + a Z_1 Z_2)$$
$$T_8 \leftarrow T_5 \times T_7 \ (= (X_1 Z_2 + X_2 Z_1)(X_1 X_2 + a Z_1 Z_2))$$
$$T_9 \leftarrow 2 \cdot T_8 \ (= 2(X_1 Z_2 + X_2 Z_1)(X_1 X_2 + a Z_1 Z_2))$$
$$T_{10} \leftarrow T_2^2 \ (= Z_1^2 Z_2^2)$$
$$T_{11} \leftarrow b \times T_{10} \ (b Z_1^2 Z_2^2)$$
$$T_{12} \leftarrow 4 \cdot T_{11} \ (= 4 b Z_1^2 Z_2^2)$$
$$T_{13} \leftarrow T_9 + T_{12} \ (= 2(X_1 Z_2 + X_2 Z_1)(X_1 X_2 + a Z_1 Z_2) + 4 b Z_1^2 Z_2^2)$$
$$T_{14} \leftarrow T_3 - T_4 \ (= X_1 Z_2 - X_2 Z_1)$$
$$T_{15} \leftarrow T_{14}^2 \ (= (X_1 Z_2 - X_2 Z_1)^2)$$
$$T_{16} \leftarrow Z_3' * T_{13}$$
$$T_{17} \leftarrow X_3' \times T_{15}$$
$$X_3 \leftarrow T_{16} - T_{17}$$
$$Z_3 \leftarrow Z_3' * T_{15}$$

Formula 2. Computing $\mathtt{ECADD}_a^{(x)}$ ($\cdot$ is negligible, $*$ is negligible if $Z_3' = 1$)

$$T_1 \leftarrow X_1^2$$
$$T_2 \leftarrow Z_1^2$$
$$T_3 \leftarrow a \times T_2 \ (= a Z_1^2)$$
$$T_4 \leftarrow T_1 - T_3 \ (= X_1^2 - a Z_1^2)$$
$$T_5 \leftarrow T_4^2 \ (= (X_1^2 - a Z_1^2)^2)$$
$$T_6 \leftarrow b \times T_2 \ (= b Z_1^2)$$
$$T_7 \leftarrow X_1 \times Z_1 \ (= X_1 Z_1)$$
$$T_8 \leftarrow T_6 \times T_7 \ (= b X_1 Z_1^3)$$
$$T_9 \leftarrow 8 \cdot T_8 \ (= 8 b X_1 Z_1^3)$$
$$X_4 \leftarrow T_5 - T_9$$
$$T_{10} \leftarrow T_1 + T_3 \ (= X_1^2 + a Z_1^2)$$
$$T_{11} \leftarrow T_7 \times T_{10} \ (= X_1 Z_1 (X_1^2 + a Z_1^2))$$
$$T_{12} \leftarrow T_6 \times T_2 \ (= b Z_1^4)$$
$$T_{13} \leftarrow T_{11} + T_{12} \ (= X_1 Z_1 (X_1^2 + a Z_1^2) + b Z_1^4)$$
$$Z_4 \leftarrow 4 \cdot T_{13}$$

Formula 3. Computing $\mathtt{ECDBL}^{(x)}$ ($\cdot$ is negligible)

New European Schemes for Signature, Integrity and Encryption (NESSIE): A Status Report

Bart Preneel

Katholieke Univ. Leuven, Dept. Electrical Engineering-ESAT,
Kasteelpark Arenberg 10, B-3001 Leuven-Heverlee, Belgium
bart.preneel@esat.kuleuven.ac.be

Abstract. In February 2000 the NESSIE project has launched an open call for the next generation of cryptographic algorithms. These algorithms should offer a higher security and/or confidence level than existing ones, and should be better suited for the constraints of future hardware and software environments. The NESSIE project has received 39 algorithms, many of these from major players. In October 2001, the project completed the first phase of the evaluation and has selected 24 algorithms for the second phase. The goal is to recommend a complete portfolio of algorithms by the end of 2002. This article presents the status of the NESSIE project after two years.

1 Introduction

NESSIE (New European Schemes for Signature, Integrity, and Encryption) is a research project within the Information Societies Technology (IST) Programme of the European Commission. The participants of the project are:

- Katholieke Universiteit Leuven (Belgium), coordinator;
- Ecole Normale Supérieure (France);
- Royal Holloway, University of London (U.K.);
- Siemens Aktiengesellschaft (Germany);
- Technion - Israel Institute of Technology (Israel);
- Université Catholique de Louvain (Belgium); and
- Universitetet i Bergen (Norway).

NESSIE is a 3-year project, which started on January 1, 2000. This paper presents the state of the project after two years, and it is organized as follows. Section 2 discusses the NESSIE call and its results. Section 3 discusses the tools which the project is developing to support the evaluation process. Sections 4 and 5 deal with the security and performance evaluation respectively, and Sect. 6 discusses the selection of algorithms for the 2nd phase. Section 7 raises some intellectual property issues. The NESSIE approach towards dissemination and standardization is presented in Section 8. Finally, conclusions are put forward in Section 9.

Detailed and up to date information on the NESSIE project is available at the project web site http://cryptonessie.org/.

D. Naccache and P. Paillier (Eds.): PKC 2002, LNCS 2274, pp. 297–309, 2002.

2   NESSIE Call

In the first year of the project, an open call for the submission of cryptographic algorithms, as well as for evaluation methodologies for these algorithms has been launched. The scope of this call has been defined together with the project industry board (PIB) (cf. Sect. 8), and it was published in February 2000. The deadline for submissions was September 29, 2000. In response to this call NESSIE received 40 submissions, all of which met the submission requirements.

2.1   Contents of the NESSIE Call

The NESSIE call includes a request for a broad set of algorithms providing date confidentiality, data authentication, and entity authentication. These algorithms include block ciphers, stream ciphers, hash functions, MAC algorithms, digital signature schemes, and public-key encryption and identification schemes (for definitions of these algorithms, see [14]). In addition, the NESSIE call asks for evaluation methodologies for these algorithms. While key establishment protocols are also very important, it was felt that they should be excluded from the call, as the scope of the call is already rather broad.

The scope of the NESSIE call is much wider than that of the AES call launched by NIST [16], which was restricted to 128-bit block ciphers. It is comparable to that of the RACE Project RIPE (Race Integrity Primitives Evaluation, 1988-1992) [22] (confidentiality algorithms were excluded from RIPE for political reasons) and that of the Japanese CRYPTREC project [4] (which also includes key establishment protocols and pseudo-random number generation). Another difference is that both AES and CRYPTREC intend to produce algorithms for government standards. The results of NESSIE will not be adopted by any government or by the European commission. However, the intention is that relevant standardization bodies will adopt these results. As an example, algorithms for digital signature and hash functions may be included in the EESSI standardization documents which specify algorithms recommended for the European Electronic Signature Directive.

The call also specifies the main selection criteria which will be used to evaluate the proposals. These criteria are long-term security, market requirements, efficiency, and flexibility. Primitives can be targeted towards a specific environment (such as 8-bit smart cards or high-end 64-bit processors), but it is clearly an advantage to offer a wide flexibility of use. Security is put forward as the most important criterion, as security of a cryptographic algorithm is essential to achieve confidence and to build consensus.

For the *security requirements* of symmetric algorithms, two main security levels are specified, named *normal* and *high*. The minimal requirements for a symmetric algorithm to attain either the normal or high security level depend on the key length, internal memory, or output length of the algorithm. For block ciphers a third security level, *normal-legacy*, is specified, with a block size of 64 bits compared to 128 bits for the normal and high security level. The motivation for this request are applications such as UMTS/3GPP, which intend to use 64-bit block ciphers for the next 10-15 years. For the asymmetric algorithms a varying security level is accepted, with as minimum about 2^{80} 3-DES encryptions.

If selected by NESSIE, the algorithm should preferably be available royalty-free. If this is not possible, then access should be non-discriminatory. The submitter should state the position concerning intellectual property and should update it when necessary.

The submission requirements are much less stringent than for AES, particularly in terms of the requirement for software implementations (only 'portable C' is mandatory).

2.2   Response to the NESSIE Call

The cryptographic community has responded very enthusiastically to the call. Thirty nine algorithms have been received, as well as one proposal for a testing methodology. After an interaction process, which took about one month, all submissions comply with the requirements of the call. There are 26 symmetric algorithms

- seventeen block ciphers, which is probably not a surprise given the increased attention to block cipher design and evaluation as a consequence of the AES competition organized by NIST. They are divided as follows:
  - six 64-bit block ciphers: CS-Cipher, Hierocrypt-L1, IDEA, Khazad, MISTY1, and Nimbus;
  - seven 128-bit block ciphers: Anubis, Camellia, Grand Cru, Hierocrypt-3, Noekeon, Q, and SC2000 (none of these seven come from the AES process);
  - one 160-bit block cipher: Shacal; and
  - three block ciphers with a variable block length: NUSH (64, 128, and 256 bits), RC6 (at least 128 bits), and SAFER++ (64 and 128 bits).
- six synchronous stream ciphers: BMGL, Leviathan, LILI-128, SNOW, SOBER-t16, and SOBER-t32.
- two MAC algorithms: Two-Track-MAC and UMAC; and
- one collision-resistant hash function: Whirlpool.

Thirteen asymmetric algorithms have been submitted:

- five asymmetric encryption schemes: ACE Encrypt, ECIES, EPOC, PSEC, and RSA-OAEP (both EPOC and PSEC have three variants);
- seven digital signature algorithms: ACE Sign, ECDSA, ESIGN, FLASH, QUARTZ, RSA-PSS, and SFLASH; and
- one identification scheme: GPS.

Approximately[1] seventeen submissions originated within Europe (6 from France, 4 from Belgium, 3 from Switzerland, 2 from Sweden), nine in North

---

[1] Fractional numbers have been used to take into account algorithms with submitters over several continents/countries – the totals here are approximations by integers, hence they do not add up to 40.

America (7 USA, 2 from Canada), nine in Asia (8 from Japan), three in Australia and three in South America (Brazil). The majority of submissions originated within industry (27); seven came from academia, and six are the result of a joint effort between industry and academia. Note however that the submitter of the algorithm may not be the inventor, hence the share of academic research is probably underestimated by these numbers.

On November 13–14, 2000 the first NESSIE workshop was organized in Leuven (Belgium), where most submissions were presented. All submissions are available on the NESSIE web site [15].

3   Tools

It is clear that modern computers and sophisticated software tools cannot replace human cryptanalysis. Nevertheless, software tools can play an important role in modern cryptanalysis. In most cases, the attacks found by the cryptanalyst require a large number of computational steps, hence the actual computation of the attack is performed on a computer. However, software and software tools can also be essential to find a successful way to attack a symmetric cryptographic algorithm; examples include differential and linear cryptanalysis, dependence tests, and statistical tests.

Within NESSIE, we distinguish two classes of tools. The general tools are not specific for the algorithms to be analyzed. Special tools, which are specific for the analysis of one algorithm, are implemented when, in the course of the cryptanalysis of an algorithm, the need for such a tool turns up.

For the evaluation of the symmetric submissions, a comprehensive set of general tools is available within the project. These tools are in part based on an improved version of the tools developed by the RIPE (RACE Integrity Primitives Evaluation) project [22]. These test include: the frequency test, the collision test, the overlapping m-tuple test, the gap test, the constant runs test, the coupon collector's test, Maurer's universal test [13], the poker test, the spectral test, the correlation test, the rank test, the linear, non-linear, and dyadic complexity test, the Ziv-Lempel complexity test, the dependence test, the percolation test, the linear equation, linear approximation and correlation immunity test, the linear factors test, and a cycle detection tool.

The NESSIE project is also developing a new generic tool to analyze block ciphers with differential [1] and linear cryptanalysis [12]. This tool is based on a general description language for block ciphers.

In September 2000, the US NIST published a suite of statistical tests for the evaluation of sequences of random or pseudo-random bits; this document has been revised in December 2000 [18]. A careful comparison has been made between the RIPE and NIST test suites.

The software for these tools will not be made available outside the project, but all the results obtained using these tools will be made public in full detail.

4   Security Evaluation

We first describe the internal process within NESSIE used to assess submissions. Initially each submission was assigned to a NESSIE partner, who performed basic checks on the submission, such as compliance with the call, working software, obvious weaknesses etc. The aim of this initial check was mainly to ensure that submissions were specified in a consistent and cogent form in time for the November 2000 workshop. It is vital for proper security assessments that the algorithms are fully and unambiguously described. This process required interaction with some submitters to ensure that the submissions were in the required form.

The next internal stage (November 2000) was to assign each submission to a pair of NESSIE partners for an initial detailed evaluation. Each submission has then been subject to two independent initial assessments. After the two initial assessments of a submission have taken place, the two NESSIE partners have produced a joint summary of their assessments concerning that submission. Based on this initial evaluation, algorithms were dismissed or subjected to further dedicated analysis.

Next, an open workshop was organized in Egham (UK) on September 12-13, 2001 to discuss the security and performance analysis of the submissions. The presenters include both researchers from the NESSIE project, but also submitters, members from the NESSIE PIB, and members from the cryptographic community at large.

Following this workshop, a comprehensive security evaluation report has been published [19]. The document gives an overview of generic attacks on the different type of algorithms. Moreover, for each symmetric algorithm it presents a short description, the security claims by the designers, and the reported weaknesses and attacks. The part on asymmetric algorithms contains a discussion of security assumptions, security models, and of the methodology to evaluate the security. For each algorithm, a short description is followed by a discussion of the provable security (which security properties are proved under which assumptions) and of the concrete security reduction.

5   Performance Evaluation

Performance evaluation is an essential part in the assessment of a cryptographic algorithm: efficiency is a very important criterion in deciding for the adoption of an algorithm.

The candidates will be used on several platforms (PCs, smart cards, dedicated hardware) and for various applications. Some applications have tight timing constraints (e.g., payment applications, cellular phones); for other applications a high throughput is essential (e.g., high speed networking, hard disk encryption).

First a framework has been defined to compare the performance of algorithms on a fair and equal basis. It will be used for all evaluations of submitted candidates. First of all a theoretical approach has been established. Each algorithm is dissected into three parts: setup (independent of key and data), precomputations (independent of data, e.g., key schedule) and the algorithm itself (that must be repeated for every use). Next a set of four test platforms has been defined on which each candidate may be tested. These platforms are smart cards, 32-bit PCs, 64-bit machines, and Field Programmable Gate Arrays (FPGAs).

Then rules have been defined which specify how performance should be measured on these platforms. The implementation parameters depend on the platform, but may include RAM, speed, code size, chip area, and power consumption. On smart cards, only the following parameters will be taken into account, in decreasing order of importance: RAM usage, speed, code size. On PCs, RAM has very little impact, and speed is the main concern. On FPGAs, throughput, latency, chip area and power consumption will be considered. Unfortunately, the limited resources of the project will not allow for the evaluation of dedicated hardware implementations (ASICs), but it may well be that teams outside the project can offer assistance for certain algorithms.

The project will also consider the resistance of implementations to physical attacks such as timing attacks [9], fault analysis [2,3], and power analysis [10]. For non constant-time algorithms (data or key dependence, asymmetry between encryption and decryption) the data or key dependence will be analyzed; other elements that will be taken into account include the difference between encryption and decryption, and between signature and verification operation. For symmetric algorithms, the key agility will also be considered.

This approach will result in the definition of a platform dependent test and in several platform dependent rekeying scenarios. Low-cost smart cards will only be used for block ciphers, MACs, hash functions, stream ciphers, pseudo-random number generation, and identification schemes.

In order to present performance information in a consistent way within the NESSIE project, a performance 'template' has been developed. The goal of this template is to collect intrinsic information related to the performance of the submitted candidates. A first part describes parameters such as word size, memory requirement, key size and code size. Next the basic operations are analyzed, such as shift/rotations, table look-ups, permutations, multiplications, additions, modular reduction, exponentiation, inversion,.... Then the nature and speed of precomputations (setup, key schedule, etc.) are described. Elements such as the dependence on the keys and on the inputs determine whether the code is constant-time or not. Alternative representations of the algorithms are explored when feasible.

The result of the preliminary performance evaluation are presented in [21]. This document contains an overview of the performance claimed by the designers, a theoretical evaluation, and performance measurements of optimized C-code on a PC and a workstation. However, due to limited resources and the large number of algorithms, it was not possible to guarantee full optimization for all algorithms. Nevertheless, it was felt that these results provide sufficient information to make a selection of algorithms for the 2nd phase of the project.

6   Selection for the 2nd Phase

On September 24, 2001, the NESSIE project has announced the selection of candidates for the 2nd phase of the project. Central to the decision process has been the project goal, that is, to come up with a portfolio of strong cryptographic algorithms. Moreover, there was also a consensus that every algorithm in this portfolio should have a unique competitive advantage that is relevant to an application.

It is thus clear that an algorithm could not be selected if it failed to meet the security level required in the call. A second element could be that the algorithm failed to meet a security claim made by the designer. A third reason to eliminate an algorithm could be that a similar algorithm exists with better security (for comparable performance) or with significantly better performance (for comparable security). In retrospect, very few algorithms were eliminated because of performance reasons. It should also be noted that the selection was more competitive in the area of block ciphers, where many strong contenders were considered. The motivation for the decisions is given in [20].

Designers of submitted algorithms were allowed to make small alterations to their algorithms; the main criterion to accept these alterations is that they should improve the algorithm and not substantially invalidate the existing security analysis. More information on the alterations can be found on the NESSIE webpages [15].

The selected algorithms are listed below; altered algorithms are indicated with a *. Block ciphers:

- IDEA: MediaCrypt AG, Switzerland;
- Khazad*: Scopus Tecnologia S.A., Brazil and K.U.Leuven, Belgium;
- MISTY1: Mitsubishi Electric Corp., Japan;
- SAFER++64, SAFE++128: Cylink Corp., USA, ETH Zurich, Switzerland, National Academy of Sciences, Armenia;
- Camellia: Nippon Telegraph and Telephone Corp., Japan and Mitsubishi Electric, Japan;
- RC6: RSA Laboratories Europe, Sweden and RSA Laboratories, USA;
- Shacal: Gemplus, France.

Here IDEA, Khazad, MISTY1 and SAFER++64 are 64-bit block ciphers. Camellia, SAFER++128 and RC6 are 128-bit block ciphers, which will be compared to AES/Rijndael [5,7]. Shacal is a 160-bit block cipher based on SHA-1 [6]. A 256-bit version of Shacal based on SHA-256 [17] has also been introduced in the second phase; this algorithm will be compared to an RC-6 and a Rijndael [5] variant with a block length of 256 bits (note that this variant is not included in the AES standard). The motivation for this choice is that certain applications (such as the stream cipher BMGL and certain hash functions) can benefit from a secure 256-bit block cipher.

Synchronous stream ciphers:

- SOBER-t16, SOBER-t32: Qualcomm International, Australia;
- SNOW*: Lund Univ., Sweden;
- BMGL*: Royal Institute of Technology, Stockholm and Ericsson Research, Sweden.

MAC algorithms and hash functions:

- Two-Track-MAC: K.U.Leuven, Belgium and debis AG, Germany;
- UMAC: Intel Corp., USA, Univ. of Nevada at Reno, USA, IBM Research Laboratory, USA, Technion, Israel, and Univ. of California at Davis, USA;
- Whirlpool*: Scopus Tecnologia S.A., Brazil and K.U.Leuven, Belgium.

The hash function Whirlpool will be compared to the new FIPS proposals SHA-256, SHA-384 and SHA-512 [17].

Public-key encryption algorithms:

- ACE-KEM*: IBM Zurich Research Laboratory, Switzerland (derived from ACE Encrypt);
- EPOC-2*: Nippon Telegraph and Telephone Corp., Japan;
- PSEC-KEM*: Nippon Telegraph and Telephone Corp., Japan (derived from PSEC-2);
- ECIES: Certicom Corp., USA and Certicom Corp., Canada
- RSA-OAEP*: RSA Laboratories Europe, Sweden and RSA Laboratories, USA.

Digital signature algorithms:

- ECDSA: Certicom Corp., USA and Certicom Corp., Canada;
- ESIGN*: Nippon Telegraph and Telephone Corp., Japan;
- RSA-PSS: RSA Laboratories Europe, Sweden and RSA Laboratories, USA;
- SFLASH*: BULL CP8, France;
- QUARTZ*: BULL CP8, France.

Identification scheme:

- GPS*: Ecole Normale Supérieure, Paris, BULL CP8, France Télécom and La Poste, France.

Many of the asymmetric algorithms have been updated at the beginning of phase 2. For the asymmetric encryption schemes, these changes were driven in part by the recent cryptanalytic developments, which occurred after the NESSIE submission deadline [8,11,23]. A second reason for these changes is the progress of standardization within ISO/IEC JTC1/SC27 [24]. The standards seem to evolve towards defining a hybrid encryption scheme, consisting of two components: a KEM (Key Encapsulation Mechanism), where the asymmetric encryption is used to encrypt a symmetric key, and a DEM (Data Encapsulation Mechanism), which protects both secrecy and integrity of the bulk data with symmetric techniques (a "digital envelope"). This approach is slightly more complicated for encryption of a short plaintext, but it offers a more general solution with clear advantages. Two of the five NESSIE algorithms (ACE Encrypt and PSEC-2) have been modified to take into account this development. At the same time some other improvements have been introduced; as an example, ACE-KEM can be based on any abstract group, which was not the case for the original submission ACE Encrypt. Other submitters decided not to alter their submissions at this stage. For further details, the reader is referred to the extensive ISO/IEC draft document authored by V. Shoup [24]. The NESSIE project will closely monitor these developments. Depending on the progress, variants such as ECIES-KEM and RSA-KEM defined in [24] may be studied by the NESSIE project.

For the digital signature schemes, three out of five schemes (ESIGN, QUARTZ and SFLASH) have been altered. In this case, there are particular reasons for each algorithm (correction for the security proof to apply, improve performance, or preclude a new attack). The other two have not been modified. It should also be noted that PSS-R, which offers very small storage overhead for the signature, has not been submitted to NESSIE.

7   Intellectual Property

An important element in the evaluation is the intellectual property status. While it would be ideal for users of the NESSIE results that all algorithms recommended by NESSIE were in the public domain, it is clear that this is for the time being not realistic. The users in the NESSIE PIB have clearly stated that they prefer to see royalty-free algorithms, preferably combined with open source implementations. However, providers of intellectual property typically have different views.

One observation is that in the past, there has always been a very large difference between symmetric and asymmetric cryptographic algorithms. Therefore it is not so surprising that NIST was able to require that the designers of the block cipher selected for the AES would give away all their rights, if their algorithm was selected; it is clear that this is not a realistic expectation for the NESSIE project.

In this section we will attempt to summarize the intellectual property statements of the submissions retained for the 2nd phase. Note however that this interpretation is only indicative; for the final answer the reader is referred to the intellectual property statement on the NESSIE web page [15], and to the submitters themselves.

Twelve out of 24 algorithms are in the public domain, or the submitters indicate that a royalty-free license will be given. These are the block ciphers Khazad, Misty1, Shacal, Safer++, the stream ciphers BMGL, SNOW, Sober-t16 and Sober-t32, the MAC algorithms Two-Track-MAC and UMAC, the hash function Whirlpool, and the public-key algorithms RSA-OAEP[2] (public-key encryption) and RSA-PSS[2] (digital signature scheme).

---

[2] This statement does not hold for the variants of RSA with more than two primes.

Royalty-free licenses will be given for the block cipher Camellia, for the public-key encryption algorithms EPOC-2 and PSEC-KEM, and for the digital signature scheme ESIGN, provided that other companies with IPR to the NESSIE portfolio reciprocate.

The block cipher IDEA is free for non-commercial use only; for commercial applications a license is required.

Licenses under reasonable and non-discriminatory terms will be given for ACE-KEM (the detailed license conditions are rather complex). Additions to the 'reasonable and non-discriminatory' terms are required for the public-key algorithms ECDSA and ECIES; it is required that the license holder reciprocates some of his rights.

For the digital signature schemes SFLASH and QUARTZ the licensing conditions are expected to be non-discriminatory, but no decision has been made yet. A similar statement holds for the identification scheme GPS, but in this case certain applications in France may be excluded from the license.

Finally, the submitters of RC6 are willing to negotiate licenses on reasonable terms and conditions.

It is clear that intellectual property is always a complex issue, and it will not be possible to resolve this completely within the framework of NESSIE. However, IPR issues may play an important role in the final selection process.

8   Dissemination and Standardization

8.1   An Open Evaluation Process

The NESSIE project intends to be an open project, which implies that the members of the public are invited to contribute to the evaluation process. In order to facilitate this process, all submissions are available on the NESSIE website, and comments are distributed through this website. In addition, three open workshops are organized during the project: the first two workshops have taken place in November 2000 and September 2001; the third one has been scheduled for November 2002.

8.2   The Project Industry Board

The Project Industry Board (PIB) was established to ensure that the project addresses real needs and requirements of industry dealing with the provision and use of cryptographic techniques and cryptographic products. The goals for the Board may be summarized as follows:

- contribute to dissemination: outwards through a member's contacts with industry and users, and also through passing NESSIE information into the member's own organization influencing products and directions;
- collaboration with the Project in formulation of the call and its goals and requirements;

- contribution to consensus building through influence and contacts in the industry and marketplace;
- identification of industry requirements from market needs and corporate strategies;
- guidance and judgment on the acceptability and relevance of submissions and evaluation results;
- support in standardization of NESSIE results;
- contribution to Project workshops;
- practical contributions to analysis and evaluation of submissions;
- identification of gaps in the scope of the submissions;
- ongoing guidance during the evaluation of the processes and validity of results.

Two meetings are held per year, but the PIB may request additional meetings to address specific issues or concerns that may arise. Membership was originally by invitation, but subsequently a number of additional companies have requested and obtained membership. Currently the PIB consists of about twenty leading companies which are users or suppliers of cryptology.

8.3   Standardization

Together with the NESSIE PIB, the project will establish a standardization strategy. It is not our intention to establish a new standardization body or mechanism, but to channel the NESSIE results to the appropriate standardization bodies, such as, ISO/IEC, IETF, IEEE and EESSI. We believe that the NESSIE approach of open evaluation is complementary to the approach taken by standardization bodies. Indeed, these bodies typically do not have the resources to perform any substantial security evaluation, which may be one of the reasons why standardization in security progresses often more slowly than anticipated.

The NESSIE project will also take into account existing and emerging standards, even if these have not been formally submitted to the NESSIE project. Two recent examples in this context come from the standardization efforts run by NIST: AES/Rijndael [5,7] will be used as a benchmark for the other 128-bit block ciphers, and the NESSIE project will study the security and performance of the new SHA variants with results between 256 and 512 bits [17].

9   Conclusion

We believe that after two years, the NESSIE project has made important steps towards achieving its goals. This can be deduced from the high quality submissions received from key players in the community, and by the active participation to the workshops.

The first two years of the NESSIE project have also shown that initiatives of this type (such as AES, RIPE, CRYPTREC) can bring a clear benefit to the cryptographic research community and to the users and implementors of cryptographic algorithms. By asking cryptographers to design concrete and fully specified schemes, they are forced to make choices, to think about real life optimizations, and to consider all the practical implications of their research. While leaving many options and variants in a construction may be very desirable in a research paper, it is often confusing for a practitioner. Implementors and users can clearly benefit from the availability of a set of well defined algorithms, that are described in a standardized way.

The developments in the last years have also shown that this approach can result in a better understanding of the security of cryptographic algorithms. We have also learned that concrete security proofs are an essential tool to build confidence, particularly for public key cryptography (where constructions can be reduced to mathematical problems believed to be hard) and for constructions that reduce the security of a scheme to other cryptographic algorithms. At the same time, we have learned that it is essential to study proofs for their correctness and to evaluate the efficiency of such reductions.

Finally, the NESSIE project is inviting the community at large to further analyze the candidates for the 2nd phase, and to offer comments on their security, performance and intellectual property status. The project is accepting comments until mid November 2002, and the final selection will be announced by December 2002.

Acknowledgments

I would like to thank all the members of and the contributors to the NESSIE project. The work described in this paper has been supported by the Commission of the European Communities through the IST Programme under Contract IST–1999–12324.

References

1. E. Biham, A. Shamir, *"Differential Cryptanalysis of the Data Encryption Standard,"* Springer-Verlag, 1993.
2. E. Biham, A. Shamir, "Differential fault analysis of secret key cryptosystems," *Advances in Cryptology, Proceedings Crypto'97, LNCS 1294*, B. Kaliski, Ed., Springer-Verlag, 1997, pp. 513–525.
3. D. Boneh, R. A. DeMillo, R. J. Lipton, "On the importance of checking cryptographic protocols for faults," *Advances in Cryptology, Proceedings Eurocrypt'97, LNCS 1233*, W. Fumy, Ed., Springer-Verlag, 1997, pp. 37–51.
4. CRYPTREC project,
   http://www.ipa.gov.jp/security/enc/CRYPTREC/index-e.html.
5. J. Daemen, V. Rijmen, "AES proposal Rijndael," September 3, 1999, available from http://www.nist.gov/aes.
6. FIPS 180-1, *"Secure Hash Standard,"* Federal Information Processing Standard (FIPS), Publication 180-1, National Institute of Standards and Technology, US Department of Commerce, Washington D.C., April 17, 1995.
7. FIPS XXX *"Advanced Encryption Standard (AES),"* Washington D.C.: NIST, US Department of Commerce, Draft, February 28, 2001.

8. E. Fujisaki, T. Okamoto, D. Pointcheval, J. Stern, "RSA-OAEP is secure under the RSA assumption," *Advances in Cryptology, Proceedings Crypto'01, LNCS 2139*, J. Kilian, Ed., Springer-Verlag, 2001, pp. 260–274.

9. P. Kocher, "Timing attacks on implementations of Diffie-Hellman, RSA, DSS, and other systems," *Advances in Cryptology, Proceedings Crypto'96, LNCS 1109*, N. Koblitz, Ed., Springer-Verlag, 1996, pp. 104–113.

10. P. Kocher, J. Jaffe, B. Jun, "Differential power analysis," *Advances in Cryptology, Proceedings Crypto'99, LNCS 1666*, M.J. Wiener, Ed., Springer-Verlag, 1999, pp. 388–397.

11. J. Manger, "A chosen ciphertext attack on RSA Optimal Asymmetric Encryption Padding (OAEP) as standardized in PKCS #1 v2.0," *Advances in Cryptology, Proceedings Crypto'01, LNCS 2139*, J. Kilian, Ed., Springer-Verlag, 2001, pp. 230–238.

12. M. Matsui, "The first experimental cryptanalysis of the Data Encryption Standard," *Advances in Cryptology, Proceedings Crypto'94, LNCS 839*, Y. Desmedt, Ed., Springer-Verlag, 1994, pp. 1–11.

13. U.M. Maurer, "A universal statistical test for random bit generators," *Advances in Cryptology, Proceedings Crypto'90, LNCS 537*, S. Vanstone, Ed., Springer-Verlag, 1991, pp. 409–420.

14. A.J. Menezes, P.C. van Oorschot, S.A. Vanstone, *"Handbook of Applied Cryptography,"* CRC Press, 1997.

15. NESSIE, http://www.cryptonessie.org.

16. NIST, AES Initiative, http://www.nist.gov/aes.

17. NIST, *"SHA-256, SHA-384, SHA-512,"* Washington D.C.: NIST, US Department of Commerce, Draft, 2000.

18. NIST, *"A Statistical Test Suite for Random and Pseudorandom Number Generators for Cryptographic Applications,"* NIST Special Publication 800-22, National Institute of Standards and Technology, US Department of Commerce, Washington D.C., December 2000.

19. B. Preneel, B. Van Rompay, L. Granboulan, G. Martinet, S. Murphy, R. Shipsey, J. White, M. Dichtl, P. Serf, M. Schafheutle, E. Biham, O. Dunkelman, V. Furman, M. Ciet, J.-J. Quisquater, F. Sica, L. Knudsen, and H. Raddum, *"Security Evaluation I,"* NESSIE Deliverable D13, September 2001, available from [15].

20. B. Preneel, B. Van Rompay, L. Granboulan, G. Martinet, S. Murphy, R. Shipsey, J. White, M. Dichtl, P. Serf, M. Schafheutle, E. Biham, O. Dunkelman, V. Furman, M. Ciet, J.-J. Quisquater, F. Sica, L. Knudsen, and H. Raddum, *"NESSIE Phase I: Selection of Primitives"* NESSIE Report, September 2001, available from [15].

21. B. Preneel, B. Van Rompay, L. Granboulan, G. Martinet, M. Dichtl, M. Schafheutle, P. Serf, A. Bibliovicz, E. Biham, O. Dunkelman, M. Ciet, J.-J. Quisquater, and F. Sica, *"Report on the Performance Evaluation of the NESSIE Candidates,"* NESSIE Deliverable D14, October 2001, available from [15].

22. RIPE, *"Integrity Primitives for Secure Information Systems. Final Report of RACE Integrity Primitives Evaluation (RIPE-RACE 1040),"* LNCS 1007, A. Bosselaers, B. Preneel, Eds., Springer-Verlag, 1995.

23. V. Shoup, "OAEP reconsidered," *Advances in Cryptology, Proceedings Crypto'01, LNCS 2139*, J. Kilian, Ed., Springer-Verlag, 2001, pp. 239–259.

24. V. Shoup, *"A Proposal for an ISO Standard for Public Key Encryption,"* Version 2.0, September 17, 2001, available from http://www.shoup.net.

An Improved Method of Multiplication on Certain Elliptic Curves

Young-Ho Park[1,*], Sangho Oh[1], Sangjin Lee[1,**],
Jongin Lim[1], and Maenghee Sung[2]

[1] CIST, Korea University, Seoul, Korea
{youngho,sangho,sangjin,jilim}@cist.korea.ac.kr
[2] KISA, Seoul, Korea
mhsung@kisa.or.kr

Abstract. The Frobenius endomorphism is known to be useful in efficient implementation of multiplication on certain elliptic curves. In this note a method to minimize the length of the Frobenius expansion of integer multiplier, elliptic curves defined over small finite fields, is introduced. It is an optimization of previous works by Solinas and Müller. Finally, experimental results are presented and compared with curves recommended in standards by time-performance of multiplication.

1 Introduction

Recent issues of implementation of elliptic curve cryptosystems(for short, ECC) are primarily focused on fast scalar multiplication on elliptic curves. Traditional 'exponentiation' methods for multiplicative groups are straightforwardly applied to scalar multiplication. Such a modification seems to be a bottleneck in accelerating multiplication on elliptic curves since doubling operation is as expensive as addition. In [4], [9], [5] and [6], multiplication on elliptic curves defined over small finite fields is carried out rapidly using the Frobenius map. As known recently in [8], in case of odd characteristic field, it is also possible to speed up scalar multiplication in a similar way. In addition, the length of the Frobenius expansion can be reduced to one half with the use of a division algorithm by a specific algebraic integer whose norm is equal to the order of a given elliptic curve. Roughly replacing doublings by the Frobenius maps together with the reduction gives the running time improvement of 400% (see [9,6]).

ECC-related standards almost all recommend to use so-called 'good' curves. Here the 'good' curves mean that they are cryptographically secure and efficient in implementation. To satisfy such two properties, commonly recommended curves may be chosen to be of compactness in that the security parameter of each curve is almost the same as its field-size. This requirement may come to extreme restriction of the use of Frobenius-based methods since the size of defining

* This work was supported by grant RND project 2001-S-092 of KISA
** This work was supported by grant No. 1999-10300-001-2 from the Basic Research Program of the Korea Science & Engineering Foundation.

D. Naccache and P. Paillier (Eds.): PKC 2002, LNCS 2274, pp. 310–322, 2002.

fields should be very small, say like a binary field. We here would like to discuss an observation in order to extend properly the concept of the compactness. For cryptographic uses of elliptic curves, their order should has a large prime factor and scalar multiplication is performed actually on a cyclic subgroup of the large prime order, rather than on the whole group. This observation indicates that the reduction method mentioned above holds a redundant factor. In this note we'll introduce a method to minimize the length of the Frobenius expansion for scalar multiplication on certain elliptic curves by cutting off the redundant and so show that this approach can widen the margin of the 'good' curve.

This paper is organized as follows: In Section 2 an introduction to elliptic curves is given and the previous works, for convenient description, are reviewed briefly. In Section 3 we describe an improved reduction method which removes the redundant. Curves for use in public key cryptography are listed in Table 3 and we compare the length of Frobenius expansion on them by using three different methods in Section 4. In Section 5 we present new 'good' curves with efficient and secure property and give a comparison of them with recommended curves in standards. In Section 6 attacks known so far against subfield curves are introduced.

2   Frobenius Map and Integer Representation

From the viewpoint of application, a class of non-supersingular curves defined over finite fields of characteristic two has attracted attention of cryptographers. In particular, we are concentrated on elliptic curves defined over small fields, say, $\mathbb{F}_{2^s}$ $s \leq 5$. The reason that we restrict the category of fields is to speed up multiplication on elliptic curves. As well-known, expensive doubling operations on non-supersingular curves defined over small fields, can be replaced by the much easier Frobenius map. Hence, in what follows, all elliptic curves mean non-supersingular curves defined over small finite fields of characteristic two and their underlying fields are extensions of the small defining field with odd prime exponents. Let $\mathbb{F}_q$ be a finite field of q elements where q is a power of characteristic 2, which is rather small. We denote by $\overline{\mathbb{F}}_q$ an algebraic closure of $\mathbb{F}_q$. Take an elliptic curve $E/\mathbb{F}_q$ given by the Weierstrass equation of the form

$$y^2 + xy = x^3 + a_2 x^2 + a_6 \tag{1}$$

where a_2, a_6 in $\mathbb{F}_q$ and $a_6 \neq 0$. Then the qth-power Frobenius endomorphism of $E/\mathbb{F}_q$ is defined by

$$\Phi : E(\overline{\mathbb{F}}_q) \to E(\overline{\mathbb{F}}_q), (x, y) \mapsto (x^q, y^q).$$

From Hasse's famous result, the number of $\mathbb{F}_q$-rational points of E is closely related to an integer t by the formula:

$$\#E(\mathbb{F}_q) = q + 1 - t$$

where t is the trace of the Frobenius endomorphism Φ satisfying the equation

$$\Phi^2 - t\Phi + q = 0.$$

Note that t should be odd for a non-supersingular elliptic curve $E/\mathbb{F}_q$. Some facts related with the Frobenius expansion of elements in $\mathbb{Z}[\Phi]$ are presented with no proof. For details, the reader can be referred to [6].

Lemma 1. *[6] Let $\rho \in \mathbb{Z}[\Phi]$, there exists an integer r, $-q/2 \le r \le q/2$, and $u \in \mathbb{Z}[\Phi]$ such that*

$$\rho = u\Phi + r.$$

In particular, if we choose $r \in \{-q/2 + 1, \cdots, q/2\}$, then r and u are unique.

Lemma 2. *For $q \ge 4$, let $\rho \in \mathbb{Z}[\Phi]$ be such that $N_{\mathbb{Z}[\Phi]/\mathbb{Z}}(\rho) \le (\sqrt{q} + 1)^2$. Then ρ has a Φ-expansion of length at most 4, where the magnitude of each integral coefficient is bounded by $q/2$.*

Theorem 1. *[6] For $q \ge 4$, let $\rho \in \mathbb{Z}[\Phi]$. Then ρ can be represented as*

$$\rho = \sum_{i=0}^{k} r_i \Phi^i$$

where $r_i \in \{-q/2 + 1, \cdots, q/2\}$ and $k \le \lceil 2\log_q \|\rho\| \rceil + 3$.

In Theorem 1, $\|\cdot\|$ means the Euclidean norm.

Algorithm 1   **(Frobenius expansion of ρ)**
Input: $\rho = r_1 + r_2\Phi \in \mathbb{Z}[\Phi]$.   **Output:** m_i is a sequence of integers such that $\rho = \sum_{i=0}^{k} m_i \Phi^i, m_i \in [-q/2 + 1, q/2]$

1)   Set $x = r_1$, $y = r_2$ and $i = 0$.
 2)   While $\|x\| > q/2$ or $\|y\| > q/2$, do the followings :
   a)   Compute $z \equiv x \pmod{q}$.
   b)   Set $m_i = \begin{cases} z & \text{if } z \le q/2, \\ z - q & \text{otherwise.} \end{cases}$
   c)   Set $h = (m_i - x)/q$, $x = y - th$, $y = h$, and $i = i + 1$.
 3) $m_i = x, m_{i+1} = y$.
 4)   Return m_i.

3   Reduction of the Length of Frobenius Expansions

For public key cryptography, the group order of $E(\mathbb{F}_{q^n})$ should have a large prime factor p. Let P be a point of $E(\mathbb{F}_{q^n})$ of prime order p. We denote $\#E(\mathbb{F}_{q^n})$ the group order of $E(\mathbb{F}_{q^n})$ and write $\#E(\mathbb{F}_{q^n}) = hp$ where h is called the cofactor of $E(\mathbb{F}_{q^n})$. The main computational problem in elliptic curve public key cryptosystems is scalar multiplication mP for a large integer $m < p$. According to

Theorem 1, the length of Frobenius expansion of m depends on the norm of m, i.e $N_{\mathbb{Q}[\Phi]/\mathbb{Q}}(m) = m^2$ which is approximately equal to q^{2n}. As in [9] and [8], by a reduction modulo $\Phi^n - 1$, they could reduce the expansion length by nearly 50% as follows:

1') $\Phi^n(Q) = Q$ implies $(\Phi^n - 1)Q = O$ for any point $Q \in E(\mathbb{F}_{q^n})$, where O denotes the point at infinity.

2') Dividing m by $\Phi^n - 1$, we obtain a remainder $\rho' \in \mathbb{Z}[\Phi]$ such that

$$N_{\mathbb{Q}[\Phi]/\mathbb{Q}}(\rho') < \frac{9 + 4q}{4} N_{\mathbb{Q}[\Phi]/\mathbb{Q}}(\Phi^n - 1) = \frac{9 + 4q}{4} \#E(\mathbb{F}_{q^n}) \approx q^{n+1}.$$

3') We have $mQ = \rho'Q$ for any point $Q \in E(\mathbb{F}_{q^n})$.

4') Replacing multiplication by m by multiplication by ρ' reduces its expansion length by nearly half.

Under the consideration of cryptographic applications, we want to utilize scalar multiplication on the subgroup $< P >$ rather than that on all points of it. In this aspect, if the cofactor h is not trivial, that is $h \geq \#E(\mathbb{F}_q) \neq 1$, then this approach for reduction has some redundant factor. Because it is achieved by modulo $\Phi^n - 1$ whose norm is the order of an elliptic curve, that is $N_{\mathbb{Q}[\Phi]/\mathbb{Q}}(\Phi^n - 1) = \#E(\mathbb{F}_{q^n})$.

To exclude the aforementioned redundant and so to minimize the length of the Frobenius expansion, we now will give an improved method which generalizes that of Müller[6] and Smart[8]. Let us consider multiplication on the cyclic subgroup $< P >$ of large prime order p, rather than on the whole group $E(\mathbb{F}_{q^n})$. Recall that the Frobenius map Φ acts on $< P >$ as a multiplication map λ, where λ is a root of the characteristic polynomial of Φ modulo p. Hence, we have $\Phi(P) = \lambda P$ and since $\Phi^2 - t\Phi + q$ is the characteristic polynomial of Φ, $\bar{\Phi} = t - \Phi$ is the conjugate of Φ. We assume that there exists an element $\alpha = a + b\Phi \in \mathbb{Z}[\Phi]$ such that

$$N_{\mathbb{Q}[\Phi]/\mathbb{Q}}(a + b\Phi) = s_p p \quad \text{and} \quad (a + b\Phi)P = O \tag{2}$$

for some small positive integer s_p. In fact, if we find $\alpha = a + b\Phi \in \mathbb{Z}[\Phi]$ such that $N_{\mathbb{Q}[\Phi]/\mathbb{Q}}(\alpha) = s_p p$ then we have

$$(a + b\lambda)(a + bt - b\lambda) \equiv 0 \pmod{p}$$

since $(a + b\Phi)(a + b\bar{\Phi}) = (a + b\Phi)(a + b(t - \Phi)) = (a + b\Phi)(a + bt - b\Phi) = s_p p$. Therefore, we have $(a + b\Phi)P = O$ or $(a + b\bar{\Phi})P = O$.

Remark 1. It is clear that there exists a positive integer $s_p \leq h = \#E(\mathbb{F}_{q^n})/p$ satisfying (2) since $N_{\mathbb{Q}[\Phi]/\mathbb{Q}}(\Phi^n - 1) = \#E(\mathbb{F}_{q^n}) = hp$. But the s_p is in general smaller than the cofactor h. (See Theorem 2 and Table 1.)

Roughly speaking, the main idea of our method is to replace $\Phi^n - 1$ by $\alpha = a + b\Phi$ by which we divide a multiplier m in order to reduce the expansion length. Since $\mathbb{Z}[\Phi]$ is μ-Euclidean for some positive real number μ (see [8]), we can divide m by α and obtain a remainder ρ with $N_{\mathbb{Q}[\Phi]/\mathbb{Q}}(\rho) < \mu N_{\mathbb{Q}[\Phi]/\mathbb{Q}}(\alpha)$.

So we replace mP by ρP. Our method gives the Frobenius expansion of ρ which is shorter than that of ρ' by the previous works and in fact, it has minimal length. It will be shown theoretically and on experiment that this method reduces the expansion length by roughly $\lfloor \log_q(\#E(\mathbb{F}_{q^n})/(s_p p)) \rfloor = \lfloor \log_q(h/s_p) \rfloor$ (see Theorem 3 and Table 3). Compared with the cofactor h, the fact that s_p is small leads us to decrease the length. But notice that it does not work on all of points of $E(\mathbb{F}_{q^n})$ but all of points of order p. This method can be briefly described as follows:

1) Find $\alpha = a + b\Phi$ such that $N_{\mathbb{Q}[\Phi]/\mathbb{Q}}(\alpha) = s_p p$ for some small positive integer s_p and $(a + b\Phi)P = O$.
2) Dividing m by $\alpha = a + b\Phi$, we obtain a remainder $\rho \in \mathbb{Z}[\Phi]$ such that

$$N_{\mathbb{Q}[\Phi]/\mathbb{Q}}(\rho) < \mu N_{\mathbb{Q}[\Phi]/\mathbb{Q}}(\alpha), \quad \text{with } 0 < \mu \leq \frac{(9 + 4q)}{16}.$$

3) We have $mP = \rho P$ for any point in the subgroup of order p.
4) Replacing multiplication by m by multiplication by ρ reduces its expansion length by a little more than that of [9] and [8].

Now we describe our method in detail. First, we give a good upper bound on s_p satisfying (2) which guarantees that s_p be a small integer.

Lemma 3. *(See [10]). Let $K = \mathbb{Q}(\sqrt{D})$ be an imaginary quadratic field. Then every non-zero ideal $\mathcal{P}$ of K has an ideal $\mathcal{I}$ with $N_{K/\mathbb{Q}}(\mathcal{I}) \leq \frac{2}{\pi}\sqrt{|D|}$ such that $\mathcal{IP} = (\alpha)$ for some $\alpha \in O_K$, the ring of integers in K.*

Theorem 2. *Let $\#E(\mathbb{F}_{q^n})$ be divisible by a large prime p and $p^2 \nmid \#E(\mathbb{F}_{q^n})$. If $D = t^2 - 4q$ has no square factor, then there exists an element $\alpha = a + b\Phi \in \mathbb{Z}[\Phi]$ such that*

$$N_{\mathbb{Q}[\Phi]/\mathbb{Q}}(a + b\Phi) = s_p p$$

for some positive integer $s_p < 1.28\sqrt{q}$.

Proof. Let $\#E(\mathbb{F}_{q^n}) = hp$ and $K = \mathbb{Q}(\sqrt{D})$. Since $N_{\mathbb{Q}[\Phi]/\mathbb{Q}}(\Phi^n - 1) = N_{K/\mathbb{Q}}(\Phi^n - 1) = \#E(\mathbb{F}_{q^n}) = hp$, it is obviously that p splits in $K/\mathbb{Q}$. Let $\mathcal{P}$ be a prime ideal of K such that $N_{K/\mathbb{Q}}(\mathcal{P}) = p$. By Lemma 3, there exists an ideal $\mathcal{I}$ such that $\mathcal{IP} = (\alpha)$ for some $\alpha \in O_K$ and $N_{K/\mathbb{Q}}(\mathcal{I}) \leq \frac{2}{\pi}\sqrt{|D|}$. Set $s_p = N_{K/\mathbb{Q}}(\mathcal{I})$. From Hasse theory, we have

$$s_p \leq \frac{2}{\pi}\sqrt{|D|} = \frac{2}{\pi}\sqrt{|t^2 - 4q|} \leq \frac{2}{\pi}2\sqrt{q} < 1.28\sqrt{q}.$$

Hence we have $\alpha \in O_K$ such that $N_{K/\mathbb{Q}}(\alpha) = N_{K/\mathbb{Q}}(\mathcal{IP}) = s_p p$ with $s_p < 1.28\sqrt{q}$. Now it remains to prove that $\alpha \in \mathbb{Z}[\Phi]$. Notice that $O_K = Z[\theta]$ where $\theta = (1 + \sqrt{D})/2$ because t is odd and $D \equiv 1 \pmod 4$. Since $\Phi^2 - t\Phi + q = 0$, we have $\Phi = (t \pm \sqrt{D})/2$ and

$$\theta = \begin{cases} \Phi - (t-1)/2 & \text{if } \Phi = (t + \sqrt{D})/2, \\ -\Phi + (t+1)/2 & \text{if } \Phi = (t - \sqrt{D})/2. \end{cases}$$

Therefore $\alpha \in O_K$ if and only if $\alpha \in \mathbb{Z}[\Phi]$, which completes the proof. $\square$

Corollary 1. *Under the condition above, assume that $D = t^2 - 4q$ has a square factor, $s^2|D$ and $D' = D/s^2$ has no square factor. Then there exists an element $\alpha = a + b\Phi \in \mathbb{Z}[\Phi]$ such that*

$$N_{\mathbb{Q}[\Phi]/\mathbb{Q}}(\rho)(a + b\Phi) = s_p p$$

for some positive integer $s_p < 1.28 s^2 \sqrt{q}$.

Proof. From the fist part of the proof of Theorem 2, we have

$$\alpha' \in O_K \text{ such that } N_{K/\mathbb{Q}}(\alpha') = s'_p p$$

with $s'_p < 1.28\sqrt{q}$. But in general $\alpha' \notin \mathbb{Z}[\Phi]$. It is easy to check that $s\alpha' \in \mathbb{Z}[\Phi]$. Put $\alpha = s\alpha' \in \mathbb{Z}[\Phi]$ and $s_p = s^2 s'_p$. Then $N_{\mathbb{Q}[\Phi]/\mathbb{Q}}(\alpha) = s_p p$, which completes the proof. $\square$

In Theorem 2, we have obtained an upper bound $1.28\sqrt{q}$ on s_p if $D = t^2 - 4q$ has no square factor. Since q is small, so is the upper bound and notice that $\log_q s_p < 1$. If $D = t^2 - 4q$ has a square factor, it is also guaranteed that there exists an element $\alpha \in \mathbb{Z}[\Phi]$ such that $N_{\mathbb{Q}[\Phi]/\mathbb{Q}}(\alpha) = s_p p$. But s_p in general increases in size. The case where $q = 16, n = 47, t = -1$ in Table 3 is an example. It is easily checked that $D = t^2 - 4q = -3^2 \cdot 7$. Since the ring of integers of $\mathbb{Q}(\sqrt{D}) = \mathbb{Q}(\sqrt{-7})$ is principal domain, we have $s'_p = 1$ and so $s_p = s^2 s'_p = 9$. The following Table 1 gives upper bounds on s_p for $q = 2^s \le 32$ where $D = t^2 - 4q$ has no square factor.

Table 1. Upper bounds on small positive integer s_p for $q = 2^s \le 32$

q	2	4	8	16	32
$\lfloor 1.28\sqrt{q} \rfloor$	1	2	3	5	7

It should be briefly pointed out that we need in advance to find $\alpha \in \mathbb{Z}[\Phi]$ satisfying (2). The problem of solving norm equations in $\mathbb{Z}[\Phi]$ can be done using the known methods such as Shanks' algorithm [7], lattice reduction method [11] or Cornacchia's algorithm [1]. In fact, this can be performed in the setup procedure for elliptic curve $E(\mathbb{F}_{q^n})$ and so it takes no costs for scalar multiplication.

Proposition 1. *Let $\alpha = a + b\Phi \neq 0 \in \mathbb{Z}[\Phi]$. If $\beta \in \mathbb{Z}[\Phi]$ then there exist $\delta, \rho \in \mathbb{Z}[\Phi]$ such that $\beta = \delta\alpha + \rho$ and $N_{\mathbb{Q}[\Phi]/\mathbb{Z}}(\rho) < \mu N_{\mathbb{Q}[\Phi]/\mathbb{Z}}(\alpha)$ with $0 < \mu \le (9 + 4q)/16$.*

Proof. Since $\Phi^2 - t\Phi + q$, we say $\Phi = (t + \sqrt{D})/2$ where $D = t^2 - 4q$. Set $N_\alpha = N_{\mathbb{Z}[\Phi]/\mathbb{Z}}(\alpha)$ and $c = -\lfloor t/2 \rfloor$. Setting $\Phi' = \Phi + c$, we change a $\mathbb{Z}$-basis $\{1, \Phi\}$ to $\{1, \Phi'\}$ and then $\mathbb{Z}[\Phi] = \mathbb{Z}[\Phi']$. Notice that $\Phi' = (1 + \sqrt{D})/2$ since t is odd. Then α can be written by $a_1 + b_1\Phi'$ in term of this new basis. For a given dividend β, we let $\gamma = \beta/\alpha$ and then we have

$$\gamma = \beta/\alpha = \beta\bar{\alpha}/N_\alpha = \frac{x_1 + x_2\Phi'}{N_\alpha}$$

where $\bar{\alpha}$ denotes the complex conjugate of α. Take $\delta = y_1 + y_2\Phi'$ with $y_i = \lfloor x_i/N_\alpha \rceil$ $(i = 1, 2)$, where $\lfloor x \rceil$ denotes the nearest integer to x. Finally, take $\rho = \alpha(\gamma - \delta)$, then since $\beta = \alpha\gamma, \alpha\delta \in \mathbb{Z}[\Phi]$, $\rho \in \mathbb{Z}[\Phi]$. It is easily checked that

$$\begin{aligned}
N_{\mathbb{Q}[\Phi]/\mathbb{Q}}(\rho)/N_{\mathbb{Q}[\Phi]/\mathbb{Q}}(\alpha) &= N_{\mathbb{Q}[\Phi]/\mathbb{Q}}(\gamma - \delta) \leq N_{\mathbb{Q}[\Phi]/\mathbb{Q}}(\tfrac{1}{2} + \tfrac{1}{2}\tfrac{1+\sqrt{D}}{2}) \\
&= \tfrac{1}{4}N_{\mathbb{Q}[\Phi]/\mathbb{Q}}(\tfrac{3+\sqrt{D}}{2}) = \tfrac{1}{4}(\tfrac{9-D}{4}) \\
&< \tfrac{1}{4}((9 + 4q)/4). \quad \square
\end{aligned}$$

Proposition 1 shows that $\mathbb{Z}[\Phi]$ is μ-Euclidean for some μ such that $0 < \mu \leq (9+4q)/16$. This improves a bound of μ by $1/4$ compared to that of [8, Theorem 5]. Our computational experiments show in Table 2 that the averages of upper bounds of μ's listed in Table 3 are roughly 70% smaller than that of Proposition 1.

Table 2. Experimental Comparison of μ for $q = 2^s \leq 32$

q	2	4	8	16	32
$(9 + 4q)/16$	1.06	1.56	2.56	4.56	8.56
Average of upper bounds of μ	0.25	0.40	0.69	1.21	2.29

Using the proof of Proposition 1, we consequently give an efficient Algorithm to compute a remainder ρ from m, q, t and $\alpha = a + b\Phi$.

Algorithm 2 (Divide m by $\alpha = a + b\phi$)

Input:	$m \in \mathbb{N}, q, t$ and $\alpha = a + b\Phi$.
Output:	$\rho = r_1 + r_2\Phi$ such that $N_{\mathbb{Z}[\Phi]/\mathbb{Z}}(\rho) < \mu N_{\mathbb{Z}[\Phi]/\mathbb{Z}}(\alpha)$.

Precomputations
1) $N_\alpha = N_{\mathbb{Z}[\Phi]/\mathbb{Z}}(\alpha) = s_p p$, $c = -\lfloor t/2 \rfloor$
2) Set $\Phi' = \Phi + c$ and $N = N_{\mathbb{Z}[\Phi]/\mathbb{Z}}(\Phi')$.
3) $a_1 = a - bc$, $b_1 = b$. (Represent $\alpha = a_1 + b_1\Phi'$).

Main
4) $x_1 = m(a_1 + b_1)$ and $x_2 = -mb_1$.
5) $y_i = \lfloor x_i/N_\alpha \rceil$ $(i = 1, 2)$.
6) $r_1' = m - (a_1 y_1 - N b_1 y_2)$ and $r_2' = -(a_1 y_2 + b_1 y_1 + b_1 y_2)$.
7) $r_1 = (r_1' + r_2'c)$ and $r_2 = r_2'$.
8) Return r_1, r_2.

Proof. From the proof of Preposition 1, if we put $c = -\lfloor t/2 \rfloor$ and $\Phi' = \Phi + c$, then $\alpha = a + b\Phi = a + b(\Phi' - c) = (a - bc) + b\Phi' = a_1 + b_1\Phi'$. Note that Putting $\beta = m$ and $T = Tr_{\mathbb{Z}[\Phi]/\mathbb{Z}}(\Phi')$ in the proof of Proposition 1, we have

$$\gamma = m/\alpha = m\bar{\alpha}/N_\alpha = \frac{m(a_1 + b_1 T) - mb_1\Phi'}{N_\alpha} = \frac{x_1 + x_2\Phi'}{N_\alpha}.$$

Since $\delta = y_1 + y_2\Phi'$ with $y_i = \lfloor x_i/N_\alpha \rceil$ $(i = 1, 2)$, we have

$$\rho = m - \alpha\delta = m - (a_1 y_1 - Nb_1 y_2) - (a_1 y_2 + b_1 y_1 + Tb_1 y_2)\Phi'.$$

Notice that $T = Tr_{\mathbb{Z}[\Phi]/\mathbb{Z}}(\Phi') = 1$ if t is odd, which justifies Algorithm 2. $\square$

According to Proposition 1, the length of Frobenius expansion of ρ obtained by dividing m by α instead of $\Phi^n - 1$ can be determined in the following Theorem.

Theorem 3. *For any integer m, let $\rho \in \mathbb{Z}[\Phi]$ be a remainder obtained by dividing m by $\alpha = a + b\Phi$ in Algorithm 2. The expansion length of ρ is at most $\lceil \log_q(\mu s_p p) \rceil + 4$.*

Proof. It follows from Theorem 1 that the length $k + 1$ of Frobenius expansion of ρ is at most $\lceil 2 \log_q \|\rho\| \rceil + 4 = \lceil \log_q N_{\mathbb{Q}[\Phi]/\mathbb{Q}}(\rho) \rceil + 4 \leq \lceil \log_q(\mu s_p p) \rceil + 4$ by Proposition 2. $\square$

For a random large integer $m \approx p$, the expansion length of ρ is in general equal to $\lceil \log_q(\mu s_p p) \rceil + 4$, and similarly that of ρ' obtained by dividing m by $\Phi^n - 1$ is in general equal to $\lceil \log_q(\mu \# E(\mathbb{F}_{q^n})) \rceil + 4$. Hence, the difference of the two lengths is roughly $\lfloor \log_q(\# E(\mathbb{F}_{q^n})/(s_p p)) \rfloor = \lfloor \log_q(h/s_p) \rfloor$. It will be exactly shown in our computational experiments.

4   Experimental Results

In this section we will first deal with a general method computing the order $\# E(\mathbb{F}_{q^n})$ of an elliptic curve E defined over a small field $\mathbb{F}_q$, which can be described as follows: Let $t_0 = 2, t_1 = t = q + 1 - \# E(\mathbb{F}_q)$, and for $l \geq 2$,

$$t_l = t_1 t_{l-1} - q t_{l-2}.$$

Then the group order of E is given as $\# E(\mathbb{F}_{q^n}) = q^n + 1 - t_n$.

Now experimental results for the previous theoretical claims are given for $q \leq 2^5$. This restriction of q allows us to use the Frobenius map for fast multiplication on elliptic curves. For reference, the larger q is hardly useful in practical implementation since it requires too much precomputation. Also, for cryptographic use, the order of each curve should have a large prime factor. We looked at extension fields $\mathbb{F}_{q^n}$ with $q^n \leq 2^{550}$ and tried to find curves whose order have a large prime factor p at least 160 bits and whose cofactor $h < 2^{24}$. The cases of its cofactor being equal to the order of the group $E(\mathbb{F}_q)$ were left out in Table 3.

In Table 3, we compared the lengths of expansion by using three different methods with 10^5 random numbers $m \in [1, p-1]$ for each curve. If one uses no reduction method, the length of expansion of m is expected to be less than or equal to $\lceil \log_q m^2 \rceil + 4$. If one uses a reduction method modulo $\Phi^n - 1$ to obtain a remainder ρ' then its expansion length of ρ' is expected to be less than or equal to $\lceil \log_q(\mu \# E(\mathbb{F}_{q^n})) \rceil + 4$. In a similar way, if one divides m by α satisfying (2) to obtain a remainder ρ, we expect that the length of expansion of ρ is at most $\lceil \log_q(\mu s_p p) \rceil + 4$. To minimize the length of expansion we applied the new reduction method to these curves, which was more efficient than the previous methods (see Table 3).

Table 3. The case $q = 2$

						The expansion length by using		
n	t	$\log_2 p$	h	s_p	μ	no reduction	$\Phi^n - 1$	α
277	1	264	15514	1	0.25	523	274	260
307	-1	289	351212	1	0.25	575	304	286

Table 3. (continue). The case $q = 4$

						The expansion length by using		
n	t	$\log_2 p$	h	s_p	μ	no reduction	$\Phi^n - 1$	α
97	1	179	58204	1	0.42	176	96	88
139	1	266	6676	1	0.42	264	138	131
163	3	316	1306	1	0.25	315	162	157
181	1	349	13036	1	0.42	347	180	173
191	-1	363	880134	1	0.42	361	190	180
239	-1	464	20082	2	0.42	462	238	231
251	-1	482	1518054	1	0.42	480	250	239
271	1	522	1645516	1	0.42	519	270	259

5   New Concept of Compactness

We begin by recalling the concept of compactness mentioned in the introduction. A compact curve has the security parameter which is almost the same with the bit-size of the underlying field. Table 4 lists a correspondence of ECC(in [12]) to RSA, where the securities of ECC and RSA are estimated in terms of the Pollard-ρ method and the general number field sieve method respectively. Curves in Table 4 are used widely in almost all standards for public-key cryptography including P1363 and ANSI X9.62. They are secure and compact. For example, the security parameter and the underlying field size of the curves in sect193

Table 3. (continue). The case $q = 8$

n	t	$\log_2 p$	h	s_p	μ	no reduction	$\Phi^n - 1$	α
						The expansion length by using		
71	-3	199	30684	2	0.58	131	70	66
71	-1	200	12790	2	0.75	131	70	66
89	3	257	1074	2	0.58	170	88	85
101	-1	288	62630	1	0.75	190	100	95
107	1	309	6856	1	0.74	204	106	102

Table 3. (continue). The case $q = 16$

n	t	$\log_2 p$	h	s_p	μ	no reduction	$\Phi^n - 1$	α
						The expansion length by using		
47	-1	166	5042178	9	1.42	82	46	42
97	3	367	2118494	3	1.25	183	96	91

Table 3. (continue). The case $q = 32$

n	t	$\log_2 p$	h	s_p	μ	no reduction	$\Phi^n - 1$	α
						The expansion length by using		
37	-5	163	7491206	4	2.25	64	37	33
41	3	183	8297610	5	2.60	72	40	37
41	9	195	1992	1	1.08	77	41	38
47	-1	220	57562	4	2.75	87	46	44
73	-3	349	120924	6	2.60	138	72	70
101	-7	491	32360	2	1.76	195	101	98
101	1	491	19424	2	2.72	195	100	98

series are 192-bit and 193-bits respectively. In particular, sect163, 233 and 283, except for sect193, include elliptic curves defined over $\mathbb{F}_2$.

As well-known in [9], multiplication on them is performed very fast using the Frobenius map, when compared with that on curves defined over large finite field. Table 5 shows that efficient implementation of curve arithmetic is essential in ECC for constrained applications such as mobile communication. In fact, the running time of multiplication on sect163r1 is not adequate for practical mobile service, say digital signature. In this context, it is natural that we focus on elliptic curves defined over small finite fields of characteristic 2 which are the Frobenius operation-available. Except for binary curves, they may not fulfill the previous concept of compactness. Here we want to expand it reasonably in order to contain them into the category of 'good' curves.

Now we note two factors which play an important role in efficient implementation of arithmetic in curves given here. One of them is the size of the underlying field. The other is the length of the Frobenius expansion for multiplication on such curves. The previous sections show how to minimize that easily. Table 6 shows that harmonizing properly two factors can give a new concept of compactness in aspects of efficiency and security. Indeed, a new curve $E(\mathbb{F}_{2^{213}})$ have a good favor over the sect193. For example, the former allows the stronger security and higher performance as compared with them of the latter. In particular, we note that no Frobenius-operation available curves defined over $\mathbb{F}_{2^{193}}$ exist.

Hence we propose to add to a family of compact curves, the Frobenius operation-available curves with the sufficiently large security parameter.

Table 4. Comparison of ECC with RSA

ECC	RSA	security($\frac{\sqrt{\pi n}}{2}$)
sect163[12]	1024 bits	2^{80}
sect193[12]	1536 bits	2^{96}
sect233 [12]	2240 bits	2^{112}
sect283[12]	3456 bits	2^{128}

Table 5. Elliptic Curve Arithmetic on mobile

1 full multiplication	CDMA3100 (ARM7 TDMI)	PentiumII 650Mhz
sect163k1	0.48 sec	1.32 ms
sect163r1	1.82 sec	5.02 ms

Table 6. Elliptic Curves for ECC

Elliptic Curves	$q = 8, n = 71, t = -3$ $s_p = 2 \; p = 199$ bits	$q = 8, n = 101, t = -1$ $s_p = 1 \; p = 288$ bits
Reduction by α (Full multiplication)	$\mathbb{F}_{2^{213}}$ (9.01 ms)	$\mathbb{F}_{2^{303}}$ (25.29 ms)
Reduction by $\Phi^n - 1$ (Full multiplication)	$\mathbb{F}_{2^{213}}$ (9.62 ms)	$\mathbb{F}_{2^{303}}$ (26.71 ms)
Elliptic Curves	sect193 [12]	sect283 [12]
With no Frobenius map (Full multiplication)	$\mathbb{F}_{2^{193}}$ (20.4 ms)	$\mathbb{F}_{2^{283}}$ (53.32 ms)

6   Attacks against Subfield Curves

Let E be an elliptic curve defined over a subfield $\mathbb{F}_q$ of $\mathbb{F}_{q^n}$, where q is a power of 2. We can consider attacks against the discrete logarithm problem(for short, DLP) on the curve E in two ways. In case of n being a large prime, the DLP is infeasible under all attacks known so far, including the GHS attack [2] and the Pollard ρ-methods [3,13]. For the others, it can be broken by taking an isogeny $E \to E'$ such that E' is defined over $\mathbb{F}_{q^n}$ and applying to the GHS attack. The underlying fields focused in this paper satisfy the former condition and are secure.

7   Conclusion

We have introduced a method of improving performance of scalar multiplication on certain elliptic curves and have presented theoretical reasons on it. The proposed method is to minimize the length of the Frobenius expansion under the consideration of cryptographic use and takes roughly the improvement of $\lfloor \log_q(\#E(\mathbb{F}_{q^n})/(s_p p)) \rfloor = \lfloor \log_q(h/s_p) \rfloor$, compared with the old reduction methods. As pointed out in previous sections, the proposed method shows that a lot of efficient curves for ECC can be optimized in aspects of compactness. To conclude, we propose the Frobenius operation-available curves for use in mobile-based ECC.

References

1. G. Cornacchia, *"Su di un metodo per la risoluzione in numeri interi dell' equazione $\sum_{h=0}^{n} C_h x^{n-h} y^h = P$"*, Giornale di Matematiche di Battaglini, **46** (1908), 33-90.
2. P. Gaudry, F. Hess and N. Smart, *"Constructive and destructive facets of Weil descent on elliptic curves"*, to appear J. Cryptology.
3. R. Gallant, R. Lambert, and S. Vanstone, *"Improving the parallelized Pollard lambda search on binary anomalous curves"*, Math. of Com., **69** (2000), 1699-1705.
4. N. Koblitz, *"CM-curves with good cryptographic properties"*, In Advances in Cryptology, CRYPTO 91, LNCS 576, Springer-Verlag (1992), 279-287.
5. W. Meier, O. Staffelbach, *"Efficient multiplication on certain non-supersingular elliptic curves"*, Advances in Cryptology, Crypto'92, 333-344.
6. V. Müller, *"Fast multiplication on elliptic curves over small fields of characteristic two"*, Journal of Cryptology, **11** (1998), 219-234.
7. D. Shanks, *"Five number theoretic algorithms"* In Proc. 2nd Manitoba Conference on Numerical Mathematics (1972), 51-70.
8. N.P. Smart, *"Elliptic curve cryptosystems over small fields of odd characteristic"*, Journal of Cryptology, **12** (1998), 141-151.
9. J. Solinas, *"Efficient arithmetic on Koblitz curves"*, Design, Codes and Cryptography, **19** (2000), 195-249.
10. I. Stewart, D. Tall, *"Algebraic Number Theory"*, Chapman and Hall, Halsted Press, 1979.

11. B. Vallée, *Une approche géométrique des algorithmes de réduction des réseaux en petite dimension"*, (1986) Thése, Université de Caen.
12. 'Standard for Efficient Cryptography'.
13. M. Wiener and R. Zuccherato, 'Faster Attacks on Elliptic Curve Cryptosystems', contribution to IEEE P1363.

An Alternate Decomposition of an Integer for Faster Point Multiplication on Certain Elliptic Curves

Young-Ho Park[1,*], Sangtae Jeong[2], Chang Han Kim[3], and Jongin Lim[1]

[1] CIST, Korea Univ., Seoul, Korea
{youngho,jilim}@cist.korea.ac.kr
[2] Dept. of Math., Seoul National Univ., Seoul, Korea
stj@math.snu.ac.kr
[3] Dept. of CAMIS, Semyung Univ., Jechon, Korea
chkim@venus.semyung.ac.kr

Abstract. In this paper the Gallant-Lambert-Vanstone method is re-examined for speeding up scalar multiplication. Using the theory of μ-Euclidian algorithm, we provide a rigorous method to reduce the theoretical bound for the decomposition of an integer k in the endomorphism ring of an elliptic curve. We then compare the two different methods for decomposition through computational implementations.

1 Introduction

Public key cryptosystems based on the discrete log problem on elliptic curves over finite fields(ECC) have gained much attention as a popular and practical scheme for computational advantages as well as for communicational advantages. As the complexity of protocols based on ECC relies mostly on the complexity of scalar multiplication, the dominant cost operation is computing kP for a point P on an elliptic curve.

Various methods for faster scalar multiplication have been devised by selecting relevant objects involving base fields and elliptic curves [1,3]. For example, by considering elliptic curves defined over the binary field, say Koblitz curves, Koblitz [5], Meier and Staffelbach [7] and Solinas [12,13] employed the Frobenius endomorphism to introduce an algorithm for faster scalar multiplication that do not use any point doublings. Extending their ideas, Müller [6] and Smart [11] came up with practical methods which are applicable to elliptic curves over small finite fields of small characteristic.

Recently, Gallant, *et al.* [3] presented a new method for faster scalar multiplication on elliptic curves over (large) prime fields that have an efficiently-computable endomorphism. The key idea of their method is decomposing an

---

* This work is supported in part by the Ministry of Information & Communication of Korea("Support Project of University Foundation Research $<'$ 00 $>$" supervised by IITA)

D. Naccache and P. Paillier (Eds.): PKC 2002, LNCS 2274, pp. 323–334, 2002.

arbitrary scalar k in terms of an integer eigenvalue λ of the characteristic polynomial of such an endomorphism(See §3). The problem with this method is how
efficiently a random integer $k \in [1, n-1]$ could be decomposed into $k = k_1 + k_2\lambda$
modulo n with the bitlengths of k_1 and k_2 half that of k where n is a large prime
number. They gave an algorithm for decomposing k into the desired form using
the extended Euclidean algorithm and did not derive explicit bounds for decomposition components. However, they expected that the bounds are approximately
near to $\sqrt{n}$ on the basis of numerous implementations.

In this paper, we present an alternate algorithm for decomposing an integer
k using the theory of μ-Euclidian algorithm. This algorithm runs a little bit
faster than that of Gallant *et al.*'s and unlike their algorithm, our algorithm
gives explicit bounds for the components. To compare the two algorithms for
scalar decomposition we give a precise analysis of all elliptic curves treated in
[3].

This paper is arranged as follows. In Section 2, we recall some basic facts on
elliptic curves and in Section 3 we briefly discuss the Gallant-Lambert-Vanstone
method for comparison with ours. Section 4 is concerned with decomposing
an integer k via μ-Euclidian algorithm in the endomorphism rings of elliptic
curves. Section 5 contains various examples of elliptic curves and then we give
explicit bounds for decomposition components. In the final section we compare
two methods to draw our conclusions.

2 Endomorphism Rings

We begin with introducing some basics to elliptic curves. Let $\mathbb{F}_q$ be a finite field
of q elements and E be an elliptic curve over $\mathbb{F}_q$ given by a Weierstrass equation

$$E/\mathbb{F}_q : y^2 + a_1xy + a_3y = x^3 + a_2x^2 + a_4x + a_6$$

with $a_i \in \mathbb{F}_q$. $E(\mathbb{F}_q)$ denotes the set of $\mathbb{F}_q$-rational points on E together with
the point at infinity O and $\text{End}(E)$ denotes the ring of $\mathbb{F}_q$-endomorphisms of E.
It is well known that (non-supersingular) elliptic curves over finite fields have
complex multiplication. Indeed, $\text{End}(E)$ is isomorphic to a complex quadratic
order.

The Frobenius endomorphism $\Phi \in \text{End}(E)$ is the morphism given by $\Phi(x, y) = (x^q, y^q)$. It satisfies the quadratic relation $\Phi^2 - t\Phi + q = 0$ in $\text{End}(E)$, where t
is called the trace of the Frobenius Φ. More importantly, t is related closely to
the order of $E(\mathbb{F}_q)$ by the formula: $\#E(\mathbb{F}_q) = q + 1 - t$. By Hasse's remarkable
work on $\#E(\mathbb{F}_q)$, we have

Theorem 1. *Let E be an elliptic curve over $\mathbb{F}_q$ and let n denote the number of*
$E(\mathbb{F}_q)$, *then*

$$|t| = |q + 1 - n| < 2\sqrt{q}.$$

For cryptographic applications, one deals with only non-supersinglar elliptic
curves E, so the endomorphism ring of E is an order in the imaginary quadratic
field $\mathbb{Q}(\sqrt{t^2 - 4q})$. Hence it is easily seen that $\mathbb{Z}[\Phi] \subset \text{End}(E) \subset \mathbb{Q}(\sqrt{t^2 - 4q})$.

3 Gallant-Lambert-Vanstone Method

Let E be an elliptic curve over $\mathbb{F}_q$ and ϕ be an efficiently-computable endomorphism in $\text{End}(E)$. For cryptographic purposes, the order of $E(\mathbb{F}_q)$ must have a large prime factor n. Let $P \in E(\mathbb{F}_q)$ be a point of prime order n. Then the map ϕ acts on the subgroup of $E(\mathbb{F}_q)$ generated by P as a multiplication by λ, where λ is a root of the characteristic polynomial of ϕ modulo n. In place of the Frobenius, Gallant *et al.* exploited ϕ to speed up the scalar multiplication by decomposing an integer k into a sum of the form $k = k_1 + k_2\lambda \pmod{n}$, where $k \in [1, n-1]$ and $k_1, k_2 \approx \sqrt{n}$. Now we compute

$$kP = (k_1 + k_2\lambda)P = k_1P + k_2\lambda P = k_1P + k_2\phi(P).$$

Since $\phi(P)$ can be easily computed, a windowed simultaneous multiple exponentiation applies to $k_1P + k_2\phi(P)$ for additional speedup. It is analyzed in [3] that this method improves a running time up to 66 % compared with the general method, thus it is roughly 50 % faster than the best general methods for 160-bit scalar multiplication. The problem we face is how efficiently a randomly chosen k can be decomposed into a sum of the required form and how explicitly upper bounds of the lengths of the components k_1 and k_2 can be given.

For complete comparison with our method we will now describe the algorithm in [3] for decomposing k out of given integers n and λ. It is composed of two steps. By considering the homomorphism $f : \mathbb{Z} \times \mathbb{Z} \to \mathbb{Z}_n$ defined by $(i, j) \mapsto (i + j\lambda)$ (mod n) we first find linearly independent short vectors $v_1, v_2 \in \mathbb{Z} \times \mathbb{Z}$ such that $f(v_1) = f(v_2) = 0$. As a stage of precomputations this process can be done by the Extended Euclidean algorithm, independently of k. Secondly, one needs to find a vector in $\mathbb{Z}v_1 + \mathbb{Z}v_2$ that is close to $(k, 0)$ using linear algebra. Then (k_1, k_2) is determined by the equation:

$$(k_1, k_2) = (k, 0) - (\lfloor b_1 \rceil v_1 + \lfloor b_2 \rceil v_2),$$

where $(k, 0) = b_1v_1 + b_2v_2$ is represented as an element in $\mathbb{Q} \times \mathbb{Q}$ and $\lfloor b \rceil$ denotes the nearest integer to b. We provide an explicit algorithm in [3] as follows:

Algorithm 1 (Finding (k_1, k_2))

Input:	$k \approx n$, the short vectors $v_1 = (x_1, y_1), v_2 = (x_2, y_2)$.
Output:	(k_1, k_2) such that $k \equiv k_1 + k_2\lambda \pmod{n}$.

1)	$D = x_1y_2 - x_2y_1, a_1 = y_2k, a_2 = -y_1k.$
2)	$z_i = \lfloor a_i/D \rceil$ for $i = 1, 2.$
3)	$k_1 = k - (z_1x_1 + z_2x_2), k_2 = z_1y_1 + z_2y_2.$
Return:	$(k_1, k_2).$

This algorithm takes two round operations and eight large integer multiplications. In [3, Lemma 2], an upper bound of the vector (k_1, k_2) obtained from Algorithm 1 is estimated by the Euclidean norm inequality :

$$\| (k_1, k_2) \| \le \max(\| v_1 \|, \| v_2 \|).$$

In the procedure of finding two independent short vectors v_1, v_2 such that $f(v_1) = f(v_2) = 0$, Gallant, *et al.* showed $\| v_1 \| \leq 2\sqrt{n}$ but could not estimate $\| v_2 \|$ explicitly. However they expected heuristically that v_2 would also be short. For this reason, they could not give explicit upper bounds of k_1 and k_2 although the lengths of components prove to be near to $\sqrt{n}$ through numerous computational experiments.

4   An Alternate Decomposition of k

We are now describing a new method for decomposing k from a viewpoint of algebraic number theory. Recall that $\text{End}(E)$ is a quadratic order of $K = \mathbb{Q}(\sqrt{-D})(D > 0)$, which is contained in the maximal order of K, denoted $\mathcal{O}_K$. Let ϕ be an efficiently-computable endomorphism in $\text{End}(E)$. Then we have $\mathbb{Z}[\phi] \subset \text{End}(E) \subset \mathcal{O}_K$. Since ϕ is in general not a rational integer, it satisfies a quadratic relation

$$\phi^2 - t_\phi \phi + n_\phi = 0. \tag{1}$$

We assume that the discriminant of ϕ defined by $D_\phi = t_\phi^2 - 4n_\phi$ is of the form $-Dm^2$ for some integer m. As usual, for a point $P \in E(\mathbb{F}_q)$ of a large prime order n we want to perform scalar multiplication kP for $k \in [1, n-1]$. Suppose now that there exists an element $\alpha = a + b\phi \in \mathbb{Z}[\phi]$ such that

$$N_{\mathbb{Z}[\phi]/\mathbb{Z}}(\alpha) = s_n n \text{ and } (\alpha)P = O \tag{2}$$

for some positive integer s_n, which is relatively small to n. We then want to decompose a scalar k using a division by α in the μ-Euclidean ring $\mathbb{Z}[\phi]$, where μ is some positive real (see Lemma 2 or [11]). First of all, the existence of such α is guaranteed from the following Lemma.

Lemma 1. *There exists an element $\alpha \in \mathbb{Z}[\phi]$ satisfying (2) for some positive integer $s_n \leq 3n_\phi$. Moreover, $s_n = 1$ when $\mathbb{Z}[\phi]$ is a principal maximal order and n splits in $\mathbb{Q}(\phi)/\mathbb{Q}$.*

Proof. Let $v_1 = (a, b)$ be the short vector constructed in [3] such that $f(v_1) = 0$. Since $f(v_1) = a + b\lambda \equiv 0 \pmod{n}$, it is clear that $(a + b\phi)P = O$. Put $\alpha = a + b\phi$ and $n' = N_{\mathbb{Z}[\phi]/\mathbb{Z}}(a + b\phi) \in \mathbb{Z}$. Then we have $N_{\mathbb{Z}[\phi]/\mathbb{Z}}(a + b\phi) = (a + b\bar{\phi})(a + b\phi) = n'$, so $n'P = (a + b\bar{\phi})(a + b\phi)P = O$. It implies that $n' \equiv 0 \pmod{n}$ and $n' = s_n n$ for some integer s_n. Since $a, b \leq \sqrt{n}$ in [3] and $| t_\phi | < 2\sqrt{n_\phi}$, we have

$$s_n n = a^2 + abt_\phi + b^2 n_\phi \leq a^2 + | abt_\phi | + b^2 n_\phi \leq n_\phi(a^2 + | ab | + b^2) \leq 3n_\phi n.$$

The second assertion follows from [14].   □

Motivated by the work of [3] we give an alternate decomposition of k in terms of ϕ in place of λ in [3]. Viewing a k as an element of $\mathbb{Z}[\phi]$ we divide k by α satisfying (2) in $\mathbb{Z}[\phi]$ and write

$$k = \beta\alpha + \rho$$

with $N_{\mathbb{Z}[\phi]/\mathbb{Z}}(\rho) < \mu N_{\mathbb{Z}[\phi]/\mathbb{Z}}(\alpha)$ for some β and $\rho \in \mathbb{Z}[\phi]$. We then compute

$$kP = (\beta\alpha + \rho)(P) = \beta(\alpha(P)) + \rho(P) = \rho(P).$$

From a representation of ρ, that is, $\rho = k_1 + k_2\phi$, it turns out that

$$kP = \rho P = k_1 P + k_2\phi(P).$$

Since $\phi(P)$ is easily computed we can apply a (windowed) simultaneous multiple exponenciation to yield the same running time improvement as in [3]. Unlike [3] our method gives rigorous bounds for the components k_1, k_2 in term of n_ϕ. To see this, we give the following theorem estimating $N_{\mathbb{Z}[\phi]/\mathbb{Z}}(\rho)$.

Theorem 2. *Let $\alpha = a + b\phi \neq 0 \in \mathbb{Z}[\phi]$. If $\beta \in \mathbb{Z}[\phi]$ then there exist $\delta, \rho \in \mathbb{Z}[\phi]$ such that $\beta = \delta\alpha + \rho$ and $N_{\mathbb{Z}[\phi]/\mathbb{Z}}(\rho) < \mu N_{\mathbb{Z}[\phi]/\mathbb{Z}}(\alpha)$ with*

$$0 < \mu \leq \begin{cases} (9 + 4n_\phi)/16 & \text{if } t_\phi \text{ is odd,} \\ (1 + n_\phi)/4 & \text{if } t_\phi \text{ is even.} \end{cases}$$

Proof. Since $\phi^2 - t_\phi\phi + n_\phi = 0$, we take $\phi = (t_\phi + \sqrt{D_\phi})/2$ where $D_\phi = t_\phi^2 - 4n_\phi$. Put $N_\alpha = N_{\mathbb{Z}[\phi]/\mathbb{Z}}(\alpha)$ and $c = -\lfloor t_\phi/2 \rfloor$. Setting $\phi' = \phi + c$ and changing a $\mathbb{Z}$-basis $\{1, \phi\}$ to $\{1, \phi'\}$, we have $\mathbb{Z}[\phi] = \mathbb{Z}[\phi']$ and

$$\phi' = \begin{cases} (1 + \sqrt{D_\phi})/2 & \text{if } t_\phi \text{ is odd,} \\ \sqrt{D_\phi}/2 & \text{otherwise.} \end{cases}$$

Then α can be written as $a_1 + b_1\phi'$ in term of this new basis. For a given dividend β, we let $\gamma = \beta/\alpha$ and then we have

$$\gamma = \beta/\alpha = \beta\bar{\alpha}/N_\alpha = \frac{x_1 + x_2\phi'}{N_\alpha}$$

where $\bar{\alpha}$ denotes the complex conjugate of α. Take $\delta = y_1 + y_2\phi'$ with $y_i = \lfloor x_i/N_\alpha \rceil$ $(i = 1, 2)$, where $\lfloor x \rceil$ denotes the nearest integer to x. Finally, take $\rho = \alpha(\gamma - \delta)$, then since $\beta = \alpha\gamma, \alpha\delta \in \mathbb{Z}[\phi], \rho \in \mathbb{Z}[\phi]$. It is easily checked that

$$N_{\mathbb{Z}[\phi]/\mathbb{Z}}(\rho)/N_{\mathbb{Z}[\phi]/\mathbb{Z}}(\alpha) = N_{\mathbb{Q}[\phi]/\mathbb{Q}}(\gamma - \delta) \leq N_{\mathbb{Q}[\phi]/\mathbb{Q}}(\tfrac{1}{2} + \tfrac{1}{2}\phi')$$

$$= \tfrac{1}{4} N_{\mathbb{Z}[\phi]/\mathbb{Z}}(1 + \phi') = \begin{cases} \tfrac{1}{4} N_{\mathbb{Z}[\phi]/\mathbb{Z}}(\frac{3 + \sqrt{D_\phi}}{2}) & \text{if } t_\phi \text{ is odd,} \\ \tfrac{1}{4} N_{\mathbb{Z}[\phi]/\mathbb{Z}}(\frac{2 + \sqrt{D_\phi}}{2}) & \text{otherwise.} \end{cases}$$

$$= \begin{cases} \tfrac{1}{4}(\frac{9 - D_\phi}{4}) \leq \tfrac{1}{4}((9 + 4n_\phi)/4) & \text{if } t_\phi \text{ is odd,} \\ \tfrac{1}{4}(\frac{4 - D_\phi}{4}) \leq \tfrac{1}{4}((4 + 4n_\phi)/4) & \text{otherwise.} \end{cases} \qquad \square$$

From the proof of Theorem 2, we can produce an efficient algorithm to compute a remainder $\rho = k_1 + k_2\phi$ from k and $\alpha = a + b\phi$. It is also composed of two steps as in [3]. As a stage of precomputations, we first compute

Precomputations

---

1) $N_\alpha = N_{\mathbb{Z}[\phi]/\mathbb{Z}}(\alpha) = s_n n$, $t_\phi = Tr_{\mathbb{Z}[\phi]/\mathbb{Z}}(\phi)$ and $c = -\lfloor t_\phi/2 \rfloor$.

2) Set $\phi' = \phi + c$. $N = N_{\mathbb{Z}[\phi]/\mathbb{Z}}(\phi')$ and $T = Tr_{\mathbb{Z}[\phi]/\mathbb{Z}}(\phi') = \begin{cases} 1 & \text{if } t_\phi \text{ is odd,} \\ 0 & \text{otherwise.} \end{cases}$

3) $a_1 = a - bc$, $b_1 = b$ (to represent $\alpha = a_1 + b_1\phi'$).

Algorithm 2 (Divide k by $\alpha = a + b\phi$)

Input:	$k \approx n$ and $N_\alpha, T, N, c, a_1, b_1$.
Output:	$\rho = k_1 + k_2\phi$ such that $N_{\mathbb{Z}[\phi]/\mathbb{Z}}(\rho) < \mu N_{\mathbb{Z}[\phi]/\mathbb{Z}}(\alpha)$.

1) $x_1 = k(a_1 + b_1 T)$ and $x_2 = -kb_1$.
2) $y_i = \lfloor x_i/N_\alpha \rceil$ $(i = 1, 2)$.
3) $k_1' = k - (a_1 y_1 - N b_1 y_2)$ and $k_2' = -(a_1 y_2 + b_1 y_1 + T b_1 y_2)$.
4) $k_1 = (k_1' + k_2' c)$ and $k_2 = k_2'$.
   Return: k_1, k_2.

Algorithm 2 takes in general two round operations and eight large integer multiplications as in Algorithm 1. But if the values t_ϕ and n_ϕ are rather small, then the values c and N are also expected to be small, which reduces 8 large integer multiplications to 6. From this observation we may expect that the proposed algorithm will be a little bit more efficient than that of [3]. In Table 1 we compare running times of two algorithms applied to Examples 1-4 in §5.1.

Table 1. Comparison of Two Algorithms(on PetiumII 866Mhz)

	$\begin{array}{c} t_\phi = 0 \\ n_\phi = 1 \end{array}$	$\begin{array}{c} t_\phi = -1 \\ n_\phi = 1 \end{array}$	$\begin{array}{c} t_\phi = 1 \\ n_\phi = 2 \end{array}$	$\begin{array}{c} t_\phi = 0 \\ n_\phi = 2 \end{array}$
Gallant's Algorithm 1	0.072 ms	0.069 ms	0.071 ms	0.069 ms
Our Algorithm 2	0.053 ms	0.054 ms	0.053 ms	0.054 ms

5   Examples and Upper Bounds

5.1   Examples

In this subsection we list up a family of elliptic curves over a large prime field $\mathbb{F}_p$ with efficient endomorphisms treated in [3] and give the characteristic polynomial of such an endomorphism in each case.

Example 1. Let $p \equiv 1 \pmod 4$ be a prime, and let E_1 be an elliptic curve defined by

$$E_1/\mathbb{F}_p : y^2 = x^3 + ax.$$

Let $\beta \in \mathbb{F}_p$ be an element of order 4. Then the map $\phi : E_1 \to E_1$ defined by $(x, y) \mapsto (-x, \beta y)$ and $O \mapsto O$ belongs to $\mathrm{End}(E_1)$. Moreover, it is easily seen that ϕ satisfies the quadratic equation

$$\phi^2 + 1 = 0,$$

so $t_\phi = 0, n_\phi = 1$ and $\mathrm{End}(E_1)$ is isomorphic to $\mathbb{Z}[\phi]$, the maximal order of $\mathbb{Q}(\sqrt{-1})$.

Example 2. Let $p \equiv 1 \pmod 3$ be a prime, and let E_2 be an elliptic curve defined by

$$E_2/\mathbb{F}_p : y^2 = x^3 + b.$$

Let $\gamma \in \mathbb{F}_p$ be an element of order 3. Then the map $\phi : E_2 \to E_2$ defined by $(x, y) \mapsto (\gamma x, y)$ and $O \mapsto O$ is an endomorphism defined over $\mathbb{F}_p$. Moreover, the quadratic equation of ϕ is given by

$$\phi^2 + \phi + 1 = 0,$$

so $t_\phi = -1, n_\phi = 1$ and $\mathrm{End}(E_2)$ is isomorphic to $\mathbb{Z}[\phi]$, the maximal order of $\mathbb{Q}(\sqrt{-3})$.

It is noted in both Examples 1 and 2 that the map ϕ can be easily computed using only one multiplication in $\mathbb{F}_p$.

Example 3. Let $p > 3$ be a prime such that -7 is a perfect square in $\mathbb{F}_p$, and let $\omega = (1 + \sqrt{-7})/2$, and let $a = (\omega - 3)/4$. Let E_3 be an elliptic curve defined by

$$E_3/\mathbb{F}_p : y^2 = x^3 - \frac{3}{4}x^2 - 2x - 1.$$

Then the map $\phi : E_3 \to E_3$ defined by

$$(x, y) \mapsto (\omega^{-2} \frac{x^2 - \omega}{x - a}, \ \omega^{-3} y \frac{x^2 - 2ax + \omega}{(x - a)^2})$$

and $O \mapsto O$ belongs to $\mathrm{End}(E_3)$. Moreover, ϕ satisfies

$$\phi^2 - \phi + 2 = 0,$$

so $t_\phi = 1, n_\phi = 2$ and $\mathrm{End}(E_3)$ is isomorphic to $\mathbb{Z}[\phi]$, the maximal order of $\mathbb{Q}(\sqrt{-7})$.

Example 4. Let $p > 3$ be a prime such that -2 is a perfect square in $\mathbb{F}_p$. Let E_4 be an elliptic curve defined by

$$E_4/\mathbb{F}_p : y^2 = 4x^3 - 30x - 28.$$

Then the map $\phi : E_4 \to E_4$ defined by

$$(x, y) \mapsto (-\frac{2x^2 + 4x + 9}{4(x + 2)}, \ -\frac{2x^2 + 8x - 1}{4\sqrt{-2}(x + 2)^2} y)$$

and $O \mapsto O$ belongs to $\mathrm{End}(E_4)$. Moreover, the quadratic equation of ϕ is given by

$$\phi^2 + 2 = 0,$$

so $t_\phi = 0, n_\phi = 2$ and $\mathrm{End}(E_4)$ is isomorphic to $\mathbb{Z}[\phi]$, the maximal order of $\mathbb{Q}(\sqrt{-2})$.

In Examples 3 and 4, computing an endomorphism is a little harder than doubling a point.

5.2   Upper Bounds on the Components k_1, k_2

Now we restrict ourselves to elliptic curves $E(\mathbb{F}_p)$ only in the previous subsection. For cryptographic applications, let P be a point of $E(\mathbb{F}_p)$ of large prime order n, so $\#E(\mathbb{F}_p) = hn$ where h is called the cofactor of $E(\mathbb{F}_p)$. Recall that for each $1 \le i \le 4, \mathrm{End}(E_i) = \mathbb{Z}[\phi]$ is the maximal order of $\mathbb{Q}(\sqrt{-D})$ where $D = 1, 3, 7$ or 2, respectively. By Lemma 1 there exists an element $\alpha = a + b\phi \in \mathbb{Z}[\phi]$ such that $N_{\mathbb{Z}[\phi]/\mathbb{Z}}(\alpha) = n$ and $(\alpha)P = O$. Finding such an α boils down to solving out a quadratic equation in $\mathbb{Z}[\phi]$. Indeed, this process can be done using the known methods such as Shanks' algorithm [9] and lattice reduction method [10]. Especially, one can also represent n, which splits in $\mathbb{Q}(\sqrt{-D})/\mathbb{Q}$, by the principal form only by using the Cornacchia's algorithm [2]. We use Theorem 2 to give explicit upper bounds on μ in the μ-Euclidean ring $\mathbb{Z}[\phi]$.

Lemma 2. *Let $\alpha = a + b\phi$ such that $N_{\mathbb{Z}[\phi]/\mathbb{Z}}(\alpha) = n$. For any integer k, there exists a remainder $\rho \in \mathbb{Z}[\phi]$ such that $k = \beta\alpha + \rho$ for some $\beta \in \mathbb{Z}[\phi]$ with*

$$N_{\mathbb{Z}[\phi]/\mathbb{Z}}(\rho) \le \begin{cases} n/2 & \text{for } E_1, \\ 3n/4 & \text{for } E_2, \\ n & \text{for } E_3, \\ 3n/4 & \text{for } E_4. \end{cases}$$

Proof. Recall that t_ϕ is even for E_1 and E_4, and t_ϕ is odd for E_2 and E_3. From the proof of Theorem 2, we get

$$N_{\mathbb{Z}[\phi]/\mathbb{Z}}(\rho)/N_{\mathbb{Z}[\phi]/\mathbb{Z}}(\alpha) \le \begin{cases} \frac{1}{4}(\frac{9-D_\phi}{4}) & \text{if } t_\phi \text{ is odd}, \\ \frac{1}{4}(\frac{4-D_\phi}{4}) & \text{if } t_\phi \text{ is even}, \end{cases}$$

which gives the desired result.   □

Finally, Lemma 2 gives explicit upper bounds on the components of k.

Theorem 3. *For any k, let ρ be a remainder of k divided by α using Algorithm 2 and write $\rho = k_1 + k_2\phi$. Then we have*

$$\max\{|k_1|, |k_2|\} \le \begin{cases} \sqrt{n/2} & \text{for } E_1, \\ \sqrt{n} & \text{for } E_2, \\ \sqrt{8n/7} & \text{for } E_3, \\ \sqrt{3n/2} & \text{for } E_4. \end{cases}$$

Proof. In case of E_1, it is easy to see that $N_{\mathbb{Z}[\phi]/\mathbb{Z}}(\rho) = N_{\mathbb{Z}[\phi]/\mathbb{Z}}(k_1 + k_2\phi) = k_1^2 + k_2^2$. Lemma 2 immediately gives $k_1^2 + k_2^2 \le n/2$, which completes the proof for E_1.

In case of E_2, we have $N_{\mathbb{Z}[\phi]/\mathbb{Z}}(\rho) = k_1^2 + k_2^2 - k_1 k_2$. If $k_1 k_2 \le 0$ then it follows from Lemma 2 that $\max\{|k_1|, |k_2|\} \le \sqrt{3n/4}$. Assume $k_1 k_2 > 0$ and $|k_2| \ge |k_1| > 0$. Then by Lemma 2, we easily deduce

$$k_1^2 + k_2^2 - k_1 k_2 = |k_1|^2 + |k_2|^2 - |k_1||k_2| = (|k_1| - \frac{1}{2}|k_2|)^2 + \frac{3}{4}|k_2|^2 \le 3n/4.$$

Hence $|k_1|^2 \le |k_2|^2 \le n$ implies that $\max\{|k_1|, |k_2|\} = |k_2| \le \sqrt{n}$, completing the proof for E_2. The other cases are also done similarly.   □

6   Comparisons of the Two Methods and Conclusion

6.1   Comparisons

In this section we compare the two methods by decomposing many integral scalars on all elliptic curves in Section 5. To protect Pohlig-Hellman attack [8] the group order of $E(\mathbb{F}_p)$ has a large prime factor n at least 160-bit. The problem of determining the group order of a given elliptic curve is not an easy task in general but thanks to an improved Schoof's algorithm one can figure out the group order of an elliptic curve. However, in the case where the endomorphism ring is known, computing the group order of $E(\mathbb{F}_p)$ is rather easy and it is explicitly given by a well known formula in [4]. Conversely, determining the elliptic curve having a given group order is not easy. For this reason, it is not easy to take 'cryptographically good' elliptic curves whose the group order has a large prime factor n and has a small cofactor. Without knowing the exact group order of elliptic curves we here decompose scalars by the two methods under the assumption that elliptic curves in consideration are good cryptographically. Indeed our method gives a decomposition of a scalar if only we know the quadratic equation satisfied by an efficient endomorphism on elliptic curves.

For each example in subsection 5.1, we considered various primes p where p is the norm of some element $\pi \in \mathbb{Z}[\phi]$ satisfying $N_{\mathbb{Z}[\phi]/\mathbb{Z}}(1 - \pi) = nh$ for a large prime n and a small h. We then decomposed 10^5 random integers $k \in [1, n-1]$. In an appendix we put a list of tables showing comparable data in two decompositions. Here we briefly describe implementation results. For Example 1 the two decompositions are identically same for 20 different primes p. In other examples different decompositions of k occurred but for most of scalars k the decompositions are exactly same and in different cases the length differences for components are within 2 bits because the ratios of maximum lengths are less than 3, so it makes no big difference in applying the simultaneous windowed techniques. On the whole, we can analyze that the two decompositions are same for more than 80 % out of all cases we have investigated. In different decompositions, the length differences are almost negligible.

6.2   Conclusion

We described an alternate method of decomposing k using the theory of μ-Euclidian algorithm. The proposed method gives not only a different decomposition of a scalar k but also produces explicit upper bounds for the components by computing norms in the complex quadratic orders. We then compare the two different methods for decomposition through computational implementations. From these we conclude that the two decompositions are same for most of cases of elliptic curves we have considered. Even in different decompositions of a same scalar, the two methods makes no big difference in a sense that the length differences of components are very small. So this shows that the algorithm of [3] runs smoothly with desired bounds for components, as expected.

References

1. Ian Blake, Gadiel Seroussi and Nigel Smart, 'Elliptic Curves in Cryptography', London Mathematical Society Lecture Note Series. 265, Cambridge University Press, (1999).
2. G. Cornacchia, *"Su di un metodo per la risoluzione in numeri interi dell' equazione $\sum_{h=0}^{n} C_h x^{n-h} y^h = P$"*, Giornale di Matematiche di Battaglini, 46, (1908),33-90.
3. R. Gallant, R. Lambert and S. Vanstone, *"Faster Point Multiplication on Elliptic Curves with Efficient Endomorphisms"*, Advances in Cryptology-Crypto 2001, LNCS 2139, Springer-Verlag (2001), 190-200.
4. K.Ireland and M.Rosen, 'A classical introduction to modern number theory', Graduate Texts in Mathematics, vol 84, Springer-Verlag, (1982).
5. N. Koblitz, *"CM-curves with good cryptographic properties"*, Advances in Cryptology-Crypto '91, LNCS 576, Springer-Verlag (1992), 279-287.
6. V. Müller, *" Fast multiplication in elliptic curves over small fields of characteristic two"*, Journal of Cryptology, **11** (1998), 219-234.
7. W. Meier and O. Staffelbach, *"Efficient multiplication on certain nonsupersingular elliptic curves"*, Advances in Cryptology-Crypto'92, Springer-Verlag (1992), 333-344.
8. S. Pohlig, M. Hellman,*An improved algorithm for computing logarithms over $GF(p)$ its cryptographic significance, "*, IEEE Trans. Inform. Theory, **24** (1978), 106-110.
9. D. Shanks, *"Five number theoretic algorithms"* In Proc. 2nd Manitoba Conference on Numerical Mathematics (1972), 51-70.
10. B.Vallée,*Une approche géométrique des algorithmes de réduction des réseaux en petite dimension"*, (1986) Thése, Université de Caen.
11. N. Smart, *"Elliptic curve cryptosystems over small fields of odd characteristic "*, Journal of Cryptology, **12** (1999), 141-145.
12. J. Solinas, *"An improved algorithm for arithmetic on a family of elliptic curves"*, Advances in Cryptology-Crypto '97, LNCS 1294, Springer-Verlag (1997), 357-371.
13. J. Solinas, *"Efficient arithmetic on Koblitz curves"*, Design, Codes and Cryptography, **19** (2000), 195-249.
14. I. Stewart and D. Tall, 'Algebraic Number Theory', Chapman and Hall, Halsted Press, (1979).

Appendix: Implementation Results

We list up tables showing comparable data in two decompositions. For each example in subsection 5.1 we considered 3 different primes p and then decomposed 10^5 random integers $k \in [1, n-1]$ for each p. Each example consists of 3 tables and each table pairs with two parts. One part in each table consists of 4 data, p, n, α and λ. The other part shows the degree of likeness in two decompositions. It contains the ratio of the same decompositions to different ones and the ratio of maximum lengths, $\max_{\{i=1,2\}}$ to $\sqrt{n}$ where $\max_1$ denotes the maximum length of the components by our method and $\max_2$ denotes that by Gallant *et al.*'s method.

Example 1: $\phi^2 + 1 = 0$

p	2435650778561789424356750646486535653413982256141
n	1217825389280894712178371297187162754778237787 81
λ	463083162867534564602873813002322039600425577 86
α	3440208842102491051764 30 + 5858472629694406217 2859 ϕ

same	different	$\max_1/\sqrt{n}$	$\max_2/\sqrt{n}$
100%	0%	0.576	0.576

p	7321851856786295141841249611588797801248802237 7
n	3660925928393147570920637235629128340232794047 3
λ	19769856633674487989568880377360877117950324 407
α	1823245032990702779880 48 + 58026156004674194 058763 ϕ

same	different	$\max_1/\sqrt{n}$	$\max_2/\sqrt{n}$
100%	0%	0.628	0.628

p	3930678888074997741808595252689014229714795666337
n	1965339444037498870904297555040731424331941753793
λ	1309814068063573440285466856760823735681467247754
α	9550037863987291956099 53+ 1026307562089254651 689328 ϕ

same	different	$\max_1/\sqrt{n}$	$\max_2/\sqrt{n}$
100%	0%	0.706	0.705

Example 2: $\phi^2 + \phi + 1 = 0$

q	1220661975006673910903067813381247142962340996767
n	3051654937516684777257672395640126525353303951 11
λ	2568307617589060328687300360227744919781368332 95
α	1342796970351349858390 5 -545581462326562493124029]ϕ

same	different	$\max_1 > \max_2$	$\max_1/\sqrt{n}$	$\max_2/\sqrt{n}$
100 %	0 %	0 %	0.517	0.517

p	9502214463242359684030598552576966651387176185739
n	3167404821080786561343537123938124336285385868 83
l	2823514850778985137378326951118188726354834645 75
α	4273079135498328131916 37 -2103701491098140564 50749 ϕ

same	different	$\max_1 > \max_2$	$\max_1/\sqrt{n}$	$\max_2/\sqrt{n}$
75%	25%	21 %	0.938	0.743

p	1021410883513058291273849827291939137569277512 23
n	1021410883513058291273844378164392483906244782 51
λ	2937762420972822110494082541513856472961323898 2
α	1929027762096972608836 89 -1760049892278345211 94641 ϕ

same	different	$\max_1 > \max_2$	$\max_1/\sqrt{n}$	$\max_2/\sqrt{n}$
74%	26%	14%	0.878	0.844

Example 3: $\phi^2 - \phi + 2 = 0$

p	12206619750066739109030678133812471429623409 96767
n	30516549375166847772576723956401265253533039 5111
λ	25683076175890603286873003602277449197813683 3295
α	13427969703513498583905 -5455814623265624931 24029 ϕ

same	different	$\max_1 > \max_2$	$\max_1/\sqrt{n}$	$\max_2/\sqrt{n}$
100%	0%	0%	0.518	0.518

p	27811890929441973874395311564036633313232309 03297
n	92706303098139912914650953243482719649855589 6781
λ	21918279997822803296613353806449073940359362 6775
α	8530330605806091877376 51 -190989728098028002 286769ϕ

same	different	$\max_1 > \max_2$	$\max_1/\sqrt{n}$	$\max_2/\sqrt{n}$
75%	25%	24%	0.982	0.640

p	95022144632423596840305985525769665138717618 5739
n	31674048210807865613435371239381243362853858 6883
λ	28235148507789851373783269511181887263548346 4575
α	4273079135498328131916 37-210370149109814056 450749 ϕ

same	different	$\max_1 > \max_2$	$\max_1/\sqrt{n}$	$\max_2/\sqrt{n}$
75%	25%	21%	0.941	0.750

Example 4: $\phi^2 + 2 = 0$

p	56363293711595169407644604885168816934193385 8747
n	28181646855797584703822270466344994215707990 8971
λ	89410463644172197664541344572565104224954335 021
α	4803045640050692328380 13-159881197071256943 510201 ϕ

same	different	$\max_1 > \max_2$	$\max_1/\sqrt{n}$	$\max_2/\sqrt{n}$
100%	0%	0%	0.753	0.753

p	68146790876522902430524762995908603350973574 6451
n	34073395438261451215262315574947704358870047 8113
λ	92899111242628958306702491539054896203949387 582
α	3513428730472869623132 79-329615032986583083 697556 ϕ

same	different	$\max_1 > \max_2$	$\max_1/\sqrt{n}$	$\max_2/\sqrt{n}$
75%	25%	13%	0.864	0.864

p	56363293711595169407644604885168816934193385 8747
n	28181646855797584703822270466344994215707990 8971
λ	89410463644172197664541344572565104224954335 021
α	4803045640050692328380 13-159881197071256943 5102 ϕ

same	different	$\max_1 > \max_2$	$\max_1/\sqrt{n}$	$\max_2/\sqrt{n}$
100%	0%	0%	0.752	0.752

Weierstraß Elliptic Curves
and Side-Channel Attacks

Éric Brier and Marc Joye

Gemplus Card International, Card Security Group
Parc d'Activités de Gémenos, B.P. 100, 13881 Gémenos, France
{eric.brier,marc.joye}@gemplus.com
http://www.gemplus.com/smart/
http://www.geocities.com/MarcJoye/

—To Erik De Win.

Abstract. Recent attacks show how an unskilled implementation of elliptic curve cryptosystems may reveal the involved secrets from a single execution of the algorithm. Most attacks exploit the property that addition and doubling on elliptic curves are different operations and so can be distinguished from side-channel analysis. Known countermeasures suggest to add dummy operations or to use specific parameterizations. This is at the expense of running time or interoperability.

This paper shows how to rewrite the addition on the general Weierstraß form of elliptic curves so that the same formulæ apply equally to add two different points or to double a point. It also shows how to generalize to the Weierstraß form a protection method previously applied to a specific form of elliptic curves due to Montgomery.

The two proposed methods offer generic solutions for preventing side-channel attacks. In particular, they apply to all the elliptic curves recommended by the standards.

1 Introduction

Elliptic curve cryptosystems become more and more popular. With much shorter key lengths they (presumably) offer the same level of security than older cryptosystems. This advantage is especially attractive for small cryptographic devices, like the smart cards.

In the last years, a new class of attacks was exploited to retrieve some secret information embedded in a cryptographic device: the so-called side-channel attacks [Koc96,KJJ99]. By monitoring some side-channel information (e.g., the power consumption) it is possible, in some cases, to deduce the inner workings of an (unprotected) crypto-algorithm and thereby to recover the secret keys. To counteract these attacks, a variety of countermeasures have been proposed (e.g., see [KJJ99,Cor99,LD99,OS00,JQ01,LS01,JT01,Möl01]).

This paper only deals with *simple* side-channel analysis (e.g., SPA), that is, side-channel analysis from a single execution of the crypto-algorithm. The more

D. Naccache and P. Paillier (Eds.): PKC 2002, LNCS 2274, pp. 335–345, 2002.

sophisticated differential side-analysis (e.g., DPA) plays the algorithm several times and handles the results thanks to statistical tools. This second type of attacks is not really a threat for elliptic curve cryptography since they are easily avoided by randomizing the inputs [Cor99,JT01].

Simple side-channel analysis is made easier for elliptic curve algorithms because the operations of doubling and addition of points are intrinsically different. Efficient countermeasures are known but they only apply to *specific* elliptic curves. Although one can always choose of an elliptic curve of the required form, it is very likely that people will select elliptic curves recommended in a standard. For example, over a large prime field, the National Institute of Standards and Technology (NIST) [NIST00] (see also [SECG00]) recommends to use elliptic curves of prime order whereas the order of the curves suggested in [OS00,JQ01,LS01] is always divisible by a small factor.

The rest of this paper is organized as follows. In the next section, we review SPA-like attacks. In Section 3 and 4, we present two different approaches to prevent these attacks for elliptic curve cryptosystems using the (fully general) Weierstraß parameterization. Finally, we conclude in Section 5. (An introduction to elliptic curves may be found in appendix.)

2   SPA-Like Attacks

The most commonly used algorithm for computing $\mathbf{Q} = k\mathbf{P}$ on an elliptic curve is the double-and-add algorithm, that is, the additively written *square-and-multiply algorithm* [Knu81, § 4.6.3].[1]

Input: $\mathbf{P}$, $k = (k_{l-1}, \ldots, k_0)_2$
Output: $\mathbf{Q} = k\mathbf{P}$

---

1. $\mathbf{R}_0 = \mathbf{P}$
2. for $i = l - 2$ downto 0 do
3. $\mathbf{R}_0 \leftarrow 2\mathbf{R}_0$
4.   if $(k_i \neq 0)$ then $\mathbf{R}_0 \leftarrow \mathbf{R}_0 + \mathbf{P}$
return $(\mathbf{Q} = \mathbf{R}_0)$

Fig. 1. Double-and-add algorithm for computing $\mathbf{Q} = k\mathbf{P}$.

Suppose that the doubling of a point and the addition of two different points are implemented with different formulæ, these two operations may then be distinguished by simple side-channel analysis, e.g., by simple power anal-

---

[1] Noting that the computation of the inverse of an point is virtually free, we can advantageously use a NAF representation for k —that is, $k = (k'_l, \ldots, k'_0)$ with $k'_i \in \{-1, 0, 1\}$ and $k'_i \cdot k'_{i+1} = 0$— and replace Step 4 in the double-and-add algorithm by $\mathbf{R}_0 \leftarrow \mathbf{R}_0 + k'_i\mathbf{P}$. The expected speedup factor is 11.11% [MO90].

ysis (SPA) [KJJ99]. When the power trace shows a doubling followed by an addition, the current bit, say k_i, is equal to 1; $k_i = 0$ otherwise.

The usual way to prevent simple side-channel attacks consists in always repeating the same pattern of instructions, whatever the processed data. This can be done by

- performing some dummy operations [Cor99];
- using an alternate parameterization for the elliptic curve [LS01,JQ01];
- using an algorithm already satisfying this property [LD99,OS00,Möl01].

In [Cor99], it is suggested to use the double-and-add-*always* variant of the double-and-add algorithm (Fig. 1): a dummy addition is performed when $k_i = 0$. The drawback in this variant is that it penalizes the running time.

There are other algorithms towards SPA-resistance (e.g., [CJ01]) but they require the elementary operations —in our case the doubling and the addition of points— to be indistinguishable. To this purpose, several authors suggested to use alternate parameterizations for the elliptic curves. In [LS01], Liardet and Smart represents points with the Jacobi form as the intersection of two quadrics in $\mathbb{P}^3$. In [JQ01], Joye and Quisquater suggest to use the Hessian form. Unfortunately, contrary to the Weierstraß form, these parameterizations are not fully general. The Jacobi form has always a point of order 4 and the Hessian form a point of order 3. This implies that the cardinality of the corresponding elliptic curve is a multiple of 4 and 3, respectively. On the other hand, standard bodies [NIST00] or companies [SECG00] recommend elliptic curves that do not all fit in these settings. For instance, they recommend to use several elliptic curves of prime cardinality over a large prime field. Rather than investigating specific forms for parameterizing an elliptic curve, we show in the next section how to perform —with the *same* formula— a doubling or an addition with the general Weierstraß parameterization.

The third approach for defeating SPA-like attacks is an application of Montgomery's binary technique [Mon87] (see also [Möl01] when memory constraints are not a concern). For elliptic curves over binary fields, the algorithm is described in [LD99]. Over large prime fields, the algorithm is described in [OS00]. This latter algorithm is unfortunately limited to the Montgomery parameterization (that is, elliptic curves with a point of order 2). We generalize it in Section 4 so that it works with the general Weierstraß parameterization.

3   Revisiting the Addition Formulæ

As given in textbooks (see also Appendices A.1 and A.3), the formulæ for adding or doubling points on a Weierstraß elliptic curve are different. The discrepancy comes from the geometrical interpretation of the addition law on elliptic curves, the so-called *chord-and-tangent rule* (see Fig. 2).

Let ℓ be the line passing through $\mathbf{P}$ and $\mathbf{Q}$ (tangent at the curve E if $\mathbf{P} = \mathbf{Q}$) and let $\mathbf{T}$ be the third point of intersection of ℓ with E. If ℓ' is the line connecting $\mathbf{P}$ and $\mathcal{O}$ then $\mathbf{P} + \mathbf{Q}$ is the point such that E intersects E at $\mathbf{T}$, $\mathcal{O}$ and $\mathbf{P} + \mathbf{Q}$.

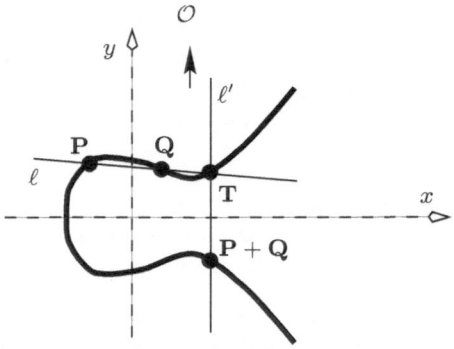

Fig. 2. Chord-and-tangent rule.

It is however possible to write the slope of line ℓ, λ, so that its expression remains valid for the addition or the doubling of points, which consequently unify the addition formulæ. This is explicited in the next proposition.

Proposition 1. *Let E be the elliptic curve over a field $\mathbb{K}$, given by the equation $E_{/\mathbb{K}} : y^2 + a_1 xy + a_3 y = x^3 + a_2 x^2 + a_4 x + a_6$. Let also $\mathbf{P} = (x_1, y_1)$ and $\mathbf{Q} = (x_2, y_2) \in E(\mathbb{K}) \setminus \{\mathcal{O}\}$ with $\mathrm{y}(\mathbf{P}) \neq \mathrm{y}(-\mathbf{Q})$. Then $\mathbf{P} + \mathbf{Q} = (x_3, y_3)$ where $x_3 = \lambda^2 + a_1 \lambda - a_2 - x_1 - x_2$, $y_3 = -(\lambda + a_1) x_3 - \mu - a_3$ with*

$$\lambda = \frac{x_1^2 + x_1 x_2 + x_2^2 + a_2 x_1 + a_2 x_2 + a_4 - a_1 y_1}{y_1 + y_2 + a_1 x_2 + a_3}$$

and $\mu = y_1 - \lambda x_1$.

Proof. The condition $\mathrm{y}(\mathbf{P}) \neq \mathrm{y}(-\mathbf{Q})$ is equivalent to $y_1 \neq -y_2 - a_1 x_2 - a_3$. Starting from the definition of λ when $\mathbf{P} \neq \mathbf{Q}$ (see Eq. (13) in Appendix A.1), we obtain

$$\begin{aligned}
\lambda &= \tfrac{y_1 - y_2}{x_1 - x_2} = \tfrac{y_1 - y_2}{x_1 - x_2} \cdot \tfrac{y_1 - (-y_2 - a_1 x_2 - a_3)}{y_1 - (-y_2 - a_1 x_2 - a_3)} \\
&= \tfrac{y_1^2 + a_1 x_2 y_1 + a_3 y_1 - y_2^2 - a_1 x_2 y_2 - a_3 y_2}{(x_1 - x_2)(y_1 + y_2 + a_1 x_2 + a_3)} \\
&= \tfrac{(y_1^2 + a_1 x_1 y_1 + a_3 y_1) - (y_2^2 + a_1 x_2 y_2 + a_3 y_2) + a_1 x_2 y_1 - a_1 x_1 y_1}{(x_1 - x_2)(y_1 + y_2 + a_1 x_2 + a_3)} \\
&= \tfrac{(x_1^3 + a_2 x_1^2 + a_4 x_1 + a_6) - (x_2^3 + a_2 x_2^2 + a_4 x_2 + a_6) - a_1 y_1 (x_1 - x_2)}{(x_1 - x_2)(y_1 + y_2 + a_1 x_2 + a_3)} \\
&= \tfrac{x_1^2 + x_1 x_2 + x_2^2 + a_2 x_1 + a_2 x_2 + a_4 - a_1 y_1}{y_1 + y_2 + a_1 x_2 + a_3} \ .
\end{aligned}$$

We see that if we replace x_2 by x_1 and y_2 by y_1 (i.e., if we assume $\mathbf{P} = \mathbf{Q}$), the above formula for λ yields $\lambda = \frac{3x_1^2 + 2a_2 x_1 + a_4 - a_1 y_1}{2 y_1 + a_1 x_1 + a_3}$, that is, the λ for the doubling (again see Eq. (13) in Appendix A.1). □

The above proposition can be particularized to the simplified Weierstraß equations (see Appendix A.3), depending on the field of definition.

Corollary 1. *Let $\mathbb{K}$ be a field of characteristic $\mathrm{Char}\,\mathbb{K} \neq 2, 3$, and let E be the elliptic curve given by the equation $E_{/\mathbb{K}} : y^2 = x^3 + ax + b$. Then for any $\mathbf{P} = (x_1, y_1)$ and $\mathbf{Q} = (x_2, y_2) \in E(\mathbb{K}) \backslash \{\mathcal{O}\}$ with $y_1 \neq -y_2$, we have $\mathbf{P} + \mathbf{Q} = (x_3, y_3)$ where*

$$x_3 = \left(\frac{x_1^2 + x_1 x_2 + x_2^2 + a}{y_1 + y_2} \right)^2 - x_1 - x_2 \tag{1}$$

and

$$y_3 = \left(\frac{x_1^2 + x_1 x_2 + x_2^2 + a}{y_1 + y_2} \right) (x_1 - x_3) - y_1 \ . \tag{2}$$

□

Corollary 2. *Let $\mathbb{K}$ be a field of characteristic $\mathrm{Char}\,\mathbb{K} = 2$, and let E be the non-supersingular elliptic curve given by the equation $E_{/\mathbb{K}} : y^2 + xy = x^3 + ax^2 + b$. Then for any $\mathbf{P} = (x_1, y_1)$ and $\mathbf{Q} = (x_2, y_2) \in E(\mathbb{K}) \backslash \{\mathcal{O}\}$ with $y_1 \neq y_2 + x_2$, we have $\mathbf{P} + \mathbf{Q} = (x_3, y_3)$ where*

$$x_3 = \left(\frac{x_1^2 + x_1 x_2 + x_2^2 + ax_1 + ax_2 + y_1}{y_1 + y_2 + x_2} \right)^2 + \left(\frac{x_1^2 + x_1 x_2 + x_2^2 + ax_1 + ax_2 + y_1}{y_1 + y_2 + x_2} \right) + a + x_1 + x_2 \tag{3}$$

and

$$y_3 = \left(\frac{x_1^2 + x_1 x_2 + x_2^2 + ax_1 + ax_2 + y_1}{y_1 + y_2 + x_2} \right) (x_1 + x_3) + x_3 + y_1 \ . \tag{4}$$

□

Over a field $\mathbb{K}$ of characteristic $\mathrm{Char}\,\mathbb{K} \neq 2, 3$, remarking that $x_1^2 + x_1 x_2 + x_2^2 = (x_1 + x_2)^2 - x_1 x_2$, our formulæ (Eqs. (1) and (2)) require 1 inversion and 5 multiplications for adding two points. Over a field $\mathbb{K}$ of characteristic $\mathrm{Char}\,\mathbb{K} = 2$, our formulæ (Eqs. (3) and (4)) require 1 inversion and 3 multiplications plus 1 multiplication by a constant for adding two points (we neglect the cost of a squaring).

When $\mathrm{Char}\,\mathbb{K} \neq 2, 3$, projective coordinates are preferred [DMPW98]. (See Appendix A.2 for a short introduction to projective coordinates.)

We now give the projective (homogeneous) version of Eqs. (1) and (2). Write $\lambda = \frac{x_1^2 + x_1 x_2 + x_2^2 + a}{y_1 + y_2} = \frac{(x_1 + x_2)^2 - x_1 x_2 + a}{y_1 + y_2}$. Owing to the symmetry of λ, we may write from Eq. (2), $y_3 = \lambda(x_2 - x_3) - y_2$, since $\mathbf{P} + \mathbf{Q} = \mathbf{Q} + \mathbf{P}$, and consequently we have $2y_3 = \lambda(x_1 + x_2 - 2x_3) - (y_1 + y_2)$. Setting $x_i = \frac{X_i}{Z_i}$ and $y_i = \frac{Y_i}{Z_i}$, we so obtain after a few algebra

$$\begin{cases} X_3 = 2FW \\ Y_3 = R(G - 2W) - L^2 \\ Z_3 = 2F^3 \end{cases} \tag{5}$$

where $U_1 = X_1 Z_2$, $U_2 = X_2 Z_1$, $S_1 = Y_1 Z_2$, $S_2 = Y_2 Z_1$, $Z = Z_1 Z_2$, $T = U_1 + U_2$, $M = S_1 + S_2$, $R = T^2 - U_1 U_2 + aZ^2$, $F = ZM$, $L = MF$, $G = TL$, and

$W = R^2 - G$. Therefore, adding two points with our unified formulæ require 17 multiplications plus 1 multiplication by constant. When $a = -1$ then we may write $R = (T - Z)(T + Z) - U_1 U_2$ and the number of multiplications decreases to 16.

4   Generalizing Montgomery's Technique

In [Mon87], Montgomery developed an original technique to compute multiples of points on an elliptic curve. His technique is based on the fact that the sum of two points whose difference is a known point can be computed without the y-coordinate of the two points.

Input: $\mathbf{P}$, $k = (k_{l-1}, \ldots, k_0)_2$
Output: $\mathrm{x}(k\mathbf{P})$

---

1. $\mathbf{R}_0 = \mathbf{P}$; $\mathbf{R}_1 = 2\mathbf{P}$
2. for $i = l - 2$ downto 0 do
3.   if $(k_i = 0)$ then
4. $\mathrm{x}(\mathbf{R}_1) \leftarrow \mathrm{x}(\mathbf{R}_0 + \mathbf{R}_1)$; $\mathrm{x}(\mathbf{R}_0) \leftarrow \mathrm{x}(2\mathbf{R}_0)$
5.   else [if $(k_i = 1)$]
6. $\mathrm{x}(\mathbf{R}_0) \leftarrow \mathrm{x}(\mathbf{R}_0 + \mathbf{R}_1)$; $\mathrm{x}(\mathbf{R}_1) \leftarrow \mathrm{x}(2\mathbf{R}_1)$

return $(\mathrm{x}(\mathbf{R}_0))$

Fig. 3. Montgomery's technique for computing $\mathrm{x}(k\mathbf{P})$.

(Observe that the difference $\mathbf{R}_1 - \mathbf{R}_0$ remains invariant throughout the algorithm: $\mathbf{R}_1 - \mathbf{R}_0 = \mathbf{P}$.)

For sake of efficiency, Montgomery restricted his study to elliptic curves of the form $by^2 = x^3 + ax^2 + x$ over a field $\mathbb{K}$ of characteristic $\neq 2, 3$. The next proposition gives the corresponding formulæ in the general case. The formulæ over a field of characteristic 2 are given in [LD99, Lemmas 2 and 3].

Proposition 2. *Let $\mathbb{K}$ be a field of characteristic* Char $\mathbb{K} \neq 2, 3$, *and let E be the elliptic curve given by the equation $E_{/\mathbb{K}} : y^2 = x^3 + ax + b$. Let also $\mathbf{P} = (x_1, y_1)$ and $\mathbf{Q} = (x_2, y_2) \in E(\mathbb{K}) \setminus \{\mathcal{O}\}$ with $\mathbf{P} \neq \pm\mathbf{Q}$. Given the point $\mathbf{P} - \mathbf{Q} = (x, y)$, the x-coordinate of $\mathbf{P} + \mathbf{Q}$ satisfies*

$$\mathrm{x}(\mathbf{P} + \mathbf{Q}) = \frac{-4b(x_1 + x_2) + (x_1 x_2 - a)^2}{x(x_1 - x_2)^2} . \tag{6}$$

Furthermore, if $y_1 \neq 0$ then the x-coordinate of $2\mathbf{P}$ satisfies

$$\mathrm{x}(2\mathbf{P}) = \frac{(x_1{}^2 - a)^2 - 8bx_1}{4(x_1{}^3 + ax_1 + b)} . \tag{7}$$

Proof. From Eq. (16) (in Appendix A.3), letting x_3 the x-coordinate of $\mathbf{P} + \mathbf{Q}$, we have

$$
\begin{aligned}
x_3(x_1 - x_2)^2 &= (y_1 - y_2)^2 - (x_1 + x_2)(x_1 - x_2)^2 \\
&= (y_1{}^2 + y_2{}^2 - 2y_1y_2) - (x_1{}^3 + x_2{}^3 - x_1{}^2 x_2 - x_1 x_2{}^2) \\
&= -2y_1y_2 + 2b + (a + x_1x_2)(x_1 + x_2) \ .
\end{aligned}
$$

Similarly, the x-coordinate of $\mathbf{P} - \mathbf{Q}$ satisfies $x(x_1 - x_2)^2 = 2y_1y_2 + 2b + (a + x_1x_2)(x_1 + x_2)$. Now by multiplying the two equations, we obtain

$$
\begin{aligned}
x_3 \cdot x(x_1 - x_2)^4 &= -4y_1{}^2 y_2{}^2 + [2b + (a + x_1x_2)(x_1 + x_2)]^2 \\
&= -4(x_1{}^3 + ax_1 + b)(x_2{}^3 + ax_2 + b) + \\
&\qquad [2b + (a + x_1x_2)(x_1 + x_2)]^2 \\
&= [-4b(x_1 + x_2) + (x_1x_2 - a)^2](x_1 - x_2)^2
\end{aligned}
$$

which, dividing through by $(x_1 - x_2)^2$, yields the desired result.

When $y_1 \neq 0$ (i.e., when $2\mathbf{P} \neq \mathcal{O}$), we have from Eq. (16) (in appendix) that $\mathrm{x}(2\mathbf{P}) = \frac{(3x_1{}^2 + a)^2}{4y_1{}^2} - 2x_1 = \frac{(x_1{}^2 - a)^2 - 8bx_1}{4(x_1{}^3 + ax_1 + b)}$. $\qquad\square$

Another useful feature of Montgomery's technique is that the y-coordinate of a point $\mathbf{P}$ can be deduced from its x-coordinate, the x-coordinate of another point $\mathbf{Q}$ and the coordinates of the point $\mathbf{P} - \mathbf{Q}$. This is explicited in the next proposition.

Proposition 3. *Let $\mathbb{K}$ be a field of characteristic $\mathrm{Char}\,\mathbb{K} \neq 2, 3$, and let E be the elliptic curve given by the equation $E_{/\mathbb{K}} : y^2 = x^3 + ax + b$. Let also $\mathbf{P} = (x_1, y_1)$ and $\mathbf{Q} = (x_2, y_2) \in E(\mathbb{K}) \setminus \{\mathcal{O}\}$ with $\mathbf{P} \neq \mathbf{Q}$. Given the point $\mathbf{P} - \mathbf{Q} = (x, y)$, if $y \neq 0$ then the y-coordinate of $\mathbf{P}$ satisfies*

$$
\mathrm{y}(\mathbf{P}) = y_1 = \frac{2b + (a + xx_1)(x + x_1) - x_2(x - x_1)^2}{2y} \ . \tag{8}
$$

Proof. Define $\mathbf{D} = \mathbf{P} - \mathbf{Q} = (x, y)$. Since $\mathbf{Q} = \mathbf{P} + \mathbf{D} = (x_2, y_2)$, we obtain from Eq. (16) (in appendix) $x_2 = \left(\frac{y_1 - y}{x_1 - x}\right)^2 - x_1 - x = \frac{-2yy_1 + 2b + (a + xx_1)(x + x_1)}{(x_1 - x)^2}$, which concludes the proof, multiplying through by $(x_1 - x)^2$. $\qquad\square$

Assume we are working on an elliptic curve over a field $\mathbb{K}$ of characteristic different from 2 or 3. We refer the reader to [LD99] for a field of characteristic 2. Within projective (homogeneous) coordinates, Equation (6) becomes

$$
\begin{cases}
\mathrm{X}(\mathbf{P} + \mathbf{Q}) = -4bZ_1Z_2(X_1Z_2 + X_2Z_1) + (X_1X_2 - aZ_1Z_2)^2 \,, \\
\mathrm{Z}(\mathbf{P} + \mathbf{Q}) = x \cdot (X_1Z_2 - X_2Z_1)^2 \,.
\end{cases} \tag{9}
$$

Hence, the addition of two points requires 7 multiplications plus 3 multiplications by a constant.

The formulæ to double a point within homogeneous projective coordinates are obtained similarly from Eq. (7). We get

$$\begin{cases} X(2\mathbf{P}) = (X_1{}^2 - aZ_1{}^2)^2 - 8bX_1Z_1{}^3, \\ Z(2\mathbf{P}) = 4Z_1(X_1{}^3 + aX_1Z_1{}^2 + bZ_1{}^3). \end{cases} \tag{10}$$

This can be evaluated with 7 multiplications plus 2 multiplications by a constant.

Consequently, the whole protected algorithm of Fig. 3 requires roughly $14l$ multiplications, $5l$ multiplications by a constant and 1 inversion for computing $x(k\mathbf{P})$, where l is the bit-length of k. This is more than in [OS00] but our method does not require specific curves. Note also that, by Proposition 3, the y-coordinate of $\mathbf{Q} = k\mathbf{P}$ can be recovered from $x(\mathbf{R}_0) = x(\mathbf{Q})$, $x(\mathbf{R}_1)$ and $\mathbf{P}$.

5   Conclusion

This paper described two alternative approaches in the development of counter-measures against simple side-channel attacks. The main merits of the proposed methods is that they are not specific to a particular class of elliptic curves. In particular, they apply to all the elliptic curves recommended in the standards.

References

CJ01.   Christophe Clavier and Marc Joye. Universal exponentiation algorithm: A first step towards provable SPA-resistance. In Ç.K. Koç, D. Naccache, and C. Paar, editors, *Cryptographic Hardware and Embedded Systems - CHES 2001*, volume 2162 of *Lecture Notes in Computer Science*, pages 305–314. Springer-Verlag, 2001.

Cor99.   Jean-Sébastien Coron. Resistance against differential power analysis for elliptic curve cryptosystems. In Ç.K. Koç and C. Paar, editors, *Cryptographic Hardware and Embedded Systems (CHES '99)*, volume 1717 of *Lecture Notes in Computer Science*, pages 292–302. Springer-Verlag, 1999.

DMPW98.   Erik De Win, Serge Mister, Bart Preneel, and Michael Wiener. On the performance of signature schemes based on elliptic curves. In J.-P. Buhler, editor, *Algorithmic Number Theory Symposium*, volume 1423 of *Lecture Notes in Computer Science*, pages 252–266. Springer-Verlag, 1998.

JQ01.   Marc Joye and Jean-Jacques Quisquater. Hessian elliptic curves and side-channel attacks. In Ç.K. Koç, D. Naccache, and C. Paar, editors, *Cryptographic Hardware and Embedded Systems - CHES 2001*, volume 2162 of *Lecture Notes in Computer Science*, pages 412–420. Springer-Verlag, 2001.

JT01.   Marc Joye and Christophe Tymen. Protections against differential analysis for elliptic curve cryptography: an algebraic approach. In Ç.K. Koç, D. Naccache, and C. Paar, editors, *Cryptographic Hardware and Embedded Systems - CHES 2001*, volume 2162 of *Lecture Notes in Computer Science*, pages 386–400. Springer-Verlag, 2001.

KJJ99.   Paul Kocher, Joshua Jaffe, and Benjamin Jun. Differential power analysis. In M. Wiener, editor, *Advances in Cryptology – CRYPTO '99*, volume 1666 of *Lecture Notes in Computer Science*, pages 388–397. Springer-Verlag, 1999.

Knu81.   Donald E. Knuth. *The art of computer programming, v. 2. Seminumerical algorithms.* Addison-Welsley, 2nd edition, 1981.

Koc96.   Paul Kocher. Timing attacks on implementations of Diffie-Hellman, RSA, DSS, and other systems. In N. Koblitz, editor, *Advances in Cryptology – CRYPTO '96*, volume 1109 of *Lecture Notes in Computer Science*, pages 104–113. Springer-Verlag, 1996.

LD99.   Julio López and Ricardo Dahab. Fast multiplication on elliptic curves over $GF(2^m)$ without precomputation. In Ç.K. Koç and C. Paar, editors, *Cryptographic Hardware and Embedded Systems*, volume 1717 of *Lecture Notes in Computer Science*, pages 316–327. Springer-Verlag, 1999.

LS01.   Pierre-Yvan Liardet and Nigel P. Smart. Preventing SPA/DPA in ECC systems using the Jacobi form. In Ç.K. Koç, D. Naccache, and C. Paar, editors, *Cryptographic Hardware and Embedded Systems - CHES 2001*, volume 2162 of *Lecture Notes in Computer Science*, pages 401–411. Springer-Verlag, 2001.

MO90.   François Morain and Jorge Olivos. Speeding up the computations on an elliptic curve using addition-subtraction chains. *Theoretical Informatics and Applications*, 24:531–543, 1990.

Möl01.   Bodo Möller. Securing elliptic curve point multiplication against side-channel attacks. In G.I. Davida and Y. Frankel, editors, *Information Security*, volume 2200 of *Lecture Notes in Computer Science*, pages 324–334. Springer-Verlag, 2001.

Mon87.   Peter L. Montgomery. Speeding the Pollard and elliptic curve methods of factorization. *Mathematics of Computation*, 48(177):243–264, January 1987.

NIST00.   National Institute of Standards and Technology (NIST). Digital signature standard (DSS). FIPS PUB 186-2, 2000.

OS00.   Katsuyuki Okeya and Kouichi Sakurai. Power analysis breaks elliptic curve cryptosystems even secure against the timing attack. In B. Roy and E. Okamoto, editors, *Progress in Cryptology – INDOCRYPT 2000*, volume 1977 of *Lecture Notes in Computer Science*, pages 178–190. Springer-Verlag, 2000.

SECG00.   Certicom Research. Standards for efficient cryptography. Version 1.0, 2000. Available at url http://www.secg.org/.

Sil86.   Joseph H. Silverman. *The arithmetic of elliptic curves*, volume 106 of *Graduate Texts in Mathematics*. Springer-Verlag, 1986.

A   Mathematical Background

A.1   Elliptic Curves

Consider the elliptic curve defined over a field $\mathbb{K}$ given by the Weierstraß equation:

$$E_{/\mathbb{K}} : y^2 + a_1 xy + a_3 y = x^3 + a_2 x^2 + a_4 x + a_6 \ . \tag{11}$$

It is well-known that formally adding the point $\mathcal{O}$ makes the set of points $(x, y) \in \mathbb{K} \times \mathbb{K}$ satisfying Eq. (11) into an Abelian group [Sil86, Chapter III]. We denote this group $E(\mathbb{K})$. We have:

(i) $\mathcal{O}$ is the identity element: $\forall \mathbf{P} \in E(\mathbb{K})$, $\mathbf{P} + \mathcal{O} = \mathbf{P}$.

(ii) The inverse of $\mathbf{P} = (x_1, y_1)$ is $-\mathbf{P} = (x_1, -y_1 - a_1 x_1 - a_3)$.
(iii) If $\mathbf{Q} = -\mathbf{P}$ then $\mathbf{P} + \mathbf{Q} = \mathcal{O}$.
(iv) Let $\mathbf{P} = (x_1, y_1)$ and $\mathbf{Q} = (x_2, y_2) \in E(\mathbb{K})$ with $\mathbf{Q} \neq -\mathbf{P}$. Then $\mathbf{P} + \mathbf{Q} = (x_3, y_3)$ where

$$x_3 = \lambda^2 + a_1 \lambda - a_2 - x_1 - x_2 \quad \text{and} \quad y_3 = -(\lambda + a_1)x_3 - \mu - a_3 \qquad (12)$$

with

$$\lambda = \begin{cases} \dfrac{y_1 - y_2}{x_1 - x_2} & \text{if } \mathbf{P} \neq \mathbf{Q} \\ \dfrac{3x_1^2 + 2a_2 x_1 + a_4 - a_1 y_1}{2y_1 + a_1 x_1 + a_3} & \text{if } \mathbf{P} = \mathbf{Q} \end{cases} \qquad (13)$$

and $\mu = y_1 - \lambda x_1$.

A.2   Projective Representations

The formula for λ involves an inversion and this may be a rather costly operation. For this reason, one usually prefer *projective coordinates*.

Within *projective Jacobian coordinates*, we put $x = X/Z^2$ and $y = Y/Z^3$ and the Weierstraß equation of the elliptic curve becomes

$$E_{/\mathbb{K}} : Y^2 + a_1 XYZ + a_3 YZ^3 = X^3 + a_2 X^2 Z^2 + a_4 X Z^4 + a_6 Z^6 \qquad (14)$$

where the point at infinity is represented as $\mathcal{O} = (\theta^2, \theta^3, 0)$ for some $\theta \in \mathbb{K} \setminus \{0\}$. The affine point (x_1, y_1) is represented by a projective point $(\theta^2 x_1, \theta^3 y_1, \theta)$ for some $\theta \in \mathbb{K} \setminus \{0\}$ and conversely a projective point $(X_1, Y_1, Z_1) \neq \mathcal{O}$ corresponds to the affine point $(X_1/Z_1^2, Y_1/Z_1^3)$.

Within *projective homogeneous coordinates*, we put $x = X/Z$ and $y = Y/Z$ and the Weierstraß equation of the elliptic curve is

$$E_{/\mathbb{K}} : Y^2 Z + a_1 XYZ + a_3 YZ^2 = X^3 + a_2 X^2 Z + a_4 X Z^2 + a_6 Z^3 \ . \qquad (15)$$

The point at infinity is represented as $(0, \theta, 0)$ for some $\theta \in \mathbb{K} \setminus \{0\}$. The affine point (x_1, y_1) is represented by a projective point $(\theta x_1, \theta y_1, \theta)$ for some $\theta \in \mathbb{K} \setminus \{0\}$ and a projective point $(X_1, Y_1, Z_1) \neq \mathcal{O}$ corresponds to the affine point $(X_1/Z_1, Y_1/Z_1)$.

Note that in projective coordinates (Jacobian or homogeneous), only the point at infinity has its Z-coordinate equal to 0. The addition formulæ in projective coordinates are derived from the affine formulæ by replacing each affine point (x_i, y_i) by a projective equivalent (X_i, Y_i, Z_i).

A.3   Simplified Equations

Two main families of elliptic curves are used in cryptography, according to the base field $\mathbb{K}$ over which the curve is defined. In this appendix, we give the corresponding simplified formulæ for each family.

Char $\mathbb{K} \neq 2, 3$

In this case, the general Weierstraß equation (Eq. (11)) may be simplified to

$$E_{/\mathbb{K}} : y^2 = x^3 + ax + b \ .$$

Taking $a_1 = a_2 = a_3 = 0$, $a_4 = a$ and $a_6 = b$ in Eqs. (12) and (13), the sum of $\mathbf{P} = (x_1, y_2)$ and $\mathbf{Q} = (x_2, y_2)$ (with $\mathbf{P} \neq -\mathbf{Q}$) is given by $\mathbf{P} + \mathbf{Q} = (x_3, y_3)$ where

$$x_3 = \lambda^2 - x_1 - x_2 \quad \text{and} \quad y_3 = \lambda(x_1 - x_3) - y_1 \tag{16}$$

with $\lambda = \frac{y_1 - y_2}{x_1 - x_2}$ if $\mathbf{P} \neq \mathbf{Q}$, and $\lambda = \frac{3x_1^2 + a}{2y_1}$ if $\mathbf{P} = \mathbf{Q}$.

Char $\mathbb{K} = 2$ (Non-supersingular Curves)

Supersingular elliptic curves are cryptographically weaker, we therefore consider only non-supersingular elliptic curves. The simplified Weierstraß equation then becomes

$$E_{/\mathbb{K}} : y^2 + xy = x^3 + ax^2 + b \ .$$

Again, from Eqs. (12) and (13), the sum of $\mathbf{P} = (x_1, y_2)$ and $\mathbf{Q} = (x_2, y_2)$ (with $\mathbf{P} \neq -\mathbf{Q}$) is given by $\mathbf{P} + \mathbf{Q} = (x_3, y_3)$ where

$$x_3 = \lambda^2 + \lambda + a + x_1 + x_2 \quad \text{and} \quad y_3 = \lambda(x_1 + x_3) + x_3 + y_1 \tag{17}$$

with $\lambda = \frac{y_1 - y_2}{x_1 - x_2}$ if $\mathbf{P} \neq \mathbf{Q}$, and $\lambda = x_1 + \frac{y_1}{x_1}$ if $\mathbf{P} = \mathbf{Q}$.

One-Way Cross-Trees and Their Applications

Marc Joye[1] and Sung-Ming Yen[2]

[1] Gemplus Card International, Card Security Group
Parc d'Activités de Gémenos, B.P. 100, 13881 Gémenos Cedex, France
marc.joye@gemplus.com
http://www.gemplus.com/smart/
http://www.geocities.com/MarcJoye/
[2] Laboratory of Cryptography and Information Security (LCIS)
Dept of Computer Science and Information Engineering
National Central University, Chung-Li, Taiwan 320, R.O.C.
yensm@csie.ncu.edu.tw
http://www.csie.ncu.edu.tw/~yensm/

Abstract. This paper considers the problem of efficiently generating a sequence of secrets with the special property that the knowledge of one or several secrets does not help an adversary to find the other ones. This is achieved through *one-way cross-trees*, which may be seen as a multidimensional extension of the so-called *one-way chains*. In a dual way, some applications require the release of one or several secrets; one-way cross-trees allow to minimize the amount of data necessary to recover those secrets and only those ones.

1 Introduction

In [10], Lamport proposed a login protocol based on the iterative use of a *one-way function*. This elegant construction was exploited in many cryptographic applications, including the S/KEY one-time password system [8], electronic micro-payment schemes [2,16], generation of sever-supported digital signatures [3] or with bounded life-span [5], and also one-time signature schemes [7,9,13,14].

Lamport's one-time password scheme can briefly be described as follows. From an initial value S_1 and a one-way function h, a user computes $S_i = h(S_{i-1})$ for $i = 2, \ldots, n$. The final value S_n is given, in a secure manner, to the remote system (i.e., the verifier). The first time the user wants to login, he will be asked to deliver S_{n-1} as password. The remote system then checks whether $S_n \stackrel{?}{=} h(S_{n-1})$. If yes, then access is granted to the user and the remote system updates the password database by storing S_{n-1}. This is a one-time password. The next time the user will login, he has to send S_{n-2} as password, the remote system then checks whether $S_{n-2} \stackrel{?}{=} h(S_{n-1})$, ... and so on until S_1 is used as password. The main advantage of this method over the fixed password solution is that replay attacks are no longer possible.

Roughly speaking, one-way cross-trees generalize the idea behind Lamport's scheme through the use of several one-way functions and several initial values.

D. Naccache and P. Paillier (Eds.): PKC 2002, LNCS 2274, pp. 346–356, 2002.

The resulting constructions naturally introduce a *pyramidal hierarchy* between the secrets (passwords) and therefore provide a simple means to allow *controllable* delegation. Lamport's scheme also presents some hierarchy but only vertical; for example, given the secret S_r anyone can compute $S_{r+1}, S_{r+2}, \ldots, S_n$. Consequently, if for some reason or other, secret S_r has been disclosed, then the security of secrets $S_{r+1}, \ldots,$ is compromised. One-way cross-trees are more flexible, the delegation is *fully* parameterizable. Such desirable property is useful for key escrow systems. It is so possible to construct a system wherein the release of some secret keys only enables to recover the messages encrypted under those keys and not all the past and future communications.

The rest of this paper is organized as follows. In Section 2, we formally define one-way cross-trees. We also derive some useful properties. Section 3 shows how one-way cross-trees allow to efficiently generate and release secrets. Some applications are then presented in Section 4. Finally, we conclude in Section 5.

2   One-Way Cross-Trees

We begin by formalizing the necessary definitions.

Definition 1. *A function $h : x \mapsto h(x)$ is said* one-way *if when given x, $h(x)$ is easily computable; but when given $h(x)$, it is computationally infeasible to derive x.*

Notation. When a function h is iteratively applied r times to an argument x, we will use the notation $h^r(x)$, that is $h^r(x) = \underbrace{h(h(\cdots(h(x))\cdots))}_{r \text{ times}}$.

$$h^0(x) = x \longrightarrow h^1(x) \longrightarrow h^2(x) \longrightarrow \cdots \longrightarrow h^n(x)$$

Fig. 1. One-way chain.

The iterative application of a one-way function h results in the generation of a *one-way chain*. Once generated, the chain is then employed in the backward direction, exhibiting the useful property that it is computationally infeasible to derive $h^{i-1}(x)$ from $h^i(x)$. One-way cross-trees generalize this concept. Loosely speaking, in a κ-ary one-way cross-tree, there are κ possible one-way directions from a given position—a one-way chain corresponds to a unary one-way cross-tree, there is only one possible one-way direction. More precisely, we have:

Definition 2. *Let $h_1, h_2, \ldots, h_\kappa$ be one-way functions and let $(I_1, I_2, \ldots, I_\kappa)$ be a κ-tuple. A κ-ary one-way cross-tree (κ-OWCT for short) is a structure T consisting of vertices and directed edges. Each vertex is labeled with a κ-tuple of the form*

$$\boldsymbol{V}_{r_1, r_2, \ldots, r_\kappa} = \left(h_1^{r_1}(I_1), h_2^{r_2}(I_2), \ldots, h_\kappa^{r_\kappa}(I_\kappa) \right), \tag{1}$$

where $r_1, r_2, \ldots, r_\kappa \in \mathbb{N}$. *The vertex corresponding to the κ-tuple $\boldsymbol{I} = (I_1, I_2, \ldots, I_\kappa)$ is called the* root *(or generator) of T. Each vertex (except the root) has at least one edge directed towards it. Moreover, each vertex (including the root) has at most κ edges directed away from it. Given an edge directed away from a vertex P towards a vertex S, vertex P is called the* predecessor *of S and vertex S is called the* successor *of P. A vertex without successor is called a* leaf. *A κ-OWCT is iteratively constructed as follows. Given a vertex labeled $\boldsymbol{V}_{r_1, r_2, \ldots, r_i, \ldots, r_\kappa}$, its κ (possible) successors are given by the vertices labeled $\boldsymbol{V}_{r_1, r_2, \ldots, r_i+1, \ldots, r_\kappa} = \bigl(h_1^{r_1}(I_1), h_2^{r_2}(I_2), \ldots, h_i^{r_i+1}(I_i), \ldots, h_\kappa^{r_\kappa}(I_\kappa)\bigr)$ with $i \in \{1, \ldots, \kappa\}$.*

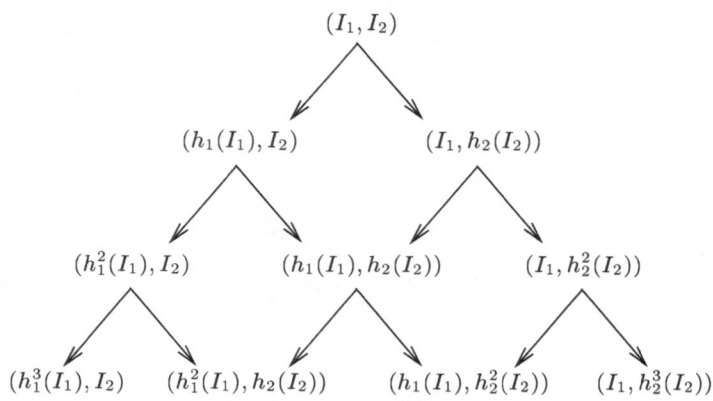

Fig. 2. Binary one-way cross-tree (2-OWCT).

Proposition 1. *Let T be a κ-OWCT. Given any κ-tuple $\boldsymbol{V}_{r_1, r_2, \ldots, r_\kappa} \in T$, it is*

(P1) *computationally infeasible to find another κ-tuple $\boldsymbol{V}_{r_1', r_2', \ldots, r_\kappa'}$ if $r_i' < r_i$ for some $1 \leq i \leq \kappa$;*

(P2) *computationally easy to find another κ-tuple $\boldsymbol{V}_{r_1', r_2', \ldots, r_\kappa'}$ if $r_i' \geq r_i$ for all $1 \leq i \leq \kappa$.*

Proof. This immediately follows from the one-wayness of T (see Eq. (1)). Finding $\boldsymbol{V}_{r_1', r_2', \ldots, r_\kappa'}$ for some $r_i' < j_i$ requires the inversion of the one-way function h_i, which is assumed to be computationally infeasible. $\square$

Definition 3. *The* weight *of a κ-tuple $\boldsymbol{V}_{r_1, r_2, \ldots, r_\kappa}$ in a κ-OWCT T is defined as $W(\boldsymbol{V}_{r_1, r_2, \ldots, r_\kappa}) = \sum_{i=1}^{\kappa} r_i$. The* depth *of $\boldsymbol{V}_{r_1, r_2, \ldots, r_\kappa} \in T$ is given by*

$$\Delta(\boldsymbol{V}_{r_1, r_2, \ldots, r_\kappa}) = W(\boldsymbol{V}_{r_1, r_2, \ldots, r_\kappa}) - W(\boldsymbol{I}), \tag{2}$$

where $\boldsymbol{I}$ denotes the root of T. Moreover, the depth *of T is defined as being the depth of the element of greatest depth.*

Definition 4. *A κ-OWCT T is said* complete *if all of its leaves have the same weight.*

Proposition 1 is the fundamental property of a one-way cross-tree. It indicates that given one element $V_{r_1, r_2, \ldots, r_\kappa}$, only the elements of the κ-*ary one-way subcross-tree* generated by $V_{r_1, r_2, \ldots, r_\kappa}$ can be evaluated. In other words, when given *one* element, no elements of lower or equal weight can be computed.

Proposition 2. *A complete κ-OWCT T of depth δ has exactly*

$$N(\kappa, \delta) = \binom{\delta + \kappa - 1}{\delta} \tag{3}$$

(distinct) elements of depth δ.

Proof. We use induction on κ. The case $\kappa = 1$ corresponds to one-way chains and we obviously have $N(1, \delta) = 1 = \binom{\delta}{\delta}$. Suppose now that $\kappa \geq 2$ and that Eq. (3) holds for $\kappa - 1$. Let $\boldsymbol{R} = (R_1, R_2, \ldots, R_\kappa)$ be the root of T. Then, the number of elements of depth δ is given by

$$
\begin{aligned}
N(\kappa, \delta) &= \#\{(h_1^{s_1}(R_1), h_2^{s_2}(R_2), \ldots, h_\kappa^{s_\kappa}(R_\kappa)) \mid \textstyle\sum_{i=1}^\kappa s_i = \delta\} \\
&= \#\{(h_1^{s_1}(R_1), h_2^{s_2}(R_2), \ldots, h_\kappa^{s_\kappa}(R_\kappa)) \mid 0 \leq s_1 \leq \delta, \textstyle\sum_{i=2}^\kappa s_i = \delta - s_1\} \\
&= \textstyle\sum_{s_1=0}^\delta N(\kappa - 1, \delta - s_1) \\
&= \textstyle\sum_{s_1=0}^\delta \binom{\delta - s_1 + \kappa - 2}{\delta - s_1} \quad \text{by the induction assumption} \\
&= \binom{\delta + \kappa - 1}{\delta} \ .
\end{aligned}
$$

$\square$

Corollary 1. *A complete κ-OWCT T of depth δ has $\binom{\delta + \kappa}{\delta}$ elements.*

Proof. Obvious, since $\sum_{d=0}^\delta N(\kappa, d) = \sum_{d=0}^\delta \binom{d + \kappa - 1}{d} = \binom{\delta + \kappa}{\delta}$. $\square$

Proposition 3. *Let T be a κ-OWCT. Given one or several κ-tuples of T, all the κ-tuples in the smallest one-way subcross-tree containing the given κ-tuples can be evaluated.*

Proof. Let $\mathcal{S} = \{V_{r_1^{(j)}, r_2^{(j)}, \ldots, r_\kappa^{(j)}} = (h_1^{r_1^{(j)}}(I_1), h_2^{r_2^{(j)}}(I_2), \ldots, h_\kappa^{r_\kappa^{(j)}}(I_\kappa))\}_{1 \leq j \leq \ell}$ be the subset of the given κ-tuples. If $\tilde{r}_i$ denotes the smallest $r_i^{(j)}$ ($1 \leq j \leq \ell$) such that $h_i^{r_i^{(j)}}(I_i)$ is a component of a κ-tuple in $\mathcal{S}$, then the one-way subcross-tree generated by $V_{\tilde{r}_1, \tilde{r}_2, \ldots, \tilde{r}_\kappa}$ will contain all the κ-tuples of $\mathcal{S}$ and is the smallest one. From the root $V_{\tilde{r}_1, \tilde{r}_2, \ldots, \tilde{r}_\kappa} = (h_1^{\tilde{r}_1}(I_1), h_2^{\tilde{r}_2}(I_2), \ldots, h_\kappa^{\tilde{r}_\kappa}(I_\kappa))$ of this subcross-tree, all its κ-tuples can be evaluated. $\square$

Alternatively, one-way cross-trees may be described in terms of integer lattices (see Fig. 3). Let T be a κ-OWCT and let $(I_1, I_2, \ldots, I_\kappa)$ be its root. Each element $(h_1^{r_1}(I_1), h_2^{r_2}(I_2), \ldots, h_\kappa^{r_\kappa}(I_\kappa)) \in T$ may uniquely be represented by the

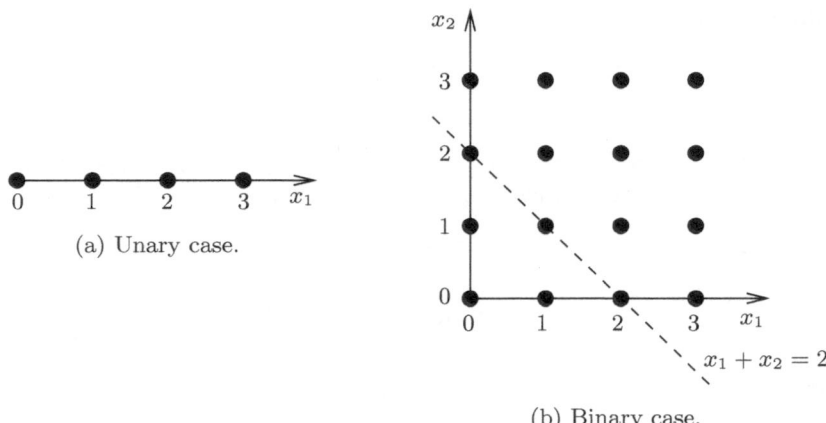

(a) Unary case.

(b) Binary case.

Fig. 3. Lattice interpretation.

integer vector $(r_1, r_2, \ldots, r_\kappa)$. We can therefore define a lattice L containing those integer vectors: $L = \{\sum_{i=1}^{\kappa} x_i\, \boldsymbol{e_i} \mid x_i \in \mathbb{N}\}$ where $\{\boldsymbol{e_i}\}$ is the standard basis—that is, $\boldsymbol{e_i}$ is a vector with a '1' in the ith position and '0' elsewhere. Figure 3 depicts the lattice analogues of a one-way chain and of a binary one-way cross-tree. The elements of depth δ correspond to the lattice vectors lying in the hyper-plan $\Pi_\delta \equiv x_1 + x_2 + \cdots + x_\kappa = \delta$. Increasing the depth of one unit means "jumping forward" away from the hyper-plan Π_δ towards the parallel hyper-plan $\Pi_{\delta+1}$. Moreover, each lattice vector $(s_1, s_2, \ldots, s_\kappa) \in L$ defines a sublattice $L_{\boldsymbol{s}} = \{\sum_{i=1}^{\kappa} x_i\, \boldsymbol{e_i} \mid x_i \in \mathbb{N}, x_i \geq s_i\}$. The one-wayness of cross-tree T implies that from the only knowledge of the κ-tuple $(h_1^{s_1}(I_1), h_2^{s_2}(I_2), \ldots, h_\kappa^{s_\kappa}(I_\kappa))$, only the κ-tuples $(h_1^{x_1}(I_1), h_2^{x_2}(I_2), \ldots, h_\kappa^{x_\kappa}(I_\kappa))$ with $(x_1, x_2, \ldots, x_\kappa) \in L_{\boldsymbol{s}}$ may be computed. Note that, although less practical in higher dimension, the lattice formulation can be useful for theoretical purposes. For example, $N(\kappa, \delta)$ (see Proposition 2) may be considered as $|L \cap \Pi_\delta|$.

3   Generation/Release of Secrets

Suppose that a sequence of n secrets $(S_1, S_2, \ldots, S_n)$ has to be generated. There are basically two ways to do it:

(M1) A first method consists in randomly choosing $S_1, \ldots, S_n$.
(M2) Another method is to randomly choose S_1 and then evaluate $S_i = h(S_{i-1})$ for $i = 2, \ldots, n$, where h is a one-way function.

In this section, we will see that κ-OWCTs unify these two approaches and offer a fine control on both efficiency and security.

3.1   Efficiency

Method (M1) is computationally more efficient while Method (M2) is more efficient in terms of storage—only S_1 has to be stored and S_i is computed as $S_i = h^{i-1}(S_1)$. Note that, in (M1), $S_1, \ldots, S_n$ can be considered as the root of a n-OWCT and, in (M2), as the elements of a 1-OWCT (one-way chain). Therefore, if the secrets are constructed as elements of a κ-OWCT where κ varies between 1 and n, we obtain a full range of possibilities, enabling to choose the best trade-off between computational speed and storage requirements.

However, one-way functions such as SHA [1] or MD5 [15] are very fast; the storage limitation is thus more restrictive. Consequently, Method (M2) seems to be optimal since it only requires the storage of one secret, but the following paragraph brings the opposite consideration.

3.2   Security Considerations

From a security point of view, Method (M1) is superior because the secrets are totally independent; in Method (M2), from a secret S_r, anyone is able to compute $S_{r+1}, S_{r+2}, \ldots, S_n$. Note that this property is sometimes desired in certain applications such as Lamport's one-time password scheme (see Section 1).

3.3   Generation/Release of Secrets in a κ-OWCT

In this paragraph, we discuss in more details how to generate and release a sequence of n secrets in a κ-OWCT T with $2 \leq \kappa \leq n - 1$. A first idea is to use the elements of T as secrets. However, special precautions must be taken: the elements in a κ-OWCT are not completely independent (see Proposition 3). Another idea is to only use the leaves of a complete κ-OWCT. Even in that case, independence between secrets is not guaranteed. Consider for example a complete 3-OWCT of depth 4 with root (I_1, I_2, I_3). The leaf $\boldsymbol{V}_{2,1,1} = (h_1^2(I_1), h_2(I_2), h_3(I_3))$ may for example be obtained from leaves $\boldsymbol{V}_{2,0,2} = (h_1^2(I_1), I_2, h_3^2(I_3))$ and $\boldsymbol{V}_{1,2,1} = (h_1(I_1), h_2^2(I_2), h_3(I_3))$ (which are also of depth 4).

Consequently, the elements of a κ-OWCT T may not be used like this as secrets, they have first to be passed through a one-way hash function H, i.e. the secrets will be

$$S_i = H(\boldsymbol{V}_{r_1, r_2, \ldots, r_\kappa}), \tag{4}$$

where $\boldsymbol{V}_{r_1, r_2, \ldots, r_\kappa} \in T$. The use of the hash function H also results in better performances since it reduces the size of the secrets.

To release a subsequence of secrets $\{S_i, \ldots, S_j\}$, it suffices to reveal their common predecessor of highest weight, say $\boldsymbol{P} \in T$. Note however that, by Proposition 3, this allows to construct all the secrets in the subcross-tree generated by $\boldsymbol{P}$. So, several elements of T must sometimes be released in order to reconstruct *only* the secrets in $\{S_i, \ldots, S_j\}$. Consequently, the secrets have to be carefully arranged into the OWCT in order to minimize the number of elements to release.

3.4   Binary-OWCT vs. OWCT of Higher Dimension

We already learned in §3.1 that a small parameter κ enhances the storage efficiency in the construction of a κ-OWCT. It is worth noting that it may also enhance the overall security, simply because the database containing the root element $\boldsymbol{I} = (I_1, I_2, \ldots, I_\kappa)$ is smaller (κ secret components have to be stored, the other ones are computed), making its maintenance easier.

Another advantage of binary-OWCTs is that each elements has at most two successors. Therefore the release of one element of depth δ enables to derive at most 2 elements of depth $(\delta + 1)$ (and hence at most 2 secrets instead of κ for a κ-OWCT).

Finally, we can remark that, contrary to OWCT of higher dimension, all the components of elements of same depth in a 2-OWCT tree are different. So, for efficiency purposes, if only the leaves of a complete 2-OWCT are used then *one-way* hash function H (see Eq. (4)) may advantageously be replaced by the XOR (exclusive OR) operator in the construction of the secrets. More explicitly, if T is a complete 2-OWCT of depth $n - 1$ with root (I_1, I_2), then secrets $S_1, \ldots, S_n$ are given by $S_i = h_1^{i-1}(I_1) \oplus h_2^{n-i}(I_2)$.

4   Applications

4.1   Key Escrow

It is well-known that *key escrow* systems are proposed to reach a balance between the user's privacy and the society security if those systems are employed by an organization or a country. Briefly, a key escrow system goes as follows. A trusted escrow agent is assumed to hold the secret key of each person in the group and it will be asked to reveal the secret key under authorized law enforcement when required. Unfortunately, the main problem in key escrow systems, especially hardware-oriented systems, is that once the personal secret key has been disclosed, all the past and future communications are no longer secure. Consequently, a scheme with time-constrained release of personal secret keys would be very useful. The proposed construction (namely, generation and release of secrets using κ-OWCTs) can successfully be applied to construct such a scheme.

Imagine a company where user's secret keys are periodically updated for security reasons, say each day. Consider a complete 2-OWCT T of depth 364. By Proposition 2, T has 365 leaves $\boldsymbol{V}_{i,364-i} = (h_1^i(I_1), h_2^{364-i}(I_2))$ with $0 \le i \le 364$. As remarked in §3.4, the XOR operator may be used to construct the secrets; therefore we define secret S_j by

$$S_j = h^{j-1}(I_1) \oplus h^{365-j}(I_2) \qquad (1 \le j \le 365) \ . \tag{5}$$

Note that the same one-way function $h_1 = h_2 := h$ has been chosen.

The scheme can therefore be described as follows. At the beginning of each year, each user A receives a tamper-proof hardware from the trusted center or key escrow agent. Note that this is also the assumption made in the original key escrow standard. In the hardware, there is a real-time clock or a counter that can be used as input to compute the sequence of numbers $\{1, 2, 3, \ldots, 365\}$. The tamper-proof device also stores a secret value I and user's identity ID_A. Define $I_1 = H(I\|1)$ and $I_2 = H(I\|2)$ where H is a one-way hash function. When user A wishes to encrypt a message m to receiver B using a shared session key K_{AB}, both the message and the session key K_{AB} are sent into the hardware and the hardware outputs

$$C = \left(j, \{K_{AB}\}_{SK_j}, ID_A, \{m\}_{K_{AB}}\right) \tag{6}$$

where $1 \leq j \leq 365$ is the number of the day and $\{p\}_k$ denotes the encryption (any encryption algorithm adopted by the hardware) of message p under secret key k. From integer j (computed from the embedded real-time clock or counter) and the identity ID_A, the hardware computes A's secret key SK_j as

$$SK_j = h^{j-1}(I_1\|ID_A) \oplus h^{365-j}(I_2\|ID_A) \ . \tag{7}$$

On the receiver's (i.e., B) side, his hardware contains the same information except that the identity is now ID_B. From the transmitted C (Eq. (6)), A's secret key SK_j can be recovered (by Eq. (7)) and thus the session key K_{AB} can be correctly extracted. If the computed session key and the entered session key are the same, then receiver's hardware starts to decrypt the ciphertext $\{m\}_{K_{AB}}$, otherwise rejects the decryption request.

Suppose now that for some reason, the wire-tapped communication initiated from A during days 30 till 116 has to be decrypted. Then the law enforcement agent submits the set of numbers $\{30, 31, 32, \ldots, 116\}$ to trusted key escrow agent and receives

$$(h^{30-1}(I_1\|ID_A), h^{365-116}(I_2\|ID_A)) = (h^{29}(I_1\|ID_A), h^{249}(I_2\|ID_A)) \ . \tag{8}$$

From this information, all the secret keys between SK_{30} and SK_{116} can evidently be recomputed. Therefore, all the session keys protected by these secret keys can be extracted and the corresponding wire-tapped ciphertexts can be correctly decrypted. Note that, from Proposition 3, only *one* release of the form $(h^r(I_1\|ID_A), h^s(I_2\|ID_A))$ is permitted. For example, if the law enforcement agent requests the secret keys $SK_{301}, \ldots, SK_{310}$, he may not be provided with $(h^{300}(I_1\|ID_A), h^{55}(I_2\|ID_A))$ because he is then also able to compute $SK_{117}, \ldots, SK_{300}$. Secret keys $SK_{301}, \ldots, SK_{310}$ must thus be released individually.

To overcome this drawback, one can for example construct a complete 2-OWCT of depth 6 with root (I_1, I_2). By Corollary 1, this OWCT has $\binom{8}{6} = 28$ elements. These elements are then numbered in a publicly known way as $E_1, E_2, \ldots, E_{28}$. We define

$$R_i = (R_{i,1}, R_{i,2}) = (H(E_{2i-1}), H(E_{2i})) \quad (1 \leq i \leq 12) , \tag{9}$$

where H is a one-way hash function. From the discussion in §3.3, we know that all of the $H(E_j)$ are independent. Therefore, R_i $(1 \leq i \leq 12)$ may be used as roots to construct 12 independent 2-OWCTs. The secret keys of user A are now given by

$$SK_{i,j} = h^{j-1}(R_{i,1}\|ID_A) \oplus h^{31-j}(R_{i,2}\|ID_A) , \tag{10}$$

where $1 \leq i \leq 12$ denotes the number of the month and $1 \leq j \leq 31$ denotes the number of the day in month i. Suppose now that the law enforcement agent requests A's secret keys used during 20th March till 10th April, then he will receive

$$(h^{19}(R_{3,1}\|ID_A), R_{3,2}\|ID_A, R_{4,1}\|ID_A, h^{21}(R_{4,2}\|ID_A)) . \tag{11}$$

The advantage of this second construction is that *one* release of a sequence of secret keys is permitted *each month* instead of each year.

4.2   Delegation

Consider as the previous paragraph that for security reasons secret keys are changed each day. Suppose an employee in a company needs to go on a business trip, and he has no special portable computer available for the access to the company. Before going on his trip, he plans to give the secret keys (for logging into his computer account, for decrypting emails, etc.) to his secretary. Since the secret keys are constructed from OWCTs, the employee has just to release some secret values and not all the secret keys. Then the secretary can compute the corresponding secret keys. She can thus decide in place of the employee according to his policy told beforehand; or if the employee can make a call to the office, she follows instructions given by him. Note that the secretary can only recover the secret keys corresponding to the period during those the employee is away from the office. She is not able to substitute the employee afterwards or to decrypt past communications.

4.3   Lamport-Like Schemes

If the elements of a κ-OWCT (with $\kappa \geq 2$) are passed through a one-way function (see Eq. (4)), they constitute independent secrets—that is, given one or several secrets, it is computationally infeasible to find another one. OWCTs provide thus a simple and efficient means to construct independent secrets. Moreover, to enhance the performance, one can attribute an element of lower weight to a secret which is more often used; the computation of this element (and thus of the corresponding secret) from the root of the OWCT is then speeded up.

Suppose that an user generates N independent secrets in a κ-OWCT ($\kappa \geq 2$). These secrets may represent the initial values of N one-way chains (see Fig. 1). Each of these chains can then for example be used to construct a micro-payment protocol with a given merchant [2,16]. The OWCT just serves as a memo to compute the initial value of a one-way chain. The advantages are (1) the user has just to remember (or store) the root of a OWCT; and (2) if for some reason one secret has been disclosed, the security of the transactions with the other merchants is not compromised. Of course, other applications based on one-way chains (e.g., [3,5,6,7,8,9,10,13,14]) may also be adapted advantageously to such a construction.

5   Conclusions

This paper generalized the concept of one-way chain. The resulting construction, called one-way cross-tree, finds interesting applications in the generation and release of secrets. In a κ-OWCT, only κ secrets have to be stored; moreover, when required, some selected secrets (and only those ones) may efficiently be released.

Acknowledgments

Sung-Ming Yen was supported in part by the National Science Council of the Republic of China under contract NSC 89-2213-E-008-049.

References

1. FIPS 180-1. Secure hash standard. Federal Information Processing Standards Publication 180-1, NIST, U.S. Department of Commerce, April 1995.
2. R. Anderson, H. Manifavas, and C. Sutherland. A practical electronic cash system. Available from URL <http://www.cl.cam.ac.uk/users/rja14/>, 1995.
3. N. Asokan, G. Tsudik, and M. Waidner. Server-supported signatures. In E. Bertino, editor, *Fourth European Symposium on Research in Computer Security (ESO-RICS '96)*, volume 1146 of *Lecture Notes in Computer Science*, pages 131–143. Springer-Verlag, 1996.
4. D. Bleichenbacher and U.M. Maurer. Directed acyclic graphs, one-way functions and digital signatures. In Y.G. Desmedt, editor, *Advances in Cryptology — CRYPTO '94*, volume 839 of *Lecture Notes in Computer Science*, pages 75–82. Springer-Verlag, 1994.
5. O. Delos and J.-J. Quisquater. An identity-based signature scheme with bounded life-span. In Y.G. Desmedt, editor, *Advances in Cryptology — CRYPTO '94*, volume 839 of *Lecture Notes in Computer Science*, pages 83–94. Springer-Verlag, 1994.
6. D. de Waleffe and J.-J. Quisquater. Better login protocols for computer networks. In B. Preneel, R. Govaerts, and J. Vandewalle, editors, *Computer Security and Industrial Cryptography*, volume 741 of *Lecture Notes in Computer Science*, pages 50–70. Springer-Verlag, 1993.
7. S. Even, O. Goldreich, and S. Micali. On-line/off-line digital signatures. In G. Brassard, editor, *Advances in Cryptology — CRYPTO '89*, volume 435 of *Lecture Notes in Computer Science*, pages 263–275. Springer-Verlag, 1990.
8. N.M. Haller. The S/KEY one-time password system. In *Proc. of the ISOC Symposium on Networks and Distributed Systems Security*, 1994.
9. L. Lamport. Constructing digital signatures from a one-way function. Technical Report CSL-98, SRI International, 1979.
10. L. Lamport. Password authentication with insecure communication. *Comm. ACM*, 24(11):770–772, November 1981.
11. M. Mambo, K. Usuda, and E. Okamoto. Proxy signatures for delegating signing operations. In *Proc. of the 3rd ACM Conference on Computer and Communications Security*, pages 48–57. ACM Press, 1996.
12. R.C. Merkle. A digital signature based on a conventional encryption function. In C. Pomerance, editor, *Advances in Cryptology — CRYPTO '87*, volume 293 of *Lecture Notes in Computer Science*, pages 369–378. Springer-Verlag, 1988.

13. R.C. Merkle. A certified digital signature. In G. Brassard, editor, *Advances in Cryptology — CRYPTO '89*, volume 435 of *Lecture Notes in Computer Science*, pages 218–238. Springer-Verlag, 1990.
14. M.O. Rabin. Digitalized signatures. In D. Dobkin, A. Jones, and R. Lipton, editors, *Foundations of Secure Computation*, pages 155–168. Academic Press, 1978.
15. R. Rivest. The MD5 message digest algorithm. Internet Request for Comments RFC 1321, April 1992. Available at `<ftp://ds.internic.net/rfc/rfc1321.txt>`.
16. R.L. Rivest and A. Shamir. PayWord and MicroMint: two simple micropayment schemes. *CryptoBytes*, **2** (1), 7–11, 1996.

RSA Key Generation with Verifiable Randomness

Ari Juels[1] and Jorge Guajardo[2]

[1] RSA Laboratories
Bedford, MA, USA
ajuels@rsasecurity.com
[2] Department of Electrical Engineering and Information Sciences
Ruhr-Universität Bochum, Germany
guajardo@crypto.ruhr-uni-bochum.de

Abstract. We consider the problem of proving that a user has selected and correctly employed a truly random seed in the generation of her RSA key pair. This task is related to the problem of *key validation*, the process whereby a user proves to another party that her key pair has been generated securely. The aim of key validation is to pursuade the verifying party that the user has not intentionally weakened or reused her key or unintentionally made use of bad software. Previous approaches to this problem have been *ad hoc*, aiming to prove that a private key is secure against specific types of attacks, e.g., that an RSA modulus is resistant to elliptic-curve-based factoring attacks. This approach results in a rather unsatisfying laundry list of security tests for keys.

We propose a new approach that we refer to as *key generation with verifiable randomness* (KEGVER). Our aim is to show in zero knowledge that a private key has been generated at random according to a prescribed process, and is therefore likely to benefit from the full strength of the underlying cryptosystem. Our proposal may be viewed as a kind of distributed key generation protocol involving the user and verifying party. Because the resulting private key is held solely by the user, however, we are able to propose a protocol much more practical than conventional distributed key generation. We focus here on a KEGVER protocol for RSA key generation.

Key words: certificate authority, key generation, non-repudiation, public-key infrastructure, verifiable randomness, zero knowledge

1 Introduction

In this paper, we consider the problem of demonstrating that a public key PK is well selected, in other words, that it has been chosen so as to benefit strongly from the security properties of the underlying cryptosystem. This problem has been typically refered to in the literature as that of *key validation*. Interest in key validation arises when a user registers a public key PK of some kind with a certificate authority (CA) or presents it for use in some other application, such

D. Naccache and P. Paillier (Eds.): PKC 2002, LNCS 2274, pp. 357–374, 2002.
© Springer-Verlag Berlin Heidelberg 2002

as a group signature scheme. The structure of PK offers only limited assurance about the strength of the corresponding private key SK. For example, in the RSA cryptosystem, it may be that the public modulus n is long, ensuring security against the general number field sieve. At the same time, one of the two component primes may be short, creating vulnerability to elliptic-curve-based factoring attacks. Thus, it is easily possible for a user to generate SK of some weak form so as to render it vulnerable to any of a range of common attacks, without the knowledge of the CA. If SK is, say, a private signing key, then a malicious user of this sort can seek to repudiate transactions based on digital signatures generated using SK, claiming that the vulnerability of SK led to key compromise. The user might, for instance, place an order for a purchase of stock, and then repudiate it if the market subsequently goes down. Weakness in a key may alternatively result because a user has made inappropriate use of the same "stale" key across multiple platforms. For example, a user might choose to make use of the same key for her magazine subscription as for her financial transactions. Finally, and probably most importantly, a weak key may be produced by bad software. Faulty or malicious software might induce a subtle weakness by using a "stale" prime in RSA keys, i.e., using the same component prime in different moduli. As demonstrated by Young and Yung [36], malicious software might create a key that appears to have been correctly generated, but is primed for theft by the creator of the software, a process dubbed "kleptography". A software package may also generate a key that is weak simply because of faulty programming. This last is of perhaps the greatest concern to security architects.

Such concerns and the liability risks they create for certificate issuers have been a recurrent issue in standards bodies for some time, and have thus served as an impetus for investigation into key validation techniques. A key validation protocol aims at enabling a user to prove to a verifying party, with minimal information leakage, that her private key SK has a particular security property that may not be evident from inspection of PK. For example, researchers have proposed protocols enabling the possessor of an RSA private key to prove to a CA with little information leakage that the corresponding public modulus n is the product of two primes p and q of roughly equal length. Such a protocol is included in the appendix to the ANSI X9.31 standard for digital signatures used in financial services applications [2].

Note, however, that an RSA key can also be constructed in such a way that it is vulnerable to any of an arbitrarily long list of special-form factoring algorithms: examples of ones popular in the literature include the so-called $p-1$ attack and $p+1$ attack [27]. Recognizing that a host of different types of attacks against the RSA cryptosystem are possible, ANSI X9.31 for example includes discussion of a range of key validation tests. It is clear from the outset, though, that this kind of *ad hoc* approach is fundamentally limited: One can always devise a new type of attack and corresponding key validation protocol to add to the list, and no set of litmus tests can guard against use of a stale key.

In this paper, we propose a novel alternative to or enhancement of key validation that we refer to as *key generation with verifiable randomness*, and denote for brevity by KEGVER. A KEGVER protocol shows not that a key is resistant to a list specific attacks, but instead that the key has been generated as an honest party would, and is therefore unlikely to be weak with respect to any known attack and unlikely to be stale. The starting point for our approach may be thought of as an ideal process in which a *trusted dealer* or *trusted third party* (TTP) generates a key pair (SK, PK) according to a universally agreed upon process, e.g., the example methods presented in the IEEE P1363 standard [1]. In this ideal process, the TTP sends (SK, PK) privately to the user and PK to the CA. The user is assured here that the privacy of her key SK is as good as if she had generated it herself. The CA is assured that the key pair (SK, PK) was generated securely, namely according to published guidelines, and therefore benefits from the full strength of the underlying cryptosystem. It should be noted that TTPs form a component of many secret sharing and key distribution schemes, e.g., [32]. The role of the TTPs in these schemes, however, is to effect a correct sharing of secrets. In our ideal process, it is to ensure correct key generation.

Of course, involvement by a TTP in real-world settings is generally undesirable and impractical. It is well known, however, that such a TTP can be simulated by the user and CA alone using fundamental cryptographic techniques known as *general secure function evaluation* [21,35]. While offering rigorously provable security characteristics, such techniques remain highly impractical, particularly for such computationally intensive operations as key generation. Our contribution in this paper is a technique that simulates the TTP efficiently in a practical sense. The one drawback to our proposal is that it involves a slight weakening of the ideal process: The user is able to influence the TTP to a small (but negligible) degree. We believe that our proposal is of great practical interest, and note that it can even be achieved in a non-interactive setting. We focus on KEGVER protocols for RSA in this paper.

A capsule description of our KEGVER protocol for RSA is as follows. The user and CA jointly select random integers x and y; these integers are known to the user, but not the CA. The user then produces an RSA modulus n. She proves to the CA that n is a Blum integer and the product of two primes, p and q. She furthermore proves that p and q lie in intervals $[x, x + l]$ and $[y, y + l]$ for some public parameter l, i.e., that they are "close" to x and y. The parameter l is selected to be small enough to constrain the user in her construction of the modulus n, but large enough to ensure that she can very likely find primes in the desired intervals. Secure, joint generation of x and y, judicious selection of l, and a number of implementation details form the crux of our work in this paper. As an additional contribution, we propose new definitions required to characterize the security of a KEGVER protocol.

1.1   Previous Work

While general secure function evaluation and zero-knowledge proof techniques are largely impractical, researchers have devised a number of efficient protocols to prove specific properties of public keys. One of the earliest such protocols is due to van de Graaf and Peralta [33], who present a practical scheme for proving in zero knowledge that an integer n is of the form $p^r q^s$ for primes p and q such that $p, q \equiv 3 \bmod 4$ and the integers r and s are odd. Boyar et al. [7] show how to prove that an integer n is square-free, i.e., is not divisible by the square of any prime factor. Together, these two proof protocols demonstrate that an integer n is a Blum integer, i.e., an RSA modulus that $n = pq$ such that $p, q \equiv 3 \bmod 4$. Gennaro et al. [19] build on these two protocols to demonstrate a proof system showing that a number n is the product of quasi-safe primes, i.e., that $n = pq$ such that $(p-1)/2$ and $(q-1)/2$ are prime powers (with some additional, technical properties). Camenisch and Michels [8] extend these proof techniques still further, demonstrating a protocol for proving that an RSA integer is the product of two safe primes, i.e., primes p and q such that $(p-1)/2$ and $(q-1)/2$ are themselves primes. While asymptotically efficient, however, this last protocol is not very practical.

Chan et al. [11][1] and Mao [25] provide protocols for showing that an RSA modulus n consists of the product of two primes p and q of large size. Liskov and Silverman [23] describe a protocol interesting for its direct use of number-theoretic properties of n to show that p and q are of nearly equal length. Fujisaki and Okamoto [15,16] present related protocols for proving in statistical zero knowledge that a committed integer lies within a given range. All of these protocols are largely superseded for practical purposes by the work of Boudot [6], who, under the Strong RSA Assumption, demonstrates highly efficient, statistical zero-knowledge protocols for proving that a committed number lies in a given range. The Boudot protocols permit proofs of very precise statements about the sizes of p and q.

Loosely stated, all of these protocols demonstrate that a committed number (or public key) lies in a particular set or language. Our aim, which may be viewed as complementary, is to show that a committed number has been selected from a given set *at random* according to some publicly specified process. Thus, these previous protocols, and particularly the Boudot protocols, are useful in the construction of our KEGVER scheme. Our focus in this paper, however, is on the additional apparatus required to make broader statements about adherence to a prescribed key-generation protocol.

A simple approach to ensuring freshness in RSA key generation is for the CA to select a random string s of, say, 100 bits, and require that the leading bits of the public key PK be equal to s. This method, however, has several drawbacks. It only ensures freshness in a narrow sense: While the CA can be assured with high probability that the user has not registered PK before, there is no assurance that the user has not re-used one of the constituent primes of the modulus before. Moreover, by constraining the form of PK, the CA naturally constrains the possible set of private keys SK, leading to some degradation in security. Finally, the required alteration to the key generation process limits compatibility with current prime generation techniques.

---

[1] The original version of this paper contained a technical flaw, and was subsequently republished as a GTE technical report.

A broader but still simple approach proposed for verification of the key generation process is to derive all underlying randomness from application of a pseudo-random number generator to a random initial seed s. Of course, this approach only provides *ex post facto* arbitration of potential disputes, as revelation of s also discloses the private key.

Distributed key generation is an area closer in spirit to our work in this paper, and can in fact serve directly to achieve a KEGVER scheme for RSA. (For discrete-log based systems, the idea is straightforward and very practical, but we do not have space enough to describe it here.) The best basis is a distributed key generation protocol presented by Boneh and Franklin [5] and further explored most recently in, e.g., [10,20,24]. In this protocol, a minimum of three players (or two, in some variants) jointly generate an RSA modulus n. At the end of this protocol, each of the players holds a share of the corresponding private key. No player learns the whole private key at any point.

To see how such a distributed key generation protocol for RSA can serve as the basis for a KEGVER protocol, consider the two-party case. The idea here is to have the CA act as one player and the user as the other. At the end of the protocol, the CA sends its private key share to the user, who is able then to reconstruct and verify the correctness of the entire private key. This approach enables the CA to be assured that n is generated according to a prescribed protocol, e.g., that p and q are generated uniformly at random from a prescribed range. Likewise, the user in this case can be assured that her private key is not exposed to the CA or to an eavesdropper. The idea for the three-party (or multi-party) case is analogous.

The main drawback to distributed key generation for RSA is that it is quite slow. Malkin *et al.* [24] present experiments involving a highly optimized version of the three-party Boneh and Franklin protocol [5]. These experiments suggest that about 6 minutes of work is required to generate a 1024-bit modulus across the Internet using fast servers. In contrast, convention generation of a 1024-bit RSA on a fast workstation requires less than a second [34]. The basic Boneh and Franklin protocol, moreover, is not secure against active adversaries, and thus would not be suitable by itself as the basis for a KEGVER protocol. Instead, it would be necessary to employ a variant with robustness against malicious players, e.g., [24]. These variants are even less efficient than that of Boneh and Franklin. It is possible to construct a non-interactive KEGVER protocol based on distributed RSA key generation by having the user simulate other players (by analogy with our discrete-log-based example above). The overall costs and complexity of such an approach remain high, however.

Since our aim is not sharing, but rather correct generation of a private key, we adopt an approach in this paper rather different in its technical details from distributed key generation. As a result, we are able to present a KEGVER protocol for RSA that is quite efficient and also has a natural, fully non-interactive variant.

1.2 Our Approach

Let us sketch the intuition behind our KEGVER protocol for RSA, expanding on our capsule description in the introduction to the paper. One common technique for generating a component prime of an RSA modulus n is to pick a random starting point r in an appropriate range, and apply a primality test to successive candidate integers greater than r until a (highly probable) prime p is found. This basic approach may be enhanced by means of sieving or other techniques, but is essentially the same in almost all systems in use today. The pivotal idea behind our KEGVER scheme is for the user and CA to generate r jointly in such a way that r has three properties: (1) r is selected uniformly at random from an appropriate interval; (2) The user knows r; and (3) The CA holds a commitment to r, but does not know r itself. The user performs the same process to derive a starting point s for a second component prime.

Ideally, we would then like the user to furnish an RSA modulus n and prove that the constituent primes p and q are the smallest primes larger than r and s. In the absence of any known practical technique to accomplish this, we adopt a slightly weaker approach. We restrict the user to selection of a modulus n that is a Blum integer, i.e., the product of primes p and q such that $p, q \equiv 3 \bmod 4$. We use well known protocols to have the user prove in zero knowledge that n is indeed a Blum integer. We then employ techniques for proofs involving committed integers, and for range proofs in particular. These enable the user to prove in zero knowledge that p is "close" to r and that q is "close" to s.

As a result of this last proof and the fact that r and s are generated jointly, the user is greatly restricted in her choice of p and q. In particular, she must choose each of these primes from a small interval generated uniformly at random. The result is that the user has very little flexibility in her choice of n, and must therefore select a modulus n nearly as strong as if she had adhered honestly to the prescribed key generation protocol. As a tradeoff against the high efficiency of our protocol, a malicious user does in fact have a little "wiggle room" in her choice of n, but this is small for practical purposes. At the same time, use of zero-knowledge (and statistical zero-knowledge) protocols ensures that the CA gains no information about the private key other than that contained in n itself.

Although we do not dilate on the idea in our paper, we note also that KEGVER can also be employed by a user as a local check against "kleptographic" attacks by an RSA key-generation module [36]. For this, the user employs a separate KEGVER module (generated by a separate entity) to check the correct behavior of the key-generation module.

Organization

In section 2, we present formal definitions for the notion of key generation with verifiable randomness, along with brief description of the cryptographic and conceptual building blocks. We present protocol details in section 3. We offer security and performance analyses in sections 4 and 5 respectively. Due to space limitations, we have omitted many details from this version of the paper. A full version is available from the authors on request.

2   Definitions

Thusfar we have described a KEGVER protocol as one in which the user, through joint computation with a CA, is constrained to produce keys in a manner "close" to honest adherence to some standard key generation algorithm. Our first task is to characterize formally this notion of "closeness". We assume for the sake of simplicity a cryptosystem in which every public key PK has a unique corresponding private key SK. We refer to a probability d as *overwhelming* in parameter l if for any polynomial *poly* there is some L such that $d > 1 - \frac{1}{|poly(l)|}$ for $l > L$. We let $\in_U$ denote uniform random selection from a set.

We begin by defining key generation and key generation with verifiable randomness. We let keygen denote a key generation algorithm that takes as input a soundness parameter t and a key-size parameter k. With probability overwhelming in t, the algorithm outputs a well-formed private/public key pair (SK, PK). The length of the public key is specified by k: For example, in our RSA-based key generation algorithm, it is convenient to let the output key length be $2k - 1$ or $2k$ bits. Let $\mathcal{PK}_k$ denote the set of public keys specified by key-size parameter k, i.e., the set of all such possible outputs PK of keygen. We assume that membership in $\mathcal{PK}_k$ is efficiently computable without knowledge of SK. We let $P_{k,t}$ denote the probability distribution induced by keygen over $\mathcal{PK}_k$ for parameter k, and let $P_{k,t}(PK)$ be the probability associated with key PK in particular.

A KEGVER protocol involves the participation of a user and a CA. The protocol takes as input a key-size parameter k and security parameters l, m, and t. Here, l and t are soundness parameters, while m is a security parameter governing statistical hiding of committed values, as we explain below. If the protocol is successful, the public output of the protocol is a public key $PK \in \mathcal{PK}_k$, and the private output to the user is a corresponding private key SK. Otherwise, the protocol fails, and we represent the public output by $\emptyset$. The probability of protocol failure when the participants are honest is characterized by security parameter l. We let $Q_{k;l,m,t}$ denote the probability distribution induced by output PK over $\mathcal{PK}_k$ by the KEGVER protocol when the two participants are honest. We say that the CA *accepts* if the CA is persuaded that PK has been properly generated; otherwise the CA *rejects* the protocol output.

Definition 1. *Let $Q_{k;l,m,t}^A$ be probability distribution induced by the output of KEGVER with fixed key-size parameter k and security parameters l, m and t over executions accepted by an honest CA when the user is represented by an algorithm A (not necessarily honest). We say that KEGVER is a μ-sound KEGVER protocol for keygen if, for any algorithm A with running time polynomial in k, we have*

$$\max_{PK \in \mathcal{P}_k} \frac{Q_{k;l,m,t}^A(PK)}{P_{k,t}(PK)} \leq \mu. \tag{1}$$

$\square$

This definition specifies the soundness of KEGVER, stating that a dishonest user can generate a given key with probability only μ times that of an honest user executing keygen. For small μ, this means that it is infeasible for a dishonest user to persuade the CA to accept the output of the protocol unless its output distribution is similar to that of keygen. Suppose, for example, that keygen is a standard RSA key-generation algorithm for which the RSA assumption [27] is believed to hold. Then if μ is polynomial in k, it is hard for an attacker to weaken her own key effectively in KEGVER.[2] We make the following observation; all quantities here are relative to key-size k, while security parameters are fixed.

Observation 1. *Suppose there exist polynomial-time algorithms A and B such that with non-negligible probability, $B(PK) = SK$ for pairs (SK, PK) distributed according to $Q_{k;l,m,t}^A$. Then if μ is polynomial, it follows that there is a polynomial-time B' such that $B'(PK) = SK$ with non-negligible probability over $P_{k,t}$, and thus that the RSA assumption does not hold on* keygen. $\square$

The other feature we want is for KEGVER is privacy. In particular, we do not want the CA to obtain any (non-negligible) information about SK other than PK. To make this notion more precise, let us consider the following experiment with an adversary A_1. Adversary A_1 engages (not necessarily honestly) in protocol KEGVER with an honest user with parameters k and m. If the protocol is successful, i.e., outputs a public key PK, then A_1 computes and outputs a guess of the corresponding private key SK at the conclusion of the protocol. Let us then consider a second adversary A_2 that is given a public key $PK \in_{Q_{k;l,m,t}} \mathcal{PK}_k$, i.e., a public key drawn from the distribution specified by $Q_{k;l,m,t}$. This adversary likewise computes a guess at the corresponding private key SK, but without the benefit of a transcript from execution of KEGVER.

Definition 2. *We say that KEGVER is private if for any polynomial-time adversary A_1, there exists a polynomial-time adversary A_2 such that for any polynomial poly there is an L such that $m > L$ implies*

$$\mathsf{pr}[A_1 \ guesses \ SK] - \mathsf{pr}[A_2 \ guesses \ SK] < 1/|poly(m)|. \tag{2}$$

$\square$

This definition states informally that by participating in protocol KEGVER yielding public key PK, a CA – or an arbitrary eavesdropper – gains only a non-negligible advantage in its ability to compute the private key SK.

We can extend this definition to consider an adversary A_1 that engages adaptively in some polynomial number of invocations of KEGVER. As we assume independent randomness for each invocation of the protocols in this paper, this extended definition is no stronger for our purposes than Definition 2.

---

[2] Of course, a malicious user seeking to weaken her own key can tailor an efficient attack algorithm A for factoring n and then promulgate A. For example, A may contain implicit knowledge of one of the component primes of n. The case for repudiation will be difficult to support in such cases, though, as A will be self-indicting.

2.1   Building Blocks

In our scheme, we work over a group $\mathcal{G}$ published by the CA, with order $o(\mathcal{G})$ unknown to the user. We describe $\mathcal{G}$ in the paper as being of "unknown order", as contrasted with a group of "known order", i.e., order known to all players. Additionally, the order $o(\mathcal{G})$ must be larger than the maximum value of the target public RSA key n to be generated by the user. Note that if $o(\mathcal{G})$ is small, this may permit the user to cheat, but will not in fact degrade user privacy. Thus it is in the interest of the CA to choose $\mathcal{G}$ with the appropriate order. In our scheme, it is convenient for the group $\mathcal{G}$ to be generated as a large subgroup of Z_N^* for an RSA modulus N with unpublished factorization. Because of exploitation of the properties of a group of unknown order, many of our sub-protocols rely for security on the Strong RSA Assumption.

The CA additionally publishes two generators of $\mathcal{G}$, denoted by g and h. These generators are selected such that $\log_g h$ and $\log_h g$ are unknown to the user. We believe that the best setup for our protocol is one in which the CA lets $N = PQ$, where $P = 2P' + 1$ and $Q = 2Q' + 1$ for primes P' and Q', and selects $\mathcal{G}$ as the cyclic group of order $2P'Q'$, i.e., the group of elements with Jacobi symbol 1.[3] The CA would then, e.g., select $g, h \in_U \mathcal{G}$. The CA proves to users that $<g>=<h>$. This is accomplished through proofs of knowledge of $\log_g h$ and $\log_h g$, as described below. Since the CA has freedom in selecting N and can therefore manipulate the orders of the groups generated by g and h, however, these proofs of knowledge require t rounds with binary challenges. (This is equivalent to a cut-and-choose proof.) This involves a non-negligible overhead, but the proofs need only be generated by the CA once and checked by each user only upon key registration.

Fujisaki-Okamoto commitment scheme: This commitment scheme, introduced in [15], is essentially a variant on the commitment scheme of Pedersen [28], but adjusted for application to groups $\mathcal{G}$ of unknown order of the form described above. The Fujisaki-Okamoto scheme is statistically hiding in a security parameter m. To commit to a value $x \in Z$, the user selects a commitment factor $w \in_U \{-2^m N + 1, 2^m N - 1\}$. She then computes the commitment $C(x, w) = g^x h^w \bmod N$. For further details, see [6,15]. Note that this commitment scheme is only certain to be hiding provided that the CA has selected g and h such that $<g>=<h>$. The Fujisaki-Okamoto commitment scheme is binding assuming the hardness of factoring, i.e., that the user cannot factor N.

Proof of knowledge of discrete log: Suppose that for some $a \in <g>$, a prover wishes to prove knowledge of $x \in Z_N$ such that $y = g^x \bmod N$. The prover may use a variant of the Schnorr proof of knowledge [31] as follows, with soundness parameter t and privacy parameter m. The prover selects $z \in_U [1, 2^m N]$ and computes $w = g^z$. The verifier computes a challenge $c \in_U [0, 2^t - 1]$. The prover

---

[3] One must select $\mathcal{G}$ carefully. For example, while certain papers, e.g., [6], state that $\mathcal{G}$ can be any large subgroup of Z_N^*, Mao and Lim [26] provide some caveats on such subgroups with prime order.

returns $r = cx + z$ (over Z). The verifier checks that elements of the prover's proof are in $<g>$. (In our setting, where N is a safe prime and $<g>$ is the cyclic group of order $2P'Q'$, as described above, the verifier checks that elements have Jacobi symbol 1). Then the verifier checks the equality $g^r = wy^c \bmod N$. The protocol is statistical zero-knowledge provided that $1/2^m$ is negligible. It is sound under the Strong RSA Assumption [15]; without breaking this assumption, a cheating prover is able to succeed with probability at most 2^{-t+1} [8]. This proof of knowledge may be rendered non-interactive if the challenge is generated as $c = H(N \parallel g \parallel y \parallel w)$ for an appropriate hash function H. Security may then be demonsrated upon invocation of the random oracle model on H. We assume use of non-interactive proofs in our protocols, and write $POK\{x : y = g^x\}$ to denote a proof of knowledge of the form described here.

Generalized proofs of knowledge of discrete log: As shown in [13,14], it is possible to construct efficient, general, monotone boolean predicates on statements of knowledge of discrete logs. Efficient proofs across multiple bases are also possible. In [8], it is observed that these general proof techniques may be applied to the setting we describe here involving groups of unknown order. We employ here the notation developed by Camenisch and Stadler [9], in which a proof statement is written in the form $POK\{variables : predicate\}$, where *predicate* is a monotone boolean formula on statements of knowledge of discrete logs, potentially over multiple bases. For example, a proof of equality of two values represented by commitments C_1 and C_2 would be written as follows: $POK\{a, r_1, r_2 : (C_1 = g^a h^{r_1}) \bigwedge (C_2 = g^a h^{r_2})\}$. More recently, Damgård and Fujisaki [30] study a generalization of Fujisaki-Okamoto committments and proofs of knowledge for these, making some minor corrections to [15]. A related generalization permits proof that one committed value is equal to the product of two other committed values [8,25].

Interval proof: An *interval proof* is a statistical zero-knowledge proof that a committed value lies within some explicitly specified interval. For commitment $C = g^x h^r$, for example, the prover may wish to prove that $x \in [0, 2^{512}]$. Boudot [6] presents two highly efficient interval proof techniques. We consider here the interval proof in [6] *without tolerance*. The goal is for the prover to demonstrate, for explicit integers a and b such that $b > a$ and on commitment C of value x that $x \in [a, b]$. We represent this by $POK\{x, r : (C = g^x h^r) \bigwedge (x \in [a, b])\}$. Soundness here depends on the Strong RSA Assumption.

Blum integer proof: As noted above, combination of the protocols in [7,33] yields an efficient proof that an integer n is a Blum integer. We denote this proof protocol by $\mathsf{Blum}(n)[t]$, where t is a security parameter. If successful, the protocol yields output 'yes', otherwise output 'no'. The protocol can be either interactive or non-interactive. The soundness of the protocol is overwhelming in t, while the computational and communication costs are linear in t.

3   Protocol

We take as our starting point the following algorithm keygen for RSA key generation. We assume that keygen takes as input an even-valued key-size parameter k (essentially half of the modulus length). We also assume the availability of a probabilistic algorithm $\mathsf{primetest}(z, t)$, that takes as input an integer z and soundness parameter t; this algorithm outputs 'yes' if the input element is prime and otherwise, with overwhelming probability in t, outputs 'no'. For technical reasons, our protocol keygen generates RSA moduli n that are Blum integers.

Algorithm $\mathsf{keygen}(e, k)[t]$
$\quad r \in_u [2^{k-1}, 2^k - 1];$
$\quad s \in_u [2^{k-1}, 2^k - 1];$
$\quad$ while $gcd(e, r - 1) > 1$ or $r \not\equiv 3 \bmod 4$
$\quad\quad$ or $\mathsf{primetest}[r, t] = $ 'no'
$\quad\quad\quad r \leftarrow r + 1;$
$\quad$ while $gcd(e, s - 1) > 1$ or $s \not\equiv 3 \bmod 4$
$\quad\quad$ or $\mathsf{primetest}[s, t] = $ 'no'
$\quad\quad\quad s \leftarrow s + 1;$
$\quad p \leftarrow r; q \leftarrow s;$
$\quad d \leftarrow e^{-1} \bmod (p - 1)(q - 1);$
$\quad$ output $(n = pq, d);$

The algorithm keygen outputs with overwhelming probability in k and t a Blum integer (and thus RSA modulus) n with a bit length of $2k - 1$ or $2k$. Note that for the sake of efficiency, one would generally use a sieving technique in practice to compute p and q. Adoption of sieving would have no impact, however, on the output of the algorithm. Another common practice is to fix a target bit length for n and adjust the intervals for p and q accordingly. We specify keygen as above for simplicity of presentation.

3.1   **KEGVER** Protocol

We are now ready to present the details of our KEGVER protocol for RSA key generation. Prior to execution of the protocol, the CA publishes key-size parameter k and security parameters l, m, and t, along with an RSA modulus N such that $|N| > 2k + 1$, and whose factorization it keeps private. The CA additionally publishes g and h of a subgroup $\mathcal{G}$ of Z_N^* such that $|o(\mathcal{G})| > 2k + 1$, and a proof $Proof_1 = POK\{a, b : (g^a = h) \bigwedge (h^b = g)\}$. As explained above, the ability of the CA to select N means that the soundness of this proof of knowledge depends upon execution with binary challenges over t rounds.

We begin by introducing a sub-protocol unigen. This protocol enables the user and the CA jointly to select a value $z \in [A, B]$ such that if at least one party is honest, z is distributed across $[A, B]$ uniformly at random. As may be seen from the properties of the building blocks, the soundness of the protocol depends on both the Strong RSA Assumption and the discrete log assumption over $\mathcal{G}$, while privacy is statistical in m. The public output of the protocol is a commitment C_z; the private output, revealed to the user, is z. We let $[A, B]$ denote the input bounds and (n, t) denote the security parameters. We write $(C_z, z) \leftarrow \mathsf{unigen}[A, B](n, t)$ to denote output of public value C_z and private value z from the protocol.

Protocol $\mathsf{unigen}[A, B](m, t)$.

1. The user checks the correctness of $Proof_1$, which demonstrates that h and g generate the same group. If $Proof_1$ is incorrect, she aborts.
2. Let $L = B - A + 1$. The user selects $v \in_U [0, L-1]$ and $w_v \in_U [-2^m N, 2^m N]$. She computes $C_v = C(v, w_v)$, and sends C_v to the CA.
3. The CA selects $u \in_U [0, L-1]$ and sends u to the user.
4. The user checks that $u \in [0, L-1]$. If not, she aborts.
5. If $v + u \geq L$, then $o = g^L$; otherwise $o = 0$. The user selects $w_o \in_U [-2^m N, 2^m N]$, computes $C_o = C(o, w_o)$, and sends C_o to the CA.
6. The user executes $Proof_o = POK\{a : h^a = (C_o/g^L) \bigvee (h^a = C_o)\}$. This demonstrates that C_o represents a commitment of g^L or of 0.
7. Let $C_{z'} = C_v g^u / C_o$, a quantity computable by both the user and the CA. The user executes $Proof_{z'} = POK\{a, b : (C_{z'} = g^a h^b) \bigwedge (a \in [0, L-1])\}$. Together, $Proof_o$ and $Proof_{z'}$ demonstrate that $C_{z'}$ represents a commitment of $(u + v) \bmod L$.
8. If the CA is unable to verify either $Proof_o$ or $Proof_{z'}$, then the CA aborts. Otherwise, the public output of the protocol is $C_z = C_{z'} g^A$, and the private output is $z = ((u + v) \bmod L) + A$.

Given unigen as a building block, we are ready to present the full protocol for KEGVER. The basic strategy is for the user and CA to employ unigen to generate r and s, private values from which the user initiates a search for primes p and q. The user then proves, by way of commitments on her private values, that p and q are "close" to r and s respectively, and then that $n = pq$ is a Blum integer. The pair $[e, k]$ is input such that e represents the public exponent and k specifies the bit length of p and q, and thus n. Security parameters are l, m and t. The public output of the protocol is $n = pq$, while the private output is (p, q).

Protocol KEGVER$[e, k](l, m, t)$.

1. $(C_r, r) \leftarrow \mathsf{unigen}[2^{k-1}, 2^k - 1](m, t)$.
2. $(C_s, s) \leftarrow \mathsf{unigen}[2^{k-1}, 2^k - 1](m, t)$. (Note that the expensive verification step 1 in unigen can be omitted here, as it was already executed in the previous invocation.)
3. The user generates a prime $p \geq r$ meeting the conditions: (1) $gcd(e, p-1) = 1$; (2) $p \equiv 3 \bmod 4$; and (3) $p - r$ is minimal. If $p - r > l$, the user aborts, and the protocol output is $\emptyset$.
4. The user generates a prime $q \geq s$ meeting the conditions: (1) $gcd(e, q-1) = 1$; (2) $q \equiv 3 \bmod 4$; and (3) $q - s$ is minimal. If $q - s > l$, the user halts, and the protocol output is $\emptyset$.

5. The user selects $w_p, w_q \in_U [-2^m N, 2^m N]$ and computes $C_p = C(p, w_p)$ and $C_q = C(q, w_q)$.

6. The user sends C_p to the CA and proves $POK\{a, b : (C_p/C_r = g^x h^b) \bigwedge (a \in [0, l])\}$, and analogously for C_q.

7. The user sends $n = pq$ to the CA and proves $POK\{a, b, c, d : (C_p = g^a h^b) \bigwedge (C_q = g^c h^d) \bigwedge (g^n = g^{ac})\}$. In other words, the user proves that C_p and C_q are commitments to factors of n.

8. The user executes $\mathsf{Blum}(n)[t]$.

9. If the CA is unable to verify one or more proofs, or if $\mathsf{Blum}(n)[t]$ outputs 'no', the CA rejects and the protocol output is $\emptyset$. Otherwise, the public output of the protocol is n and the private output, obtained by the user, is (p, q).

Non-interactive variant of KEGVER: The protocol KEGVER can be rendered non-interactive by having the user execute all proofs non-interactively and generate the value u in unigen as $H(C_v)$ for an appropriate hash function H. In this case, we really have two algorithms KEGVER$_{user}$ and KEGVER$_{CA}$, where KEGVER$_{user}$ produces a public key PK and proof transcript T, and KEGVER$_{CA}$ decides whether to accept or not to accept a key/transcript pair (PK', T'). To guard against reuse of stale keys, a CA may require that the hash function H be keyed uniquely to that CA. Of course, this does not prevent intentional subsequent use of stale keys with CAs that do not adopt such a precaution.

Definition 1 must be altered for the non-interactive case. In particular, we define the probability $Q^A_{k;l,m,t}$ so that the probability distribution over keys PK' yielded by polynomial-time attack algorithm A also produces an accompanying transcript T' accepted by the CA. The algorithm A can of course run KEGVER$_{user}$ or some variant algorithm any number of times polynomial in k.

4 Security

If $<g>=<h>$, the protocol KEGVER is statistical zero-knowledge with privacy dependent on the parameter m used for the construction of commitments [6,15]. Details on simulator construction for the CA are available in security proofs for the underlying primitives as presented in the literature. If the proof protocols in KEGVER are to be realized non-interactively (as is better for most practical purposes), then the zero-knowledge property depends additionally on a random oracle assumption on an underlying hash function used for challenge generation [29]. In the case that $<g>\neq<h>$, the commitments of the user may not in fact be statistically secure. Hence, the privacy of KEGVER also depends on the soundness of $Proof_1$. The soundness of all proof protocols depends on the challenge sizes and also, for non-interactive proofs, on the random oracle assumption.

The new and critical security issue we focus on here is the choice of security parameter l and its impact on the soundness bound μ of Definition 1. To address this issue, we require use of a number theoretic conjecture regarding the density of primes. Most relevant here the view of prime density offered by Gallagher [17]. Gallagher shows that number of primes in the interval $(x, x + \lambda \ln x]$ is Poisson distributed with mean λ as $x \to \infty$.

The security of our construction depends on a slightly different quantity. In particular, our aim is to find a value l such that for a random k-bit value r, the interval $[r, r + l]$ with overwhelming probability contains a prime p such that $p \equiv 3 \bmod 4$ and $gcd(e, p - 1) = 1$. For this, we make two heuristic assumptions. Our first assumption is that the distribution of primes in the range used to construct RSA moduli is roughly Poisson distributed in accordance with the conjecture of Gallagher. We assume, second, that e is an odd prime constant (as is the case in most applications). Finally, let d_1 denote the probability density of primes p of general form; let d_2 denote the probability density of primes p such that $p \equiv 3 \bmod 4$ and $e \nmid (p-1)$. We assume, as one would naturally expect, that $d_2/d_1 = (e - 1)/2e$. Let X be a Poisson-distributed random variable with mean λ. The probability that $X = 0$ is $e^{-\lambda}$. Thus we obtain the following conjecture.

Conjecture 1. For large r, the probability that the interval $[r, r + l]$ contains no prime $p \equiv 3 \bmod 4$ such that $e \nmid (p - 1)$ is at most $e^{-\lambda}$ for $l = \lambda \ln r(\frac{2e}{e-1})$ or, equivalently, for $\lambda = \frac{l}{\ln r}(\frac{e-1}{2e})$.   □

This conjecture yields the following observation on the best parameterization of λ and l in accordance with Definition 1. It is easy to see that this observation extends to the non-interactive variant of KEGVER.

Observation 2. *Suppose that* $\lambda = \omega(\ln \ln r) = \omega(\ln k)$, $t = \omega(\ln k)$ *and* $\lambda \frac{2e}{e-1} \ln r < l = O(k^c)$ *for some constant c. Then the failure probability for an honest user, i.e., the probability that an honest user cannot find suitable primes p and q in* KEGVER *is negligible in k, and the soundness bound μ is polynomial in k.*   □

Example 1. Let us consider a concrete example involving the generation of 512-bit primes (i.e., roughly a 1024-bit RSA modulus) and public exponent $e = 3$. Choosing $\lambda = 57$ yields a failure probability for an honest user in KEGVER of less than 2^{-80} by Conjecture 1. This corresponds to $l = \lambda \frac{2e}{e-1} \ln r < 60, 687$. Clearly, given that at most one in four integers has the form $p \equiv 3 \bmod 4$, the maximum number of primes p in an interval of this size is at most 15,171. It follows then that our KEGVER protocol is μ-sound for $\mu < 15, 171^2 = 230, 159, 241$. This assumes that the soundness parameter t is large enough so that the ability of an attacker to cheat in any zero-knowledge proof is negligible, e.g., $t = 100$.

Stronger concrete security bounds: The concrete security bounds demonstrated in Example 1 above are deceptively weak. First, we note that μ is a bound on the ability of an attacker to distort the output distribution of KEGVER. For this, the ideal strategy is for a malicious user to choose a prime p in the interval $[r, r + l]$ such that the preceding prime p' is as close as possible to p. In fact, though, the aim of a malicious user is entirely different, namely to generate a key that is weak with respect to some attack algorithm or algorithms. Hence, the attacker is much more tightly constrained than our analysis according to Definition 1 suggests at first glance.

We can achieve substantially stronger concrete security bounds by relaxing Definition 1 in a probabilistic sense across intervals. We do not dilate formally on the idea here. Instead, we note simply that in Example 1 above involving generation of 512-bit primes with $l = 60,687$, the average number of primes of the form $p \equiv 3 \bmod 4$ in the interval $[r, r + l]$ is about 86, and the distribution of such primes is very tightly concentrated around this mean. In fact, under the Gallagher conjecture, the probability that the interval contains more than 250 such primes is well less than 2^{-80}. Thus, given a sufficiently large soundness parameter t (e.g., $t = 100$), the soundness bound $\mu < 250^2 = 62,500$ is a more accurate one for our purposes in Example 1.

5   Performance

One of the desirable features of KEGVER is that it places the bulk of the computational burden (primarily in the protocol Blum) on the user, rather than the CA. This preserves the usual balance of computational effort by the two parties. In particular, RSA key generation, which the user must perform in any case, is a computationally intensive task. In contrast, certification of an RSA key by a CA is, in its basic form, a relatively lightweight operation.

We can substantially reduce the computational requirements for the CA through use of such techniques as batch verification, as introduced in [12], and improved in many subsequent works such as [3], combined with addition chains, as explored in, e.g., [4]. We estimate that such enhancements would yield a speedup for the CA of approximately a factor of six. An additional protocol modification we can exploit is elimination of square-freeness proof protocol of van de Graaf and Peralta [33]: It can be proven that the KEGVER protocol itself implicitly enforces the condition of square-freeness with high probability. Due to space limitations, we omit proof of this fact from this version of the paper.

Given these observations, we can express the computational cost of the protocol very roughly in terms of the number of modular exponentiations required by the two parties (disregarding small added costs, such as the fact that Fujisaki-Okamoto commitments require exponents slightly longer than the modulus). Given soundness parameter $t = 100$, the computational requirement for the user in KEGVER is the equivalent of about 153 full modular exponentiations. The overall computational cost for the CA to the equivalent of roughly 10 full modular exponentiations. The transcript size for the full protocol is about 37kB.

We have created an implementation in C of a non-interactive variant of the KEGVER protocol for 1024-bit RSA modulus generation. Timing experiments took place on a Pentium III processor running Windows NT 4.0, with 64 Mbytes of RAM and running at 500 MHz. We compiled our code under gcc version 2.95.3 through use of the UNIX emulation environment Cygwin version 1.3.2. For multiprecision arithmetic, we used the GNU MP library, version 3.1.1. We note that the GMP library computes exponentiations via the sliding-window method for exponentiation [27] which provides roughly a 20–30% speed-up over the binary method for exponentiation. In addition, we implemented routines for double exponentiation using the method of simultaneous multiple exponentiation attributed to Shamir in [18]. Due to time constraints in the construction of the prototype, triple exponentiations were implemented simply through one call each to the double exponentiation and the single exponentiation routines, with multiplication of the partial results. In addition, in all of the computations by the CA (verifier), we employ the Chinese Remainder Theorem (CRT).

Table 1. Time Critical Proofs/Protocols in KEGVER

Proof/Protocol	# times called	Prover (sec)	Verifier (msec)
unigen	2	2.7	509
rangeproof (long)	(2)	(2.4)	(438)
rangeproof (short)	2	1.7	343
Blum Proof	1	1.3	201
KEGVER	–	10.9	2.05 sec

Table 1 summarizes the timings of the critical proofs and protocols in KEGVER. We denote the range proofs by the generic label rangeproof; the label "long" indicates a relatively expensive proof over a large interval, and "short", one on a small interval. The second column in Table 1 indicates the number of times that the specified protocol is called by KEGVER (either user or verifier). There are two calls to unigen; these include two range proofs, whose timings are provided in the next row. (Parentheses indicate that the associated calls and timings are subsumed by calls to unigen.) There are also two independent invocations of short range proofs, one for each of the primes in the RSA modulus. These latter proofs correspond to Step 6 in KEGVER. We observe that roughly 86% of the time required for unigen is in fact accounted for by an invocation of the associated (long) range proofs. Together, invocations of the cryptographic protocols unigen,Blum, and rangeproof (short) account for about 92% of the time required to perform KEGVER, the remainder accounted for by non-cryptographic operations. This is true for both the user and CA. For further details on our experiments, we refer the reader to the full version of this paper.

We did not implement batch verification or addition chains in this prototype. Additionally, we employed a range-proof protocol known as SZKrange$^+$ [22] in lieu of the Boudot protocol; the latter is about twice as fast in this setting. (We did this not for technical reasons, but due to intellecutal property concerns regarding the Boudot protocol.) Through use of batch proofs and the Boudot protocol, we believe it possible to achieve roughly a factor of 10 improvement in the performance of the verifier (i.e., CA) protocol. This would reduce the execution time to about 205 msec, making KEGVER highly practical.

Acknowledgments

Thanks to Markus Jakobsson, Burt Kaliski, Ron Rivest, Bob Silverman, and the anonymous referees of this paper for their comments and suggestions.

References

1. IEEE Std. 1363-2000. *Standard Specifications for Public-Key Cryptography*. The Institute of Electrical and Electronics Engineers, 2000.
2. ANSI X9.31 2001. *Digital Signatures Using Reversible Public Key Cryptography for the Financial Services Industry (X9.31)*. American National Standards Institute (ANSI), 2001.
3. M. Bellare, J.A. Garay, and T. Rabin. Fast batch verification for modular exponentiation and digital signatures. In K. Nyberg, editor, *Advances in Cryptology – EUROCRYPT '98*. Springer-Verlag, 1998. LNCS no. 1403.
4. D. Bleichenbacher. Addition chains for large sets, 1999. Unpublished manuscript.
5. D. Boneh and M. Franklin. Efficient generation of shared RSA keys. In B. Kaliski, editor, *Advances in Cryptology – CRYPTO '97*, pages 425–439. Springer-Verlag, 1997. LNCS no. 1294.
6. F. Boudot. Efficient proofs that a committed number lies in an interval. In B. Preneel, editor, *Advances in Cryptology – EUROCRYPT '00*, pages 431–444, 2000. LNCS no. 1807.
7. J. Boyar, K. Friedl, and C. Lund. Practical zero-knowledge proofs: Giving hints and using deficiencies. *Journal of Cryptology*, 4(3):185–206, 1991.
8. J. Camenisch and M. Michels. Proving that a number is the product of two safe primes. In J. Stern, editor, *Advances in Cryptology –EUROCRYPT '99*, pages 107–122. Springer-Verlag, 1999. LNCS no. 1592.
9. J. Camenisch and M. Stadler. Efficient group signature schemes for large groups. In B. Kaliski, editor, *Advances in Cryptology – CRYPTO '97*, pages 410–424. Springer-Verlag, 1997. LNCS no. 1294.
10. D. Catalano, R. Gennaro, and S. Halevi. Computing inverses over a shared secret modulus. In B. Preneel, editor, *Advances in Cryptology – EUROCRYPT '00*, pages 445–452. Springer-Verlag, 2000. LNCS no. 1807.
11. A. Chan, Y. Frankel, and Y. Tsiounis. Easy come - easy go divisible cash. In K. Nyberg, editor, *Advances in Cryptology –EUROCRYPT '98*, pages 561–575. Springer-Verlag, 1998. LNCS no. 1403. Revised version available as GTE tech. report.
12. L. Chen, I. Damgård, and T.P. Pedersen. Parallel divertibility of proofs of knowledge (extended abstract). In A. De Santis, editor, *Advances in Cryptology – EUROCRYPT '94*, pages 140–155. Springer-Verlag, 1994. LNCS no. 950.
13. R. Cramer, I. Damgård, and B. Schoenmakers. Proofs of partial knowledge and simplified design of witness hiding protocols. In Y.G. Desmedt, editor, *Advances in Cryptology – CRYPTO '94*, pages 174–187. Springer-Verlag, 1994. LNCS no. 839.
14. A. de Santis, G. di Crescenzo, G. Persiano, and M. Yung. On monotone formula closure of SZK. In *35th Annual Symposium on Foundations of Computer Science (FOCS)*, pages 454–465. IEEE Press, 1994.
15. E. Fujisaki and T. Okamoto. Statistical zero knowledge protocols to prove modular polynomial relations. In B. Kaliski, editor, *Advances in Cryptology – CRYPTO '97*, pages 16–30. Springer-Verlag, 1997. LNCS no. 1294.
16. E. Fujisaki and T. Okamoto. A practical and provably secure scheme for publicly verifiable secret sharing and its applications. In N. Koblitz, editor, *Advances in Cryptology – CRYPTO '98*, pages 32–46. Springer-Verlag, 1998.
17. P.X. Gallagher. On the distribution of primes in short intervals. *Mathematika*, 23:4–9, 1976.

18. T. El Gamal. A public key cryptosystem and a signature scheme based on discrete logarithms. *IEEE Transactions on Information Theory*, 31:469–472, 1985.

19. R. Gennaro, D. Micciancio, and T. Rabin. An efficient non-interactive statistical zero-knowledge proof system for quasi-safe prime products. In *Proceedings of the Fifth ACM Conference on Computer and Communications Security*, pages 67–72, 1998.

20. N. Gilboa. Two party RSA key generation. In M. Wiener, editor, *Advances in Cryptology – CRYPTO '99*, pages 116–129. Springer-Verlag, 1999. LNCS no. 1666.

21. O. Goldreich, S. Micali, and A. Wigderson. How to play any mental game. In *STOC '87*, pages 218–229. ACM Press, 1987.

22. A. Juels. $SZKrange^+$: Efficient and accurate range proofs. Technical report, RSA Laboratories, 1999.

23. M. Liskov and B. Silverman. A statistical-limited knowledge proof for secure RSA keys, 1998. Manuscript.

24. M. Malkin, T. Wu, and D. Boneh. Experimenting with shared generation of RSA keys. In *1999 Symposium on Network and Distributed System Security (SNDSS)*, pages 43–56, 1999.

25. W. Mao. Verifiable partial sharing of integer factors. In *Selected Areas in Cryptography (SAC '98)*. Springer-Verlag, 1998. LNCS no. 1556.

26. W. Mao and C.H. Lim. Cryptanalysis in prime order subgroups of Z_n^*. In K. Ohta and D. Pei, editors, *Advances in Cryptology - ASIACRYPT '98*, pages 214–226. Springer-Verlag, 1998. LNCS no. 1514.

27. A.J. Menezes, P.C. van Oorschot, and S.A. Vanstone. *Handbook of Applied Cryptography*. CRC Press, 1996.

28. T. Pedersen. Non-interactive and information-theoretic secure verifiable secret sharing. In J. Feigenbaum, editor, *Advances in Cryptology - CRYPTO '91*, pages 129–140. Springer-Verlag, 1991. LNCS no. 576.

29. D. Pointcheval and J. Stern. Security proofs for signature schemes. In U. Maurer, editor, *Advances in Cryptology – EUROCRYPT '96*, pages 287–398. Springer-Verlag, 1996. LNCS 1070.

30. I. Damgård and E. Fujisaki. An integer commitment scheme based on groups with hidden order, 2001. IACR eArchive.

31. C.P. Schnorr. Efficient signature generation by smart cards. *Journal of Cryptology*, 4:161–174, 1991.

32. A. Shamir. How to share a secret. *Communications of the ACM*, 22:612–613, 1979.

33. J. van de Graaf and R. Peralta. A simple and secure way to show the validity of your public key. In C. Pomerance, editor, *Advances in Cryptology – CRYPTO '87*, pages 128–134. Springer-Verlag, 1987. LNCS no. 293.

34. M. Wiener. Performance comparison of public-key cryptosystems. *Cryptobytes*, 4(1), 1998.

35. A.C. Yao. Protocols for secure computations (extended abstract). In *FOCS '82*, pages 160–164, 1982.

36. A. Young and M. Yung. Kleptography: Using cryptography against cryptography. In W. Fumy, editor, *Advances in Cryptology - EUROCRYPT '97*, pages 62–74. Springer-Verlag, 1997. LNCS no. 1233.

New Minimal Modified Radix-r Representation with Applications to Smart Cards

Marc Joye[1] and Sung-Ming Yen[2]

[1] Gemplus Card International, Card Security Group
Parc d'Activités de Gémenos, B.P. 100, 13881 Gémenos Cedex, France
marc.joye@gemplus.com
http://www.gemplus.com/smart/
http://www.geocities.com/MarcJoye/
[2] Laboratory of Cryptography and Information Security (LCIS)
Dept of Computer Science and Information Engineering
National Central University, Chung-Li, Taiwan 320, R.O.C.
yensm@csie.ncu.edu.tw
http://www.csie.ncu.edu.tw/~yensm/

Abstract. This paper considers the problem of finding a minimum-weighted representation of an integer under any modified radix-r number system. Contrary to existing methods, the proposed transformation is carried out from the left to the right (i.e., from the most significant position). This feature finds numerous applications and especially in fast arithmetic techniques because it reduces both time and space complexities, which is particularly attractive for small devices like smart cards.

1 Introduction

A *modified radix-r representation* (MR-r) of an integer N is a sequence of digits $N = (\ldots, c_2, c_1, c_0)$ with $-r < c_i < r$. Unlike the (usual) radix-r representation (i.e., with $0 \leq c_i < r$), such a representation is not unique. The radix-r representation is a special case of MR-r representation.

In the theory of arithmetic codes [vL82] or for fast implementation of cryptosystems [Gor98,MvOV97], it is of interest to have a representation such that the number of nonzero digits (i.e., the *arithmetic weight* [CL73]) is minimal. In the binary case (i.e., when $r = 2$), a well-known minimal representation is given by the so-called *nonadjacent form* (NAF), that is, a representation with $c_i \cdot c_{i+1} = 0$ for all $i \geq 0$. In [Rei60], Reitwiesner proved that each integer has exactly one NAF. Clark and Liang [CL73] later addressed the general case and extended the notion of NAF to an arbitrary radix $r \geq 2$:

Definition 1. *A* MR-r *representation* $(\ldots, c_2, c_1, c_0)$ *is said to be a generalized nonadjacent form (GNAF) if and only if*

(G1) $|c_i + c_{i+1}| < r$ *for all i ; and*
(G2) $|c_i| < |c_{i+1}|$ *if $c_i \cdot c_{i+1} < 0$.*

D. Naccache and P. Paillier (Eds.): PKC 2002, LNCS 2274, pp. 375–383, 2002.

As one can easily see, this form coincides with the definition of the NAF when $r = 2$. Moreover, as for the NAF, it can be proven that this form is unique and has minimal arithmetic weight [CL73].

However, the GNAF is not the only representation with minimal arithmetic weight. For example, $(1, 0, 1, 0, -1, 0)$ and $(1, 0, 0, 1, 1, 0)$ are two minimal MR-2 representations for 38.

Our Results

This paper considers a new *minimal* MR-r representation and presents an efficient algorithm to compute it. This new representation, unlike the GNAF, presents the nice property to be obtained by scanning the digits *from the left to the right* (i.e., from the most significant digit to the least significant one). This processing direction is of great importance since only for that direction a table of precomputed values may be used to speed up the exponentiation, at least for exponentiation algorithms processing one digit at a time [BGMW92]. A subsequent advantage is that the exponent need not be recoded in advance, which results in better performances in both running time and memory space. This is especially important for small devices like the smart cards. Moreover, only for that direction, further speedups may be obtained if the element to be raised up presents a special structure [Coh93, pp. 9–10]. Finally, this processing direction also solves an open problem introduced in [WH97, § 3.6].

2   New Minimal Representation

Throughout this paper, for convenience, $-a$ will sometimes be denoted as $\bar{a}$ and $\langle S \rangle^k$ will represent $S, S, \ldots, S$ (k times).

2.1   Elementary Blocks

Given the radix-r representation $(\ldots, c_2, c_1, c_0)$ of an integer N, the corresponding GNAF can easily be obtained as follows [CL73]: compute the radix-r representation of $(r + 1)N$, $(\ldots, b_2, b_1, b_0)$, then the GNAF is given by $(\ldots, c'_2, c'_1, c'_0)$ where $c'_i = b_{i+1} - c_{i+1}$. So, if the radix-r representation of $(r + 1)N$ is known, we are done. This computation can be carried out by right-to-left adding $N = (\ldots, c_2, c_1, c_0)$ and $rN = (\ldots, c_2, c_1, c_0, 0)$ according to the standard carry rule [Knu81, p. 251]:

$$\begin{cases} \kappa_0 = 0 \\ \kappa_{i+1} = \left\lfloor \dfrac{c_i + c_{i+1} + \kappa_i}{r} \right\rfloor \end{cases}, \tag{1}$$

$b_0 = c_0$ and $b_{i+1} = c_i + c_{i+1} + \kappa_i - r\kappa_{i+1}$ for $i \geq 0$. Left-to-right algorithms to add integers also exist [Knu81, Exercises 4.3.1.5 and 4.3.1.6]. However, they do not consistently output one digit per iteration; delay may occur when the sum of two adjacent digits is equal to $r - 1$. For that reason, an *on-line* (i.e., digit-by-digit) left-to-right computation of the GNAF seems to be impossible.

This paper considers a quite different approach: instead of trying to obtain the GNAF, we are looking for other minimal forms that may be efficiently evaluated from the left to the right. Our technique relies on the following observation:

Proposition 1. *Let* $(\ldots, c_2, c_1, c_0)$ *be the radix-r representation of an integer N, and let $(c_{f+1}, c_f, \ldots, c_{e+1}, c_e)$ be a subchain of digits of this representation such that*

(E1) $f > e$;
(E2) $c_e + c_{e+1} \neq r - 1$;
(E3) $c_j + c_{j+1} = r - 1$ *for* $e < j < f$;
(E4) $c_f + c_{f+1} \neq r - 1$.

Then all but the first and the last digits of the corresponding GNAF are entirely determined.

Proof. We note from Eq. (1) that, since $\kappa_i = 0$ or 1, the value of the carry-out κ_{i+1} does not depend on the carry-in κ_i for $i \geq e$. Indeed, we have $\kappa_{e+1} = \lfloor \frac{c_e + c_{e+1}}{r} \rfloor$ by Condition (E2); hence $\kappa_{j+1} = \kappa_{e+1}$ for $e \leq j < f$ by induction from Condition (E3); and $\kappa_{f+1} = \lfloor \frac{c_f + c_{f+1}}{r} \rfloor$ by Condition (E4). Therefore, if $(\star, c'_f, \ldots, c'_{e+1}, \star)$ denotes the digits corresponding to the GNAF, it follows that

$$c'_j = b_{j+1} - c_{j+1} = c_j + \kappa_j - r\kappa_{j+1}$$
$$= \begin{cases} c_j + (1 - r)\kappa_{e+1} & \text{for } e + 1 \leq j \leq f - 1 \\ c_f + \kappa_{e+1} - r\kappa_{f+1} & \text{for } j = f \end{cases} \tag{2}$$

where $\kappa_{e+1} = \lfloor \frac{c_e + c_{e+1}}{r} \rfloor$ and $\kappa_{f+1} = \lfloor \frac{c_f + c_{f+1}}{r} \rfloor$. $\square$

A subchain of radix-r digits satisfying Conditions (E1)–(E4) will be called a *radix-r elementary block*. From Proposition 1, two types of elementary blocks may be distinguished.

Definition 2. *Let* $0 \leq d, b, e \leq r - 1$, $c = r - 1 - d$ *(that is, $c + d = r - 1$) and $k \geq 0$. An elementary block of the form*

$$(b, d, \langle c, d \rangle^k, e) \quad \text{with } b + d \neq r - 1 \text{ and } e + d \neq r - 1 \tag{3}$$

will be referred to as a Type 1 *radix-r elementary block; and an elementary block of the form*

$$(b, d, \langle c, d \rangle^k, c, e) \quad \text{with } b + d \neq r - 1 \text{ and } e + c \neq r - 1 \tag{4}$$

as a Type 2 *radix-r elementary block.*

Notice that a Type 1 elementary block contains an odd number of digits (and at least 3) while a Type 2 elementary block contains an even number of digits (and at least 4).

Based on this definition, we can now present the new recoding algorithm.

378 Marc Joye and Sung-Ming Yen

2.2 General Recoding Algorithm

From Proposition 1 (see also Eq. (2)), the GNAF corresponding to a Type 1 elementary block $(b, d, \langle c, d \rangle^k, e)$ is given by[1]

$$G_1 = (\star, d + \lfloor \tfrac{e+d}{r} \rfloor - r \lfloor \tfrac{b+d}{r} \rfloor, \langle c + (1-r) \lfloor \tfrac{e+d}{r} \rfloor, d + (1-r) \lfloor \tfrac{e+d}{r} \rfloor \rangle^k, \star) \ . \quad (5)$$

By definition of a Type 1 elementary block, we have $b + d \neq r - 1$ and $e + d \neq r - 1$. Hence, Eq. (5) respectively simplifies to

$$G_1 = \begin{cases} (\star, d, \langle c, d \rangle^k, \star) & \text{if } b + d < r - 1 \text{ and } e + d < r - 1 \\ (\star, d+1, \langle -d, -c \rangle^k, \star) & \text{if } b + d < r - 1 \text{ and } e + d \geq r \\ (\star, d-r, \langle c, d \rangle^k, \star) & \text{if } b + d \geq r \text{ and } e + d < r - 1 \\ (\star, -c, \langle -d, -c \rangle^k, \star) & \text{if } b + d \geq r \text{ and } e + d \geq r \end{cases} \quad (6)$$

Similarly, the GNAF corresponding to a Type 2 block $(b, d, \langle c, d \rangle^k, c, e)$ is given by

$$G_2 = \begin{cases} (\star, d, \langle c, d \rangle^k, c, \star) & \text{if } b + d < r - 1 \text{ and } e + c < r - 1 \\ (\star, d+1, \langle -d, -c \rangle^k, -d, \star) & \text{if } b + d < r - 1 \text{ and } e + c \geq r \\ (\star, d-r, \langle c, d \rangle^k, c, \star) & \text{if } b + d \geq r \text{ and } e + c < r - 1 \\ (\star, -c, \langle -d, -c \rangle^k, -d, \star) & \text{if } b + d \geq r \text{ and } e + c \geq r \end{cases} \quad (7)$$

Here too, we see the difficulty of converting a radix-r representation into its GNAF by scanning the digits from the left to the right. If an elementary block begins with $(b, d, c, d, c, d, \ldots)$ with $b + d < r - 1$, the output will be $(\star, d, c, d, c, d, \ldots)$ or $(\star, d+1, -d, -c, -d, -c, \ldots)$ depending on the two last digits of the elementary block; if $b + d \geq r$, the output will be $(\star, d - r, c, d, c, d, \ldots)$ or $(\star, -c, -d, -c, -d, -c, \ldots)$. However, as stated in the next lemma, these outputs may be replaced by *equivalent* forms (i.e., forms having the same length and the same weight, and representing the same integer) so that the two last digits of an elementary block do not need to be known in advance.

Lemma 1. Let $0 \leq d \leq r - 1$ and $c = r - 1 - d$. Then

(i) if $d \neq r - 1$, $(d + 1, \langle -d, -c \rangle^k)$ and $(\langle d, c \rangle^k, d + 1)$ are equivalent MR-r representations;

(ii) if $d \neq 0$, $(d - r, \langle c, d \rangle^k)$ and $(\langle -c, -d \rangle^k, d - r)$ are equivalent MR-r representations.

Proof. With the MR-r notation, $(d + 1, \langle -d, -c \rangle^k)$ represents the integer

$$N = (d+1)r^{2k} + \sum_{j=0}^{k-1} (-dr - c)r^{2j}$$
$$= (d+1)r^{2k} + \sum_{j=0}^{k-1} (cr + d + 1 - r^2)r^{2j}$$
$$= dr^{2k} + \sum_{j=0}^{k-1} (cr + d)r^{2j} + 1 \quad \text{since } \sum_{j=0}^{k-1} r^{2j} = \tfrac{r^{2k}-1}{r^2-1}$$

which is thus also represented by $(d, \langle c, d \rangle^{k-1}, c, d + 1)$. We also note that $(d + 1, \langle -d, -c \rangle^k)$ and $(\langle d, c \rangle^k, d+1)$ have the same arithmetic weight since their digits are identical, in absolute value. The second equivalence is proved similarly. □

---

[1] The '$\star$' indicates that the digit is unknown.

Consequently, GNAFs G_1 and G_2 (see Eqs (6) and (7)) can respectively be replaced by another equivalent form, which we call *generalized star form* (GSF), respectively given by

$$S_1 = \begin{cases} (\star, \langle d, c \rangle^k, d, \star) & \text{if } b + d < r - 1 \text{ and } e + d < r - 1 \\ (\star, \langle d, c \rangle^k, d + 1, \star) & \text{if } b + d < r - 1 \text{ and } e + d \geq r \\ (\star, \langle -c, -d \rangle^k, d - r, \star) & \text{if } b + d \geq r \text{ and } e + d < r - 1 \\ (\star, \langle -c, -d \rangle^k, -c, \star) & \text{if } b + d \geq r \text{ and } e + d \geq r \end{cases} \qquad (8)$$

and

$$S_2 = \begin{cases} (\star, \langle d, c \rangle^k, d, c, \star) & \text{if } b + d < r - 1 \text{ and } e + c < r - 1 \\ (\star, \langle d, c \rangle^k, d + 1, -d, \star) & \text{if } b + d < r - 1 \text{ and } e + c \geq r \\ (\star, \langle -c, -d \rangle^k, d - r, c, \star) & \text{if } b + d \geq r \text{ and } e + c < r - 1 \\ (\star, \langle -c, -d \rangle^k, -c, -d, \star) & \text{if } b + d \geq r \text{ and } e + c \geq r \end{cases} \qquad (9)$$

The outputs now behave very regularly; an elementary block $(b, d, c, d, c, d, \ldots)$ will be recoded into $(\star, d, c, d, c, d, \ldots)$ if $b + d < r - 1$ or into $(\star, -c, -d, -c, -d, -c, \ldots)$ if $b + d \geq r$. We have just to take some precautions when outputting the last digits of the corresponding GSFs. The following example clarifies the technique.

Example 1. Suppose that the radix-4 GSF of $N = 208063846$ has to be computed. Its radix-4 representation is $(30121230311212)_4$. Then, by adding artificial beginning and ending 0's and decomposing this representation into elementary blocks, the corresponding GSF is easily obtained from Eqs (8) and (9) as follows.

Radix-4 representation:	0 0 3 0 1 2 1 2 3 0 3 1 1 2 1 2.0
Elementary blocks:	0 0 3 0 1
	0 1 2 1 2 3
	2 3 0 3 1
	3 1 1
	1 1 2 1 2.0
Corresponding GSF blocks:	$\star\, 0\; 3\; 0\; \star$
	$\star\, 1\; 2\; 2\; \bar{1}\; \star$
	$\star\, 0\; \bar{3}\; 0\; \star$
	$\star\, \bar{3}\; \star$
	$\star\, 1\; 2\; 1\; 2\; \star$

Radix-4 GSF representation:	3 0 1 2 2 $\bar{1}$ 0 $\bar{3}$ 0 $\bar{3}$ 1 2 1 2

□

In the previous example, it clearly appears that, from the definition of an elementary block, the two first digits of an elementary block are the two last ones of the previous block. This also illustrates that the decomposition into elementary (and thus GSF) blocks always exists. Note also that the values of the first and last digits of the corresponding GSF are given by the adjacent GSF blocks.

So, by carefully considering the two last digits of each possible elementary block, we finally obtain the desired algorithm. Two additional variables are used: variable β_i plays a role similar to the "borrow" and τ keeps track the value of the repeated digit (d in Definition 2).

```
INPUT:  (n_{m-1}, ..., n_0)        (Radix-r representation)
OUTPUT: (n'_m, n'_{m-1}, ..., n'_0) (Radix-r GSF representation)
```

$\beta_m \leftarrow 0$; $n_m \leftarrow 0$; $n_{-1} \leftarrow 0$; $n_{-2} \leftarrow 0$, $\tau \leftarrow 0$

for i **from** m **down to** 0 **do**

    case

        $n_i + n_{i-1} < r - 1$: $\beta_{i-1} \leftarrow 0$, $\tau \leftarrow n_{i-1}$

$$n_i + n_{i-1} = (r-1): \beta_{i-1} \leftarrow \begin{cases} 0 & \text{if } \beta_i = 1,\ n_{i-1} = (r-1-\tau) \\ & \text{and } n_{i-1} + n_{i-2} < r - 1 \\ 1 & \text{if } \beta_i = 0,\ n_{i-1} = (r-1-\tau) \\ & \text{and } n_{i-1} + n_{i-2} \geq r \\ \beta_i & \text{otherwise} \end{cases}$$

        $n_i + n_{i-1} \geq r$: $\beta_{i-1} \leftarrow 1$, $\tau \leftarrow n_{i-1}$

    endcase

    $n'_i \leftarrow -r\beta_i + n_i + \beta_{i-1}$

od

Fig. 1. Left-to-right radix-r GSF recoding algorithm.

To verify the correctness of the algorithm, it suffices to check that each type of elementary block is effectively transformed accordingly to Eqs (8) and (9). The next theorem states that the proposed algorithm is optimal in the sense that the resulting representation has the fewest number of nonzero digits of any MR-r representation.

Theorem 1. *The GSF of a number has minimal arithmetic weight.*

Proof. This is straightforward by noting the GSF is obtained from the GNAF where some subchains were replaced according to Lemma 1. Since these transformations produce equivalent subchains, the GSF has the same arithmetic weight as the GNAF and is thus minimal.   □

Remark 1. We note that, as in [CL73], the proposed algorithm can be extended to transform an arbitrary MR-r representation into a minimal one.

2.3   Binary Case

In the binary case (i.e., when $r = 2$), the algorithm presented in Fig. 1 is slightly simpler. Using the same notations as in Fig. 1, if $n_i + n_{i-1} = 1$, we can easily verify that

$$\beta_{i-1} = \left\lfloor \frac{\beta_i + n_{i-1} + n_{i-2}}{2} \right\rfloor \tag{10}$$

is a valid expression for β_{i-1}. Moreover, this expression remains valid when $n_i = n_{i-1} = 0$ (i.e., in the case $n_i + n_{i-1} < 1$) because if $n_{i+1} = 0$ then $\beta_i = 0$ and if $n_{i+1} = 1$ then, by Eq. (10), we also have $\beta_i = 0$; therefore Eq. (10) yields $\beta_{i-1} = 0$. Similarly when $n_i = n_{i-1} = 1$ (i.e., $n_i + n_{i-1} \geq 2$), we can show that Eq. (10) yields $\beta_{i-1} = 1$, as expected. The radix-2 GSF recoding algorithm thus becomes [JY00]:

INPUT: $(n_{m-1}, \ldots, n_0)$ (Binary representation)
OUTPUT: $(n'_m, n'_{m-1}, \ldots, n'_0)$ (Binary GSF representation)

$\beta_m \leftarrow 0$; $n_m \leftarrow 0$; $n_{-1} \leftarrow 0$; $n_{-2} \leftarrow 0$
for i from m down to 0 do
$\quad \beta_{i-1} \leftarrow \lfloor \frac{\beta_i + n_{i-1} + n_{i-2}}{2} \rfloor$
$\quad n'_i \leftarrow -r\beta_i + n_i + \beta_{i-1}$
od

Fig. 2. Left-to-right binary GSF recoding algorithm.

3   Applications

Minimal representations naturally find applications in the theory of arithmetic codes [vL82] and in fast arithmetic techniques [Boo51,Avi61]. In this section, we will restrict our attention to fast exponentiation (see the excellent survey article of [Gor98]).

The commonly used methods to compute g^k are the generalized "square-and-multiply" algorithms. When base g is fixed or when the computation of an inverse is virtually free, as for elliptic curves [MO90], a signed-digit representation further speeds up the computation. These algorithms input the MR-r representations of exponent $k = (k_m, \ldots, k_0)$ (i.e., with $-r < k_i < r$ and $k_m \neq 0$) and of base g, and output $y = g^k$. This can be carried out from right to left (Fig. 3a) or from left to right (Fig. 3b).

INPUT: $k = (k_m, \ldots, k_0), g$ INPUT: $k = (k_m, \ldots, k_0), g$
OUTPUT: $y = g^k$ OUTPUT: $y = g^k$

$y \leftarrow 1$; $h \leftarrow g$ $y \leftarrow g^{k_m}$
for i from 0 to $m-1$ do   for i from $m-1$ down to 0 do
$\quad y \leftarrow y \cdot h^{k_i}$ $\quad y \leftarrow y^r$
$\quad h \leftarrow h^r$ $\quad y \leftarrow y \cdot g^{k_i}$
od   od
$y \leftarrow y \cdot h^{k_m}$

        (a) Right-to-left (RL).   (b) Left-to-right (LR).

Fig. 3. Modified exponentiation algorithms.

Using Markov chains, Arno and Wheeler [AW93] precisely estimated that the average proportion of nonzero digits in the radix-r GNAF (and thus also in the radix-r GSF) representation is equal to

$$\rho_r = \frac{r-1}{r+1} \ .$$ (11)

The LR algorithm can use the precomputation of some g^t for $-r < t < r$ while the RL algorithm cannot! One could argue that the exponent may first be recoded into a minimal MR-r representation and then the LR algorithm be applied. However this also requires more memory space since each digit in the MR-r requires an additional bit (to encode the sign for each digit). Consequently, since only the LR algorithm is efficient, the proposed (left-to-right) general recoding algorithm (Fig. 1) will also bring some advantages because, as aforementioned, the exponent need not be pre-recoded into its MR-r representation. This feature is especially desirable for small devices, like smart cards.

Another generalization of exponentiation algorithms is to use variable windows to skip strings of consecutive zeros. Here too, the proposed recoding algorithms offer some speedups. Indeed, as a side effect, while having the same weight as the GNAF, the GSF representation has more adjacent nonzero digits, which increases the length of the runs of zeros. This property was successfully applied by Koyama and Tsuruoka [KT93] to speed up the window exponentiation on elliptic curves. We note nevertheless that the zero runs of their algorithm are generally longer than those obtained by the GSFs.

4   Conclusions

In this paper, a new modified representation of integers for a general radix $r \geq 2$ is developed. Like the nonadjacent form (NAF) and its generalization, the proposed representation has the fewest number of nonzero digits of any modified representation.

When developing fast computational algorithms for hardware implementation, especially for some small devices which have very limited amount of memory, the problem of extra space requirement cannot be overlooked. Scanning and transforming the original representation from the most significant digit has its merit in not storing the resulting minimum-weighted result, hence memory space requirements are reduced. Finally, this solves a problem considered to be hard (see [WH97, § 3.6]), i.e., to obtain a minimal modified radix-4 representation by scanning the digits of the standard representation from the left to the right.

Acknowledgments

The authors are grateful to the anonymous referees for their useful comments. Sung-Ming Yen was supported in part by the National Science Council of the Republic of China under contract NSC 87-2213-E-032-013.

References

Avi61.   A. Avizienis, *Signed-digit number representations for fast parallel arith-metic*, IRE Transactions on Electronic Computers **EC-10** (1961), 389–400, Reprinted in [Swa90, vol. II, pp. 54–65].

AW93.   S. Arno and F.S. Wheeler, *Signed digit representations of minimal Hamming weight*, IEEE Transactions on Computers **C-42** (1993), no. 8, 1007–1010.

BGMW92.   E.F. Brickell, D.M. Gordon, K.S. McCurley, and D.B. Wilson, *Fast exponentiation with precomputation*, Advances in Cryptology – EUROCRYPT '92, Lecture Notes in Computer Science, vol. 658, Springer-Verlag, 1992, pp. 200–207.

Boo51.   A.D. Booth, *A signed binary multiplication technique*, The Quaterly Journal of Mechanics and Applied Mathematics **4** (1951), 236–240, Reprinted in [Swa90, vol. I, pp. 100–104].

CL73.   W.E. Clark and J.J. Liang, *On arithmetic weight for a general radix representation of integers*, IEEE Transactions on Information Theory **IT-19** (1973), 823–826.

Coh93.   H. Cohen, *A course in computational algebraic number theory*, Springer-Verlag, 1993.

EK94.   Ö. Eğecioğlu and Ç.K. Koç, *Exponentiation using canonical recoding*, Theoretical Computer Science **129** (1994), no. 2, 407–417.

GHM96.   D. Gollmann, Y. Han, and C.J. Mitchell, *Redundant integer representation and fast exponentiation*, Designs, Codes and Cryptography **7** (1996), 135–151.

Gor98.   D.M. Gordon, *A survey of fast exponentiation methods*, Journal of Algorithms **27** (1998), 129–146.

JY00.   M. Joye and S.-M. Yen, *Optimal left-to-right binary signed-digit recoding*, IEEE Transactions on Computers **49** (2000), no. 7, 740–748.

Knu81.   D.E. Knuth, *The art of computer programming/Seminumerical algorithms*, 2nd ed., vol. 2, Addison-Wesley, 1981.

KT93.   K. Koyama and Y. Tsurukoa, *Speeding up elliptic cryptosystems by using a signed binary window method*, Advances in Cryptology – CRYPTO '92, Lecture Notes in Computer Science, vol. 740, Springer-Verlag, 1993, pp. 345–357.

MO90.   F. Morain and J. Olivos, *Speeding up the computations on an elliptic curve using addition-subtraction chains*, Theoretical Informatics and Applications **24** (1990), 531–543.

MvOV97.   A.J. Menezes, P.C. van Oorschot, and S.A. Vanstone, Handbook of applied cryptography, ch. 14, CRC Press, 1997.

Rei60.   G.W. Reitwiesner, *Binary arithmetic*, Advances in Computers 1 (1960), 231–308.

Swa90.   E.E. Swartzlander, Jr. (ed.), *Computer arithmetic*, vol. I and II, IEEE Computer Society Press, 1990.

vL82.   J.H. van Lint, *Introduction to coding theory*, Springer-Verlag, 1982.

WH97.   H. Wu and M.A. Hasan, *Efficient exponentiation of a primitive root in* $GF(2^m)$, IEEE Transactions on Computers **C-46** (1997), no. 2, 162–172.

Author Index